The Practical Woodworker

The Practical Woodworker

Edited by Bernard E. Jones

 Ten Speed Press

1☉

TEN SPEED PRESS
P O Box 7123
Berkeley, California 94707

Library of Congress Catalog Number: 83-40022
ISBN: 0-89815-106-6 (paperbound), 0-89815-111-2 (clothbound)

Cover Design by Brenton Beck

Printed in the United States of America

3 4 5 — 90

Table of Contents

Introduction

TAKEN together with THE COMPLETE WOODWORKER (Ten Speed Press, 1980) this volume completes a reference and instructional set for woodworkers of all skill levels. Comprehensive in scope, thorough in detail, and clear in presentation, this set provides a standard work on the complete techniques of hand woodworking. Originally published just when modern machine methods and artificial materials were replacing hand methods carefully learned over thousands of years, THE COMPLETE WOODWORKER and THE PRACTICAL WOODWORKER show European hand-craftsmanship at its best. In addition to a discussion of hand tools and techniques, a large number of plans and designs for furniture and other structures are found in both volumes.

The following discussion of the plan and contents of each book is included to help the readers use them to their best advantage. THE COMPLETE WOODWORKER is a concise, but complete, general reference volume on the basic tools and skills of woodworking. The clearly and logically presented information provides answers to most inquiries. Supplementing this, THE PRACTICAL WOODWORKER gives a fuller and more detailed discussion of hand woodworking methods, as well as more illustrations. However, for many essential tasks (hammering, gluing, finishing...), there is no more instruction required than is presented in THE COMPLETE WOODWORKER. Therefore, such sections are not duplicated in THE PRACTICAL WOODWORKER.

In addition to expanding on the material in THE COMPLETE WOODWORKER, THE PRACTICAL WOODWORKER gives detailed instructions on many advanced techniques

(woodturning, wood carving...) not found in the first volume, as well as hundreds of pages of plans and designs. Using these plans and the methods described, any conscientious woodworker can make the fine and useful items described, ranging from chairs and tables to greenhouses.

Certain chapters deserve a brief note. Chapter 1, "The Workshop and Its Equipment," gives a very helpful discussion of something easily overlooked until we experience the frustration of trying to work in a makeshift location. Much of successful woodworking depends on having a workspace suited to what must be done, and work surfaces that aid, rather than hinder, accurate work. Any trouble or expense involved in making a proper work-space will be amply repaid in the greater ease of work done there. Similarly, Chapter 2, "Tools for Measuring and Marking," emphasizes the importance of this first step in woodworking. If work is not clearly, accurately and consistently measured and marked, it is impossible to do fine work at all. More error and difficulty arise with measuring and cutting (in my experience) than in any other part of woodworking. The next six chapters offer a comprehensive view of cutting and planing wood to size and shape. These are followed by five chapters on the joints used in fine woodworking, from simple half and lap joints to mortise and tenon. The section on techniques closes with clear and detailed chapters on wood turning and carving, inlay, marquetry, veneering and fretwork; all important in producing truly fine furniture and other woodwork.

The second half of THE PRACTICAL WOODWORKER consists of numerous chapters on individual items, complete with drawings and plans as required. Chapter 20, "Tool Chests," is of use to anyone who wants to store their tools safely while keeping them conveniently at hand. This is followed by chapters on "Garden Lights" (as the English call cold frames) and "Greenhouses" which show how to easily construct these important garden aids. A chapter showing the correct manner of building doors and windows is followed by an extensive presentation of the most useful and popular furniture—dressers, tables of all kinds, chairs, cupboards, cabinets, kitchen queens, wardrobes, roll-top desks and writing desks. There is also a chapter on fancy boxes which provides many ideas for work on a small, but always useful, item. The last chapter is a very detailed and helpful list of woods; including their origins, botanical names, characteristics and uses.

Finally, a word about the editor and the production of this volume might be of interest. Bernard E. Jones was a prolific and highly thought of editor of technical manuals in the early years of this century. His skill in finding expert craftsmen to write each of the chapters, and in editing their work to fit the volume made this book possible, as well as preserving much knowledge of craftsmanship that otherwise might have disappeared with the decline of hand woodworking as a commercial method. THE PRACTICAL WOODWORKER was conceived as a complete guide to woodworking, and an attempt was made to include as much material as possible. Unfortunately, even a fine editor could not prevent having articles of uneven quality, or the inclusion of trivial chapters intended to bulk up a work of unlimited scope. By deleting those chapters that are trivial, of inferior quality, or which duplicate those of THE COMPLETE WOODWORKER without offering much new information, we have produced another standard reference that should be in the hands of every woodworker.

Steve Herold
Berkeley, California
March 1983

The Workshop and its Equipment

Arrangement of Small Workshop.—
The workshop at home is generally a spare room, maybe a surplus bedroom or a room in the basement, but failing the necessary accommodation in the house, a small shed is often erected, as will be described on later pages.

A general view of a room equipped as a small workshop is presented by Fig. 1. The two windows shown help to make a well-lighted and ideal workshop. Fig. 2 is a plan of a similar room measuring about 12 ft. by 9 ft.

In cases where it would be more desir-able and convenient to have a workshop erected in wood the same plan would serve, the wall thickness, of course, being less, and the dimensions of the workshop being modified to suit requirements. A specially built workshop could have a skylight.

Fig. 1.—Typical Small Workshop

1

Lighting the Workshop.—Windows facing north or east are usually preferred, but where this scheme is rigidly carried out to the exclusion of other windows the workshop is very cheerless, and such a system should therefore be avoided when possible. Where a workshop has sky-lights, these should be fitted with blinds so that the direct rays of the sun may be

for general purposes is best constructed of red or white deal throughout. The advantage of a soft wood top is that, although more readily damaged than one of hardwood, it can be easily trued up providing that it is sufficiently thick for the purpose. The type of bench shown is designed for heavier and perhaps rougher work than those about to be

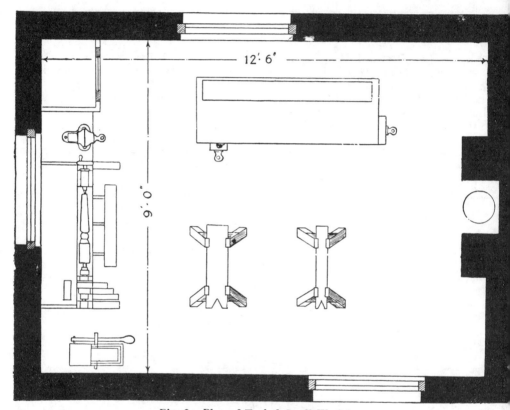

Fig. 2.—Plan of Typical Small Workshop

kept off the work or the operator. Artificial lighting may be by electricity, gas, acetylene, or oil, the first-named being the best and the last the worst. The light should be so arranged that the worker faces the light more or less, and therefore does not cast a shadow on his work.

BENCHES

Suitable Timber.—A common form of bench is shown in Figs. 3 to 9, and

described. The benches, shown by Figs. 10 to 24 should preferably be built of hardwood with the exception of the well-board which may be of deal. Suitable hardwoods are beech and sycamore and even birch. The legs, rails and other parts of the frame may also be of hardwood, although good red or white deal would be found quite suitable both in strength and durability for these parts. If hardwood is used, some of the scantlings

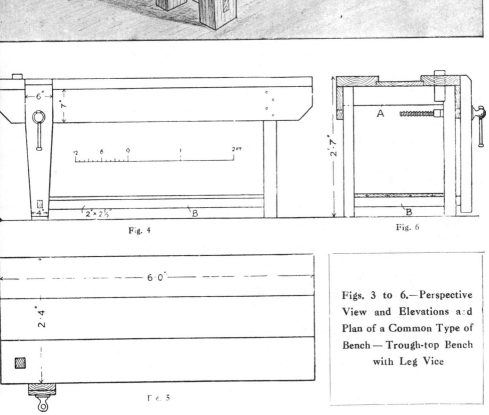

Fig. 4

Fig. 6

Fig. 5

Figs. 3 to 6.—Perspective View and Elevations and Plan of a Common Type of Bench — Trough-top Bench with Leg Vice

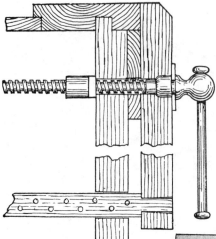

platform (*see* Figs. 3 to 9, already referred to) is fitted with the "Dolly" form of vice, a leg vice of which the cheek is vertical and has a steel screw with box and runner below with pinholes and iron pin for adjustment. The top is formed of two 9 in. by 2 in. deal boards, the lower inner edges of which are rebated to receive a board 11 in. by 1 in. which forms the well or trough. Three of the legs are made of 3 in. by 2½ in. stuff, but the leg to which the vice is attached is stouter—4 in. by 2½ in. It is very important that this leg should have a tenon at the upper end fitting into a mortise made in the underside of the top, as illustrated in Fig. 8, so that when work

Fig. 7.—Method of Fitting
Iron Bench Screw

could be less in size than those shown in the illustration.

A Common Type of Bench.—The common form of bench provided with a

Fig. 9.—Fixing Runner to Cheek of Vice

is screwed up in the vice the leg cannot be pulled forward by the action of the vice ; if this is not done, after a time the leg and side of the bench are gradually forced forward, even when the top is strongly screwed to the side, so causing the latter to split. The top ends of the legs should be mortised and haunched as shown in Fig. 8 to receive the bearers (A, Fig. 6). The lower ends of the legs should be connected to the rails by ordinary stub-mortise and tenon joints, and the platform should be made of ¾ in. grooved and tongued boarding, machine-prepared floor-boarding being suitable for this purpose. The construction of the bottom of the runner and cheek will be clearly understood from Fig. 9. An enlarged sectional detail of the arrangement for fitting and connecting the iron screw is given by Fig. 7 or this page.

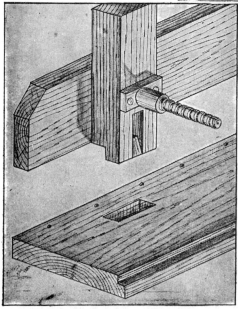

Fig. 8.— Construction of Top of Leg

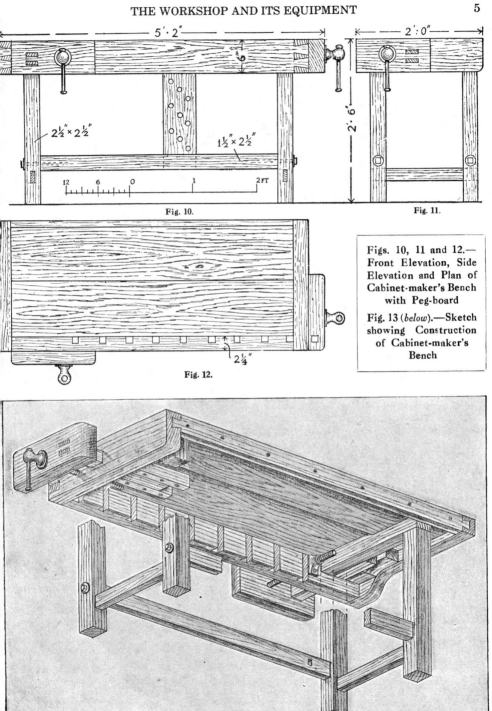

Fig. 10.

Fig. 11.

2½″ × 2½″

1½″ × 2½″

12   6   0   1   2 FT

5′·2″

2′:0″

2′:6′

Fig. 12.

2¼″

Figs. 10, 11 and 12.—
Front Elevation, Side
Elevation and Plan of
Cabinet-maker's Bench
with Peg-board

Fig. 13 (below).—Sketch
showing Construction
of Cabinet-maker's
Bench

Fig. 13.

Fig. 14.—Sketch of Cabinet-maker's Bench with Tool Drawer

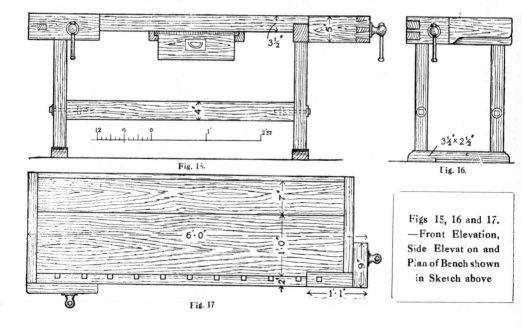

Fig. 15.

Fig. 16.

Fig. 17

Figs 15, 16 and 17.
—Front Elevation,
Side Elevation and
Plan of Bench shown
in Sketch above

Cabinet-maker's Bench.—One form of cabinet-maker's bench is illustrated by Figs. 10 to 13. The top is constructed as follows : The two end pieces and the front cheek (which has the slots made in it for the stop) are dovetailed together at the angles, as shown in Figs. 10 to 13. The back piece is 1 in. thick and is lap-dovetailed into the end pieces, as shown at Fig. 13. The planing board and wellboard of the top are rebated together and

through the mortise and securing with a key wedge may be adopted.

A peg board for holding long pieces of timber for planing is shown fixed to the front of the bench (*see* Fig. 10). When a long piece of board is screwed up in the vice at one end, the other end is liable to drop when the pressure of the plane is applied, and to keep this end up a peg is put in one of the holes shown and the board rested on it. A number of holes

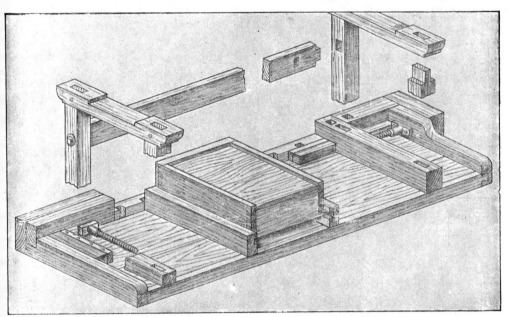

Fig. 18.—Sketch showing Construction of the Bench illustrated on preceding page

their ends tongued into grooves made in the end pieces. The front cheek, after being notched for the stops, is glued and screwed to the planing board. The cross rails are connected to the legs by stub-mortise and tenon joints and fixed wedged. If desired, as an alternative arrangement, the tenons could go right through and be pinned. The longitudinal rails have short stub tenons and are additionally secured by a bolt and nut, the latter being inserted in a mortise made in the rail, as clearly shown in Fig. 10. This method makes a very sound job, but, if desired, the old method of making a long tenon pass

are necessary to accommodate various widths of work.

Another example of a cabinet-maker's bench is shown in Figs. 14 to 18. It is fitted with an end vice for cramping up and holding work. The construction is generally similar to the preceding bench, but different in one or two details. The peg board is omitted, but a drawer for tools is shown. On the sides of the drawer are screwed small fillets which slide in grooved runners screwed to the underside of the bench. The legs are supported on base pieces which also act as end rails.

Portable Bench.—Figs. 19 to 23 are

illustrations of a small portable bench which will be found very suitable where the available. The top consists of a planing or working board and a well. Sizes for general purposes are figured on the illustrations. Two ledgers are screwed to the underside of the top, and to these the top rails of the leg framings are attached with strong 3-in. butt hinges. The drawings clearly show the construction of the leg framing. A block of wood is screwed to the top; this has a hole bored through it, as have also the upper ends of the struts, and thus the three parts can be held firmly together by a bolt and nut, a wing or butterfly nut

Fig. 19.—Sketch of Portable Bench

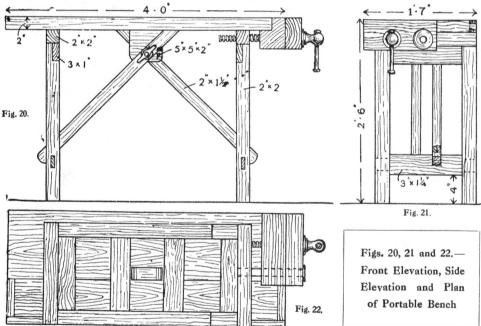

Fig. 20.

2"×2"

3 × 1"

5×5×2"

2" × 1½"

2"×2

Fig. 21.

3"×1¼"

Fig. 22.

Figs. 20, 21 and 22.—
Front Elevation, Side
Elevation and Plan
of Portable Bench

use of a bench is only occasionally required and a proper workshop is not being the most convenient. The lower ends of the struts are notched over the

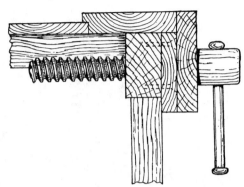

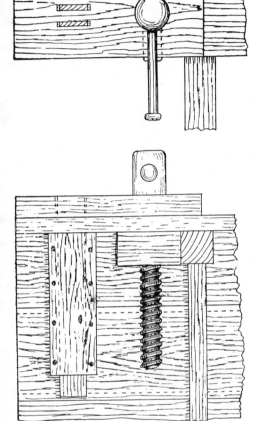

Figs. 24, 25 and 26.—Front Elevation, Vertical Section and Plan Looking Up, showing Method of Fitting a Wooden Vice. (*See* Fig. 27.)

bottom side rails of the legs and bolted to them, the bolts being preferably cranked as shown in the drawing.

Bench Fitted with Drawer and Cupboard.—The bench, shown by Fig. 28, is an extremely handy form, provided with three drawers and a cupboard. One or two of the drawers can be fitted up to hold chisels, gouges, bits and other of the smaller tools. The bottom drawer can be made to contain hollows, rounds, bead planes, metal planes and other of the small planes.—The cupboard can be fitted with shelves, so as to accommodate jack plane, trying plane, saws and other of the larger tools.

If the bench is made a fair size, say

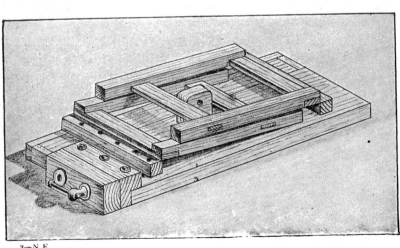

Fig. 23.— View of Underside of Portable Bench, showing Legs Folded Up. (*For details, see preceding page*)

2—N.E.

about 5 ft. 6 in. long and 2 ft. 3 in. wide, it will contain all the tools for ordinary

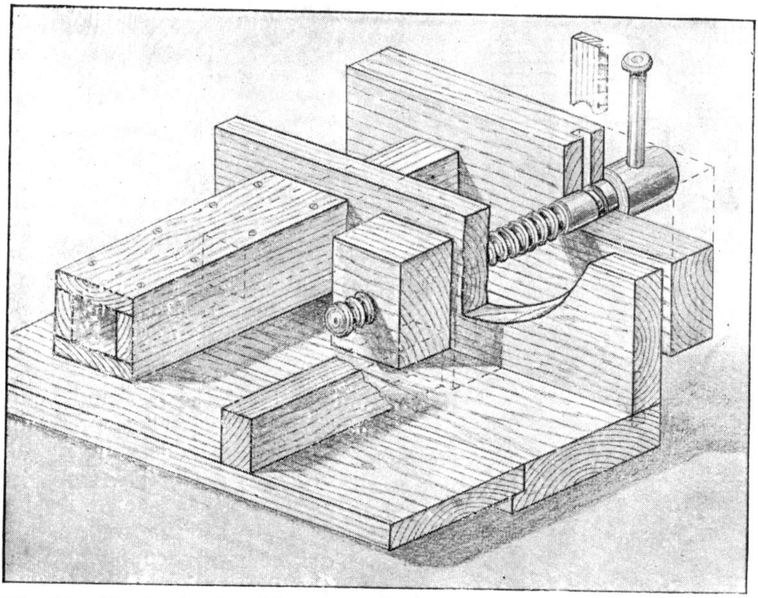

Fig. 27.—Sketch showing Method of Fitting Wooden Vice. (*See* Figs. 24 to 26)

woodworker. The vice can be fixed to the underside of the top with two or three bolts and wing nuts, and consequently can be quickly detached.

Bench Vices. —The vice illustrated by Figs. 24 to 27 represents one constructed almost entirely of wood, the screw and nut usually being made of beechwood. The cheek and runner are best made of some kind of hardwood, all the other parts being of red and white deal. Formerly the

requirements, without any tool chest, cupboard, or outside rack being necessary. This bench will be found especially useful and suitable for anyone who has not a proper workshop and has to make use of a room which, during part of the day, has to be employed for other purposes. By using a simple iron stop that can be screwed level with the top and a small iron vice as illustrated it is possible for the bench to form a piece of furniture when not in use by the

Fig. 28.—Sketch of Bench Fitted with Drawers and Cupboard

wooden screw type of vice was more used than any other, but it has been superseded since the introduction of metal screws and nuts (or boxes). The drawings fully and clearly show the construction. The sizes of the parts vary, of course, according to requirements. The screw and cheek are held together by means of a hardwood key which is inserted in a mortise made from the bottom edge of the cheek. The end of the key is hollowed so as to fit into the groove turned in the shank of the screw; this is shown in Fig. 27.

back of the cheek, holes being made to receive the bolt heads so that they sink a

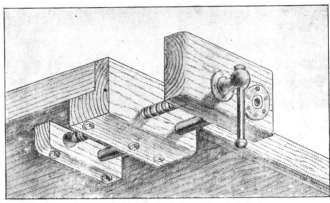

Fig. 29.—Vice with Steel Screw and Wooden Jaws

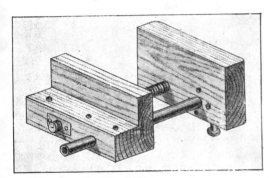

Fig. 30.—Detail of Vice (looking from Back)

little below the surface. These are indicated at Fig. 30. The block is fixed to the top of the bench by three coach bolts. Bolts and nuts can be used, in which case the heads are sunk $\frac{3}{8}$ in. below the surface of the top and pieces of wood fitted in the holes, glued and planed off flush with the top surface. This vice, if carefully made, will be found to work parallel, because of the strong connection be-

The vice illustrated by Figs. 29 and 30 is an improvement on the one above described and illustrated. It is provided with a steel screw and nut and a runner is formed of a piece of strong $\frac{3}{4}$-in. to $1\frac{1}{8}$-in. gas pipe or steam tubing, screwed at one end so as to fix into a 3-in. or 4-in. iron flange, in which four to six holes have been drilled and countersunk to receive stout screws. The flange may be more firmly fixed to the cheek by using range screws (or bolts) and securing with a nut at the

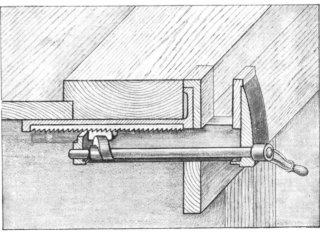

Fig. 31.—Instantaneous-grip Vice

tween the runner and cheek. It is quite suitable for either a side vice or end vice.

Instantaneous-grip Vice.—Fig. 31 shows a type of instantaneous-grip vice which has been much used for many years. It is very strong and serviceable, although much more expensive than home-constructed vices. The action is as follows : Upon raising the handle, the bar and screw cam is turned ; the diameter of the latter gradually decreasing causes the semi-nut (which has a rack on its upper side) to lower and disengage from the long rack, whereupon the front jaw slide can

Fig. 32.—Useful Vice for Curved Work

be drawn out the desired distance ; the work is then placed in position and the jaw pushed close to it. When the handle is pressed down, the cam raises the semi-nut in contact with the rack ; and the further movement of the handle forces the jaw to the work by the screw action of the cam. The top edges of the jaw are kept below the surface of the planing plank about 1 in., this allowing of both of the jaws being lined with hardwood, which is secured to them by screws. This wood lining prevents the edges of the tools being damaged by coming into contact with the metal. Photographic

illustrations in later chapters show a different type of instantaneous-grip vice.

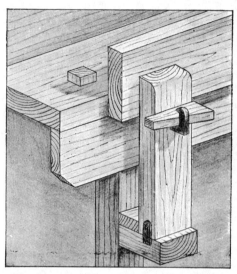

Fig. 33.—Improvised Vice for Small Work

Other Kinds of Vices.—For curved work a vice whose jaws stand above the level of the bench top is very useful, as shown in Fig. 32 ; it is made with two long cheeks and a runner at the bottom with holes and pins for adjustment, the

Fig. 34.—Cleat for Holding Boards whilst Planing, etc.

inner cheek being screwed to the side of the bench.

Fig. 33 shows an improvised form of vice which will be found useful for holding small work and when planing the edges

Fig. 35.— Clamp for Use on Table

of boards and for similar operations. A long iron bolt is forged into a hook form at its head end as shown. A hole is bored through the cheek of the vice large enough for the shank of the bolt to work in freely. The side of the bench and leg are bored

for the cheek to rest upon, and a piece of iron screwed on each side of the cheek will prevent the cheek from slipping side-

Fig. 36.—Underside of Clamp

ways. For tightening the work a hardwood wedge is driven between the vice cheek and the forked nut head. The bottom of the cheek can be adjusted by

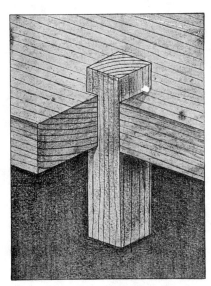

Fig. 37.—Ordinary Bench Stop

Fig. 38.—Wedge Bench Stop

so that the bolt passes through and is fastened at the back of the leg with a nut. A block is fastened to the leg of the bench

pieces of wood varying in width. Several wedges of different size will be found useful for different thicknesses of work.

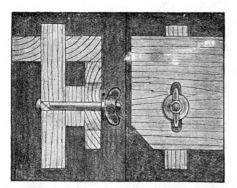

Figs. 39 and 40.—
Vertical Section and
Front Elevation of
Adjustable Bench
Stop. (*See* Fig. 41 *at
foot of page*)

Fig. 34 shows a
cleat, which is a
triangular - shaped
piece of wood,
screwed to the top
edge of the bench ;
it will be found
very useful for
holding b o a r d s,
etc., the edges of
which are to be
planed. This ar-
rangement will
hold the work fast
as long as there

sunk so that it can be firmly secured to
the board with a couple of stout screws.
The board may be fixed to the table top
by four hardwood buttons or clips and
bolts with wing nuts, one of which is shown
in Fig. 36.

Bench Stops.—The simplest form of
bench stop is made by screwing a thin
strip to the bench top as shown in Fig. 34.
This form is especially useful when planing
short wide boards, such as panels, etc.

Fig. 37 shows a simple form of stop
which has probably been used more than
any other kind.
It is generally
made from a piece
of hardwood
about 2 in. sq.
fitting tightly into
a mortise made
through the top
of the bench. To
prevent splitting
the top, care
should be taken
to make the
breadth of the
mortise the same
as the stop. The
two sides of the
mortise having
the end grain

Fig. 42.—Spring Stop

is a pressure forward, but any back pressure will,
of course, directly loosen the work.

In cases where it is not desirable or convenient
to set up an ordinary bench and it is only required to do light work on a table, and without
injury to it, the contrivance shown by Figs. 35 and
36 will be found convenient. A board about
9 in. wide and 2 in. thick and long enough to
project about 3 in. at each end over the table top
is required ; a piece the same length and about
4 in. wide and $1\frac{1}{2}$ in. thick is nailed or screwed to
the board as indicated in the illustrations. Before fixing the edge piece, a strong G-cramp
should be passed through a mortise made in it,
the lower end of the cramp being fitted into a
recess made in the underside of the planing board
so that the surface of the metal is a little below
that of the board. The lower end of the cramp
should have been previously drilled and counter-

Fig. 41.—Sketch showing Adjustable
Bench Stop

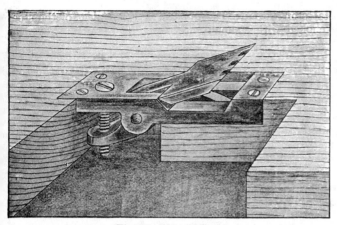

Fig. 43.—Metal Stop

kind a piece of work can be firmly held between them and flat on the top of the bench. When holding work in this manner one stop is put in the bench top and the other in the end vice. The two stops are placed the proper distance apart and when the end screw is tightened the work is gripped between them.

Fig. 43 shows a cheap and effective form of metal stop. The view is given partly in section so as to show how the stop is fitted and fixed to the top of the bench. The stop piece, shown open and inclined, is raised or lowered by means of a screwdriver inserted in the head of the large screw. The general action will be clearly understood from the illustration.

Another good form of a metal adjustable stop, known as Morrill's pattern, is shown by Fig. 44. The view is given partly in section so as to show the fitting of the stop to the bench top, ready for screwing. The illustration clearly shows the construction of the stop.

should fit tightly to the stop. The adjustment is made by simply striking the stop upwards or downwards with a mallet.

Fig. 38 is an improvement on the last-mentioned kind of stop. It is formed of a pair of wedges ; to keep them together and allow them to slide, a slot is made in the front portion so that the shank of a round-headed screw can work freely in it, the screw holding firmly in the back wedge. A washer, as shown, will prevent the head of the screw from catching in the slot.

An adjustable stop that has proved most satisfactory for general use is shown by Figs. 39, 40 and 41. A slot is made in the side of the bench, so that a ½-in. bolt can work freely in it, the bolt passing through a block and the stop which have been bored to receive it. A wing nut (with a washer at the back) is fitted to the screwed end of the bolt.

Fig. 42 is a sectional view of a spring stop. This kind is largely used by cabinet-makers, and especially for benches with end vices, as by using two stops of this

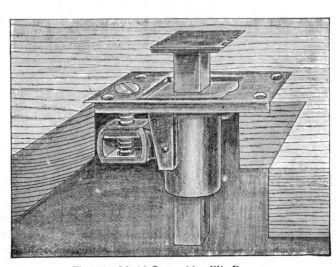

Fig. 44.—Metal Stop : Morrill's Pattern

The disadvantages of metal stops are that they are liable to get choked with

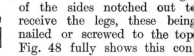

Fig. 45   Fig. 46

Figs. 45 and 46.—Front and End Elevations of Sawing Stool

sawdust and chips of wood, and, secondly, tools are often driven against them and their edges damaged.

SAWING AND OTHER STOOLS

Figs. 45 to 48 illustrate the ordinary strong form of stool which is very useful for sawing upon and for a great variety of other purposes. It is generally made of scantling, the legs being from 2 in. by 2 in.

Fig. 47.—Sketch of Sawing Stool

to 3 in. by 3 in. and the top 3 in. by 2 in. to 4 in. by 3 in. The legs should incline both ways as shown.

The upper ends of the legs of the stool should be cut as shown and the edges of the sides notched out to receive the legs, these being nailed or screwed to the top. Fig. 48 fully shows this construction.

The bracing piece at each end should be cut to fit and then nailed or screwed to the legs. The bottom ends of the legs should be scribed ("scribing" will be described in detail later), and then sawn to fit the floor. For general purposes red

Fig. 48.—Method of Fixing Legs of Sawing Stool

or white deal will be found a quite suitable material for stools.

Fig. 49 shows a somewhat similar stool but having a much broader top in which a holdfast or other form of cramp can be fixed (*see also* Fig. 1 on an earlier page). This cramp will allow of broad material being held and more conveniently sawn off, and will also be found serviceable for many other purposes.

Mortising Stools.—The making of small mortises can usually be done at the bench, but when a number of mortises of large size have to be made through material 3 in. to 5 in. wide they are more conveniently and quickly worked by using a mortising-stool, the ordinary kind of which is shown by Fig. 50. As will be seen, the edges of the legs run up and project above the bed, forming "horns," and work placed on the bed between these can be held firmly if desired by pushing in a wedge, hand-tight, between the work and the horns. The size of the stool and sizes of materials will vary according to requirements. The legs may be from 2 in. to 3 in. thick and 7 in. to 11 in. wide ; the bed may be 3 in. to 4 in. thick and 4 in. to 7 in. broad. The length may vary from 3 ft. to 5 ft. ; height to top of bed about 1 ft. 6 in.

Stool for Small Work.—Fig. 51 shows a light and handy form of stool suitable for small work. It can be made of boarding $\frac{3}{4}$ in. to $1\frac{1}{4}$ in. thick and 6 in. to 9 in. wide. To make it rigid, a block is fixed in each inner angle, also two struts, as clearly shown in the illustration.

Fig. 49.—Sawing Stool with Wide Top

Fig. 50.—A Type of Mortising Stool

Fig. 51.—Handy Stool for Small Work

Fig. 52.—Timber Rack

TIMBER RACKS

Fig. 52 shows a useful form of timber rack. It is made with vertical standards, from 3 in. by 3 in. to 4 in. by 3 in., mortised or bored to receive bearers. which may be pieces of round iron or old gas or steam piping (as shown in the upper part of Fig. 52), 1 in. to $1\frac{1}{2}$ in. in diameter ; or they may be of timber. 2 in. by 4 in. or 3 in. by 4 in., with tenons fitting into mortises as illustrated.

Fig. 53 shows a much handier, and at the same time stronger, kind of rack. Holes are cut into the brickwork about

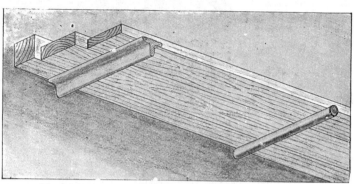

Fig. 53.—Timber Rack consisting of Metal Cantilevers

3 ft. to 4 ft. apart and 4½ in. to 6 in. deep ; pieces of T-iron, H-iron, or strong piping are inserted and held firmly in the wall by wedging it with pieces of tile or slate, and plastering with cement. It will be obvious that timber can be more quickly stacked or removed with this form of rack than with others.

Timber is better if stacked with small strips of wood (called " skids ") between the layers, as shown in the bottom part of Fig. 52, thus allowing the air to circulate all round the timber and enabling it to season better.

Sometimes boards are stacked edgeways, in which case the rack may consist of a horizontal bar with vertical strips fixed to it, the boards lying in the slots between the strips.

Tools for Measuring and Marking

RULES

THE common type of rule used by woodworkers is the four-fold "two-foot," of which two varieties are shown : Fig. 3, a cheap type ; Fig. 4, with brass edge plates to the joints and also with bevelled

tenths, etc., of an inch are seldom used. Measurements in rough carpentry are considered accurate enough if given in eighths, but very often the phrases " bare eighth " or " full eighth " are used when the measurement is slightly under or

Fig. 1.—Transferring Measurement from Rule

Fig. 2.—Accurate Measuring with Bevelled-edge Rule

edges. Figs. 5 and 7 show rules with slides for measuring board thicknesses, taking the depth of rebates, etc.

Woodwork measurements in subdivisions of an inch are given in eighths; twelfths,

above the division. Thus, if two carpenters were working together, one cutting whilst the other was fixing the work, one would observe to the other that he

19

wanted a piece of wood, say, " 2 ft. 6⅝ in. bare." In cabinet work, finer measurements are required, and they are commonly given to the nearest sixteenth, " bare " or " full " if necessary.

The ordinary sub-divisions of each inch in a four-fold rule are therefore eighths, but in some rules other divisions and scales are given, particularly in bevel-edged rules as Fig. 4. The pivot joints of good-class rules are often divided into degrees so that the legs of the rule can be set at any angle, rules being com-

monly used to do the work of adjustable bevels. (*See* Fig. 9.)

The bevel-edged portions of the rule are not only useful because of the scales on them but also because the bevel leads to greater accuracy by bringing the divisions of the rule nearer the surface to be marked, as illustrated in Figs. 1 and 2. Of course, the non-bevelled rule can be turned on its edge for accurate marking, as in Fig. 11.

A few years ago the two-fold " two-foot " (Figs. 7 or 9) was largely used,

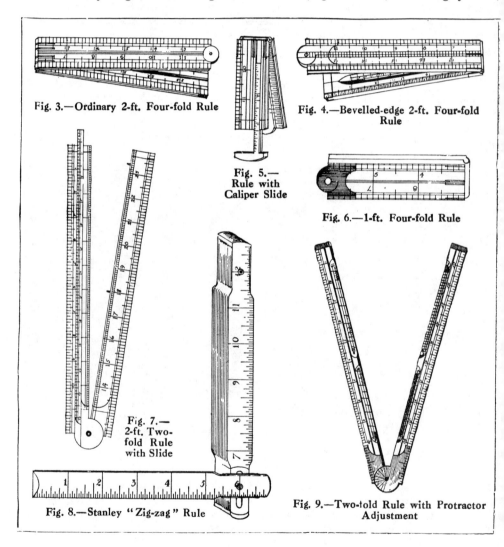

Fig. 3.—Ordinary 2-ft. Four-fold Rule

Fig. 4.—Bevelled-edge 2-ft. Four-fold Rule

Fig. 5.— Rule with Caliper Slide

Fig. 6.—1-ft. Four-fold Rule

Fig. 7.— 2-ft. Two-fold Rule with Slide

Fig. 8.—Stanley "Zig-zag" Rule

Fig. 9.—Two-fold Rule with Protractor Adjustment

but is now practically out of date owing to being clumsy for carrying about; however, it is convenient for bench work. On the whole, the ordinary four-fold "two-foot" with square edges is mostly used, and is found accurate enough for almost every purpose. Four-fold "three foots" or "four-foots" are preferred by some woodworkers. On the other

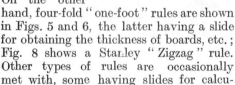

Fig. 10.—Measuring-off a Board for Length

hand, four-fold " one-foot " rules are shown in Figs. 5 and 6, the latter having a slide for obtaining the thickness of boards, etc.; Fig. 8 shows a Stanley " Zigzag " rule. Other types of rules are occasionally met with, some having slides for calcu-

little difficulty in using a rule, but one or two workshop hints will prove useful. There are two ways of measuring a length — roughly and accurately. In the rough method the rule is taken in one hand and stepped along the surface to be measured, say a board, the termination of the rule on the board being judged at each step by the eye, or marked by a rub with the brass end of the rule. Fig. 10 shows the more accurate method, the length of the rule being ticked off on the surface of the board and the process repeated until the end of the board is reached.

The thickness of a board is measured

Fig. 11.—Accurate Measuring with Rule on Edge

lating or drawing geometrical figures, but these are not of much use.

Using the Rule.—Of course, there is

Fig. 12.—Measuring Thickness of Board

as in Fig. 12. This method is better than using the end of the rule, as the corners get worn. The rule shown in Fig. 5 is also useful for getting the thickness of the boards, the method of using it being obvious. The slide rule in Fig. 7 is useful for obtaining the depth of grooves, etc. Fig. 13 shows a simple method of divid-

board and so that, say, figures 2 and 11 coincide with the edges of the board. Mark the board at figures 5 and 8 ; the board will thus be divided equally into

Fig. 13.—Dividing Board into Three Widths

Fig. 14.—Lining-down with Rule and Pencil

Fig. 15.—Taking Width of Recess with Pinch-rod—Two Laths, one sliding on the other

ing the width of a board into two or more equal parts. Suppose a board 7 in. wide is to be sawn into three strips. Lay the rule in a slanting direction across the

three parts. Lines parallel to the edges are then drawn as shown in Fig. 14.

Other methods of measuring and drawing parallel lines will be given later.

STRAIGHTEDGES

Straightedges are used in woodworking for testing and marking. They are of various sizes, a useful size for small jobs being about 3 ft. long, 2½ in. wide, and ¼ in. thick. Fig. 17 shows a typical example.

A straightedge may be tested for accuracy in three ways: (1) Hold another straightedge against it. (2) Place the straightedge on a flat surface and draw a line (see Fig. 18); turn the straightedge over

Fig. 16.—Sighting Straightedge for Accuracy

and compare the edge with the line, then, if they coincide, the straightedge is accurate. (3) Spy down the edge of the straightedge (Fig. 16). Note that a good straightedge should be straight " both " ways : (*a*) the flat surface should be straight and (*b*) the edge should be straight.

softer the pencil and the more H's the harder. The degrees are thus :—BB, B, HB, H, HH—Of late years a new degree F has been manufactured and is between HB and H. For general work F is the best—H being a little too hard and HB a little too soft. Of course any one of these three degrees is near enough for ordinary use.

Fig. 19 shows the ordinary method of sharpening the pencil, the length of the point being about an inch ; if too long, the lead is apt to break and if too short or dumpy inaccurate work is likely to result. A chisel is more useful than a pocket-knife for sharpening pencils.

Sometimes the pencil is sharpened to a chisel point as Fig. 20 ; this will last longer and give fine. lines, but is not so convenient to use, and cannot be conveniently used for writing.

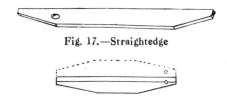

Fig. 17.—Straightedge

Fig. 18.—Testing Straightedge Geometrically

Fig. 21.—
Reel for
Chalk
Line

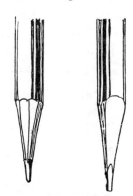

Figs. 19 and 20.—Shapes of
Pencil Points

PENCILS

Any ordinary pencil is suitable for woodwork. " Carpenters' pencils," which were largely used a few years ago, are oval in section and last longer than the ordinary type, but they are clumsy and do not assist accurate work.

Pencils are made in various degrees of hardness and those by good makers have the degree of hardness printed on them. The degrees vary in good makes from 6B to 6H—the more B's there are the

CHALK LINES

A chalk line is sometimes found **very** useful for marking long lengths. A cotton line is the best as it holds the chalk-dust better. A reel, as shown in Fig. 21, is often used to hold the line.

The line is chalked by fastening one end (or getting someone to hold it) and rubbing the line with a piece of chalk. To use the line (*see* Fig. 22) fasten one end at the correct point and pull the other end until the line is taut ; then, as near the middle

Fig. 22.—Chalk Line in Use

of the line as possible, pull the line a few inches away from the surface and let it go. A straight chalk line will thus be flicked on the surface. For use on white wood, a " chalk line " may be charged with black lead.

In Fig. 22 a short line is shown being marked in order to illustrate the method clearly.

PINCH ROD

Fig. 15 shows the method of obtaining the width of an opening by using a "pinch rod." The latter consists of two laths (or rules) which are held so that they touch each side of the opening and are then gripped together.

MARKING KNIVES AND AWLS

For bench work, and any work demanding accuracy, a marking knife is preferable to a pencil. Fig. 23 shows a usual type, one end being chisel shaped and the other pointed, the latter for ordinary marking, and the former for cutting into the surface of the wood a little, as in tenoning and. dovetailing. Fig. 24 shows a marking knife with a handle which can be gripped better and is more convenient to use, while Fig. 25 shows a handled marking awl.

Fig. 23 represents the type in general use and is good enough for all practical purposes.

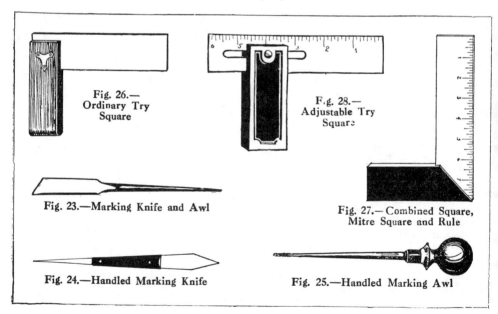

Fig. 26.—Ordinary Try Square

Fig. 28.—Adjustable Try Square

Fig. 23.—Marking Knife and Awl

Fig. 27.—Combined Square, Mitre Square and Rule

Fig. 24.—Handled Marking Knife

Fig. 25.—Handled Marking Awl

SQUARES

The most commonly used square in woodworking is the type shown in Fig. 26

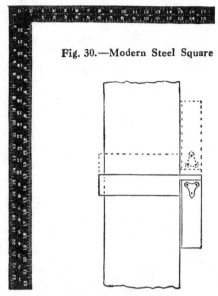

Fig. 30.—Modern Steel Square

Fig. 29.—Testing Try Square

with the blade 6 in. long, the blade being of steel and the stock usually of ebony lined with brass on the inside face to prevent wearing. This square is made in various sizes, the 12 in. being largely used.

Fig. 27 shows a mitre square and rule combined ; this square can be used for lines at 90° or 45°. An adjustable try square is shown in Fig. 28.

Steel squares (Fig. 30) are nowadays used largely by woodworkers, but chiefly on roof work and to a lesser degree in staircasing. Fig. 31 shows how this square is used for getting the length of a rafter when the span and rise are given. In the illustration the span would be 16 ft. and the rise 6 ft., and the length of the rafter the distance between the points on the legs of the square, or 10 ft. If a fence were now screwed on the square lineable with A C, the square would be suitable for marking the top and bottom bevels for the rafters (see Fig. 33 and 34).

3—N E.

Ellis's patent steel square (Fig. 32) has a metal adjustable fence and other improvements.

Crenelated squares are useful for setting-out work, particularly carpentry. They have a series of notches in the blade, as illustrated clearly in Fig. 35. A pencil or marker is placed in a crenelation (or notch) and the square glided along the timber, thus making a mark parallel to the edge of the timber.

Wooden squares of a larger size than the metal type are often very useful for squaring frames, etc. A handy size for a square of this type is with the blade about 2 ft. long. The illustration (Fig. 36) shows the square with blade and stock pulled apart to show the joint. They are usually made of baywood (mahogany).

A square may be tested for accuracy as in Fig. 29. Select a board having a straight edge and, holding the stock firmly

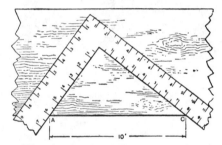

Fig. 31.—Obtaining Length of Rafter with Steel Square

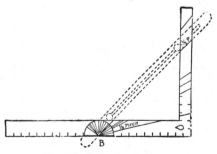

Fig. 32.—Ellis Steel Square

against the edge of the board, draw a line across the board ; turn the square over and if the edge of the square coincides with this line then the square is accurate. If not, draw another line, and the amount of inaccuracy will be half the angle betwee.' the two lines. In

of course, the under edge must not be used because that will remain out of square. When a metal square gets out

Fig. 33.—Adjusting Gauge of Steel Square

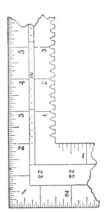

Fig. 35.—Crenelated Steel Square

Fig. 36.—Construction of Wooden Square for Framing-up

Fig. 37.—The "3, 4 and 5" Rule of Constructing and Testing Squares and Right Angles

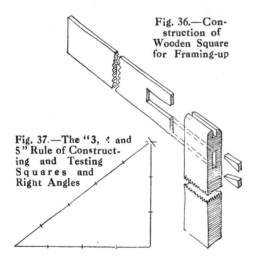

Fig. 34.—Marking Rafter Bevels with Steel Square

the case of a wooden square that has been accidentally knocked inaccurate, the top edge of the blade may be " shot " with the trying-plane until correct, when,

of truth (with dropping on the ground usually) the best remedy is to buy a new one.

Another method of testing squares,

or of drawing square angles, is by means of the " 3, 4 and 5 rule " (Fig. 37). Set off four units (inches, feet, or any other unit) along the line ; strike off three units from one end to intersect five units set off from the other end. A triangle is equal to the square of the hypotenuse," that is, $3^2 + 4^2 = 5^2$. This rule is very useful for large angles.

Figs. 38 and 39 show the method of using the square for marking lines on timber. The chief point to be watched is that

Fig. 38.—First Position in Using Try Square

Fig. 40.—Testing Square Edges with Try Square

Fig. 39.—Second Position in Using Try Square

Fig. 41.—Using Adjustable Bevel

thus obtained with sides in the proportion of 3 : 4 : 5. This must be a right-angled triangle because " the squares of two sides of a right-angle triangle must be the stock of the try-square should be kept tightly against the edge of the timber.

In testing a piece of timber for squareness the try-square is held as Fig. 40.

Keep the stock tightly against the flat side of the timber—do not use the stock against the edge. Hold the timber to-

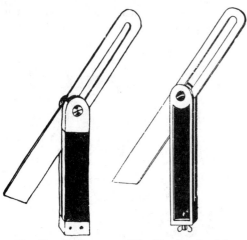

Fig. 42.—Ordinary Adjustable Bevel

Fig. 43.—Bevel with Double-wing Nut

bench. Apply the square at intervals of about 1 foot, or glide the square along the timber.

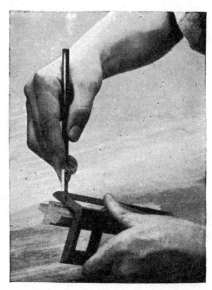

Fig. 45.—Using Square Template on Glazing Bar when Use of Try Square is Inconvenient

Fig. 47.—Using Mitre Template in Paring a Mitre

Fig. 46.—Mitre Template

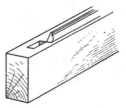

Fig. 48.—Mitre in Joint-making for which Mitre Template is used

Fig. 44.—Bevel with Single-wing Nut for Tightening

wards the light, as shown, for small work ; in this way the smallest inaccuracy can be seen. When testing large pieces of timber one end can be rested on the

BEVELS

Bevels are necessary for marking and testing angles that are not right angles.

The ordinary type of bevel is shown in Fig. 42, the blade being slotted so that its length can be adjusted for various purposes and also so that the blade will shut into the stock when not in use.

The blade is secured in the required position by tightening the screw with a screwdriver. The method of adjusting correct the bevel is screwed up tightly. Fig. 43 shows a wing nut for tightening up, the nut being at the end of the stock. Fig. 44 shows a bevel with a single-wing nut instead of the usual screw.

For rough work a bevel may be dispensed with and the rule used instead ; the rule is very handy and quickly set,

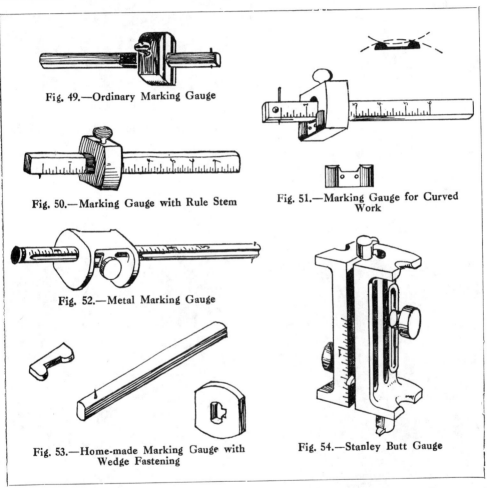

Fig. 49.—Ordinary Marking Gauge

Fig. 50.—Marking Gauge with Rule Stem

Fig. 51.—Marking Gauge for Curved Work

Fig. 52.—Metal Marking Gauge

Fig. 53.—Home-made Marking Gauge with Wedge Fastening

Fig. 54.—Stanley Butt Gauge

the bevel is first to set it to the correct angle ; then tighten the screw and compare with the desired angle. It will usually be found that the bevel has altered a little in screwing up. The blade should therefore be tapped gently on the bench and the bevel again compared with the angle desired. When but is easily knocked out of the correct angle and is therefore unsuitable where accuracy is required.

TEMPLATES

A template in woodworking can mean either a pattern (say, of thin wood or paper) or a tool-guiding appliance used in marking or cutting angles. The latter kind of template includes the "mitre template" and the "square template."

Fig. 46 shows the ordinary brass mitre template which is used for mitreing and scribing joints, while Fig. 47 shows it in use. Care should be taken not to chisel too much off the joint—beginners have a tendency to do this. Take a little off at a time and gently tap the template backwards. But even at the finish leave the joint a little full here because this is the most noticeable part of the joint and it will easily crush up a little. Remember you can always take a little more off but you cannot put a little more on. Fig. 48 shows part of a mitred-and-tenoned joint showing where the end of the moulding has been cut with the aid of the mitre template.

Templates are also made in wood, but brass is better, as the chisel is bound to slip a little into the wood template occasionally, and thus destroy its accuracy.

Square templates are chiefly used for joiners, but it is not essential for most woodworkers. Fig. 45 shows the square template being used to square a line round a moulded sash bar.

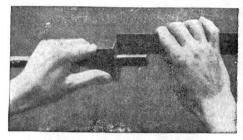

Fig. 55.—Setting Marking Gauge

Templates are used for dovetailing, etc., and mitre blocks and boxes are also forms of mitre templates ; all these will be dealt with in later chapters.

GAUGES

Marking Gauges.—Gauges are used for marking parallel lines. The simplest

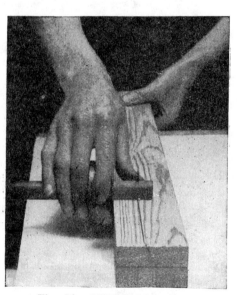

Figs. 56 and 57.—Holding and Using Marking Gauge : Note Disposition of Fingers

marking as in the case of window bars or other pieces of wood where it is awkward to use a square. It is a useful tool

type is the marking gauge, varieties of which are shown in Figs. 49 to 54. The ordinary workshop type (Fig. 49) consists of four parts : stem, head, fastening screw, and marker. The stem and head are usually of beech and the screw of

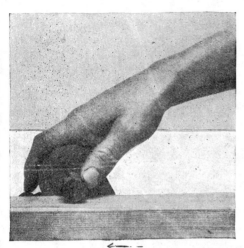

Fig. 58.—First Position of Marking Gauge : Arrow shows Direction of Stroke

boxwood. Various methods of fastening the head to the stem are in use (see Fig. 53 for another method) but the screw is the best. The marker is simply a pointed bit of steel.

In setting the gauge it is taken in the left hand (Fig. 55), the screw loosened, and the head adjusted to the correct distance from the point by using the rule as shown. After the screw is tightened the gauge should again be tested ; it will probably have moved a little in tightening, when, if so, the head can be shifted a slight amount by tapping the end of the stem on the bench.

It is very often desired to gauge a line down the centre of a board. The obvious method is to measure the board, divide by two, and set the gauge ; this takes too long and is not so accurate as from the description it would seem to be. Instead, guess half the width of the board, set the gauge accordingly and mark the distance from each side ; two points near the centre of the board will thus be obtained and the gauge is then set accurately mid-way between them.

The method of holding the gauge is

shown in Figs. 56 and 57. Hold it in the right hand with the thumb near the top of the stem, the first finger on the head, and the rest of the fingers on the stem. The chief thing to bear in mind is that the head of the gauge must be pressed continually against the edge of the timber from which you are gauging. Do not let the marker dig deeply into the wood ; this is avoided by giving the gauge a slight rotary movement as shown in Figs. 58 and 59. At the beginning of the stroke the stem should be touching the wood at its far corner ; as the gauge is pushed forward the point should be gradually pressed down into the wood, as shown in Fig. 59.

Fig. 50 shows a gauge with a scale on the stem. This is occasionally an advantage, but for good work simply setting the head to this scale is not accurate enough.

Fig. 51 shows a gauge with a metal plate attached to the face of the head ; this enables the gauge to be used for either concave or convex work, as shown in the small sketch. Note also that this gauge has a small screw in the stem for adjusting the marking point.

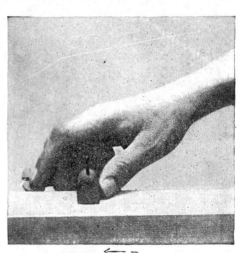

Fig. 59.—Final Position of Marking Gauge

A metal marking gauge is shown in Fig. 52 ; this has a point marker at one end and a roller marker at the other.

The latter makes a fine mark, and is useful across the grain and in knotty timber.

A home-made gauge is shown in Fig. 53, and in this a wedge is used for fastening, the wedge being made of such shape and size that it cannot fall out when the gauge is put together.

The " Stanley Butt Gauge " shown in Fig. 54 is a special type used chiefly in America for fitting butt hinges. The gauge has two bars ; one bar has two points on it, one for gauging the edge of the door and the other for gauging the door casing, in which second case the end of the gauge head is used as a guide. The marking point on the other bar is used for gauging the thickness of the hinge. This gauge may be carried conveniently in the pocket.

Cutting Gauges. —This type of gauge (Fig. 62) is similar to a marking gauge except that it has a cutter instead of a marker. It is especially suitable for dovetailing, where it is an advantage to cut into the wood a little. Thin wood may be cut into strips, or small rebates may be made with a cutting gauge in firstclass condition. The cutter is usually held in the stem by a small wedge.

Fig. 61 shows a combined marking, cutting, and pencil gauge. The last named is very useful for chamfering, because if an ordinary marking gauge were used the marks would be left on the timber after the chamfers were made.

Mortise Gauges. —A mortise gauge (Fig. 63) is similar to a marking gauge, but it has two points for marking two lines simultaneously. This, of course, saves

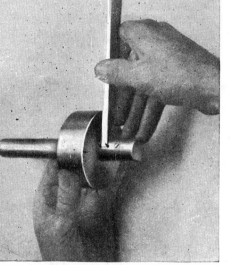

Fig. 60.—Setting Mortise Gauge to Width of Chisel

much time when marking mortise and tenon joints. One point is attached to the stem as in a marking gauge and the other point is attached to a slide that works in the stem, and is adjusted by a screw at the bottom of the stem. Either a thumb screw or a flush screw is used, it being preferable to have the screw flush with the bottom of the stem (Fig. 63), as a projecting screw is liable to get out of order. Fig. 66 shows an inferior type of mortise gauge in which the slide is actuated by simply pulling or pushing it to the desired position ; this is more difficult to set accurately than the preceding types.

Fig. 60 shows how the mortise gauge is held when setting for mortising. The two points are adjusted to the correct distance apart by holding the mortising chisel against them. The head is then screwed up at the correct distance from them. In marking a mortise in the centre of a piece of timber the points should be set to the width of the chisel, the head " loosely tightened " as near the required position as can be guessed, and the points pricked into the timber from each side. Finally the gauge is adjusted by tapping slightly on the bench, and the screw in the head is then tightened up.

COMPASSES, DIVIDERS AND TRAMMELS

Compasses and Dividers. —The " compasses " used in woodworking are really dividers. Fig. 67 shows the usual shape and Fig. 68 illustrates a pattern with sensitive adjustment.

Fig. 61.—Combined Marking and Cutting
Gauge

Fig. 62.—Ordinary Cutting Gauge

Fig. 63.—An Ordinary Type of Mortise
Gauge: Flush Screw at End of Stem

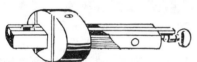

Fig. 64.—Mortise Gauge with Projecting
Wing Nut

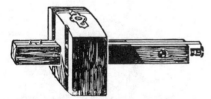

Fig. 65.—Square-stock Mortise Gauge
with Projecting Screw

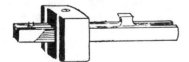

Fig. 66.—Mortise Gauge without Fine
Adjustment

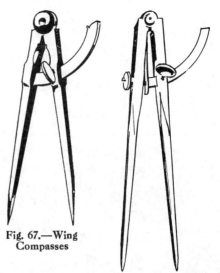

Fig. 67.—Wing
Compasses

Fig. 68.—Wing Compasses
with Sensitive Adjustment

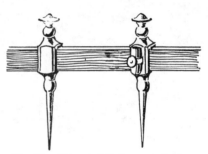

Fig. 69.—Trammel Points attached to
Lath

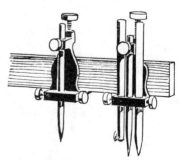

Fig. 70.—Stanley Adjustable
Trammel Points

Compasses are used for drawing circles and other geometrical work, but the most common use to which they are put in practical work is scribing. Fig. 71 shows a piece of skirting that has to be fitted to an uneven floor. The skirting board is loosely nailed into position (or otherwise temporarily held) and the compasses vertical scribing distance constant, it is better to rest the wing on the floor when using; if this is done and the compasses kept vertical a mark will be made on the board at a constant distance from the floor. The skirting is then chopped or planed to this line, when it will be found to fit the uneven surface of the floor accurately.

Fig. 71.—Scribing Skirting Board to Floor

Fig. 74.—Wait's Attachments Forming a Trammel

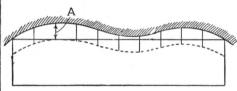

Fig. 72.—Scribing by the Spiling Method

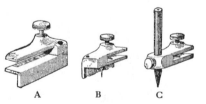

Fig. 73.—Wait's Rule Attachments

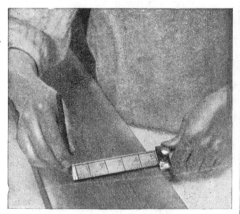

Fig. 75.—Wait's Attachment in Use for Lining-up a Board (attachment should be in close contact with edge of board)

set to the greatest width of the gap between the floor and the board. The compasses are then drawn along with one point on the floor while the other marks the board. In order to keep the

This method of scribing is used in numerous cases where linings, framings, plinths, etc., have to be fitted to uneven surfaces. Care should always be taken that the compasses should be set and held in the precise direction that the board has to be moved up to fit into its final position; this is more clear in Fig. 72. Sometimes

Wait's rule attachments (Fig. 73) are useful for drawing circles and parallel lines. Fig. 73 (A) is for use on a rule

Fig. 76.—Ordinary Spirit Level

Fig. 78.—Spirit-level Tubes: Correct and Incorrect Settings.

Fig. 77.—Spirit Level with Side Openings

Fig. 79.—Section through Spirit Level

the compasses are dispensed with and parallel lines are drawn; along each of these parallel lines the scribing distance A (Fig. 72) is set. A freehand line through the points thus obtained will show the wood that must be removed. This method is sometimes called "spiling," a small strip of wood the length of A being used.

Trammel points are used for drawing large circles. A pair of these are shown in Fig. 69; they need only be screwed to a strip of wood at the correct distance apart. Fig. 70 shows a pair of Stanley trammel points; both points are ad-

Fig. 80.—Using Spirit Level with Side Openings above Operator's Head

justable for height, and one end has a pencil and a roller marker as well as a trammel point. A trammel for drawing ellipses will be dealt with later.

as a gauge; it is shown in use at Fig. 75. (B) Fig. 73 is attached to the rule and forms a centre point; (c) Fig. 73 is to hold a pencil. The last two attachments are shown in use in Fig. 74; a bradawl often replaces the small point shown at B (Fig. 73).

SPIRIT LEVELS, PLUMBS, ETC.

Spirit Levels are used for testing horizontals. When purchasing a spirit level avoid getting a fancy or flimsy article. The chief points of a good level are: (a) it should be as long as possible without being inconvenient; (b) it should be strongly made; (c) it should have a quick bubble. The reasons for these three points should be obvious; the longer the level the more accurate the work; it should be strongly made to withstand occasional knocks—a metal plate along the bottom is an advantage; a slow bubble is not as accurate and takes longer to use than a quick bubble. Fig. 76 shows a cheap level; its chief fault is that it has no openings in the side so that the bubble can be seen when the level is held high up. This seems a slight matter, but in practice it is a great inconvenience not to be able to use the level at the height of the eyes or even above the head. Fig. 77 shows a better type with side openings.

A section of the level showing the tube in position is shown in Fig. 79. The tube is of glass and is nearly filled with methylated spirits. The bubble is the amount the tube is *short of being full;*

this means that when the tube is tilted the spirit runs to the bottom and the *bubble runs to the top*. Beginners have difficulty in accounting for the latter phenomenon, but if it is not understood a level cannot be used quickly and satisfactorily.

Sometimes the tube gets broken, but it can easily be replaced with a little

tube. Press the tube gently into the plaster until the bubble comes to rest exactly in the centre. Note that the tube is slightly curved in length, and take care to fix it with the round or convex side upwards. When the tube seems to be correctly placed, mark round the level with a pencil on to the board ; reverse the position of the level, keeping

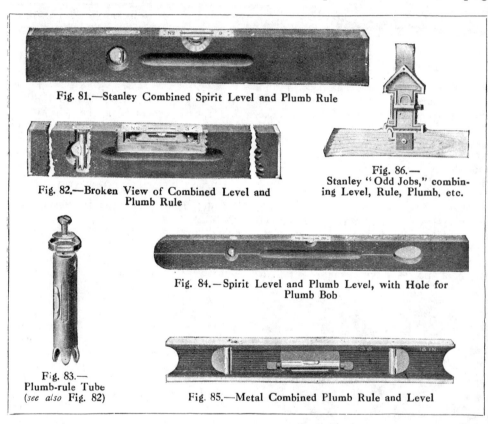

Fig. 81.—Stanley Combined Spirit Level and Plumb Rule

Fig. 82.—Broken View of Combined Level and Plumb Rule

Fig. 86.—Stanley " Odd Jobs," combining Level, Rule, Plumb, etc.

Fig. 84.—Spirit Level and Plumb Level, with Hole for Plumb Bob

Fig. 83.—Plumb-rule Tube (*see also* Fig. 82)

Fig. 85.—Metal Combined Plumb Rule and Level

care. Tubes (Fig. 78) can be bought separately from local dealers.

In fixing a new tube proceed as follows : Set a piece of smooth wood level on the bench or in the vice, testing it by means of a level of proved accuracy. Unscrew the plate off the top of the level to be repaired and scrape away the plaster-of-paris in which the broken tube was embedded. Mix some fresh plaster-of-paris with water and put a little in the groove (chiefly at the ends) that holds the

to the pencil lines. Place the top plate in position and see whether the bubble is correct with it. If everything is all right let the plaster set a minute or two and then screw the top plate down.

In using the level greater accuracy is obtained if it is used on the top of a parallel straightedge, particularly if the surface to be levelled is rough or not straight.

The Stanley Company manufactures numerous patterns of spirit levels ; for exampie, Fig. 81 shows a combined spirit level and plumb rule, the small vertical tube being used for " plumbing " vertical work. Fig. 82 is a broken view of this rule showing how the levels are fixed in position. Both level and plumb tubes are made so that they can be ad-

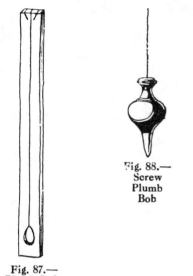

Fig. 88.—
Screw
Plumb
Bob

Fig. 87.—
Plumb Rule

justed ; notice the small springs under the level tube, which can be screwed down at each end and any slight inaccuracy that arises in the level thus corrected. The vertical tube (shown enlarged in Fig. 83) is adjusted by means

of the set-screw and the slotted cup. Notice the slight convex curve on the tube glass.

A level with plumb level and hole for a plumb bob is shown by Fig. 84, and a metal combined plumb rule and level by Fig. 85. Stanley fittings for use with levels include level sights for levelling at a distance and pitch adjusters for setting surfaces to any desired inclination. The Stanley " Odd Jobs " tool No. 1, illustrated in Fig. 86, combines level, rule, plumb, gauge, etc.

A Plumb Rule and Bob can easily be made. Fig. 87 shows a common design. A convenient size is 3 ft. 6 in. by 3 in. by $\frac{5}{8}$ in. Three saw cuts are made in the top for fastening the string. Lines are gauged down the centre of the rule and a hole formed near the bottom for the bob to swing into. A bob may be made by casting one in a sand mould and then boring a fine hole through it for the string. Turned lead bobs can be bought. Fig. 88 shows an iron or brass bob with the top to screw off so that the string can be threaded through it and the top screwed on again. They are neater in appearance than lead bobs.

" Plumb up " means vertical or pointing to the centre of the earth ; " level " means tangential to the earth's surface, and therefore, at any point, a plumb line is at right angles to a level line.

In a later chapter detailed instructions on making a spirit level will be given.

Saws and Sawing

The Cross-cut Saw.—Hand saws may be divided into two classes, cross-cut saws and rip saws. As the names imply, the cross-cut saw is for cutting across, and the rip saw for cutting or ripping, with or along, the grain.

A cross-cut saw is shown in Fig. 1. The blade is of steel and varies in thickness, diminishing towards the end and the back, while the usual length is 26 in. A tapered blade is lighter, easier to handle, and clears itself in the saw kerf. The thickness varies, as shown by the numbers in Fig. 3, the smaller the number the thicker being the blade at that part; "E" means easy or bare and "T" tight or full.

Usually the back of the saw is straight (*see* Fig. 2), but the skew-back shape as in Fig. 1 is very common.

The shape of the teeth is shown at Figs. 7 to 9. Such a tooth-shape has been found to be of the best proportions for biting into the wood and yet sawing smoothly. The shape shown in Fig. 5 would cause the saw to stick and jump, and would make the sawing difficult and dangerous. On the other hand, the shape shown in Fig. 6 would not bite enough. Fig. 4 shows a mean between the two.

If the saw simply consisted of a blade with teeth stamped out as shown in Fig. 7 the saw could hardly be used at all, because (*a*) the "point" of each tooth would be an *edge* and therefore would not cut the fibres easily, and (*b*) the saw "kerf" (the cut made by the saw) would be so narrow that the saw blade would " bind " or rub on its sides.

If the teeth are filed on the slope they will appear as in Fig. 8. *Points* are thus formed on the teeth instead of *edges*, thus enabling the saw to cut better. If, next, the teeth are pressed alternately to one side and then to the other, as in the plan Fig. 9, the teeth will be wider at the cutting points than the thickness of the saw. A wide saw kerf will thus be made, through which the saw blade can pass easily to and fro. This bending of the teeth is known as " setting " the saw.

If any hard metal point (a nail) is dragged across a piece of timber a scratch results. Each tooth of a saw is like a sharp nail; *see* Fig. 12, which shows a piece of wood with a row of nails knocked into it and bent alternately to each side to demonstrate the " set " of a saw. It is obvious that if the nail points are sharp and if this instrument is dragged backwards and forwards across a piece of wood it will ultimately make a groove, or possibly cut the timber in two. In some such way the saw acts. Fig. 13 is an enlarged section of the saw kerf showing how the points of the teeth scratch their way through the wood while the other parts of the teeth remove the centre portion of the kerf. The amount of " set " on the saw determines the amount of clearance. More set is required for soft woods than for hard woods, and more for wet woods than for dry woods. A saw for use on wet soft wood should therefore have considerable set.

Cross-cut hand-saw teeth are usually about six to the inch. The hardened and tempered steel blade of the saw should admit of being bent so that the tail nearly touches the handle, and of springing back straight so that there is no buckle in the saw. Any buckling of the blade may be easily seen by looking along the edge of the teeth.

The saw handle should be of a good

workers guide the saw with the knuckle instead of the thumb.

Beware of two mistakes in sawing: (a) using short strokes, (b) pressing on the saw. Use as long strokes as possible; do not saw too quickly; do not press on the saw, but rather let it work by its own weight. If the saw is forced, it will require harder work and will be more difficult to guide. Simply pull the

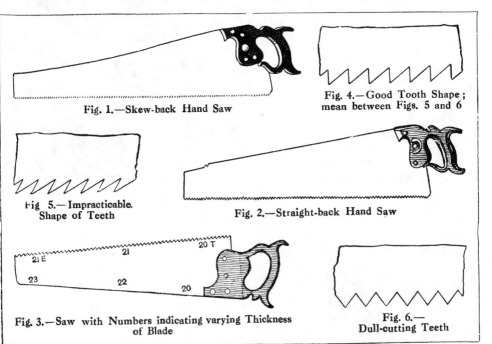

Fig. 1.—Skew-back Hand Saw

Fig. 4.—Good Tooth Shape; mean between Figs. 5 and 6

Fig 5.—Impracticable. Shape of Teeth

Fig. 2.—Straight-back Hand Saw

Fig. 3.—Saw with Numbers indicating varying Thickness of Blade

Fig. 6.— Dull-cutting Teeth

shape for gripping firmly and easily, and should be attached to the blade by saw screws. If the blade ever becomes loose these screws should be tightened up with a brace and a forked bit (see Fig. 38 on a later page).

Using Cross-cut Saws.—The most difficult part in sawing is starting the saw. Guide the saw by putting the thumb against it as in Figs. 10 and 11. Take two or three up strokes to get a start. If you try to start by a down stroke there will be a danger of the saw jumping and damaging the work or cutting your finger. This method of starting the saw is applicable to all varieties of saws. Some

saw slowly backwards and push it slowly forwards in long strokes. This is the easiest method, and the safer, more accurate, and quicker in the long run.

Fig. 15 shows the method of sawing the end off a board—the latter resting on sawing stools, etc. The waste piece of board is supported by the left hand to prevent it from splitting a piece off the board. As the board is being cut this " short end " should be held in such a way that the kerf is widened, thus assisting the saw and preventing it from binding.

Sometimes a long board has to be cross

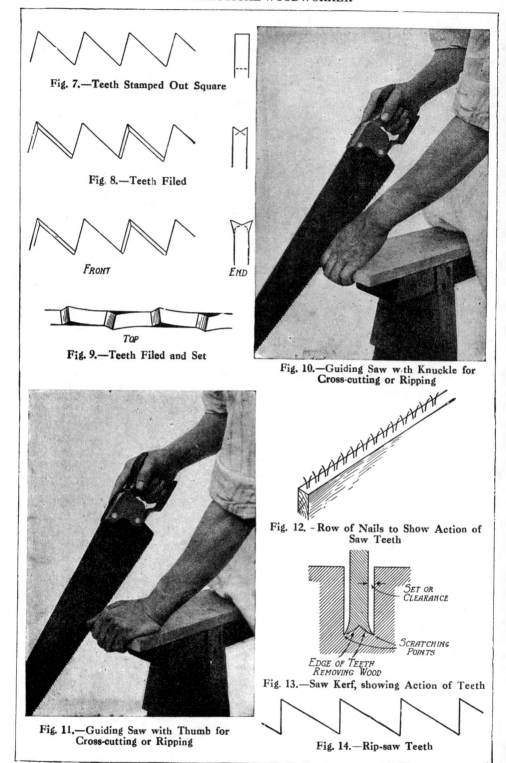

Fig. 7.—Teeth Stamped Out Square

Fig. 8.—Teeth Filed

Front

End

Top

Fig. 9.—Teeth Filed and Set

Fig. 10.—Guiding Saw with Knuckle for Cross-cutting or Ripping

Fig. 12. - Row of Nails to Show Action of Saw Teeth

Set or Clearance

Scratching Points

Edge of Teeth Removing Wood

Fig. 13.—Saw Kerf, showing Action of Teeth

Fig. 11.—Guiding Saw with Thumb for Cross-cutting or Ripping

Fig. 14.—Rip-saw Teeth

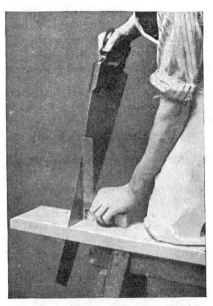

Fig. 15.—Method of Sawing End off Board to P.event Splitting

Fig. 16.—Testing Squareness of Cutting

Fig 17 —Cross-cutting Long Board near Middle

Fig. 18. Sawing End off Long Board : Only one Trestle available

cut in the middle (Fig. 17). In this case it is better if someone holds the work at one side of the saw. Notice that if the assistant drops the board slightly or lets it move towards the worker, the saw kerf will partly close and the saw will bind.

Fig. 18 shows the method of sawing the end off a long board when only one sawing stool is available.

The Rip Saw.—This saw is for cutting in the direction of the grain. Of course, a cross-cut saw can do this, but a rip

Using Rip Saw.—Three methods of using the rip saw are shown in Figs. 23 25 and 26. Fig. 23 shows the usual method; follow the same instructions as for cross-cutting. Fig. 25 shows a method of rip sawing favoured by cabinet-makers chiefly. Fig. 26 shows the method of ripping a piece of wood held in the vice; this method is, of course, only suitable for short lengths. Figs. 20 and 24 show two common faults.

Fig. 19.—Front View showing Saw Blade and Elbow in Same Plane

Fig. 20.—Defective Sawing: Saw Too Upright

saw does it more rapidly, as the teeth are especially designed for cutting with the grain. The shape of the teeth is shown in Fig. 14, the front of the tooth being vertical. There are usually four teeth to the inch, and the length (28 in.) is greater than that of the cross-cut. Otherwise the general appearance of the two is much the same.

Owing to the use of machinery, rip saws are now little used and the average craftsman does not possess one, the cross-cut being employed for all kinds of rough sawing.

The Panel Saw.—This saw has come more and more into use of late years, owing largely to the introduction of machinery and machine sawing for large stuff. It is the most useful all-round saw that a woodworker possesses. It can be used for cross-cutting, ripping, tenoning, and most other purposes. If a man can only afford one saw, this is the saw to get. Though it cannot be said to be as quick as a rip saw for ripping big stuff, or as a cross-cut saw for cross-cutting, or as handy as a tenon saw for small work, it will do the work of all three

Fig. 21.—First Position of Saw when Starting

Fig. 22.—End of First Up-stroke

Fig. 23.—Correct Slope for Saw

Fig. 24.—A Common Defect : Using Saw at too little slope

and leave the cut finer than the " rip " or the " cross-cut." Its length is usually 22 in., with teeth about the same size as those of the tenon saw.

Tenon Saws.—This saw (Fig. 27) gets its name from the fact that it is largely used for sawing tenons, for which purpose it is especially suitable owing to its length, size of its teeth, thinness of blade, etc. Along the top edge of the blade is

the top block of the hook with the left hand and firmly held (*see* Fig. 37). A piece of timber insecurely held when sawing means time wasted, inaccurate work, buckled saws, and possibly cut fingers.

Fig. 34 shows a wider type of bench hook. Owing to the top piece stopping off short, there is less likelihood of mutilating the bench with the saw.

In using the tenon saw, one or two

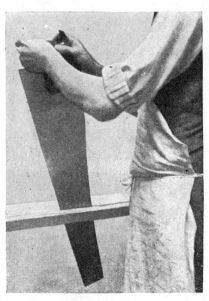

Fig. 25.—Method of Ripping largely used by Cabinet-makers

Fig. 26.—Ripping Short Length in Vice

a strip (called the " back ") of grooved steel or brass into which the blade fits ; this gives strength and rigidity to the thin blade, thus enabling greater accuracy in sawing to be obtained. The tenon saw is often known as a " back " saw for obvious reasons.

Using the Tenon Saw.—This saw is used chiefly for bench work. In sawing, a bench hook is often used for holding the timber. The bench hook may be cut out. of the solid (Fig. 32) or made by nailing two small blocks on a strip of wood about 10 in. long ; see Fig. 33. When sawing, the bench hook is hooked against the front of the bench and the timber to be sawn is pressed against

up strokes should first be made. Start sawing with the saw inclined at about 30 degrees (Fig. 35) and during sawing gradually bring the handle down until the saw is level and the strokes are level (Fig. 36).

Tenon saws are 12 in. to 18 in. in length, the usual size in use being a 14 in. The number of teeth to the inch is about ten.

Adjustable " back " or tenon saws are occasionally met with ; see Fig. 31. Both the top and bottom edges of the blade have teeth, and the steel rib can be adjusted anywhere down the blade, thus adapting the saw for any depth of cut. These saws do not seem to have "caught on," and the trained craftsmen seldom possesses one.

Dovetail saws (Fig. 28) are similar in shape to a tenon saw but smaller—10 in.

is the usual size—and with finer teeth, about 12 to the inch. Usually, as shown, the handle is not closed : the shape of the handle and the size are the only features

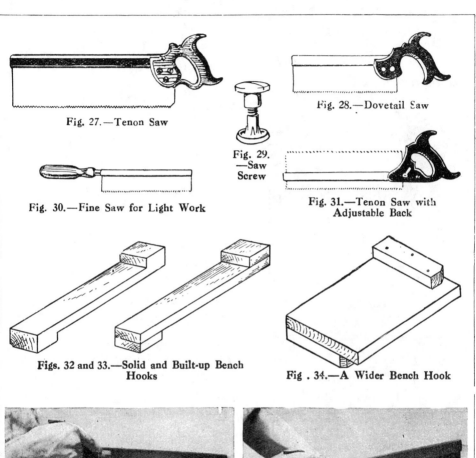

Fig. 27.—Tenon Saw

Fig. 28.—Dovetail Saw

Fig. 29.—Saw Screw

Fig. 30.—Fine Saw for Light Work

Fig. 31.—Tenon Saw with Adjustable Back

Figs. 32 and 33.—Solid and Built-up Bench Hooks

Fig. 34.—A Wider Bench Hook

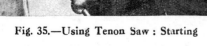

Fig. 35.—Using Tenon Saw : Starting

Fig. 36.—Tenon-sawing : the Cutting continued

that distinguish it from a tenon saw. As the name implies, a dovetail saw is used chiefly for cutting dovetails and for other small work.

Fig. 37.—Using Bench Hook for Sawing

Fig. 38.—Tightening Saw Screw with Brace and Forked Bit

The handles of all the foregoing types of saws are fastened to the blades by saw screws. If the handle becomes a

little loose it can be remedied by tightening these screws. Some of these screws have to be tightened by means of a forked brace-bit (*see* Fig. 38). A better type of saw screw that can be tightened with an ordinary screwdriver is shown in Fig. 29.

A small hardwood-handled light brass-backed saw is shown in Fig. 30. It is suitable for small work, such as cutting beading.

The Bow Saw.—This tool is not so largely used as formerly owing to the use of band saws ; it is used for cutting shaped work by hand. The saw (Fig. 39) may be bought, or can be readily made as given in the details in Fig. 41.

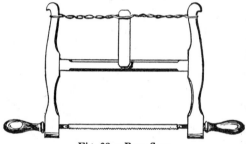

Fig. 39.—Bow Saw

Fig. 41 shows a form of bow saw which has stood the test of everyday workshop use for fifty years, and is still as useful as ever. By redrawing the squares shown at the left-hand side the worker should easily get the correct shape for the arms. The bow saw frame is made of beech, the arms being of $1\frac{1}{8}$-in. thick stuff at the handles, tapering to $\frac{5}{8}$ in. full at the top ends, all sharp edges being rounded off. The centre bar is of $\frac{3}{4}$-in. square stuff. The right-hand centre-bar joint is shown in section to explain clearly how the pivoting joint is formed. The bar shoulders, instead of being cut square, are rounded as at A to suit the corresponding hollows, which are cut out right across the inner sides of the arms ; also, the bar tenons are merely stump-tenons $\frac{3}{8}$ in. or so long, rounded from the extreme ends to the shoulders as at B, and they are made a working fit for the shallow sockets in

Fig. 40.—Using Bow Saw

Bow-saw handles and blades can be obtained separately from tool dealers. The saw when in use is stretched tightly by means of the tourniquet arrangement; if the blade is not stretched when in use it easily breaks, besides being difficult to saw with. The blade should be slackened when not in use.

Fig. 40 shows the bow saw in use. If a closed pattern (like a keyhole) has to be cut out in a piece of timber the blade has to be unfastened, inserted through the starting hole bored in the timber, and again fastened. This is troublesome, and therefore a keyhole saw (Figs. 42 and 44) or a compass saw (Fig. 43) is often used. The former is often

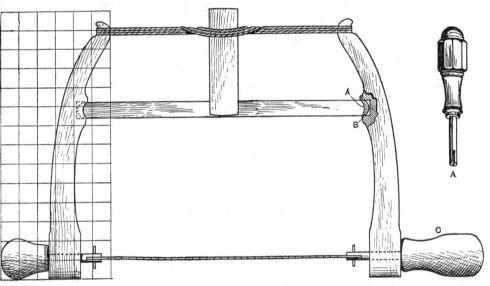

Fig. 41.—Details of Home-made Bow Saw; A, Alternative Design for Handle

which they work. The bar joint thus made forms a knuckle joint facilitating the saw tension, and also permits much latitude in using saws of varying lengths.

To give good control over the saw, the handle is made rather short and stumpy looking, shaped something like c, and the clip holes are bored right through and the ends riveted over iron end washers.

Fig. 42.—Using Keyhole Saw

called a pad saw—the handle being called a pad and being sometimes adapted to take a variety of tools ; the blade fits into the handle when not in use.

A patent iron-handle pad saw is shown in Fig. 46 ; the wide end of the blade is shaped for use as a screwdriver.

Sometimes the compass-saw handle is made with an adjustable handle so that various blades for different classes of work may be used. A compass saw with three blades—one for sawing metal— is shown in Fig. 45.

The use of fretwork saws will be ex-

Saws become dull chiefly by sawing gritty timber, " catching " nails, etc. A dull saw on examination will show a speck of white on each tooth " point," whereas a tooth in good condition should have a sharp point.

Saw Setting.—The saw may or may not require setting. If it saws easily, making a wide saw kerf, it will not require that treatment. The saw may be set after being sharpened, but the other way is the more usual.

A saw may be set in a number of ways. The average workman uses a saw-set,

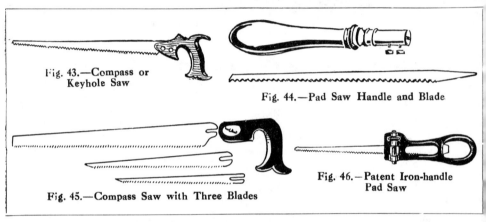

Fig. 43.—Compass or Keyhole Saw

Fig. 44.—Pad Saw Handle and Blade

Fig. 45.—Compass Saw with Three Blades

Fig. 46.—Patent Iron-handle Pad Saw

plained when an example of fretting is given in a much later chapter.

SETTING AND SHARPENING SAWS

Most tool dealers set and sharpen saws at a small cost, and many woodworkers prefer to send their saws to them rather than themselves tackle a job which is regarded as difficult. Some workers sharpen their own saws four or five times until, owing to lack of skill, the teeth have become uneven, and the saws have then to be sent to the saw expert. Saw sharpening is not really difficult, and the following instructions, which apply to most kinds of saws, should enable anyone to sharpen saws easily and efficiently.

the simplest type of which is shown in Fig. 47 and consists of a handled piece of steel containing a number of slots or notches, which are of various sizes to suit different thicknesses of saws. A slot is fitted over a tooth and the saw-set handle pressed downwards until it is judged that the tooth has been bent enough ; that is, until it has been given enough set. This process is repeated with every alternate tooth on one side of the saw (see Fig. 51). The remaining teeth are then set from the other side.

In this method of setting the operator can only guess that each tooth has an equal amount of set. Some saw-sets of this type are therefore provided with a gauge (Fig. 48), which is so adjusted that when the tooth is bent sufficiently the gauge touches the side of the saw blade. In this way each tooth is given the same amount of set.

Plunger saw-sets are now largely used iron block and hitting the teeth with a hammer is the oldest and most rapid method, though it is only recommended

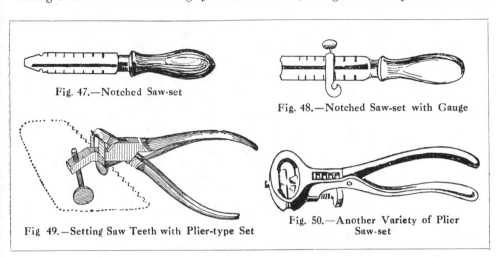

Fig. 47.—Notched Saw-set

Fig. 48.—Notched Saw-set with Gauge

Fig 49.—Setting Saw Teeth with Plier-type Set

Fig. 50.—Another Variety of Plier Saw-set

(see Fig. 50). On pressing the handles together the plunger is pressed against the tooth; when the handles are released the plunger springs back. The saw-set can be adjusted for various sizes of teeth by turning the revolving disc, which is numbered for different sizes of saws. There are numerous variations of this for use by the expert or for one who has a lot of saw setting to do. The average woodworker seldom uses this method. Fig. 53 illustrates the block and Fig. 54 the special saw-setting hammer. The iron block is about 7 in. or 8 in. long, with the top edges bevelled off as in the illustration. The bevelled edges should

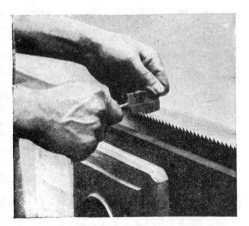

Fig 51.—Using Notched Saw-set

Fig. 52.—Using Plier Saw-set

type of saw-set, Figs. 49 and 52 showing two varieties in use.

Setting saws by placing them on an be of different slopes so that they will do for different sizes of teeth. The saw is then held flat on the block with the teeth projecting over the bevel and each alternate tooth struck with the hammer. The saw is then turned over and the pro-

at different angles; B is a steel wedge, and C is a casting to hold the block and wedge. Fig. 56 shows the saw-set in use.

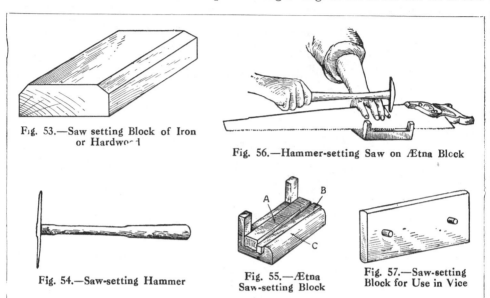

Fig. 53.—Saw setting Block of Iron or Hardwood

Fig. 56.—Hammer-setting Saw on Ætna Block

Fig. 54.—Saw-setting Hammer

Fig. 55.—Ætna Saw-setting Block

Fig. 57.—Saw-setting Block for Use in Vice

cess repeated. The bevel edge with the most slope and the largest end of the hammer should be used for big teeth.

A block of iron, about 5 in. long, with a rounded top edge, as Fig. 57, is sometimes used fixed in the vice, the pins in the side preventing the block being

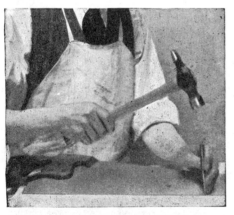

Fig. 58.—Setting Saw Teeth with Hammer and Punch

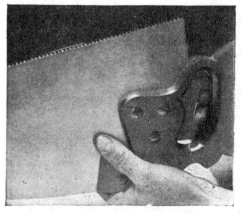

Fig. 59.—Needle Gliding between Points of Properly Set Teeth of Saw

A saw-set of the above type, called the Ætna, is illustrated in Fig. 55, in which A is a steel block with the edges bevelled

knocked down in the vice by the hammering.

A method of setting saws on the above

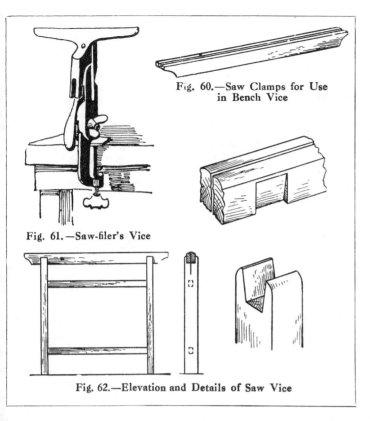

Fig. 60.—Saw Clamps for Use in Bench Vice

Fig. 61.—Saw-filer's Vice

Fig. 62.—Elevation and Details of Saw Vice

about 2 in. by 1 in. in section (*see* Fig. 60). The saw blade is placed between these two strips and the whole tightened up in a vice. The saw should not project more than about $\frac{1}{2}$ in., or the teeth will spring or "give" when filing, but when using the saw-set of the plunger type the teeth must project more to accommodate the saw-set. Fig. 61 shows another type of saw vice.

The ordinary woodworker's bench vice is rather low for saw sharpening. A more convenient type of saw clamp of suitable height is shown in Fig. 62 ; the clamp pieces fit into tapered slots in the top of the stand, and when driven into position with a few taps from a hammer bind the saw blade tightly between them.

On sighting along the teeth of a dull

lines is to use a piece of *hardwood*, as Fig. 58. Place the saw on it, and hit each tooth with a nail punch and hammer. Each tooth will be bent a little—varying with the strength of the blow—but the hardwood will prevent the teeth being bent too far or getting broken. This method is very convenient when the workman has not a saw-set to hand or for the amateur worker who does not wish to go to the expense of buying one. A hardwood block similar in shape to Fig. 53 could be used.

When an ordinary hand saw has been properly set it will allow a needle to glide down the teeth as shown in Fig. 59 (which is reproduced from a straight, untouched photograph).

Sharpening Saws.—In order to hold the saw whilst sharpening, various devices are used, the simplest consisting of two pieces of wood the length of the saw and

Fig. 63.—Topping Saw Teeth with Flat File

or badly sharpened saw it will be seen that the teeth are not in a straight line, but they are uneven. Therefore the first step in sharpening is to straighten—

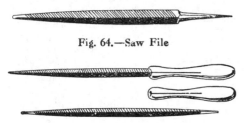

Fig. 64.—Saw File

Fig. 65.—Double-ended Saw File

or reduce to an even slightly convex curve—the line of the teeth, and this is done by running a file (preferably a flat one) over the points of the teeth. It is convenient to fit a flat file in a groove cut in a piece of wood, and then if this wooden guide is held against the side of the blade, the file will be kept level and the points of the teeth consequently filed more accurately, or a large file may be used without mounting it, as in Fig. 63.

A three-cornered or triangular file, incorrectly known sometimes as a "three-square" file (Fig. 64), is required for the actual sharpening. Such files are made in various sizes, a 4½ in. file being suitable for hand saws and a 3½ in. for tenon saws. A double-ended saw file (Fig. 65) is very convenient and the one generally favoured. An 8 in. file is a convenient size ; though rather large for panel and tenon saws, it may be used to sharpen them as well as the hand saw.

The section of the file is an equilateral triangle, and the size of the file will not alter the angles of the file, which are 60° in every case

Begin sharpening at the handle end of the saw. The file is held level but pointing towards the handle end of the saw. (Some saw sharpeners advise that the file should be inclined a little, about 15 degrees, but this does not matter much, and it gives the teeth an uneven appearance.) The position to hold the file may be determined by laying it between the teeth so that it

will file the teeth and yet preserve the former shape. The position of the file is shown in Figs. 66 and 67.

File down into each alternate gap between the teeth until the white specks (denoting dullness) on the teeth points to the left of the file are *nearly* removed. The file should only be used on the forward strokes. Two or three strokes of the file will be required for each tooth.

The tooth to the left of the file is the one that is being sharpened, but, of course, the side of the tooth to the right will also be filed a little. It is for this reason that the white specks on the teeth do not need to be entirely removed whilst doing the first side of the saw ; they will be entirely removed when filing from the other side.

Sometimes, when a workman is in a hurry, he does not bother to set the saw or to run the "flatting" file over the teeth points, but simply gives each gap one or two strokes of the file. This is a quick method, and an equal amount is taken from each tooth.

When the saw has been filed from one side, it is turned round and filed from

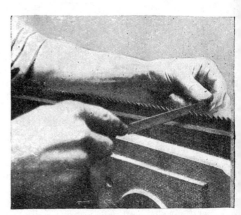

Fig. 66.—Filing Saw Teeth

the other ; taking care that the file again points towards the handle end of the saw.

If the file were held at right angles to the saw blade the gap between the teeth would be exactly 60°, but by pointing the file towards the handle this angle is increased to about 64°. A good angle for the front (leading edge) of the teeth of a cross-cut saw is about 75°. The teeth angles will thus be as shown in Fig. 68.

The front edges of the rip-saw teeth are at about 90° to the edge (87° is shown in the diagram). The angle between the teeth will be about 62°, thus giving the shape as in Fig. 69.

The teeth of the rip saw are filed in the same manner as for a cross-cut saw,

Fig. 67.—Plan showing Angle of Saw File

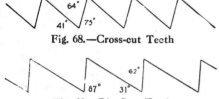

Fig. 68.—Cross-cut Teeth

Fig. 69.—Rip Saw Teeth

but the file is not pointed so much towards the handle (from 3° to 5° out of square is about right), whilst for a cross-cut, tenon, or panel saw the file should be pointed about 20° to 30° out of square. The more the file is held out of square the finer will be the point and the keener the cutting, but the teeth will be weaker and more quickly dulled. Some experts contend that for rip saws the file should be held at 90° to the blade, each tooth then acting as a small chisel; but as the grain of timber is always more or less curved it is better generally to point the file towards the handle as before stated. For saws that are used mostly for cross-cutting soft wood a fine sharp tooth that will easily cut its way through soft fibres is desired, and this is obtained by holding the file more obliquely to the saw blade, say about 60° (30° out of square). For hardwood the teeth are better if less acute, and the file is held at about 70°

to 75° to the face of the saw (15° to 20° out of square)

Panel, tenon, dovetail, and compass saws are sharpened as for a cross-cut saw, but it is desirable to use a little

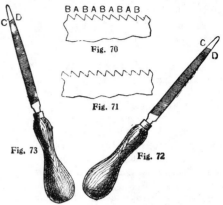

Figs. 70 to 73.—Diagrams showing Effects of Varying the Angle at which Saw File is Held

finer file. Pad saws are made with the blade tapering quickly towards the back edge, and therefore do not require setting.

If the above instructions are followed, no difficulty should be experienced in sharpening all the ordinary types of saws, but the beginner often finds that the teeth after being filed are not even and regular. Let it be assumed that the teeth, after filing, are similar to those shown in Fig. 70, while, properly filed, the angles should be alike, as in Fig 71. Teeth A (Fig. 70) are supposed to be filed with their points towards the filer and teeth B away from the filer. The file in the first place is held at an angle similar to that shown by Fig 72, and in the second place at that shown by Fig. 73. The greater pressure in each case is on the angle C, which tends to widen the roots of the teeth A, as the filing also tends towards the points of these teeth both in the face and back filing. With such filing the teeth on one range will (as will be seen) have a faster cut than on the other range, and if such filing is continued, eventually every alternate tooth will be filed out, or the saw gets into such a condition that it will be useless. The aim should be to hold the file at correct angles in each case and to avoid undue pressure with the thumb at the angles c (Figs. 72 and 73), for it will be clearly seen that the teeth A get most of the filing unless this is guarded against. Ease the pressure at the angle C, and increase it a little at D, so that the faces of the teeth (in each case) get their due amount of filing.

Accurate Sawing: Waste Caused by the Saw Kerf.—If a piece of wood exactly 6 inches long is sawn into halves exactly in the centre it might be thought that two 3 in. pieces would result. A little reflection will make obvious that each piece will be 3 in. long *less half the thickness of a saw kerf*. This does not matter on rough work but for good joinery, cabinet work, etc., if any joint has a gap the size of half a saw cut it is a bad job.

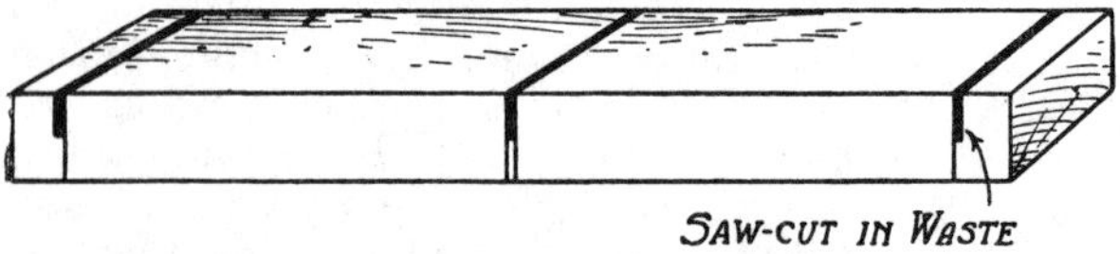

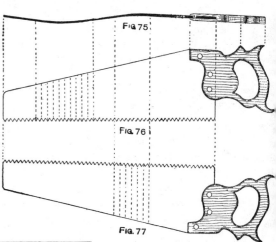

so that *half the line is left on the piece that is wanted*. This will conduce to accuracy Remember that a few extra seconds spent on accurate sawing will save minutes of fitting and planing afterwards. Get into the habit of cutting a piece exactly right length the first time.

Figs. 75 to 77.—Top, Front and Back of Buckled Handsaw

SAW-CUT IN WASTE

Fig. 74 —Sawing in the Waste

Suppose two pieces of wood exactly 1 ft. long each had to be cut out of a piece 2 ft. 6 in. long. First look to see if the ends of the piece are good or shaky, and square a line over one end to avoid any defects. Measure 1 ft. from the squared line and square another line; square another line over about a " bare eighth " (the thickness of the saw kerf) from this line. From the last line measure 1 ft. and square another line over the timber. If now the ends are sawn off with the saw kerfs in the waste wood and the centre sawn between the two lines the resulting pieces will be exactly 6 in. long (*see* Fig. 74).

It is clear from the above that the saw kerf should be in the waste wood, or the piece of timber wanted will be a little short. A good rule, when the timber is marked with pencil, is to try to saw

Buckled Saws.—The blade of a saw often gets buckled—that is, permanently bent—particularly when the teeth have little set and the tool is used on wet timber. Fig. 75 shows the plan of a buckled saw Fig. 76 the front side, and Fig. 77 the back side. The curvature or buckle can be hammered out of the saw. A joiner's hammer with a slightly round face should be used so that the blade will not be marked. Saw experts use special hammers. The blade of the saw should be laid, hollow side down, on a block of iron, and the convex side hammered as shown in Figs. 75 and 76. The dotted lines show where the blade should be hammered. The saw shown will have to be hammered on both sides as indicated. In general it is better to have a buckled saw put right by an expert, as it is necessary to know beforehand the effect of every blow of the hammer

The Plane

A PLANE in its simplest form consists of a blade fitted into a wooden or metal stock. The blade projects slightly below the bottom of the stock, and on being pushed over the surface of a piece of wood acts like a chisel and cuts into the wood, thus removing a shaving. Planes usually have a wedge or other device to hold the blade in position.

Though planes are not used as much as formerly, because of the introduction of machinery, particularly in modern well-equipped workshops, most wood-workers possess at least three planes : jack plane, trying plane, smoothing plane. These are known as the " bench planes," and are part of the necessary equipment of every woodworker.

The jack plane is used for rough work. If a piece of timber has to be planed the surface is first roughly " jacked " over, the trying plane is then used to make the surface straight and out of twist, and lastly the work is smoothed by the smooth-ing plane. In the case of a door or piece of framing, the jack and trying planes are used before the work is framed up and the " smoother " afterwards.

Jack Plane.—A jack plane (Fig. 1) is about 16 in. or 17 in. long, and the cut-ting iron is usually $2\frac{1}{8}$ in. or $2\frac{1}{4}$ in. wide. The stock and wedge are made of beech. The handle, which forms part of the body of the plane, is made from a separate piece of wood and glued in a slot formed at the top of the stock. Handles of planes are often broken—usually through knock-ing the plane accidentally off the bench on to the floor—in which case a new handle can be bought for a few pence, the old handle chiselled out of its slot, and the new one glued in.

Most planes are made of beech ; in fact, all the wooden planes may be said to be of this timber ; metal planes often have fittings and handles of rosewood or ebony. Beech is well adapted for planes ; it is close grained, fairly hard, does not readily twist, and wears evenly.

On looking at the grain at the end of a plane the annual rings of the wood are easily seen. Crossing the annual rings, and nearly at right angles to them, are fine white lines called the medullary rays (*see* Fig. 2). If these white lines are at right angles to the sole, the plane will wear better and more evenly than if the lines were not upright. Of two planes that are about equal in other respects, choose the one with the more vertical medullary rays.

A plane should be " oiled " before using ; this makes it heavier, lessens the friction, and thus makes the plane work easily. A reasonably heavy plane is better than a light one, as it works more solidly and does not require so much pressing down on to the work. If the plane, therefore, has not been oiled, or is too light, it should be soaked in raw lin-seed oil or other suitable oil until it is a suitable weight. This is usually done by suspending it in an oil tank. If this is inconvenient the cutter and wedge are

55

taken out, the bottom of the mouth of the plane is stopped with putty, and the mouth filled with oil. After a few days the oil will have soaked into the plane ; add more oil until sufficient has been edge of the blade. The back iron enables the plane to work better by increasing the stiffness of the blade and breaking the shavings as they are cut by the blade (*see* Fig. 5).

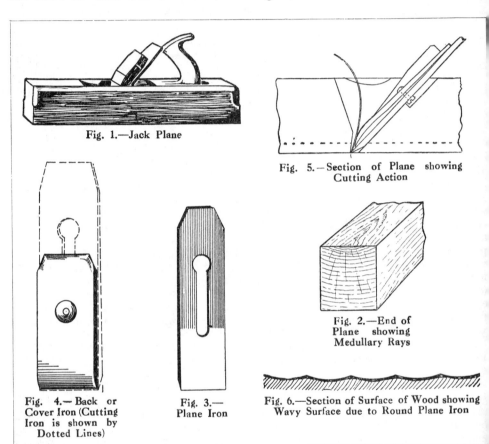

Fig. 1.—Jack Plane

Fig. 5.—Section of Plane showing Cutting Action

Fig. 2.—End of Plane showing Medullary Rays

Fig. 4.— Back or Cover Iron (Cutting Iron is shown by Dotted Lines)

Fig. 3.— Plane Iron

Fig. 6.—Section of Surface of Wood showing Wavy Surface due to Round Plane Iron

absorbed. Planes are sometimes french-polished, but this is not necessary.

The plane iron, or cutter, is shown in Fig. 3, and, as described in the chapter on sharpening, is made of steel and iron, the steel being used to give a keen edge and the iron to give toughness to the blade and also enable it to be quickly sharpened.

Besides the cutter there is also a " back iron " (Fig. 4). This is screwed to the blade, the edge of the back iron being set back a little from the cutting

The amount that the back iron is se back from the cutting edge is important for a jack plane it should be a bare $\frac{1}{8}$ in The amount of " set back " is greates for the jack plane ; for the trying plan a slightly less amount is better, $\frac{1}{16}$ in being usual, and for a smoothing plan a bare $\frac{1}{16}$ in. is used. The jack plane i for the roughest work, and therefore th set back is greatest for this plane ; th smoothing plane being used for finish'.n off the work, and therefore for removin fine shavings, is set the finest.

The cutting iron of the jack plane should be ground slightly convex—about

Fig. 7.—Edge of Jack Plane Iron

Fig. 8.—Edge of Trying Plane Iron

Fig. 9.—Edge of Smoothing Plane Iron

smoothing plane blade is straight, but with the corners taken off. These shapes

Fig. 12.—Unscrewing Plane Irons : Incorrect and Dangerous Method

a bare ⅛ in. (see Fig. 7). This makes the plane work freely. Of course, this convexity of the plane iron causes the surface of the work to be wavy and uneven (see Fig. 6, which shows the unevenness exaggerated for clearness). This unevenness is afterwards removed by the trying plane and smoothing plane.

Fig. 8 shows the shape of the cutting iron for the trying plane, and Fig. 9 the shape of the smoothing plane iron. It

of the trying plane and smoothing plane blades are not held to definitely, the smoothing plane often being of the shape shown for the trying plane. The main object is to remove the corners so that marks are not made on the surface of the wood whilst planing.

Taking Plane Apart.—When the jack plane requires sharpening it first has to be taken apart. The wedge and irons are loosened in two ways, as shown by Figs.

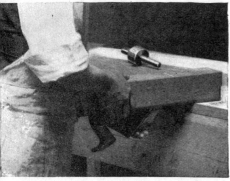

Fig. 10.—Loosening Plane Iron by Striking Plane on Bench

Fig. 11.—Loosening Plane Iron by Hitting End of Plane with Hammer

will be seen that the trying plane blade edge is the same shape as the jack plane, but with not as much curvature. The

10 and 11. The easiest method is shown at Fig. 10 ; take hold of the wedge and plane irons with one hand and the plane

with the other, and hit the top of the front end smartly on the bench. This

Fig. 13.—Unscrewing Plane Irons; Usual Method

Fig. 14.—Unscrewing Plane Irons by using Plane Wedge

will loosen the wedge, and the wedge and irons are then withdrawn. Fig. 11 shows

the other method, which consists o striking the front end of the plane sharpl with the hammer. Whilst doing this th plane should be held with the thumb i the mouth on the irons and wedge, t prevent them dropping.

Now unscrew the back iron from th plane iron. This is usually accomplishe by grasping the top end of the irons i the left hand and resting the cutting en on the bench (Fig. 13). Do not hold th irons in the left hand as shown in Fig. 12 as the screwdriver is liable to slip an

Fig. 15.—Unscrewing Plane Irons by usin Bench Hook

damage the hand. Sometimes the bac iron screw is so tight that it cannot b loosened easily. In this case place the iro so that the back projection of the screw fit into the groove in the back of the wedg —the latter resting on the bench (se Fig. 14). By this method both hands ca be used to the screwdriver if desired. hole in the top of the bench or in th bench hook (see Fig. 15) will do instea of the wedge. An even better plan fo very stiff irons is to screw them up i the vice ; this will help to squeeze the irons together and loosen the screw ; use the screwdriver with both hands.

When the blade is sharpened the irons

with the left hand and the blade inserted (Fig. 18). The latter is pushed forward until the correct amount projects beyond the sole of the plane, as can be seen by

Fig. 16.—Putting Plane Irons in Position

Fig. 18. — Inserting Blade in Plane after Sharpening

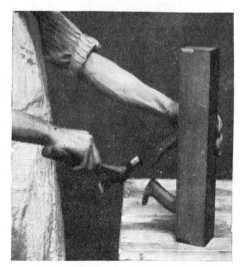

Fig. 19.—Fastening Wedge in Plane

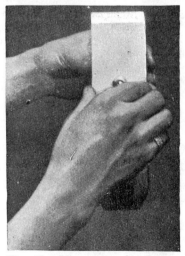

Fig. 17.—Plane Irons in Correct Position

are put together (see Figs. 16 and 17) by sliding the back iron up the plane and screwing together ; the plane is then held

sighting along the sole, as shown in Fig. 20. The wedge is now inserted with the right hand—the thumb of the left hand meantime keeping the blade in position —and then tightened with one or two taps from the hammer (Fig. 19). Whilst

Fig. 20.—Sighting Along Sole of Plane for Projection of Blade

if it takes off a correct thickness of shaving, an experienced workman can set the iron very quickly and correctly, often the first time and without trying it on the timber.

After years of wear and with repeatedly hitting with the hammer, the top end of the plane gets badly damaged. To prevent this a striking button, usually made of boxwood, may be fixed in the top end of the plane (*see* Fig. 21).

Adjusting a New Plane.—Planes, when first bought, or when using a new back iron or blade, and particularly when in the hands of an amateur or an apprentice, do not work easily. One of the chief faults is " choking up," that is, the shavings, instead of issuing freely from the mouth, stop up the mouth. The usual reason for this is that the back iron does not fit closely at the edge on to the plane iron, and, when planing, a shaving inserts itself in the small opening ; an obstruction is thus formed and other shavings tend to stop in the mouth. The obvious cure is to file the back iron carefully until it fits the blade closely. The back iron should also be thin at the edge and smooth, so as to offer the least possible resistance to the shavings.

tightening the wedge the iron may have slipped a little ; sight down the sole of the plane ; if the iron does not project enough give it a slight tap with the hammer ; if it projects too much hit the top end of the plane gently (as when loosening the wedge). One or two adjustments like this may be necessary ; finally, when the correct amount of iron projects beyond the sole, tap the wedge again with

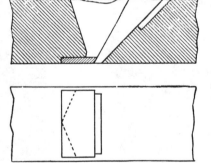

Fig. 22.—Re-mouthing Plane ; An Alternative Mouthpiece is Shown Dotted

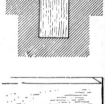

Fig. 21.—Striking Button in Plane

the hammer, and so make sure that the irons are securely held in the plane. Though at first one or two adjustments of the plane may be required as above, or the plane may have to be tried to see

If the back iron is adjusted as described, the blade only allowed to project a little beyond the sole. and a smear of oil put on the sole of the plane—particularly if planing a highly resinous wood

Fig. 23.—Cutting Sole of Plane for Mouthpiece

like pitchpine—the plane will probably work all right.

" Clattering " is another defect, but it usually accompanies choking up, and if the latter is remedied the former defect is usually cured also. But sometimes "clattering" (anyone who has had a plane that " clatters " will know what this is—the plane, instead of removing shavings, clatters over the wood) is due to the blade not bedding down solidly on wood stock. If this is the case the wood should be carefully pared with a chisel until the blade beds properly.

There is often a temptation when a plane which has a narrow mouth chokes, as in a new plane, to chisel the mouth wider. This should be avoided.

Shooting and Re-mouthing a Plane.—After using for many months the sole of a plane wears uneven, and it then requires " shooting." This is done by taking a few fine shavings off the sole with

the trying plane. Repeated shooting and wearing of the plane will cause the mouth of the plane to become wider, as illustrated in Fig. 5, which shows that the width of the mouth is greater along the dotted line. When this happens the plane requires re-mouthing, as shown in Fig. 22. Notice that the mouthpiece extends a little beyond the ends of the mouth. Boxwood is generally used for re-mouthing a plane. A plane does not work well when it has a wide mouth because the wood just in front of the cutting edge is not pressed upon by the sole of the plane. Figs. 23 and 24 show the sole of the plane being chiselled to receive a new mouthpiece. The method of using a jack plane will be dealt with in the next chapter.

Trying Plane.—This plane (Fig. 25) is very similar to the jack plane, the only differences being the shape of the handle —which is of the closed type—and the size. The trying plane is made long— average length about 22 in.—so that it will plane the wood straight. A short plane would sink into hollows, whereas a long plane cannot do so, but removes the lumpy parts and thus makes a level surface. The materials, methods of setting and taking apart, are the same as

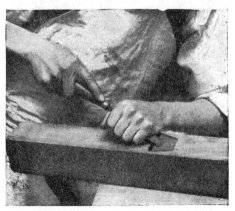

Fig. 24.—Chiselling Recess for Mouthpiece

for a jack plane, but the iron is wider— usually $2\frac{1}{2}$ in.—and the cap iron is set back only a $\frac{1}{16}$ in. from the cutting edge of the blade.

A special type of trying plane is called a *jointer* or *panel* plane, the length being from 26 in. to 30 in. As the name implies, this plane is used for making joints—the

are used. The smoothing plane is often used for convex curves if there is not much to do, but a hollow-soled compass plane is better. Concave work cannot

Fig. 25.—Trying Plane

Fig. 26.—Smoothing Plane

longer the plane, of course, the greater the tendency to plane the wood straight.

Smoothing Plane.—A smoothing plane (Fig. 26), as the name suggests, is for smoothing or finishing a surface. As the plane is not required to straighten the timber it is of a convenient size for holding and using. The usual size is about 8 in. long with 2¼ in. cutter.

The method of taking apart, re-assembling, and adjusting is the same as for the jack plane, except that owing to the shape of the smoothing plane the back end of the plane is hammered or knocked

be done with a smoothing plane, and therefore a compass plane is essential, though for small work a spokeshave (really a small compass plane) may be used.

Fig. 29 shows a wooden compass plane. Sometimes a stop for adjusting roughly to various curves is attached. In using this type of plane always keep the nose of the plane tightly against the work.

Adjustable compass (or circular) planes (Figs. 30 and 31) have an adjustable metal sole ; these are preferable to the wooden type, as they can be more accur-

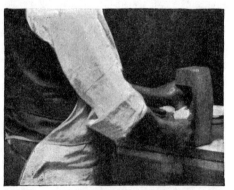

Fig. 27.—Loosening Plane Irons by Striking Back of Plane on Bench

Fig. 28.—Loosening Plane Irons by Hitting Back of Plane with Hammer

on the bench when loosening or setting (*see* Figs. 27 and 28).

COMPASS AND TOOTHING PLANES

When hollow or round surfaces have to be worked, planes with curved soles

ately adjusted to the curve either concave or convex. Fig. 31 shows a later and better variety than Fig. 30. The sole of the plane is adjusted to the correct curvature in each case by the screw at the top.

Toothing Planes.—In making a glued

joint between two surfaces, or in veneering, the surfaces are " toothed " with a toothing plane. The toothing simply roughens the surfaces, thus enabling the glue to adhere better. The plane in shape

Fig. 29.—Wooden Compass Plane or "Round Sole"

is similar to a small smoothing plane, the difference is in the blade, which is upright, has no cap iron, and is grooved at the back. Fig. 32 shows the blade, which has a series of V-shaped grooves at the back. When the blade is sharpened, like an ordinary plane blade, the edge will consist of a series of small teeth something like the edge of a saw. When the plane is used the teeth scratch the wood and give a better surface for holding the glue. The plane is used after the manner of an ordinary smoothing plane, but is pushed over the wood in all directions, with and across the grain.

REBATE AND BULL-NOSE PLANES

Rebate planes (see Fig. 33) are usually

available the rebate is cut out by using the saw with the table raised, and the rebate is then cleaned up with the rebate plane.

Rebate planes are made in various

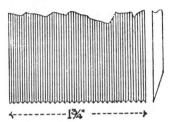

Fig. 32.—Blade of Toothing Plane

widths, ranging from $\frac{1}{4}$ in. to $1\frac{3}{4}$ in. A useful size is $1\frac{1}{4}$ in. The plane consists of three parts : body, blade, and wedge. There is no cap or back iron. The planes have either square or skew mouths. The latter type is the better—a skew mouth lets the shavings escape easily, thus preventing " choking," and a skew blade cuts better than a square one.

Rebate planes are not convenient tools for making rebates, but only for " cleaning up " rebates that have been cut by some other method. These methods will be described later, and include the circular saw, spindle, fillister, plough-cutting gauge.

Special rebate planes are used for some jobs. Suppose, for example, a "stopped " rebate had to be cut as in Fig. 33a. The best way to proceed would probably be to cut about 6 in. near the " stopped end " with the chisel and the rest with a

Fig. 30.—Stanley Adjustable Compass Plane

called " rabbit " planes in the workshop, and are used for making rebates, or " rabbits." Where a circular saw is

Fig. 31.—Victor Adjustable Compass Plane

plane. As, however, the rebate plane would not work close up to the stopped end, a special plane with its blade close to the nose is used. This plane (*see* Fig. 34) is called a *bull-nose* plane, and is made of metal. It is 3 in. to 4 in. in length, and is very useful. It should form part of every woodworker's kit.

The screw on the top of the plane enables it to be adjusted for any required depth of rebate. These planes are not much used, as a combination of the use of rebate plane and plough enables any

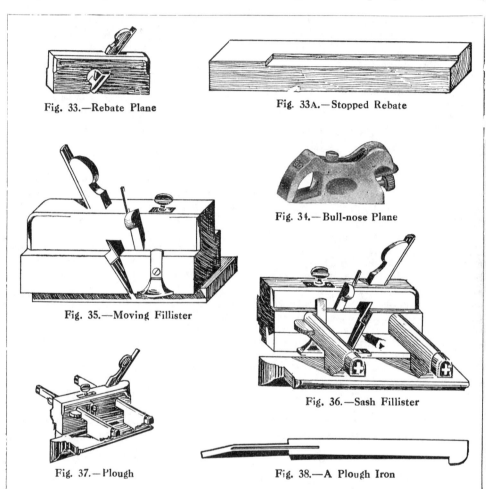

Fig. 33.—Rebate Plane

Fig. 33A.—Stopped Rebate

Fig. 34.—Bull-nose Plane

Fig. 35.—Moving Fillister

Fig. 36.—Sash Fillister

Fig. 37.—Plough

Fig. 38.—A Plough Iron

FILLISTERS AND PLOUGH

FILLISTERS are planes for making rebates. They consist essentially of a rebate plane with a movable fence, on the principle shown in Figs. 35 and 36. Two types are shown. The *Moving fillister* shown in Fig. 35 has a fence sliding on the sole of the plane, and the fence of the *Sash fillister* (Fig. 36) slides by means of stems through the body of the plane.

rebate to be cut, and a plough is necessary for making grooves.

THE PLOUGH (Fig. 37) is used for making all sizes of grooves and rebates. The blade, or " bit " is fastened into the body of the plane by a wedge ; a side fence works on stems after the manner of the sash fillister, and a screw on the top of the plane determines the depth of the groove or rebate. A set of six or eight " bits " of various sizes is supplied with each plane (see Fig. 38). The method of using the plough is shown in Fig. 39. Take care to adjust the fence parallel to the " fin " of the plane.

JOINTING, MOULDING AND BEADING PLANES

Jointing or *matching* planes are made in pairs—one to cut the groove and the other the tongue (see Figs. 40 and 40A). A separate pair is required for each thickness of board. When making a tongued and grooved joint with match-

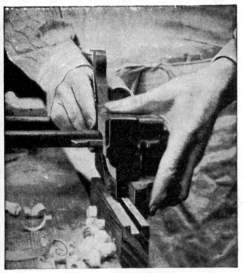

Fig. 39.—Using Plough

ing planes the joint should first be " made " (planed with the trying plane and adjusted to a fit), as the tonguing plane takes off an equal amount throughout the length of the board, and therefore if the pieces fit before being tongued and grooved they will fit afterwards.

Though moulding planes are not used in the workshop as much as formerly, a set of these planes is usually provided for " sticking " (moulding) short lengths, when it would not be worth while to " set up " a machine. The chief moulding planes are hollows and rounds, bead and ovolo planes.

A full set of hollows and rounds consist

of 18 pairs, but about three " rounds " (see Fig. 42A) of various sizes are usually sufficient, except for very rare jobs. Hollows (Fig. 42) can be dispensed with if necessary, as the round portions of mouldings may be worked by the ordinary planes and then glass-papered to a finish.

Bead planes (Fig. 43) may be had in sizes to make beads from $\frac{1}{8}$ in. to 1 in. Planes for making small mouldings of

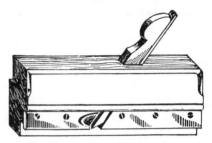

Fig. 40.—Grooving Plane

Fig. 41.—Blades for Matching Planes

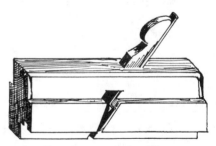

Fig. 40A.—Tonguing Plane

standard patterns as Fig. 44 may be obtained, but these mouldings and others can be made without special planes, as will be described later.

METAL PLANES

Two or three metal planes have already been described, but there are numerous other types, chiefly of the Stanley make.

An exceedingly useful metal plane is the block plane (Fig. 45). It is about the size of a small smoothing plane, and can be used with one hand (*see* Fig. 46) ; it is thus very convenient for planing

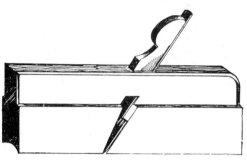

Fig. 42.—Hollow Plane

mitres as well as useful for all kinds of small work. The width of the mouth can be adjusted by means of the screw at the front. The blade is secured in position by means of the cap, propelled backwards and forwards by the screw at the back, and adjusted sideways by the lever at the back. The blade of the block

Fig. 43.—Bead Plane and the Beading Cut by it

plane is used with the bevel upwards, and the inclination of the blade is 20 deg. as against 45 deg. in ordinary planes.

Fig. 47 shows a block plane having the cutter at an even lower angle—12 deg. This angle enables the planes to be used with ease across the grain on hardwoods.

Large metal planes are not as largely used as was expected when they were introduced. The chief objection is that the metal " drags " on the wood, thus making the metal plane tiring to use.

They are also more expensive and quite as liable to get out of order or get broken as, or even more than, wooden ones. The

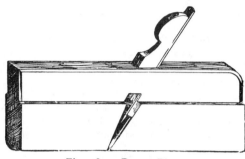

Fig. 42A.—Round Plane

average woodworker in this country nearly always has the three bench planes of wood, frequently an iron smoothing plane, usually a metal bull-nose and very often a block plane. Other metal planes are often met with, but though often very useful can hardly be said to belong to the average woodworker's equipment.

In order to avoid the excessive friction of the iron sole of metal planes, the sole is often corrugated as in Fig. 48. Another method of avoiding the " drag " of the metal is to have a plane with metal fittings and a wooden sole as in Fig. 49, which shows a Bailey jack plane and Fig. 50 a smoothing plane.

Fig. 44.—Ovolo Plane and Ovolo Moulding Cut by it

Fig. 51 shows a rebate plane with a square iron ; the front part of the plane is movable and secured by the screw at the top. This plane is very suitable for shooting the shoulders of tenon joints, and is sometimes called a shoulder plane.

Fig. 52 is a small metal plane about

A Bailey adjustable jack plane is shown in Fig. 53. The illustrations give a plan and side elevation ; a view of the seat for the blade, showing the screw for

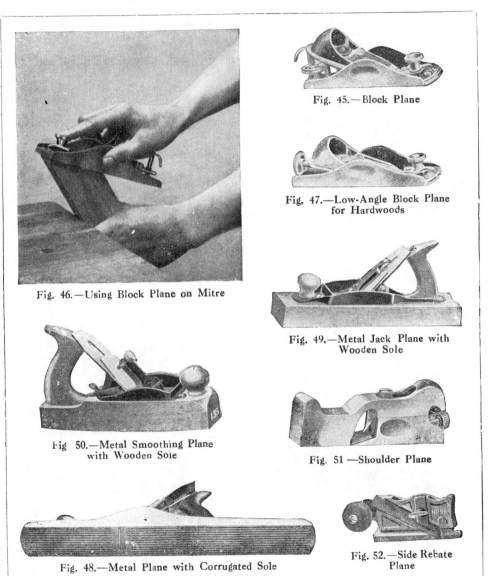

Fig. 45.—Block Plane

Fig. 47.—Low-Angle Block Plane for Hardwoods

Fig. 46.—Using Block Plane on Mitre

Fig. 49.—Metal Jack Plane with Wooden Sole

Fig. 50.—Metal Smoothing Plane with Wooden Sole

Fig. 51 —Shoulder Plane

Fig. 48.—Metal Plane with Corrugated Sole

Fig. 52.—Side Rebate Plane

4 in. long for planing the vertical sides of rebates ; it has a reversible nosepiece, so that it will work closely up into corners when required.

propelling the blade and the lever for lateral adjustment the cap ; the plane irons ; and the iron, cap, and seat together. The method of adjusting the

Fig. 53.—Bailey Jack Plane, showing Parts Separated

blade of metal plane is shown in Fig. 54.

Fig. 55 shows a cabinet-maker's edge plane; with the blade right at the end it can be worked close up into corners. A cabinet-maker's block plane with machined sides and suitable for fine work or with a shooting board is shown in Fig. 56.

Fig. 57 shows a block plane having a handle at the back so that the plane may be gripped and used comfortably.

Other special planes will be dealt with as they are required—notably the veneerer's and inlayer's toothing planes and router planes.

Fig. 56.—Cabinet-maker's Block Plane

Fig. 57.— Handled Block Plane

Fig. 55.—Edge Plane

7—N.E.

Fig. 54.—Adjusting Blade of Block Plane

SPOKESHAVES AND ROUTERS

A spokeshave may be described as a small double-handled plane for planing

The method of using the spokeshave is shown in Fig. 62. Always work " with the grain," as shown in Fig. 63, the arrows showing the directions in which the

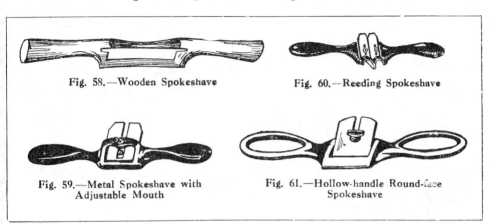

Fig. 58.—Wooden Spokeshave

Fig. 60.—Reeding Spokeshave

Fig. 59.—Metal Spokeshave with Adjustable Mouth

Fig. 61.—Hollow-handle Round-face Spokeshave

curves. It is made of either metal or wood, both types being largely used.

A wooden spokeshave is shown in Fig. 58. It consists of only two parts, the stock and the blade. The latter is sharpened with a finger-slip oilstone, as fully illustrated on another page, and is

Fig. 62.—Using Spokeshave

adjusted to take off the correct thickness of shaving by tapping the prongs, or the front, of the blade, with the hammer.

spokeshave should be pushed in order to avoid plucking up of the grain.

There are about four kinds of wooden spokeshaves : round faced for quick curves, flat faced for flat curves, brass-plated spokeshaves to prevent the mouth wearing, and spokeshaves with adjustable blades operated by thumb-screws.

Many varieties of metal spokeshaves may be obtained, with straight or raised handles, adjustable cutters, and types for quick curves (see Figs. 59 and 61).

A small spokeshave is usually better than a large one, as the small one will work both quick and large curves, whereas a large one is generally suitable only for big work.

A router is a tool after the manner of a spokeshave, but used for cutting trenches, reeds, and mouldings away from the edge of the timber or on curved work. Fig. 64 shows a router used for planing the bottom of trenches, say for shelving, stairs, etc. Special routers are mentioned on later pages.

Some routers have an adjustable fence so that grooves parallel to the edge of the timber can be cut.

Reeding and moulding tools are made in many varieties and consist usually of a two-handled body like a spokeshave, a sliding fence, and a number of adjustable blades for cutting various forms of mouldings, beads, and reeds. A reeding tool without a fence, but capable of taking for light routing out. A tool that is sometimes used for secret nailing is shown in Fig. 67. A $\frac{1}{4}$-in. chisel when attached to the body turns up a small shaving as

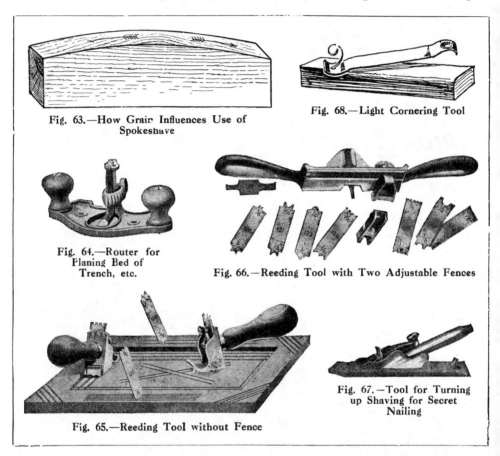

Fig. 63.—How Grain Influences Use of Spokeshave

Fig. 68.—Light Cornering Tool

Fig. 64.—Router for Planing Bed of Trench, etc.

Fig. 66.—Reeding Tool with Two Adjustable Fences

Fig. 67.—Tool for Turning up Shaving for Secret Nailing

Fig. 65.—Reeding Tool without Fence

various sizes of reeding tools, is shown in Fig. 65. A reeding spokeshave is shown by Fig. 60.

Fig. 66 shows a reeding tool with two adjustable fences—one for straight and one for curved work. It is also suitable

shown on a later page; when the nail is driven the shaving is glued and pressed back into position.

Fig. 68 shows an American tool for easily removing a corner from a long strip.

Planing

THE object of planing is to make a piece of timber straight so that it does not twist, in order that it will fit into the required position, and also to make it smooth so that it may be painted, varnished, polished, etc.

rough," that is, make the surface fairly straight and smooth.

Figs. 1 and 2 show the method of using the jack plane. At the beginning of the stroke the left hand will have to press hard on the end of the plane, this pressure

Fig. 1.

Fig. 2.

Figs. 1 and 2.—Using Jack Plane, Beginning and End of Movement

Suppose a piece of timber, say about 3 ft. long, 4 in. wide, and 2 in. thick, is going to be used in the construction of a door or a piece of framing. Select the better side and place the timber on the bench and against the bench stop. First use the jack plane and take off " the

being released towards the end of the stroke. The right hand pushes the plane forward. If the plane takes off too much or too little—" too much iron " or " not enough iron "—the blade should be adjusted as described in the preceding chapter.

71

A common fault in planing is taking too much off the end near the bench stop. To avoid this try to take less off this

be tested for straightness with a straight-edge or by sighting as in Fig. 40 (p. 35). The piece of timber shown in that photo-

Fig. 3.

Fig. 4.

Figs. 3 and 4.—Testing across a Planed Surface

end and more at the beginning of the stroke. Generally, take as little off as possible ; remember you can always plane a little more off, but you cannot put any on.

There is also a tendency to plane the surface round (convex in direction of length). With a piece of timber about 3 ft. long, it will be impossible to plane the surface hollow with a jack plane, except to a very slight extent

graph is being sighted for straightness of edge. Shut one eye when sighting and simply " spy " along the edge of the wood ; in this way the slightest irregularity can be detected. Sighting is a better and more usual method of testing than using a straightedge.

For straightness across the board the surface may be tested by holding the plane cornerwise as in Fig. 3 ; if the

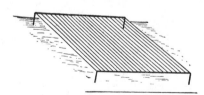

Fig. 5.—Plane Surface

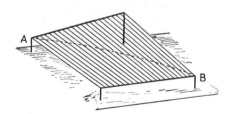

Fig. 6.—Twisted Surface

depending on the projection of the blade. The best method of planing straight and avoiding planing round is to try to plane hollow. The surface can

board is round or hollow light can be seen under the corner of the plane. A better method is to use the blade of the square as shown in Fig. 4.

Twist.—Besides being straight the timber should be *out of twist*—that is, the surface should be a plane, or flat, surface. Beginners usually have some

These strips may be about 18 in. long by 2 in. wide by ¼ in. thick : the upper parts of the strips are usually bevelled to make the top edges thinner. If the surface

Fig. 7.—Using Winding Strips

little difficulty in understanding what a plane surface (or a surface out of twist) really means. Suppose we have two rods perfectly level (as tested with a spirit level) ; *see* Fig. 5. Now suppose strings were connected, close together, from rod to rod : a plane surface would be thus formed. Consider now that only one of these rods was level and the other sloping and were connected by strings ; we should thus get a twisted surface as in Fig. 6. Note that the strings and rods are *straight*—that is, all the edges

twists, the winding strips will appear as in Fig. 9. It will be seen that the winding strips exaggerate the twist and thus make it easy to detect. The amount of twist may easily be estimated. Suppose that the right-hand end only of the back strip projects above the front one ½ in. (as in Fig. 9) and that the width of the wood is 4 in. and the length of the winding strips 16 in. The proportion of length of winding strips to width of surface is thus 4, and the amount of twist will therefore have been magnified four times ; the amount

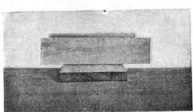

Fig. 8.

Fig. 9.

Figs. 8 and 9.—Winding Strips on Plane and Twisted Surfaces respectively

of the surface are straight yet the surface itself is twisted.

A surface is tested for twisting by using a pair of winding strips as in Fig. 7.

of twist of the surface is therefore ⅛ in. Fig. 9 shows the surface with the amount of twist exaggerated for clearness.

To take the surface out of twist it will

obviously be necessary to plane away the two thin wedge-shaped portions shown.

The workman does not calculate the amount of twist as given above, but guesses the amount to be planed off, then tests again, and so on until the surface is correct ; but an understanding of the above theory will enable a more

Fig. 10.—Observing whether a Small Surface is Twisted

twist though the edges are straight (*see* Fig. 6), but a twisted surface must be curved somewhere. For example, a line as A B (Fig. 6) passing on the surface from corner to corner will be convex. If a straightedge could be put in all directions on a surface so that it touched the surface at all points, then that surface would be

Fig. 11.—Face and Edge Marks

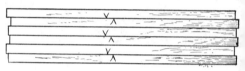

Fig. 12. – Edge Marks, showing how Pieces are arranged in Pairs when Setting Out

F g. 13.

Fig. 14.

Figs. 13 and 14.—Edge Planing, with and without using Vice.   Note Position of Fingers

accurate guess to be made. It is not often that an experienced man needs to use the winding strips more than twice on the same surface.

It has been shown that a surface may

out of twist. As, however, timber is usually very narrow in proportion to its length, any method of testing for twist with a straightedge is usually not reliable. (The surfaces of stonework are often taken out of twist with a straightedge alone, because stone surfaces are usually broader in proportion to length than timber surfaces.)

The jack and trying planes are often

Fig. 15.—Using Smoothing Plane

used instead of winding strips ; the planes are laid on their sides with the jack plane nearest the eye.

Another method of testing for twist, suitable for small stuff, is shown in Fig. 10. This method, which simply consists in holding the surface in a suitable position and looking at it, requires a little practice and care to use successfully.

After the " rough " has been taken off with the jack plane the trying plane is used for straightening and taking out of twist. When the latter has been accomplished the surface is "face marked" as shown in Figs. 11 and 12. The edge is now ready for planing.

Squaring the Edge.—Select the better edge, and place the timber, if it is thin, in the vice, or, if it is thick enough to stand up whilst planing, put it on the bench (*see* Figs. 13 and 14). Hold the plane as shown with the tips of the fingers of the left hand gliding along the side of the wood, so that the sole of the plane can be held steadily at right angles to the surface already planed. Test for straightness as in Fig. 40 (p. 35) and for squareness to the " face " by using a square. Hold the square and timber towards the light so that any light may be seen between the edge of the timber and the

blade of the square. Either glide the square along the timber or test at intervals of about 6 in. If not square, plane the prominent parts ; if correct, mark a " face edge mark " as in Fig. 12. This mark is usually a **V** pointing to the face side.

Planing to Correct Width and Thickness.—The third side, or rather the second edge, has now to be planed. Set the marking gauge to the required width of the piece of wood and gauge *on the face side, from the face edge.* Plane the third side (or second edge) to the gauge line ; this will make the third side straight and the wood parallel. Test the edge with the square from the face side.

We now come to the last side or back. Set the gauge to the desired thickness and gauge both edges from the face side. Plane to the gauge lines. The timber is now said to be " trued up," that is, it is (1) straight, (2) out of twist, (3) square, and (4) the desired size.

In making any article, the pieces for the framework are first " trued up " ; they are then " set out " for mortising, tenoning, moulding, etc., after which operations the framework is fastened together and finished off. This finishing varies with the class of work, rough work being simply planed ; painted work being usually planed and glasspapered ; and

Fig. 16.—Using Metal Smoothing Plane

polished hardwood being planed, scraped, and glasspapered.

Thin stuff is not planed out of twist as it can be easily bent to the correct position ; panels and similar stuff are simply planed smooth and to even thickness.

A surface is planed smooth by using the smoothing plane ; the method of holding and using is shown in Fig. 15. In order to produce a smooth surface having no rough or " plucked up " grain, the two main points to be observed are to set the plane fine and to plane " with the grain." Remember that to set the plane " fine " the iron should project as little beyond the sole as is consistent with removing a suitable shaving, and

up, as it were, of a number of cylinders encasing each other. Of course, these cylinders are not straight or truly circular in section, but for the purposes of explanation let it be supposed that they are as in Fig. 18. If a slice is cut off the trunk as Fig. 19, the grain of the surface will simply be a number of parallel straight lines. Now cut the trunk obliquely, and the section will be a number of ellipses, as in Fig. 20.

The surface in Fig. 19 may be planed in either direction, but the cut surface in Fig. 20 must be planed in the direction

Fig. 17.—Section of Tree

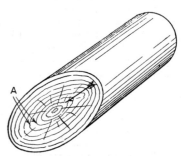

Fig. 18.—Imaginary Tree

Fig. 19.—Obtaining Straight Grain

Fig. 20.—Tree Trunk Cut Obliquely

the set back of the cap iron should be as little as convenient. The blade should be kept sharp.

Fig. 16 shows a metal smoothing plane in use.

As the smoothness of the finished surface depends largely on planing with the grain, and as this is not understood thoroughly even by the majority of experienced workmen, the nature and cause of the grain of timber will now be explained.

Planing and the Grain of Timber.— On examining the section of a tree trunk as in Fig. 17 it is found to consist of annual rings. The tree is therefore made

of the arrow or it will " pluck up " ; planing in the direction of the arrow is called planing " with the grain," and planing in the reverse direction is " against the grain." If the surface is planed against the grain the blade of the plane tends to dig in the wood at the corners marked A, and a rough surface results.

Consider now an actual tree trunk ; Fig. 21 shows the elevation of the trunk and Fig. 22 the plan of the end. Saw he trunk on the line A B. On taking away the portion cut off the view of the cut surface of the trunk will be as in Fig. 23. The direction in which the wood should be planed is shown by the arrows.

A rectangular piece of wood is shown in Fig. 24, the arrows showing the direction for correct planing. Note that if the surface were planed in the wrong edge to tell the correct direction for planing; this can be detected by looking at the grain on the surface and seeing how it rises to the surface.

The average woodworker spends a large proportion of his time in planing, and it is well worth while to understand the above theory of graining, as it will lead to better and quicker work But even the experienced craftsman is some-

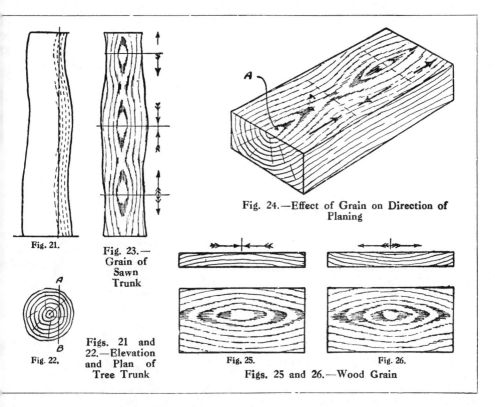

Fig. 21.

Fig. 22.

Fig. 23.—
Grain of
Sawn
Trunk

Figs. 21 and
22.—Elevation
and Plan of
Tree Trunk

Fig. 24.—Effect of Grain on Direction of
Planing

Fig. 25.

Fig. 26.

Figs. 25 and 26.—Wood Grain

direction there would be a tendency to pluck out the small piece A.

The directions for planing do not depend on the shape of the grain lines, but on how the grain rises to the surface of the wood; for example, in Figs. 25 and 26 the surfaces of the two boards are very much alike, but the grain on the edges show that the graining rises to the surface in a different manner. The arrows show the direction for planing. It is, however, not necessary to observe the times very hazy about grain; his usual method is to plane the timber regardless of grain, and then plane the plucked-up parts in the reverse direction, if necessary. This method may be excused for painted work; but for hardwood—say mahogany—if the grain is plucked up badly—and this is commonly done—much work with the plane and scraper is necessary before it is remedied. It is obviously a great advantage in planing curly-grained stuff to know, before the plane is put on the wood, which way the grain goes. The method of testing it in it to hold the strip is often used (*see* Fig. 31); the strip is thus kept in a

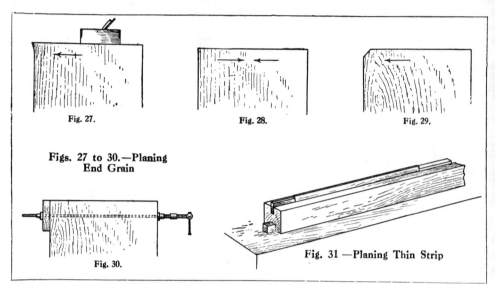

Fig. 27.   Fig. 28.   Fig. 29.

Figs. 27 to 30.—Planing End Grain

Fig. 30.

Fig. 31 —Planing Thin Strip

with the plane and the subsequent working up is wasteful of time, labour, and material.

suitable position and can be planed with greater ease.

Planing End Grain.—It might be said that there is one wrong method of planing end grain, and three correct ones, each of the latter being specially suitable under given circumstances.

If a piece of wood is planed on the end by pushing the plane along the *end* as if it were the *edge* of a board a small piece will probably be knocked off at the end, as shown in Fig. 27. The usual method is to plane from each end as in Fig. 28. Another way is to take a small corner off the far end with the chisel and then plane straight through as shown (*see* Fig. 29). The small bevel prevents any breaking. Of course, this method cannot be used where the end must be left perfectly square. Fig. 30 shows a further method, which consists in fastening (probably with a cramp) a bit of wood at the far end to prevent splitting and then planing straight through.

Planing Thin Strips and Panels.— When planing thin strips, particularly on the edge, a piece of timber with a groove

Fig. 32.—Testing Thickness of Panel with a " Mullet "

Panels are tested for thickness by means of a " mullet " or " mulleting piece " (*see* Fig. 32). This is a small piece of wood that is grooved at the same time as the framework, and therefore if the panels fit the mullet they will fit into their proper grooves.

In ordinary mechanical language. the " mullet " is a notch gauge.

In planing panels and suchlike stuff the object is to make them smooth and of even thickness so that they will fit neatly into their grooves. As the top of the bench is often rough and uneven, a " panel board " is sometimes used (*see* Fig. 33). This is merely a wide board about 4 ft. or so long, with a butting strip to act as a stop at one end. This strip is better than the bench stop when planing wide stuff.

In planing panels, and smoothing up generally, some workmen begin planing near the bench stop and work backwards ; they argue that every time the plane is put down and a shaving begun a slight mark is made on the wood, and that in planing from the bench stop and working backwards these marks are avoided. This generally is not a matter of much consequence, but on the whole this method of beginning at the bench stop

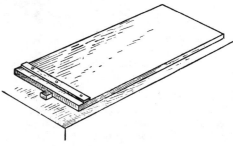

Fig. 33.—A Panel Board

end may be recommended, but for " smoothing " only.

The use of special planes will be dealt with later in connection with the processes for which they are required.

Rebating

THE terms "rabbet" and "rabbit" mean the same thing as rebate and are often used. But rebate is probably the original and more correct word. The cutting of rebates is often necessary in woodwork, generally in the formation of joints. It means the cutting of a step or shoulder along the edge of a piece, as in Fig. 1, in most cases transversely to the grain. Usually the end of another piece fits into this at right angles, as in Fig. 2. The advantage of the rebate in such a case is that the outer surfaces of

Fig. 1.—Rebate

the parts remain flush, when if simply depending on nails or screws and a plain butt joint they might easily be forced more or less out of position by a blow or severe pressure.

Generally the lines of a rebate are marked before commencing to cut. The wood has usually been planed to the required thickness, width and length, so that the lines can be gauged. Sometimes the rebated end is not finished to length but is left roughly sawn so that the end grain can be trimmed flush after the parts

are together. In such a case the distance in of the rebate from the end cannot be marked with a gauge, but lines must be

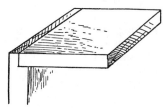

Fig. 2.—Rebated Joint

squared across. When the lines are marked a cut is made with a tenon saw slightly outside of the line, as in Fig. 3 and nearly or quite to the depth of the rebate. This makes it easy to rough away most of the wood with a chisel and finish with a rebate plane. That

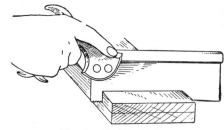

Fig. 3.—Cutting Rebate

is the way of working when no special planes are available, and it is a quite satisfactory method to adopt for just occasional rebating.

80

A chisel may be used in the vertical position (Fig. 4) or horizontally (Fig. 5). The first is generally more convenient on narrow pieces and the second on wide ones. As a precaution against chiselling

used carefully. Special planes, such as the fillister, trenching or grooving plane, router, and plough, can be set to cut to a required depth and will go no deeper, so that lines are unnecessary. More will

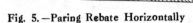

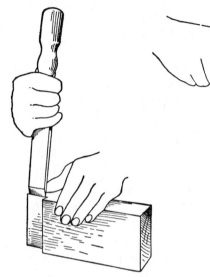

Fig. 4.—Chiselling Rebate Vertically

Fig. 5.—Paring Rebate Horizontally

be said about the use of these planes a little further on ; some of them have already been referred to.

A rebate plane is used as in Fig. 7. As it is an open-sided plane it cuts close to the shoulder of the rebate. It usually has a skew mouth, that is, the cutter moves forward in a diagonal position instead of at right angles with the sides of the plane body as in most other planes. This enables it to make a cleaner cut across grain and reduces risk of splitting away the farther edge of the work. The usual width of the rebate plane is $1\frac{1}{4}$ in., but narrower ones are made for planing grooves of less width. Strictly speaking, a rebate has a shoulder at one side only

or planing below the gauge line it is usual to cut down exactly to it, as in Fig. 6, before the intermediate surface is levelled. Chisel and plane can then be used to reduce to the level required without continual examination to see when the line is reached, for it is easy to see when the bevelled portion at each edge has been removed, and the chief thing to be careful about is to get a

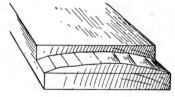

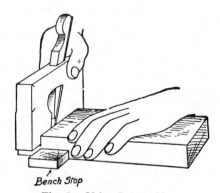

Fig. 6.—Ensuring Correct Depth of Rebate

Fig. 7.—Using Rebate Plane

straight surface from one to the other. With a plane this is done almost automatically ; but a chisel, of course, may go too deep in the intermediate part if not

and is open at the other, as in all the examples shown. When it does not occur at the end or edge of a piece but at an intermediate place, necessitating a shoulder at each side, it becomes a groove or trench, but a rebate plane can be used for planing it. Rebates and grooves, however, are not always planed. In many cases they can be cut entirely with a chisel. If they are short it may be quicker

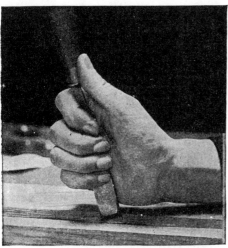

Fig. 8.—Cleaning Inner Angle of Rebate with Chisel

to finish with a chisel than to change from chisel to plane, for a skilled worker can cut as straight with a chisel as with a plane on a short distance. In either case it is advisable to test for straightness with the edge of a try square blade or with the side of the chisel itself.

A chisel is often used for cutting the shoulder of a rebate, or the sides of a groove, exactly to the scribed or gauged line, as a sawcut to the line is rather too rough and inaccurate for some work. Therefore $\frac{1}{16}$ in. or so is left for chiselling and the chisel is used in the vertical position already illustrated. It is set exactly on the line and forced down to the depth of the rebate in a series of cuts, with a slight diagonal or side movement of the chisel simultaneously with the downward movement. In a rebate (though not in a groove) a rebate plane could be used on the end grain, but as a rule a chisel is preferable. End grain is not easy to plane, and the risk of splitting at the far edge is consider-

able. The shoulder of end grain cann be chiselled till after the main body material is cleared out of the rebat A chisel is necessary also for cuttin well down into the angle of the rcba in finishing the latter, for the saw often stopped slightly short of the f depth, or if it is not the plane cann always clear shavings completely out the angle unless the fibres of end gra are severed by drawing the edge of t chisel along. Fig. 8 shows the inn angle of a long rebate being " cleaned the chisel being drawn first along o side of the rebate and then along t other side.

On very wide pieces a chisel lying its face, as in Fig. 5, may not be lo enough to reach across, perhaps not ev half way if worked from opposite sid In such cases, of course, a plane is esse tial, and some of the roughing must done with the chisel face upwards in tilted position.

When a rebate runs parallel with t grain a sawcut need not be made. M of the material can be roughed out wi a chisel, and a rebate plane can be us

Fig. 9.—Using Temporary Guide whilst Making Rebate

in the ordinary position on the horizon face and lying on its side to plane t other face. Or a strip of wood can ailed temporarily or clamped to the ne as a guide for the side of the plane to york against (*see* Fig. 9).

Rebate planes are not restricted to he wooden pattern shown in Fig. 7. There is some variety in the shapes and izes of metal ones. The ordinary bull-ose and the badger plane (a large rebate lane open at one side only ; *see* Fig. 10) an be used on rebates of greater width han the rebate plane. So also can the ack and other ordinary planes if the urface next to the shoulder of the rebate as first been finished with a plane that uts right up to it. But rebates are sually limited to about the width of rebate plane. If much wider they would robably not be called rebates, but would e for the purpose of making halved or

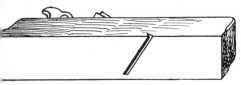

Fig. 10.—Sole of Badger Plane

alf-lap joints, while if wide and not onstituting joints it would in many ases be better to build them up by putting piece or pieces on rather than to cut way solid wood.

Use of Fillister Plane.—A plane pecially designed for cutting rebates s the fillister (Figs. 35 and 36, page 93) ; t differs from the rebate plane in having side fence, and in its more elaborate orms it is adjustable for depth of cut and as a slitting cutter in advance of the main utter, so that even across grain it can e used without making a sawcut or narking lines for planing to. But it is sed mainly for cutting rebates with the rain, which are often required in joinery, n window sashes, for instance, and in ther framework.

There are three types of fillister—the ash fillister (Fig. 36, page 93) which ooks very much like a plough, and is esigned for planing a rebate on the pposite side of the wood to that which the

fence slides against. There is the moving fillister (Fig. 35, page 93), intended for planing rebates on the same side as the fence ; and there is the standing fil-lister, which is not adjustable.

A rebate with the grain may be started by ploughing a groove with a plough at the distance and to the depth required

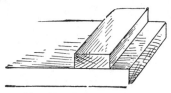

Fig. 11.—Built-up Rebate

and clearing the remainder of the rebate with any planes that are available. If necessary two or more grooves may be ploughed side by side. There are a few other planes intended primarily for cutting grooves, but these are suitable also for finishing rebates. But, as already men-tioned, all special planes for work of this character can be dispensed with by a beginner or by anyone who does such work only occasionally. Their value also has been reduced by the fact that where such work is turned out in quantity it is not done by hand but by machine. A great deal of rebating and groov-ing can be done with a circular saw which is provided with a rising and falling table. It is set so that the top of the saw stands up to the correct distance for

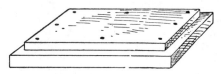

Fig. 12.—Built-up Rebates

cutting to the depth required, and a fence on the table acts as a guide in pushing the wood over the saw.

Built-up Rebates.—A rebate may be built up instead of cut in the solid. Ex-amples are shown in Figs. 11 and 12, the attached pieces being nailed or screwed on. The method in Fig. 11 is common in

some rather rough classes of work, and
where it can be adopted it often economises
both material and time. The method in
Fig. 12 is an alternative to cutting a
rebate all round a piece of wood. The
smaller piece is planed to width and
length and nailed on the other. A rebate
at the ends, or at the sides only, could be
formed similarly, but as a rule it is better
to cut it in the solid. The rebate in
a door frame, into which the door fits,
is often built up. The lid of a box or
chest often fits a rebate which is built
up, as shown in Fig. 13.

Fig. 14 is an instance of a rebated joint
where the parts are not at right angles.
The bead shown is not an essential feature
of it, but beads are often used in such

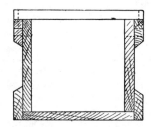

Fig. 13.—Section of Box showing
Built-up Rebates

places to avoid the unsightly appearance
of a joint in a plain surface. The wood
may shrink and the joint open slightly,
but the beads make this almost unnotice-
able. Instead of a bead the edges of the
joint are sometimes chamfered. This
type of rebate usually runs with the
grain.

Occasionally a shallow rebate may be
cut round the edges of a large piece to
avoid planing down the entire surface
to a thickness required. A rebate may
or may not be wanted, but a certain
uniform thickness at the edges is important
and the piece of wood available may be
considerably thicker and perhaps not
uniform in thickness. Or it may be
warped and a lot of planing would be
necessary to make it true on both faces.
Some work can be avoided by planing
one face true, gauging from this, and
going round the edges of the other face

with a rebate plane. In large boxed-up
foundry patterns this is common.

The inner edges of panelled frames are
sometimes rebated instead of grooved.
Glass in a wood frame nearly always fits
in a rebate. The advantage is that it

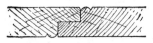

Fig. 14.--Rebated Joint

can be inserted after the frame is together
and can be replaced if broken. But in
a rebate the inserted panel or glass requires something to keep it from falling
out. This may take the form of a
nailed-in moulding or bead, as dotted in
Fig. 15

Rebates are not invariably straight
but may have to follow a curve. The
equivalent of a rebate often occurs in
turned work and is easily cut, but it is
comparatively rare in bench work and is
more troublesome, because it must generally be cut rather tediously with gouge
and chisel, assisted perhaps with tools
of the router class, which are made in
considerable variety of form. There is
one kind (Fig. 66, page 99), made in spokeshave form, with an adjustable fence to
keep the cutter at a fixed distance from
the edge of the work. It can be used for
curved rebates or grooves. Another is
the side router. Routers are used chiefly
for finishing work already roughed with
a chisel. Compass rebate planes, which
have curved soles and sides, are also used.

Stopped Rebates.—Instances sometimes occur when a rebate must have a
stopped end instead of running the full

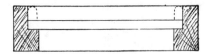

Fig. 15.—Rebated and Beaded Frame

length of the edge it is cut in. Fig. 16 is
an example in cabinet work where the appearance of a rebate at the front edge is
considered objectionable, and therefore it
is stopped and the corner of the fitted-in

piece notched to suit, so that, viewed from the front only, the method of jointing is concealed. Occasionally there are other reasons for stopping a rebate, and sometimes the stop may be formed by building-up methods. In rebated frames, for in-

the corners were mitred it would go through on all four pieces alike. When the corners are tenoned or halved methods of forming the rebate may vary. A safe method for a beginner is to put the frame together and mark and cut the rebate

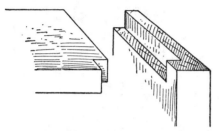

Fig. 16.—Stopped Rebate

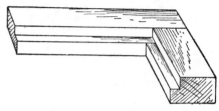

Fig. 17.—Method of Jointing Rebated Frame

stance, as in Fig. 15, the rebate must stop at the inner corners. This does not necessarily mean that it cannot be planed through in preparing the pieces. On the two pieces that fit between the rebates would go full length. On the other also it might be stopped, or it might be planed through and made good afterwards. If

afterwards, mainly with a chisel, but using suitable planes as far as possible ; the same method of cutting would be adopted for the stopped rebate in Fig. 16. In the case of a rebated frame the neatest way is to plane all pieces through and modify the joint so that the rebate is stopped, as in Fig. 17.

Grooving, Ploughing and Tongueing

A GROOVE may be wide and shallow, as in Fig. 1, or narrow and deep, as in Fig. 2. The first is used in framing and boxing up and fitting the ends of shelves into

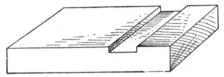

Fig. 1.—Trench or Groove

uprights, and similar work where pieces alike in thickness or nearly so are united at right angles, as in Fig. 3. The second is used mainly in the edges of boards to receive thin tongues or strips of wood,

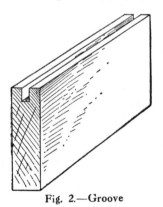

Fig. 2.—Groove

projecting and fitting a similar groove in the next board, as in Fig. 4. Both types of groove are very commonly em-

ployed in woodwork. The difference in their proportions makes it necessary to adopt different methods in cutting them. The first can be treated in a number of different ways. Without special tools it can be cut in the way described for rebates. It is first marked out by squaring lines across with penknife or scriber to indicate the width of groove, and its depth is marked with a gauge. Two cuts are then made with a tenon saw, allowing a little for chiselling exactly

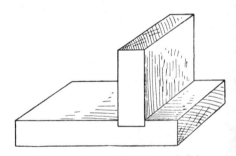

Fig. 3.—Grooved (or Housed) Joint

to the lines, and the wood between the sawcuts is cleared out with a chisel and finished with a rebate plane. In wood about an inch thick grooves of this kind seldom exceed $\frac{1}{4}$ in. in depth. In thinner wood they would often be less, for deep grooves weaken the piece in which they are cut.

The trenching or grooving plane (Fig 4A) is designed specially for grooves of this class. Like the fillister for rebates, it is adjustable for depth and has a slitting cutter for the side of the groove. It is a narrow plane, ranging from $\frac{1}{4}$ in. to $\frac{3}{4}$ in. wide, but, of course, can be used in wider grooves. The side rebate is another plane used for planing the edges of grooves in widening them. There is also a great variety of other planes of the rebate and shoulder and router class which can be used in most grooves of moderate size. The sash fillister can be used also in a groove which its fence allows it to reach to, and the same is true of the plough when a groove runs with the grain.

plough has the advantage of adjustability and it possesses a set of cutters of different widths. It can be set to cut to a certain depth, and has an adjustable fence at one side which acts as a gauge in keeping the cutter at a fixed distance from the edge of the wood, so that when the plough is set for the work it will cut the groove without any necessity for marking out or measuring. It will not cut across grain, like the fillister and trenching planes, though it is occasionally used on end grain, but practically all its work is in cutting narrow grooves with the grain.

Fig. 4A.—Trenching Plane

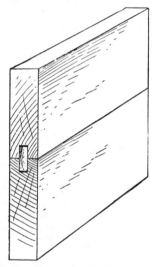

Fig. 4.—Grooved and Tongued Joint

The Plough. — In hand work the plough is the only suitable plane for making grooves for tongues, as shown in Figs. 2 and 4. An exception to this, however, is the matching planes (Figs. 40 and 41, page 94). These are made in pairs, for this work only, and are not adjustable like the plough. One forms a groove of definite size in the edge of a board and the other forms a tongue to fit it on the edge of another board. The tongue then is not a separate strip like the example in Fig. 4. But very little of this kind of ploughing and tongueing is done by hand now, and matching planes are seldom used. A

Sometimes it is convenient to use it in commencing wide grooves and rebates. Fig. 39, page 94, shows a plough in use. When used on considerable lengths of wood it is best to work it in a series of comparatively short strokes, just as with the ordinary surface planes. But ploughing is commenced at the front end of the wood and gradually worked backwards.

Grooves for the reception of tongues are required on so large a scale that most of this work is done by machinery. Boards for partitions, large panels, floor boards, and boarding for covering large surfaces, could not be grooved and tongued economically by hand, and so the latter is restricted to small amounts in details of joinery and other work, where it is seldom a case of fitting a number of boards edge to edge but of making grooves in pieces which are not of the proportions available in prepared boards.

The plough illustrated in Fig. 37, page 93, is only one of a number of types. But in all alike there is a set of interchangeable cutters, ranging from about $\frac{1}{8}$ in. to $\frac{9}{16}$ in. in stages of $\frac{1}{16}$ in. There is a vertical metal plate running the length of the plane, less in thickness than the narrowest cutter. The lower edge of this plate is the sole of the plane and bears on the bottom of the ploughed groove,

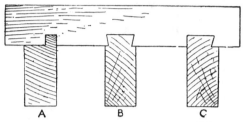

Fig. 5.—Three Types of Grooved Joint

enabling the thickness of shaving to be adjusted suitably. The fence determines the distance of the cutter, and of the groove it cuts from the side of the wood. The fence may have either screw or wedge adjustment, the type shown in Fig. 37, page 93, being adjusted by means of wedges. To set the plane the wedges are loosened, the plane set, and the wedges tightened by tapping them with the hammer. The depth of the groove is determined by a vertically sliding stop at the side of the metal plate. This is raised and lowered by turning the thumb-screw seen on the top of the plane. When the stop bears on the upper surface of the work the plough ceases to cut the groove any deeper.

Returning to grooves of the class shown in Figs. 1 and 3, which usually run across grain, there are some variations in the form they may take. Fig. 5 shows three ways in which such a groove may be modified, each having some advantage of its own. The width of the groove shown at A represents only about one-third the thickness of the piece fitted into it. This is done sometimes in corner or edge joints as an alternative to a rebate ; or it may be employed when the fitted-in piece comes so near an edge that a full width groove would leave very short and consequently weak grain beyond. Another, and sometimes the chief advantage, is that the piece fitted in is secure from lateral displacement by having

a shoulder to bear against on each side instead of only on one side as in an ordinary rebate. The plough is suitable for cutting such a groove when it runs with the grain. If across grain a plough could not be used because it would tear up the surface too badly. The groove could be sawn and chiselled and finished with other planes, or a special plane called a dado groove could be used, or a narrow trenching plane.

The grooves at B and C in Fig. 5 are dovetailed, so that the inserted piece cannot pull directly out, but must be slid in or out in the longitudinal direction of the groove. There may be a double-sided dovetail, as at B, or a single-sided one, as at C. These are rather troublesome to cut, and are only adopted in high-class work when the additional security they afford is very desirable. The groove would first be cut in the ordinary way to the width of its narrowest part and then undercut with a chisel to the extent of the vee. The parts fitting into them are treated similarly, the dovetail being usually cut with a chisel. Grooves of this kind can be built up by nailing on strips that have had their edges bevelled, or the grooves may be machine-cut.

Figs. 6 and 7 show methods of jointing boards edge to edge when it is considered desirable to have more than the ordinary

Fig. 6.—Rebated and Tongued Joint

Fig. 7.—Double-tongued Joint

provision against an open crack right through the joint, which might occur if the tongue in an ordinary tongued joint became split. In Fig. 6 the joints in the opposite faces of the boards are not opposite each other. In making this joint by hand one edge of each board has a tongue and the other a corresponding groove. The tongue is formed by cutting two rebates which are dissimilar in distance in from the edge. On the other edge the groove may be ploughed either before or after the single rebate has been cut. Fig. 7 has its cuter joints opposite each other but has a tongue and groove side by side on each edge of the board. In this case two rebates and a groove are cut in each edge. As a rule, of course, the edges would be machine-cut, a revolving cutter of the correct profile being employed and a large number of boards done.

Besides the various grooving planes already mentioned there are combination and universal planes. These are provided with a large number of cutters and adjustments which adapt them for a great many different operations, They are entirely of metal, and necessarily rather complicated and expensive compared with the single purpose planes. Some are limited to various grooving operations,

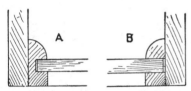

Fig. 8.—Two Methods of Securing Drawer Bottom

such as ploughing, rebating, slitting, matching, with perhaps beading. Others include different kinds of simple moulding, and chamfering. As many as 50 or 60 different cutters may be supplied with a plane of this class, the large number, of course, being accounted for, not being of different shapes, but because the commonly used shapes are in sets of different widths or curves. The best plane of this type is the Stanley Universal plane which will be described later in a special chapter.

Grooves, like rebates, are sometimes built up instead of cut out. Fig. 8 shows two examples where a drawer bottom fits in a groove which is not cut in the sides of the drawer itself but in attached pieces. At A a separate strip is grooved and attached to the side of the drawer. At B two strips are used and the groove is not ploughed at all, but is formed by

the space between them. These methods are generally adopted for strength when the sides of the drawer are too thin to be ploughed deeply enough, or when the drawer has to contain heavy articles.

Fig. 9.—Usual Method of Fixing Drawer Bottom

The ordinary method, with no building up, is shown in Fig. 9. Fig. 10 shows a method of fitting panels into frames when a flush surface is required on one side, and a groove central with the thickness of the panel would come too close to the edge of the frame. The edge of the panel is rebated so that the projecting tongue and the ploughed groove it fits into are as far as possible from the edge of the frame.

Varieties and Uses of Tongues.— A tongue is a strip of wood for fitting into a ploughed groove. In cross section it is generally about $\frac{7}{8}$ in. by $\frac{1}{4}$ in. It is usually long enough to go in as a single piece the full length of the joint, but there is no objection, as a rule, to making up the length by inserting two or more shorter strips end to end. As a separate tongue must go halfway into each of the pieces

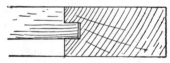

Fig. 10.—Flush Panel

it unites its width must be nearly double the depth of the ploughed groove in the edge of each piece; it should not be quite double or there might be some risk of its preventing a close joint between the pieces. When it is formed solid on the edge of one piece and fits into a groove in the other it should still not quite reach to the bottom of the groove. This is indicated in preceding illustrations where tongues fitting in grooves are shown.

A tongue is not used because it is of any value in holding parts together. Its purpose is partly to keep the outer surfaces flush by preventing side movement in relation to each other, and partly to avoid an open crack right through the joint if the latter is not quite close. Wood is liable to shrink or to swell as it loses or acquires moisture, and therefore absolutely tight joints are not always possible or desirable. A tongue in the joint allows shrinkage, but it is a barrier to a direct passage through.

In work where grooving and tongueing is done on a large scale tongues are sawn to size on a circular saw. Width and thickness must be exact, but length is anything that happens to be convenient. If sawn by hand some amount of planing is necessary afterwards to get the thickness exact and uniform, but the edges can generally be left as sawn. Usually the thickness of the board they are cut from would represent the width of the tongues, and this would be quite near enough without gauging and planing to width. Exceptions might occur in very fine and exact work or when the tongues are wider than they are wanted. In thickness a tongue should be a reasonably close fit in its groove but not so tight as to require driving in.

The grain of a tongue usually runs lengthwise, but exceptions to this are sometimes made. It may run either crosswise or diagonally, in which case, of course, the loose tongue is very weak transversely and can easily be snapped off anywhere. But when inserted this weakness does not matter ; in fact, unless the joint is very short the tongue has to be inserted in short lengths, because long ones across grain are unobtainable. The advantage of having the grain across instead of lengthwise is that it cannot split down the middle as a tongue with longitudinal grain might. Tongues with cross grain may be cut from a board the same thickness as the tongue, or a thicker board may be used and the strips sawn down into two or more afterwards.

The advantage of diagonal grain is that longer strips can be cut diagonally than at right angles across a board, and there is also slightly less risk of breakage, because there is a greater length of grain to split when it is diagonal than when it is direct across the strip.

The tongued joint may be glued or may be simply put together without glue, the latter being commonest. A joint is glued when a single piece would be preferred if it could be obtained wide enough. The reason for gluing is to make a practically solid piece. But the risk of shrinkage makes it impossible to glue

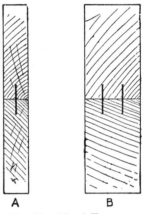

Fig. 11.—Metal Tongues

up very great widths and at the same time prevent them from warping and splitting. Therefore a number of narrow pieces, each free to shrink independently of the others, is the best way in many cases, and the joints are not glued.

When glue is used in edge joints there is no great advantage in using a tongue as well, and in the majority of such cases it is omitted. To make a good glue joint it is necessary to have the wood surfaces in tight contact everywhere with only a thin film of glue between. This is done by pressing and sliding the parts over each other to squeeze all superfluous glue out, and then usually by clamping until the glue is dry. When a tongue has to be inserted one of the grooved pieces is held in the vice, as in making an ordinary edge glue joint, and the tongue is glued in and secured with a few nails to keep it from moving endwise while the other piece is being adjusted on it. Plenty of glue is applied to the edges of both pieces, and they are fitted together and the upper one slid a few inches each way with as much downward pressure as possible and finally adjusted with its ends flush with .the ends of the lower piece. Then clamps are applied to keep the joint squeezed together and it is laid aside for a few hours to dry.

Metal tongues are sometimes used instead of wood. They do not require a ploughed groove, but can be inserted in a sawcut, which is usually made with a circular saw. They are not only strong themselves, but the narrow groove they require diminishes risk of breaking the ledges of wood on each side of the groove. A central tongue may be used, as at A in Fig. 11, or if the joint is wide two tongues may be inserted, as at B. In very wide joints two wooden tongues are sometimes used similarly.

Shooting and Mitre Cutting

Shooting Square Work.—When it is required to joint-up thin boards to form panels, etc., this may be done by overhand planing, or shooting as it is sometimes termed. Each board is fixed in turn in

a straightedge is applied it will touch both of them, as illustrated by Fig. 2.

Construction of Shooting Boards. —The method described above is difficult and requires a deal of skill, and is not con

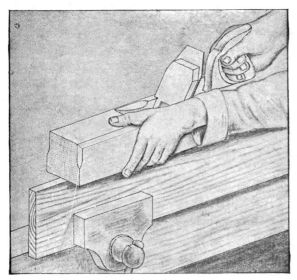

Fig. 1.—Overhand Planing or Shooting

Fig. 2.—Testing Jointed Boards with Straightedge

the vice and the edges planed straight and square as shown in Fig. 1 (*see* also Figs. 13 and 14, p. 103). When one piece is placed on the other the surfaces forming the joint should touch each other the whole length, and the broad surfaces should be in one plane, so that when

venient where much jointing and thin-edge planing is required ; therefore the shooting is generally done with the help of a shooting board, which in size may vary according to the purposes for which it is required. A useful size is made by having a 9-in. or 11-in. by $\frac{7}{8}$-in. board for the base. A piece 5 in. to 7 in. wide and ¾ in. thick is fixed on the top of this. The length may be from 2 ft. 6 in. to 4 ft. A stop made of hardwood is housed into the top board, as shown in Fig. 3. Shooting boards are liable to warp, as shown exaggerated at Figs. 4 and 5, which causes the plane to shoot the edges of the work out of square ; this can be obviated by screwing ledges to the underside

are tried together their face sides are not in one plane, as shown in Fig. 9 ; whereas, if the face of one piece is placed downwards on the shooting board and the other piece upwards, they come together, as shown in Fig. 10.

Shooting Edges at an Angle.— When it is required to plane edges at an angle other than a right angle, if the material is ¾ in. or more in thickness the

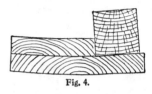

Fig. 4.

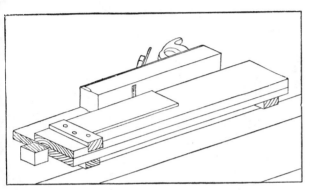

Fig. 3.—Using Shooting Board

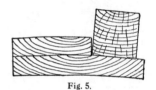

Fig. 5.

Figs. 4 and 5.—Faulty Construction of Shooting Boards

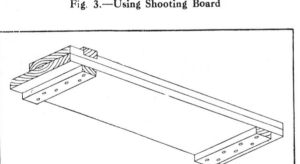

Fig. 6

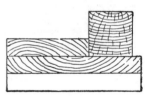

Fig. 7.

Figs. 6 and 7.—Shooting Board prevented from Warping by Ledges

(hardwood being the best for the purpose) and so keeping the board true, as shown at Figs. 6 and 7.

Using the Shooting Board.— It sometimes happens that the edges of the work are not shot quite square owing to the shooting board wearing or warping or to the face of the plane not being at right angles to the side that is on the rebate of the shooting board (Fig. 8). Then if the face side of each piece is placed on the shooting board and planed, when they

work is frequently done by overhand planing. A bevel is then set to the required angle and applied to the ends of the stuff, as shown at Fig. 11, and marked. The work is then planed to the lines and also to fit the bevel (Fig. 12) which is frequently applied during the process of planing.

Shooting Block.— For thinner material a shooting block is more convenient. Where there are only one or two pieces to be done, just one or two blocks of

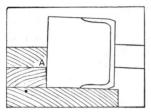

Fig. 8.—Shooting Out of
Square

Fig. 13.—Built-up Shooting Block
for Bevelling Edges and Ends of
Work

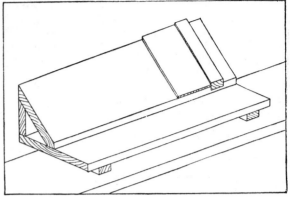

Fig. 13.

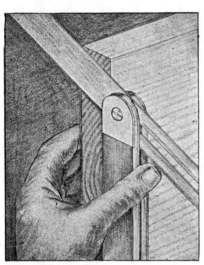

Fig. 11.—Applying Bevel to End of
Board for Marking

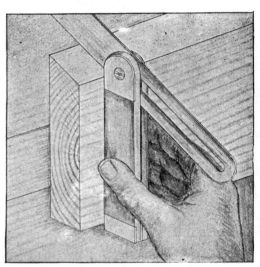

Fig. 12.—Testing Planed Edge with
Bevel

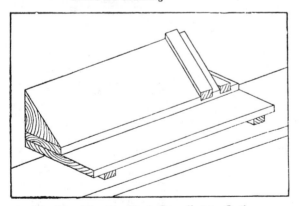

Fig. 14.—Movable Block Dowelled to Ordinary
Shooting Board

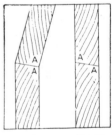

Fig. 9.   Fig. 10.

Fig. 9.—Placing Boards Together so
that Adjacent Angles are Equal

Fig. 10.—Placing Boards Together so
that Opposite Angles are Equal

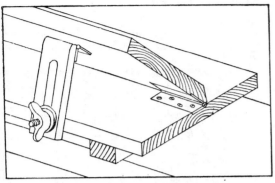

Fig. 16.—Adjustable Shooting Block

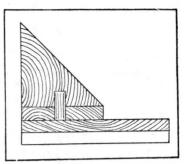

Fig. 15.—Section through Movable Block showing Dowel

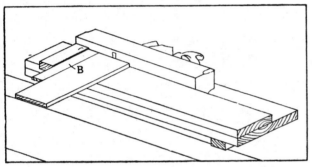

Fig. 17.—Shooting End-grain

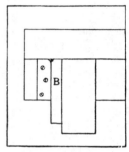

Fig. 18.—Using Piece to Prevent Breaking of Corner

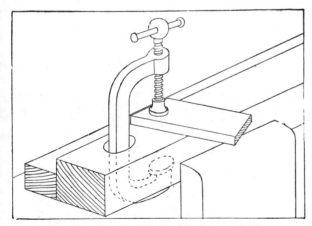

Fig. 20.—Shooting Block with Adjustable Stop

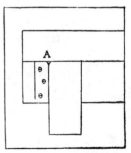

Fig. 19.—Faulty Method, Corner Broken

wood cut to the particular angle and temporarily screwed to the shooting

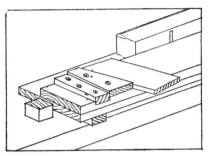

Fig. 20A.—Shooting Ends at an Angle

block will probably be found sufficient. But when there are a number of pieces to be done accurately, then it will generally pay to have a more or less permanent block. Fig. 13 shows a block built up. Figs. 14 and 15 illustrate a solid triangular piece trued up to the desired angle; by means of three or four dowels it can be made readily to fit on or be taken off an ordinary shooting board. Fig. 16 shows one end of a very useful and simple form of adjustable shooting block which can be set to any angle within its limits.

Shooting End Grain.—Fig. 17 shows

stop becomes worn and does not properly support the corner of the work, and

Fig. 21.—Ordinary Mitre Block

the fibres forming it become broken, as at A, Fig. 19, by the plane-iron edge.

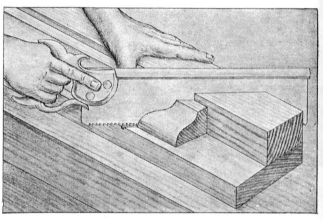

Fig. 22.—Cutting Mitre

Therefore it is a good plan to have an

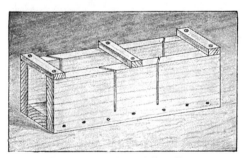

Fig. 23.—Ordinary Mitre Box

the operation of shooting end grain square to an edge. After a time the end of the

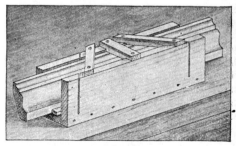

Fig. 24.—Moulding in Position in Box

intervening piece, as shown at B, Figs. 17 and 18, then the end of the work and this piece are shot together, which prevents the corner of the work being damaged. This matter has already been alluded to in the chapter on general planing.

Shooting Ends at an Angle.—When it is required to shoot ends at an angle a wedge-shaped piece can be cut to the proper form and fastened to the ordinary shooting board, as shown at Fig. 20A.

A very convenient kind of shooting block with adjustable stop is represented by Fig. 20. The block is bored and pared so as to receive a strong form of **G-cramp**, which will hold the stop firmly

Fig. 26.—Mitre Trimming Machine

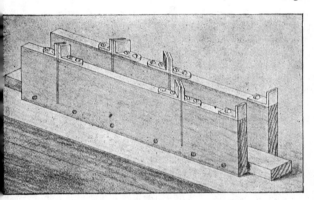

Fig. 25.—Adjustable Guides to Box

at any desired angle, and which can be quickly altered as found necessary.

CUTTING MITRES

Mitre Cut or Mitre Block.—In Fig. 21 is shown the ordinary mitre cut made of two pieces of wood ; these are fastened together by a little glue and also are nailed from the underside of the base. This is a very useful form of mitre cut for general purposes, particularly for small mouldings, and the work and block can be held together by the left hand, as shown in Fig. 22.

Mitre Box.—The ordinary mitre box is shown in Fig. 23. This is used for deeper and larger mouldings than can be cut by the mitre block. Fig. 24 shows a cornice moulding in position. This kind of mitre box can be used for different

sizes of mouldings by inserting a fillet of the proper width, as shown.

Fig. 25 illustrates a mitre box with metal guides, which are screwed upon the edges as illustrated ; they can be adjusted to suit any thickness of saw ; as they greatly reduce the wear of the cuts in the box, truer mitres can be cut for a much longer period. The metal guides can also be obtained for cutting square ends, and may be

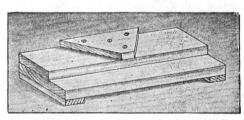

Fig. 27.—Ordinary Mitre Shoot with Solid Fence

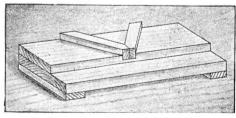

Fig. 28.—Mitre Block with Two Stops

used at the end of the box as shown or in pairs at the top of the cuts.

Metal Mitre Cut.—There is a number of excellent, and, of course, expensive, mitreing machines on the market, but probably one of the handiest is illustrated by Fig. 26. It will cut mouldings of a good size and mitres at any angle within the compass of the machine. It cuts mitres true and smooth, obviating any necessity of shooting. A much later chapter will deal in detail with the use of this and similar simple machinery.

Fig. 30.—Improvised Shooting Block

Shooting Blocks.—A very useful improvised block is shown at Fig. 30. A piece of wood is screwed to the top of the bench and its surfaces well planed so that it is quite square with the side of the bench; then a fillet is screwed to the side of the bench almost touching the screw and at the mitre angle with the piece s. The upper end A may be thicknessed out as shown. Then by holding the plane on the skew so that the iron cuts the mitre whilst the other part of the sole of the plane is kept firmly on the piece s, as will be seen, the bench vice can be brought into use to hold the moulding firmly.

Fig. 29.—Shooting Mitre

SHOOTING MITRES

Mitre Shoots.—The two common kinds of mitre shoots are shown in Figs. 27 and 28. The base is shown battened, or ledged, underneath so as to prevent warping, which would cause untrue mitres. The hardiest kind is that shown by Figs. 28 and 29, because the work and the mitre stop can be grasped firmly together, as shown at Fig. 29.

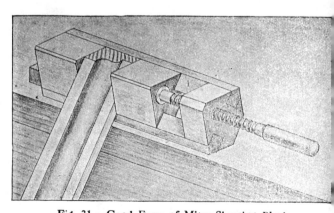

Fig. 31.—Good Form of Mitre Shooting Block

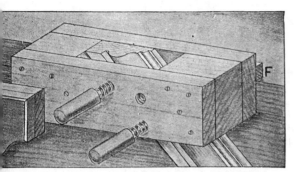

Fig. 32.—Another Kind of Mitre Shooting Block

and use the plane so that the mitre of the moulding is cut by the iron and not the sur- face of the block.

During recent years many accurate mitreing appliances constructed of steel have been introduced. For example, Fig. 33 shows an appliance especi- ally made for use with a steel plane, and it will be noted that the angle of mitre is adjustable. Still other appli- ances will be mentioned in

Fig. 31 illustrates a most useful ind of shooting block which will old mouldings of different sizes. If esired, this kind can be bought eady-made with either a wooden or teel hand-screw.

The shooting block shown by Fig. 2 has its advantages, being simple o make and also suitable for being eld firmly in the bench vice. To revent slipping, a fillet F can be fixed t the back of the block so as to rest n the top of the bench as shown.

Of course, in using this kind of lock great care must be taken to have he plane irons set very fine and to hold

Fig. 33.—Metal Shooting "Board"

connection with special applications of mitreing discussed in later chapters.

Halved, Lapped, Notched and Housed Joints

Unless woodwork joints are neatly and well made, the best after-finish cannot conceal a clumsy effect, nor can proper strength and durability be expected. The careless worker often relies on tightening with the cramp, or on slight alterations when fitting, but by far the most satisfactory and least time-wasting way is to follow sound and craftsmanlike principles from the start.

The number of different joints employed in woodworking is surprisingly large. Joiners, carpenters, cabinet-makers, wheelwrights and many other trades each have their own favourite methods, and, oddly enough, often have distinctive ways of making what is really the same joint. Even national variations are met in the work and tools of one country as compared with another.

It is here proposed to deal with many descriptions of jointing in such detail as to be practically helpful. Fully illustrated instructions will be given for constructing all the ordinary kinds of joints employed by skilled artisans, besides numerous others of an unusual and unique type.

Halved Joints.—Figs 1 to 17 show simple examples, in wood of rectangular section, of joints commonly met with in carpentry and cabinet work. They are very easy to make, and, in some cases

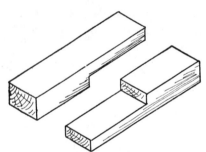

Fig. 1.—Straight Half-lap Joint

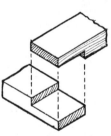

Fig. 2.—Angle Half-lap Joint

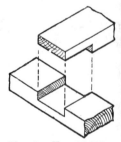

Fig. 3.—Tee Half-lap Joint

are quite as suitable as more difficult joints. The straight half-lap joint (Fig. 1) can be used for lengthening posts or rails in hut-building, etc., also for forming wall plates, joists and rafters for roofs, floors, and temporary structures. It is readily set out. A marking gauge, marking knife (or pencil) and square are employed in setting out the pieces. As the name of the joint indicates, the depth of each piece cut away is half the thickness of the wood, and in cutting down with the tenon saw care should be taken to keep inside the line ; the four cuts are made with a tenon saw. The terms " halved " and " lap " are often used interchangeably ; but, as a matter of fact, while a halved joint is always a lapped one, a lap joint is not invariably with a flush face. A familiar instance is the Oxford frame, and the centre of a barrow-wheel may also be cited. In making Tee and cross half-joints, the parts should be gauged to a width, so that they may be set out with the cer-

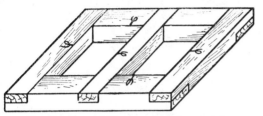

Fig. 4.—Lapped Frame with Tee-stretcher

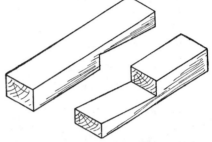

Fig. 6.—Straight Bevelled Half-lap Joint

halved. Fig. 2 shows the angle half-lap joint, suitable for corners or angles in framework, and in framed grounds for the fixing of joinery.

Tee and Cross Half-lap Joints.—

The Tee half-lap (Fig. 3) is useful where a rail meets a post, or post meets sill, in the framework of huts. Fig. 4 shows a square frame halved at the angles, and with a Tee stretcher fitted at the middle. The sinking for the Tee joint is marked out for the width and gauged for depth ; then, after making the usual saw-cuts, the waste is removed with a paring chisel,

tainty of fitting truly. When marking for the width of sinking, care must be taken that the saw kerfs are not too far apart. It is better to have the slot too narrow rather than too wide, and fit the joint afterwards by planing the opposite piece or paring the joint. But this precaution should not be depended upon to give good work. It is only suggested that it is better to have the joint a little tight rather than a little

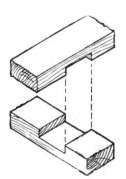

Fig. 5.—Cross Half-lap Joint

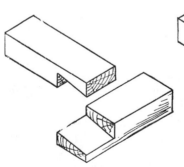

Fig. 7.—Angle Bevelled Half-lap Joint

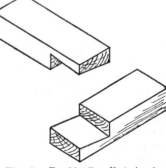

Fig. 8.—Double Bevelled Angle Half-lap

used either horizontally or vertically, as proves most convenient.

The cross half-lap (Fig. 5) is obviously a double Tee, and is very handy where pieces are required to cross each other

slack. The former can be remedied, but the latter cannot. The aim should be to saw the joint right first time, and so that the pieces can be fitted together " hand-tight."

Bevelled Half-lap Joints. — Examples of this useful joint are shown by Figs. 6, 7, and 8. It is occasionally employed for heavy framing work, wall plates, sills and binders, to withstand a pulling stress, also in good half-timbering for the exterior of Elizabethan-style

regarded as a Tee half-lap modified to resist a lateral pull (*see* Figs. 9 and 10). It is extensively used in cabinet work. The pin part should be made first, commencing as for an ordinary lap joint, then sawing the shoulders to the necessary angle and carefully finishing with the

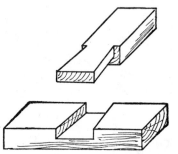

Fig. 9.—Dovetailed Tee Half-lap

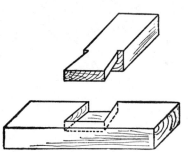

Fig. 10.—Stopped Dovetailed Half-lap

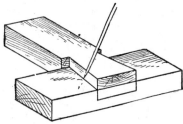

Fig. 11.—Marking Sinking from Pin

Fig. 12.—Sawing Dovetail Socket ; note Saw-kerfs in Waste Wood

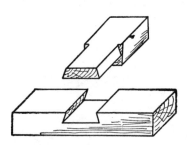

Fig. 13.—Dovetail Half-lap for Upward Pull

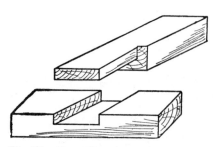

Fig. 14.—Dovetailed Acute-Angle Half-lap

houses. The marking down and across is similar to the simpler form of lap, but a tapered piece of wood is used as a template for the depth, instead of the gauge, though the latter is sometimes used as well, to give the right starting point for the taper.

Dovetail and Diagonal Half-lap Joints.—The dovetail half-lap may be

chisel. The pin half is next held over the piece for the socket, the sinking accurately ma ked, as in Fig. 11, squared down, sawn sparely so as to fit the pin tightly (*see* Fig. 12), and the waste chiselled out. Fig. 13 illustrates a similar joint designed to resist an upward pull. An adaptation of dovetail and half-lap joints will be seen in Fig. 14, which

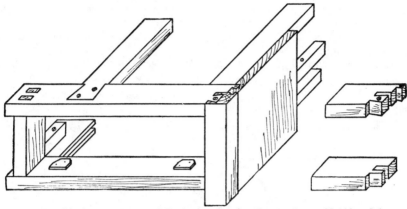

Fig. 15.—Portion of Chest of Drawers, showing Dovetail and Half-lap Joints

shows the same kind of joint as in Fig. 10, but not having the two pieces at a right angle; this is known as diagonal halving. Fig. 17 is a cross diagonal joint.

The corners of the frame illustrated in Fig. 18 are secured by bevelled half-lapping, while in the centre are two diagonal crosspieces or braces. To set out the latter, the sliding bevel is used to take the exact angle, which is then transferred to the first portion of the cross. The second piece is then laid on the first and marked in. The marked piece is now gauged for depth and cut; the other being next laid in position in the halving and marked to fit in the usual way. To insert the completed cross into the frame, one is laid on the other and the positions marked for all the cuts, the depths on both frame and cross-ends being then gauged.

In Fig. 16 we show the application of the ordinary form of the ship-lap joint (there is a more complicated form of this

joint which will be described later); this is only suitable for use between two absolutely fixed posts or something similar,

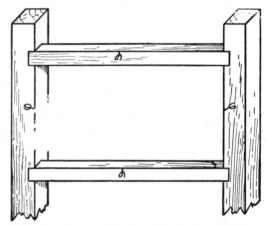

Fig. 16.—Posts and Rails with Ship-lapped Joints

but in such positions it is a handy way of fixing rails or uprights. The reason why it is necessary that the timbers between which this joint is used must be rigidly fixed is, the joint being made on the slope and fixed with nails, these latter have the tendency to force the posts or other timbers apart, thus destroy-

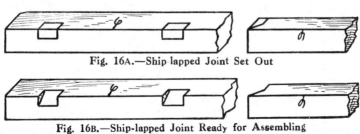

Fig. 16A.—Ship-lapped Joint Set Out

Fig. 16B.—Ship-lapped Joint Ready for Assembling

ing the stiffness and also opening the back part which should fit close up to them.

The ship-lap joint consists of a bevel lip fitting into a sloping recess, and the setting out is as shown in Fig. 16A, while the two parts after cutting are shown in Fig. 16B. This is really a carpenter's joint, and is rarely applicable to any other branch of woodworking, though exceptions occasionally crop up. This joint

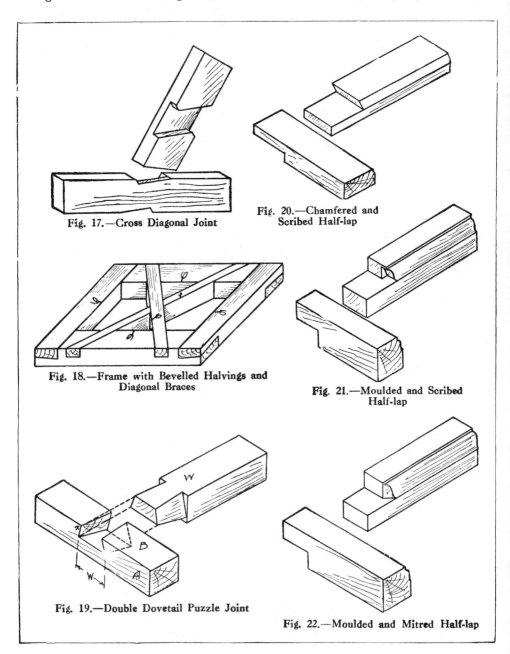

Fig. 17.—Cross Diagonal Joint

Fig. 20.—Chamfered and Scribed Half-lap

Fig. 18.—Frame with Bevelled Halvings and Diagonal Braces

Fig. 21.—Moulded and Scribed Half-lap

Fig. 19.—Double Dovetail Puzzle Joint

Fig. 22.—Moulded and Mitred Half-lap

is also largely localised, being very common in the south of England, but rarely seen in the Midlands and the North.

A puzzle joint, dovetailed both ways,

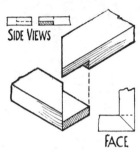

Fig. 23.—Plain Mitred Half-lap

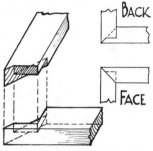

Fig. 24.—Stopped and Mitred Half-lap

manner and the other piece next marked, keeping the lines full for fitting. It is as well if the joint is fitted tight. Sur-

is shown by Fig. 19. It is of the same kind as seen in Fig. 14, with the difference that the two pieces have to be separated by a slanting, downward pull; this causes the apparent dovetail on the face B. The joint is made by first gauging the edge A half-way down; on this line the width w is set out, and the dovetail is marked on faces A and B. The bevel

prisingly many people are deceived by this joint.

Moulded and Chamfered Half-lap. —Figs. 20, 21, and 22 show moulded and chamfered pieces with half-lap joints,

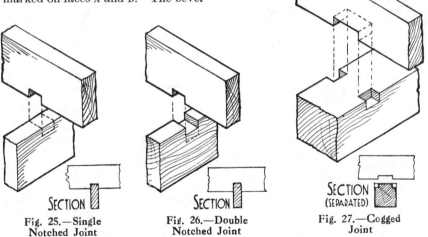

Fig. 25.—Single Notched Joint

Fig. 26.—Double Notched Joint

Fig. 27.—Cogged Joint

x is then transferred to the opposite edge, w is squared over to the same edge, and the work is gauged down at the point where the bevel and square lines intersect. Cutting out is done by sawing down and chiselling out the waste in the ordinary

Figs. 20 and 21 being scribed and Fig. 22 mitred. The scribing and mitreing referred to will be discussed later when dealing with mortise and tenon joints. Figs. 23 and 24 are examples of mitred half-lap joints, that seen in Fig. 24 being stopped

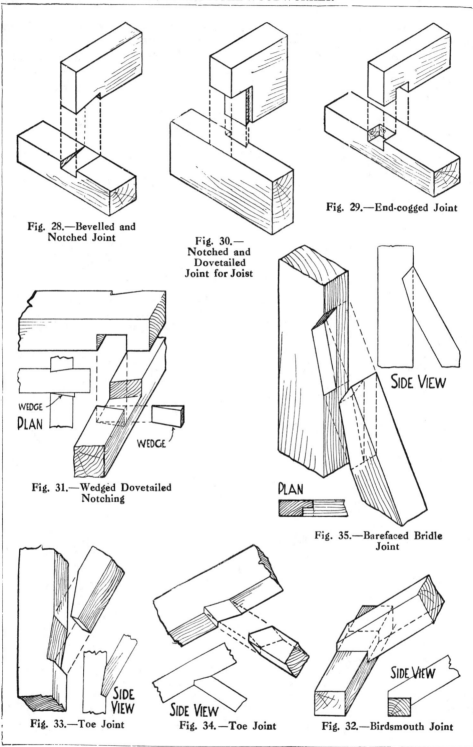

Fig. 28.—Bevelled and Notched Joint

Fig. 29.—End-cogged Joint

Fig. 30.—Notched and Dovetailed Joint for Joist

WEDGE

PLAN

WEDGE

Fig. 31.—Wedged Dovetailed Notching

SIDE VIEW

PLAN

Fig. 35.—Barefaced Bridle Joint

SIDE VIEW

Fig. 33.—Toe Joint

SIDE VIEW

Fig. 34.—Toe Joint

SIDE VIEW

Fig. 32.—Birdsmouth Joint

to prevent the end grain of the wood showing, as would be required for picture frames.

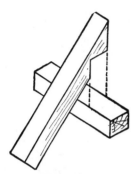

Fig. 36.—Falling Birdsmouth Joint

Fastening Halved or Lap Joints.
—For securing all manner of halved or lap joints glue, nails, screws, or a combination of such can be employed. Much, of course, depends on the particular purpose, the nature of the strain to be met, and whether or not appearance has to be studied.

Notched Joints.—Numerous varieties of these are illustrated by Figs. 25 to 39. Though sometimes met with in ordinary woodworking, their chief use is in con-

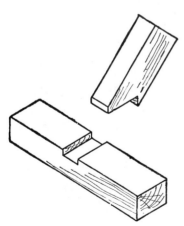

Fig. 37.—Sunk Birdsmouth Joint

structive carpentry, such as the framework of wooden buildings, cycle sheds, photographic and cinema studios etc..

also in the making of rough benches and brackets. Figs. 25, 26, and 27 are examples of single and double notching, employed for fitting joists into floor

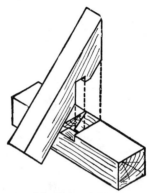

Fig. 38.—Notched Birdsmouth Joint

binders. The depth having been marked with a gauge or template, and the width from the work itself, the rest is merely a matter of sawing and chiselling. Fig. 27 is also known as a cogged joint, and is used with extra heavy beams. Figs. 28 and 29 are end-notched joints, employed at the ends of joists, or when a cross rail is notched on to a wall plate or head piece in framed or stone buildings.

Fig. 30 shows the end of a roof joist or purlin notched into a beam or rafter in such a way as to withstand a tensile

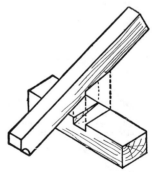

Fig. 39.—Bevelled and Notched Joint

pull. This is a good manner of binding a building. Fig. 31 illustrates another method of jointing to resist a pull by driving a wedge into the joint This may be considered as a cross half-lap, modified into a locking and wedged dovetail.

Figs. 32 to 39 show more kinds of notching, which can be used, graded from the simple to the rather complex,

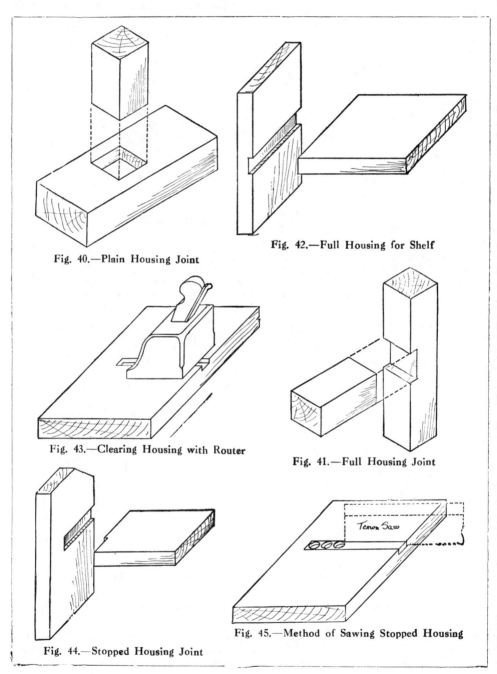

Fig. 40.—Plain Housing Joint

Fig. 42.—Full Housing for Shelf

Fig. 43.—Clearing Housing with Router

Fig. 41.—Full Housing Joint

Fig. 44.—Stopped Housing Joint

Fig. 45.—Method of Sawing Stopped Housing

to suit the greater or lesser importance of the work in hand. It is thought that the drawings are sufficiently explicit to render explanation needless, inasmuch as the joints are all derived from one or other of those already described. Some of them, it will be seen, may if desired be formed with the saw alone, but generally the chisel also is needed. The main thing necessary is to make sure of careful angling and accurate fitting.

Housed Joints.—Housing may be defined as sinking the end of one piece into a notch or groove cut in another for its reception. It is chiefly used for the ends of shelves, and for posts, rails, etc. Figs. 40 to 42, 44, and 46 to 52 illustrate different housing joints. Fig. 40 shows [illegible]ost housed into a sill; though this

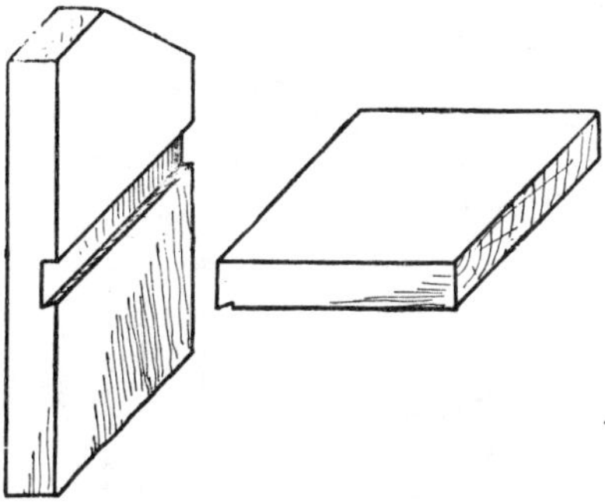

Fig. 46.—Dovetailed Housing Joint

ought only to be done when the top also is fixed, otherwise the depth is insufficient for rigidity. The recess may be set out from the bottom of the post itself, and is then chiselled away like a mortise, keeping well inside the marked lines to ensure a tight fit.

Fig. 41 is typical of the rail and post joint, as in the case of a door post and head for a hut framework or partition. It is fastened by nailing from the back.

Figs. 42, 44, and 46 to 48 show five methods of housing shelves into the upright ends of a bookcase or cabinet. In setting out the parallel lines for the sinking should always be marked exactly to the thickness of the shelf. Then, for the plain housing (Fig. 42) having gauged to the depth, the lines are sawn down, with the saw kerfs inside the waste wood, to the gauge marks. The core or waste is next taken out nearly to the depth with a narrow chisel, and the trench is often finished with a router, or "old woman's

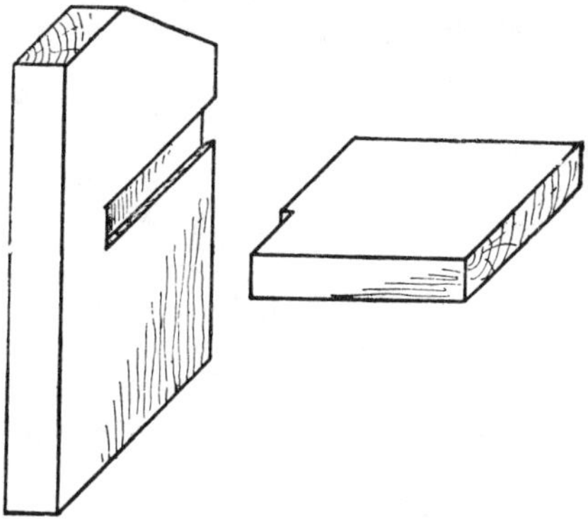

Fig. 47.—Dovetailed and Stopped Housing

tooth," to a flat bottom as shown by Fig. 43. The chisel in the router is adjustable to any desired depth. By the foregoing method the sinking is left visible on the front edge of the upright; it looks decidedly better if this is avoided

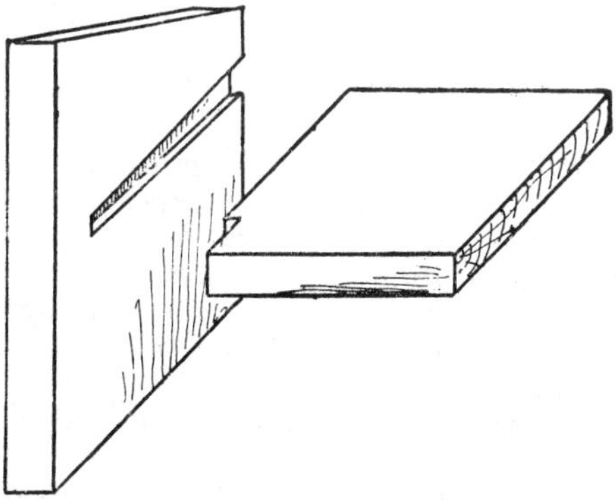

Fig. 48.—Tapered, Dovetailed and Stopped Joint

by "stopping," as seen in Fig. 44. The latter may be done by gauging the width of the stopped end, and using the saw slantwise on the marked parallel lines till the cut reaches the stop and is the right depth at the other end; the sinking is then finished with a chisel. Another way is to get a start for the tenon saw by boring three or four holes with a centre bit to the width and depth of the groove, these holes being afterwards cut out square with the mallet and chisel. The saw can now be inserted and the groove finished off with the router (*see* Fig. 45).

A stronger joint, to resist an endways pull, is obtained by dovetailing or bevelling one edge of the housing, as seen in Figs. 46 and 47, the first being plain and the second stopped. The best method,

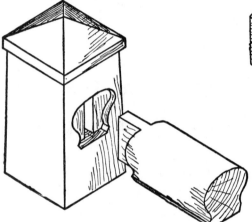

Fig. 49.—Housed and Tenoned Joint

however, as used for good furniture, is a stopped, dovetailed and tapered joint (*see* Fig. 48). When well fitted, glued, and driven in from the back this makes a perfect joint, both as regards strength and appearance. This joint requires no nailing.

A type of tenoned and housed joint used between a newel post and hand-rail is illustrated by Fig. 49. In a thick newel post, shrinkage is almost certain to occur, which causes the joint at the shoulder to open. This defect is prevented by housing the whole of the hand-rail into the post to a depth of about ⅜ in., which permits the post to shrink or expand at will. To do this a mortise and tenon is first made. The tenon is inserted and the rail marked round with a marking awl, the housing

for the rail being finally cut wi'h mallet, chisel and scribing gouge.

The housed joint between the pulley

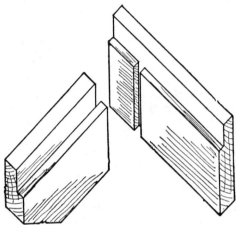

Fig. 51.—Trenched Joint

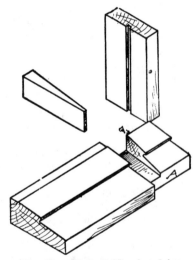

Fig. 50.—Wedged Housing Joint

stile and bevelled sill of a double-hung sliding-sash window frame is shown by Fig. 50. The housing is tapered, and is cut wider than the thickness of the stile, in order to allow the insertion of a wedge behind the latter, as indicated. The trenching is often set out, squared over, and cut before rebating and bevelling the sill, so that the try-square and gauge may be used. The pieces notched at the sides marked A are cut out for the reception of the outside and inside linings,

is nailed from the upper side of the head.

Fig. 52 illustrates the housed trenching

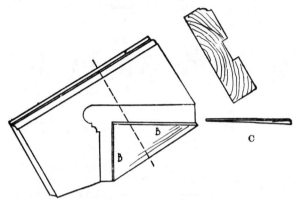

Fig. 52.—Trenched Housing for Stairs

which form the box for the sash-weights to slide up and down in.

Fig. 51 shows the joint between the head and side of an ordinary inside door casing to be fixed in a brick or stone opening. This joint is fitted tightly and

of a stair string to receive the step ends. It will be noticed that the sides marked B are out of parallel in order to admit a glued wedge C besides the step end, to ensure a good fit on the top side of the tread and a rigid fixing.

Edge and Angle Joints

Glue Joints.—What are known as glue joints are those which depend chiefly, or, at any rate, to a large extent, on gluing for their adhesion and strength, though not necessarily to the exclusion of other factors. These comprise butt, slotted screw, tongued and grooved, feathered, and keyed joints. They are mostly used to join up boards to a greater

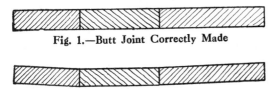

Fig. 1.—Butt Joint Correctly Made

Fig. 2.—Butt Joint Badly Made

width than can be obtained singly, and for angles.

Glued Butt Joints.—This is the simplest form of glue joint, consisting of two (or more) boards planed straight and square on adjacent edges and glued together, as shown in section by Fig. 1. It is not nearly so easy as it looks. In making such a joint, especially when a fairly long one, the patience and skill of the novice, and sometimes of the professional, are taxed to the utmost, and it often happens that when the two boards fit closely together they are not straight on the face, appearing instead as in Fig. 2. The remedy, of course, is further careful planing.

Should the wood be over ¾ in. thick,

the joints are best made with the boards fixed in the bench vice, the trying plane being held with the fingers of the left hand under the plane face, and the finger tips running along the face of the board so as to act as guides and keep the plane iron in the middle, either for the whole length of the board or for a portion only, as may be needed, and for good jointing aim should always be made for the final shaving to be the full length of the board. The feet should be placed to facilitate walking in the direction of the length.

The trying plane used for jointing should be in good condition. The cutting iron should be as thin as possible and only very slightly round on the edge, while the back iron should be set down to within the merest trifle of the cutting edge of the front iron. The shavings taken off will then be no thicker than the thinnest tissue paper. Rough, "near enough" work will not answer; indeed, the joints must fit exactly together, and this is achieved when no light can be seen through the joint. This is most important.

For thinner boards and very short joints there is no better way than the "underhand" method of using the plane. This necessitates the employment of a shooting board (*see* Fig. 3 and also the chapter on mitreing), a handy appliance which should be found in every workroom. The main portion A may be 9 in.

wide by 1 in. thick ; it must be straight and out of twist. The part B on which the plane works should project about 3 in., and is screwed to the under side

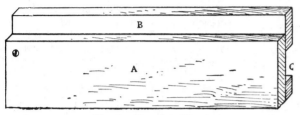

Fig. 3.—Shooting Board

of A. The strip C, of the same thickness as B, is merely to make the board level. Fig. 4 is a sectional view, with the plane and work in position.

One of the pieces to be jointed should be laid on the shooting board face upwards, while its fellow must be " shot " face downwards, to counteract the state of things indicated in Fig. 2, which might be caused by the curvature of the plane making the edges slightly out of square.

The edges of the boards should be tested with the try-square, and by holding the two surfaces in contact between the worker and the light. The parallelism of the boards when together should also be verified by laying a straightedge across.

The glue employed for the joints must be of the best quality and comparatively freshly made. It should be used as hot as possible.

A great many people undoubtedly make it too thick, under the impression that it will be stronger, whereas the exact reverse is the case. The glue should run off the brush like thin paint.

Undoubtedly the best way to put glue joints together is by " rubbing " ; that is to say, the two edges are glued liberally, and then the two boards are rubbed to and fro in contact, as shown in Fig. 5, so as to rub as much of the surplus glue out of the joint as possible, and incidentally to rub it well into the pores of the wood. For joints of any length assistance is required, otherwise it is difficult to keep the boards flush at the sides and

ends. As the to and fro movement becomes stiffer, proving that the glue is beginning to set, the boards are brought finally into correct adjustment, and should

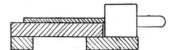

Fig. 4.—Section of Shooting Board in Use

then be no more interfered with till set hard.

When more than two boards are to be joined at one time (as in Fig. 1), the upper joint should be made first ; then, while these two boards are held vertically, the under edge can be glued, as well as the upper edge of the next board, and the two already joined rubbed down on the single one. If the contrary order is adopted, the first joint is sure to be broken. It is, however, better to let one joint set before making another. A glued joint is sufficiently set for careful handling in two hours, and is practically at maximum strength in two days.

The correct numbering of the joints as

Fig. 5.—Rubbing a Glue Joint

they are fitted up is very important, so as to ensure that the tested surfaces are those that will be glued. The system shown in Fig. 6 cannot fail to give satisfaction. It consists of straight marks and crosses made over each joint, so that each adjacent half is alike, but reversed. All numbering is best done before the jointing, and invariably on the best side of the wood.

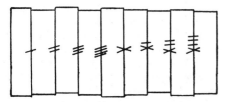

Fig. 6.—Correct Way of Numbering Joints

Steel dogs (Fig. 7) are very useful to strengthen the joints when set, especially in compound work. They cannot be depended on to pull the joints together, but are of much help towards holding them after rubbing so that they may be more freely handled. Fig. 8 shows the dog in use.

After making the joints the boards should be stood aside very carefully, so that the air can circulate freely between them. Fig. 9 illustrates a series of six joined boards, set away to dry with strips between. These strips must be parallel and should bed evenly on each board. They may be employed singly for short joints, but for anything over 3 ft. long it is best to have two strips between each board.

Slotted Screw Joint.—This is a butt joint having hidden screws driven into keyhole slots (see Fig. 10). It is used principally by cabinet-makers. The

Fig. 7.—Steel Dog

Fig. 8.—Method of Using Dog

screws are inserted at intervals along the edge of one of the boards to be jointed, leaving the heads projecting about ¾ in. Holes are bored in the edge of the other board so that the screw heads will fit into

them, and slots are made leading from the holes, as shown, of the right size to take the shank of the screws. On placing the two boards together with the screw heads in the holes, and then forcing the top board to the right, the head of each screw will, as it were, dovetail itself into the wood and hold the joint together. When driving in the screws they must be made to lean slightly so that they will draw the joint together rather than apart ; thus the left-hand screw in the illustration is wrongly inserted, the other being correct. It is also usual before finally gluing the joint, and after it has been tried up, to give the screws half a turn, thus ensuring a close joint.

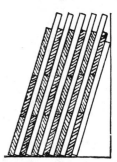

Fig. 9.—Stacking Boards after Gluing

Rebated Joint.—In this joint (Fig. 11) an open groove is cut at each edge to be joined, usually with a rebate plane. The edges require to be as carefully trued up as for the ordinary butt joint, and are glued in much the same way.

Tongued or Feathered Joints.—Either tongued or matched joints are now generally insisted on in preference to the glued butt. The first is illustrated in section by Fig. 12. A groove of equal width and depth has to be cut in both pieces with a " plough." This is a plane having a narrow iron, an adjustable fence to keep the groove at the right distance from the edge of the work, and usually also a device for regulating the depth.

To use the plough the fence is set by means of the two wedges to bring the iron in the middle of the wood (unless otherwise desired), while the gauge for the depth is adjusted by means of the thumbscrew at top. The board is then fixed in the bench vice, and, holding the plough as shown in earlier pages, working is started to and fro on a portion at the

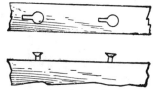

Fig. 10.—Details of Slotted Screw Joint

far end till almost deep enough. Next, stepping backwards, another short section is done, and so on, till the near end is reached. Lastly, one or two pushes are given along the entire length. Unless the grooves are made true, the effect of the finished joint will be as indicated exaggeratedly by Fig. 13, and the tongue will be of more trouble than use.

The tongues, or feathers, are thin planed-up wooden-strips, usually cut parallel with the grain, though some prefer them cut cross. Opinion is divided as to which is best. If good three-ply wood is available it makes excellent tongues, combining the advantages of both the parallel and cross varieties, but to prevent the grain stripping the outside ply should be parallel with the wood to be glued up.

For a perfect joint it is requisite that the tongue should fit just closely in the

SECTION

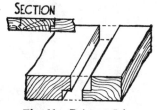

Fig. 11.—Rebated Joint

grooves without being tight, and be slightly less in width than the combined depth of the two grooves, so as not to bind when the joint is glued up. Such

a joint is shown sectionally by Fig. 14, and it will generally prove more difficult to divide than the surrounding wood. To make tongued joints easy to rub when gluing, the tongues should be planed slightly uneven in thickness, so that one edge fits tightly while the other will be loose enough to allow the board to be rubbed to and fro. The tight edge is obviously inserted first.

To glue the tongue, lay it on the joint and rapidly cover one side with glue, then turn it over and do the other side, after which it should be tapped into its

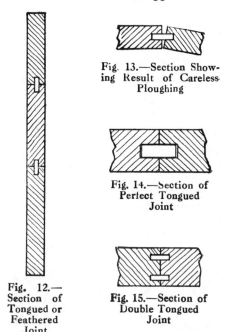

Fig. 12.—
Section of
Tongued or
Feathered
Joint

Fig. 13.—Section Showing Result of Careless Ploughing

Fig. 14.—Section of Perfect Tongued Joint

Fig. 15.—Section of Double Tongued Joint

groove. Then the two edges of the board are glued with the projecting tongue and the joint rubbed quickly.

In very thick material it may be advisable to use double tongues, as shown sectionally in Fig. 15, which is preferable to using a single thick one. In that case, the two grooves should be ploughed from the same side of the wood, otherwise they will probably fail to coincide, and crippled tongues would result.

Rebated and Filleted Joint.—This may be regarded as an open-grooved

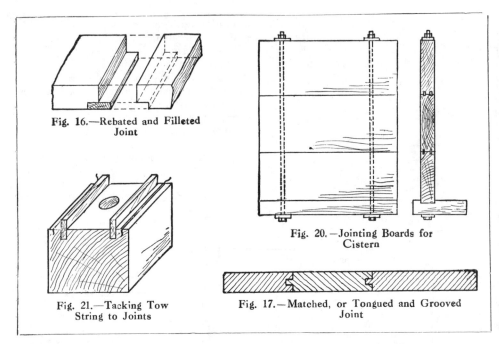

Fig. 16.—Rebated and Filleted Joint

Fig. 20.—Jointing Boards for Cistern

Fig. 21.—Tacking Tow String to Joints

Fig. 17.—Matched, or Tongued and Grooved Joint

tongued joint. It is suitable for work of which only one side shows, and which is not subjected to a bending strain. It is illustrated by Fig. 16.

Matched Joints.—This type of joint (Fig. 17) is also known as grooved and tongued ; but, while the groove on one

board is cut with a plough as before, the tongue is formed on the other board itself by means of a tonguing plane, which cuts a rebate on each edge, leaving a projecting piece between. The two are usually sold together as " matching planes " (*see* Figs. 18 and 19). The

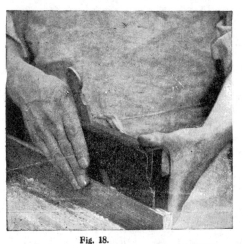

Fig. 18.

Fig. 19.

Figs. 18 and 19.—Using Matching Planes

boards should be accurately shot and fitted before the matching is done, when, if the planes are in good condition, the joint will fit as well as it previously did.

Watertight Joints for Cistern.— Figs. 20, 21, and 22 show a method employed for constructing wooden cisterns, suitable for the water storage of a country house. The thickness of material may be from 1½ in. to 4 in., according to the size of the tank. Red deal, elm, oak, and pitch pine are suitable woods to use for this kind of work. The planking should all be brought to the same thickness, the groove being ploughed from both faces with the same setting. This can only be done when the timbers have been machined to thickness.

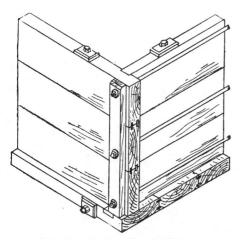

Fig. 22.—Bolting End of Cistern

Having made and fitted the joints, two lengths of tow string are tacked to them, as shown by Fig. 21, the whole being given two coats of priming paint before putting together.
· In boring the holes for the long bolts it is better to bore from each edge to ensure true alignment. The end of the tank is put together in a similar way, being then fitted between and housed into the sides and bottom to an equal depth. Two or three lengths of tow should also be nailed on to the bottom of the grooves.

The end is kept in position by long bolts passing through the sides, and through stout pieces planted at the ends of the latter, as in Fig. 22, in order to

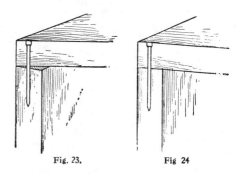

Fig. 23.   Fig 24

distribute the pressure and keep the sides straight.

Angle Joints.—When nailing together end and side pieces, as for the angles of a box, care should be taken to select nails of the right length. For nailing into the end grain, the length should equal from 2½ to 3 times the thickness of the first piece of wood. The distance apart should be at least equal to the thickness of nail, and it is better to slope the nails slightly towards each other ; this is known as " lock nailing." Figs. 23 to 26 show the result of badly fitting nailed butt joints.

In cutting the ends of boards care

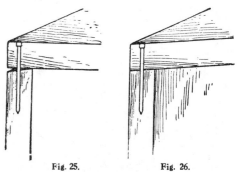

Fig. 25.   Fig. 26.

Figs. 23 to 26.—Examples of Badly Fitting Nailed Joints

should be taken that the tenon saw is kept at a right angle to the stuff. It is much better to shoot the ends on the shooting board, ascertaining at the same time that opposite sides are of equal length, to ensure a true rectangle in the finished box.

When using this joint in furniture making it is better to nail and glue it; also, if the job permits, fixing glued

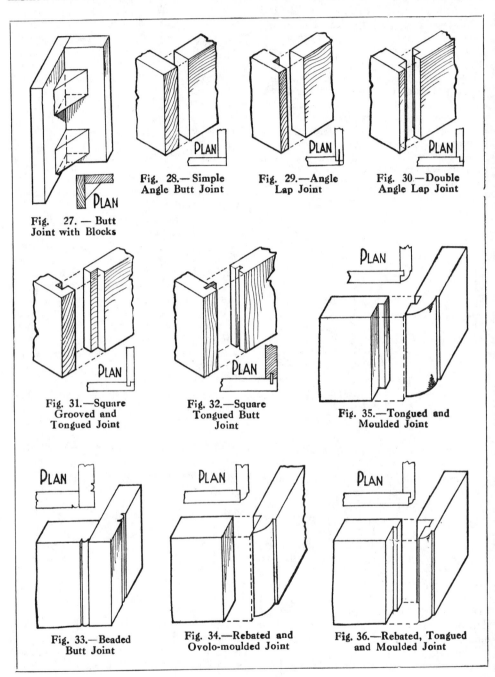

Fig. 27. — Butt Joint with Blocks

Fig. 28.— Simple Angle Butt Joint

Fig. 29.—Angle Lap Joint

Fig. 30—Double Angle Lap Joint

Fig. 31.—Square Grooved and Tongued Joint

Fig. 32.—Square Tongued Butt Joint

Fig. 35.—Tongued and Moulded Joint

Fig. 33.—Beaded Butt Joint

Fig. 34.—Rebated and Ovolo-moulded Joint

Fig. 36.—Rebated, Tongued and Moulded Joint

blocks into the internal angles, as in Fig. 27. Fig. 28 shows a simple angle butt joint ready for nailing or screwing. Fig. 29 illustrates the use of a rebate in one piece to receive the end of the other ; this gives more surface for gluing and resists an inward pressure better, also it

especially if a very ,hin hardwood cross tongue is employed.

Ornamental Angle Joints.—Sometimes, as for furniture, both butted and tongued joints are finished with a bead or moulding. Figs. 33 to 36 are typical examples. These joints are otherwise

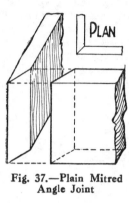

Fig. 37.—Plain Mitred Angle Joint

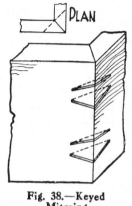

Fig. 38.—Keyed Mitreing

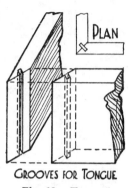

GROOVES FOR TONGUE

Fig. 39.—Tongued Mitreing

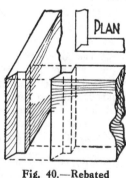

Fig. 40.—Rebated Mitreing

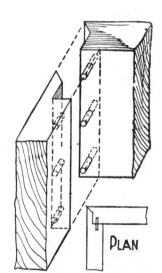

Fig. 42.—Rebated and Dowelled Mitre Joint

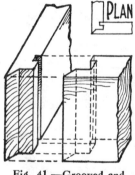

Fig. 41.—Grooved and Tongued Mitreing

may be nailed in two directions if desired. A slight variation of the previous example, but a little stronger, is shown by Fig. 30.

The grooved and tongued angle joint seen in Fig. 31 is a very good form, but there is a danger of the short end-grain lap breaking off. It is, however, strong and serviceable when used as a side angle joint and glued. Fig. 32 illustrates an excellent joint,

made in the same way as already described.

Mitred Argle Joints. —Figs. 37 to 39, and 40 to 42, show six methods of joining the ends of boards to form mitred angles. The plain mitreing (Fig. 37) and the keyed mitreing (Fig. 38) are used for skirting or plinth boards. Where extra strength is required with no details of the jointing showing, as in a plinth base for heavy furniture, such as a wardrobe on which the carcase stands, the joints illustrated by Fig. 39 and Figs. 40 to 42 are employed. The appearance of the tongued mitre joint (Fig. 39) when

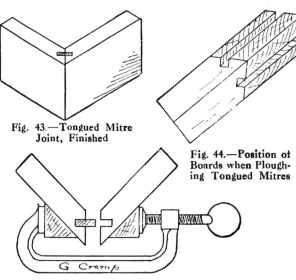

Fig. 43.—Tongued Mitre Joint, Finished

Fig. 44.—Position of Boards when Ploughing Tongued Mitres

Fig. 45.—Method of Clamping Tongued Mitre

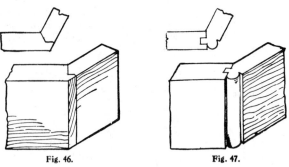

Fig. 46.

Fig. 47.

Figs. 46 and 47.—Obtuse Angle Joints: Rebated and Tongued

finished is shown by Fig. 43. Fig. 44 indicates how the pieces are put together in the bench vice when grooving with the plough in order to have a face at 90°

for the fence. By gluing triangular pieces to the face of each board a good seating may be provided so as to cramp up the joint effectively, as seen in Fig. 45. The rebated and dowelled joint shown in Fig. 42 is specially adapted for thick work, and gives particularly strong results. These joints can also be used for friezes, fascias, etc., on furniture and joinery fixings.

Obtuse Angle Joints. —Figs. 46 and 47 show

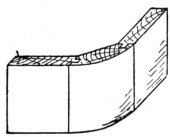

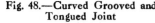

Fig. 48.—Curved Grooved and Tongued Joint

two ways of dealing with a joint at an obtuse angle for either side or end grain. The rebating, grooving and moulding are discussed elsewhere, and need not here be explained. Fig. 48 illustrates a composite grooved and tongued angle joint, planed to a curve, as might be useful for skirting, a bottom stair, or a plinth to furniture.

It must be borne in mind that the strength and rigidity of all this kind of jointing depends wholly upon a good tight fit and the best quality glue, properly applied.

Dowelled Joints

Uses of Dowelled Joints.—In a dowelled joint, holes are bored in line at a right angle with the two surfaces to be connected, and into these are inserted glued wooden pins. When properly done, the result is very strong and rigid, besides being quickly executed and effecting a saving of material; but if carelessly carried out it readily comes apart. In some cases dowels are used for parts intended to be removable, as in cornice

Fig. 1.—Wheel-wright's Dowel   Fig. 2.—Ordinary Dowel

fitments, piano fronts, and extra leaves for dining tables. Another typical use of this joint is by the wheelwright, who inserts dowels into the ends of the curved wooden sections, or felloes, where they meet; not to hold the felloes to the wheel, but simply to keep them flush at the joints. The felloes are really held on the wheels by wedges inserted in the tenons formed on the ends of the spokes, and also by the iron tyres. The kind of

dowel used for wheels is nearly spindle-shaped, as shown in Fig. 1. When, however, the dowels are required to hold the parts together entirely, by the aid of glue alone, they must be cylindrical, as in Fig. 2.

Making Dowels.—These should be of sound, well-seasoned, straight-grained material, preferably hardwood, and usually beech. A convenient method is to saw blocks two or three times the required length, and to split them into roughly rectangular sticks. The latter are then planed, first to a square section, next hexagonal, and finally circular. A handy

Fig 3.—Dowel Box

device to hold the sticks while planing is illustrated by Fig. 3. The dowels are then cut to length, and the square ends trimmed as seen in Fig. 2, to facilitate driving in. This is best done with a dowel-pointer used in the brace, but a knife or chisel can be employed. Some workers flatten one side of the dowels, or cut a narrow **V**-groove along them, to allow the escape of air and surplus glue, but others consider this unnecessa y, and do not recommend it.

The dowels can be gauged to size and shaped up by passing them through a round hole in a piece of wrought-iron plate, letting the hole remain as left by

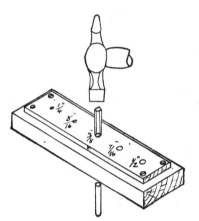

Fig. 4.—Dowel Plate, showing Method of Use

the drill. Fig. 4 shows such a dowel plate, mounted on a 1-in. thick hardwood block with various sizes of holes. The wooden base serves to keep the dowel vertical as it is driven through

the iron plate. Dowels can also be turned in the lathe, or they may be purchased. They should not be too smooth ; a slight roughness improves the strength of the joint.

Marking Boards for Dowelling.— For dowelling the edges of two boards together, first see that the surfaces meet

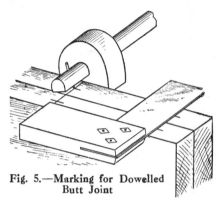

Fig. 5.—Marking for Dowelled Butt Joint

truly, as if for an ordinary glued butt ; then fix them back to back in the bench vice. Mark the centre of each board lengthways with the gauge, from opposite sides, and measure off the positions for

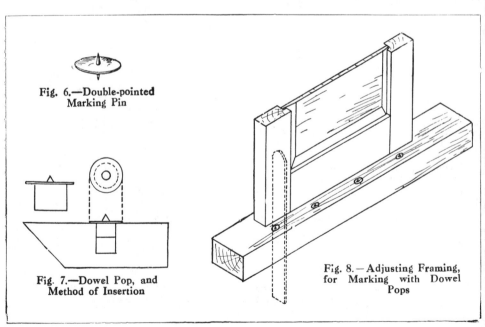

Fig. 6.—Double-pointed Marking Pin

Fig. 7.—Dowel Pop, and Method of Insertion

Fig. 8.—Adjusting Framing, for Marking with Dowel Pops

the dowels, from an inch or two to a foot distant, according to the work. Square these marks across the edges, and where the squared lines cut the gauged lines will be the points for boring. This method is illustrated by Fig. 5.

It is not always practicable to mark the two edges together, as, for instance, when a piece of woodwork is already partly made up. In such a case, some workmen use a kind of double drawing-pin (Fig. 6), having a point each side. One point is driven into the fixed portion where the dowel is to come, and the other piece to be joined is laid over the projecting point and tapped gently down. This obviously gives two marks exactly in line.

Dowel Pops.—Another good plan for marking the centres when boring dowel holes, used in Yorkshire, is to employ "dowel pops" (Fig. 7), of various sizes, usually cast in brass. Suppose it is the base of a

Work.—One method often adopted when making a length of panelling, such as is illustrated by Fig. 9, is to set out as 'or mortise and tenon joints (that is, by marking the width of one piece on the edge of the other), and then to measure and make fresh marks inside these at the proper distances for the dowels, squaring them across. A gauge mark is also made along the length of the wood to give the distance from the edge. The points where the inner lines cross the central line will then be the places to insert the point of the

Fig. 9.—Length of Panelling to be Dowelled

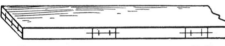

Fig. 11.—Old Way of Setting Out Rail

wardrobe that requires dowelling. The holes are bored at suitable places in the base, away from shakes or knots, and the dowel pops are inserted, resting on their thin flanges. Next the framing is placed in position, resting on the projecting points of the pops, as shown in Fig. 8, measuring the equality of each side space and testing for flushness with a straightedge. A sharp tap is lastly given with a mallet on the top of the framing, when the points of the pops make impressions at the bottom of the latter, showing clearly where to bore for the dowels.

Marking Dowels for Panelled
16—N.E.

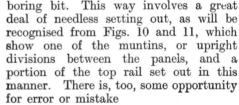

Fig. 10.—Old Way of Setting Out Muntin for Dowelling

boring bit. This way involves a great deal of needless setting out, as will be recognised from Figs. 10 and 11, which show one of the muntins, or upright divisions between the panels, and a portion of the top rail set out in this manner. There is, too, some opportunity for error or mistake

A much better plan is to set out the timber as shown by Figs. 12 and 13, the first being the rails and the second the stiles and muntins. The marks indicated are all that are necessary, with the exception that the lines on the muntins (the middle pieces in Fig. 13) must be squared over as a guide to cutting off, while those on the middle rail will need squaring over on to the other edge of the wood. The muntins might, of course, be in two pieces, to obviate the waste of the two or three inches at the middle rail, as well as for convenience in converting. The setting out of the actual holes is done by means of a dowelling template, made as illustrated in Figs. 14 and 15, the stock being of hardwood and the tongue of brass. The full length may be about 3 in., and the other parts in proportion. The tongue may be about $\frac{1}{8}$ in. thick, and the series of small holes

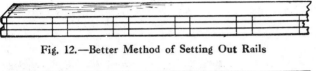

Fig. 12.—Better Method of Setting Out Rails

Fig 13.—Better Method of Setting Out Stiles and Muntins

shown should be drilled truly, for on this will depend, in a great measure, the accuracy of the work set out with the tool. The tongue is screwed in the stock as shown in the section (Fig. 15), and both parts of the latter must be in the same plane, so that the tool can be used from either side, as occasion requires. In drilling the holes in the tongue it is also necessary to get them an equal distance from either end, and equally spaced, for the same reason.

The method of using the template is explained by Fig. 16. The tongue is placed level with one of the squared-over marks and the stock against the face side, when the dowel hole can be marked through a hole in the plate with a fine bradawl. The correct hole to use, in the present instance is that indicated by a cross at the left of the illustration. To finish the marking, slide the template to the right, as shown by the dotted lines, and mark through the corresponding hole at the other end. This is the manner of setting out for the muntins ; that for the top or bottom rails is done as shown at the right, the two crossed holes being marked with the template in one position.

When setting out on, or for, wider rails, the template can be moved along, using the holes already marked as a guide,

until the whole ground is covered ; thus Fig. 17 shows a wide rail set out for six dowels, while Fig. 18 shows the end of a thicker rail, in the setting out of which two rows of holes in the template are used, alternately near the face and the back. This will be found much preferable to using stouter dowels.

When making panelling with dowelled joints, do not forget the grooves in which the panels will fit. The dowels should be kept well clear of these, as shown by the dotted lines in Fig. 19. It will, of course, be understood that the dowel holes must be bored before the grooves are made, otherwise there would be great difficulty in getting them correct.

Dowelling Chairs, Tables, etc.— For dowelling the legs of tables or chairs or the rails of a cabinet framing into the stiles, a template may be made from a piece of thin zinc, the exact size of the end to be joined. Three small holes are pierced in this, and it is then laid in position on the leg or stile and the holes

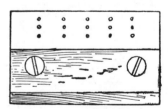

Fig. 14.—Plan of Metal Dowelling Template

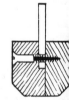

Fig. 15.—Section of Metal Dowelling Template

Fig. 16.—Method of Using Template for Setting Out

pricked through, as shown by Fig. 20. The other side of the template is used for marking the end of the rail. The holes should be irregularly spaced, certainly not all in line.

Dowelling Doors.—To mark the centres for dowels in light doors, such

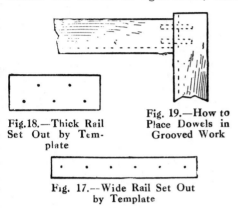

Fig.18.—Thick Rail Set Out by Template

Fig. 19.—How to Place Dowels in Grooved Work

Fig. 17.—Wide Rail Set Out by Template

as those of sideboards, cupboards in wash-stands, chiffoniers, etc., the wooden template illustrated by Fig. 21 will be found useful. It should be of hardwood and equal in length to the width of the door rail, the projecting part being as wide as the thickness of the rails and stiles. The holes should be the same distance from each end. In use, it simply needs to be held on the ends of the rails, which it fits, while marking the holes with the bradawl, being then transferred

dowel holes should fit those in the template as nearly as possible, without being actually tight.

Dowelling Felloes on Wheels.—

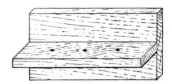

Fig. 21.—Wooden Dowelling Template for Doors

Fig. 22.—Faulty Method of Marking Felloes for Dowels

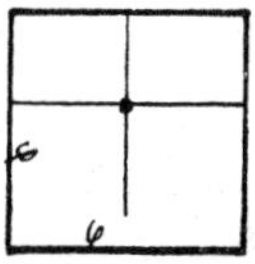

Fig. 23.—Correct Method of Marking Felloes

Fig. 22 shows the method often adopted to obtain the boring mark for dowels in wheel felloes, which may sometimes be useful for other circular work. With this it is necessary, however, for all the felloes to be true to size, a comparatively rare state of things. Therefore, a better way of getting the correct spot is that indicated in Fig. 23, where the face side

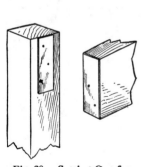

Fig. 20.—Setting Out for Dowels in Table or Chair

Fig. 25.—Felloes Correctly Dowelled

Fig. 24.—Felloes Joined, with Dowel Too Low

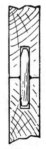

Fig. 26.—Section of Perfectly Dowelled Joint

Fig. 27.—Joint with Bent Dowel, through Faulty Boring

to the side edges of the stiles, to mark the corresponding holes near the top and bottom.

The bradawl employed for marking

and the inside of the felloe are gauged from, the crossing of the lines being the right spot for boring. The holes should be bored at a right angle to the end of the felloe. It will be noticed that the mark is higher up in Fig. 23 than in Fig. 22. The former is correct, for if the

Fig. 28.—Diagram showing Various Faults in Dowels

Fig. 29.—Plan showing Holes Before and After Opening

dowel is too low down there is a risk of splitting off the lower corner of the felloe, where the grain is cut across. Figs. 24 and 25 will make this clear.

Boring Holes for Dowels.—The bit for boring dowel holes should be in good working order. a short-length twist bit being best. The right size for most work is $\frac{5}{16}$ in., though the $\frac{1}{4}$-in. or $\frac{3}{8}$-in. size may occasionally be found convenient. The bit must be kept truly vertical to the surface, or the joint will be unsatisfactory. Till expertness is gained, a try-square applied to the drill

the right depth and parallel with the sides of the wood, so that the dowel exerts its full holding power without being crippled in any way. Fig. 27, on the other hand, shows the effect of one of the holes being bored slightly out of parallel ; in such a case the joint has to be forced together and held until the glue has set. Even then the dowel is crippled and its holding power much diminished.

Besides being parallel with the sides of the wood, it is equally important that the holes should be truly at a right angle to the joint the other way. Fig. 28 shows a series of four holes bored for dowels, that on the extreme right being as it should be. The second is bored correctly in the lower part but badly in the upper, therefore the dowel will be more or less crippled in putting the joint together. In the third, the dowel will be quite straight when in place, but it will have to be bent to get it to enter,

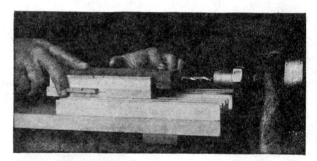

Fig. 31.—Method of Using Boring Fitment

Fig. 30.—Fitment for Boring Dowel Holes in Lathe

will be of assistance as a test. Fig. 26 is a section of a perfectly dowelled joint, where the two holes are bored to exactly

and will probably be injured in doing so ; the fault here is that both holes are bored badly, though in such a way that one compensates the other. This kind of compensation is very undesirable, but sometimes cannot be avoided. In the last case, the extreme left, the holes partly miss each other, either through faulty setting out or extremely careless boring. When this occurs, the holes should be plugged up and re-bored, for if left as it is the dowel will prove worse than useless.

The holes must be bored to a correct depth, a little over half the length of the dowel, to allow for glue and any trifling roughness at the bottom. Thus, with dowels 2¼ in. long, the holes should be 1¼ in. deep. With a good twist bit this may be gauged by counting the turns given, after testing the depth of the first hole. Another way is to place a wooden stop over the bit, or to use a metal bit gauge (*see* Chapter on Boring), to check it at the right distance down. A cylindrical piece of hardwood may be used, bored along the middle and furnished with a set screw to tighten it. It is as well to open or countersink the tops of the holes very slightly, as indicated by the second hole in Fig. 29, and seen sectionally in Fig. 26, this helps considerably in putting together and forms a sinking for surplus glue. The opening can be done with a snail or rose bit used in a brace.

Boring Dowel Holes in the Lathe.

—If a lathe is available it forms an ideal appliance for making dowelled joints, obviating a great deal of the setting out, dispensing with a template, and, what is perhaps the best recommendation of all, boring the holes absolutely straight and true. The necessary fitment can readily be constructed to fit any lathe, and may be adapted to any thickness or width of material. The only parts which cannot very well be manipulated in the lathe are extra long pieces, owing to the room required but in such cases the two methods are easily worked together, the long portions being bored in the ordinary way, as already described, and the shorter ones for the same job being drilled in the lathe.

The complete fitment is illustrated in Fig. 30, and the method of using it in Fig. 31 ; while Figs. 32 to 34 explain how it is made. Fig. 32 is a plan, and Fig. 33 a section, of the fitment in position on the lathe ready for work, the lettering being similar in each. The lathe bed is shown at A, while B is a clamp for bolting the fitment in place (two are required, one near the front and the other near the back). At C are cross-pieces, and to these the actual bed of the fitment, D, is screwed

from underneath. On the top of the bed and level with the sides are fixed the two pieces E, provided with longitudinal and parallel grooves. In these grooved pieces slides the adjustable holder shown in Fig. 34. This latter consists of the two side pieces F, on the bottom of which are formed projections that will just fit into the grooves in E, these projections being nearer to one side than the other, as indicated. On the top of the pieces F are screwed strips G, level with the outside edges. To keep the two side portions of the holder in position, and yet allow them to be divided easily and quickly, so that they will fit into any of the

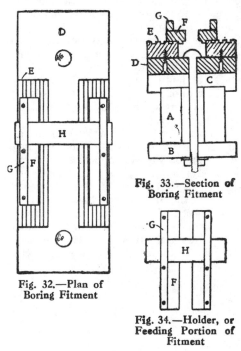

Fig. 32.—Plan of Boring Fitment

Fig. 33.—Section of Boring Fitment

Fig. 34.—Holder, or Feeding Portion of Fitment

grooves in E, a cross-bar H is sunk into the pieces F, so that it is level with their upper surfaces and passes under the strips G, thus retaining them rigid and parallel, and at the same time permitting a lateral adjustment.

The fitment must be so fixed on the lathe that the centres are midway between the pieces F when the latter are in any pair of grooves. In the section (Fig. 33) the guides are completely inside, that is as close together as possible ; while in the plan (Fig. 32) they are in the middle groove.

The wood to be bored lies in the rebates formed by the pieces F and G, therefore the whole fitment must be built up according to the lathe, so as to bring the surface of F about ⅜ in. below the actual lathe centre, when it will be right for working on any thickness of material from ¾ in. to 1¼ in.

To use the fitment the sliding piece should be placed in suitable grooves to bring the holes the correct distance from the edges, and then fed up to the drill, as in Fig. 31, working from each of the pieces G, and, if more than two holes are wanted, resetting after the first boring. The face side of the material must be downwards during the boring operations, and a guide mark should be made to act as a depth gauge. For boring rails or other horizontal parts, another sliding holder, similar to Fig. 34, is required, in which, however, the pieces G are shortened at the front, so that the wood to be bored can rest directly across F. The rails must be set out on the side opposite where the holes are to be. The marks are then placed to the inside of the shortened pieces G, and the fitment used as before.

The best tool for boring in the lathe is an ordinary twist drill. This will be found to act very quickly and easily ; the sizes also will fit the stock dowels better than

is the case with twist bits. The drill, of course, needs to be fixed in a chuck.

Gluing Dowels.—The parts being bored and ready to put together, the dowels cut off and trimmed, and the glue at hand (which should be slightly thinner than usual), the holes in one piece are

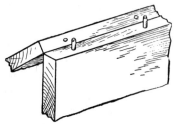

Fig. 35.—Parts of Dowel Joint in Position for Gluing

glued inside, using a round stick instead of a brush. The dowels are also touched with glue at one end, and then driven gently home into the glued holes. The other part is now held against the first, as shown in Fig. 35, the two edges and the projecting halves of the dowels being rapidly brushed with glue, allowing a little to run into the holes. Lastly, the pieces are fitted promptly together with pressure, and cramped up tightly till set.

Some workers prefer " cold " or liquid glue for dowelling, since it does not set so quickly, but more time must elapse before the joints can be depended on to bear usage.

Mortise and Tenon Joints

The Mortise and Tenon Joint.—This joint, in one or other of its numerous forms, is the most important and probably the most used of all where strength and rigidity are required. It is of great value to carpenters, joiners, cabinet-makers, cart and coach builders, wheelwrights, shipwrights and aircraft workers. An advantage of this kind of joint is that it seldom needs reinforcing by metal fastenings.

The making of simple mortise and

Closed Mortise and Tenon.—One of the most common forms of this joint is the ordinary closed tenon, so called because the tenon is surrounded by wood on all four sides. Fig. 1 shows the setting out of the mortise, Fig. 2 the setting out of the tenon, Fig. 3 the mortise made, Fig. 4 the tenon cut, and Fig. 5 a section of the complete joint secured by a pin. though the latter is often omitted.

Using Mortise Gauge.—Save in exceptional cases, it is usual for the tenon

Fig. 1.—Closed Mortise Set Out

Fig. 3.—Closed Mortise Made

Fig. 5.—Section through Closed Mortise Joint, showing Pin

Fig. 2.—Tenon Set Out

Fig. 4.—Tenon Cut

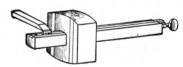

Fig. 6.—Setting Mortise Gauge

tenon joints in material of rectangular section will first be dealt with; then a number of examples will be given showing their application in different kinds of work, with hints for setting out and making.

to be one-third the thickness of the material, or thereabouts. While it is certainly possible to do the setting out merely by measurement, it saves much time and trouble to employ a mortise gauge (Fig. 6), for marking the two parallel lines on opposite faces of each piece, and on the end of the tenon portion. Except for large mortises, the width consists of single cuts with the chisel, hence the gauge requires setting to the

Fig. 7.—Beginning with Chisel on Bored Mortise

width of the latter by turning a nut at the end of the gauge stem, which regulates the distance between the two marking pins. The arrangement for setting the pins, however, varies in different patterns of gauges. The sliding stock is then moved till its face is the correct distance from the inner pin, and the screw tightened up. The lines indicating the length of the mortise and tenon respectively are measured and squared over on all four faces.

An ordinary marking gauge may, with a little care, be used to set out mortises and tenons by marking single lines from opposite sides, if the exact position for these is first measured centrally and the gauge set accordingly. This, however, presupposes that the wood is of uniform thickness and with truly parallel sides. It is better if only a marking gauge is available to set the gauge twice and work from one side only.

Cutting the Mortise.—The easiest way of making a mortise is to bore out part of the waste before using the chisel. A small piece of work may be held in the bench vice, while longer or very heavy pieces are best laid on two trestles. The back side should always be done first, and both sides should be bored from if the mortise goes right through the wood. It will be noticed in Fig. 7 that a third hole is bored. This is advisable in a longer mortise; in fact, as much of the

wood as possible should be bored away, thus reducing the chisel work.

One often sees the method of mortising shown in Fig 8 recommended, a small wedge-shaped piece being taken out in the middle and continued each way until the ends of the mortise are reached, when these are cut down square. This method is not a good one, as the chisel has to be reversed between each stroke, and it is impossible to remove so much of the waste wood as is desirable.

A better way is to commence nearly close up to the end of the mortise nearest the worker, cutting perpendicularly and as far in as the chisel will enter without using undue force. Then move the chisel back without reversing, and make another cut, removing the loose wood at the same time. Bring the chisel back to its first position, making another perpendicular cut, then take in a further piece towards the other end, and so on, till the whole length of the mortise has been done. The successive strokes are indicated in Fig. 9, and shown in plan by Fig. 10. By this

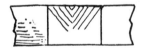

Fig. 8.—Incorrect Method of Chiselling

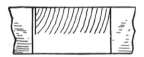

Fig. 9.—Correct Method of Chiselling

Fig. 10.—Plan of Correct Chiselling

method practically the whole of the wood is removed as it is cut away, while the work is done very quickly and cleanly.

Faults in Making Mortises.—Fig. 11 represents in section lengthways a series of mortises, of which N is the only perfect one. Here the ends are straight through from top to bottom—a result, unfortunately, but seldom found, even in the best work. At o is seen the most usual product, in which the ends of the mortise are both cut under, as a rule purposely on the principle that the tenon

Fig. 11.—Faults in Mortising (Endways)

Fig. 12.—Faults in Mortising (Sideways)

will fit at each side and nothing else matters. That is true to a certain extent ; but if the undercutting is overdone there is a risk of driving out the wood at the back when fitting together.

The faults shown at P and R are caused by carelessness or want of judgment, and the remedy is fairly obvious. The section shown in s is sometimes made intentionally, and is called a wheelwright's mortise. The idea is that the

tises of a bad shape at the ends than at the sides, but the latter also is by no means uncommon. In Fig. 12 are illustrated a series of sideways sections of finished mortises, of which T alone is satisfactory. The effect of U is that the holding pin cannot be so strong, owing to the tenon and the sides of the mortise not being in close contact ; but in v the case is different, there being grave danger of splitting the work when putting the joint together. The slovenly cutting seen at w has very little influence on the completed joint ; nevertheless, it should be avoided. In x the faults are glaringly apparent, and the wood will almost certainly split. The last two mortises are tapered, being wider at the top than at the bottom. In one case the right-hand side of the mortise has been made sloping and in the other both sides are inaccurately cut.

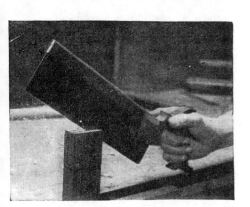

Fig. 13.—Starting Tenon

Fig. 14.—Making Tenon—after Reversing Wood

tenon being forced into the mortise causes the wood, as it were, to clinch itself, and needs no further fixing ; but the notion is rather far-fetched, and such a joint cannot be very secure.

There is more excuse for making mor-

The last-mentioned batch of faults will only occur in the larger mortises. The narrow ones, being cut to the width of the chisel, must come out the full width, but it is just possible to make the mistakes shown at v and w,

Sawing the Tenon.—Figs. 13 and 14 illustrate the commencement of sawing a tenon. The first shows the slight cut across the corner at the face side

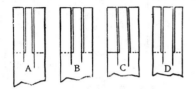

Fig. 15.—Various Faults in Sawing Tenons

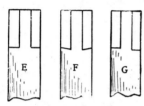

Fig. 16.—Various Faults in Cutting Tenon
Shoulders

or edge, and the second indicates the position of the saw leading from this cut to the opposite side, after the timber has been reversed. This latter cut should gradually be run down on the side

ing at the face side is to have the finishing cut there also. In the case of very long tenons the wood may have to be reversed four times instead of two,

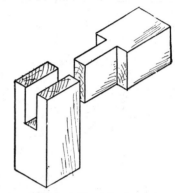

Fig. 19.—Finished Slot Mortise Joint, ready
for Fixing

but it is better if the cuts begin and finish on the face side.

In making a shoulder cut the saw at first is held with its point down, the hand being then gradually lowered until the saw is horizontal, and the cutting proceeded with until it meets the tenon

Fig. 17.—Slot Mortise
Set Out

Fig. 18.—Setting
Out Tenon for
Slot Mortise

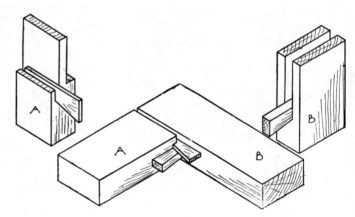

Fig. 20.—Adjustable Slot Mortise and Tenon Joint

of the tenon nearest the operator, when the timber may be again reversed and the cut continued to the shoulder lines; or the cut may be finished at the second operation. The object of start-

cut, when the "cheek" will drop off. Unless it is a "barefaced" tenon, the other side is then done in the same way.

Faults in Sawing Tenons.—It is usually impressed on beginners that they must learn to cut to the lines, and, of course, the advice is good ; but it is quite possible to obey it literally and yet be far from correct, especially when sawing

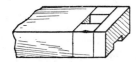

Fig. 21.—Closed Haunched Mortise

Fig. 23.—Tenon with Secret Haunching

Fig. 22 — Haunched Tenon

tenons. In Fig. 15 are shown a series of tenons sawn in, but with the shoulders uncut ; and of these only one is right, though all are sawn to the lines. Thus A is cut on the inside of the lines, which will make the tenon too thin ; B is inside one line and outside the other, while C commences in the same way and crosses the lines. The correct method is seen at D, where the cuts are made on the outside of each line, leaving the tenon the full thickness to fit properly in the mortise.

Fig. 16 illustrates the right and the wrong way of cutting shoulders for tenons. Thus, E is correct ; each shoulder is sawn in exactly to the mark, and will

as the term is ; in consequence they will fit on the outside only, and if any considerable amount of cleaning off is required the result will be an open shoulder. At G the cutting is worse still, one shoulder being sawn on the one side of the mark and the other on just the opposite, the effect being that only one shoulder will fit.

Slot Mortise and Tenon.—In this joint, also known as the " open " type, the mortise is merely a slot cut in the end of a piece of timber, so that the tenon can be driven in from the side. Fig. 17 shows the setting out of such a mortise, and Fig. 18 the setting out of the tenon, while Fig. 19 illustrates the finished joint ready for fixing together. It is often used in making door frames.

Adjustable Slot Mortise and Tenon.—Fig. 20 illustrates the familiar device employed to stretch the canvas for oil paintings. The shoulder is grooved out against the face of tenon with a $\frac{1}{8}$-in. chisel and sloped to fit a $\frac{1}{8}$-in. wedge, as shown at A on the left ; while the slot mortise is made with a sloping end to receive a wedge full width, as at B on the right. The canvas is then tacked on to the frame and the wedges driven up till the required tension is obtained.

Haunched Mortise and Tenon.—In cases where the end of the mortised piece has to be cut off level with the tenoned piece, and a slot mortise is not suitable, the joint is " haunched," that is, the mortise is made shorter than the

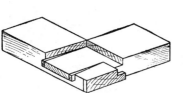
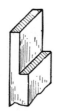
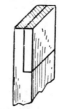

Fig. 24.—Cut-away View of Wedged Haunched Tenon

Fig. 25.—Barefaced Tenon Cut

Fig. 26.—Setting Out Barefaced Tenon

Fig. 27.—Section of Barefaced Mortise and Tenon Joint

fit on the inside as well as on the outside. The shoulders at F are started at the lines but the cutting is continued " under."

actual width of the tenon, as in Fig. 21, while the tenon itself is cut away, as in Fig. 22. The tenon is first sawn the full width, as for the ordinary type, then the haunch is marked off and the small block of waste sawn away. The recess in the mortise to receive the haunch is sawn to the lines with the end of the tenon saw and finished with the chisel. Another form, known as secret haunching, is shown by Fig. 23 ; in this the haunch does not show on the end. Haunched joints are often secured by wedges at each side of the tenon, for which purpose the ends of the mortise are made a little

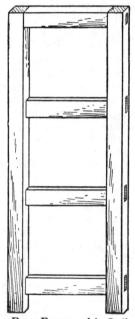

Fig. 28.—Door Frame, with Ordinary and Barefaced Tenons

wider and slanting outwards, as seen in the cut-away view (Fig. 24).

Barefaced Tenons. — A barefaced tenon has only one shoulder, the other side being flush with the face, as indicated by Fig. 25. Fig. 26 shows how the tenon is set out, the setting out for the mortise being readily understood from the section of the complete joint (Fig. 27). The barefaced tenon is used when one side of a rail has to be flush with the stile or post, while the other side is set back ; as, for instance, when it is desired to fix matchboarding across the

lower rails of a frame, such as is shown in Fig. 28. In that case the lower rails have barefaced tenons, while the top rail is the same thickness as the stiles, and has ordinary tenons. The barefaced joint is also useful when a stouter tenon is desirable than the thickness of the material would otherwise allow, as in the rails connecting table tops.

Stub or Joggle Tenon.—When a tenon does not pass right through the material it is known as a stub or joggle tenon. These are only employed to keep the tenoned piece laterally in position, and are seldom required. Fig. 29 is typical of such.

Oblique Mortises and Tenons.— These are more difficult and require careful setting out. Fig. 30 illustrates a rectangular frame in which two oblique braces are inserted. Fig. 31 shows the method of setting out the rails (note that the face marks are both on the inside) ; while Fig. 32 shows the top rail tenoned and haunched. The bottom rail (Fig. 33) does not require haunching. The stiles should be set out as a pair in the same way as the rails ; one is shown in Fig. 34 with the mortises set out, including that for the brace, while Fig. 35 shows the cut mortises. In actual practice, however, only the mortises for the rails would at first be set out and made. The frame would then be knocked together, so that the braces can be laid on i in the position they will eventually occupy, when the mortises can readily be marked on the stiles and rails, as well as the shoulder lines on the braces, after which it is only necessary to square the various lines across to get the complete setting out.

Fig. 36 shows one brace after the various marks have been squared over and connected, and also gauged for cutting the tenons ; while Fig. 37 shows the same brace after the tenons are cut. Before inserting the braces it is necessary to cut the tenons at the longest point to a right angle with the shoulders, and also to cut them parallel with the latter, thus bringing them to the shape seen in Fig. 38. The reason for cutting the oblique tenons as described is to give them a much firmer abutment, and also to simplify making the mortises, as will be understood by reference to Fig. 39, where the method temporarily to the face of the work, so that the bit may be held vertically and enter at a right angle. This is illustrated by Fig. 40, where A is the stile to be

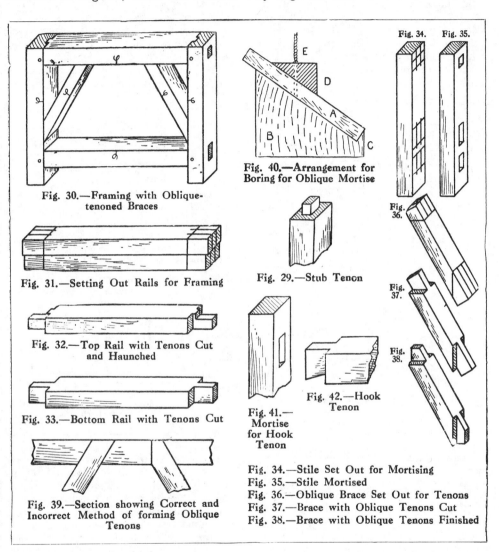

Fig. 30.—Framing with Oblique-tenoned Braces

Fig. 31.—Setting Out Rails for Framing

Fig. 32.—Top Rail with Tenons Cut and Haunched

Fig. 33.—Bottom Rail with Tenons Cut

Fig. 39.—Section showing Correct and Incorrect Method of forming Oblique Tenons

Fig. 40.—Arrangement for Boring for Oblique Mortise

Fig. 29.—Stub Tenon

Fig. 41.—Mortise for Hook Tenon

Fig. 42.—Hook Tenon

Fig. 34.—Stile Set Out for Mortising
Fig. 35.—Stile Mortised
Fig. 36.—Oblique Brace Set Out for Tenons
Fig. 37.—Brace with Oblique Tenons Cut
Fig. 38.—Brace with Oblique Tenons Finished

recommended is seen on the right, and the direct way on the left, both being in section.

In making oblique mortises it is a good plan to support the piece at a suitable angle in a box or cradle, or on an inclined plane, fixing a wedge-shaped block mortised, B an inclined plane having a stop C, D a block secured to the stile, and E the bit. Or, in some cases, the stile and block might be clamped in the bench vice at the required angle, placing a piece of waste at the back of the hole to prevent splintering.

Hook Tenon.—Figs. 41 and 42 show respectively the mortise and tenon forming a hook or dovetail joint. The mortise is made on the bevel at one end, or rather side, the tenon being cut to fit. Since the mortise obviously has to be the full width of the tenon, a space is left into which a pair of folding wedges can be inserted which hold the joint very firmly together, while, at the same time, it may easily be unshipped if desired.

It is often made long enough to project on the other side, and a hole is cut to receive a tapered key or peg.

Tusk tenons are also employed in general carpentry, especially in collapsible bookcases, garden frames, etc., in which case the tenon is often made thicker, and the hole for the peg or wedges cut through the face side of the wood, instead of through what may be called the flat or top of the tenon.

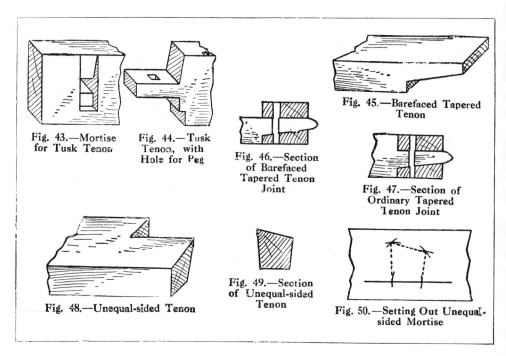

Fig. 43.—Mortise for Tusk Tenon

Fig. 44.—Tusk Tenon, with Hole for Peg

Fig. 45.—Barefaced Tapered Tenon

Fig. 46.—Section of Barefaced Tapered Tenon Joint

Fig. 47.—Section of Ordinary Tapered Tenon Joint

Fig. 48.—Unequal-sided Tenon

Fig. 49.—Section of Unequal-sided Tenon

Fig. 50.—Setting Out Unequal-sided Mortise

Tusk Tenon.—Fig. 43 shows the mortise made ready to receive a "tusk" tenon, while Fig. 44 shows the tenon ready for insertion. This kind of joint is used in building construction for the framing of floor joists. It will be noticed that though the mortise is so small as to weaken the joist very little, yet the tenon takes a very strong bearing owing to the recess made below the mortise and the sloping cut above it. As a rule the setting out of this joint is done by placing the tenon in the middle as regards the depth of the joists and allowing it to be one-seventh of the depth only in thickness.

Tapered Tenons.—Some workers have a particular fancy for the tapered tenon; but while there are undoubtedly a few points in its favour for special purposes, it is not advised for frequent use. Great care must be taken in setting out to get the tenons accurate, for if too tight they will act as wedges and split the wood, while if too slack they depend entirely on the pin for security. In Fig. 45 is shown a barefaced tapered tenon, such as would be used for framing up the bottom of a wheelbarrow or farm cart, while Fig. 46 is a section of the joint finished. A similar tapered joint, but with the ordinary double shoulders, is shown by Fig. 47. In all cases the upper side should be parallel with the face of the wood.

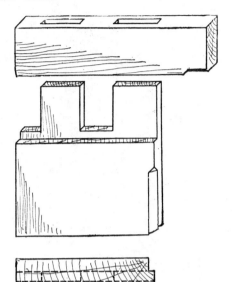

Fig. 51.—Double Tenon Joint for Bottom Rail of Door (shown on its side)

Unequal-sided Tenons—An unequal-sided barefaced tenon is shown by Fig. 48, and in section by Fig. 49. The mortise is set out as illustrated by Fig. 50, in which the straight line represents the face. On this is marked off the width of the tenon in the proper position, then, with a sharp pair of compasses, the width of the tenon is taken from back to front at each side and transferred to the wood, using the points already marked to work from, and striking arcs as shown. Next, the diagonals of the tenon are taken each way and transferred to the wood as before, lastly connecting the points where the arcs cut each other, as indicated by the dotted lines. A mortise made to these marks will be found to fit the tenon exactly.

Double Tenons.—In the case of wide timbers, such as the middle and bottom rails of panel doors, it is not desirable to run the tenons the whole width, which would not make either a strong or satis-

factory job on account of the excessive shrinkage which would take place, leaving the tenons slack. Furthermore, the stile is weakened by having such a wide mortise. To overcome these disadvantages double tenons are used. Fig. 51 shows the double-tenoned joint between the stile and bottom rail of a 2-in. house door. Fig. 52 shows the setting out for the tenons, and also for the muntin mortise in the middle. It is a good rule to limit the width of the tenon to six times its thickness. The haunch at the bottom edge is to allow of enough end grain wood being left in the stile to wedge against. The small tongue forming the lower haunch, and the one between the tenons, are to keep the rail from warping and also prevent light coming through the door should the joint open a little. It is a merit of double tenons that four wedges may be used, instead of only two.

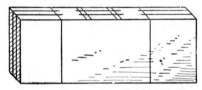

Fig. 52.—Setting Out Double Tenons

Fig. 53.—Double Tenon for Middle Rail (on Left)

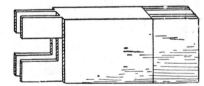

Fig. 54.—Compound Double Tenon for Mortise Lock

The middle rail of a door should be haunched in the centre alone, as seen on the left in Fig. 53 : the two haunches required for the lower rail being shown on the right for comparison. The dotted lines indicate where the grooves for the panels will come, and, in actual practice,

rails only of doors to be fitted with mortise locks. When it is known which way the doors will hang, these tenons would be made on the lock side alone;

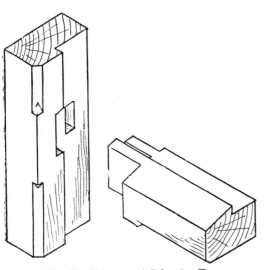

Fig. 55.—Double-tenoned Joint for Transom Rail

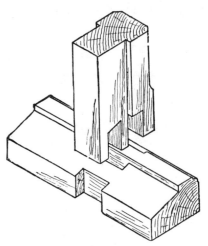

Fig. 57.—Tenoned and Bridled Joint

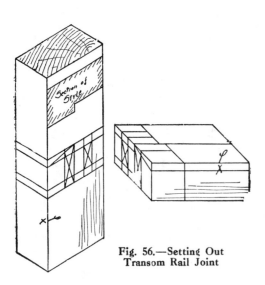

Fig. 56.—Setting Out Transom Rail Joint

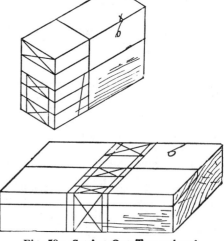

Fig. 58.—Setting Out Tenoned and Bridled Joint

these should be made before the shoulders are cut.

Fig 54 illustrates another form of doub e tenon, set out on the right and made on the left, as used in the middle

but in the absence of definite information it is best to prepare both sides, as shown. It is also advisable to cut the mortise for the lock in the rail itself be'ore putting the door together.

Fig. 55 shows the joint between transom rail and stile of an outside cottage door frame, rebated, weathered and chamfered, where, on account of the great thickness, a different kind of double tenon is called for. It will be noted that the tenons are not the same length, and that the near one is bevelled on its top edge to corre-

not a double tenon, is seen in Fig. 57. This shows a post tenoned and bridled into the sill, as in the case of a French window. When finished, the shoulder lines are, of course, vertical. Fig. 58 indicates how this joint is set out on the square. Wedges can be inserted from the bottom side of the sill into the middle

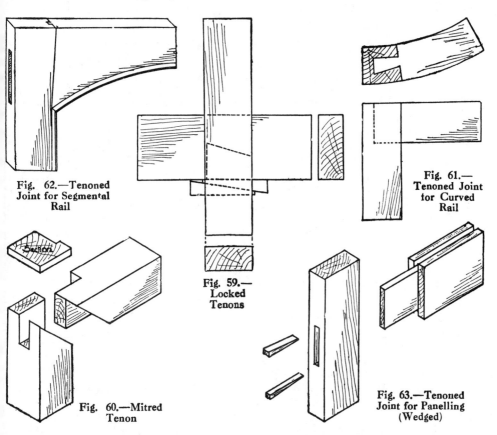

Fig. 62.—Tenoned Joint for Segmental Rail

Fig. 61.—Tenoned Joint for Curved Rail

Fig. 59.—Locked Tenons

Fig. 60.—Mitred Tenon

Fig. 63.—Tenoned Joint for Panelling (Wedged)

spond with the weathered slope of the transom rail. When setting out for rebated and grooved framing, it is well to let the tenons coincide with the grooves and with the edge of the rebate. In this case the near tenon finishes level with the rebate. Fig. 56 illustrates how to set out shoulder and gauge lines in the square stuff, for all tenons and mortises should be cut before rebating, chamfering or moulding is begun.

A somewhat related type of joint, though

tenon, and it is advisable that an oak pin should be driven through the whole joint from front to back. Previous to wedging up, the joint should be well coated with thick paint.

Locking Tenons.—Fig. 59 shows the method of tenoning when the rails are continued through a post in such a manner that the latter is continued in one piece from top to bottom. An example of this kind can be seen in the doorpost and transom rail of a vestibule, and sometimes in a large casement window. The tenons are made first in the usual way, being then cut and bevelled to fit each other, as indicated by the dotted lines, thus forming a locked joint. The mortise is cut wider than the rail, in rail, being then rested on the end of the stile, flush to the face, and marked round with an awl. The stile can now be gauged and the mortise slotted with tenon saw and chisel.

Fig. 62 shows how the segmental top

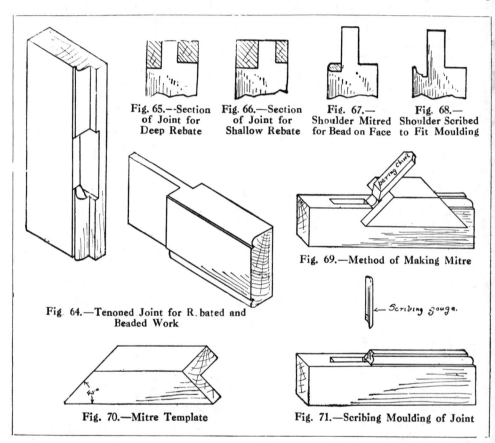

Fig. 65.—Section of Joint for Deep Rebate

Fig. 66.—Section of Joint for Shallow Rebate

Fig. 67.— Shoulder Mitred for Bead on Face

Fig. 68.— Shoulder Scribed to Fit Moulding

Fig. 69.—Method of Making Mitre

Fig. 64.—Tenoned Joint for R. bated and Beaded Work

Fig. 70.—Mitre Template

Fig. 71.—Scribing Moulding of Joint

order to let the bevelled tenons pass each other into position, and the extra space is filled up with a pair of folding wedges glued before insertion.

Mitred Tenon.—A mitred tenon may sometimes be needed in picture and other frames. A typical instance is shown by Fig. 60, the section displaying the rebate for the glass and picture.

Tenons for Curved Work.—Fig. 61 illustrates the joint for a door or window rail, curved in plan with the stile. The dovetail tenon is first cut on the curved

rail of a glazed panel door is jointed to the stile. The bevelled shoulder will be noted from the full width of the stile at the top to the depth of the quirk in the moulding, which has been struck on the solid material. The shoulder lines should be marked on the square stuff, and the tenon cut before the curved cut is made and rebated to receive the glass. It will be seen that the tenon is haunched.

Tenons for Grooved, Beaded, or Moulded Work.—Fig. 63 shows the joint between rail and stile in ordinary

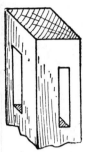

Fig. 72.— Mortises for Table-leg Joint

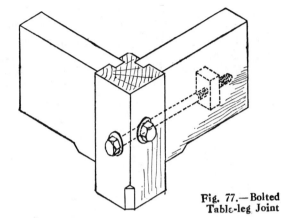

Fig. 77.—Bolted Table-leg Joint

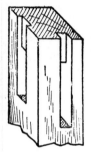

Fig. 73.— Haunched Mortises in Table Leg

Fig. 74. — Rail with Haunched and Mitred Tenon

Fig. 75.—Top View of Table-leg Joint

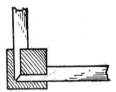

Fig. 76.—Section of Table-leg Joint

panelled framing, as in a door or dado frame. It will be noted that the tenon is narrower by the depth of both the top and bottom grooves in the rail made to receive the panels.

Fig. 64 shows the middle rail tenoned into the rebated and once-beaded stile of a cupboard frame. This kind of joint requires tenon shoulders of unequal length. The following general principles will make the procedure to be followed in such cases clear. Thus, when there is only a rebate to be considered the shoulders are cut to fit into the rebate, and the tenon so cut as to bring one side level with the latter. Fig. 65, for instance, illustrates the joint in section for a deep rebate, and Fig. 66 that for a shallower one. When there is a moulding on the side opposite the rebate, both shoulders have to be longer, so that one fits to the rebate while the other is mitred or scribed to fit

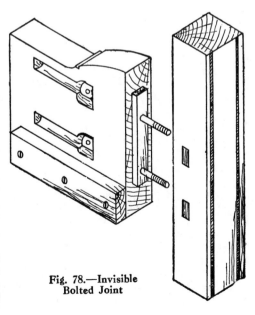

Fig. 78.—Invisible Bolted Joint

the moulding. Fig. 67 shows a shoulder mitred to fit a corresponding bead on the mortised head, and Fig. 68 shows the scribed joint to fit to a moulded head. Returning to the joint illustrated in Fig. 64, the method of mitreing is in-

in two directions at right angles is shown by Fig. 72. Barefaced tenons are used, and the mortises continued till they meet. Fig. 73 shows the leg with the haunchings cut, while Fig. 74 illustrates one of the rails tenoned and haunched,

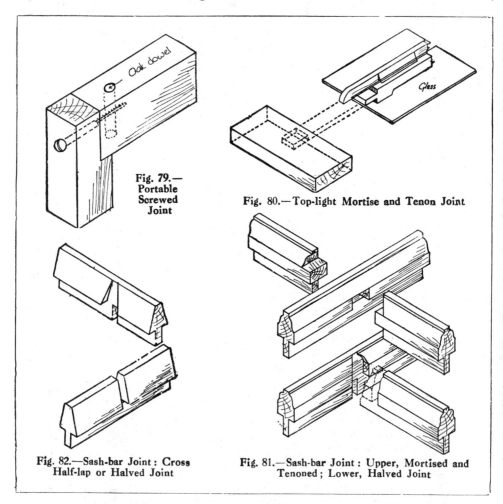

Fig. 79.—Portable Screwed Joint

Fig. 80.—Top-light Mortise and Tenon Joint

Fig. 82.—Sash-bar Joint : Cross Half-lap or Halved Joint

Fig. 81.—Sash-bar Joint : Upper, Mortised and Tenoned ; Lower, Halved Joint

dicated by Fig. 69. This is done with a paring chisel, guided by a template (Fig. 70) cut to an angle of 45°. The method of using this mitre template is shown in Fig. 47, page 36. Fig. 71 shows the scribed portion being shaped with a scribing gouge.

Table-leg Joints.—A table leg or corner post mortised to take side rails

the end being mitred to get the advantage of as much length as possible. Fig. 75 is a top view of the finished joint, and Fig. 76 a section showing the mitred ends of the tenons, which should be kept just short enough not to touch each other.

Bolted Table-leg Joints.—Fig. 77 shows a bolted barefaced tenon joint, suitable to connect the rails and leg of a strong table or work-bench. This method is often employed in portable buildings to allow of the structure being taken down and stored away in pieces. The wooden framework of machinery is also mostly put together in this fashion, and many examples may be met with when visiting a flour-mill or an up-to-date dairy. The hole for the bolt is made after the tenoned rail is inserted into the mortise, and the nut is then sunk into the back of the rail. Great care should be exercised in fixing the nut true and firm, so that it will not shift when the bolt is withdrawn.

Another type of joint, with bolts arranged not to show from the outside, is illustrated by Fig. 78. The bolts have cylindrical heads with holes drilled through. This enables a nail punch to be inserted and the bolt screwed into the nut, which is sunk into the post and plugged up with the same kind of wood, selected to follow the graining. This joint is often met with in wooden bedsteads. The tenon is only needed to take the dead weight off the bolts, the latter themselves sufficing to hold the joint tight.

Portable Screwed Joint.—Fig. 79 shows a portable joint, just notched or stub-tenoned together, and held in position with a long round-headed screw. A hardwood dowel is glued and driven through the rail to receive the thread of the screw, which acts like the nut on a bolt. This joint is suitable for light framework, such as a meat-safe or dog kennel.

Sash-bar Tenon Joints.—Sash-bars require special treatment. Fig. 80 illustrates the joint between a rebated and chamfered sash-bar and the bottom rail of a skylight. It will be seen that the portion above the glass is continued over the bottom rail.

When making a long skylight, such as the glass covers for garden frames, it is better to let the tenon go right through the top and bottom rails and to wedge them up in the ordinary way, long tenon and short tenon alternately.

Figs. 81 and 82 give two methods of jointing moulded and rusticated sash-bars. The first is mortised and tenoned together, and is mostly used with thick bars, which are here shown scribed. The second is really a variation of the half-lap joint, with moulded and sloping sides cut to fit.

Fox-wedged Mortise and Tenon Joints.—In certain work it is not expedient for the tenons to go through the wood for wedging, and equally impossible to use pins. In such cases, carpenters and joiners generally adopt the method

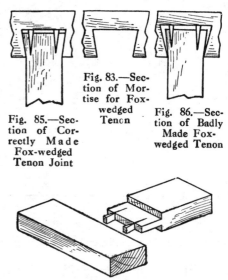

Fig. 85.—Section of Correctly Made Fox-wedged Tenon Joint

Fig. 83.—Section of Mortise for Fox-wedged Tenon

Fig. 86.—Section of Badly Made Fox-wedged Tenon

Fig. 84.—Fox-wedged Tenon Ready For Driving In

known as " fox " or secret wedging. This consists of making the mortise wider on the inside than the outside, by the thickness of the two wedges, as shown sectionally in Fig. 83. The rectangular tenon is made a little shorter than the depth of the mortise and saw kerfs are cut in the end ; then the parts are glued, the wedges inserted, as in Fig. 84, and on knocking the tenon in the wedges are forced home by coming against the inside of the mortise. In consequence, the tenon is expanded into what is practically a dovetail, as illustrated by Fig. 85.

Fox-wedged joints are more or less successful according to whether the wedges and the sloping sides of the mortise are correctly made, and it often turns out that they are not. One common cause of failure is shown sectionally by Fig. 86, where the wedges are not large

spandril frame under the stairs in a hall. If the tenons had to be cut out of the solid rail parallel to the bottom, the mortise holes would be so acute as to be almost useless ; they would also be extremely difficult to cut. This is overcome by inserting two loose tenons, as in-

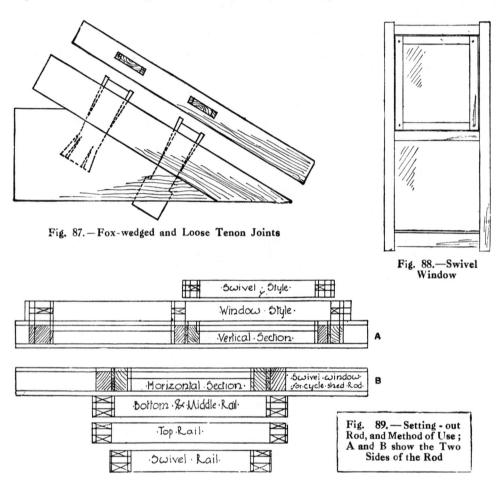

Fig. 87.—Fox-wedged and Loose Tenon Joints

Fig. 88.—Swivel Window

Fig. 89. — Setting - out Rod, and Method of Use ; A and B show the Two Sides of the Rod

enough to expand the tenon to the full extent of the mortise, with resulting looseness. When, on the other hand, the wedges are too thick, there is risk of breaking off the sides of the tenon, or even of splitting the rail.

Fig. 87 shows a good way of joining the sloping piece and bottom rail of a triangular panelled frame, such as the

dicated, one being fox-wedged while the other is shouldered and slipped in from the bottom. The whole can then be glued and cramped up, which gives a very strong joint

Use of the Setting-out Rod. — For repetition work a setting-out rod saves much time. As an example, Fig. 88 is the elevation of a small swivel window for a cycle shed in 1½-in. thick material. All stuff should first be planed straight, true and square, and to the right width and thickness. The setting-

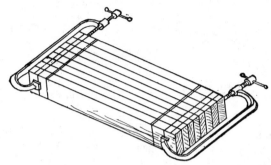

Fig. 90.—Cramping Work while Setting Out

out rod is next prepared in 2 in. by ½ in. wood, planed up smooth and with straight, parallel edges. Fig. 89 shows both sides of the rod when set out, allowing for the rebating and jointing. The same illustration also indicates how to apply the rod to the squared pieces, transferring the shou'der lines from rod to stuff. The gauge lines and bevelling are also shown. Setting-out work will be dealt with in the chapter on drawing, and in numerous examples later.

The pieces should first be mortised and tenoned ; secondly rebated and the bottom rail weathered ; thirdly fitted together joint by joint and finally glued, wedged up, and c eaned off with the smoothing plane.

ensures accuracy, and makes all identical parts, such as stiles, rails, muntins, etc , equal in length.

Wedging Mortise and Tenon Joints.—All kinds of tenons used in joiners' work are best secured with glue and wedges, unless they are of sufficient thickness to make a pin more suitable. As a rule, joints where glue is employed should be wedged, while others should be pinned. There are exceptions, but they are few, and rarely found in practical work.

In Fig. 91 are given sectional examples of how and how not to cut out the "wedging" for a mortise and tenon joint. Thus at H a double tenon is inserted in mortises where the wedging is cut out very abruptly. so that the wedges have not a fair opportunity. At I is seen the opposite extreme, a parallel wedging, which is very unlikely to make a strong joint. The correct wedging is shown at J ; it reaches nearly through the wood with an easy taper, hence correctly-made wedges will fit throughout the whole length.

At L, in Fig. 92, is illustrated a properly-cut wedge. Too often they are made as at M, or at even a greater angle, which will not be satisfactory in use.

Pinning Mortise and Tenon Joints.—For ordinary pinning, the joint is well cramped up while boring the hole through the tenon and the two cheeks of the

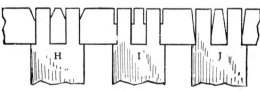

Fig. 91.—Section through Tenons and Mortises ; Correct and Incorrect "Wedgings" to Mortises

Fig. 92.—Right and Wrong Forms of Wedges

It is more convenient, when a number of similar, or nearly similar, pieces have to be dealt with, to clamp them at the ends, as seen in Fig. 90, while the setting-out markings are squared across. This

mortise, for doing which a brace and bit is used. A slightly-tapering wooden pin, a shade larger than the hole, is then driven tightly in and cut off flush. This does not make so strong a joint as " draw-boring," to be next described.

Draw-boring.—The best method of pinning is first to bore the hole through

the holes into line and thereby tightening up the joint. The steel pin is lastly removed and a wooden one substituted.

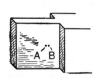

Fig. 93. — Diagram showing Where to Draw-bore the Tenon

Fig. 94.—Draw-bore Holes Out of Line

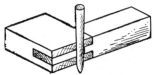

Fig. 95.—Driving Draw-bore Pin through Joint

the mortise only. The joint is then put together and the position of the hole marked on the tenon by inserting the point of the bit. Next, the pieces are taken apart, and a mark is made on the tenon a trifle nearer the shoulder, as at B in Fig. 93, where A is the one originally made. The tenon is now supported on a piece of waste, the bit inserted at B and a hole bored. On again putting the joint together the holes a e obviously out of line, as seen in Fig. 94. A tapered steel pin, specially supplied for the purpose, is driven through, as in Fig. 95, which naturally has the effect of forcing

In the case of a slot mortise shown on an earlier page (*see* Fig. 19), the hole in the tenon should not only be closer to the shoulder, as before described, but should, in addition, be a little farther away from the inner edge, so as to force the tenon up to the end of the mortise. This is usual y a trap for the inexperienced.

The displacement of the central hole in draw-boring must be only of the slightest, or there is a risk of splitting the pin, or possibly of breaking the tenon. A few trials will soon show how much to allow.

Scarfing and Other Joints

Scarfing Joints.—Scarfing joints are used to connect timbers in length, and might better be termed splicing joints. They are numerous, varying from the simple to the elaborate, according to the part they have to play. Thus, for a wall plate, a common halving joint is all that is needed; while in heavy constructional carpentry, as for lengthening posts, beams, struts, tie-pieces, etc., something much more substantial and secure is essential.

The joint should always be selected

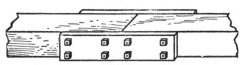

Fig. 1.—Butt Joint with Fish-plates

to suit the particular work in hand. Thus, in the case of a tie beam there is a pulling or tensile strain; a girder is subject to a bending strain; a column to compression, while any of the foregoing might also have to resist a shearing strain, or sliding pressure

Fig. 1 illustrates a very simple form of scarfed joint, in which the two pieces are merely butted together and held in position by a couple of fish-plates bolted on the sides. It is satisfactory for work not subject to vibration, and supported entirely by a wall or by columns at short intervals. If movement is likely, the bolts will wear the wood and the joint

will fail. Since stout plates and bolts are imperative, it is only suitable for heavy work. When plates projecting outside are inadmissible, the joint may

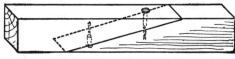

Fig. 2.—Butt Joint with Central Fish-plate

be made as in Fig. 2, a slot being cut in the middle at each end and a single plate inserted. This takes longer, and is not so strong.

Splayed Scarf Joint.—Fig. 3 shows a splayed scarf joint, or plain splice. It is easy to make, but is only used in light work, as, for instance, the joint between the ash bend and straight in the leading edge of an aeroplane, for splicing broken cart shafts, broken oars, etc. In dry work the pieces are secured by screws and glue; while, where wetting is likely,

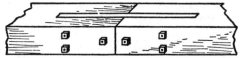

Fig. 3.—Splayed Scarf Joint

bolts, iron plates and screws are necessary. The splice should be at least 9 in. long, or, better still, 1 ft. If the pieces are equal in size the setting out may be done by measuring off the required distance, squaring over, and connecting the lines diagonally; otherwise one piece should be cut first and the other marked

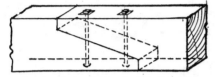

Fig. 4.—Splayed Scarf with Shoulders

by it, laying them out in a straight line while doing so.

Splayed Scarf with Shoulders.— Fig 4 shows a splayed scarf joint with shoulders and bolt fastenings. This is suitable for heavy work and will resist a lengthways push better than the simple splayed joint.

Birdsmouth Splay Joint.—Fig. 5 illustrates the birdsmouth splay joint,

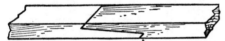

Fig. 5.—Birdsmouth Splay Joint

Fig. 6.—Setting Out Birdsmouth Splay Joint

Fig. 7.—Finished Parts of Birdsmouth Splay Joint

which to some extent resists a bending stress. Fig. 6 shows the setting out, and Fig. 7 the two parts ready for putting together. If several of these joints are required it is worth while making a template, especially with timber of unequal size.

An elaboration of the preceding is the splayed scarf with folding wedges and inclined shoulders (Fig. 8). The hardwood wedges pull the pieces together tight, helping to take any tensional stress

that may be put on, and thus relieving the bolts. It is used in bridge building, shoring, strutting, etc. Fig. 9 shows the employment of the same joint in an

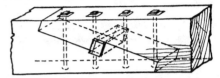

Fig. 8.—Splayed Scarf with Folding Wedges

aeroplane, for the main plane spar, which is too long to be in one piece. It is cut, fitted in close contact, glued, wedged and dowelled, as shown, forming a very strong joint indeed. This and all other aeroplane joints are wrapped round with glued tape, for extra strength.

Slot Mortise and Tenon Scarf.— This joint (Fig. 10) is one of the strongest and most useful in carpentry, and is suitable for splicing very large timbers. Although easy to make, it is important that the parts should fit correctly without being tight, otherwise there is a difficulty in putting together. Fig. 11 shows how to set out the joint. The width is divided into four parts, and a series of equal lengths are measured off, usually six inches each. In Fig. 11 only three of these are shown to save space, but in Fig. 10 four have been used, two in the middle and one at each end, the joint being thus 2 ft. long. Obviously it could be made longer by having five divisions, three being in the centre, as shown by Fig. 12. The best way of putting together is to drop one piece into position while the other is

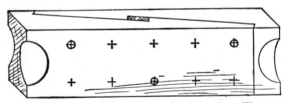

Fig. 9.—Splayed Scarf Joint for Aeroplane Work

lying in place. Fig. 13 shows the two parts ready for doing so. Pins and draw-boring are mostly used for fixing, though bolts are sometimes employed.

When boring the pin-holes, prior to marking, two should be bored through the slot mortises in each piece. This type of joint may be further strengthened, if desired, by making certain members pointed, as indicated by the dotted lines.

Tabled Joint.—Fig. 14 shows a tabled joint, practically a hook halving. It is easy to make, and is useful where longi-

lapping 1 ft. at each side of the joint and having four bolts run through. The fish-plates should be the same width as the beam, so that the bolts may be placed zigzag, while the thickness of the plates should be about one-quarter the depth of the beam. Like the preceding joint, certain parts may be pointed if preferred, as shown dotted in Fig. 15.

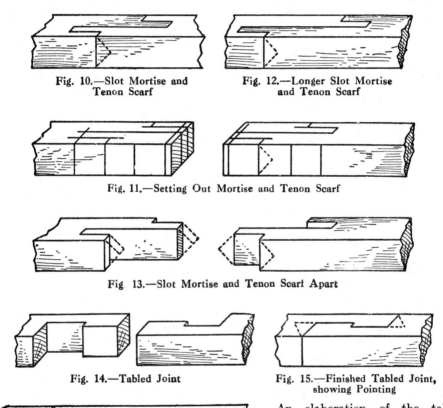

Fig. 10.—Slot Mortise and Tenon Scarf

Fig. 12.—Longer Slot Mortise and Tenon Scarf

Fig. 11.—Setting Out Mortise and Tenon Scarf

Fig 13.—Slot Mortise and Tenon Scarf Apart

Fig. 14.—Tabled Joint

Fig. 15.—Finished Tabled Joint, showing Pointing

Fig. 16.—Tabled Joint with Folding Wedges

An elaboration of the tabled joint, with folding wedges, used in heavy engineering work, is shown by Fig. 16. Another one, very similar, but having a vertical check to prevent side motion, is illustrated by Fig. 17. When well made this is very effective and needs no other fastening than the folding wedges, but if constructed in a slovenly manner it cannot be recommended. Fig. 18 shows the pieces apart. The seating for the wedges should be so cut as to allow a

tudinal stresses (tension and compression) are encountered, but not so good for a lateral bending strain. It is greatly improved by the addition of wooden fish-plates at the top and bottom, over-

slight amount of draught, so that the parts will be forced together when the wedges are driven in.

Double-splayed Scarf Joint.—A double-splayed scarf joint with shoulders at top and bottom is illustrated by Fig. 19. It should only be used when there is substantial support immediately underneath, and should be fixed by bolts and straps, as seen sectionally in Fig. 20.

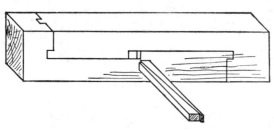

Fig. 17.—Joggle Halving Joint

posts, each piece has what are actually two stopped rebates cut in it, as shown by Fig. 22, one quarter of the area of each section being cut away at alternate corners.

Hammer-headed Key Joint.—This strong and useful joint, illustrated by Fig. 23, consists of a slot so cut in the two pieces as to accommodate a hammer-headed key, sufficient space being left for the insertion of four folding wedges, which pull the joint up tight. In making it great care should be exercised. The key should first be made, in hard wood of a non-splitting nature, and the recess marked direct from the key, making allowance for wedges and fitting. When placing the wedges, note that they are in contact from top to bottom of the hole

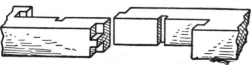

Fig. 18.—Parts Cut for Joggle Halving

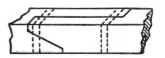

Fig. 19.—Double-splayed Scarf Joint

Fig. 20.—Section of Bolts and Straps for Double-splayed Joint

Fig. 21.—Double-splayed Joint Apart

If bolts are employed without straps, and there is the least movement, the wood will gradually wear away and the joint loosen. The two pieces, ready for fixing, are shown by Fig. 21. To set out, divide the length into five parts, taking two parts for each splay and leaving one in the middle for the square. The total length may vary from eighteen to thirty inches.

MISCELLANEOUS JOINTS

Double-halved Longitudinal Joint. In this, which is very suitable for heavy

on their sloping sides, otherwise they will tend to tilt the joint out of truth.

Fig. 24 shows the application of a hammer-headed key joint to a circular-headed frame.

A simpler joint for connecting two light curved pieces end to end, when no great strain is expected, is by means of a double dovetail key (*see* Fig. 25).

Screwed Joints for Curved Work.—When part of the woodwork is hidden behind brick or stone on one side, and has plaster or wood linings on the other, an easy way for joining curved pieces is by a screwed-on overlapping piece, as shown by Fig. 26. This method is very extensively used in the building trade.

The joint where the straight side of a

Handrail Bolts and Dowels —A very strong type of joint, used in handrailing, heavy curtain poles, wooden

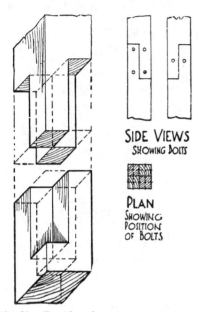

SIDE VIEWS
SHOWING BOLTS

PLAN
SHOWING
POSITION
OF BOLTS

Fig. 22.—Double-halved Longitudinal Joint

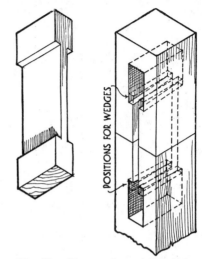

Fig. 23.—Hammer-headed Key Joint

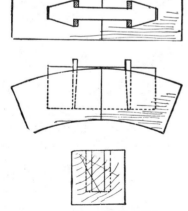

Fig. 24.—Hammer-headed Joint on Curved Frame

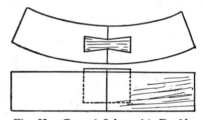

Fig. 25 —Curved Joint with Double Dovetail Key

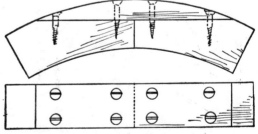

Fig. 26.—Lapped and Screwed Joint in Curved Frame

window or other frame meets the curved head may be treated as in Fig. 27. Here glue is employed as well as screws.

curb fenders, etc., is shown by Fig. 28. The bolt holds the pieces close, while the dowels prevent rotation. The nuts are circular, with grooves cut round the edges, to facilitate tightening with hammer and punch.

Screw Dowel for Walking-stick.—

of the screw shank, and continued forward with a smaller bit so as to allow the thread to catch. The holes must be big enough or the stick will split ; but, on

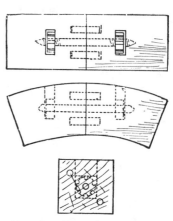

Fig. 28.—Curved Head Jointed with Handrail Bolts and Dowels

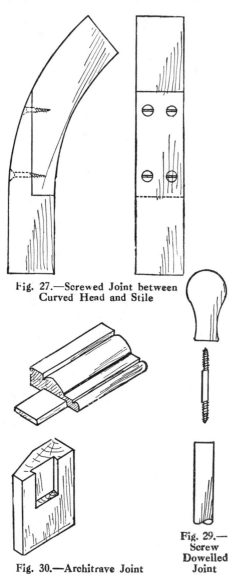

Fig. 27.—Screwed Joint between Curved Head and Stile

the other hand, if made too large, the pieces will soon come apart, as most people have had melancholy experience. The joint is fixed by glue.

Architrave Joint.—Fig. 30 shows a good way of jointing the bottom end of an architrave with the plinth block

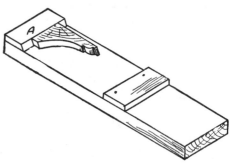

Fig. 31.—Planing Board for Short Breaks in Mouldings

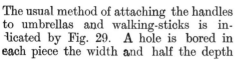

Fig. 30.—Architrave Joint

Fig. 29.— Screw Dowelled Joint

The usual method of attaching the handles to umbrellas and walking-sticks is indicated by Fig. 29. A hole is bored in each piece the width and half the depth

of a door or window. It is held in position by glue and screws.

Short Breaks in Moulding.—Fig. 31 illustrates the planing board used for making short breaks in mouldings, as when continuing a cornice round a pilaster. A small piece of moulding, or several such, has to be cut, which is too short to be held in the vice or on an ordinary shooting board. In such cases it can be planed by placing on the special board against the bevelled stop A, as shown,

nailed. The same principle can be adapted for cornices, picture and dado rails, etc. ; it is also often employed in cabinet-making, where rounded corners are required instead of the sharp arris of the mitre.

Simple Scarfing Joints.—In making furniture and fittings boards are some-

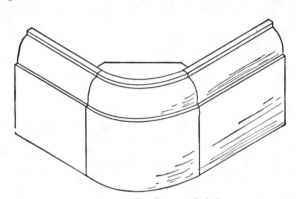

Fig. 32.—Joint for Curved Skirting

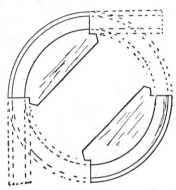

Fig. 33.—Method of Making Joint for Curved Skirting

and nailing it down, punching the nails in a little.

Joint for Curved Skirting, etc.— An excellent and very substantial method of jointing skirting or other mouldings round circular corners is shown by Fig. 32. A block of wood is turned in the lathe to the same profile as the moulding, and is then cut as indicated in Fig. 33, rebating it at each side to receive the straight pieces. In fixing, the back part of the corner block is sunk into the brickwork, plugged and

times required to be lengthened where, from the fact that the work is otherwise supported, simpler methods than those previously dealt with will very well suffice. In mantel-boards and small shelves, for instance, two or three dowels will answer quite satisfactorily ; in table-tops mere gluing and cramping will do ; while in further cases, rebates, grooves and tongues, half-lapping, or adaptations of some of the other joints already described may be used.

Boring Tools and Their Uses

THE BRADAWL

THE chief boring tools are the bradawl, the gimlet, and the brace and bit. For small holes, say up to about ⅛ in. or 3/16 in., the bradawl (or sprigbit) is generally

by boring part-way with the bradawl Screw holes in softwoods are bored in th same way. Holes for nails or screws in hardwoods are bored with the bradaw only if they are very small, the brac

Fig. 1.—
Ordinary
Bradawl

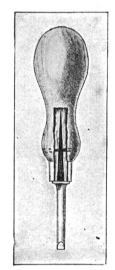

Fig. 2.—Section of
Bradawl having Pin
through Tang

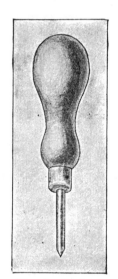

Fig. 3.—Bradawl
Secured by
Ferrule

Fig. 4.—Section of
Bradawl Secured by
Ferrule

used, particularly if the holes are only a few in number. When nailing softwoods, say with nails up to about 2 in. to 2½ in. in length, and if there is a danger of splitting owing to the nails being near the edge, the nails are " given a start "

and bit being generally used for large ones.

The common type of bradawl is shown in Fig. 1. It consists of three parts the handle (preferably ash, but often beech), the ferrule of brass, and the blade or prong or bit). The blade has a tang which fits into the handle. Between tang and blade is a shoulder which prevents the blade being driven into the handle. Fig. 2 shows a section of a

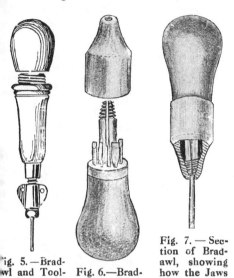

Fig. 5.—Bradawl and Tool-pad with Wing-nut Adjustment

Fig. 6.—Bradawl and Tool-pad

Fig. 7. — Section of Bradawl, showing how the Jaws Grip the Blade

bradawl having a pin passing through the handle and tang and thus preventing the blade from being easily withdrawn from the handle, this being a decided advantage.

Fig. 3 shows an even more securely fixed blade than the type shown in Fig. 2. After the tang is driven into the handle the cup-shaped ferrule is driven on the handle and holds against the shoulder of the blade (see Fig. 4). The tang is then fastened with one or two pins.

There is a number of types of bradawls with detachable blades, as shown in Figs. 5, 6 and 7. Sometimes these elaborate bradawls are known as " tool-pads." The " bits " (or tools) often comprise a small screwdriver, gimlets, reamer, etc.

In the type shown in Fig. 5 the " bits " are kept in the hollow handle, which is usually made of boxwood and has a screw top. The various bits are quickly fixed in the jaw or chuck by means of

the wing screw. Care should be taken not to hit the handle of this tool-pad with the hammer, as being hollow it is easily split.

Fig. 6 shows another variety of bradawl and tool-pad. The shanks of the tools fit into the jaws, the top of which is screwed and tapered. On screwing the cap into position the jaws are forced together and grip the shank of the bit, as indicated in Fig. 7.

Using the Bradawl.—Before using, the bradawl should be sharpened. This is usually done by filing the end bevelled from both sides, the bevels being about $\frac{1}{4}$ in. long. The end, of course, is an *edge*, like a chisel, not a point. A *pointed* bradawl is a mere pricker ; it cannot bore. A saw file is generally used for sharpening, though the bradawl could be ground on a grindstone or flagstone if desired. A

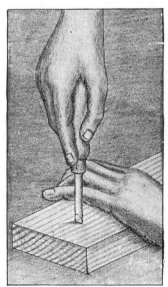

Fig. 8.—Correct Method of Using Bradawl

keener edge may be given by a few rubs on an oilstone, but this is usually not considered worth the trouble.

The cutting edge of the bradawl should be held across the grain (Fig. 8) and pressed into the timber. Whilst pressing on the bradawl it should be slightly rot&ced to and fro with an arc-like movement ; it should not be turned completely round as in the case of a gimlet. Very often it is driven into the wood with the hammer, as in Fig. 9. This method undoubtedly requires less effort on the part of the workman, but there is a

being held by the left hand and the handl of the bradawl grasped with the righ hand, which exerts a lifting action an at the same time a slight arc-like motion

If the bradawl is driven into a piec of timber with its edge in the directio of the grain it acts as a wedge and th

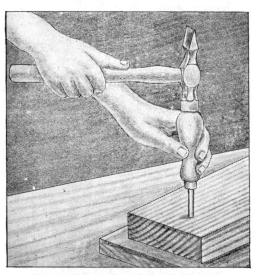

Fig. 9.—Driving Bradawl with Hammer

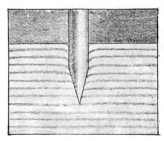

Fig. 12.—Boring Action of Bradawl

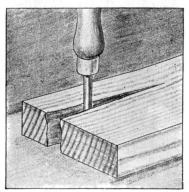

Fig. 11.—Timber Split with Bradawl owing to Incorrect Usage

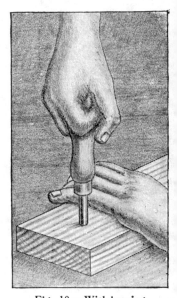

Fig. 10.—Withdrawing Bradawl

likelihood of the handle of the bradawl being split, and there is also difficulty in withdrawing the tool.

The usual method of withdrawing the bradawl is shown in Fig. 10, the timber

wood is likely to split, as in Fig. 11. the edge of the blade is held across th grain there is no wedge action tendin to split the wood and the edge also cut the fibres, thus making a cleaner an larger hole than when the edge of the blade is parallel with the grain. Besides this cutting action there is also a crushing

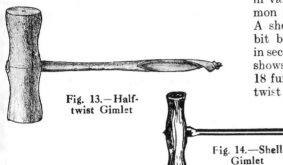

Fig. 13.—Half-twist Gimlet

Fig. 14.—Shell Gimlet

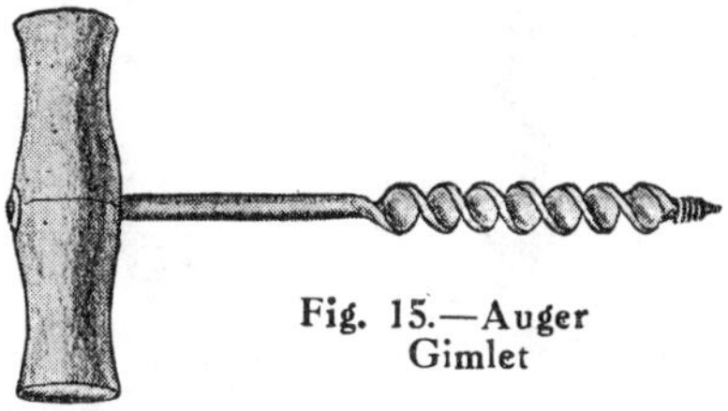

action, the fibres being compressed and bent downwards, as indicated in Fig. 12.

GIMLETS

A gimlet is a self-contained boring tool (like a bradawl), but having a twisted or threaded point that forces its way into the wood. In boring a hole with a bradawl continuous pressure has to be applied, but in the case of a gimlet, after it has once been started, the worm end " eats " its way into the timber. The handle is therefore shaped so that

a fair amount of turning effort can be applied.

The steel portion of the gimlet is made in various shapes. Fig. 13 shows a common form known as a half-twist gimlet. A shell gimlet is shown at Fig. 14, the bit being a straight shank, half circular in section, with a twist at the end. Fig. 15 shows an auger bit, and Figs. 16, 17 and 18 further illustrate an ordinary form of twist gimlet in course of use.

Using the Gimlet.—
To bore a hole with a gimlet it has to be turned con-

Fig. 15.—Auger Gimlet

stantly in one direction (like the hands of a clock). Fig. 16 shows the usual way of holding when starting to bore. The gimlet is at first rotated and pressed down at the same time. When the point and the cutter have entered the wood, and provided the wood is not too hard or

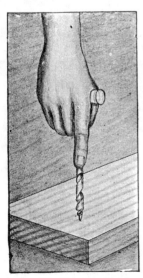

Fig. 16.—Starting Gimlet

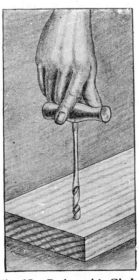

Fig. 17.—Boring with Gimlet

Fig. 18.—Withdrawing Gimlet

the gimlet dull, the gimlet can be turned more quickly by the thumb and finger, as indicated in Fig. 17.

worker possesses a brace and bits or handdrill and two or three bradaw gimlets are hardly necessary, and, in fa

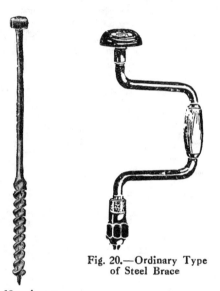

Fig. 20.—Ordinary Type of Steel Brace

Fig. 20A.— Wooden Brace

Fig. 20B.—Scotch Brace

Fig. 19.—Auger, Gedge's Pattern

inadvisable. The chief advantages of t gimlet are its small size and small price

The gimlet is withdrawn by grasping the handle (Fig. 18) and using a combined lifting and rotating action; this will bring out the core and leave a cleaner hole. The process just described often has to be repeated several times when boring hardwood or thick softwood.

Care should be exercised in the use of all gimlets when boring near the end of the wood, as they exercise a splitting action. This is especially the case when they become worn and blunt and thus do not cut properly; extra effort is then exerted which brings into play the wedge-like form of their ends, which tends to force the fibres apart instead of cutting them, thus splitting the timber.

Gimlets do not appear to be as much used nowadays as formerly. If a wood-

Fig. 21.—Examples of Ratchet Braces and Fittings

An *auger* (Fig. 19) might be describe as a large gimlet used for boring lar and long holes in carpentry, etc. T handle may either fit through a hole e auger shank or the latter may be ṣaped like a brace bit and fit into a ṣecial adjustable handle.

Fig. 22.—Further Examples of Ratchet Braces and Fittings

BRACE AND BITS

A brace is a tool for holding and rotating ṣits for boring holes and other purposes. The common simple type is shown in Fig. 20. It consists of three parts : the jaws (or chuck), the head, and the crank. Formerly the bit was fastened in the jaws by means of a thumbscrew, as in the old-fashioned wooden brace in Fig. 20A, or by a spring catch as in Fig. 20B, but the usual type of jaws on modern braces is as shown in the illustration. The bit is inserted between the jaws, which grip the bit between them when the jaw cap is screwed down on to the jaws. This latter operation is accomplished not by turning the jaw cap, but by holding it still with the left hand and turning the crank of the brace with the right hand.

Very often the jaws are serrated, as shown in Figs. 21 and 22, in which case they are known as " crocodile jaws," to get a better grip on the bits.

The power of the brace depends on the " sweep " of the crank—the bigger the sweep the more powerful being the brace. The sweep is the diameter of the circle that the crank describes. A 10-in.

sweep is a usual size, though 8 in. is fairly common. Other sizes of braces may be also obtained. Though more turning power can be exerted when the crank is large, it is found in practice that a 10-in. sweep gives enough power for all ordinary purposes. The handle of the crank and the head are usually made of rosewood. In good makes the head runs on ball-bearings.

Many braces, in fact, probably the majority in use by professional workmen, are now fitted with a ratchet. Stanley ratchet braces are shown in Figs. 21 and 22 ; the letters in the illustrations show to which braces the various fittings belong, parts A belonging to brace A, etc. The ratchet is simply a catch or

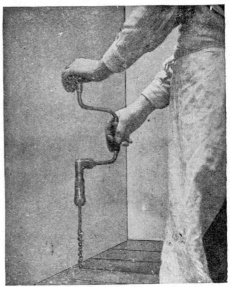

Fig. 23.—Boring Hole with Ratchet Brace in Floor near Wall

device which, at will, enables the crank to be rotated without rotating the jaws and bit. This adds greatly to the utility of the tool. Fig. 23 shows a hole being bored in the floor near a wall with a ratchet brace and a twist bit. A hole could not be easily bored in this position with an ordinary brace, as the crank of

forming part of the tool, the bit can be turned at a higher speed than with a brace, and, further the turning of the handle of the drill does not have a strong tendency to pull the drill and bit out

Fig. 23A.—Sectional View showing Ratchet and Jaws

Fig. 23C.

Figs. 23B and 23C.—Angular Bit Stock and How to Use It

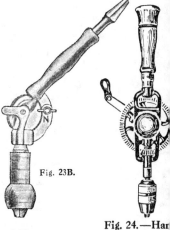

Fig. 23B.

Fig. 24.—Hand Drill

the brace could not be turned continuously. With the ratchet brace, the ratchet may be so adjusted that on turning the crank clockwise the bit is turned. When the crank has thus been turned as far as possible, that is, until it comes in contact with the wall, it may be turned backwards, during which latter turn the bit remains stationary. The crank is again turned clockwise and turns the bit, and so on until the hole is bored. The ratchet may also be adjusted so that the ratchet misses on a clockwise turn and grips on the anti-clockwise turn. Fig. 23A gives a pictorial view showing how the ratchet works; the crocodile jaws are also clearly shown in the illustration.

Figs. 23B and 23C show an angular bit stock; it is an alternative to the ratchet brace in awkward positions; N (Fig. 23B) is the clamp.

HAND DRILL

This tool (Fig. 24) is better for many purposes than the brace, and deserves to be better known. Owing to the gearing

of its correct direction. These are two decided advantages. The tool is recommended to both amateurs and skilled craftsmen.

BRACE BITS

There are many varieties of bits, different patterns having been found necessary for boring holes under differing conditions, such as size of hole and kind

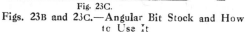

Fig. 25.—Shell Bit

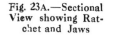

Fig. 26.—Spoon Bit

of timber. Other bits are necessary for drilling and enlarging holes in metal fittings for woodwork and for other purposes.

Shell Bit.—This bit (Fig. 25) is the simplest and mostly used type of bit.

It is employed only to bo e small holes (up to about ⅜ in. diameter) generally for screws and nails. It is sharpened by

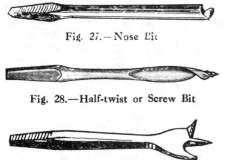

Fig. 27.—Nose Bit

Fig. 28.—Half-twist or Screw Bit

Fig. 29.—Centre Bit

filing the end. This bit has less tendency than any other type of bit, when boring a hole through a piece of wood, to splinter the back side, but even with this it is better to safeguard against splintering by holding a scrap of timber to the other side of the wood. This warning applies particularly to such jobs as boring the holes for a keyhole.

The shell bit has to be forced into the wood by continual pressure. If the hole

is deep or in hardwood it is customary, after boring a little distance, to withdraw the bit whilst still turning in the same

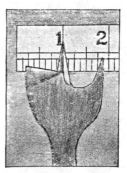

Fig. 30.—Obtaining Size of Centre Bit

direction, so that some of the " core " is withdrawn. If it is attempted to bore a deep hole without withdrawing some of the core at intervals the bit will get very hot and the brace difficult to turn, there being also a possibility of boring an unsatisfactory hole.

Spoon Bit.—Fig. 26 shows this bit to be similar to the shell bit except that the cutting end is spoon-shaped. It is a little quicker in action than the ordinary

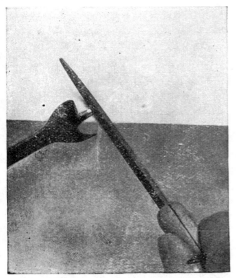

Fig. 31.—Sharpening Point of Centre Bit

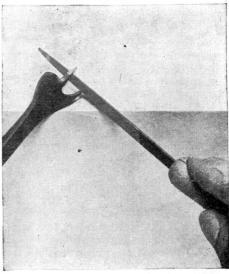

Fig. 32.—Sharpening Nicker of Centre Bit

shell bit, but the end is soon damaged by "running against" a nail.

Nose Bit.—This is another variety of shell bit (*see* Fig. 27) possessing the same merits and demerits. Both spoon and nose bits are useful for boring with the grain, and the shape of the end enables the core of the hole to be easily withdrawn.

Half-twist Bit.—This bit (Fig. 28) is often known as a "screw bit" because it is used in "boring for screws," for which it is particularly suited. It is self-propelling, and is therefore not fatiguing to use. As the bit starts at a point and gradually thickens in the shank it exerts

Fig. 33.—Removing Burr on Nicker of Centre Bit

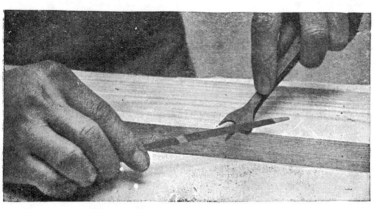

Fig. 35.—Filing Cutter of Centre Bit

should be *slightly less* than $\frac{7}{8}$ in. so that the side of the cutter will not rub or scar the side of the hole, thus giving a clean cut. The size of a centre bit should therefore be determined, as in Fig. 30, or a trial hole bored and measured.

As there are a wedge-like action when boring, and care is therefore necessary to avoid splitting the wood.

Centre Bit.—This bit is of a distinct type from the preceding bits, its action in cutting a hole being quite different. A centre bit (Fig. 29) consists of three parts : the centre pin, which forms an axis or guide when cutting the hole ; the outside point or "nicker," which marks the rim of the hole and cuts the wood fibres ; the cutter or scoop, which removes the wood after the manner of a revolving chisel. The "size" of a centre bit is twice the distance from the centre pin to the nicker. For example, in Fig. 30 the distance from the centre of the bit to the nicker is $\frac{7}{8}$ in. and therefore the size of the bit is $1\frac{3}{4}$ in. The distance from the centre pin to the outside of the cutter

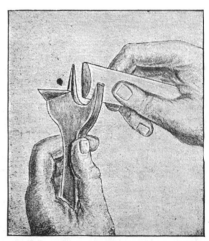

Fig. 34.—Using Finger Slip to Sharpen Centre Bit

three parts to a centre bit there must be three operations in sharpening. First

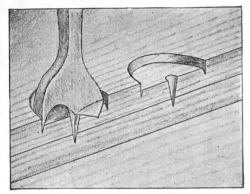

Fig. 36.—Boring with Centre Bit : First Operation, shown partly in section

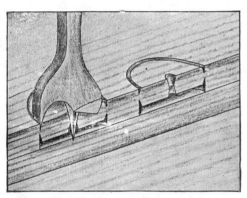

Fig. 37.—Boring with Centre Bit : Second Operation, shown partly in section

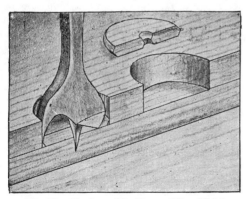

Fig. 38.—Boring with Centre Bit : Third Operation, shown partly in section

the point should be sharpened by filing. as in Fig. 31, if necessary. Fig. 32 shows how the nicker is filed—on the *inside*, not on the outside. If the latter were filed the size as well as the cutting properties of the bit would be spoiled. The nicker should also be sloping on the edge so as to cut easily. Sometimes the " burr " on the outside is carefully removed on the oilstone, as in Fig. 33, or the nicker finished with a " finger slip," as in Fig. 34, but these last two operations are hardly necessary except in very high-

Fig. 39. —Twist Bit : Jennings' Pattern

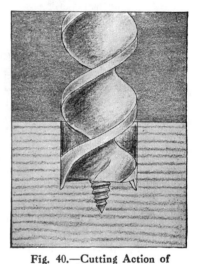

Fig. 40.—Cutting Action of Twist Bit

class work. Lastly, the cutter is filed, as in Fig. 35. The filing must be done on the top side of the cutter, otherwise the bit will not " bite " into the wood when in use.

A hole may be bored with a centre bit right through a piece of wood without splitting if a piece of wood is held against the wood where the bit comes through, as recommended when boring with the shell. It is usual, however, to bore from both sides of the wood. Figs. 36, 37 and 38 show a slight variation of the usual method of boring from both sides. Preferably the work is placed on or against a piece of waste wood, though this could be dispensed with. The hole is bored

Fig. 41.—Filing Cutter of Twist Bit

Fig. 42.—Filing Nicker of Twist Bit

until the centre point projects a little through the back of the wood, as shown in Fig. 36. The work is then bored from the other side a little so that the nicker makes a circular cut, as indicated in Fig. 37. The work is turned back to its first position and the boring continued, when a circular piece should come out as shown. If the bit is sharp and held at right angles to the face of the work the hole will be true and smooth.

The ordinary type of centre bits have to be forced into the wood by constant pressure, but a special type with a screw centre point may be obtained. This is occasionally used for large holes, and as the screw end tends to pull the bit into the wood the work is made easier.

Twist Bits.—These bits have both a twisted point and a twisted shank. When the bit "gets a start" it forces its way

into the wood. No pressure is usually required on the head of the brace and it is only necessary to turn the crank. The worm point "eats its way" into the wood, this action being assisted by the spiral shank. The cutters at the end of the bit cut the wood after the manner of a centre bit—though this action varies a little with the type of twist bit used. Compare, for example, a Jennings' twist bit and a Gedge's twist bit. Twist bits are self-clearing, as the cuttings ascend the spiral shaft to the top of the hole.

In the Jennings' twist bit (Fig. 39) the end works on the principle of the centre bit, but has two nickers and two cutters—and, of course, a screw centre point. Fig. 40 is a sectional view of a piece of wood partly bored, showing the front edge of one cutter and the edges of the nickers. This twist bit is sharpened with a file

Fig. 43.—Twist Bit : Gedge's Pattern

Fig. 44.—Twist Drill Bit

Fig. 45.—Wood Countersinks

after the manner of a centre bit; *see* Fig. 41, which illustrates how a cutter is sharpened, and Fig. 42, which shows a nicker being filed.

There are other twist bits of slightly varying design, but they usually belong to either of the two preceding classes. A dowel bit is a short twist bit. Fig. 44

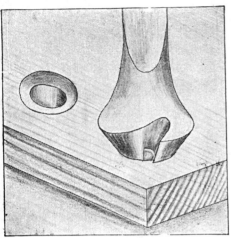

Fig. 46.—Using Wood Countersink

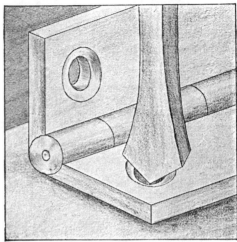

Fig. 50.—Using Iron Countersink

Fig. 47.—Countersink for Brass

Fig. 49.—Iron Countersink

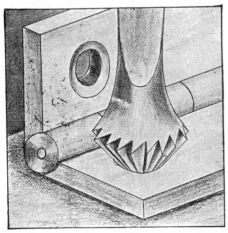

Fig. 48 —Using Countersink on Brass Hinge

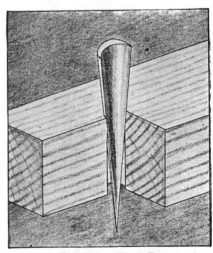

Fig. 51.—Using Wood Reamer

Gedge's bit (Fig. 43) is a twist bit very similar to the preceding but with a different shape of cutter end, which is formed by two curved wings. It is sharpened with a small round (rat-tail) file.

shows a twist drill bit that is very useful for boring hardwood in any direction of the grain without much fear of splitting

Countersinks.—These bits are of various types, and are used for countersinking screw holes in wood or metal. Fig. 45 shows two types of countersinks for *wood*. The ordinary type is shown in use in Fig. 46. It will be seen that the bit has one cutter only. This bit should be sharpened with a rat-tail file. Fig. 47 represents a countersink for brass ; it is shown in use on a brass hinge in Fig. 48, from which illustration it will

Reamers.—These are used for enlarging holes already made. There are three chief types. Fig. 52 shows a reamer for wood, which is after the manner of a tapering shell bit and should be sharp on the edges. Fig. 51 shows the wood reamer in use.

A metal reamer (Fig. 53) is like a long pyramid in shape and has four cutting

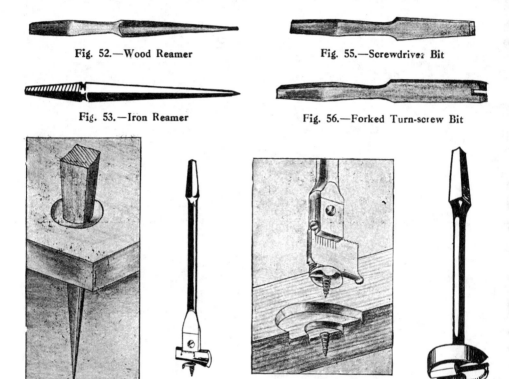

Fig. 52.—Wood Reamer

Fig. 55.—Screwdriver Bit

Fig. 53.—Iron Reamer

Fig. 56.—Forked Turn-screw Bit

Fig. 54.—Using Iron Reamer

Fig. 57 —. Expansion Bit (Clarke's Patent)

Fig. 58.—Boring with Steer's Screw Adjustment Expansion Bit. The Wood is shown in Section.

Fig. 59.— Forstner Bit

be seen that the bit has a number of cutters ; these should be sharpened, when required, with a small saw file. Very often this bit is used for countersinking timber, particularly hardwood, as it usually leaves a cleaner hole than the wood countersink.

A countersink for iron is shown in Fig. 49, and in use, countersinking the holes in an iron hinge, in Fig. 50. It is sharpened with a file or on the grindstone.

corners. In Fig. 54 the end of the reamer is shown enlarging a screw hole in a metal hinge. This reamer though supposed to be specially for iron is also suitable for brass, etc.

A special reamer for brass, semi-circular in section and tapering in length like the two former types, is sometimes used. It is, however, not necessary, and the iron reamer will do the work equally well.

Screwdriver Bit.—This bit is shown in Fig. 55 and is very useful for driving screws, particularly if the screws are numerous or large in size. The chief difficulty when using the brace and screwdriver bit is not to turn the brace or screw but to keep the bit in the nick of

Expansion Bits.—The ordinary type of expansion bit (Clarke's patent) is shown in Fig. 57. The principle is quite simple : an adjustable wing cutter slides in a groove ; the projection of this cutter gives the radius of the hole, the cutter being fixed in any desired position by means of

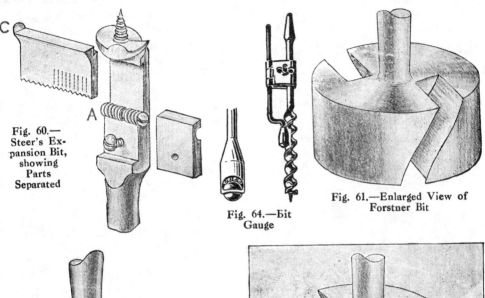

Fig. 60.—Steer's Expansion Bit, showing Parts Separated

Fig. 64.—Bit Gauge

Fig. 61.—Enlarged View of Forstner Bit

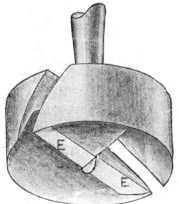

Fig. 62.—Forstner Bit, showing Cutting Edges

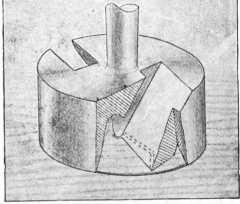

Fig. 63.—Sectional View of Forstner Bit, showing Cutting Action

the screw. It is better when dealing with tight screws to use the ratchet and turn the crank backwards and forwards through a small arc.

A forked screwdriver bit is shown at Fig. 56, and is used for tightening saw screws and other screws of the same kind, as already shown in the chapter on saws and sawing.

a screw. One expansion bit will cut holes within certain limits only, two useful sizes being a small one cutting holes between $\frac{1}{2}$ in. and $1\frac{1}{4}$ in. and a larger one boring from $\frac{7}{8}$ in. to 3 in.

In the screw-adjusting expansion bits (see Figs. 58 and 60), turning the side screw A with a screwdriver modifies the distance of the circular cutter C.

Forstner Bit.—This bit (Fig. 59), unlike other bits, is guided not by its centre but by its circular rim. It will bore any arc of a circle, and will bore in any direction regardless of grain or knots and leave a smooth surface. It is particularly useful for recessed work.

not many holes the two following methods may be used : (1) count the number of turns of the brace to bore the first hole

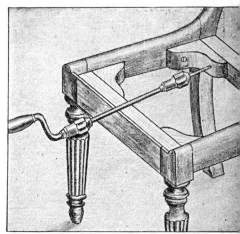

Fig. 68.—Using Extension Bit

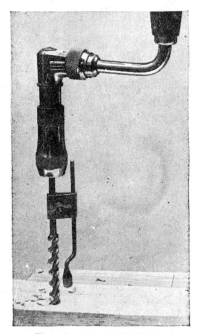

Fig. 65.—Using Bit Gauge

Fig. 66.—Dowel Sharpener

Fig. 67.—Extension Bit

A small three-cornered, or flat, file is used for sharpening it. Figs. 61 to 63 illustrate clearly the action of the bit; E indicates the two cutting edges.

Bit Gauges. — When boring holes, say for dowels, they have to be of a certain depth. The correct depth can be obtained in various ways. If there are

Fig. 69.—Disc Cutter in Use

of correct depth and give the other holes a similar number of turns ; (2) mark the bit with chalk, a pencil or a file.

Fig. 64 shows a gauge (and enlarged

detail) for attaching to the side of a bit, and Fig. 65 shows the gauge in use. Bit gauges for countersinking are also used, so that the countersinking will accurately receive the head of the screw.

Fig. 70.—Extension Bits

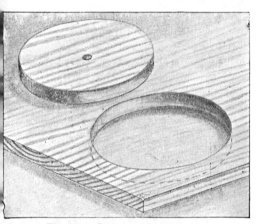

Fig. 71.—Circular Disc Cut Out

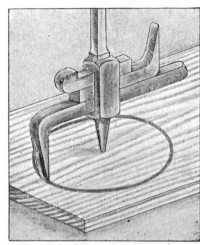

Fig. 72.—Cutting Circular Recess or Disc with Disc Cutter

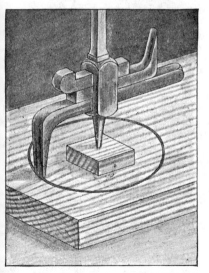

Fig. 73.—Method to Avoid Making Hole in Centre of Recess

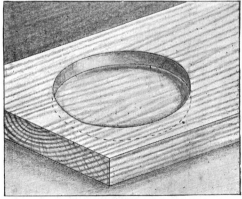

Fig. 74.—Circular Recess as Cut with Disc Cutter

Other Bits and Devices.—A bit for pointing the ends of dowels is shown in Fig. 66.

Figs. 67 and 70 show various patterns of extension bit holders. These will extend the brace bit, enabling it to be

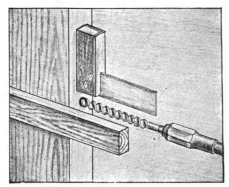

Fig. 75.—Boring at Right Angles to Edge

Fig. 76.—Boring Mitre

used for boring through walls, floors, etc., where the ordinary bit will not reach. Fig. 68 gives an example of their use.

A disc cutter bit is often found useful for cutting small wheels and discs. It consists of a centre point and a sliding nicker which can be adjusted according

to the size of disc required. Fig. 69 shows the cutter being used to cut a hole (or alternatively, a disc) from a thin board. Fig. 71 shows the finish of the operation. The disc cutter is also useful for cutting circular recesses that are too large for a centre bit. The circular side is first cut, as in Fig. 72, by chiselling. If it is desired to avoid a mark in the centre a piece of waste wood should be used, as in Fig. 73. The finished recess is shown at Fig. 74.

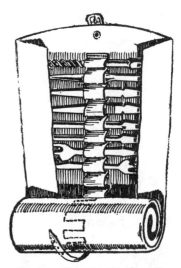

Fig. 77.—Case for Holding Bits

Boring at Right Angles to an Edge. —When boring for mortise locks and similar purposes care has to be exercised so that the bit goes in the right direction. This is best tested by a straightedge, as shown at Fig. 75. The bit must also fit the blade of a try-square as shown.

Boring at an Angle to a Mitre.—To bore accurately a hole at a mitre is somewhat difficult; but it can easily be done by a guide piece, as shown at Fig. 76.

A case or roll for holding bits is shown in Fig. 77. Some woodworkers prefer a case with longer pockets so that the bits cannot come in contact with, and damage, each other.

Wood Turning

THE production of circular shapes by revolving the wood in a lathe and operating on it with suitable cutting tools is termed wood turning. It differs from woodwork at the bench as widely as two crafts can differ which deal with the same material. Turned articles may vary extremely in shape and in size, and these variations require different methods of securing in the lathe, different speeds of rotation according to their weight, different arrangements of grain, and in many cases more or less complicated building up preparatory to turning.

In wood turning one of the first things to learn is how to avoid accidents. A revolving piece of wood demands precautions which are quite unnecessary in operating on a stationary piece. As the cutting tools are held and manipulated by hand, it is not always possible to hold them so firmly that centrifugal force cannot affect them. The alternative is to take care that they are caused to approach the work in a manner that avoids risk. Only experience can thoroughly teach this. The wood turner has often to work with tools extremely close to a dangerous position, and it is at such times that he needs to be cautious and to hold them with extreme firmness and steadiness. If the tool is forced out of position it may damage or even completely spoil the work, and in serious cases the operator himself may suffer some injury. Another point is that either with or without a tool accident the work may be thrown out of the lathe

owing to it not having been adequately secured. Unlike a bench worker, a beginner at the lathe may have acquired considerable skill and then meet with an accident which causes him to lose confidence in his ability to use the turning tools safely. An experienced turner, however, never has mishaps, and while experience is being gained there are always some ways of working which are safer than others. The beginner should do more scraping and less actual cutting with gouge and side chisel, and he should reserve these latter for surfaces where they can be safely used with comparatively little skill.

Turning Tools.—Sharp tools are as necessary at the lathe as at the bench. A tool too dull to cut at the bench can be forced to scrape or tear at the lathe, but the result is a rough surface produced with difficulty. Time spent in properly grinding and sharpening tools is never wasted. The tools used at the lathe are very few compared with those required for bench work. Fig. 1 shows all the main forms of cutting tools, and nearly all the work can be done if necessary, with the gouge and side chisel alone. It is desirable, however. to have at least two different sizes of these tools, large ones for large work and quick removal of material, and small ones for small work. For average work a gouge and side chisel $\frac{5}{8}$ in. wide are suitable. The sizes obtainable range from $\frac{1}{4}$ in. to 2 in. In Fig. 1, A is a turning gouge, B a side chisel. C a facing chisel, D a round-nose

171

chisel, and E a diamond-point chisel. The gouge is ground on the outside, and is ground back at the sides more than an ordinary firmer gouge, so that viewed from the front and side it appears as in Fig. 2. The side chisel is ground as in Fig. 3, usually with some amount of slope, as

coachmaker's chisel, long and thick, with its end ground semicircular. The diamond point is used for right-hand and left-hand scraping where an ordinary chisel could not be held at right angles to the surface. Sometimes instead of a double edge, two separate tools, as in

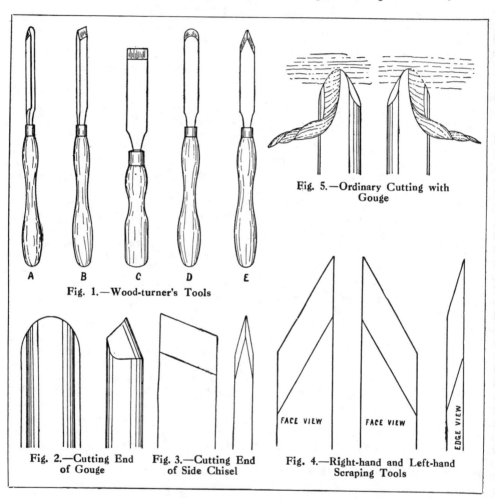

Fig. 5.—Ordinary Cutting with Gouge

Fig. 1.—Wood-turner's Tools

Fig. 2.—Cutting End of Gouge

Fig. 3.—Cutting End of Side Chisel

Fig. 4.—Right-hand and Left-hand Scraping Tools

shown in the face view, though some prefer an edge at right angles. so that both points can be used for parting. The firmer chisel is used for scraping, and does not differ in any way from an ordinary bench chisel, except that the angle of sharpening is often more obtuse. The round-nose is used for scraping concavities. It is a

Fig. 4, are employed, one for right-hand and one for left-hand scraping. The side chisel also may be used as a substitute.

All turning tools, with the exception of the firmer chisel, are long and stout with long handles, the latter being desirable to give plenty of leverage and power to resist varying stress at the cutting end. The gouge is the only tool used exclusively for cutting. The side chisel is occasionally used for scraping, and the other tools invariably for scraping, that is, they are approached in a horizontal position, and operate by a scraping action. The gouge

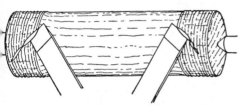

Fig. 6.—Method of Using Side Chisel

is held at a suitable angle to cut shavings. It is generally used with a lateral sliding movement to right or left so that it cuts, as in Fig. 5, the movement being towards the side on which the shaving is being cut. This is better than making a direct frontal cut with the point or middle portion of the cutting edge only, though the latter method is suitable occasionally. The side chisel is used similarly, as in Fig. 6, on cylindrical articles of small or moderate diameter, and produces a very smooth surface. On large diameters it is better to scrape with a firmer chisel, and on flat surfaces it is impossible to use the chisel as in Fig. 6, the reason being that the upper point must not be allowed to touch the surface or it will dig in with more or less disastrous results. The main use of the chisel, however, is for parting or for cutting incisions or ends, as in Fig. 7. The cuts have to be made so that the shavings are thin enough on one side of the chisel to be forced away by its wedge-like action. Thus in making a division at some distance from either end of a cylindrical piece as seen to the left in Fig. 7, a number of cuts are made side by side until there is sufficient clearance to allow the chisel to go as deeply as required. Similarly, if it is necessary to remove a considerable amount from an end to obtain the desired length, it must be done gradually by a number of shavings, each perhaps about $\frac{1}{16}$ in. thick, for no amount of force would remove a thick slice at one

stroke of the chisel. The gouge is used in a position sloping up to the work, as in Fig. 8, and the side chisel also when used for the purpose shown in Fig. 6. The scraping tools are held horizontally or nearly so, as in Fig. 9. The exact position of the hands often varies somewhat with different workmen. A good practice adopted by many is to keep the forefinger of the left hand below the rest to clasp it and the tool together. Others use the left hand palm downwards on the tool instead of the reverse way as illustrated. In all cases the right hand grasps the end of the tool handle as shown.

Rest.—Turning tools cannot be used without a support or rest for them to bear on, for the downward pressure on the cutting edge is much more than could be resisted by the hands alone. The work, of course, revolves towards the operator, and the support should be as near the cutting edge as possible. If far back there is more leverage for the hands to resist, and varying thicknesses of shaving and varying stress make this dangerous. Therefore the rest must be kept as close to the surface of the work as convenient. The wood-turner's rest is quite different from that of the metal-turner. The usual design is shown in Fig. 10. It consists of two main parts—the rest itself and its base, which is clamped to the lathe bed. The rest itself, shown in the upper part of the figure, has a rounded top edge for the tool to rest on, and from there its surface

Fig. 7.—Method of Using Chisel for Cutting Ends and Divisions

slopes downwards away from the work. It is provided with a post which fits into a socket in the base, and when adjusted for height and for horizontal angle it is clamped by a set-screw. The base also can be adjusted to any angle on the lathe bed, and moved in or out to suit the diameter of the work. It has a slot, as shown, which receives a suitable bolt for clamping. Adjustments for height do not

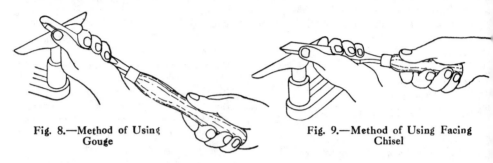

Fig. 8.—Method of Using Gouge

Fig. 9.—Method of Using Facing Chisel

vary much, but some amount of adjustment is necessary. On face-plate work. that is, flat disc-shaped articles, the top of the rest must usually coincide with, or be very slightly below, the lathe centre height, when the face of the work is being operated on. In turning the edges of such work, and in cylindrical articles between centres, the turner adjusts to any height he finds convenient, his own height in relation to the lathe having something to do with it. Usually the top of the rest is kept a little above the lathe centre height.

Fork Centre.—Another feature peculiar to the wood-turner's lathe is the fork centre (Fig. 11), which is screwed into the mandrel nose for turning articles between centres. Its forked end is forced into the

average work the fork is sufficient and it is quickly adjusted and quite reliable.

Centring Work for Turning.—In preparing a piece of hard wood for turning, it is necessary to make a saw-cut to receive the fork centre, as in Fig. 12, or cut a recess with a chisel; but in softwood this is not necessary. The piece of wood prepared for turning is, of course, sawn square in the first place and then its corners are generally removed, as shown in Figs. 12 and 13, sometimes by sawing, sometimes with a hatchet or pared off with a chisel. This saves the gouge some work in roughing down to diameter. A piece secured between centres in the lathe is shown in Fig. 13. It is driven by the fork centre at the left-hand end, and is supported at the other end by the fixed dead centre in the poppet. The point of this centre is forced into the end sufficiently to keep the wood securely between the centres. A little oil is necessary at the dead centre before the

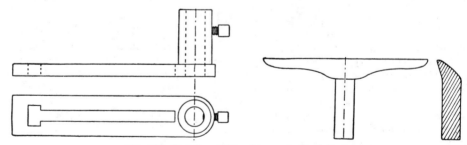

Fig. 10.—Details of Wood-turner's Tool Rest

end grain of the work and revolves the latter with the mandrel. For very heavy and large work something more secure is often necessary; but for small and

lathe is started. A small hole with a bradawl is often bored as a guide for the dead centre to enter, otherwise it may shift considerably to one side in screwing up. Sometimes a centre punch is used instead of a bradawl. The fork centre end of the wood is treated similarly when no saw-cut is made. It has the advantage of indicating the exact centre as well as providing a guide for the points. To size, and mark the exact centres on its ends. A simple way to do this without measurement is to rule pencil lines diagonally from corner to corner on the ends, so that their point of crossing gives the centre. This is done while

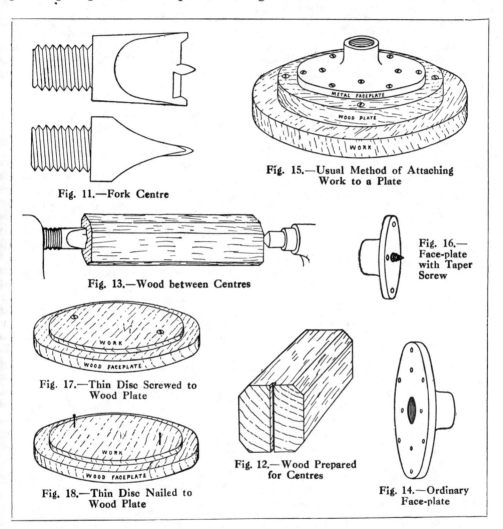

Fig. 11.—Fork Centre

Fig. 15.—Usual Method of Attaching Work to a Plate

Fig. 13.—Wood between Centres

Fig. 16.—Face-plate with Taper Screw

Fig. 17.—Thin Disc Screwed to Wood Plate

Fig. 18.—Thin Disc Nailed to Wood Plate

Fig. 12.—Wood Prepared for Centres

Fig. 14.—Ordinary Face-plate

guess the centre when putting the wood in the lathe may involve waste in turning, or may result in failure of the piece to hold up to diameter, a flat being left on one side after the piece is reduced to size. It is economical, therefore, to saw the wood just large enough to turn to the required the wood is square before its angles are removed.

Work between centres almost invariably has its grain running as shown in Fig. 13. All the simplest work in turning is done in this way, and the beginner should start with small work between centres. The fact that the length of the piece is much greater than its diameter does not necessarily mean that the finished article is similarly proportioned. In many cases a number of articles all alike are wanted which can be turned most expeditiously together in a stick and cut off in a number of comparatively short lengths. Such lengths, however, are usually greater than their diameter. If the diameter is greater than the length, it would as a rule be best to turn them with the grain running the other way. In such a case they would not be made between centres.

Face-plates.—When articles of a thin disc-like character have to be turned, the use of the sliding poppet with its dead centre is dispensed with. The work then is screwed, or otherwise secured, to a face-plate, which screws on to the mandrel nose, the fork centre also being dispensed with. The face-plate and work revolve with the mandrel, and as the overhang or extension outwards from the mandrel end is slight, no support in place of the dead centre is necessary. Moreover, the attachment of the work to the plate holds it in quite a different way from the between centre method shown in Fig. 13. In the latter, the fork centre has no hold at all independently of the pressure of the dead centre at the other end of the work. But a piece of wood screwed to a face-plate is secure without such pressure, and the absence of the dead centre support allows unobstructed turning of the flat front face as well as the edge or diameter of the work. Fig. 14 shows an ordinary face-plate, which is usually of cast-iron, though small ones are often of brass. It screws on in the mandrel nose up to the shoulder, and the direction in which the mandrel revolves tends to tighten it, so that there is no risk of it running off. It is provided with a number of screw holes, and the screws, which are put through from the back, must, of course, be short enough not to come through to the front face of the wood. The work may be screwed directly to the metal plate, but much more frequently a disc of wood, larger in diameter than the metal, is interposed, as in Fig. 15. This wood plate usually remains more or less permanently on the metal face, being changed only when worn out or of unsuitable diameter for the work in hand. Its advantages are that it can be refaced when out of truth, diameters can be marked on it, or recesses cut for chucking the work, and screws or nails can be put through the work into it if screwing from the back is undesirable. Moreover, a large diameter for the attachment of large work can be obtained in this way with less weight than a metal plate of similar diameter.

In Fig. 15 screws are shown put into the work outside the diameter of the metal plate. This is the usual way when a wood plate is used. In some cases the screws must be within the radius of the metal, but this does not involve removal of the wood plate. The metal plate is always provided with plenty of holes, and these need not all be used for the attachment of a wood plate. Pieces of work of small and moderate size do not need more than two screws to hold them to the plate, and in many cases a single screw in the centre is sufficient. Fig. 16 shows a plate provided with a central taper screw for small work, the screw being a part of the plate itself. This is sufficient to hold a block of wood of moderate size, and is quicker than putting an ordinary screw in with a screwdriver. It will be seen that the plate is provided with screw holes as well, which can be used if necessary. Plates of this kind sometimes have thin wood faces put on, though it is more usual to attach the work directly to the metal face. The thickness of the work must always be more than the length of the taper screw, and a considerable body of wood around is necessary to prevent splitting. Risk of the latter is minimised by boring a hole of suitable size before screwing the work on the plate. Very small and thin work cannot be put on the taper screw of a plate of the kind shown in Fig. 16, and neither can they be attached by screws put through from the back of the plate, because they could only penetrate for so short a distance that they would not hold the work securely enough. They must be put through from the front, as in Figs. 17 and 18, and their points must not penetrate far enough to reach the metal. When the methods of attachment shown in Figs. 17 and 18 are adopted, it is evident that little or nothing can be

Fig. 19.—Wood in Cup Chuck

removed from the front face by turning, the work being usually planed to thickness before it is put on the plate. This, indeed, is often the quickest way, the face being merely glasspapered in the lathe and tools used only for turning to diameter.

In some cases the face is not a plain one, but may be recessed or dished or turned to any required contour across the face be-

the back face of the work with the tool. If the work is screwed direct to a metal plate, then it is always desirable to have the plate smaller in diameter, so that in turning the edges there shall be no risk of damage to the cutting tool through contact with the metal.

Cup Chucks.—The cup chuck, or bell chuck, is another variety, not so much used as the fork centre or face-plate, but often required for some kinds of work. It screws over the mandrel nose in the same way as the face-plate, but is shaped so that the end of a piece of wood can be driven a tight fit into it (*see* Fig. 19). The inside diameter of the chuck is usually about 2 in., and the wood to be turned must fit this whether the finished diameter beyond the chuck is smaller or larger. The cup chuck can be used in conjunction with the dead centre of the poppet, in which case it

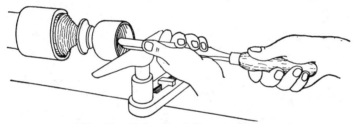

Fig. 20.—Example of Cup-chuck Work

sides having the edge turned. The screws then must be arranged to come in a zone where little or no material has to be faced off. The nails in Fig. 16 are shown only partly driven in. The turning can frequently be done with their heads standing out as shown, and it makes it easier to remove the work from the plate. They can be pulled out with pincers. If driven completely in, the work must be prised off. When a wood face-plate is used, it is usually of larger diameter than the work. In some cases it is convenient to have the plate smaller than the work, as when the edge of the latter is rounded or turned to a contour which would be difficult or impossible with a plate extending beyond the diameter of the work. Or sometimes, to avoid the trouble of re-chucking, it is an advantage to be able to get right round to

is merely a substitute for the fork centre; but usually the work is allowed to run without this support, for the advantage of the cup chuck is that the end of the work can

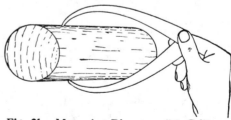

Fig. 21.—Measuring Diameter with Callipers

be got at, as in Fig. 20, which would not be possible if the poppet was used. As the wood is supported only at the end where the chuck is, its length must be limited, otherwise the outer end would not run truly under the pressure of the turning tool. The length permissible, however, is ample for the majority of small articles, and in many cases a number can be turned and cut off one at a time from a single piece of wood. The end of the wood is driven into the chuck with a hammer, and after the work is finished and cut off, the

work in the lathe has to be turned to definite sizes, and measurement is necessary at frequent intervals during its reduction. In work between centres all diameters have to be calipered. The callipers may be set to the size required, and the work reduced until the callipers will just pass over it with light pressure, as

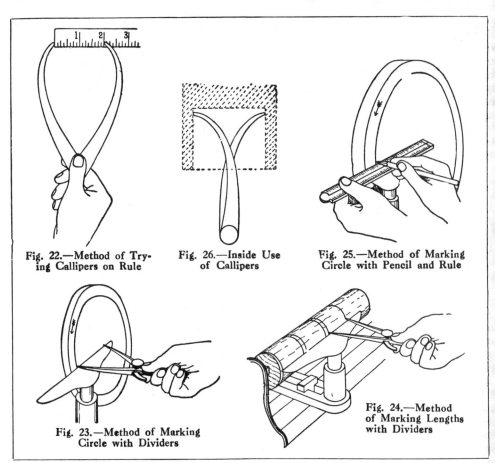

Fig. 22.—Method of Trying Callipers on Rule

Fig. 26.—Inside Use of Callipers

Fig. 25.—Method of Marking Circle with Pencil and Rule

Fig. 23.—Method of Marking Circle with Dividers

Fig. 24.—Method of Marking Lengths with Dividers

stump is forced out of the chuck by inserting the end of a suitable rod of iron behind it, through the screwed end of the chuck, and hammering it so that the wood is punched out. Before driving the wood in, it is pared roughly circular with a chisel to suit the chuck, or sometimes it is put between centres and turned.

Measurement and Testing.—Most

in Fig. 21, or the callipers may be adjusted to the work and its size found by trying them on the rule, as in Fig. 22. The first method, of course, is the proper one to adopt when reduction must be made to an exact size. The callipers are set to that size on the rule, and the work is alternately reduced and tested until it is right. On small diameters tests can be made while the lathe is running, but as a rule it is best to stop the lathe for calliper-ing the work. On the face-plate diameters can be measured direct with the rule across the front face, and if there is much thickness a small try-square can be used to see that the edge is at right angles with the face. But frequently the edge is not a simple one at right angles. It may have various diameters which must be tested, so that the callipers are sometimes neces-sary in measuring face-plate work. Next to the rule, therefore, callipers are the most important measuring instrument used in wood turning. As diameters vary greatly, more than one size of callipers is necessary, unless the lathe-centre height is so small that nothing above a very limited diameter can be turned in it. A pair of callipers of that capacity may then suffice for everything.

Lengths between centres or thicknesses on the face-plate can be measured direct with the rule, or where a number of similar measurements have to be made, it is sometimes preferable to set a pair of dividers to the size. Thus diameters on the face-plate may be struck with them, as in Fig. 23, or lengths between centres marked as in Fig. 24.

For large diameters on the face-plate, trammels are sometimes used. But rule and pencil, as in Fig. 25, are suitable for most of this work. A pencil circle can be put on and its full diameter measured, and then if it is slightly over or under size, an incised circle can be made correctly with the point of the side chisel. In any case, if the measurement is important, a rule is used across the full diameter before the work is finally passed. Its end is kept flush on one side with the forefinger of the left hand, and its further extremity is moved in a slight arc, so that it passes to and fro over the centre of the circle, and the full diameter can be noted. If measurement was made without this pre-caution, the rule might not be exactly across the centre, and the diameter would appear slightly less than it actually was.

A straightedge, or the edge of a steel-bladed square, is used a great deal in testing for straightness, both between centres and on the face-plate. Without this test a flat surface on the face-plate might be slightly concave, or convex, or variable. The same defects might not be possible lengthwise in a cylindrical article between centres, because calliper tests would show variations in diameter ; but it is much quicker to use callipers only at places some distance apart, and test for straightness between. A tapering article must necessarily be done in this way, the large and small diameters being turned at the ends and the work tested for straight-ness between those points, for calliper tests along a tapering body are out of the question. Instead of making repeated straightedge tests on large work between centres, a good method is to reduce to diameter at the ends, and at one or two intermediate points, if the length is very great, and then plane a flat along the whole length down to the level of the finished diameter. This flat can be seen while the work is revolving, and the turner has thus a guide to tell him when he has reduced to diameter at all parts of the length.

A great proportion of turned work, how-ever, is not of the plain character that makes these methods possible. In most cases a number of different diameters have to be callipered, and measurements from one point to another lengthwise are necessary. The latter may be made direct with a rule ; but if a number of similar articles have to be turned, it is more con-venient to mark the distances on a strip of wood, and transfer from this to the work. In some cases the first article turned can be used as a pattern for the others, being held close to the revolving wood, and pencil lines run round the latter at the important points. Curves and mouldings may be turned to the eye, or templates may be made for testing. A template may be of thin wood or cardboard or thick paper. The required contour is marked on it and cut so that the template can be tried against the work, and the latter turned until it fits. Calliper tests or other means of measurement are usually necessary in conjunction with the template, otherwise the latter would not give correct results.

A template does not necessarily represent the entire contour of a piece of work. It is often more convenient to make templates for small portions only perhaps two

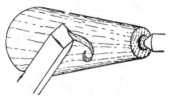

Fig. 27.—Method of Turning in Direction to Avoid Tearing Grain

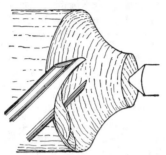

Fig. 28.—Method of Reducing Large to Small Diameter

or three separate ones for a contour which is continuous but has portions which do not require fitting to a template, and which would make the fitting slower and more tedious if they were included in the template. Templates are necessary for curves where the eye cannot be trusted, or where mechanical accuracy is demanded, as when the curve must be of definite radius.

Callipers have sometimes to be used for inside measurements as in Fig. 26. Ordinary callipers are reversed, being closed and the arms slid past each other, as shown, so that the points can enter a cavity and measure its interior diameter. The diameter at the entrance can be measured with a rule, but it may be necessary to ascertain the size at some distance farther in, and for this purpose inside callipers are required. The ordinary callipers, shown in Figs. 22 and 26, which are intended primarily for outside measurements, are not suitable for measuring small

inside diameters unless in rather shallow recesses. This is because the curvature of their arms prevents them from penetrating when the points are set to only a short distance apart. In such cases, callipers intended specially for inside measurements are the only kind that can be used. These have straight arms with slightly hooked points. This makes them useless for ordinary outside measurements, because the inner edges of the arms come in contact with the work before the points have advanced far enough to reach to the full diameter. Another kind of calliper is made for both purposes. They are double in character, the pivot being midway instead of at the extremity. The arms in one direction are straight, and those on the other side of the pivot are curved, and they are constructed so that the inside and outside points are always identical in extension, which is useful when work is being done where inside and outside parts have to fit each other and must be alike in diameter. It is comparatively seldom, however, that inside callipering in wood turning is necessary.

General Work.—In turning, as in bench work, cutting against the grain must be avoided. Thus in the case of a tapering article, as in Fig. 27, the side chisel must move from the large towards the small end, and not in the reverse way. Similarly, in turning down from a large to a small diameter, as in Fig. 28, the gouge

Fig. 29.—Method of Boring with Narrow Chisel

Fig. 30.—Handle between Centres

would cut best if held on its side as shown, the cut beginning at the large part and proceeding to the small diameter. This gives better results than holding the gouge on its back at right angles to the surface being cut, the reason being that the cutting edge. as illustrated, makes a clean slicing cut, the material moving past

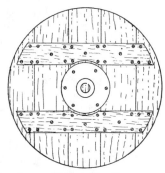

Fig. 31.—Large Plate with Cleats across Back

it diagonally and with the grain sloping in a direction which makes it impossible for it to tear up. In face-plate and in cup-chuck work central apertures of small diameter cannot be roughed out with a gouge, as the latter could not be held in a position to avoid risk of catching and severely jolting the work. Such apertures, therefore, must be sunk entirely by means of scraping tools, either a chisel of suitable width, or a round-nose if the recess is concave at the base. An instance of the latter has been already illustrated in Fig. 20. A tool handle turned in the cup chuck would be bored with a narrow chisel, as in Fig. 29, perhaps $\frac{1}{8}$ in. wide, and it would not be allowed to penetrate to the full depth required for the point of the tool tang to reach, but only as far as the diameter of the hole made by the chisel suited the tang. The remainder would be bored with a brace and small bit.

An alternative method of turning a tool handle is shown by Fig. 30, and this is the best way if the handle is a long one. It is turned between centres, and the hole bored with a brace and bit afterwards. Considerable skill is necessary then to bore the hole exactly parallel with the handle. If it slopes to either side, the tool and handle will not be in a line, which looks bad. The ferrule must be at the dead-centre end, as shown in Fig. 30, otherwise it could not be put on until after

the handle was removed from the lathe and cut off. It is fitted by calliper measurement to drive on tight, and the handle is generally replaced in the lathe for finishing after the ferrule is on. Only a very slight amount, or nothing at all, is cut off the end beyond the ferrule, as it is usually not necessary, and the impression left by the dead centre is a guide for starting the boring.

Face-plate Work.—Work attached to the face-plate must generally be screwed, and screw holes in it are unavoidable. As the screws usually enter at the back of the work and do not go right through it, the holes made are seldom objectionable. If desired, they may be plugged after the work is finished. In some circumstances glue is used as a means of attaching work to the plate. It is not done by gluing direct, but by gluing paper to the plate, and then gluing the work on the paper. A very secure hold is obtained in this way, and a clean, easy removal of the finished work from the plate. The only objection is the interval of an hour or two for the glue to dry before the turning can begin. The method is suitable not only for small, light articles, but even for moderately large and heavy ones. One advantage of the absence of

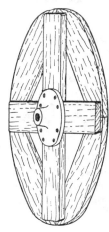

Fig. 32.—Skeleton-type Plate for Very Large Diameters

screws is that the risk of turning down on a screw and spoiling the edge of the tool is avoided. A piece of paper as large in area as the back of the work is used only when comparatively small blocks of wood are attached to the plate. For larger work the paper and glue are used only in places some distance apart.

Rings built up in segments are often attached by gluing, and in these it is sufficient to use a piece of paper under each end joint of the first layer. A ring built in six segments, for instance, would require six patches of paper glued to the plate in positions corresponding with the joints of the first layer of segments. Each piece of paper might be from 2 in. to 4 in. square, depending on the size of the work. The pieces would not be less in width than the segments, and would extend about an equal distance along them, the joint being midway on the paper. To obtain a close joint in gluing the paper to the plate, superfluous glue is squeezed out by pressing the edge of a steel square, or other suitable article, on the paper and drawing or pushing it from the centre out to the edges. The paper then is in close contact with the wood, and the gluing on of the work can proceed immediately after. When the turning is finished the work is prised off with a chisel. It is slightly lifted in this way all round before being finally forced completely off. The paper causes separation without splinters of wood from either the work or the plate adhering to the other, as would be the case if wood was glued directly to wood.

A simple disc of wood on a metal face-plate to facilitate attachment of work is only suitable for comparatively small diameters. If more than 10 in. or 12 in. in diameter, cleats would have to be screwed to the back to stiffen and keep it from warping. Plates much above that diameter, of course, are too large to be cut from a single piece of board. They must be made up of two or three pieces edge to edge to give the required width, as in Fig. 31, and cleats then may be the chief or only means of holding them together. But pieces edge to edge with cleats across the back are in the largest plates often superseded by the method shown in Fig. 32. This, it will be seen, does not give a continuous surface across the entire plate, but only a ring of variable width from the

circumference inwards, and perhaps a small portion at the centre, the latter being usually necessary in order to have a centre from which to strike circles. This skeleton type of plate is sufficient for work of large diameter, for, apart from the fact that such work often consists of rings without central parts, it is not necessary for a solid piece of work of large diameter to fit against a plate over its entire area.

A plate with an outer ring of surface only is sufficient both for attachment and for providing a bearing surface for the work. Therefore very large plates are seldom made with surfaces continuous from centre to periphery. Work not large enough to be put on such a plate is better in any case on a smaller one. Sometimes large work requires a plate fully up to its own diameter, and sometimes a plate much smaller will do, or may even be desirable to permit of getting at the back of the work and so avoiding re-chucking. A plate made as in Fig. 32 is usually of the largest diameter that the lathe will take, but in some cases there may be other similarly built of smaller diameter.

In preparing pieces of wood for turning suitable allowances in size must be made. They must be sufficient but not excessive. Discs of wood to go on the face-plate are generally sawn circular to a slightly larger diameter than the finished one. If a band-saw is not available they may be cut with a keyhole-saw or a bow-saw. Occasionally in small diameters with no band-saw the corners are cut off with a tenon-saw, and the roughly octagonal piece made circular by the turning ; but this is rougher work for the gouge than turning a similarly octagonal piece between centres. One reason is that the diameter, and consequently the flats, are often greater, and another is that some of the angles present almost end grain to the tool, and this is harder to cut than grain running the other way. If a number of discs of small diameter are wanted, a piece of wood long enough from which to cut a number may be planed, and circles marked on it for sawing.

In work between centres and in cup chuck work, the wood put in the lathe must be longer than the finished article. There are instances where pieces between centres can be cut to finished length before turning; but as a rule it is necessary to allow for cutting off at both ends. At the fork-centre end especially, an inch or two must nearly always be wasted, because the mark of the centre in the end is not wanted, and the turning tools cannot be allowed to go too near in cutting down the end of the work. At the dead-centre end the side chisel or other tools can go quite close to the stationary centre with no risk at all, and very little need be cut off at that end. In finishing the turned article it is usual to cut down to a very small

fresh grain, which loses some of its moisture and shrinks. This, of course, occurs transversely to the fibres, shrinkage in length being negligible. Thus a large disc on the face-plate will become elliptical through shrinkage. In large work where dimensions are important, shrinkage must be guarded against, and warping also. More or less elaborate building up is necessary in such cases.

Shrinkage and warping are minimised by using well-seasoned wood, and by allowing intervals of time where possible between preparation for the lathe and final reduction to size. As soon as the turning is finished, the article should be

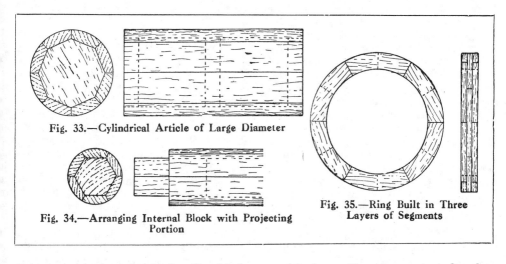

Fig. 33.—Cylindrical Article of Large Diameter

Fig. 34.—Arranging Internal Block with Projecting Portion

Fig. 35.—Ring Built in Three Layers of Segments

diameter with the point of the side chisel and the wood is then taken out of the lathe and the waste ends sawn off. When a number of small articles are turned on one length of wood between centres, the same method is adopted of cutting down between each to as small a diameter as possible without risk of breakage, and finishing with a saw after it is taken out of the lathe. In cup-chuck work the finished article can be cut completely off with the side chisel while the lathe is running, the article removed being enclosed in the left hand at the last moment.

Built-up Work.—Shrinkage of wood to be turned has to be considered, the same as in bench work. Turning exposes

varnished or otherwise protected unless the work is of a rough class, in which no ultimate finish of this sort is intended. The character of the turned article also is a factor which may decide its treatment. Very small articles cannot shrink appreciably unless extreme accuracy in size is important. In most work between centres shrinkage need not be considered. Large diameters between centres are built up as much to reduce weight and material as to avoid shrinkage, warping, or splitting. The method of building up is shown in Fig. 33.

There is, of course, the alternative of solid building, often done because the diameter required is greater than the thickness of wood available. An advantage in the latter kind of building up is that the pieces are better seasoned throughout their thickness, and consequently cracks are not liable to occur on the exterior, as is the case with a very thick section of unbuilt-up wood. But for very large diameters a hollow interior, as in Fig. 33, is preferable to solid wood. Interior blocks are prepared, the number depending on the length of the article, and round these, staves or lags are nailed or screwed. The greater the diameter the greater should be the number of staves, and consequently of flats, on the blocks. Octagon blocks are shown in Fig. 33, but often more flats than this are desirable. The number is decided by marking out an end view on a board, and settling what thickness of wood to use for the staves and how thin they may be reduced at their edges. Fig. 34 shows a hexagon block with grain running the same way as that of the staves. This is suitable for a smaller diameter than that of Fig. 33. Fig. 34 shows the hexagon block projecting some way beyond the ends of the staves. This is often done when the article has to be turned to a smaller diameter there, and to reduce the staves sufficiently would necessitate making them extremely thick in other parts. The projecting block, therefore, is turned to the diameter. Work of this sort often occurs in making patterns for columns, cylinders, and large pipes. Flanges or mouldings of larger diameter than the main body are generally made as rings to fit over the latter, shallow grooves being turned to receive them. The rings may have to be fitted in halves, or sometimes they can slip over an end and bear against a shoulder on the body. In pattern-making the entire article is usually in halves for convenience of moulding. Cylindrical articles built in the way illustrated are not necessarily parallel. Taper can be provided for by cutting the blocks to suit.

In face-plate work segmental building up is common. A ring built of segments is shown in Fig. 35. Here also the number of segments to the circle varies according to diameter, six being generally

the minimum, but six is exceeded only in very large diameters. Too few to the circle means short grain at their ends. Six is suitable for most work, and is very convenient for marking out, as dividers or trammels set to a radius are at the same time precisely a sixth of the circle. Segmental building up depends for its strength on layers with overlapping joints. The first layer with its six end joints must have these joints covered and held together, and the construction stiffened by bringing the end joints of the next layer midway between those of the first. In Fig. 35 three layers are shown. This is stronger than two only; but a much greater number than this is sometimes needed to build up to the depth of ring required. If the ring is attached to a solid plate, the latter, of course, holds the first layer, and in some cases where the depth is very shallow a single layer may make up the thickness required, though in good work more than one layer would be used. In an independent ring, as in Fig. 35, two layers are the minimum. Rings built in this way cannot become elliptical by shrinkage, and are as strong in one direction as in another, as the grain almost follows the circle. Only the principle of building up is shown in Fig. 35. A sectional view has to be marked out full-size first of all, and then the number of layers and widths and radii of the segments can be obtained. They are usually glued together, nails being sometimes used as well; but nails must not be in places where there is any risk of turning down on them.

Re-chucking. — Re-chucking means the removal and replacement of a piece of work on the face-plate, in order to turn some part which cannot be got at with the work in its original position. Thus if opposite faces of a disc have to be operated on, the disc must be reversed on the plate after the first face is finished. It might be supposed that this would be necessary in nearly all work, but as a matter of fact the majority of articles can be turned without re-chucking. In metal turning re-chucking is very common, and is simpler than in wood turning. It is simpler because the metal-turner uses a variety of adjustable chucks which grip the work, and it is an easy matter to bore a central aperture, or turn an outer

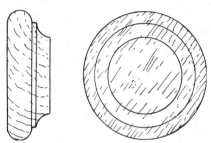

Fig. 36.—Example in which Back can be Turned without Re-chucking

diameter, and use this as a means of reversing the work centrally on the plate. In wood turning the work is not held by a concentric grip, but almost always by screws. The jaws of a metal chuck would generally be in the way and the risk to the cutting tools would be considerable. Moreover, a grip tight enough to hold the work securely would generally leave its marks on the surface gripped, and this would be objectionable. Therefore the work must be rescrewed to the plate when reversed.

As it is nearly always highly important that the re-chucked work should run true with the portion already turned, it would not do simply to set it to a circle on a plain plate and screw it there. It would inevitably get more or less out of centre during the screwing, and although with a great deal of care it could be readjusted until true, it would be a tedious and unsatisfactory method. Therefore the surface of the plate must be recessed to receive the work and keep it central while the screws are inserted ; and this is also some guarantee that it cannot be accidentally forced out of centre during turning, as might happen if it depended on screws only to keep it in correct position. Most articles turned on the face-plate simply have to be flat on the back, and no turning need be done there, the surface being planed true before screwing to the plate.

There are cases also where the back face

need only be turned near the edge, an example of which is shown in Fig. 36, where the edge is rounded. In such cases re-chucking is generally avoided by using a face-plate of smaller diameter than the work, so that the edge of the latter stands out sufficiently for the tool to be used right round to the back as far as necessary. A rounded edge, as in Fig. 36, and all convex surfaces are finished by scraping with a chisel, the chisel being swung round to follow the curve.

Concave surfaces can be finished only with a round-nose. As it is desirable to make wood face-plates last as long as possible, they are never recessed deeper than can be avoided, and the larger the plate the stronger is the objection to turning a recess in it. When a plate has been recessed for re-chucking a piece of work, it generally has to be levelled down to the base of the recess before it can be used for other work, and this repeated a few times soon makes it so thin that it has to be discarded. Very large plates, therefore, are scarcely ever recessed, but work is chucked on them by putting on instead of reducing. The portion put on usually consists of blocks at intervals in a circle of the required diameter, perhaps three, four or six of them. They are screwed or nailed on and turned, just as a recess would be turned, the intervals between the blocks not making much difference, except that the tool must be approached carefully and held steady. Either the inner or outer diameter of a ring of blocks may be turned,

Fig. 38.—Method of Centring Work by a Stud Fitting in Recess on Plate

Fig. 37.—Blocks Put on Large Plate to Serve Same Purpose as Recess

according to whether they fit inside or outside the work. An example is shown in Fig. 37.

In some work re-chucking can be done by means of a small central hole, either in the work or the plate, and a corresponding stud to fit it on the other. In such a case, if the projecting stud was required on the face-plate, the latter would never be turned down to leave a stud standing out. The stud would be a nailed-on piece. On the other hand, a small hole, say, 1 in. or a little more in diameter, in the centre of the plate would not be so objectionable as a recess of large diameter. For a small hole would not interfere with the attachment of other work, all of which would be large enough to cover the hole and bear on the surface around. A disadvantage of the hole would be that the centre from which to strike circles would be lost, and the hole would have to be plugged in order to get a new centre. Central holes and studs of small diameter would be the best method of chucking work on the face-plate, except for the one objection that for large work they are not accurate enough. Where accurate chucking is important, it is best to fit the work to the plate at as large a diameter as possible, and the larger and heavier the work the more essential this becomes.

The stud of small diameter is very common in pattern-making. Large numbers of bosses, as in Fig. 38, are required, and these are almost always provided with studs for correct centring on the pattern. As the boss and stud must be concentric, the boss is chucked by its stud on the face-plate, as shown. Sometimes the block of wood for the boss is put on the plate and turned to provide the stud on the solid wood, and then re-chucked to turn the front of the boss ; but a more expeditious way is to nail the stud on the block and attach to the plate without any need for actual re-chucking.

Glasspapering and Finishing.—Work is glasspapered in the lathe while revolving, but to avoid a scratched surface, the glasspaper should be constantly moved from side to side rather than held stationary. Glasspaper is used on flat rubbers the same as for bench work, when the shape of the work permits. For flat faces on the face-plate, the glasspaper would be wrapped on a flat rubber, and also for straight cylindrical surfaces between centres. Convex and concave outlines are generally done without a rubber. It might be supposed that varnishing and polishing could be done advantageously with the work revolving, but this is not the case. Small articles can be polished best while revolving, but large surfaces cannot, and the application of varnish with a brush, except on very small work, always has to be done with the lathe stopped. The reason is that a lathe, no matter how slowly it is running, brings fresh surface under the brush too rapidly for the varnish to be taken up by the wood, and the varnish in the brush is exhausted immediately. The result is a wet patch where contact begins, and a mere trace of varnish or none at all beyond that.

Turned work is comparatively free from tool marks, and very little glasspapering is necessary before varnishing. In rubbing down successive coats, the glasspapering should be very light. It is done with the lathe running, and is simpler and quicker, especially when the contour of the work is intricate, than glasspapering stationary work.

Tool Sharpening.—The sharpening of tools is dealt with specially in an earlier section, but a few notes dealing particularly with turners' tools may now be given. The wood-turner usually keeps an oilstone specially for sharpening the turning gouges. A stone used for the gouge as well as for other tools would soon get worn so concave by the gouge that it would not be suitable for chisels and other flat tools. The gouge soon wears a deep groove, and this is an advantage, because it can then be sharpened more quickly than on a flat surface, and the groove acts also as a guide, so that less attention is required to keep the gouge from moving too much to one side and slipping off the stone. In a stone of ordinary width, say, $1\frac{3}{4}$ in., there is room for at least two grooves side by side, and often three are formed, the first and largest in the middle and a smaller one on each side. It does not take long to start a groove if the gouge is kept constantly on the same line, and once very slightly started the gouge follows it easily afterwards. The groove, of course, begins and ends slightly short of full length of the stone, starting from the surface near the ends and going down to its full depth along the middle portion of its length, where the pressure is greatest. But no matter how deep the groove becomes, it is always necessary to give a rolling motion to the gouge as it travels backwards and forwards along the stone. It is necessary that the edge should be sharpened not only at the point, but equally all round its curve.

An oil-stone slip is used to remove burr from the inside, and, of course, must never be tilted, but lie flat in the channel and move parallel with it. This is analogous to the turning over of an ordinary chisel on the stone and rubbing the burr off. In both cases this operation, though it should be frequently repeated, requires only a few light strokes compared with the rubbing down on the other side where the grinding angle is. For rough turning some turners think the use of a slip unnecessary, and do not use it, holding that the burr becomes removed almost immediately by the turnings after the cut is begun.

The side chisel is ground and sharpened equally on both sides. The round-nose requires a rolling motion like the gouge, and is sharpened on the same stone as the gouge. Being flat it does not require the use of a slip, but is laid on a flat stone, the same as an ordinary chisel, for rubbing the face. In grinding, also, the gouge and round-nose must be given a constant rolling motion to grind uniformly and neatly to their curves. As grinding is not so often necessary as sharpening, the grindstone or emery-wheel is not usually allowed to become grooved. This can be prevented by moving the gouge constantly across the face of the grindstone from one side to another, so that it has no chance to wear a groove. This is not so easily done on an oilstone where the hands are employed in moving the tool backwards and forwards, and too close an approach to one side or one end results in its slipping off the stone.

Removal of Chucks, etc. — Face-plates, cup chucks, and fork centres screw on to the mandrel nose in the opposite direction to that in which the lathe runs, so that

the tendency is for them to tighten rather than come off when the lathe is running. The way to remove a face-plate is to grasp the belt cone or the belt of the lathe with the left hand and unscrew the plate with the right hand, the latter being generally pulled by its upper edge and a pushing action exerted on the former, so that they are forced in opposite directions. As soon as the plate is loose enough to unscrew freely, it is supported beneath by the right hand, and the farther side of the belt is pulled downwards to revolve the mandrel in the reverse direction to its ordinary running. The plate then comes off in the right hand. A very heavy plate may have to be supported with both hands, while another person turns the lathe in its reverse direction.

In putting a plate on it should not be run up to the shoulder so that it stops with a jerk, or there may be trouble in getting it off again. Even without this a plate sometimes becomes jammed so tight on the mandrel that the hands cannot unscrew it. In such a case the usual method is to start it with a hammer, but this jars the lathe and should be avoided if possible. A short stout piece of rod to serve as a punch is used in conjunction with the hammer. In order to use it on the plate, there is generally a suitable hole drilled in the exterior of the boss of the plate, or a notch is cut in the edge of the plate. The end of the punch is inserted there at a suitable tangent to jar the plate in the direction of unscrewing. Occasionally, and especially in large lathes, a lever is inserted between the under edge of the belt pulley and the base of the headstock, and its projecting end pressed downwards to prevent the pulley and mandrel from turning while the plate is being loosened. But if the plate is very tight this is scarcely any more effective than holding the pulley with the left hand. The same lever is sometimes used in large lathes as a brake for stopping quickly. In small lathes the left hand is generally pressed on the belt cone to stop the lathe after the driving power has ceased.

Repetition Work. — In commercial work where very large numbers of similar articles are constantly required, both the lathes and the methods become modified. Knives of various shapes are attached to carriages, and take the place of the ordinary turning tools and the ordinary tool-rest. They automatically turn to diameters and lengths. Plain round rods are not turned in lathes at all, but are rounded to the required diameter by being pushed or drawn through special machines. Lathes are made intended only for face-plate work, the ordinary bed and sliding poppet being absent. On the other hand, two lathes may be fitted on a single long bed, the headstock and poppet of the smaller one being removable if the full length of the bed is wanted for the large one. The headstock of a lathe may have a screwed nose at each end of the mandrel so that a face-plate can be put on either end, the one at the back being intended for large plates and work. At the front the swing is limited to the height of the centre above the lathe bed. At the back the plate projects beyond the end of the lathe bed, and a radius from the centre down to the floor is available. The tool-rest, then, is on a stand separate from the bed.

In some ordinary lathes the headstock can be reversed if necessary, or turned at right angles for face-plate work too large to clear the bed.

Copying lathes are a highly specialised variety. They are used for turning irregular shapes, generally ovals which are not uniform in the longitudinal direction. The tool advances and retires automatically, its carriage being oscillated by a revolving metal pattern of the article to be produced. Articles of very irregular contours can thus be produced automatically in large numbers all alike, such as gunstocks, boot trees, wheel spokes, adze and hammer handles. Some of these machines are made to turn out two articles simultaneously from one pattern.

Spiral Turning.—Most cheap reproductions of antique spiral turned work are the product of automatic or semi-automatic lathes, but all the original specimens, and also the really high grade copies, are a combination of lathe work and carving.

An example of this is shown by the table leg (Fig. 39). Fig. 40 shows the leg turned preparatory to having the spiral formed on it. It will be observed that the necks are sunk to the same depth as it is intended to cut the twist, say, 1 in. Referring to Fig. 39, it will be seen that the twist begins and finishes on opposite sides of the cylinder. This is the usual practice, and in calculating the size and the number of the twists required to obtain this effect and to fill a given space, the workman does not reckon for so many complete twists, but so many twists and a half. Between A and B (Fig. 39) the neck of the twist is $\frac{3}{4}$ in. wide, and circumscribes the cylinder four and a half times.

To set out the spiral, divide the circumference of the cylinder by four equidistant longitudinal lines. Multiply the number of twists desired (four and a half) by four, and divide the length of the cylinder by the product (eighteen). Spin pencil lines round the cylinder at the points thus obtained (*see* the enlarged view of the cylinder, Fig. 41). A flexible straightedge is made by folding a piece of stout paper so as to obtain a firm edge to rule by, and by beginning at A (Fig. 41) and ruling a continuous line diagonally across the divisions until B is reached, a left-handed spiral may be developed. Now, if two lines are laid down parallel with this and $\frac{3}{8}$ in. on each side of it, the setting out will be complete. In the event of the job having no squares, it will not matter at what point the spiral begins, and the setting out of a twist of this description would be completed by ruling a single additional line $\frac{3}{4}$ in. away from the first. It is usual to cut twists in pairs, consequently for a set of table legs two would be required for each hand. To mark out a right-handed twist, a beginning may be made at the same point, and the line carried round in the opposite direction.

When a number of pieces have to be cut the spiral may be readily reproduced in the following way: Wind a perfectly straight strip of stout paper round that part of the cylinder which is set out to form the bead. The paper must be just wide enough to cover the bead part, and long enough to reach its entire length. Secure it with a couple of pins, and trim one end of it quite fair with the annular line at that part of the cylinder. This strip forms a template. To use it, spin a pencil line round one end of the cylinder to be marked out. Pin the trimmed end of the template securely quite fair by this line and revolve the job, when the strip will automatically take up the correct position on the cylinder, and the twist may be marked out by running a pencil along both sides of the strip. To reverse the hand of the twist, turn the paper over, pin and wind in the opposite direction.

For " setting in " the twist a saw fitted

these the neck should be nicely hollowed. A chisel may now be taken to round up the bead, and if followed by a cabinet-maker's file (not a rasp).

If the work is being done on a treadle lathe glasspapering is effected in the following manner : The foot is worked so as to swing the flywheel backwards and forwards, the hand holding the glasspaper being carried to and fro along the twist. Should a power machine be employed it will have to be run " dead slow," and after glasspapering the job in one direction, the belt will need to be crossed and the motion reversed to obtain a uniform finish.

Reeding.—Formerly this class of work

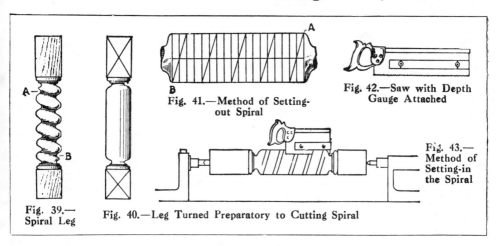

Fig. 39.—Spiral Leg

Fig. 40.—Leg Turned Preparatory to Cutting Spiral

Fig. 41.—Method of Setting-out Spiral

Fig. 42.—Saw with Depth Gauge Attached

Fig. 43.—Method of Setting-in the Spiral

with a depth-gauge is shown by Fig. 42, the method of fixing the gauge being that which is usually employed in the shops where spiral cutting is frequently done. The idea of punching holes through a tenon saw, however, may not commend itself to the occasional operator, in which case he will have to devise some temporary means of securing the gauge to the saw blade. The gauge in this instance will be set $\frac{3}{4}$ in. from the saw teeth. The operation of " setting in " the twist is shown by Fig. 43, constructional lines being omitted for the sake of clearness. Success with this is dependent on getting a perfectly fair start. A carver's gouge may be used to remove the surplus timber between the saw-cuts, and on reaching the bottom of

was done entirely by hand. The turned material was longitudinally pencil-lined, dividing the job into equal width spacing, depending on the number of reedings, and the work finished with wood-carving tools, the principal tool used for the purpose being the ordinary carving **V** or parting tool.

A later and quicker way is to operate on the work with horizontal cutters whilst it is supported between the lathe centres. This method of course necessitates special attachments for the lathe.

Example of Wood Turning.—An outline of the usual procedure in making an article such as a wooden stool is shown by Figs. 44 to 47.

When the square for the seat is

mounted on the screw chuck, start the lathe, and with the compasses scribe a circle of the size required. The corners may then be removed by a single cut with

bit. In " setting up " see that the end of the frame arrests the forward movement of the block before it reaches the point of the bit. A cardboard template may be

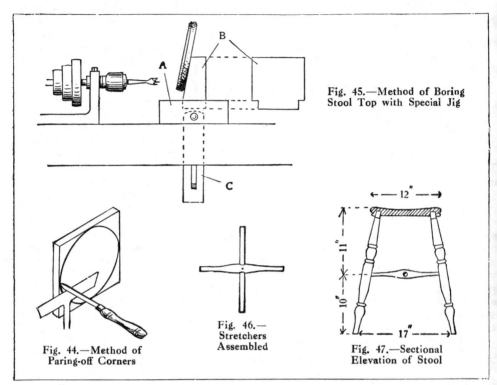

Fig. 45.—Method of Boring Stool Top with Special Jig

Fig. 44.—Method of Paring-off Corners

Fig. 46.— Stretchers Assembled

Fig. 47.—Sectional Elevation of Stool

the parting tool (Fig. 44). The point of the parting tool should be spread a little to give clearance, or the tool will become unduly hot and the temper may be drawn. As the corners of the square will fly off with considerable force, care should be taken to keep out of the " line of fire," and to protect any windows that may be in the vicinity.

Fig. 45 illustrates a fit-up for boring the stool top. A is a square frame, put together like the four sides of a box, and is held in position by a wedge passing through the leg C. The wooden block shown by B slides in this frame, and determines the angle and depth to which the holes are bored. The stool top is held by the hands in the position shown, and together with the block is fed towards the

used for marking the positions of the holes. The boring of the legs and stretchers presents no special difficulty. They may be bored in the lathe or by hand, whichever is preferred. The hole in the stretcher should be bored from both sides to prevent breaking through.

In fitting up, the glue should be used very hot, and special attention should be paid to the holes. The stretchers are put together as shown by Fig. 46. These are not glued, but are secured with a brad. The legs are next assembled round the stretchers, the brad in which is placed towards the bottom. The legs are then driven into the holes in the top, and the stool is ready to be stained and varnished.

A part sectional elevation of the stool with dimensions is shown by Fig. 47.

Veneering

THE process of veneering has been very unjustly condemned at times, and is frequently referred to in terms of contempt, it being believed in some quarters that veneering is synonymous with cheap and shoddy work. These impressions, in some cases, have doubtless arisen because of the abuse of veneering, and in others from a wrong impression of its particular purpose. In these circumstances it may be advisable to deal with the proper uses of veneering before dealing with the particular processes involved.

When veneering was in vogue a good deal more than it is to-day, much cheap and shoddy work was produced with inferior wood groundworks and bad veneer. Instances are common where orange-box and egg-box wood has been sold to cabinet-makers, who used it instead of the more expensive pine or American whitewood for groundworks, and then veneered it with cheap knife-cut veneer worth about ½d. a square foot. It was work of this kind that was largely responsible for the suspicion with which veneered work was viewed, and it may be said here that when veneering is used to conceal bad wood and poor construction, it is being used in a wrong way, and the resultant work may properly be termed "shoddy." In this connection reference should be made to the shoddy inlaid mahogany bureaux, of which many thousands exist. Instead of mortising the carcases together, the drawer rails are simply butted between the carcase ends. with 3-in. French nails

driven through the ends into the rails. The nails were punched in, and the holes stopped with plaster-of-paris before knife-cut veneer was laid over the ends, concealing the holes and also the imperfections of the wood always found in cheap timber. Veneering of this kind is always unsatisfactory, as it "blisters" very easily, and when this occurs it cannot be easily remedied. Cheap wood frequently contains a lot of resin, and knots shrink away from the veneer with disastrous results.

In the proper use of veneering good, sound wood is used for the groundwork, with good figured veneer. In some cases Honduras mahogany is veneered with wood of another kind, and the work generally when properly done is superior to, and more costly than, ordinary solid wood. This leads naturally to an excellent reason for veneering. If "curl" timber is to be used in panels, for example, the cost of the wood would be prohibitive, and it would not last nearly as long as the same "curl" timber cut into veneer and used in conjunction with plain panel boards. It may be said, generally, that the more richly figured woods cannot be used in the solid because the contrasting grains and erratic growth—which give such a beautiful effect—are conducive to twisting and warping. This timber, however, when cut into very thin layers and properly treated and glued or veneered on panel boards, gives the rich effect desired, and "stands" far better than the solid curl or figured wood. Satinwood,

191

for example, can only be used " in the solid " for thin facings or mouldings owing to its poor standing power. The more richly figured it is the more it costs, and for this reason even mouldings in satin-wood work are frequently made with mahogany groundworks and thin satin-wood facings. Economy in working on material is not the particular object aimed at, but rather increased durability.

Another " proper " use of veneering is in connection with curved work, such as circular and elliptical tables and cabinets. With such work, the rails of a circular table, for instance, or even a complete rim, it will be understood that " building up " in layers is far better than cutting solid rails, which are fitted between the legs. The latter method, if employed, causes weakness due to the inevitable short grain in parts, and the end grain is objectionable in appearance, as it has no figure and will not polish and look well. In both of these cases veneering is resorted to for decorative purposes, and as in the case of a built-up rim, the construction may be seen inside the rim. The veneering is obviously employed to enhance the appearance of the table. There is no attempt to deceive, and the maximum strength is obtained. This point also applies to quartered veneering, which may frequently be seen to advantage in old-fashioned piano cases and bedsteads of burr walnut. These, obviously, could not be made from solid wood, and if they were, it would only be at the expense of much labour and wood, and additionally, the wood would twist so much as to make the work valueless in a very short time. It will thus be seen that veneering is quite legitimate when used for " quartering " or for geometrically arranged units of contrasting woods in panels, drawer fronts, etc.

The durability of veneering is sometimes questioned ; but the best test of this factor is the examination of old work, particularly that of the eighteenth century and the Victorian era. There are few who have not at some time admired the fine veneers and veneering of that typical piece of Victorian furniture, the parlour table, either circular or elliptical. even though at the same time it may be regretted that the design was not so good as the workmanship.

At this stage it may be advisable to mention briefly the methods employed in cutting veneers. The old cabinet-makers evidently cut them by hand, as the examination of old work shows much of the veneer to be almost $\frac{1}{8}$ in. thick, with a very rough back caused by large-toothed saws. The advent of very large circular saws brought about the introduction of saw-cut veneers of moderate thickness, whilst the improved circular saw is really a very flat cone or drum with small sections of saw bolted all round. The flat cone gives the necessary rigidity and prevents buckling, and thus enables saw-cut veneers of twenty or more to the inch to be produced. A later development was the introduction of knife-cut veneer. The log is simply fixed in a large lathe, and is made to rotate against a large firmly-set knife, which takes off the veneer in one long roll. For purposes of convenience the sheet is cut into smaller ones 2 ft. or 3ft. wide, which are known generally as sheets. The wood used for veneer is, of course, chiefly in logs or balks, and bone-dry seasoning is not essential. With knife-cut veneer cutting, very dry wood is too brittle, and it is therefore the practice to first cut the veneer and then to dry the sheets in specially constructed drying rooms.

The advantages attaching to " saw-cut " and " knife-cut " veneers are not generally appreciated. It may be said of the former that a finer finished surface may be obtained by the use of saw-cut veneer than is the case when knife-cut veneer is used. Against this must be set the extra cost of saw-cut veneer, and the fact that extra labour is entailed, as saw-cut veneer cannot usually be laid by hand. The extra thickness of saw-cut veneer is its chief advantage, which prevents undue absorption of glue. With thin veneer, and particularly with figured veneer, the glue will penetrate right through the leaf. It will be understood that a " gluey " surface is undesirable for polishing, as e stain—bichromate of potash, for stance—only takes readily to a really ean wood surface. This drawback is t very apparent when the work is ished ; but the penetration of glue in e case of thin veneers undoubtedly duces the lustrous qualities of the wood,

The absorption of glue leads up to an important process which is very necessary when dealing with veneers with very open grains. Among the latter are included bird's-eye maple, Hungarian ash, and occasionally pollard oak. The first-named wood being marked with small

Fig. 1.—French Cabinet with Veneered and Marqueter.ed Decoration

nsequently producing a flat, uninterest-g effect. If a piece of figured wood were ed for both knife-cut and saw-cut neers, and then laid, cleaned up and lished, one would have no difficulty in cking out the knife-cut piece, it being much less "deep" and lustrous in pearance.

" eyes," the glue penetrates right through the wood, and as is usually the case with very light-coloured woods, the glue shows unsightly in the grain when the work is polished. To obviate this tendency, light-coloured open grained woods are specially treated. The underside of the veneer is first toothed level, and then it is carefully covered with a thin layer of glue-size and whiting. When this dries it forms a thin skin which usually effectually prevents the glue soaking through the veneer when it is laid. Some cabinet-makers prefer to mix whiting and ochre, for instance, with the glue, matching the finished colour of the surface, so that if some should penetrate it will not show in contrast to the natural wood. The first is probably the better method, because, as indicated previously, more lustre is obtained if the veneered surface is kept perfectly free from glue.

Before proceeding to describe the actual methods and tools used in veneering, it may be well to mention that veneering is divided into two distinct processes, namely, " hand " and " caul " veneering. The first is done with a veneering hammer, a very simple tool which can easily be made by a woodworker ; the second method briefly consists in the application of pressure applied by means of hand-screws or cramps, and " cauls." Both methods will be described in detail later.

Hammer veneering is generally used for knife-cut veneer, and it may be success-fully employed in practically all cases where only a single piece is to be laid. Built-up patterns such as those to be described and illustrated later cannot be laid with a veneering hammer, as the mois-ture in the glue causes the pieces to swell quickly, thus causing the built-up pattern to " cockle up " and smash when the hammer is applied. For this reason " marqueteried " patterns cannot be laid with a veneering hammer, although they are frequently cut in knife-cut veneer. The illustration (Fig. 1) shows a fine cabinet with a " marqueteried " panel, and it will readily be understood that when the pattern leaves the marquetry cutter, with all the various pieces glued on to a sheet of paper, any dampness would cause the groundwork veneer to stretch unduly, with disastrous results to the insets. The marqueteried panels sold by various firms are glued down on paper, and for the reasons indicated they have to be laid with cauls and the application of pressure. The cabinet illustrated belongs to the

early Louis XVI. period. Later Louis XV work is characterised by fine " diaper ornament, some of which is cut as ma quetry, whilst other diaper patterns a made up with small lozenge- or diamon shaped pieces of veneers with intersecti lines of ebony, boxwood, etc., the wh forming a charming surface decoration

Probably the most important part veneered work is that in connection wi the groundwork, as the proper selecti and treatment of this part determine t durability of the veneering when t latter is properly done. The two woo most chiefly used are American yell pine and Honduras mahogany. It essential that groundworks should be fr from sap and imperfections such as shak and knots. The best wood is that gen ally termed " panel wood." Panel boar do not shrink or warp to any great exter as the " medullary rays " practically r parallel to the surfaces and act as stiffeni agents. Fig. 2 shows the panel boar in a log, and as the boards are cut nea the outside there is a tendency for t boards to " cast," which is due to t oblique medullary rays and the tenden of the boards to go " round " on the he side. Panel boards cannot, of cour always be used, and therefore steps mu be taken to counteract the natural te dency of the boards to curve.

Fig. 3 shows an ideal arrangement f a groundwork. This is built up wi narrow strips of wood, with the heart si alternating all through. One pulls agai the other, and no distinct " casting " tak place. It is usual when a groundwo of this kind is utilised to veneer the grou work on both sides. When a plain sin board is used, the veneer should be plac on the heart side, as the boards have natural tendency to go round on the he side (see Fig. 4). An additional reason that if veneer is laid with a hammer expands somewhat after being glued a damped, and shrinks somewhat during t drying. This causes the wood to hollow on the face side, and if the grou work is already round it pulls the surfa almost straight.

Three-ply wood has come into vog

ınd this material may be used to advan-
:age. It can be obtained in almost any
:hickness and also with from three to seven
ayers. The principle is to place each layer
with the grain running at right angles
:o the layer below. Shrinkage and warp-
ıge are thus counteracted. Old French
bed panels were made in a similar way.

up, if necessary, and planed to thickness;
the toothing plane is brought into use.
This tool has a body similar to a smoothing
plane, and a single-toothed iron is set
upright in the stock. The iron is made
with a series of serrations on the face side,
so that when ground and sharpened, the
cutting edge resembles that shown by

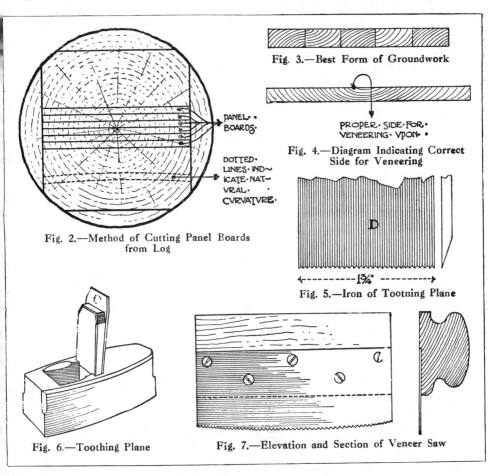

Fig. 3.—Best Form of Groundwork

PROPER· SIDE· FOR·
VENEERING· VPON· ·

Fig. 4.—Diagram Indicating Correct
Side for Veneering

PANEL· ·
BOARDS·

DOTTED·
LINES· IND~
ICATE· NAT~
VRAL· ·
CVRVATVRE·

Fig. 2.—Method of Cutting Panel Boards
from Log

D

Fig. 5.—Iron of Tootning Plane

Fig. 6.—Toothing Plane

Fig. 7.—Elevation and Section of Veneer Saw

The groundwork was first prepared, and
then veneered each side, with the veneer
grain placed across the grain of the groundwork. An outside layer was then put on
each side in the same direction as the
groundwork, thus forming a five-ply panel,
which would keep flat and sound for
generations.

The groundwork having been jointed

Fig. 5. Various degrees of coarseness
can be obtained in these irons, a fairly
coarse one being the best for groundworks.
The fine ones are used for levelling down
saw-cut veneers before they are scraped
and glasspapered. The toothing plane
(Fig. 6) should first be used diagonally on
the groundwork, that is, from opposite
corners ; then it is toothed in the direction

of the other diagonal before it is completed by toothing from end to end of the wood, in the same direction as the grain. Whether the veneer is to be laid with a veneering hammer or cauls, proper toothing is essential, and the groundwork is then ready for sizing.

It should be mentioned here that all groundworks, and particularly soft ones, such as pine or American whitewood, should be sized after toothing. It is usual to prepare the size with a small quantity of liquid glue mixed with water. This should be well rubbed into the toothed groundwork with a brush, and then allowed to dry. A little experience is necessary before one can do this really

first step. The leaf to be laid should be free from shakes, and it may be cut from the sheet by using the edge of the toothing plane-iron (like a saw) against a straight-edge. Chisels are sometimes used ; but unless great care is taken they will cause the veneer to shatter and break when cutting across the grain. A veneer saw such as is shown in Fig. 7 is the tool generally used by expert cabinet-makers.

It should be distinctly understood that there is a right and a wrong side to veneer, and particularly knife-cut veneer. If both sides of the leaf are carefully examined, it will be noticed that the " pores " of the wood are slightly depressed on one side, with corresponding projections on

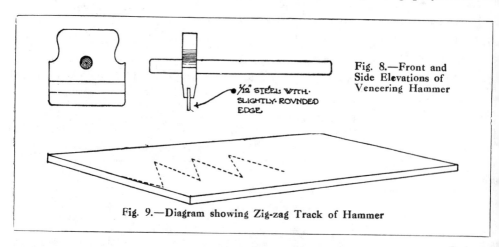

Fig. 8.—Front and Side Elevations of Veneering Hammer

½″ STEEL WITH SLIGHTLY ROVNDED EDGE

Fig. 9.—Diagram showing Zig-zag Track of Hammer

well, as occasionally the size is made too strong, which prevents it sinking properly into the wood, with the result that it can be distinctly seen as a layer when dry. Should this occur, a fine toothing plane should be used to roughen the surface again before the veneer is laid.

When circular or curved groundworks are employed, a certain amount of end grain is inevitable. Sizing in such instances is imperative, as otherwise the glue for veneering would be absorbed by the groundwork, and peeling and blistering would result.

Assuming that knife-cut veneer is to be laid with a veneering hammer on a flat surface, the selection of the veneer is the

the other side. The leaf should be laid with the depressions downwards, so that the slightly raised parts can be removed when the surface is cleaned up.

The proper side having been selected, the groundwork should be well covered with glue. The knife-cut veneer is then pressed flat with the hands, and the outer surface damped with a cloth. A little glue is then dabbed on with a brush here and there, and a hot flat-iron is then passed all over the surface until the glue underneath runs freely. A veneering hammer such as shown by Fig. 8 is then brought into play, the veneer being squeezed down with the steel edge. It should be remembered that it is necessary to rub out as much glue as possible from underneath the veneer, and this can best be effected by rubbing away from the centre of the veneer with a "zig-zag" motion, such as is indicated in Fig. 9. The glue should first be pushed from the centre towards one end, and then from the centre to the other end, until as much as possible is rubbed out. If this is done properly the veneer will then be laid flat and without blisters.

During the whole process of laying, it is essential that the outside of the veneer should be kept moist. A frequent cause of failure is that the surface is kept too wet. To obviate this, the outer surface should be kept moistened with size, as after the ironing is effected and rubbing takes place, the size dries slightly and practically closes the pores of the wood, thus preventing blisters. These latter are more frequently caused by air underneath the wood than the absence of glue, as is generally supposed, and, as has been previously indicated, can best be obviated by the application of size rather than water as a dampening agent during the ironing and laying. Of course, blisters may occur, and for the reasons indicated above, a blister should be carefully slit with a thin-bladed knife in the direction of the grain, and a little glue inserted. The whole is then rubbed, the glue and air being rubbed out simultaneously.

When the veneer is laid and stood aside to dry, the air should be kept away from the surface. If a single piece only is being handled, the veneered side can be laid flat on the bench or floor ; or if two are handled, the surfaces can be placed together with a sheet of paper in between and cramped or hand-screwed.

The hammer-veneering practice in connection with knife-cut veneers varies but little when curved work is required to be veneered. Examples of the latter frequently occur in cabinet work, such as, for example, bowed fronts in chests of drawers and dressing-tables, writing-tables, and sideboards. On the smaller side there are clock cases with curved heads, jewel boxes, and caskets. With work which is only slightly curved, such

as bow drawer-fronts, the veneer will bend quite easily, and lay without blisters if the surface is damped with size instead of water. With the small work, however, involving "quicker" curves, it sometimes happens that fractures in the veneer occur whilst bending. To avoid difficulties of this sort the usual plan is to use the veneer with the grain of the groundwork, which enables the veneer to be laid with comparative ease.

The next type of veneering to be dealt with is that generally termed "caul" veneering, and, as has already been indicated, it is employed in all cases where marqueteried patterns or built-up designs are employed. Its use is general also in connection with saw-cut as distinct from knife-cut veneer. The former kind is usually too "strong" for treatment by the hammer method, and chiefly for this reason caul veneering is almost inevitable when the veneers are laid in large pieces. The narrow cross-bandings used round drawers and panels, or very small pieces of saw-cut veneer, can, of course, be laid with a veneering hammer or even the thin side of an ordinary hammer ; but if the veneer is at all buckled, hammering is quite unsuitable. The chief requirement for caul veneering is a fairly good number of hand-screws, and if there are not sufficient of these, large and small cramps can with a little ingenuity be pressed into the service.

Veneering on a large scale simply consists of labour-saving appliances, by the use of which many surfaces can be veneered at one time. In the large firms a gluing machine, which quickly spreads the glue quite evenly over the groundwork, is usual, and then quite elaborate systems are adopted for heating the cauls and applying the necessary pressure. These are, it will be readily understood, quite simple operations in themselves ; and, as a matter of fact, the use of the above-mentioned plant is not justified unless working on a large scale.

For simple caul veneering a good example is a pair of bureau ends. It is presumed that these have been prepared and sized as already described. The underside of the veneer is then slightly toothed and the following apparatus prepared : say twelve bearers about 2 in. square, and a " caul " slightly larger than the surfaces to be veneered, made of ¾-in. pine or whitewood accurately planed and gauged to thickness. It will be seen (Fig. 10)

pressure is first applied to the middle, and as the hand-screws are tightened up at each side, pressure is brought to bear over the whole area. The bearers should be placed in pairs at intervals of 6 in. or 7 in. (*see* Fig. 12). It is well to test the whole bearers, caul, and ends before the actual

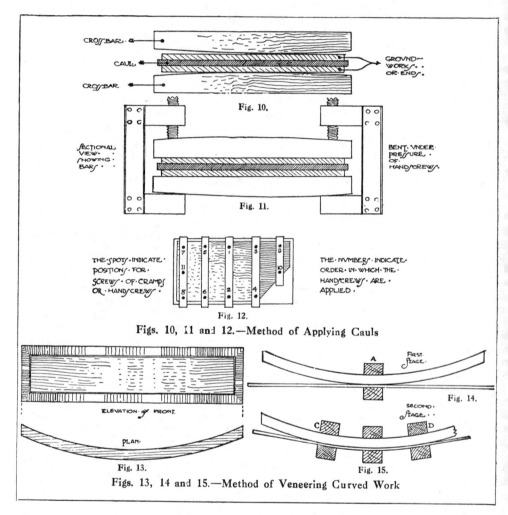

Figs. 10, 11 and 12.—Method of Applying Cauls

Figs. 13, 14 and 15.—Method of Veneering Curved Work

that the bearers are " round " on the underside. The amount of curvature is rather exaggerated in the diagram, but ¼ in. should be sufficient in a 21-in. length. It will be seen by referring to Fig. 11 that when pressure is applied by means of hand-screws to the bearers or cross-bars, the

veneering is done, so that the bearer faces can be planed flatter or rounder as occasion requires. The hand-screws should always be " set " near the proper size, so that time should not be lost after the caul has been heated. Probably the chief mistake made by beginners is in connection with he glue. Both surfaces should be well covered with glue, and then set aside until t is quite " chilled." When a spread surface is really " chilled," the hand can be aid quite flat on the glue, and then taken off without sticking in any way. If this s not done the glue will at once grip the veneer, and any alteration of position is almost impossible without splitting the sheet. Even supposing the veneer could be dropped into the exact position, it would at once cause the veneer to swell rapidly, and cause buckles. A bad after-effect is also occasioned, as after the glue dries the veneer contracts to its original size, thus causing the surface to go hollow.

The caul is heated on both sides, pre-ferably over a blaze of shavings in a fireplace, until the hand cannot com-fortably be placed on both sides. The procedure generally is as follows : (1) Cover the groundworks with glue and allow to chill. (2) Place the veneers in position, and pin down each sheet with two fine veneer pins. (3) Cover each sheet of veneer with a sheet of newspaper. (4) Thoroughly heat the caul on both sides and place between as indicated in Fig. 10. (5) Place two cross-bars in position at the middle of the ends, and hand-screw together until the glue runs out at each side. (6) Place a second and third set about 6 in. from the centre bar, and hand-screw similarly. (7) Place the remainder of the bars in position, and hand-screw. (8) When all is properly hand-screwed, test all the hand-screws and tighten wherever possible. (9) Add hand-screws at each end on the middle parts of the cross-bar.

The work having been completed in the manner indicated above, it may be stood aside to dry, twelve to twenty-four hours elapsing before the hand-screws are re-moved. Should any glue have penetrated the veneer, the paper prevents it sticking to the caul. With very " figury " veneers a good deal of glue penetrates, causing the paper to stick to the surface. This can, however, be easily removed by tooth-ing it down with a toothing plane. Should blisters be suspected, the parts may be tapped with the knuckle, when the sound

will indicate their position. As in the case of hammer veneering, they can be rectified by slitting the veneer with a thin knife and inserting glue, afterwards applying a very small caul or square piece of wood with hand-screw, in preference to rubbing down with hammer.

The second example of caul veneering is that where a curved surface has to be

Fig. 16.—Example of Built-up Veneer

negotiated, such as illustrated in the drawer front shown in Fig. 13. The practice is very similar, a thin wooden caul of $\frac{1}{4}$-in. or even $\frac{3}{16}$-in. whitewood being used in conjunction with a few cross-pieces of $\frac{7}{8}$-in. wood about $1\frac{1}{4}$ in. wide. The method employed is as follows : (1) Cover the groundwork with glue, and allow to chill.

(2) Place and pin the veneer in position, and heat the caul. (3) Cover with paper, and place on the caul. (4) Put blocks A (Fig. 14) in position, and hand-screw as indicated in diagram. (5) Put blocks c

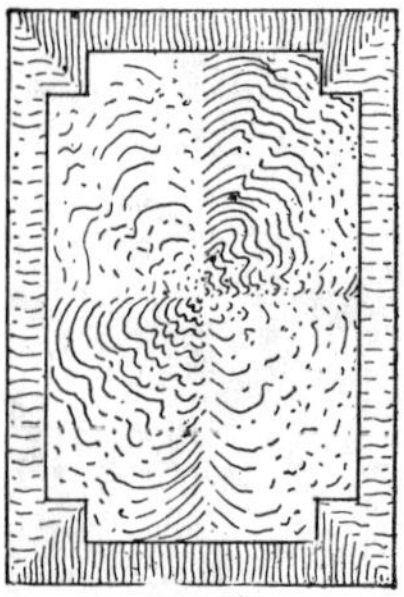

Fig. 17.

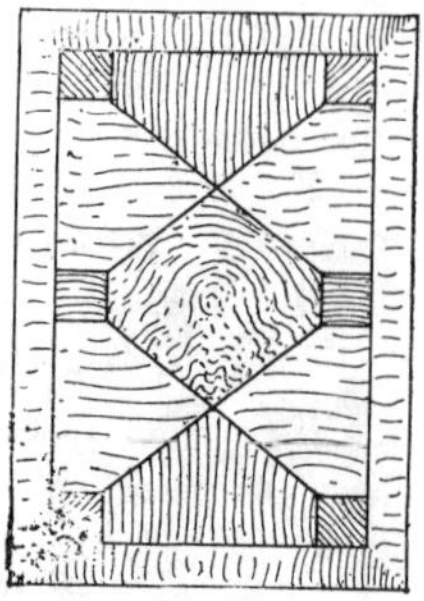

Fig. 18.

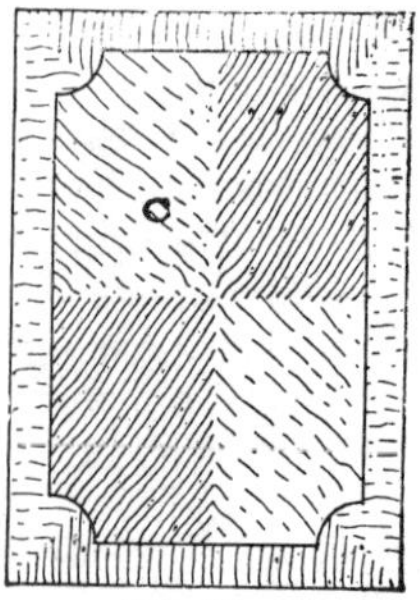

Fig. 19.

Figs. 17, 18 and 19.—Examples of Decorative Veneer Work

and D (Fig. 15) in position, and hand-screw. (6) Follow with the succeeding blocks, and hand-screw. (7) Carefully examine the edges, and adjust the hand-screws as necessary. (8) Set aside to dry for twelve to twenty-four hours.

In cases where the drawer is made prior to veneering the front, it is advisable to cramp the ends of the caul down by cramping over the back and front. Care must be taken to ensure that the pressure is along the drawer sides, as otherwise the dovetails may be strained and weakened. With an example such as is illustrated, decorated with mosaic stringing and cross-banding, a cutting gauge should be set to the margin required, and the veneer cut by working off the edges of the front. The surplus veneer can be easily removed if it is heated with an old file to soften the glue. The stringing is then cut a little longer than the finished length on one side and glued against the veneer by rubbing with a hammer. One end is then mitred with a chisel and the second length

fitted, the process being continued all round. Cross-bands of saw-cut veneer are next prepared, and the long sides are then rubbed down in two or three short lengths with a hammer. All four mitres are now cut with a very sharp chisel, and the end pieces may then be fitted and glued down between them.

A very popular and effective method of decoration consists of building up geometrical patterns in veneer, with mosaic lines or stringing between the various pieces of veneer. Such an example is the top of a portable dressing case now in the Victoria and Albert Museum, a corner being shown by Fig. 16. This dates from the eighteenth century, and the figuring and lustre of the wood is actually improved by the natural toning effected by age. A few simple examples of similar veneering are illustrated by Figs. 17, 18 and 19. These could well be utilised with but slight alteration for drawer fronts, door panels, tops of writing-cases, and other small work of a similar character. The more decorative side of veneering is

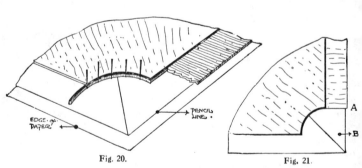

EDGE OF PAPER

PENCIL LINES

A

B

Fig. 20.

Fig. 21.

Figs. 20 and 21.—Method of Fitting Curved Corners

dealt with in the next section. The practice in most examples is very similar. Fig. 19 can be taken as a specimen to be executed in well-figured saw-cut mahogany veneer.

The design is first to be drawn on a piece of strong cartridge paper that has been damp-stretched on a plain piece of wood or an old drawing-board. Four pieces of veneer are then cut with the grain running from corner to corner, and the two inside edges planed true and square on a small shooting-board, with either a small metal block plane or a shoulder plane. This piece is then planed to width and length. The next step is to cut the hollow corner. This may be marked with a pair of compasses, and then cut

banding and the quartered part ; these may be purchased in small quantities, and are about $\frac{1}{16}$ in. square. A short length should be cut for one side, and then glued down to the paper by rubbing with the flat end of a small hammer. One end is then mitred ready for the hollow corner. As these lines are rather brittle, a small piece should be put into hot water for a couple of minutes to render bending easier. One end is then mitred to fit the straight length, and pressed round the curve with a hammer. In the case of a

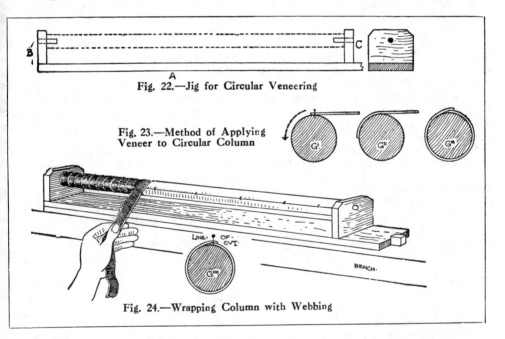

Fig. 22.—Jig for Circular Veneering

Fig. 23.—Method of Applying Veneer to Circular Column

Fig. 24.—Wrapping Column with Webbing

very carefully just outside the line with a fine fret-saw. To finish the edge cleanly a half-round file should be used ; or alternately, a strip of rounded wood with fine glasspaper wound round. This piece of veneer when finished to shape is then glued down to the paper, and the other quarters cut and glued in the same way.

If great care is exercised, it is sometimes quicker to fasten the four veneers together with two fine veneer pins, and then plane the edge and hollow out the corners, afterwards separating them and gluing down. The design shows a line between the cross-

very small or " quick " curve, veneer pins should be inserted occasionally as indicated by Fig. 20. A straight length is then laid, and so on until the line is laid all round. The cross-banding is next dealt with. This should be cut from the end of a leaf with a sharp cutting gauge in lengths which should have one edge shot true on the shooting-board. It is then glued on the underside, and rubbed down with a hammer. The straight piece should be cut square at A (see Fig. 21), and then the piece marked B is cut and fitted. Repeat for the other parts.

So far only ordinary hammer and " caul " veneering have been dealt with. The fine possibilities of veneering in cabinet-work, however, are so many, particularly in small work, that it may be well to deal with one or two special processes of veneering, which, with but little adaptation, may be applied to a large number of varied jobs.

As an example, the method of veneering a circular column or pillar will be taken, and this is identical with the method of veneering a circular pedestal, say 18 in. in diameter. The only difference is one of size, this applying also to the stand used for revolving the work, which is described and illustrated later. Supposing a column 4 ft. long by 2 in. in diameter is required to be veneered, the first essential is to prepare a satisfactory groundwork. Good straight-grained timber must be used for this purpose in order to prevent casting later, and the rounding of the material should preferably be done on a lathe. Failing the use of the latter, the groundwork can be rounded up with planes. If this procedure is adopted, a circle should be set out with dividers at each end of the piece, and then planed an octagonal shape before being finally rounded to the circle lines. It should now be carefully toothed all round, taking care to remove all slight ridges, which may be detected by simply feeling the surface with the hand. It is next sized as previously described, and stood aside to dry.

The next step is to prepare a simple apparatus which will enable the column to be easily revolved. This is shown by Fig. 22. The piece A represents a length of deal or whitewood rather longer than the column to be veneered. Piece B is a square piece firmly fastened with screws or nails to one end, with a $\frac{3}{8}$-in. dowel glued in the position indicated. Piece C is to act practically as a sliding head-piece, and is secured to the bottom part by means of two screws. The dowel in piece C is left dry. The column is inserted as indicated by simply withdrawing the right-hand dowel and then pushing it into a hole bored into the column. This allows the column to revolve freely.

It should here be mentioned that columns and circular pedestals are usually veneered with either thick knife-cut veneer or thin saw-cut veneer in order to prevent splitting. Thick veneer can be used, even when marqueteried ; but special precautions must be taken, which will be briefly mentioned later. Knife-cut veneer having been selected, it should be damped slightly to prevent splitting. The groundwork or column is then well covered with glue, and set aside to thoroughly chill. This should be tested before the veneer is placed on it, and when the hand can be put on any part and removed without the glue adhering, the fixing of the veneer can be proceeded with. The diagram G^1 (Fig. 23) shows one edge of the veneer secured with pins, the latter being driven in every 6 in. or so. It is then slowly revolved in the direction of the arrow indicated, the hands being rubbed along to press the veneer down as the column is revolved. A sectional view would then be as indicated in diagram G^{11}, and the process continued until the veneer is rolled all round as in diagram G^{111}, overlapping the edge as indicated. The overlapping part is then pinned down. Strong webbing is the next essential, one end of which is tacked to the left-hand end of the column. The latter is now slowly revolved, and the webbing bound firmly tight down the column. This is indicated in Fig. 24, and when it is bound completely in its length the end is tacked at the right-hand end, and the column removed from the stand.

A shaving blaze is then made, and the column carefully revolved in the flames until it is well heated all over to melt the glue. The webbing is thoroughly wetted, causing it to shrink, which causes the glue to be pressed out. It is then heated again and damped, and set aside to dry. The necessary pressure is, of course, executed by the dampened webbing, and the action will be better understood if one notices the varying degrees of tautness in a clothes-line. In dry weather it hangs limply, but when thoroughly wetted in a shower of rain it becomes taut. Diagram G^{1111}, (Fig. 24) shows the section of the column after the webbing has been removed after an interval of eight to ten hours. The overlapping of the veneer has been purposely enlarged. A clean joint is formed by cutting through the two thicknesses at one time with a keen-edged knife against a straightedge. The glue is then softened by ironing and damping, when the surplus outside veneer can easily be removed. It is necessary to lift one edge all along to remove the inside surplus piece, and when this has been taken out, a little glue is inserted all along and the veneer rubbed down with a hammer. If this is carefully done, the joint will be scarcely perceptible when the column is scraped and glasspapered.

It will be understood that the process described can be applied with a little adaptation to other veneering problems.

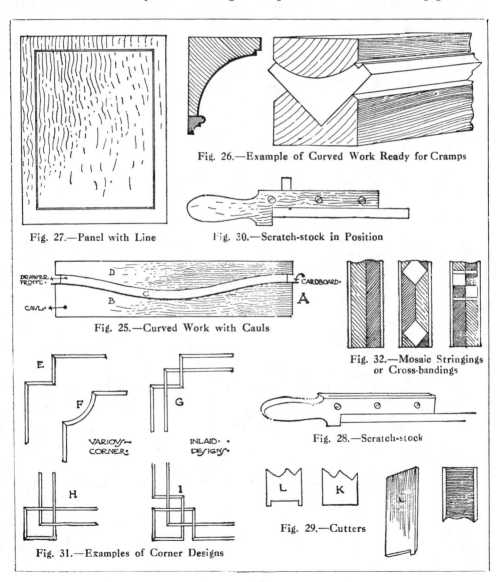

Fig. 26.—Example of Curved Work Ready for Cramps

Fig. 27.—Panel with Line

Fig. 30.—Scratch-stock in Position

Fig. 25.—Curved Work with Cauls

Fig. 32.—Mosaic Stringings or Cross-bandings

Fig. 28.—Scratch-stock

Fig. 29.—Cutters

Fig. 31.—Examples of Corner Designs

The semi-circular lid of a casket could, for instance, be veneered in this way ; and, as has been previously indicated, a large cylinder or pedestal would only need a larger stand for revolving the groundwork, the other operations and their sequence being identical with those described and illustrated.

The next practical process of veneering to be dealt with is that necessitating the use of a curved caul. This process is particularly useful when one has to veneer curved drawer-fronts, table-rails, and work of a similar character. Fig. 25 shows a drawer-front ogee in shape, which would be about 4 in. or 5 in. wide. Curved drawer-fronts of this type are usually band-sawn from thick timber, and if a number are sawn from a thick block, waste pieces— indicated by B and D—will be obtained. The drawer-front is first rasped and filed perfectly true, and then the curved surface of B is filed exactly to fit the drawer-front. The usual steps, namely, sizing, gluing, and pinning down the veneer, are then proceeded with, when the curved surface of B is made very hot. The veneer is then covered with a piece of newspaper, and the whole placed together as indicated in Fig. 26 and firmly hand-screwed. In some cases a thin piece of cardboard can be utilised with advantage. It is inserted between the newspaper and the piece B (Fig. 25), and because of its relative softness a better pressure is exerted all over the drawer-front. Whenever veneering of this type is to be done in the manner described, the whole should be tested first by hand-screwing together and carefully observing the edges to see that the uniformity of pressure aforementioned is obtained. Any defects should be remedied by filing away the high parts of the groundwork, and again testing.

It will be seen that practically any shape can be dealt with in the manner described, whether for drawers, rails, or small panels. It cannot be said that this process is more effective than the one where a thin caul is used, such as was described earlier ; but, as already indicated, if one has the waste wood for the curved cauls it is a more convenient way.

Most cabinet-makers, be they amateurs or journeymen, at an early stage wish to become proficient in inlaying lines, bandings and stringings. These materials are very much used in inlaid cabinet-work, and, used with discretion and with proper regard to proportion, they much enhance the appearance of furniture, particularly that made of mahogany and satinwood. The materials may be purchased from most cabinet-makers, timber and veneer merchants. Square lines of ebony, box, holly, and other stained woods can be obtained in lengths of about 3 ft., ranging from $\frac{1}{16}$ in. to $\frac{1}{8}$ in. square. The mosaic stringings are in similar lengths up to $\frac{3}{8}$ in. to $\frac{1}{2}$ in. wide with various designs, such as chain, loop, herring-bone, and various geometrical devices. The cross-bandings are made from $\frac{1}{8}$ in. to 1 in. wide, with one or two lines on each side. Mosaic stringings and cross-bandings are always made a bare $\frac{1}{16}$ in. thick, which is equal to the average thickness of saw-cut veneer. This thickness is very useful when inlaying veneered work, it only being necessary to remove just the thickness of the veneer, so that the stringing or cross-banding can be laid in level with the surface.

Fig. 27 represents a small panel which is to be inlaid with a single boxwood line about $\frac{3}{4}$ in. from the edges. Fig. 28 shows a scratch-stock used for inlaying. It is simply made from a piece of $\frac{7}{8}$-in. mahogany or beech, cut to the shape shown, with a saw-cut through the stem as illustrated. One or two screws are then put in, so that the cut part can be pressed together in order to secure the steel cutter. The steel cutter for a small line is illustrated by c (Fig. 29). This is made from $\frac{1}{16}$-in. steel filed to the shape shown, the projecting piece exactly equalling in size the line to be inlaid. To obtain a proper cutting-edge, the small piece is filed like a chisel bevel, and then secured in the scratch-stock with the screws. Fig. 30 shows the scratch-stock in position, the groove being cut by working the stock backwards and forwards to scrape away the groove. This action is repeated until all four grooves are cut, when the corners are finished off eatly with a chisel, and picked out clean ith a marking awl or sharp point.

Various designs can be made on drawer-onts, panels, etc., by varying the corner. he simplest one is shown at E (Fig. 31), nd this is known as a broken corner. F is nown as the "hollow" corner, the groove eing cut with a gauge, and the wood icked out with an awl. G is an elabora-on of E, and, as will be seen, it is effected y the introduction of a second line. H is n effective treatment with double lines, nd I indicates an elaboration of the one hown in H.

The best procedure is to "set out" the nes and corners with a sharp pencil, and hen to work out the grooves with the cratch-stock before finishing the corners vith a chisel. In order to prevent the vood tearing where the lines cross, these rooves running across the grain should e cut first. It is then a comparatively imple matter to scratch the remaining rooves in the same direction as the grain f the wood or veneer, as the case may be. 'he grooves having been completed, the ines are carefully cut with butt or mitre oints, and glued into their respective rooves. The practice necessary to inlay mosaic stringings or cross-bandings such as are illustrated in Fig. 32 is almost identical to that previously described. If solid wood is to be inlaid, a cutter should be made as shown by K (Fig. 29), which cuts away the whole groove in one operation. Should, however, the surface to be inlaid be veneered, a cutter is made with two teeth as shown by L. Two narrow channels are then scratched, and the strip of veneer remaining in the middle is removed by heating it with a file to soften the glue, when it can be easily removed with a chisel.

Some little practice is required to get the groove exactly the size required, and it is advisable to make the cutter slightly smaller than the groove required. Should the stock not be worked exactly square, the groove will be made slightly larger than the size of the cutter. The groove when properly made should just grip the sides of the cross-banding, when it can be mitred, glued, and rubbed down easily with a hammer.

It should be mentioned that a scratch-stock can be improvised by making a cut in the end of a marking gauge, to receive a cutter which is secured as before with screws. The stock illustrated is, however, very easily made, and better than an improvised gauge.

Inlay and Marquetry Work

Inlaying.—Inlaying consists of recessing a design in wood, ivory, etc., and laying in another shade or kind of wood for decorative purposes.

Inlaying dates back to the times of the early Egyptians, who practised the art several centuries before the Christian era. They were particularly skilful in the use of gold and ivory. Amber also was employed, being brought from the North Sea by the Phœnicians. Specimens of Egyptian inlaid work may be seen in the British Museum, and also in the Louvre in Paris, that have survived the centuries, and prove most interesting records of an ancient art. Ebony and ivory were favourite media, used in chairs and thrones. There are numerous Biblical references to inlaying, including the description of King Solomon's throne, which was, we read, "a great throne of ivory, and overlaid with the best gold." The Greeks also devised ornaments consisting of small particles of stone pieced together to form conventional representations of animal and human figures.

Its execution is by no means easy, and it requires considerable skill, especially in more advanced work. Yet in the ordinary inlaying which concerns woodworkers generally, and cabinet-makers especially, the work does not present such great difficulties as some workers believe. Some of the more difficult inlaid work, in which very intricate designs are introduced, is quite beyond the ordinary woodworker, as the whole surface which is being treated is covered with a thin veneer, in which the design is worked out. This form of inlaying requires very expensive tools, and often many coloured woods, so that the general worker is deterred from undertaking such work himself, and passes it on to expert inlayers. In such cases a piece of veneer of the same size as the surface which is to be treated is sent to the inlayers, and is returned with the inlaid design inserted, the various pieces being held together by a piece of paper glued on the outer face. The sheet of veneer is then glued to the groundwork and when the glue is dry, the paper is removed and the surface cleaned off.

There is no reason, however, why the woodworker should not decorate his work by the aid of simple inlaid designs. Such inlaying might be applied in almost any kind of furniture or fittings, and would greatly enhance both the value and appearance.

The woods used for inlaying may vary from $\frac{1}{16}$ in. to $\frac{3}{16}$ in. in thickness, but that about $\frac{1}{8}$ in. thick will be found very suitable. The woods employed should be selected with a view to forming a contrast with the groundwork which is being inlaid, and the choice will, of course, to a great extent be governed by the wood in the groundwork.

The colour treatment is an important matter, and should, if possible, be obtained through the use of natural-coloured woods.

for those artificially stained often give very unsightly effects. The natural coloured woods most suitable for the purpose may be classed as follows : White tints are obtained with white holly, sycamore, and maple ; yellow with satinwood, lancewood, canary, and light oak ; red with rosewood, mahogany, and padouk ; brown with dark oak, satin walnut, and birch ; and for black tints ebony should be used.

Having set out the design full size on a piece of paper, the pieces of wood to make up the design are cut out to the shape required. A very fine fret-saw would be found very useful in this operation, and the shapes may be transferred from the paper pattern by means of carbon paper. The pieces are then fitted together to form the complete design, care being taken that good joints are obtained. The pieces to form the complete design are then glued directly to the paper pattern, and the edges are also glued together. Another piece of paper is then glued over the top, and the whole is cramped between two pieces of board until the glue is dry. The inlay is then removed, and the piece of paper at the back on which the design was originally marked is stripped off. The inlay is then placed in position on the groundwork, and is scribed round the edges with a marking or scribing point. The wood in the groundwork must next be cut away to a sufficient depth to receive the inlay, care being taken to work exactly to the scribed lines. The cutting is accomplished with chisels and gouges, and a router would also be found most useful in removing the surplus wood. The inlay is now glued in position, and cramped until the glue is set, when the surface is cleaned off by scraping and glasspapering.

Any straight joints could be easily shot on an ordinary shooting board. An iron plane should be used, and in some cases several pieces of veneer could be worked at the same time. If, however, only one piece is planed at a time, it might be found desirable to cover it with a thin piece of wood while working the plane. A pattern is also found very useful when cutting several veneers to a certain shape and size.

The pattern should take the form of an aperture in a sheet of cardboard, as when made in this manner it enables the worker to examine the grains of the veneers without removing the pattern.

Another item is that all end grain veneers should be protected round the edges with small stringings, in which the grain runs lengthwise. This is very important, especially in drawer fronts and similar positions, as the end grain veneers would be very liable to split.

Figs. 1, 2 and 3 show three inlaid designs which would be simple to execute and would be very suitable for panels or large flat surfaces. Other simple forms of inlaying are given in Figs. 4, 5 and 6, which show the application of inlaid stringings and bandings.

Fig. 4 shows a form of stringing inlay suitable for a panel, tea-tray, or any flat surface to which such a form of decoration might be suitably applied. The outer edge in this design is inlaid with a banding about $\frac{1}{2}$ in. wide ; inside this is a narrower banding about $\frac{1}{4}$ in. wide, and a simple geometrical design is inlaid directly in the centre.

A simple inlaid stringing for applying to the front of a drawer is shown in Fig. 5. The stringing in this case might vary in width from $\frac{1}{4}$ in. to $\frac{1}{2}$ in., and should be set from $\frac{1}{2}$ in. to $\frac{3}{4}$ in. in from the outer edge. Another case in which good effects are created with inlaid stringings and bandings is illustrated by Fig. 6, which shows the top portion of a cabinet in which inlaid bandings have been introduced.

In the application of such inlaid designs as those illustrated by Figs. 1, 2 and 3, the designs are first set out full size on a piece of paper. The size to which the designs are set out must, of course, be governed by the size of the surface which is being treated ; but the inlay should not appear to be too large or over-done. The design (Fig. 1), shown enlarged by Fig. 7, would be most suitable for a long vertical rail or panel. The enlarged design which is shown by Fig. 8 would also be very suitable for application in a similar position. Both designs are very flexible, and may be increased or diminished in length to meet

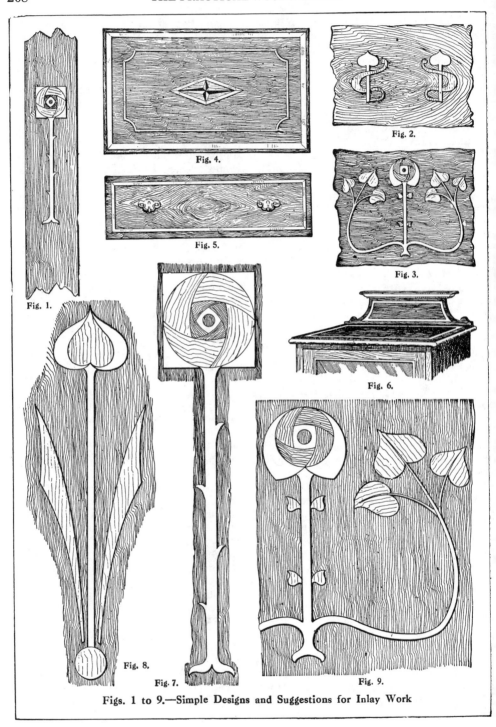

Fig. 4.

Fig. 2.

Fig. 5.

Fig. 3.

Fig. 1.

Fig. 6.

Fig. 8.

Fig. 7.

Fig. 9.

Figs. 1 to 9.—Simple Designs and Suggestions for Inlay Work

almost any requirements. In the design (Fig. 7) three kinds of wood are introduced, while in that shown by Fig. 8 only two kinds are used. The designs shown (Figs. 2 and 3) are most suitable for square

Fig. 10.—Method of Making Bandings of Two Kinds of Wood

or oblong panels or surfaces. In that shown by Fig. 2 only two kinds of wood are used. A part of the design which is shown by Fig. 3 is shown again to an enlarged scale by Fig. 9. Three kinds of wood are employed to execute this design.

Various forms of inlaid stringings and bandings are often used ; but that most commonly met with simply consists of a strip of one kind of wood. Other kinds of bandings consist of two, or even three, kinds of wood made up in geometrical patterns. The method employed to make up these kinds of bandings is illustrated in Fig. 10, which shows a banding composed of a number of oblong pieces of two kinds of wood. A number of strips are first cut and glued up edge to edge, a dark and light strip being used alternately. When the glue is dry, one edge is planed straight and square, and strips of the width required for the banding are cut from the edge as shown. To allow for the insertion of the stringings and bandings, the wood is routered away to the required depth, and they are glued into the groove and well pressed in position.

In inlaying a small geometrical design, similar to that shown by Fig. 4, to the centre of a panel, the inlay should first be built up on a piece of paper as already described for the other designs ; the outer edges should then be scribed round, and the wood routered away in a similar manner.

A router suitable for the purpose might be purchased from any tool merchant, but a very simple home-made tool is shown by Fig. 11. It consists of a wood stock

to which a cutter and iron fence are fitted. The stock should be of beech, about 11 in. long by 2 in. wide and 1 in. deep in the centre, handles being formed at each end as shown. The iron fence is shown by Fig. 12. A slot is formed in the centre, and it is secured and adjusted on the stock by means of a bolt and fly-nut. It will be found advisable to provide a number of cutters of various widths as shown by Fig. 13. The cutter passes through a slot cut in the middle of the stock, and is held in position with a wedge as shown in Fig. 11.

Marquetry Cutting.—The method of inlaying by cutting the pattern in several veneers at one operation, and afterwards letting one into the other, is one that allows much greater freedom and elaboration of design than can be obtained by inlaying in the solid. The wonderful work of the French craftsmen during the periods of Louis XIV. and XV. affords striking evidence of the possibilities of the craft in the hands of a capable worker. The furniture of this period reached a degree of richness and beauty that has never been surpassed, the work of known craftsmen such as Riesener being preserved as national treasures in both the London Wallace collection and the Jones collection at the Victoria and Albert Museum. The designs are chiefly floral forms worked

Fig. 11.—Simple Router

Fig. 12.—Fence   Fig. 13.—Cutters
for Router

up by means of shading and the introduction of grained pieces to produce a highly shaded effect, although in the later work the patterns partake frequently of a more conventional character. Of this later style, Figs. 14 and 15 are illustrations of the top and front of a lace-box in French marquetry, which gives very clearly an idea of the possibilities of the process. One ordinary length of time; while in the process under consideration, to the careful fret-worker, the work presents nothing out of the way to accomplish.

Fig. 14.

Fig. 15.

Figs. 14 and 15.—Top and Front of Box with Marquetry Decoration

will readily perceive that to inlay such a pattern as this in the solid would be an undertaking that would require an extra-

Veneers employed for marquetry are either saw-cut or knife-cut, the former being the thicker, and usually the better

o employ, though for a design in which many woods are employed the thinner veneers can be more conveniently used. n commercial work, marquetry sawing is

8 in. wide, the seat being 1 ft. 8 in. from the ground.

In carrying out a design in marquetry a full-size drawing requires to be made

Fig. 16.—Marquetry-cutter's Stock

Fig. 17.—Method of Sawing

one on a long stool that is commonly alled a "donkey." This is illustrated y Fig. 16, the worker sitting astride it, ne wood being gripped in the vice at the nd, which can be tightened at will by the ressure of the foot on the treadle under- eath. The chief advantage of such an ppliance lies in the fact that the work un be released for turning about, for onvenience of cutting, by just relaxing

first with the woods that are going to be employed marked clearly thereon for reference. The sheets of veneer that represent the different varieties of wood in the design are then glued together, with a sheet of brown paper interposed between each, to allow of easy separation after- wards. Thin glue only should be employed, and it will be found best to arrange to set the grain of each piece alternately in

Fig. 18.—Detail Design of Front of Box (Fig. 15)

e pressure of the foot. The stool, as ill be seen, is of such simple construc- on that the home-worker could easily ut it together. It is 2 ft. 4 in. long and

opposite directions, so as to minimise curling when dry. Some form of press is necessary in marquetry at this stage, and also for later operations. An old-fashioned linen or similar form of press serves admirably ; but failing the possession of such an article, a couple of hand-screws will be necessary. The work is set between two pieces of hardwood, technically termed cauls, that are gripped together by two or more of these screws. One-inch mahogany is best for the purpose, as this wood is less liable to warp than others. A simple method of clamping up, dispensing with the hand-screws, is by means of two battened pieces of hardwood that are tightened up with four stout bolts and nuts.

The sheets of veneer, after gluing together, require to be screwed up tightly by one or other of these means, so that every portion of each sheet shall come in actual contact with the next one, otherwise the woods will be liable to split in the sawing. After drying, a tracing of the pattern is pasted to the uppermost sheet, to serve as a guide in the sawing. An ordinary fret-saw frame is sufficient for the amateur worker's requirements, one with sufficient sweep being necessary to cover the whole sheet. In commercial work a fixed saw is often used, the work being moved about so that it cuts along the lines of the pattern required. The fewest possible number of holes should be made for the reception of the saw, which requires to be very fine. Fig. 17 shows the normal position of the worker's hands during the sawing. The design that is being cut is a reproduction of that on the front of the box (Fig. 15), an enlarged outline of which is given by Fig. 18. In this particular design there are a few pieces only that will become detached before the sawing out is completed ; but whatever sections are required, these need to be carefully placed on one side. When all the sawing is completed, the next thing is to separate the sections. This can usually be done by inserting the thin blade of a knife at the edges where they join, and so split the paper. In case of any difficulty, as in the instance of fragile delicate shapes, the best plan is to put the work in the press for some hours, between several thicknesses of damp blotting or old newspaper, when they can

very easily be separated. The portion in the woods required are retained and fitted into the other parts ; then the next process is to glue down to a solid ground.

It will be found by far the best plan to employ a good wood for the foundation for which purpose Honduras mahogany is considered the most suitable. White wood and yellow pine is sometimes used for common work ; but it is liable to give trouble when gluing hardwoods to it, as the softer material absorbs more of the glue. Resinous woods, such as yellow deal and pitch-pine, must never be used.

When the pattern is somewhat intricate and in many sections, the different portions are frequently placed over the working design and secured with very fine pins in their correct position. The upper surface of the whole is then given a coating of thin glue, and a sheet of paper pressed down over the pins, in actual contact everywhere with the veneers, and allowed to dry. After this the pins may be removed, and the complete design can then be very readily glued to the foundation wood. In doing this the veneer as well as the ground should be glued, and when laid in place be covered with a few sheets of newspaper to prevent it sticking to the press. Care must be taken to obtain an even pressure all round, to ensure all the superfluous glue being squeezed out the work being left in the press until quite dry. In cases where white or very light coloured woods are employed in a design the glue should be whitened with powdered flake white, so that it does not show a very conspicuous mark round the edges the forms.

When dry the work should be taken from the press, and the paper that covers the surface of the pattern removed with a steel cabinet-scraper. A smoothing plane, the iron of which has been very finely set, can be employed for a start in the case of the thicker veneers ; but when they are very thin the scraper alone should be used. The direction of stroke of the scraper should, of course, be varied to suit the direction of grain of the inlay

EXAMPLES OF INLAID AND MARQUETRY WORK

Inlaid Photograph Frame. — As an elementary piece of veneering and inlaying the photograph frame shown by Fig. 19 will be found to be an instructive as well as an interesting piece of work. As the

execution. The method of solid inlaying may be adopted, or veneers may be used. If veneers are used the worker has a wider choice of colours, and three or four or even a greater number could be introduced. If three colours are used, one should be used for the flower and bamboos, one for the stems, leaves, etc., and the remaining

Fig. 19.—Inlaid Photograph Frame

surfaces to be covered are quite small, little difficulty will be experienced in laying the veneers ; but at the same time several processes are involved which may be applied to larger work. It will be observed that the frame outline is very simple.

The design allows for much variety in

one for the background. If four colours are used, the leaves could be separated from the stems, and the centre of the flower could be a different colour from the petals.

The most appropriate wood for the background would be rosewood, padouk, or dark walnut. Oak or satinwood could be used for the stems and leaves, and holly for the flower and bamboos. The veneers used should be about $\frac{1}{16}$ in. thick, and they must be glued to a $\frac{3}{16}$-in. background, which should, preferably, be of mahogany. The background may be cut from a piece of wood 8 in. by $6\frac{1}{2}$ in., and should be marked out as shown in Fig. 20. When the veneers have been cut and fitted they are glued in position on the background, and the work should be cramped between two boards until the glue is dry. It would be a good plan to leave the shaping

opening and the outer shape being left until last.

Another method would be to simply overlay the ornament. In this case the ornamental parts are cut from $\frac{1}{16}$-in. wood, and are glued to a $\frac{3}{16}$-in. background.

The back of the frame is made up as shown in Fig. 22. Small fillets, to allow the photograph and glass to be inserted, and a wood back are fitted behind the opening, being fixed in position with screws, as shown in Fig. 23. A strut or leg is hinged to the wood back to support

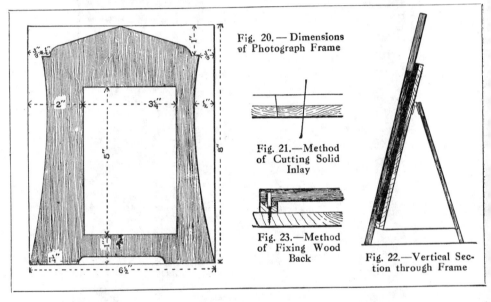

Fig. 20. — Dimensions of Photograph Frame

Fig. 21.—Method of Cutting Solid Inlay

Fig. 23.—Method of Fixing Wood Back

Fig. 22.—Vertical Section through Frame

of the background until after the veneers are glued in position.

In the case of solid inlaying, the light wood for the inlay is cut directly into the dark background. Wood $\frac{3}{16}$ in. thick should be used. and the cutting, which is done with a fret-saw, should be on the bevel, as shown in Fig. 21. The two boards are cut together, and great care must be taken to work the bevel in the right direction. The piece which is going to be inserted must be undercut, so that it is wedge-shape with the thickest part of the wedge upwards. The whole of the inner portion of the frame should be cut and glued up first, the cutting of the

the frame, and a piece of tape is arranged between the back and strut.

Inlaid Finger-plates. — The photographic reproductions (Figs. 24 to 29) show a series of inlaid finger-plates. Figs. 24, 25 and 26 are of mahogany, inlaid with a satinwood line, and a centre of green sycamore with a conventional ornament in satinwood. Figs. 27, 28 and 29 are of ebony.

For making the groove for the satinwood line a scratch-tool gauge is used. A level piece of board is fixed on the bench to work on and the plate is put on with two small screws through the holes. Although this method is suitable for straight lines,

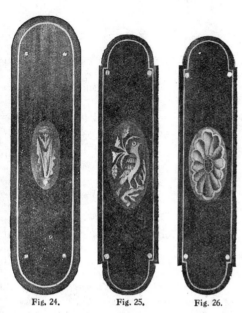

Fig. 24.   Fig. 25.   Fig. 26.

Figs. 24, 25 and 26.—Inlaid Finger-plates with Rounded Ends

it is hardly practicable for completing the grooves across the grain round the circular ends ; but it will scribe an impression if used carefully. To do this, one of the screws must be taken out to allow the end to overhang, and the impression is made the required depth by scraping out with a $\frac{1}{16}$-in. chisel. When the groove is completed, the centre oval is to be put in. These when bought are always glued on paper to keep them from getting broken in handling. They are inlaid with the paper side out, to be cleaned off. To get the oval in true position, a pencil line is marked lengthwise through the centre to correspond with a similar line on the plate. The mark is cut to the required depth with the sharp point of a knife, and the waste pared away with a chisel. It can be made quite level by reversing the chisel and scraping. The inlay should lie in nearly level ; just a shade high to allow for scraping to a clean surface. The plate is shown at this stage by Fig. 30, ready for gluing in the inlay.

The glue must be quite hot, sufficiently strong, but not thick, and the work should be done quickly in a warm place. In the case of the curved satinwood line, a length of the satinwood is necessary about 1 in. longer than will go right round. There will have to be one join where the two ends meet, which must be on the straight. The line is well-brushed over with glue, and worked round into the groove as quickly as possible, pressing it in with a hammer, the end being nipped off with the point of a knife to make the join.

To glue in the " oval centre," the paper side must be wetted with a rag dipped in hot water and the other side glued, also the sunk place on the plate, and it is put in immediately and pressed over with the hammer to force out the surplus glue. It must be fully assured that no part is inclined to rise before it is put away in a dry place to set.

A rub over with linseed oil will greatly improve the colours of the woods, and show up to advantage the varying shades in the grain of the mahogany. When there is time, it is best to leave them a few days after being oiled, before polishing.

Inlaid Trays.—Figs. 31 and 32 show two modern trays of French manufacture

Fig. 27.   Fig. 28.   Fig. 29

Figs. 27, 28 and 29.—Inlaid Finger-plates with Shaped Ends

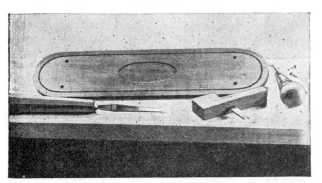

Fig. 30.—Finger-plate Ready for Inlay

narrow strip is fixed (by means of small screws) at the bottom of this framing all round, for the bottom to rest on. One face of the strip for the ends will require to be planed at a slight slant. The ends of the tray bottom require to be finished off similarly, so as to obtain a good fit.

A tray that would probably stand wear better than the foregoing would be obtained by carrying the tenons right through the ends, and then securing with hardwood pegs, in which case the bottom could very well be grooved into the sides and ends.

in the South Kensington Museum, which are considered quite the finest in this style of work that has been produced, not only in the beauty of their inlays, but in the general design and construction, which is of the simplest. The superb inlays are such, of course, that would need a practised hand to undertake ; but the construction, as will be described, is such that even an ordinary worker could produce an article on similar lines.

The inlaid tray shown by Fig. 31 is of quite simple construction. Two sides are cut with a short tenon at each extremity that fits into the ends of tray which are set slightly slanting. Then a

The rim of the tray shown by Fig. 32 is obtained by preparing a curved moulding in four parts, the moulding being of any suitable section and being grooved for fitting round the bottom of the tray.

Should a difficulty arise in obtaining the wood of a suitable width for the bottom, two boards will require to be butted together with the greatest care, so that the joining line is practically imperceptible. Three channels should be cut in the under side of the bottom across the grain for

Fig. 31.—Inlaid Tray with Plant Design

the purpose of letting in three hardwood strips ; these are to prevent the material warping. On drying, the bottom is planed quite level, and then the inlaying on the face of the work is proceeded with.

Chessboard in Marquetry. — For the art of marquetry, perhaps no more suitable object could be found for decoration than a chessboard, which is in itself a decorative object, since the checkers of the board represent the very simplest form of contrast. Moreover, wood is the most natural material to employ for this purpose, and is, as a matter of fact,

Fig. 32.—Inlaid Tray with Butterfly and Flower Design

Fig. 33.—Chessboard in Marquetry Inlay

generally employed, though other substances have been used.

The "game and playe of the chesse" is so ancient that any association with it and the ultra-modern developments of decorative art seems out of place. A suggestion is therefore given for a border treatment of the board in Italian arabesque of the simpler kind, fairly easy to cut, and to be worked in some lighter coloured wood than the checkers, so that the play may not be confused by any extraneous ornament asserting itself too strongly (see Fig. 33). It would be possible, of course, to .decorate the checkers also without destroying the contrast between the black and white. Indeed, this has been done by means of inlay in the blacks and engraving in the whites, forming an extremely rich effect. This, however, would necessitate a considerable degree of skill, while the present decorative scheme is fairly easy of attainment.

As regard material, the whole board with its border may be done in ebony and ivory, though this would be expensive. An alternative treatment would be ebony and whitewood, with some wood of medium strength of colour, such as mahogany, canary, or box, for the background of the ornament. The range of wood veneers is, however, a wide one. There is also an almost endless variety of dyed veneers.

The veneers must be fastened firmly together for the process of cutting. This may be done by means of placing glued paper between them; but it is sometimes difficult to separate the pieces afterwards. A better way, in certain circumstances, is to fasten them with small wire nails, placing sheets of greased paper between each veneer.

It will be obvious that in a design of this character the ornament and groundwork will be cut at one operation, the two pieces afterwards fitting exactly. Therefore in fastening the veneers together place the coloured woods alternately.

Box in Marquetry.—The box illustrated by Fig. 34 is of the simplest possible construction, as perfectly plain spaces are the most suited to marquetry ornamentation. The opening of the lid is at the line immediately above the keyhole. The feet may be attached either by means of glue or small screws. In this instance also, as in the case of the

Fig. 34.—Box in Marquetry Inlay

chessboard, the principal ornamental *motif* is made to repeat thereby effecting a saving of labour. There are, therefore, six panels of the same design for the back and sides, with two others for the top.

![Letter-case decorated with marquetry]

Fig. 35.—Letter-case Decorated with Marquetry

Although it may seldom happen that practical workers discover much aptitude for original design, yet it may be pointed out that this art of marquetry inlay offers many opportunities to the craftsman for the carrying out of his own ideas and the exercise of his own individuality. Especially is this so in the case of the simpler geometrical patternings which form a distinctive feature of the art. The box illustrated has therefore been designed with the idea of combining the more simple geometrical forms with some foliated ornamental device almost equally simple.

Letter-case in Marquetry.

A letter-case, or cover for a blotter decorated with a marquetry panel in the centre, is shown by Fig. 35. The cover which would look very well in oak or walnut, $\frac{1}{4}$ in. or $\frac{3}{8}$ in. thick, has a canvas or leather bag, and also a simple inlaid border along the top and bottom. It is closed, when not in use, by means of a simple metal clasp.

The centre panel of the cover is intended to be executed in veneers the separate pattern for which is given by Fig. 36, a key to the woods employed being given underneath; these are ebony box, mahogany whitewood, and canary, the material employed being very thin, not more than $\frac{1}{32}$ in., which is the usual thickness of veneer.

All the veneers are cut out at the one sawing, so that the sections forming the mosaic exactly fit one another. It will be found the best to saw away the outside

	CANARY
	WHITEWOOD
	MAHOGANY
	BOX
	EBONY

Fig. 36.—Pattern of Centre Panel of Letter-case

sections first, consisting of the background, lower part of the blotter, and sleeve, before proceeding with the inner details. It is unnecessary to drill any holes for the reception of the saw, as in all cases, with the exception of the features which will be dealt with later, all the cutting can be started from the sides. In this connection, it may be noted that in cutting out the letters on the background, a saw-cut may be made connecting them, as this will not be perceptible in the finished work. As each section is sawn out it is placed on the working drawing in its proper position ; then, when all the sawing is done, proceed to separate the layers.

Next prepare the boards forming the back and front covers, the shape of the centre part being marked out in the centre of the one forming the front. This space has next to be sunk very slightly to receive the veneers. Make a chisel or knife-cut all round, then break the grain inside with the chisel and remove the waste, making the depression an equal depth throughout, that is the thickness of the veneer, and then make level all over.

In inlaying spaces so large as this, after the ground has been levelled all over, it is sometimes pricked with a pointed tool at intervals, to form a better attachment for the glued veneers, which are now fitted, and then glued in and placed under a weight to harden.

In the execution of the features, the thin dark parts shown in the working pattern are carefully cut away in the sawing, the very fine grooves left in the work being filled in with dark wax after the sections have been glued in their place, and then scraped flat.

The top and bottom borders are now proceeded with, careful cutting of the alternate light and dark triangles, with the underneath sections, being indispensable, together with the accurate marking and chiselling out of the recesses to receive them. When they have been glued in and have hardened go over the whole with a smoothing-plane, the iron of which has been very finely set, then finish with a cabinet scraper.

There now remain the corners to be rounded off and the canvas back to be cut and secured with small round-headed brass nails the shanks of which have been cut short ; or another way would be to thin the edges of the leather with a knife, making a slight cut down the covers where they are glued on, and a thin shaving off all the way down, so that the edge of the leather is on a level with the wood and then does not easily become caught and torn up.

The brass clasp is of very simple design, and includes a catch bent up of wire that hooks on a brass pin inserted in the back of the cover. The inside of the letter-case is lined with a suitably coloured leather paper, and pockets or straps are included to hold the stationery according to requirements.

Woodcarving

WOODCARVING is classed as one of the arts, but it is an art in the exercise of which a more than usual amount of manipulative skill is called for in addition to the possession of artistic feeling.

The object of this section is to teach the craftsmanship side of the subject only, and for this purpose the whole of the progressive processes employed in carving a panel will be detailed, and later examples of incised and pierced carving.

As a preliminary, a brief consideration of the woods used and the tools employed in carving will be made.

Woods Used for Carving.—There are dozens of varieties of wood that can be carved, but it will be found that in ordinary woodcarving use is not made of more than about sixteen different kinds. These sixteen are favourites because their structure is such that the carver's tools leave a clean, sharp cut, or because their grain is so straight as to enable the wood to be worked with the least amount of trouble and risk of splitting. All woods used for carving must be thoroughly seasoned, and where time and convenience allow it is desirable for the carver himself to stock the wood for a year or two, so that when using it he can be sure that it is thoroughly dry. The woods in most general use are oak, Italian and American walnut, lime, holly, pearwood, chestnut and mahogany. Bog-oak is often used for carving, and in Ireland the carving of this wood is one of the peasant industries, the work produced being small but of good quality. Bog-oak is so called from the fact that it is found embedded in the decaying vegetable matter of the bogs, and the oak itself has often entered on the first stage of putrefaction. Other suitable woods are sycamore, satinwood, sandalwood, boxwood and ebony, but these are not used to the same extent as those mentioned first.

Tools.—Woodcarving tools are varied in shape, both in length and in section, but they can be classified into various types.

The classification here adopted is as follows : The tools are divided into four types, referable to the shape of their stems, namely (*a*) straight tools, (*b*) curved or bent tools, (*c*) spoon-bit tools, and (*d*) tools of special shape. Types *a*, *b*, and *c* are shown by Figs. 1 to 4, and type *d* by Figs. 5 and 6.

Type *a* consists of those tools which are, viewed from the edge, quite straight. They are, of course, of various sections, and are used for all ordinary work. Indeed, it is only necessary to supplement this type when doing special work, such as under-cutting, pierced work, carving that is in high relief, or work which requires to be deeply sunk from the surface. These tools can be obtained either of the ordinary shape as regards their width, as in Fig. 7, or as spade tools (Fig. 8). They also can be had shouldered (Fig. 9) or unshouldered (Fig. 10).

Type *b* consists of tools so shaped (*see*

Fig. 2) as to enable them to flow easily along internal or concave curves. It is obvious that a tool quite straight in its length would always have the line of pressure

Fig. 1.—First Type Carving Tool

Fig. 2.—Second Type Carving Tool

at too acute an angle with the grain; and if the tool made any progress at all, it would move in a series of jumps, which would leave a rough and uneven surface. But by bending the tool the line of force is directed in such a manner that it leaves the tool free to move along the surface in a way that allows the edge to cut evenly.

The above description also applies to tools of type c (Figs. 3 and 4), which, however are so shaped that they can cut curves of greater depth and less radius, thus working in less space.

Type d (Figs. 5 and 6) are tools which are of quite a special nature, and can be used only for a specific purpose. All these types can be had either shouldered or unshouldered, and type a can b had as spade tools, in addition to the ordinary shape (see Fig. 8). It is recommended that only shouldered tools should be used. They are stronger and far more serviceable than the others (see Figs. 9 and 10). An

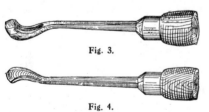

Fig. 3.

Fig. 4.

Figs. 3 and 4.—Third Type Carving Tools

objection to unshouldered tools is that the tang drives into the handle without any check, and almost invariably splits it.

The various sections of carving tool are shown in Fig. 11. The tools are made in widths varying from $\frac{1}{32}$ in. to $1\frac{1}{2}$ in. and 2 in. The choice of tools suitable fo

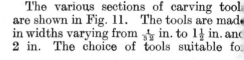

Fig. 5.

Fig. 6.

Figs. 5 and 6.—Fourth Type Carving Tools

general work or to any particular class o work is a matter needing much judgmen and care.

Tool handles vary in size, in shape, an in the kind of wood from which they ar made. They are known and regulated by the size of the ferrule, and vary from $\frac{3}{8}$ in. outside diameter of the ferrule to $\frac{5}{8}$ in. The woods most generally used fo tool handles are box, rosewood. beech hornbeam, and mahogany. Of these. bo and beech are the most lasting. Al handles should be ferruled, and the handl itself should be about $\frac{3}{8}$ in. thicker than the ferrule. The length of a handl should be $4\frac{1}{2}$ in. or 5 in. If longer, they are, except for the very large tools, clumsy and awkward to use. If shorter, there i much loss of power in using them. A goo plan in selecting handles for a set of tool is to have them in various woods, and marked distinctly with respect to th

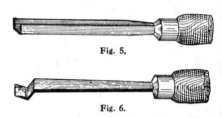

Fig. 7.—Ordinary Chisel

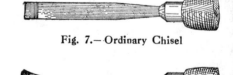

Fig. 8.—Spade Chisel

position and number of the rings that ar often turned on them. If all are of the sam wood, they can be stained in differen colours; the object being to enable th worker to distinguish the tools easily when they lie grouped together.

Fig. 9.   Fig. 10.

Figs. 9 and 10.—Shouldered and Unshouldered Tools

Fig. 11.—Cutting Edges and Sections of Carving Tools

It is important to have the handle fixed to the blade in a proper manner. The tools are generally bought with the handle fixed. But even then it is advisable to know when the tool is handled in a business-like manner. To begin with, in most cases the blade should be in perfect alignment with the handle. Especially is this the case with the setting-in tools. It is not so much a necessity with V-tools and fluters, because the force transmitted through these tools does not, as a rule, proceed in a perfectly straight line, but moves in the direction of a curve. A tool whose blade is so fixed in the handle that it forms a concave curve on its face side is often of greater advantage in getting round a concave curve than one in which the blade is in perfect alignment with the handle. But in all tools to which force has to be applied by other means than mere hand pressure, the blade must be fixed quite straight. To retain all the force given by the mallet, it is necessary that it should be directed by the shortest possible route, which is a straight line.

Other necessary tools are mallets and cramps. All roughing out should be done with the mallet, and bosses, cornices, and other work intended to be fixed at a height from the eye should invariably be finished with the mallet. When the carver is engaged on these classes of work the mallet should never leave his hand; for the cut left by the chisel with the mallet behind it is always the most effective when

looked up at from the ground. Further, by the free and continuous use of the mallet the work is got over in half the time it would otherwise take.

It is a general practice of wood-carvers to use the half-closed palm of the hand as a sort of mallet, and for light work this is a good custom, although its continued practice eventually results in a deformation of the hand.

Supplementary tools are punches, files,

LIST OF WOOD-CARVERS' ESSENTIAL TOOLS

No. on Sheffield
Tool List.

No. 1.—Straight Chisel, $\frac{1}{4}$ in. wide, chiefly used for setting in.

No. 3.—Straight Gouge, $\frac{1}{16}$ in., $\frac{1}{8}$ in., and $\frac{1}{4}$ in. wide, for grounding small spaces.

No. 3.—   ,,   ,, $\frac{3}{8}$ in. wide.

No. 4.—   ,,   ,, $\frac{3}{8}$ in. wide, for setting in, grounding, and modelling.

No. 5.—   ,,   ,, $\frac{3}{16}$ in. and $\frac{5}{16}$ in. wide, for setting in and grounding.

No. 5.—   ,,   ,, $\frac{1}{2}$ in. wide, for setting in, grounding and modelling.

No. 7.—   ,,   ,, $\frac{3}{8}$ in. wide, for grounding and modelling.

No. 8.—   ,,   ,, $\frac{1}{8}$ in. and $\frac{1}{4}$ in. wide, for modelling.

No. 8.—   ,,   ,, $\frac{3}{4}$ in. wide, for grounding and modelling.

No. 11.—   ,,   ,, $\frac{3}{16}$ in. wide, for modelling.

No. 21.—Spoon-bit Chisel, Square, $\frac{1}{8}$ in., $\frac{3}{16}$ in., and $\frac{3}{8}$ in. wide for grounding.

No. 28.—Spoon-bit Gouge or Front-bent Gouge, $\frac{1}{4}$ in. and $\frac{1}{2}$ in. wide, for modelling.

No. 39.—Straight V-Parting Tool, $\frac{5}{16}$ in. wide, for outlining and modelling.

rasps, rifflers, and a few other tools which ordinarily have a place in the woodworker's kit.

Preliminary Work.—The first procedure is to select the piece of wood, cut it to a suitable size and plane it up. Next the design is traced on tracing (transparent) paper, pinned to the panel at one end, and the carbon paper placed underneath. It is then pinned at the other end, and the outline of the design traced over with a style or a hard pencil; the shading may be ignored. The work, which for the purpose of the present example is a panel design as shown by Fig. 12, is now ready to be tooled. The cut-out portions on each edge require taking out first. Fix the panel in the bench screw, and cut but a good wood-carver does as much work as is possible with his carving tools, and relies as little as he possibly can on tools that may be termed artificial aids.

The work is now secured to the carving

Fig. 12.—Design for Carved Panel *(see also Fig. 36, p. 1357)*

out the pieces with a bow saw close to the line (*see* Fig. 13). They will be rough from the saw, and this roughness will be removed by means of the carving tools. It may be thought that a spokeshave or a bull-nose plane would do this work better; bench, three methods being here mentioned. The first, and the one employed with this panel, is with carver's cramps. A piece of cardboard, thick leather, or paper should be used to prevent the cramp marking the surface of the wood. A second method, and one that has the advantage of leaving the whole surface of the panel quite clear and unencumbered, is the use of a carver's screw, which is screwed through a hole in the bench from the underside into the panel, and tightened with a wing-nut. A third method is by means of clips and screws which grip the edge of the panel, and are screwed into the bench top.

Fig. 13.—Photograph showing Preparatory and " Bosting in " Stages

Wasting Away.—The next process is known as " wasting away," " bosting in," " roughing out," etc. " Bosting in " consists in cutting away that part of the wood on which there is no design, and which when finished is known as the " ground." On this ground the design stands in relief.

First, the depth to which the ground is to be taken is decided upon. In this case the depth has been fixed at ⅜ in. It will be noticed that the margin is not raised, but consists of a chamfer taken from the level of the ground, as shown in Fig. 14,

which represents a section of the finished carving. Thus along the edge of the panel will be drawn two lines, B representing the depth of the ground, and A the depth of the chamfer (see Fig. 15).

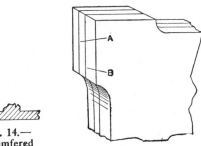

Fig. 14.— Chamfered Edge of Panel

Fig. 15.—Panel Marked for Depth of Ground, etc.

Now proceed to cut away the ground with the two gouges, taking short quick strokes, beginning so that each succeeding cut is with the grain. In this panel the first cut inside the design was made at the lower end, and the work proceeded upwards. This work of roughing out should be well done, each cut being made as though it were the final one, avoiding the temptation to permit slipshod work merely because it will be subject to further tooling.

Fig. 13 shows the " bosting in " carried out from one side only; the other part of the panel will be done from the other side when the panel is turned round. The uncut half shows the design traced on in outline only. It will be seen that the cuts are made obliquely across the grain. Do not cut with the grain if it can possibly

Fig. 16.—Making Sloping Cut

Fig. 17.—Beginning the Cut

be avoided; a uniform depth is more easily maintained by cutting across. Make all the cuts a uniform depth as far up to the design as possible. When the tool is used at an ordinary angle, as in

Fig. 16, a sloping cut is made. To make the cut that is necessary, hold the tool nearly perpendicular at the beginning of the stroke, as in Fig. 17.

The value of the photographic illustrations is enhanced because of the way

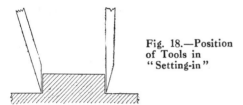

Fig. 18.—Position of Tools in "Setting-in"

in which the various stages are linked together. Thus in Fig. 13 two stages are shown : the preparatory stage and the "bosting in." Next is shown the "bosting in " and the "setting in."

The following are the materials and tools used to get the panel up to the stage shown in Fig. 13 : Panel in oak, 16⅞ in. by 12³⁄₁₆ in. by ¾ in., and to plane and square up this panel, a jackplane, tryplane, rule and square. For tracing the design : Tracing paper, carbon paper, H pencil or style, drawing pins, and straightedge. For cutting out : Bow saw, carving tools No. 5 by ⅜ in., and No 4 by ⅝ in. Cramps, screw, or slips, and carving tools No. 8 by ¼ in. and No. 7 by ⅜ in. are also wanted.

Setting In.—The " roughing out " may now be continued over the whole panel, to get it ready for " setting in." This consists of cutting along the edge of the design vertically, down to the depth required for the groundwork.

The tools required, in addition to those specified for the first stage of the work, are a mallet and the following carving tools : No. 3 by ¼ in. ; No. 3 by ⅜ in. ; No. 4 by ¼ in. ; No. 4 by ⅝ in. ; No. 5 by ³⁄₁₆ in., and No. 6 by ⅜ in.

In " setting in " the definite form of outline is given to the design. Hitherto it has been more or less vague and shadowy, suggestive only ; now it is being carried a step farther, giving it definition and clearness.

The tools used may be applied either side to the outline, the chief requirement

being that of fitting the curve accurately. Much care must be exercised on this part of the work.

In cutting a concave curve, such as the inside edge of the stalk, a tool slightly " quicker " in curve than the curve of the stalk should be used. This is to prevent the corners of the tool cutting into the stalk. One object that should be kept in view is to use as few tools as possible, within reason, of course. A multiplication of tools is confusing and inconvenient, and time is wasted in trying to find a tool that exactly fits any particular curve. A narrow tool is preferable to a wide one, and many light, continuous blows to one heavy " dead " blow.

The value of the " wasting away "

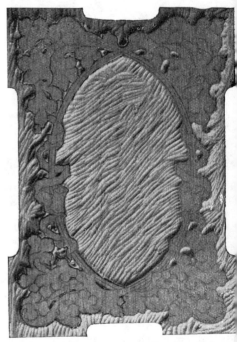

Fig. 19.—Photograph showing Panel after " Setting-in "

process will be evident by the ease with which the " setting in " is done, and the manner in which the chips fall away from the design, showing that the lateral pressure is proceeding in that direction, and not through the design itself, where would tend to damage that portion through which it passed. Some of the smaller indentations on the design may be passed by, and a major cut made including these, and this arrangement will stand until all the surplus wood has been taken away to form the ground. This procedure saves the outstanding and thinner parts of the design whilst the heavy work of cutting the ground is proceeding.

In " setting in " hold the tool so that the face nearest the design is inclined slightly towards the design, as in Fig. 18. In one case is shown the tool with its front face to the design, and in the other the back face (the ground surface) to the design. Note that it is the face of the tool, and

Fig. 20.—Photograph showing Panel " Set in " and " Ground Out "

not the tool itself, that should be slightly inclined towards the design. Set in to a uniform depth, and with a continuous cut, not in separate attempts, which produce a ragged edge. Connect all the cuts made into a continuous whole by inserting the corner of the tool into each preceding cut.

Throughout the whole work make those cuts which lie across the grain before those cuts are taken with the grain. This is to prevent undue splitting, especially of the corners. Fig. 19 shows the panel after the " setting in " has been done.

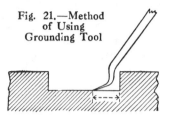

Fig. 21.—Method of Using Grounding Tool

The next stage is that of " grounding."

Grounding.—As shown in the photograph (Fig. 19) the panel is shown with one half " set in." the other half being " wasted away." In Fig. 20 the whole of the panel is shown " set in " and one-half " grounded out." This grounding is shown in various stages. The lower part of the panel is shown with the ridges left by the " wasting away " process, just taken off with a No. 5 gouge. The upper part shows the ground-work taken to a level surface. This is also shown well in the centre part of the panel. Six tools are used to cut the ground. Their sizes and the number of curve are : No. 3 by $\frac{1}{16}$ in. ; No. 3 by $\frac{1}{8}$ in. ; No. 4 by $\frac{1}{4}$ in. ; No. 3 by $\frac{3}{8}$ in. ; No. 5 by $\frac{3}{8}$ in., and a $\frac{1}{8}$-in. tool known as a " grounding tool." It is curved near the cutting edge to enable it to cut a larger surface than a straight-bladed tool can ; and to do this it has to be held more perpendicularly than the ordinary tool. Fig. 21 shows the angle at which it should be held. Notice the respective distances of the cutting edge from the wall of the carving lying immediately behind when the tools are placed in their cutting position.

Special attention is called to the fact of the tools being flat in section. For " wasting away " the tools used were quick gouges. These made deep cuts with sharp ridges between. The tools now used have to flatten the ground by reducing these ridges. The first tool used is the quickest of the six—the No. 5 curve by $\frac{3}{8}$ in. wide. This speedily brings the ridges down to a more or less level surface. Judgment as well as skill in tool manipulation are here necessary, because a stronger cut than usual will make the tool dip below the general ground level.

Some carvers use a router at this stage. It consists of a flat piece of wood, through which is fixed a cutting iron nearly at right angles to the wood, and projecting under to the depth it is proposed to take the ground. This tool, well used, ensures a perfectly level surface. It is certainly a saver of time and labour. If a router is used a little depth should be left to cut down with the carving tools, to get a tooled surface finish.

There are only three curved tools : the one already mentioned (No. 5) and a flatter one (No. 3), and one between, a No. 4. Of No. 3 curve there are three tools of varying widths, from $\frac{1}{16}$ in. to $\frac{3}{8}$ in. ; this is to fit the varying spaces. The No. 4 curve tool is for use in some of the smaller spaces ; being a little more curved, its corners do not catch in the wood and make a nasty cut. It is a mistake to suppose that a quite flat tool (No. 1 on a tool list) is necessary to finish off the ground. It is not necessary to get a surface that is as flat and smooth as a surface finished with a plane, and, moreover, a No. 1 tool is much too difficult a tool to use to get such a surface, because of its corners catching in the wood. A wide surface such as in this panel is a good test of a carver's ability, because it is rather difficult to keep uniformly level. The general tendency is to leave it raised in the centre.

In cutting the centre, begin at the edges and work the wood down towards the centre. It is possible that the " setting in " has not been done deeply enough, and the chips do not come off quite clean, a ragged edge being left where the horizontal cut is deeper than the vertical incision. This must be re-set in ; in fact it is rather a good plan to go over the outline with the setting-in tools again very lightly, so that a sufficient depth is obtained for cleaning off to a smooth surface. It is as well not to put the final finish to the surface of the ground now,

as in the course of modelling the tool at some points cut up the surface, and this can be better dealt with by leaving a little depth for the final finishing.

Modelling.—" Modelling " is the term applied to the process of treating the hitherto flat surface of the design so that the variation of surface may produce effect. So far the work has been entirely mechanical. Anyone possessed of an average manual dexterity may do the " wasting away," " setting in " and the " grounding," quite successfully and without trouble or difficulty. But for " modelling " higher faculties than mere manual skill are brought into operation. Successful modelling is only possible to a mind ripened and cultivated by an art training.

Every carver must understand what is meant by the term " modelling," and what the real object is, in so treating the plain surface of the design. It is, as previously stated, to produce an effect ; but the real question is, " What kind of an effect is it good to produce ? " An answer to this can be made in a general manner ; much must be left to each individual operator. But a few words of advice are possible and, always bearing in mind their general and not too close and particular application, they are now given. It will be noticed that the design, although obviously based on a natural form, is yet only approximately like it. In using this natural form as material for the building of the design, the type has been altered in shape according to the laws governing convention in the art. These laws require, most of all, that the type chosen as the motif must be altered to conform (1) to the requirements of the material, and (2) to the necessities of the space available for the ornament. It is obviously impossible for a spray of leaves to be taken from the tree on which it grows to fit a space of the shape of panel with symmetry, order and fitness ; hence requirement No. 2.

It is equally impossible, although perhaps not so generally recognised, that a natural form can be faithfully reproduced in such a material as wood in its entirety ; hence requirement No. 1. Therefore, as nature cannot be followed in the treatment of the design, the carver's own ideas must necessarily be followed. It is here that infinite possibilities of good work and of bad work open up. The artistic mind will recognise that something more than clean,

clever, smooth cutting is required. The mechanical type of mind can see the necessities of the form only, and produces a work that is altogether lacking in life and nervous vigour. The consideration of this leads to the knowledge that to model work correctly there must be some perception of what are the leading features or characteristics of the natural form used in the design and emphasise them. As already mentioned, each mind differs in its interpretation of design ; and it is therefore obvious that varied results can be obtained from the same design. The treatment given here is a suggestion only. Keen observation, close comparison, and the use of intelligent thought will keep the work within the limits of reason and fitness.

The tools necessary for getting the modelling of this panel up to the stage shown in Fig. 22 are a $\frac{3}{16}$ in. No. 5 ; $\frac{1}{8}$ in. No. 6 ; $\frac{1}{4}$ in. No. 8 ; $\frac{1}{8}$ in. No. 4 ; $\frac{1}{4}$ in. No. 4, and a $\frac{1}{4}$ in. No. 39. First go over the design very carefully for any correction that may be necessary in its outlines. Then carefully consider those parts that must be lower than the remainder, such as the stalks, the underlying parts of the leaves, where a part of the leaf turns over. This should be done with judgment, to get all these lower parts to their approximate ultimate level. Approximate is stated because these levels will have to be varied from the first result, because of the effect produced by the treatment of the leaves. This latter causes a different value to be given to the underlying parts as the work proceeds. The top right-hand corner of the panel shows the work at this stage.

In treating the stalk, take note of the tendency to dip it too suddenly where it disappears under a fold of the ribbon or a leaf, producing an effect, when looked at in side elevation, as shown in Fig. 23, and avoid it. The true treatment should be as in Fig. 24 ; the stalk almost level, or with the slightest perceptible rise   Always

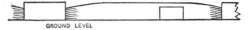

Fig. 23.—Section of Incorrect Method of Carving Underlying Stalk or Leaf

Fig. 24.—Section of Correct Method

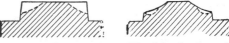

Fig. 25.—Section of Lobe in First Stage in Modelling

Fig. 26.—Section of Second Stage

throughout the modelling process look at the work from all possible points of view, what appears to be in good proportion and direction from some points may be quite wrong from others.

The next stage is to take the leaves

approximately to their ultimate shape. The lower right-hand corner shows this stage. The $\frac{1}{4}$ in. No. 4 tool is used first to lower the edges, then $\frac{1}{4}$ in. No. 8 to give the central prominences or bumps existence by cutting a hollow channel along the edges of the leaves and across the neck of each lobe. Fig. 25 shows a section of a lobe, with one side cut down with tool e. Fig. 26 shows this section still further reduced, this giving the centre of each lobe prominence. Fig. 27 gives a plan of one leaf, showing by dotted lines what is meant by cutting down the neck of each lobe. The panel should be treated up to this stage in all its parts before anything further is attempted. It will always be found better and more economical, as far as time is concerned, to work each stage in its entirety before proceeding to

Fig. 27.— Plan of Leaf

the next. Thus even if half a dozen panels were being carved at the same time, and providing there was sufficient bench room, it would be well to have them all cramped down and work the whole of them through each stage before proceeding to the next.

Fig. 28 shows a full-size detail of the entwined ribbon.

Fig. 29 shows the work carried much farther. This figure is, perhaps, the most valuable, as well as the most interesting, of the series. It shows in the top left corner the design "set in" ready for surface variation. In the top right corner this is advanced a stage and much of the lowering has been done. The lower left corner shows this taken farther still, and the lower right corner gives an illustration of the finished design. The ribbon work is taken to a stage just short of the finishing point. Thus in this illustration are

included all the stages relative to the process of "modelling." Such illustrations show much more clearly how the ultimate result is arrived at than any description possibly could. In fact, short of an actual demonstration, such an illustration shows the best possible methods that are employed in "modelling."

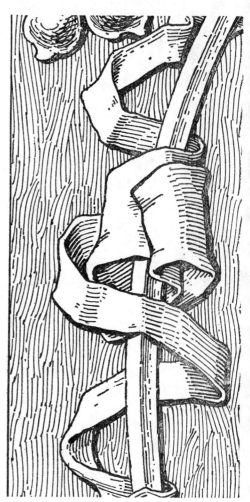

Fig. 28.—Full-size Detail of Entwined Ribbon Work

The tools actually used are a $\frac{1}{4}$ in. No. 4 ; $\frac{3}{16}$ in. No. 7 ; $\frac{1}{8}$ in. No. 7 ; $\frac{3}{8}$ in. No. 5 ; $\frac{1}{8}$ in. No. 3 ; $\frac{3}{16}$ in. No. 5 ; $\frac{5}{16}$ in. No. 3 ; $\frac{1}{4}$ in. No. 8 ; $\frac{1}{4}$ in. No. 39 ; $\frac{1}{4}$ in. No. 28. Most of them are small tools, that is, small in width. There is one type of tool introduced that is somewhat new ; that is the spoon-bit tool. This type has been used for grounding (No. 21 by $\frac{1}{8}$ in.) ; but

Fig. 29.—Photograph showing Portion Fully Modelled

that was flat in section. This tool for modelling is curved in section. Its use is necessitated by the deep and sudden cutting round and between the lobes of the leaves, to get the sudden contrasts between height and depression, between high light and deep shadow, necessary to good work.

The sudden dippings and equally sudden but graceful swellings give the life and vigour to the work. It is a very difficult matter to get the " bossiness " characteristic of Gothic work, which permanently influences this design, without thinness and mere " knobbiness." The elevations should swell gradually and broadly, not quickly and suddenly ; or they look thin and scraggy. They should be fat rather than lean. In modelling, the surface contour should be looked at from all points of view, so that it shall be as perfect as

possible. Not, bear in mind, perfect in finish, although this is desirable, but, rather, perfect in proportion of mass and grace of curve. Another point is that the elevations should not be thin and sudden, as shown in Fig. 30, which is a section of one of the lobes. The better section is given by Fig. 31, which shows a much fuller centre and much narrower channels cut on each side.

Another hint is to vary the contour so that a continuously varying play of light and shade is possible. Take the edge of a leaf, let it swell up from its source to its highest point, and sink again to its lowest point, with lesser variations, twists, and curls between. Subordinate the stalks,

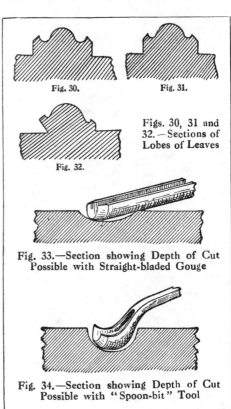

Fig. 30.

Fig. 31.

Figs. 30, 31 and 32.—Sections of Lobes of Leaves

Fig. 32.

Fig. 33.—Section showing Depth of Cut Possible with Straight-bladed Gouge

Fig. 34.—Section showing Depth of Cut Possible with " Spoon-bit " Tool

but make them clear and distinct and firm in outline and direction. Do not have all the leaves the same height, and do not give them equal values of light and shade.

Some may have their centres left high and their edges low, leaving a greater comparative height of centre lobe. Others may have only a slight difference between the highest point in the centre lobe and the lowest point in the edge, showing a slightly

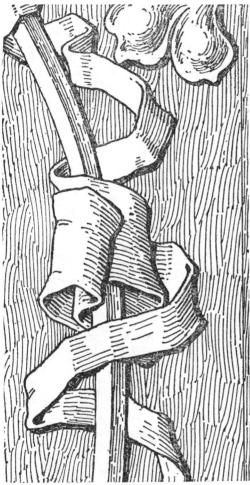

Fig. 35.—Full-size Detail of Entwined Ribbon Work

graduated swelling curve connecting the edge and the centre. The edges of many of the leaves, notably those edges that stand high, are slightly undercut. This gives a deeper shadow, which emphasises the value of the leaf, and by cutting away the visible " wall " of the leaf makes it

look lighter because now only the edge is plainly visible, and not the whole of the wood constituting the wall of the leaf. Fig. 32 shows how much undercutting is done.

In the whole of the modelling a clean, neat, light touch will be found to be absolutely essential. In the earlier portion of the work the hand and arm had a good deal of free play ; a fair amount of force could be used. In the modelling portion, the hand, arm, and fingers are not allowed any free play. Their actions are restrained by reason of their short-stroke, and by reason of the great variation of contour.

The spoon-bit gouges can work to a greater depth within a shorter distance than the ordinary straight-bladed gouge, as shown by Figs. 33 and 34. Fig. 33 shows the ordinary gouge working, and illustrates the depth that can be got with a definite length of stroke. Fig. 34 shows the same with regard to the spoon-bit gouge, and it can be seen that, because of the bend in the tool, the ratio of the depth of the cut to the length of the stroke is increased considerably. These tools are more difficult to use at first than are the straight-bladed tools, but practice will overcome this difficulty. A full-size detail of the entwined ribbon on the right-hand side of the panel is shown by Fig. 35.

The reproduction of a photograph (Fig. 36) shows the panel finished.

The tools required to finish the panel are just the same as already mentioned. Mention may be made of the spoon-bit tools and their scope and use. They are necessary in getting the hollows in the carving deep enough without extending the width of the cut. This cannot be done with the ordinary straight-bladed tool without so extending the width of the cut, and in addition cutting the surface roughly. This design has many deep depressions of small plan measurement, and their presence makes the spoon-bit tool a necessity. The object of these depressions is to get an effective play of light and shade. The depth gives blackness of shadow, and the high lights of the resulting prominences, contrasted with these, and combined with secondary shadows and half-tones, give an effect that is characteristic of fourteenth- and fifteenth-century Gothic carving.

A note of warning may be given here. Some students have a tendency to be done with a skilful use of the straight-bladed tool. To get the leaves to lie over effectively and produce good, strong curves and flowing surfaces, most of the edges are reduced nearly to the ground level.

Fig. 36.—Photograph showing Panel Completed

carried away with the value of the spoon-bit tool, and get many more tools of this kind than they will ever find a use for; some even get sets of these tools. Really only very few of these tools are necessary, and very much work of this kind may be But, necessarily, some of the leaf edges are raised, and if not otherwise treated, would show a comparatively high wall; this tends to a clumsy effect if left. To remedy this, the leaf edge is cut away far enough under to put it behind the line of vision or to just coincide with it. This lightens the edge of the leaf, intensifies the depth of shadow, and "lifts" the leaf off the ground.

In modelling the panel no part should be quite finished off before the rest is taken up to nearly finishing point. That is to say, the whole surface should be worked up in stages, these stages being applicable perfection of surface finish. Thus, in finishing the surface of the leaves, the eye should be on the level of the leaf, to see how nearly the surface curve fits the carver's idea of a good, sweeping, flowing curve. Test the curves of the raised "boss" in each lobe from all points of view, and note how the convex curves fit the concave curves and flow into them.

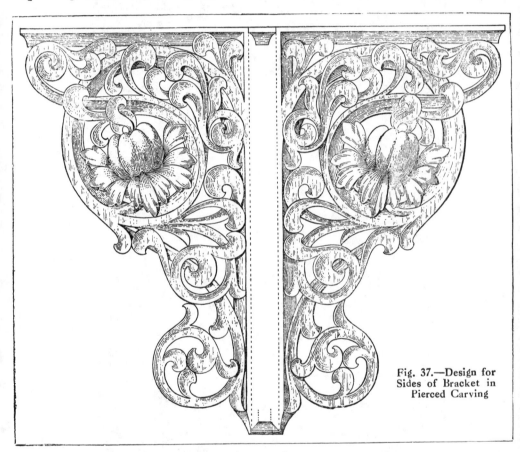

Fig. 37.—Design for Sides of Bracket in Pierced Carving

to the whole panel, one stage after another. This ensures a harmony and unity in the ultimate appearance that cannot be obtained by the treatment of finishing one part before the other portions are brought up to nearly finishing point. The degree of finish that is considered necessary differs in the opinion of different people naturally. Perfection of form is what should be aimed at rather than

A surface of this kind may have the tool marks left on it, only they are not so evident as to interfere with the perfection of form already mentioned. Without this perfection no amount of smooth surface finish can make a good job of the carving.

Before finally finishing the panel, place it at a distance of 5 ft. or 6 ft., in a good side light, and carefully note any lack of balance in the lights and shadows. There may be a little latitude allowed in the symmetry of the lights and shadows, providing this does not produce bad balance. But balance is the most important, and any transgressions of this essential principle of ornament should be rectified at once. The finish of the surface may then be proceeded with. When the carving is

Fig. 38.—Design for Centre Piece of Bracket in Pierced Carving

finished, no treatment other than waxing, or fuming and waxing, is necessary.

PIERCED CARVING

Pierced carving is well explained by its name. It is that form of carving which, instead of having a definite groundwork, has what would normally be the groundwork completely cut away with a saw.

What is left is the design, and this is modelled in the usual way.

Now, as wood is a material that is not equally strong across its width and along its length, it follows that this form of carving, which must necessitate the complete removal of much of the wood, needs to be employed with much judgment and restraint, or a result will follow that is weak both constructionally and artistically.

Some of the considerations that operate in deciding what are suitable designs, and what is the suitable treatment for pierced work, are as follows :

The pierced portions (which in ordinary relief carving is the ground) must not be too large in extent. As a precaution, and to see whether the ground spaces are too great, it is advisable to blacken them in with the pencil, and the design will give a better idea as to the suitability of these spaces as regards their size. The reason for this is that the pierced portions always give a blacker shadow than ordinary groundwork, and thus tend to bring themselves under notice, and, in consequence, appear to be bigger than they really are.

The amount of wood cut away need not necessarily be as large as the space shown on the design. A stalk, for instance, may for reasons of strength be quite thick at the back, and just thinned down to its normal thickness at the front edge.

The thickness of the wood makes for a greater appearance of relief in pierced work than in flat relief carving. This has to be kept in mind in conceiving the design, in respect, especially, to the balance and proportion that should exist between the various parts.

Figs. 37 and 38 show the design for a bracket. Later illustrations show photographs of a bracket in the various stages of the carving, and they will present a series of lessons only slightly less valuable than an actual demonstration of the work.

The first thing that has to be decided is the wood to use. Oak would be a very suitable wood for the execution of this particular example. The dimensions of the various pieces are : Two pieces for the back, 1 ft. 3½ in. by 9½ in. by ¾ in., one piece for the support, 1 ft. $3\frac{1}{2}$ in. by 8 in. by $\frac{3}{4}$ in. ; also one piece for the top (which is not carved), 2 ft. by 1 ft. by $\frac{3}{4}$ in. It will be seen that the back piece is made in two parts. This is because the wood is the more easily obtained in narrower than wider widths, and because it is much more easily worked in a narrow width. The two pieces are jointed together with a groove-and-tongue joint glued when the carving is finally completed. These pieces may, for economy, be cut one out of another, the actual marking out for the brackets and back piece being a simple matter. The thickness ($\frac{3}{4}$ in. finished) will be found quite sufficient ; the thickness of wood when pierced and carved tends to appear to be much thicker than it really is.

First prepare the wood by planing it to thickness and shooting one edge. This operation may be done whilst the board is in one piece, and it can be cut into smaller pieces afterwards. Then put on the square lines of the top end, and trace the design.

Tracing the Design.—Take a tracing of the design on ordinary tracing (transparent) paper. Do this carefully as regards the outlines ; but there is no need to put in the shading lines. To fix the tracing, make the top square line coincide with the one already drawn on the wood, and the upright line copied from the design with the back edge or with the line drawn on the wood, which represents this back edge. Then pin this tracing along the back edge, and, inserting the carbon paper black side downwards, pin along the top and front edges, and begin to trace.

Students will do well to spend some time in earnestly and seriously studying the design to understand it thoroughly well. No amount of subsequent good work will atone for a wrong interpretation of a design. Keep to the lines so far as possible, and do not fall into the mistake of supposing that any kind of work will do now, or that this part of the work is not of so much consequence as the later stages. Work as carefully now as if finishing the bracket. Bad work at this stage makes

bad results follow at every subsequent stage.

Fig. 39 shows the separate pieces, two of them with the design already traced on, and the other piece with the design on tracing-paper fixed with pins, and the carbon paper inserted ready for tracing the design. In tracing this bracket design, it must be remembered that it is to be carved on both sides. Therefore great accuracy will have to be exercised in fixing the design, so that both sides will coincide when the piercing has been done. After the outline has been traced, it is as well to pencil the parts that are to be cut out with the saw. This prevents subsequent confusion as to which is design and which is groundwork.

The bracket is now ready for actual work on it to be done with brace and bits, saws, and carving tools.

Boring Holes.—The first step to be taken in pierced carving is to bore holes so that the saw may be inserted to cut away the surplus wood, and for this suitable tools and a bench are required. For pierced carving tools, which may properly be called supplementary tools, are necessary. The ordinary tools are chisels, gouges, V-tools, veiners, etc. But to execute some forms of wood carving many other tools are necessary. Thus in pierced carving the following tools are also required : a ratchet brace ; several bits, namely, $\frac{1}{8}$ in. shell bit, $\frac{1}{4}$ in. shell bit, $\frac{5}{16}$ in. shell bit, $\frac{3}{8}$ in. shell bit, $\frac{1}{2}$ in. centre bit, $\frac{3}{4}$ in. centre bit ; a bow saw (a 10 in. will do), and the keyhole saw.

The wood may be bored on a saw stool or wooden packing box ; but a much better way is to have it held in a joiner's bench screw, and hold the brace and bits horizontally when boring the holes. The work should be fixed high enough to get the chest in use so that it may support the brace.

Fig. 40 shows the pieces of wood partially bored. One of the pieces is shown just traced ; the second shows those parts bored that necessitate the use of the smallest bits, in this case the $\frac{1}{8}$ in. and $\frac{1}{4}$ in. shell bits. These are as small bits as it is desirable to use, as with a smaller bit the saw could not be threaded through. It is desirable that all the holes should be bored with one bit that can possibly be

This procedure also encourages the use of system in executing the work. It must be laid down, as an almost invariable

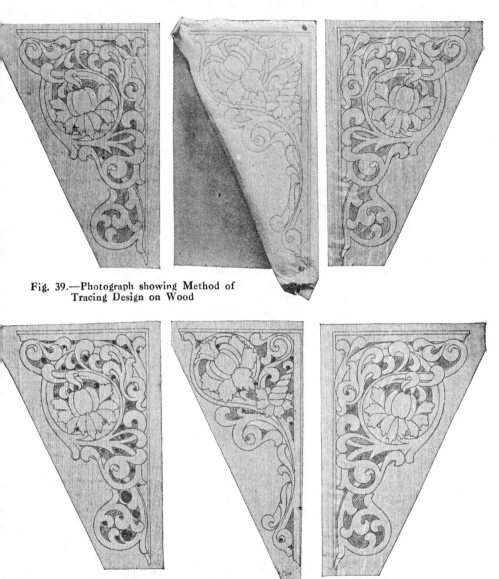

Fig. 39.—Photograph showing Method of Tracing Design on Wood

Fig. 40.—Photograph showing One Piece Traced, One Piece Partially Bored, and the Third Piece Wholly Bored, Ready for Sawing

done at one time whilst it is in the brace. This is to save the continual changing of bits that would otherwise take place.

rule, that each stage of the work should be finished before the next is begun. Even if several panels or pieces of work have to be done, it is always best to do the work of one stage on all the panels before proceeding to the work of the next stage.

The ¼ in. shell bit is the smallest to make holes through which the saw (whether bow saw or keyhole) can be threaded. Nevertheless, some of the spaces are too small to get the ¼ in. bit into. This can be obviated by using a smaller bit, say ⅛ in. bit, and then cutting away the wood that lies between with the carving tools.

But another method may be pursued. It may be said that the result of, and, indeed, the reason for, pierced carving lies in the fact that the pierced portions give deeper shadows than if the ground had been there, although even it might have been taken for a great depth. In a small space, however, if the ground is taken a good depth, the whole of the cut-out space is in shadow, and therefore the necessity for cutting right through may be avoided. The holes may be or may not be bored as desired, but the space need not necessarily be cut right through.

In Fig. 40 the work of the smaller bit may be noted, and to facilitate the further work of the carving tool, the holes are bored in pairs. The third piece in the photograph shows where the other bits have been used. It may be stated that the largest bit that the space will allow should be used. Thus it is possible to use many bits of varying size up to ¾ in. in this case. The two largest bits used in this piece of work are centre bits, ½ in. and ¾ in., and the spaces vary sufficiently to necessitate the use of all the sizes of bits between the two extremes of ⅛ in. and ¾ in. Sometimes in a small space a succession of bit-holes may save much labour with the saw. The bits can take out the greater amount of the wood, leaving only a few corners to be cut out with a carving tool. Where the design has thin stalks, which does sometimes occur, then the bits used should be smaller than the available space, so that additional strength may be given to the stalks by leaving a greater thickness of wood at the back, the front edge being thinned down to make the requisite size of stalk. In boring the

holes, it is most essential that the brace and bit are kept level and at right angles to the face of the wood. Otherwise the line of the hole will pierce the stalk or leaf or other member of the design, and produce inequalities of line that will damage the appearance of the work when finished.

Another point that should be noted is that in boring there is a tendency on the part of the bits to break the wood away at the back of the panel. With centre bits, this tendency may be made non-existent by boring from the face until nearly through, when the point of the centre bit will pierce through to the back; the wood can then be turned round and the holes bored from the back. But with shell bits this cannot be done. The best way to get over the difficulty is to have a piece of deal firmly fixed to the work at its back, and keep it there until all the boring is completed. The result is that the deal gets broken, and the oak pieces remain intact. Twist bits and screw bits may also be used.

Respecting the outline of the edges of the brackets, the boring for them may be done now; but they are, as a rule, left until the pierced design has been carved and the pieces are ready to be made up.

Sawing.—The next stage of the work is that of sawing. There is a choice of a keyhole saw, a fret saw, and a bow saw (already illustrated on earlier pages of this work). The cutting shown in Fig. 41 has been done with a keyhole saw, which is thicker and stronger than a fret saw, and makes a coarser cut, but possesses the advantage of quickness in use, there being no threading and unthreading of the blade, as there is with both the fret saw and the bow saw. To a fretworker, the fret saw will naturally appeal; it is clean in its action, and there is a less amount of cutting with the chisel afterwards.

For sawing, fix the wood firmly in the bench screw. Now insert the saw in the larger spaces, and cut towards the angles, keeping as close to the line as possible, and having the saw at right angles to the face.

In using a keyhole saw, do not take too

long a stroke, or the point will catch either in the wood or on its face, by reason of being pulled too far through.

The centre piece in Fig. 41 shows the beginning of the sawing, and the piece to the right hand the sawing completed. There are some small portions which, although they are bored, are not, necessarily, cut through with the saw. They may be cut down to about half the depth, just as if they were ordinary groundwork, still with the hole quite through. The advantage of the hole is that it helps with the dark shadow. A hole cut right through

Respecting the two other pieces, the back is generally trimmed off, and, in fact, this trimming is really a necessity in most cases, as the members of the design need thinning to show thin edges only. If, however, it is thought necessary not to have any tearing of the back edges, use the board that was employed during the boring operations, and tack it, or cramp it, firmly to the bracket pieces, and cut it along with the oak. A clean edge will show itself when the board is removed. In going round a quick corner, the saw often sticks. In such a case use a touch

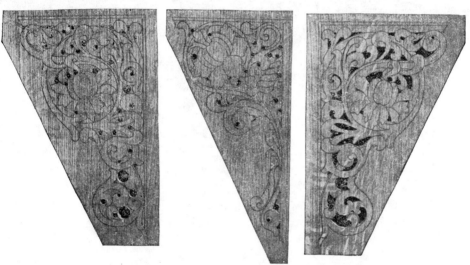

Fig. 41.—Photograph showing Boring and Sawing of Bracket

piece of wood gives a darker shadow. When placed under ordinary conditions, than if it was only cut down as groundwork.

Make the saw cuts as continuous as possible, and take great care where they meet, in angles. so that there is no over-stepping of the cut on the design. The back edge may possibly appear to be quite too ragged and untidy, caused by the saw pushing its way through. This really does not matter, as in the case of the entre bracket it is carved both sides, and consequently any tearing that occurs will quite easily be cut away in the modelling.

of oil to reduce the friction, and so make the saw run more easily.

Modelling.—The first thing to be done after the sawing is to clean up the edges. Cut well into the angles, which in the case of the very acute angles will be rough, and perhaps will be found awkward to do. If it is found impossible to cut them clean for the whole of the depth, cut them for as far as may be found possible. In the case of stalks, as already mentioned, it may not be necessary to thin them down to their surface thickness ; but it may be advisable to leave them thicker, and only thin them on their front edges. The wood should lie on a flat, smooth board whilst cleaning off, and all should be securely cramped down to the bench. This only will prevent splintering at the back.

It will be noticed on glancing at the photograph of the work in this stage (Fig. 42) that the front edge has been sawn. This is necessary, inasmuch as the design comes over the outline, and requires lowering in various places along it. This sawn outline, too, requires cleaning off in the same way as already described.

The surface is now ready to begin modelling. First of all, study the design

proportion, it may be necessary that some portions of the design will have to be taken lower than others. This part of the work may be called "arranging the masses," and is of greater importance than the later work of finishing the surface, because the effect produced by the carving depends more on its general contour and perfect proportion of parts than on any pleasing surface treatment. A glance at Fig. 42 will show where the lowest parts are.

Stalks, as a rule, are subordinate members, and require sinking to greater depths

Fig. 42.—Photograph showing Partial Sawing, Complete Sawing, and Two Stages in Modelling of Bracket

and get to know its plan, general arrangement, and intention. Then wherever any portion of the design passes under any other portion, set this in with whatever tool will fit the curve of this particular member. Generally it will be found necessary to use the mallet to do this, although, as a rule, no member should be taken to a great depth. Take particular care that in thus setting in, the "line" of the design is not broken. That is to say, the member that goes under another should have its disappearing and reappearing points in line.

For the purposes of good balance and

than other members. The flower is the chief point of interest in the design, and should be placed in considerable prominence. The stalks, which, although subordinate, yet are of value, giving the lines of direction, should be carefully cut to keep their curves intact and shapely. A large part of the foliage ends on the outlines or the borders of the design. These will have to be very carefully "set in," graduating the depth of the setting in to the fall of the curve, remembering that the margins are curved in section, the curve falling inwards. In getting this curve, take special care to get it good in direction as regards its length. Where the ends of petals fall on this hollowed edge, some cutting against the grain will inevitably take place, and sufficient time should be spent to cut these places clean and make them workmanlike. Do not slur them over, and depend on the surface carving to produce the necessary effect.

In cutting the masses to their respective shapes, opportunity will be provided, by the lowering of the surface in parts, to still further correct any deviations from a good curve of outline. In blocking out

in which the masses are arranged. Another part shows the sawing of the outer edge done, and the " setting in " only of the design, ready for the modelling. The other portion of the illustration shows a part of the work only sawn on its interior, thus connecting the work at this stage with that at the immediately preceding stage. Having got the work to this stage, correct all inequalities of curve in the outline. As some of these may not have been reached, and probably cannot be reached by the carving tools, files may be

Fig. 43.—Shape of Spoon-bit Tools for Use in Quick and Deep Curves

Fig. 44.—Photograph showing the Parts of Bracket entirely Sawn, some Parts Partially Modelled, and One Part with Modelling nearly Finished

the centre bracket, which is carved on both sides, it must be remembered that in cutting from both sides there is a danger of cutting some of the members too thin. Thus some modification of the cutting must be resorted to, and the relief in this centre bracket will not be so great as on the back, unless a piece of wood of thicker dimension is used ; and this is subject to the probability of appearing too bulky to look well.

Fig. 42 shows clearly the work up to this stage, including part of the work done in the preceding stage. One part of the illustration shows the beginnings of modelling,

used to correct them. The use of the files in this connection should be rigidly limited to the edges, and should not in any circumstances be applied to the surface carving.

The carving tools proper will now be required. To get into the corners formed by the overlaying of the design on the edges or margins, right- and left-hand skew gouges will be necessary, or, at any rate, desirable ; and it will be an added convenience if these are what are known as spoon-bit tools of the shape shown by Fig. 43.

The modelling of all three pieces being

by now much farther advanced, what now remains to be done is just surface work.

The piece in the middle is now partially " set in " and cut down, the piece on the any up to the present, and it represents the last step but one in the work of modelling. It is at this stage that the ability of a wood-carver is the most severely

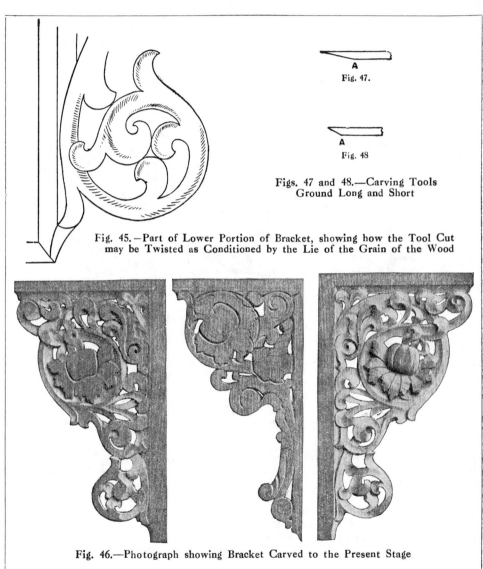

Fig. 47.

Fig. 48

Figs. 47 and 48.—Carving Tools Ground Long and Short

Fig. 45.—Part of Lower Portion of Bracket, showing how the Tool Cut may be Twisted as Conditioned by the Lie of the Grain of the Wood

Fig. 46.—Photograph showing Bracket Carved to the Present Stage

left is roughly massed, and the right-hand piece is taken to that point when all that remains to be done is to supply the surface work. In Fig. 44 the third piece is the one that has been taken the farthest of tested. No attempt should be made to hide, by entire removal, the means whereby the members have been modelled. It should be seen that the carving has been done by the carving tool, and not by a smoothing machine. What should be counted as the essential ideal is to produce a perfection of form, a perfect balance of mass, an effective comparison of elevation and depression, a judicious contrast of light and shade, rather than a perfect technique, and an accurate rendering of the form.

The tools used to get the work up to the point shown by Fig. 44 are (as per Sheffield tool list, $\frac{3}{8}$ in. by 3 in. $\frac{3}{8}$ in. by 4 in., $\frac{1}{4}$ in. by 4 in. $\frac{3}{8}$ in. by 5 in. $\frac{1}{4}$ in. by 5 in., $\frac{1}{4}$ in. by 5 in. $\frac{3}{8}$ in. by 7 in. $\frac{1}{4}$ in. by 7 in. $\frac{5}{16}$ in. by 25 in. $\frac{1}{4}$ in. by 21 in. $\frac{5}{16}$ in. by 39 in., $\frac{1}{8}$ in. by 4 in. One of these tools is a spoon-bit tool necessary to cut the hollow on the larger curved stalk at those points where the smaller leaves lie on it.

Compare, first of all the right-hand portion of the bracket with that part which is at the left hand in the photographic reproduction (Fig. 44). The first operation is to emphasise the depressed parts, and take them down to their lowest point. First set them in with tools of suitable curve. Thus, to take the most prominent member, the centre flower take suitable tools and set in along the line that has already been cut in with a **V**-tool. Reduce the inner end of the petals to the depth of the setting in. This particular part will need to be rather deeply cut to give the contrast necessary to the balance of the whole thing. In thus sinking the inner ends of the petals opportunity will be provided to give effective twists to the petals.

In sinking the various depressions to their ultimate depth, take care that they are not sunk too far to render it impossible to get a good curve. This warning is necessary, as it sometimes does happen that a depth is reached which makes it impossible to cut the member to a good curve. Especially is this the case with the upper part of the large stalk, where the small leaves are lying on it. If this is not particularly seen to, a lumpy and irregular surface is produced that gives a very bad effect. This stalk needs to be lowered in all its length, besides the hollow that is contained in it.

It is desirable to take the work from the bench from time to time, and hold it up in the position it is to occupy when finished, so that no mistake will be made in shaping the masses the wrong way, giving thereby ill-balanced effects of light and shade. Note particularly how the little curves of the leaves hold a deep shadow, and try to cultivate the ability to see these shadows and the high lights that lie close to them. It is an ability that can be cultivated by concentration. The twisting of the stalks and the leaves and, in fact, any member is often determined by the lie of the grain. For example, note the curled ending to the scroll at the bottom of the bracket. Taking the cut of the tool as from the top (*see* Fig. 45) in the direction of the curve then the twist leans towards the outside on the outer part, and towards the inside when the inner part is reached.

Finishing the Surface.—A stage when the finishing of the surface has been done has now been reached. This is shown in Fig. 46. The right-hand piece is now finished as regards its surface. The left-hand piece is taken up to that point where only the surface finishing is needed, whilst the centre piece is taken up to that stage already mentioned as the "arranging of the masses."

One very important point is the selection of the right tools for finishing, and a rigid adherence to the use of these particular tools. The best tools to use are the spade tools shown by Fig. 8. (p. 1346). These are lighter, and are capable of being used in places that the ordinary tool cannot reach. Some workers keep complete sets of spade tools for the sole purpose of "modelling." When this is done, a point that might be mentioned is, that the tools have what may be described as a "long" grind. This is shown in Fig. 47 in contradistinction to a "short" grind, shown in Fig. 48. The advantage of a "short" grind is that it gives strength, and the position of the edge A near to the cutting edge is useful in giving leverage to the tool when doing heavier work. But for finishing the surface, no heavy work is needed, and thus a lighter tool and a lighter and thinner cutting edge is made possible. This is especially useful in cleaning off the edges. A thicker tool would not easily get in

The extreme edge or arris should be cut off with a flat tool. This not only gives

Fig. 49.—Photograph of Back of Brackets showing the Edges of the Carving Cut

Fig. 50.—Photograph of One Part of the Bracket showing the Intensification of the Shadow Caused by Cutting Away the Back

Fig. 51.

Fig. 52.

Figs. 51 and 52.—Photographs showing Carved Parts of Bracket Finished and Ready for Putting Together

without leaving bruises. But a thin tool can be more easily manipulated, and cleaner work may result from their use.

a smooth appearance, but makes the direction good, and gives an opportunity for correcting any slight inequality of outline that has crept into the work. Take care in doing this to get the angles well cut ; a slight deviation at an angle will often produce awkward effects. Where the leaves are lying on the stalk, or on the hollow edge, great care has to be taken to get the angles cleanly done and well cut. Here the tools will necessarily have to be taken against the grain, and consequently sharp tools are essential. Moreover, the vertical setting-in cut must be deep enough, and the horizontal cut must never be cut below the level of the deepest part of the vertical cut.

Carving the Back of the Work.—

Owing to the fact that the relief extends the full depth, or rather, the thickness of the wood, some of the members of the design must present at some point in their contour a thick and clumsy edge if not treated in some way that will remove this awkward appearance. There is a way in which this can be done, by cutting the superfluous wood away from the back. Fig. 49 shows a view of the back thus treated. The right-hand side piece shows it just begun, and the left-hand piece shows it finished. The treatment adopted in this case is quite simple and quite easy of accomplishment. It only involves the use of three tools, viz., $\frac{5}{8}$ in. by 4 in., $\frac{1}{2}$ in. by 5 in., and $\frac{3}{8}$ in. by 6 in.

If the carved pieces were seen at both sides, then the style of treatment would be much more full of work. But as they go against a wall, all that is necessary is to cut them, so that from the front they help in making the appearance lighter. The difference in appearance is seen in Fig. 50, which should be compared with Fig. 46. The shadows at the back are intensified, and a greater contrast is; therefore, possible. The edges, too, are lightened, and this also helps to make the work look lighter. Much care is required in dealing with the stalks, because of their lightness. They require thinning down, but not so much that their strength is materially diminished. It would be better to cut away the wood at the sides only, in the case of any part of the work that would, by cutting all the wood away at the back, interfere with the strength.

In actually cutting the back, repeatedly take up the wood and look at it whilst in its intended ultimate position.

The whole of the carved parts of the bracket, finished and ready for putting together, are shown in Figs. 51 and 52. The backs of both side brackets will be finished at the back, whilst the centre bracket will be carved both sides. The front edge of this centre bracket will be carved, and some judgment will be required in carving it, so that it does not look thin and insignificant.

Making Up and Finishing. — In

making up, the first step is to join the two

Fig. 53.—Photograph of Bracket Complete

side brackets together. This is best done by making a groove-and-tongue joint. The top edge of the joined pieces should now be planed true and square, and likewise that of the central bracket. Smooth up the sides with a finely set smoothing or panel plane. In fixing the bracket, the underside of the shelf should be trenched with a stop-tapered dovetail trench. To fit this, a tapered dovetail will be cut on the top of the central bracket, and it will be glued in from the back. The back edge of the shelf should be rebated to receive the back top edge, and this will be screwed up with brass screws in cups. The back edge of the shelf will require stop-rebating.

The completed bracket is shown by Fig. 53.

CHIP CARVING

Chip carving, as the name implies, consists of the formation of design by the siderable use of, providing as it does a simple method of decorative treatment. To the carver experienced in ordinary woodcarving chip carving will be a very simple operation, but to the novice, apart from its utility, its practice will be found

Fig. 54.—Design for Chip Carving Based on the Decagon

Fig. 55.—Pattern
Incised

Fig. 56.—Pattern with
Ground Removed

Fig. 57.—Pattern with
Ground Stamped

removal of chips which are cut away from the wood in straight lines. From time immemorial it has formed the chief ornamental decorative art of primitive peoples, but even so it is still made con- to be of great educational value for the development of accuracy and precision, and the acquirement of the necessary knowledge of wood cutting.

The practice of chip carving may be

carried out entirely with a knife, and many workers use this tool only, but the use of a small selection of ordinary carving tools not only considerably facilitates the work but increases its scope.

The knives used are of the short-bladed variety with either straight, curved, or angular blades. When knives alone are used, the actual process of carving con-

the knife and the work is reduced, until the correct face of the part being cut is obtained.

The principal hand tools of the chisel variety that are used for chip carving are the **V**-tool and the skew chisel. Compared with the knife the **V**-tool saves a vast amount of work, for one stroke of this tool is the equivalent of three of the knife.

Fig. 58.—Sideboard Ornamented with Incised Work

sists of merely two operations—setting-in and cutting-out. The wood is removed by first setting the limit and then cutting it away by a slicing action of the tool. The first cut is made with the knife almost straight, and the second cut with the knife inclined at an angle of about 45°. With each successive cut. the angle between

The chief objection to its use is the danger of splitting the corners when cutting across the grain. Other useful tools are the straight spade chisel and the veiner.

The designs for chip carving are mostly of a geometrical character, and a fair knowledge of geometry is essential for their proper setting out. Much of it appears of a complicated nature in the complete design, but mostly it will be found, upon study, to resolve itself into elementary geometry and may easily be produced by means of compasses and rule. Fig. 54 shows a design of this nature which is based on the setting out of the ten-sided figure or decagon. For such a design as this, if desired, instead of the decagon having plain bands, a rim could be run along the centre of each band.

Floral designs which are not of a geometrical nature also lend themselves to the art of the chip carver, but there is

A carver's **V**-tool is the most suitable for the first stage in the actual incising ; a $\frac{1}{4}$-in. tool is a most convenient size to use. Besides this will be required a couple of carver's gouges, a $\frac{1}{2}$-in. and a very small one being convenient sizes for general work. An admirable stamp for matting the ground after it has been cut away can be made by cutting the point off a large French nail, then filing cross-lines across the flat end. Of course, a large variety of matting punches that give various textures can be purchased ; but the simplest are generally the most effec-

Fig. 59.—Hall-stand Ornamented with Relief Carving

by no means the latitude with this class of design allowable as with ordinary carving.

WOOD INCISING

Wood incising is a simple means of enriching flat surfaces in wood to produce a general effect of carving, though very much easier to execute. It is of such a nature that after a few trials to enable one to manage the tool, good results may be produced from the start.

tive, and the one suggested is to be recommended.

The wood employed for incising requires to be of close grain, and not too soft Material like pine and deal is wholly unsuitable, it being wellnigh impossible to obtain absolute clean incisions. Among the woods that can be thoroughly recommended are sycamore and satin walnut the latter especially giving little trouble with well-sharpened tools.

The piece of wood to be incised must

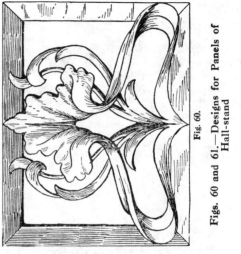

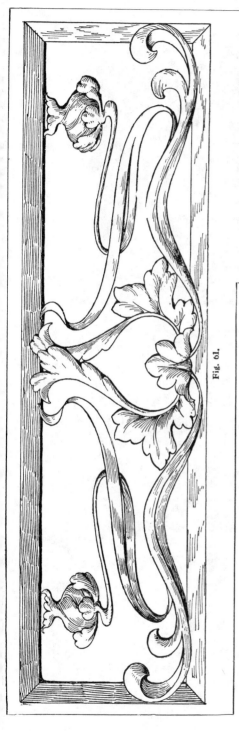

Figs. 60 and 61.—Designs for Panels of Hall-stand

Fig. 60.

Fig. 61.

have the design clearly drawn out on its surface, and needs to be rigidly fixed during the working. A small board can, of course, be conveniently held in the vice, or cramps may be used ; but whatever method is adopted, the work must be rendered perfectly immovable, and in such a position, if possible, that it may be got at from all sides.

Figs. 55, 56 and 57 show the three stages in the production of the ordinary variety of incised work, each of which can be adopted as a complete method, though the third is the most effective.

Before beginning on the actual work, it is wise to practise a few strokes on a waste piece of the same wood that is to be incised so as to be able to gauge the amount of pressure necessary and obtain a little facility in the use of the tool. A deep cut is not necessary, and will make it difficult to obtain uniformity in the line ; a shallow cut that is continuous throughout is what should be striven for. After all the outlines have been gone over in this way, veins and inner lines being delineated in thinner strokes, the next stage in the work is to cut away the ground with the gouge right up to the incised lines. With just ordinary care, this will be found quite a simple operation. In the case of very

Fig. 62.-
Carved
Over-
mantel

Fig. 63.—
Corner
Cabinet
with
Carved
Doors

small spaces, if one does not possess a carving tool small enough, a makeshift may be made by rubbing a stout knitting needle flat at one end on a stone, then finishing off on an oilstone. Such a tool set in a handle will be found extremely

work that is not to be stamped, will be found rather to improve the appearance, contrasting with the smooth raised portions. When the ground has been gone over as described, the design will, of course, stand out in relief. If it is desired to

Fig. 64.—Design for One Panel of Corner Cabinet

useful for very small work ; but the greater part will be done with the gouges.

While it is not essential to obtain an absolutely smooth ground, it should be of regular depth throughout ; a few gouge markings, however, even in the case of

" matt " the ground, the stamp is next brought into use, the end being stamped in rows round the pattern, close up to it, until the markings meet in the middle of the spaces. Naturally this operation will, of course, lower the ground still further and impart a greater appearance of relief, while affording striking contrast.

Fig. 58 is an example of a piece of furniture to which this class of decoration has been applied.

to any piece of furniture previously designed for the purpose, it may be welcome to the handicraftsman, who will, of course, understand that neither the lines of construction nor the identical ornament depicted need be slavishly

Fig. 65.—Design for Second Panel of Corner Cabinet

EXAMPLES OF CARVED FURNITURE

Hall-stand Ornamented with Carving.—The half-tone reproduction (Fig. 59) shows a well-designed hall-stand with carved panels. Because of its unlikeness

followed. The sticks, etc., pass through a well, their lower ends being received by a metal tray which drops flush into the bottom shelf. The panels should be carved to some simple designs, those shown (*see* Figs. 60 and 61) being very suitable and, if thought desirable, the small ones may form the fronts of drawers, which will contain gloves, brushes, etc.

Carved Overmantel.—Fig. 62 shows an overmantel that, although plain, is yet pleasing in effect, and will harmonise with most schemes of modern house decoration. The framing is square without mouldings, except the moulded caps to the stiles. It is rebated for the panels and the mirror. The mirror is 30 in. by 21 in., bevelled 1 in. The two upright panels are 21 in. by 8 in. by $\frac{1}{2}$ in.; and the top panel 48 in. by 6 in. by $\frac{1}{2}$ in. The framing is of 3-in. by 1-in. stuff, with 2-in. by 1-in. muntins. The base is of $4\frac{1}{2}$-in by 1-in. stuff, quite plain and square. There is no shelf, the only elaboration is in the carving of the panels, and even this is as plain as possible. The carving is flat and simple in character, and the groundwork is unpunched.

Corner Cabinet with Carved Doors. —The carved ornament of the cabinet shown by Fig. 63 is based on a style that had its vogue about three centuries ago. The majority of readers will probably be pleased with the quaint effect which its employment and the general lines of the cabinet have produced. Half-scale drawings of the carved panels, which measure 10 in. square, are shown by Figs. 64 and 65. Grotesque animals have long been a favourite with the wood carver.

KNIFE CARVING

All the essential tools and appliances for knife-carving are a suitable knife and a stone for keeping it in good order, no special work bench being necessary. The curved form of knife shown by Fig. 66 will be found the most generally useful. With regard to the material to use, any close-grained stuff is suitable, that is, a wood that will not easily split. A beginner should preferably select a wood that is not too hard, pear being an excellent variety, it having the advantage that it is soft, and therefore easy to work. The Swiss peasant carvers are the most facile wielders of the knife, as most of their carving displays much character and extreme skill of execution. One of the knife-carved articles that originated from this source is the wooden nut-crackers in the form of a bear, shown by Fig. 67, carved in walnut. The article stands by itself and forms, in addition to its useful qualities, an interesting ornament.

A more modern design for nut-crackers that works on the same principle is shown by Fig. 68. These are intended to be used in connection with a nut-bowl shown by Fig. 69, which will be found to form a quaint and interesting table ornament. The front view of these crackers is shown by Fig. 70, though, if it is intended to employ them in connection with the bowl, it will be necessary to bring the feet together, as in Fig. 69, and insert two short dowels for standing in position on the raised edge of the bowl.

In starting to carve such a subject as this, a full-size drawing of both front and side views should be made, afterwards proceeding to plane up a piece of wood in width and breadth sufficient to take the design. The general outline of the front view should be set out on the wood, as shown by Fig. 71. Then saw round the out-lines with a fret-saw, which will result in a block of wood shaped as shown by Fig. 72, the first stage in the actual carving being to form the general shape, as seen from the side, and indicated by the dotted lines. The general shape having thus been obtained, it will be found a comparatively straightforward operation to proceed to the working up of the forms by sinking parts here and there to throw others into relief, etc. Those workers who may prefer to execute the work without the aid of a saw must strive for a good general shape first, without concentrating their attention on details, going at the work boldly at the start, removing as large chips as one can safely do rather than to chip off small fragments, as a bolder effect is thus obtained. Fig. 73 gives some idea of the general form to aim for in a very early stage of the carving, before proceeding to the details, care being taken at this stage not to cut away too much of the wood, so as to have plenty for finishing off. The hole A into which the movable jaw is

Fig. 67.—Swiss
Nut-crackers,
Knife-carved

Fig. 70.—Front Elevation
of Crackers

Fig. 69.—Carved Bowl with Nut-crackers

Fig. 71.—Outline Set
Out on Wood

Fig. 66.—Knives for
Carving

Fig. 68.—Nut-crackers for Bowl

inserted is pierced straight through, the inside being smoothed with glasspaper. Even in the early stages of the work a beginner should pay particular attention should be kept sharp by frequent recourse to the oilstone. Finally, all finishing should be done with the knife alone, without the aid of files or glasspaper,

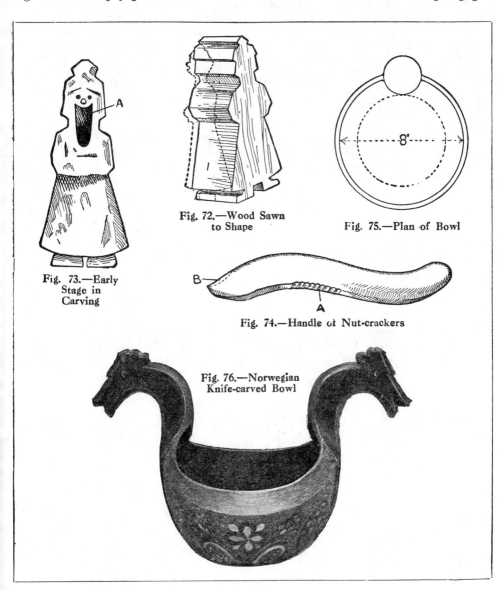

Fig. 72.—Wood Sawn to Shape

Fig. 75.—Plan of Bowl

Fig. 73.—Early Stage in Carving

Fig. 74.—Handle of Nut-crackers

Fig. 76.—Norwegian Knife-carved Bowl

to keep the work clean—that is, clean cut —without any appearance of raggedness, which is rather difficult to eliminate in the afterwork. To this end the knife which are apt to produce a rounded uninteresting surface.

The handle of the crackers is shown by Fig. 74. The shape shown should be accurately sawn out, and the small amount of carving of the jaw neatly executed to coincide with the upper part. The series of cuts, shown by A, are intended to form a surface for gripping the nuts. Also the hollowed-out part at B is to serve the same purpose. The handle portion should be nicely rounded off so as to be comfortable to hold, then it is slipped through the slot in its correct position, and drilled almost through, the handle being then removed and the hole in this slightly enlarged, so that a wooden peg, when slipped through, while fitting tightly into the other holes, will allow the handle to move easily.

Referring again to the bowl shown by Fig. 69, a suitable size for this would be 8 in. in diameter, the plan being given by Fig. 75. As the raised portion, where the figure is stood, will prevent the bowl being wholly turned in a lathe, the depression is hollowed by carving, though if a worker possesses a lathe it will be found of great assistance to turn out the wood up to the dotted line, then removing the rest with a gouge. This bowl, to present a good appearance, should be nicely smoothed up, making it of regular thickness as far as possible throughout.

Fig. 76, the original of which is in the South Kensington Museum, shows an old Norwegian bowl carved wholly in one piece of wood, which imparts an excellent suggestion for a similar treatment on more modern lines for a nut-bowl of quaint form.

Fretcutting and Pyrography

FRETCUTTING

FRETCUTTING is the practice of producing open woodwork in ornamental patterns.

The tools necessary for its execution by hand are comparatively few, the principal one, for light work, being a light iron frame with saw-blade. For heavier work the key-hole saw or bow saw are used. A 14-in. saw-frame (iron) is a suitable size. Tension may be secured in two ways— by the top clamp or by a screw in the handle operated by a turn of the wrist after the saw is threaded up. A suitable cutting-board and cramp are also necessary. A wood cutting-board with a **V**-shaped opening will be found quite adequate. Metal cutting-tables are liable to injure saw-blades. For boring holes in the wood an archimedean drill is required. A bradawl or other pointed instrument should not be used, as it is likely to split the wood. The best kind of drill stock is that which has a spring in the handle, because it assists in the withdrawal of the bit and prevents side-jerking, a common cause of broken drill bits. A small screwdriver hammer, small brads or nails, a tube of liquid glue, a dozen or more saws, glasspaper, and the outfit is complete.

Saw-blades can be had at extremely low prices ; but if the worker is desirous of turning out really good work, a good saw-blade is absolutely necessary. For turning sharp corners a medium blade with sharp, well-defined teeth is recommended. Saw-blades having short, closely-set teeth, are much too slow for general work. Those saws with rounded backs, which enable corners to be turned without leaving behind them any visible trace, are to be recommended.

To begin the actual work the design is pasted on the wood, and it is necessary to note that the grain must run lengthwise of the pattern, not across it. The paste must be applied thinly and evenly on the design (not on the wood), and the design deftly laid on the wood, the pattern being smoothed down with the palm of the hand or a soft rag so as to exclude all air and force out wrinkles. A paste made of starch boiled to a thick jelly, in which a small piece of gum arabic has been dissolved, is the best adhesive. It adheres to the wood firmly, but can be removed easily by the finest glasspaper. A few drops of oil of cloves added to the paste will preserve it.

The holes are drilled in the waste portions of the design—if possible opposite some projecting point, and the saw threaded up. The work is then firmly held down to the cutting-table with the left hand, and the fingers spreading over the work at the back of the saw. The cutting is then proceeded with, the hand-frame being held perfectly upright with a firm grip, so as to completely control its movements. Use a steady, regular stroke, feeding the work gradually to the saw, otherwise the edges of the fret will be irregular. Some workers move both the saw-frame and the wood ; but to the beginner this is a dangerous operation. as

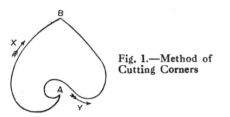

Fig. 1.—Method of Cutting Corners

it requires skill, only acquired by practice, to perform the double action perfectly. The worker quickly learns to keep the saw upright, and the left hand soon accustoms itself to holding down and feeding the work to the saw. If the worker possesses a treadle fretsaw, he has the advantage of having both hands free to guide the work, and the saw is always in an upright position, consequently there is only the guiding of the wood to the saw with which he has to contend. One important point is that in all cases the saw teeth must be placed downwards, otherwise the upward stroke brings the dust up through the saw line, and if the pattern is pasted to the wood, it raises it, and, naturally, the effect of this deters the most experienced cutters from following the line of the pattern.

There is no doubt that the beginner's first difficulty lies in the turning of corners accurately. There are two methods given here which will help. Suppose that in cutting a hole the saw begins at A (Fig. 1) and cuts to the corner B, by way of the

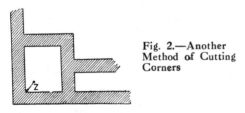

Fig. 2.—Another Method of Cutting Corners

arrow X. The saw may then be drawn back, beginning again at A sawing to B in the direction indicated by the arrow Y. Another method, and a much quicker one.

is when the saw reaches the corner Z (Fig. 2), to withdraw it a little and cut its own width in the waste portion towards the line. The small hole thus formed allows the saw to be turned without any breakage, the corner being cut clean and perfect. The beginner, however, after a little practice, will be able to turn corners without the use of these two artifices ; but, of course, much depends on the quality of the saw-blade.

The cutting of the outside of the design is usually left until all the inside of the design has been finished. The only exception to this is when most of the inside is to be cut away, as is the case with overlay borders. In these circumstances it is always advisable to cut the outside

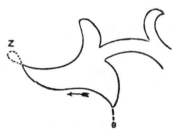

Fig. 3.—Method of Sawing Delicate Points

first, because if the inside were cut away it would leave the work weak across the grain, and it would require exceptionally gentle handling afterwards.

Outside the points are in some respects more difficult to turn than corners. However, the beginner may easily overcome the difficulty by making a round turn in the waste wood opposite, and, keeping well on the outside of the line, proceed to cut again. This is shown in Fig. 3 by the dotted line Z. Long, tapering points require care in cutting, otherwise they are liable to snap off. To do this successfully the work must be drawn to the corner of the V-slot in the table, and the wood pressed well down and fed up only as little as possible.

When the work has been cut out it is ready for finishing off. If there are slots and tenons for the fixing of a shelf or support these should be measured previously, as it is desirable to have a perfect fit without relying too much on nails and glue. Tenons might be made a shade longer, and taken off afterwards with a small plane or chisel.

The outside edges of shelves and other work having a continuous straight cut are often left uneven, and if these cannot be altered or made correct by using the saw they are best left alone. A small plane might be sometimes used with advantage ; but the worker is not advised to use metal templates which are either screwed or fixed with pin-points to the wood. The saw, when travelling along the side of a template, is liable to be pushed out of truth, thus sawing out of the vertical, and its edge is either dulled or broken by constant friction. A better method in place of templates is to draw a sharp knife-blade along the line, making a groove for the saw to run in. These methods, however, are never used by those experienced in fretcutting.

The glasspapering must be done thoroughly on both sides of the work, whether it is to be seen or not. The swarf or roughness round the frets is first removed, and then the design, if it has been pasted on. Water should not be used, as it warps the wood ; glasspapering is the only effective method to be employed. At this stage the worker will probably see his work much clearer, and any small diversions from the line of the pattern will be easily noticed, and in all probability he will attempt to remedy this with files. Such an attempt will most likely result in making it worse, because files are not adaptable to woodwork, especially when they are used across the end grain of delicate frets. Strips of glasspaper glued on shaped pieces of thin wood are more suitable, but not to be altogether recommended.

Straight sawing requires practice, and if the beginner has mastered the earlier stages of sawing straight lines and curves it should not be difficult for him to turn out fair work by his first attempts.

So far it has been assumed that the fret has been of a plain character, such as a bracket, in which case the shelf and support would, of course, require to be fixed.

If nails are used in any piece of fretted work it should be remembered that all hammering must be reduced to a minimum. Holes should be drilled with a fine bit in the back of the work, and the nails gently driven through into the shelf or other portion which is desired to be fixed. All joints, except those intended to be taken apart for cleaning, should have a touch of glue given them as an extra security. Screws also are more serviceable than nails, and have the advantage of making the work more superior, besides allowing for the work to be taken to pieces when required. Clock cases should invariably be screwed, so as to allow for the regulating or repairing of the timepiece. A wooden vice is a handy tool for assisting the worker to fit up his work, because all parts may be securely held in position while being nailed or screwed.

Overlays, such as those which form rebates for photo frames, mirrors, etc., should be cut from woods not more than $\frac{1}{16}$ in. thick, otherwise a heavy and clumsy appearance is given to the article. These thin woods should always be cut between two waste pieces and nailed together with fine nails, the design being pasted on the uppermost piece. Any holes which are to be pierced should be drilled with a sharp bit, using only sufficient pressure to force it through the wood. The outside is then sawn with a No. 1 saw-blade, and the inside, which is secured with the nails, is sawn last.

If the overlay is an ornament with interior fretting, this should be cut first, and the outside left until the last. Afterwards it should have the swarf cleaned away from the bottom edges with No. 1 glasspaper, and without further attempting to clean it, it should be glued into position under pressure.

PYROGRAPHY

Pyrography or poker-work is a method of decorating wood by charring or carbonising the surface by means of hot tools.

The process is one that is absolutely permanent, and extremely useful for the decoration of small articles in wood. It has the advantage of not necessitating the manual labour required for carving

Fig. 4.—Shield Design for Panel

and similar processes. Poker-work can be greatly improved by the addition of wood stains that may be applied with a brush. Perhaps one of the chief characteristics which contribute to the effect of the work is the softness of line resulting, for the poker point not only makes a black line where it touches the wood, but darkens it slightly on each side. The line forms an effective definition to stained surfaces, and prevents the stain from spreading.

The outfit necessary for the work consists of a hollow metal point, attached by a screw to a cork handle, through the middle of which runs a metal tube, communicating at one end with the interior of the point, and at the other with a length of rubber piping, leading to one of the two openings in the cork of a glass bottle containing benzoline. Another length of tube goes from the second of these holes to a pair of hand bellows fitted with a rubber reservoir. A small spirit lamp is also provided.

Some outfits are constructed to dispense with the spirit lamp, by means of an arrangement to burn the benzoline gas, and

others have the liquid contained in a metal receiver in the tubing, with an appliance of the same kind fitted to it; but these are not recommended. It is convenient to have one or two extra points which cost about seven shillings each.

The method of working the poker is as follows: When the point has been heated in the flame of the lamp for a few moments, and the bellows kept in action, the vapour of the benzoline is forced through the tube into the hollow in its interior, and a glowing heat is thus maintained, when the design can be burnt into the wood as easily as drawing it with a pencil.

The best woods for poker-work are holly, sycamore, and pure white chestnut. If desired, made-up articles, such as photograph frames, boxes, mirrors, chessboards, brushes, panels, letter and newspaper racks, trays, tables, etc., can be obtained with patterns ready traced on them. On no account should wood that has been previously polished or varnished be used.

The illustrations (Figs. 4 to 9) show the very wide range of effect which it is possible

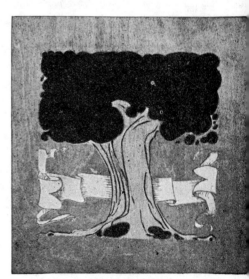

Fig. 5.—Tree Design for Panel

to produce by burning an outline to the design and afterwards filling in certain parts with stain.

Fig. 4 shows a shield design for exhibiting the owner's monogram or initials on

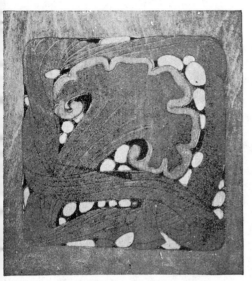

Fig. 6.—Panel Design with Strong Contrasts

a chest-front or top. It has the recommendation of being simple but effective ; the background in the original was stained a light green, the shield in pale mauve, and the leaves scorched a brownish black by means of a blowpipe, which will be referred to later. This scheme is thoroughly harmonious ; care must be exercised to introduce only those colours which harmonise with the velvety brown of the scorched wood. The tree design (Fig. 5) is intensely rich in effect, the foliage being burnt a jet black, and the ground colour a dark green. The ribbon, which greatly assists the decorative composition, is left the natural colour of the wood, a straw colour. Fig. 6 is somewhat more complex in design, but shows well the capability of the process for producing strong portions of light.

Large surfaces of jet black may be produced in the following manner : Obtain two blowpipes, one with a nipple and one from which the nipple has been removed. Connect the one without the nipple to a gas supply by means of an indiarubber tube, which will give, when lit, a very small gas-flame. The other blowpipe is held in the left hand, the small flame being

directed on the work by means of a blast of air from the mouth. The small tongue of flame will be found manageable enough to work in the smallest surfaces as well as the large ones, and will produce a rich velvety black, which cannot be obtained really satisfactorily by means of the poker point alone.

The stains for filling in the design may be the ordinary water-colour ones, although for bright effects aniline dyes are better, taking care only to select those of known permanence. Ready-made greens and violets usually are not ; but many colours are. Transparent oil colours thinned out with turpentine may also be used, as long as they are used thinly, and do not obliterate the poker outline.

The design (Fig. 7) is stained all over a deep brown, with the exception of the shield, which is dark green, and the eyes of the dolphins, which are white. The stork design (Fig. 8) would make an interesting cabinet detail.

For the production of a panel such as that shown by Fig 9, the work should be commenced by drawing a careful outline of the design on the panel, taking great

Fig. 7.—Another Design with Strong Contrasts

pains to get the main forms correct and the essential details ; but not necessarily adding all the small shading lines such as those of the hair and the tail feathers of the bird. Much of this by a fairly proficient worker can be put in direct. When the pencilling is satisfactory, start by putting the outline of the face and features in boldly, with the poker point, in a telling line that will readily assert itself. It is best to try the point first on a piece of spare wood, to see that it is working properly. The hand holding the mirror and lines of the hair are done in a similar manner, taking special pains in this latter to

"eyes" of the tail feathers being put in before the lines of the feathers are indicated, and in working them, keep well outside the pencil lines so that the light portions are not lost when the lines behind are put in. Put in the neck and upper wing feathers dark, a flat point being the best for large surfaces.

This design is one that would colour admirably; a harmonious combination of peacock green, blue and red-brown is one that would look particularly well. The light parts can be left the natural colour of the wood,

Fig. 8.—Stork Design for Panel

Fig. 9.—Design for Panel for Mirror Frame

obtain an even effect, while thickening the line out in certain places to produce the effect of shading. The peacock is executed in finer lines throughout, the or toned down slightly with very pale warm brown tone should the white colour of the wood be too glaring and necessitate it.

Tool Chests

PORTABLE TOOL BOXES

TOOL CHESTS are an obvious convenience, and are usually made by the workmen in all trades for convenience in storing their tools.

The box (Fig. 1) should be large enough to hold the hand-saw and the panel-saw in the lid. A useful size is 2 ft. 7 in. long,

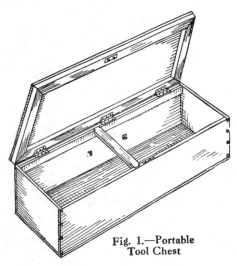

Fig. 1.—Portable
Tool Chest

11 in. wide, and 7 in. deep, outside measurements. This is just large enough to take a 26-in. hand-saw and a 22-in. panel-saw. The box may be made a little narrower if the panel-saw is put with the rest of the tools in the body of the box. The sides, top, and bottom are made of $\frac{1}{2}$-in. stuff, preferably pine. The sides are dovetailed together, and the bottom then screwed on. Pieces $1\frac{1}{4}$ in. by 1 in. are screwed to the top to strengthen it, form a deep panel to hold the saws, and to afford good fastening for the hinges. The latter are three 3-in. brass butts. A strip $1\frac{1}{2}$ in. by $\frac{3}{8}$ in. is screwed to the inside top edge of the back to receive the hinges and to strengthen the back.

A handle is bolted to the back of the box for carrying purposes. To strengthen the back and front whilst carrying, a $1\frac{1}{2}$-in. by $\frac{1}{2}$-in. strip is dovetailed to the top edge of the front side and to the strip at the top of the back. This strip is removable, and is only placed in position when the box is to be carried. The box is fitted with a reliable box lock. The saws are held in the lid panel by cleats for the blade ends, and by wooden turn-buttons (about 2 in. by $\frac{3}{4}$ in.) through the holes in the handles. The box should be given two coats of black paint, with the initials of the owner lettered in white on the top of the lid.

Alternative Design.—Fig. 2 is a photograph of an alternative design of box.

The framework of this may be $\frac{5}{8}$-in. cypress dovetailed at the corners, a suitable size being $34\frac{1}{2}$ in. by 16 in., one half being 3 in. deep, the other 2 in. A rebate joint as shown enlarged in Fig. 5 joins the two parts, and prevents strain on the hinges when the case is closed. The tongue on the wider half measures $\frac{1}{4}$ in. by $\frac{1}{4}$ in., and a $\frac{3}{16}$-in. bead is also wrought on this edge to improve the appearance of the job.

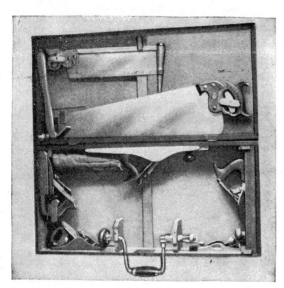

Fig. 2.—Alternative Form of Portable Tool-box

The sides of the framework are covered in with $\frac{3}{16}$-in. plywood. The bar across the middle of each side is a strengthening member, which should only be omitted if the sides are of thicker stuff, say $\frac{1}{4}$ in. The sides are secured by gluing and screwing, $\frac{3}{4}$-in. brass button-head screws at 3-in. spacing being used.

As the photograph shows (Fig. 2), the brace is utilised as a carrying handle, two slots being cut in the deeper side of the chest to accommodate it, while the two brackets shown transmit the weight of the chest solidly to the chuck-neck and handle-neck respectively. The methods of accommodating the planes and saws will be obvious from the illustrations, Figs. 2

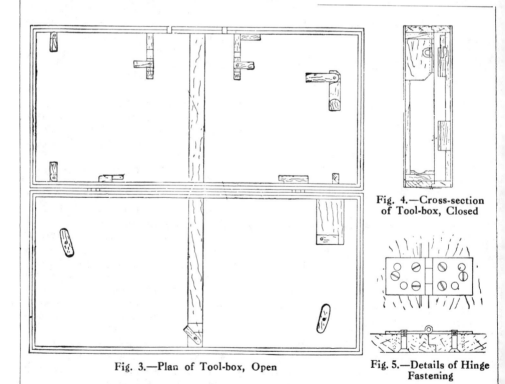

Fig. 3.—Plan of Tool-box, Open

Fig. 4.—Cross-section of Tool-box, Closed

Fig. 5.—Details of Hinge Fastening

and 3. Attention may be drawn to the position of the square in the corner behind the rip-saw, the blade fitting into a saw-cut in the block shown. The handle of the smoothing plane fits into a shaped block lined with baize, wherein it is held by the turnbutton. All the planes, in fact, are secured by blocks appropriately shaped to hold one end, suitable turn-buttons fastening the other. All blocks attached to the three-ply sides are secured by screwing through from the outside plus gluing. Fig. 4 shows a cross-section of the box.

No special provision is made in building

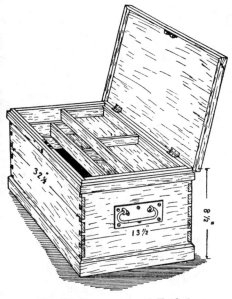

Fig. 6.—Patternmakers' Tool-chest

the chest for the smaller odd tools, as the actual selection of these carried naturally varies very much with the nature of the work to be done, and therefore the con-struction of fitments likely to suit every possible grouping is impossible. The case is fitted with a lock and key; but for ordinary securing, a couple of strong hooks and eyes are fitted. The hinges for strength's sake are backflaps, and are secured as shown in Fig. 5. In addition to the ordinary wood-screws attaching the hinges, two $\frac{3}{16}$-in. Whitworth counter-

sunk screws are tapped through each flap from the inside, and the projecting points riveted over, thus rendering it impossible for the contents of the chest to be got at by tampering with the hinges. For greater protection against hard usage, iron corner-plates should be screwed to the eight corners of the chest.

No dimensions other than the external sizes have been given, as these will natur-ally differ according to the actual tool-carrying requirements of the individual maker.

PATTERNMAKERS' TOOL-CHEST

A tool-chest to hold patternmakers' tools is shown in Fig. 6.

The largest tool likely to require accom-modation is the jack plane, for which a box 18 in. long would be sufficient. But if a hand-saw is included it would require to be not less than 31 in. inside measure-ment. A trying plane is large and could not be dispensed with. A tenon saw is continually wanted, and if kept in the box must be easy to get at. The box should be long enough to take the longest tool, and should be less in depth than it is in width. A depth of 10 in. and a width of 12 in. should be ample; in fact, the depth might be cut down to 8 in. and still leave room for all the tools a pattern-maker requires, provided they are suitably arranged in the box. This, of course, means that the tools must be packed in on top of one another, and the lower ones be inaccessible until those above are removed.

A plain interior with no fittings of any kind is scarcely desirable even when it is important to cut down the size. A simple arrangement is to fit two sliding tills, as shown in the illustration, for small tools, including the paring tools, and reserve the body of the box for large ones. These tills can be lifted out or slid to the back or the front of the box as required, their width being half that of the box. The ledges on which they slide are nailed or screwed to the ends, the lower ones being an additional thickness on the upper, so that the lower till is about $\frac{1}{2}$ in. shorter than the upper to allow of lifting out. The tills should not be very deep, or they will occupy too much of the interior space. A depth of $1\frac{1}{2}$ in. for the top one and $2\frac{1}{4}$ in. for the other is sufficient. They can be dovetailed or simply nailed.

The body of the box itself should be dovetailed. Either hard or soft wood can be used as preferred. A suitable thickness for the box is about $\frac{5}{8}$ in. Tills need not be more than $\frac{1}{4}$ in. to $\frac{3}{8}$ in. thick. The sides and ends are prepared first, and are planed to thickness, width, and length. The length, both of sides and ends, will be the overall measurement if the corners are to be dovetailed ; the width will be the inside measurement. Sometimes the sides are screwed or nailed temporarily face to face, while the edges and ends are planed and the dovetails marked and cut, as this is a little quicker than dealing with each piece separately. The ends are treated similarly except that the dovetail lines on them are usually transferred direct from the sides which they have to fit, each end in this case having its dovetails marked and cut separately. The dovetails may be measured and their angles marked with a bevel, or they may be simply divided and marked by free-hand, the lengths, of course, which correspond with the thickness of the wood, being gauged on both sides of the pieces in all cases. If this method is adopted each joint, at the time the transference of the dovetail lines to the end pieces is made, must have a number or other mark pencilled on each piece to show the position for fitting together.

When the sides and ends are fitted they are glued and nailed, and then the bottom is nailed on. It is important at this stage to see that the dovetailed frame is square, for the nailing on of the bottom fixes it unalterably. A piece for the cover is prepared similar in length and width to the bottom. There is the choice, however, of making the cover longer and putting its border strip across the under surface instead of on the end grain as illustrated.

Plinths are nailed round the bottom and top edges as shown, those at the top being $\frac{1}{2}$ in. or so below the top edge, and the border round the cover coming down to meet them when the cover is closed. Those at the bottom may be protected and strengthened by corner pieces of sheet-iron screwed on. The bottom, and the cover also, may be stiffened with battens across the grain. The grain of the bottom need not necessarily run lengthwise, as that of the cover and sides does. It may be composed of a number of short pieces with grain the other way.

Sometimes the under surface of the cover does not bear directly on the top edge of the box, but has a depth of 1 in. or more, so that saws and other suitable tools can be attached to the inside of the cover, and allow the latter to be closed with the box filled level with its top edge with other articles. The same effect can be produced by keeping the top till 1 in. below the top edge of the box and not packing tools above that mark. A plain flat cover, with the usual border, can then be used and still have fittings for the attachment of tools ; but attachment in this way is scarcely convenient for tools in constant use, and is a matter of taste rather than convenience for tools seldom used.

When the box has to be packed for travelling, plenty of cotton waste or paper or other suitable material should be used to keep the tools immovable, as it must not be assumed that the box will always be handled carefully and kept the right side up. The cover also should be screwed down instead of merely locked.

WOODWORKERS' TOOL CHEST

In constructing the tool chest shown in perspective by Fig. 7, and cross-section by Fig. 8, the length must be sufficient to accommodate a rip-saw. This will make the chest 2 ft. 9 in. long internally, and if it is made 1 ft. 8 in. wide by 1 ft. 9 in. deep, it will be found convenient for all purposes.

The material for the outside case should be good white deal or yellow pine, and as the chest may have to stand some rough usage, it should not be less than 1 in. thick. In gluing up the front, back, and ends to obtain the necessary width the joints should be tongued or dowelled, the former being the better method. In dovetailing the chest together, the number of tails should not be stinted, and they should not be more than $1\frac{1}{2}$ in. apart, as in Fig. 9, as the closer they are the stronger will the chest be. Care should be taken that the joints (see Fig. 10) do not come immediately opposite those in the ends.

The plinths run all round the chest, and should be 6 in. and $2\frac{1}{2}$ in. wide and 1 in. thick, respectively, with one edge finished with a plain bevel. The plinths, or skirting, can be mitred at the corners, but it will be stronger to dovetail them. The top plinth, or rib under the lid, must be kept down about $\frac{3}{4}$ in. from the top of the chest, so as to form a rebate for the lid to shut on. The bottom should be 1 in. thick, tongued and grooved, and nailed on crosswise; that

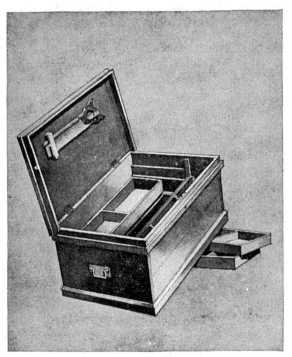

Fig. 7.—Woodworkers' Tool Chest

is, the grain to run from the front to the back of the chest.

The lid should be made from the same kind and thickness of material as the chest, with the joints tongued and grooved, and the ends clamped (Figs. 10 and 12); that is, the lid should be tenoned, and the clamp mortised through and glued and wedged. The lid should be fitted so as to overhang the chest all round about $\frac{1}{16}$ in., and be hung with a pair of strong brass butts, and the lock (which should be a spring one,

self-acting) put on, after which the rim of the lid can be mitred together at the corners, and grooved in the front and the ends (see Figs. 13 and 14).

For the inside of the chest good yellow deal or pine is recommended, which can be finished by staining. If desired, a more fancy wood can be used. As shown in Figs. 15, 16, and 17, the chest is divided in width into three parts; A, for bead-planes, plough, etc., this is 7 in. wide, and is covered by the sliding tills; B, for miscellaneous tools, best planes, or anything which is not in everyday use; and C (which is $3\frac{1}{2}$ in. wide inside) is the saw till. These compartments are divided by the two partitions shown, that between A and B being 9 in. high, and that between B and C 1 ft. 2 in. The three tills G, H, and J slide to and fro to give access to the compartments beneath, and when in place at the back of the chest, form a covering for compartment A; a sliding ledge D beneath the tills, when pulled out as shown by dotted lines, covers compartment B. The bench-planes, etc., can be packed away on the sliding board between the tills and the highest partition.

Fig. 16 shows one end of the chest with the cleats fixed, between which the partitions fit, and which are about 1 in. wide by $\frac{1}{2}$ in. thick. Those which hold the partition between B and C should be fixed

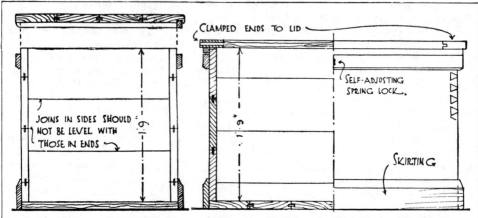

JOINS IN SIDES SHOULD NOT BE LEVEL WITH THOSE IN ENDS

Fig. 8.—Cross-section of Tool-chest

CLAMPED ENDS TO LID

SELF-ADJUSTING SPRING LOCK.

SKIRTING

Fig. 10.—Half Longitudinal Section and Front Elevation of Tool-chest

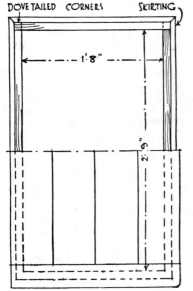

DOVE TAILED CORNERS   SKIRTING

1' 8"

2' 9"

Fig. 11.—Half Plans of Lid and Chest

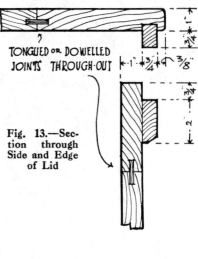

TONGUED OR DOWELLED JOINTS THROUGH OUT

Fig. 13.—Section through Side and Edge of Lid

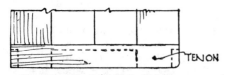

TENON

Fig. 12.—Clamped End of Lid

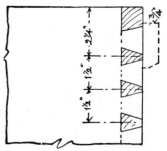

Fig. 9.—Dovetailing Sides Together

first, $\frac{1}{2}$ in. apart, the one nearest the back of the chest reaching nearly to the top, the other, nearest the front, stopping at the same height as the partition. The back partitions having been placed in position, the horizontal cleats can be fixed,

the top edges of which must be $9\frac{1}{2}$ in. from the bottom of the chest, and they must run from the back of the chest to the long upright cleat, as shown in Figs. 16 and 19. On these the sliding ledge D works, which is 9 in. by $\frac{3}{4}$ in., clamped at the ends,

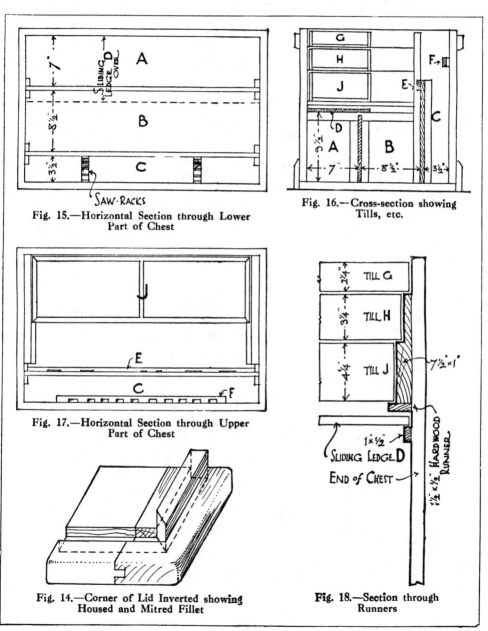

Fig. 15.—Horizontal Section through Lower Part of Chest

Fig. 16.—Cross-section showing Tills, etc.

Fig. 17.—Horizontal Section through Upper Part of Chest

Fig. 18.—Section through Runners

Fig. 14.—Corner of Lid Inverted showing Housed and Mitred Fillet

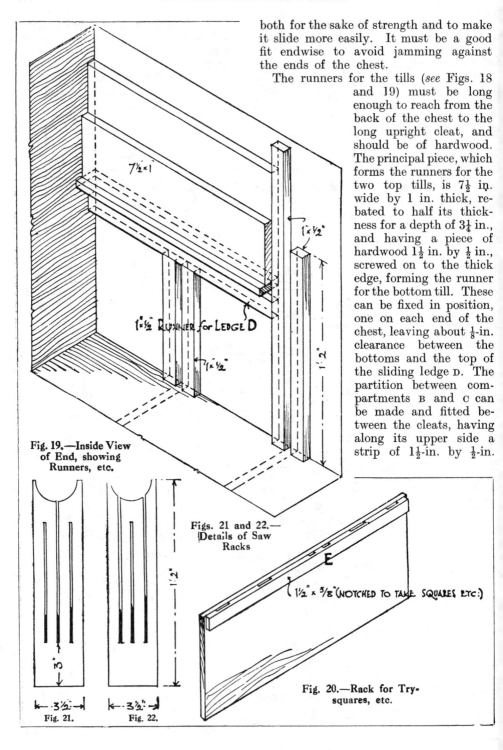

both for the sake of strength and to make it slide more easily. It must be a good fit endwise to avoid jamming against the ends of the chest.

The runners for the tills (*see* Figs. 18 and 19) must be long enough to reach from the back of the chest to the long upright cleat, and should be of hardwood. The principal piece, which forms the runners for the two top tills, is $7\frac{1}{2}$ in. wide by 1 in. thick, rebated to half its thickness for a depth of $3\frac{1}{4}$ in., and having a piece of hardwood $1\frac{1}{2}$ in. by $\frac{1}{2}$ in., screwed on to the thick edge, forming the runner for the bottom till. These can be fixed in position, one on each end of the chest, leaving about $\frac{1}{8}$-in. clearance between the bottoms and the top of the sliding ledge D. The partition between compartments B and C can be made and fitted between the cleats, having along its upper side a strip of $1\frac{1}{2}$-in. by $\frac{1}{2}$-in.

Fig. 19.—Inside View of End, showing Runners, etc.

Figs. 21 and 22.— Details of Saw Racks

Fig. 21.

Fig. 22.

Fig. 20.—Rack for Try-squares, etc.

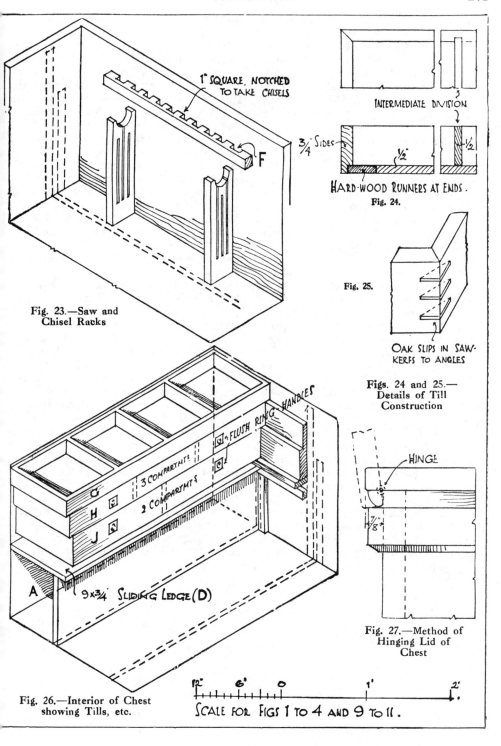

1" SQUARE, NOTCHED TO TAKE CHISELS

F

3/4" SIDES

Fig. 23.—Saw and Chisel Racks

INTERMEDIATE DIVISION

HARD-WOOD RUNNERS AT ENDS.
Fig. 24.

1/2"   1/2"

Fig. 25.

OAK SLIPS IN SAW-KERFS TO ANGLES

Figs. 24 and 25.—
Details of Till
Construction

HINGE

7/8"

Fig. 27.—Method of
Hinging Lid of
Chest

FLUSH RING HANDLES

3 COMPARTMTS

2 COMPARTMTS

½" FLUSH RING

G
H
J

A   9 x ¾" SLIDING LEDGE (D)

Fig. 26.—Interior of Chest
showing Tills, etc.

12"   6"   0   1'   2'

SCALE FOR FIGS 1 TO 4 AND 9 TO 11.

deal, cut to fit between the cleats on each end of the chest, fixed level with the top edge, on the side nearest the front of the chest, and notched about $\frac{1}{8}$ in. at intervals. The slots thus formed can be used for squares, etc., the stocks resting on top of the partition and the blades hanging down inside the saw till (*see* Fig. 20).

The saw-racks (Figs. 21, 22, and 23) are 1 ft. 2 in. long, $3\frac{1}{2}$ in. wide, and 1 in. thick, shaped at the top ends, and with three slots made in each. The middle slot, in Fig. 21, runs from the top to within 3 in. of the bottom, the remainder stopping the same distance from the bottom, and about $1\frac{1}{2}$ in. from the top. In the other (Fig. 22) the middle slot is stopped at both the top and the bottom, and the other cuts through at the top end. These two racks are fixed at about 8 in. from each end, by screwing through the horn at the top to the front of the chest, as shown in Fig. 23. The partition being then put into its place, screws can be put through it into each saw-rack, which will hold all in place. In placing the saws in the racks, the points are inserted in the closed slots, and the handle ends dropped into the open slots, one saw pointing one way and two the opposite.

A piece of hardwood, 2 ft. long and 1 in. square, with a series of notches cut into it wide enough to take the various chisels, etc., and with about $\frac{1}{8}$ in. of solid wood left between each, can be screwed to the front of the chest just above the top of the partition (leaving an equal space at each end to allow room for the hand to be inserted to remove the saws) to furnish a resting-place for the larger chisels, the handles being just inside the front of the chest,

the blades hanging in the saw till (*see* F Fig. 23).

The three sliding tills are of the same width, namely, 9 in. outside, but vary in depth. They should be of $\frac{3}{4}$-in. stuff, with $\frac{1}{2}$-in. bottoms and divisions, the rims dovetailed together, or mitred, as in Figs. 24 and 25. The fronts and back should be rebated to receive the bottoms, the grain of which should run across the width of the tills. At each end the bottom should be of hardwood. The divisions should be trenched into the sides, forming in G, H, and J respectively two, three, and four compartments (*see* Fig. 26). One of the bottom divisions should be fitted up for the brace and bits, with racks for the bits fitted round the brace, by which means one division can be made to accommodate the former and a whole set of the latter. Other divisions can be fitted with racks for small chisels, gouges, gimlets, bradawls, and various other tools.

Turn-buttons to take the tenon and dovetail saws can be screwed to the underside of the lid, so that when it is closed they will be in position between the top till and the front of the chest. The sliding ledge D can be grasped underneath with the fingers when it is desired to draw it forward, and it should have a couple of thumb-holes cut in its top by which to push it back. Each till should have a pair of flush-rings inserted in the front, so that it can be pulled forward without touching the others.

Owing to the rib under the lid running round the box the method of hinging will be as shown in Fig. 27. A strong iron handle on each end of the chest will make it complete.

Garden Lights

SIMPLE GARDEN FRAMES

THE simplest form of cold frame is a small box or packing-case with a sheet of glass over it. These are useful enough, and have the merit of convenience and mobility, and a specially suitable reference to individual plant requirements. But the garden creates problems that these useful makeshifts do not touch.

box by means of butt hinges, and the whole thing is complete.

A window sash has no means of clearing its upper surface of water because the glass is surrounded by a raised wooden border; in other words, the stiles and rails. Therefore a properly-constructed sash for a cold frame should have one rail finishing under the glass; and further, the sash should have a fall, as in a roof,

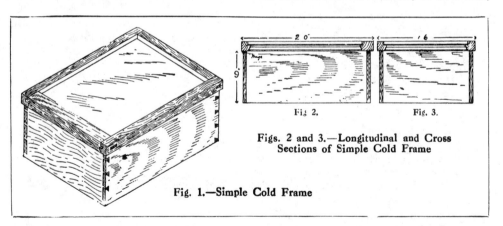

Fig. 2.   Fig. 3.

Figs. 2 and 3.—Longitudinal and Cross Sections of Simple Cold Frame

Fig. 1.—Simple Cold Frame

Cold frames can be of all sizes and shapes. Old sashes can be used in making them. To do this, a box can be made as shown in Figs. 1, 2, and 3, which give particulars of how to fit up a box for a single-light sash. It is not necessary that this box should be made to take to pieces, as it is small enough to be easily portable. The sash can be hung to the

to enable water to run off. Figs. 4, 5 and 6 show such a small frame. The bottom rail finishes on its upper surface just at the beginning of the glass rebate.

The joint at the junction of the top rail and stile is shown by Fig. 7, and the joint at the junction of the stile and the bottom rail by Fig. 8. Dowels should be u3ed for fixing the joints, white-lead paint being used as a binding medium.

Sometimes it is required to have the sash so that it can be taken off, and in this case a slide arrangement is necessary.

When the sash is loose it is apt to be caught by the wind and blown off. This is easily guarded against by fixing wooden buttons on the frame, as shown in Fig. 10. In the case of a frame with a hinged

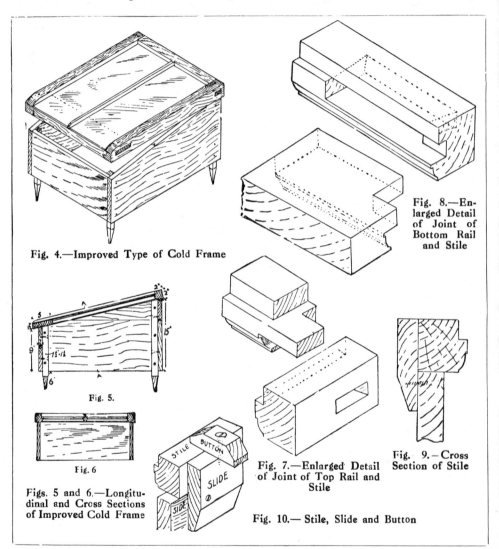

Fig. 4.—Improved Type of Cold Frame

Fig. 8.—Enlarged Detail of Joint of Bottom Rail and Stile

Fig. 5.

Fig. 6

Figs. 5 and 6.—Longitudinal and Cross Sections of Improved Cold Frame

Fig. 7.—Enlarged Detail of Joint of Top Rail and Stile

Fig. 9.—Cross Section of Stile

Fig. 10.— Stile, Slide and Button

This is shown by Fig. 9, which is a section of the stile of the sash, side of the frame and slide piece. It as an advantage to have this slide piece even if the sash is hinged, because it makes the cold frame more air-tight, and consequently warmer.

sash a stick is needed to keep the sash raised when necessary. For a larger cold frame the sash will require bars.

In glazing a frame, each succeeding upper square of glass should overlap the next lower one by about $\frac{3}{4}$ in., and each pane should be tacked at its lower end to prevent slipping. The sash, if of any size, should have a handle fixed on the top rail to assist in moving it. To protect the glass from stones, wire-netting of ¾-in. mesh may be stretched across.

For fixing the cold frame, stakes are driven into the ground so that they lie in the angles of the frame, and the latter is screwed to them.

light, 3 ft. long by 4 ft. wide ; two lights, 6 ft. long by 4 ft. wide; and three lights, 9 ft. long by 4 ft. wide. With the larger lights : One light, 4 ft. long by 6 ft. wide ; two lights, 8 ft. long by 6 ft. wide ; and three lights, 12 ft. long by 6 ft. wide.

The lights are made as shown in Fig. 12. It will be noticed that the bottom rail is thinner than the stiles and top rail, this being to allow the glass to come over it, so that the water will run away, while

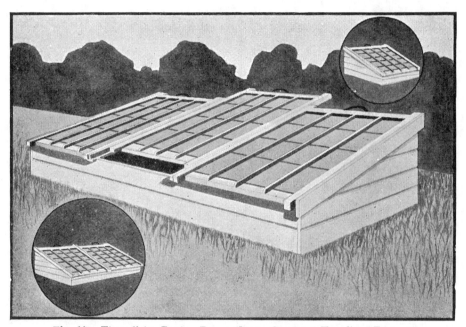

Fig. 11.—Three-light Garden Frame (Inset, One- and Two-light Frames)

GARDEN FRAMES OF SPECIAL CONSTRUCTION

Specially constructed garden frames are usually made with one, two or three lights. A three-light frame is shown by Fig. 11, and the insets in this figure show frames with one and two lights. The constructional work of these frames is of a fairly simple character.

The frames shown have sliding lights, and prove very satisfactory in use. The lights may be either 4 ft. by 3 ft. or 6 ft. by 4 ft. With the smaller lights frames can be made to the following sizes : One

a throating should be cut in the under-side to prevent the water running back and into the frame. A tie rod of ½-in. round iron, fixed across the light, as shown in Fig. 12, will greatly strengthen it.

The body for a three-light frame is shown in Fig. 13 ; but the construction in the case of a one-light or two-light frame is almost identical. A section through the frame is given by Fig. 14, and the sectional dimensions for a frame to suit either the smaller or larger lights are given in Figs. 15 and 16. Grooved-and-tongued boards not less than 1⅛ in. thick should be used. Those for the

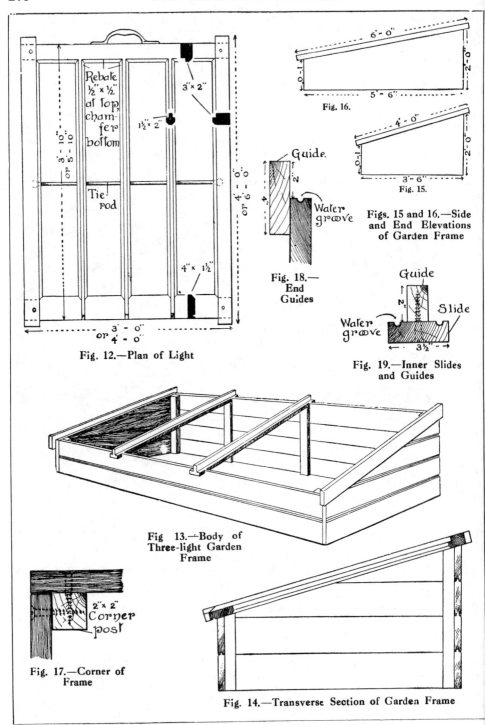

Rebate ½" × ½" at top, chamfer bottom

3" × 2"

1½" × 2"

Tie rod

4" × 1½"

3'-10" or 5'-10"

4'-0" or 6'-0"

or 3'-0" or 4'-0"

Fig. 12.—Plan of Light

6'-0"

5'-6"

2'-0"

1'-0"

Fig. 16.

4'-0"

3'-6"

2'-0"

1'-0"

Fig. 15.

Figs. 15 and 16.—Side and End Elevations of Garden Frame

Guide.

Water groove

Fig. 18.— End Guides

Guide

Slide

Water groove

3½"

Fig. 19.—Inner Slides and Guides

Fig 13.—Body of Three-light Garden Frame

2" × 2" Corner post

Fig. 17.—Corner of Frame

Fig. 14.—Transverse Section of Garden Frame

sides are cut to shape, and 2-in. corner posts are screwed $1\frac{1}{8}$ in. in from the ends, as shown in Figs. 14 and 17. Water grooves could be cut at the top edges of the sides, as clearly shown in Fig. 18. The front and back boards are screwed to the corner posts which have been previously fixed to the sides, as shown in Fig. 17. In two-light or three-light frames the front and back could be strengthened with cross-battens, as shown in Fig. 13.

In two-light or three-light frames the inner slides and guides are formed as shown in Figs. 13 and 19, water grooves

corners of the ends and frames. The frames of glass measure 1 ft. 6 in. square, and the length of the frame could be extended according to the number of frames available.

Fig. 21 shows the sectional dimensions of the frame to which the ends and inner frames should be made. The ends (Fig. 22) are of $\frac{1}{2}$-in. boards, preferably grooved and tongued, and held together with two battens 1 in. square nailed in position. Two wood stakes 1 in. square are fitted to each end for fixing in the earth ; they are pointed, and project about 6 in. The inner frames (Fig. 23) are of wood 1 in.

Fig. 20 —Extensible Garden Frame

being cut in the slides. For the guides at the ends see Fig. 18.

Deal may be used in constructing the frames ; but being exposed to the weather all the joints should be put together with white-lead paint.

EXTENSIBLE GARDEN FRAME

An extensible garden frame of simple construction is shown by Fig. 20. The frame is made in parts, and could be fitted up on any desired spot. There must be two wood ends, and a number of inner frames, which are covered with loose sheets of glass. The glass is not fixed in any way, but simply rests on the ends and frames, and is held at the bottom by small metal clips, which are fitted at the

square, half-lapped and screwed together at the top, as shown in Fig. 24, and kept from spreading by a cross batten, which should be 1 in. deep by $\frac{1}{2}$ in. thick, screwed in position. The bottom ends of the frames are cut to a point as shown. The metal clips could be of either thin iron or steel 1 in. wide, and shaped as shown by Fig. 25. The clips are let in flush with the edges of the ends and frames, each being fixed with two screws.

The wood and metal parts of the frame should be kept well painted.

HAND LIGHT

A hand light has many advantages over the larger garden frame, and by its use seeds may be raised on the site they are

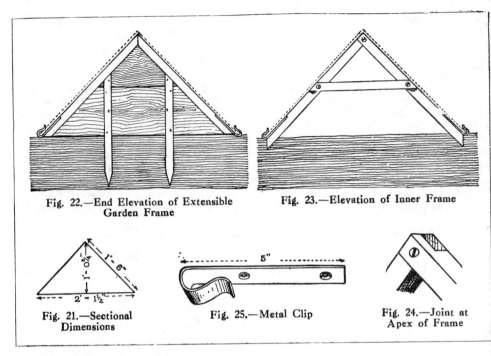

Fig. 22.—End Elevation of Extensible
Garden Frame

Fig. 23.—Elevation of Inner Frame

Fig. 21.—Sectional
Dimensions

Fig. 25.—Metal Clip

Fig. 24.—Joint at
Apex of Frame

permanently to occupy. It may be used for forcing vegetables and small salads in their permanent positions, and with glass on each side the contents of the light receive a maximum amount of heat and sunshine which is very beneficial.

Fig. 26 is a general view of the light, and Figs. 27 and 28 are side and end elevations. A cross section is shown by Fig. 29. The ends A (Fig. 30) are made from ½-in. boards to the sizes given in Fig. 31. The boards should, preferably, have grooved-and-tongued edges, and they are held together with two battens B. The battens are 2½ in. wide by ½ in. thick, and the upper edges project ½ in. above the

Fig. 26.—Hand Light

edges of the ends to form rebates for the glass. Two small battens C (Fig. 31), which are 4 in. long by 1½ in. wide by 1 in. thick, are fixed to the ends 1 in. in from the edges to carry the side rails D. The side rails are 2 ft. 5 in. long by 4 in. deep by 1 in. thick. The top edges are bevelled to match the ends, and they are fixed to the battens C. Small angle-plates fixed in the corners between the battens C and the side rails D would greatly strengthen the work. The top rail E is 2 ft. 10 in. long by 2½ in. deep by 1 in. thick. Notches are cut in the underside to fit over the ends of the light, and the ends of the rail are rounded.

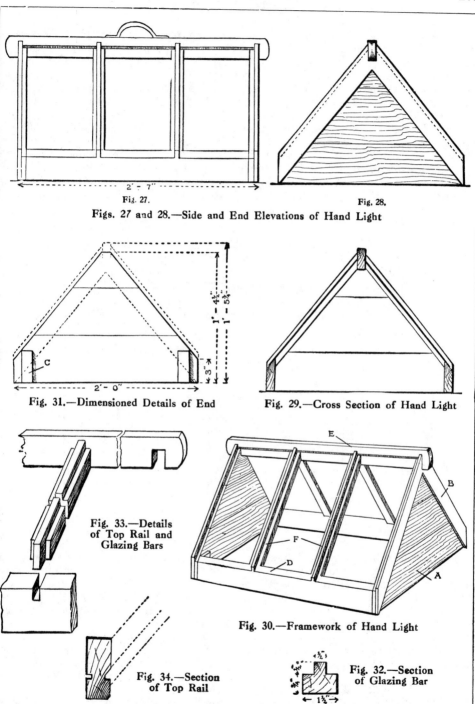

Figs. 27 and 28.—Side and End Elevations of Hand Light

Fig. 27.

Fig. 28.

Fig. 31.—Dimensioned Details of End

Fig. 29.—Cross Section of Hand Light

Fig. 33.—Details of Top Rail and Glazing Bars

Fig. 30.—Framework of Hand Light

Fig. 34.—Section of Top Rail

Fig. 32.—Section of Glazing Bar

The glazing bars F, two of which are fitted at each side of the light, are of a section similar to that shown by Fig. 32. These bars simply butt against the top rail, and are notched into the side rails, as shown in Fig. 33. Grooves are cut in the top rail in a line with the rebates in the glazing bars and ends to form a fixing for the glass. A square groove is first cut, and this is then bevelled at the bottom edge to correspond with the slope of the glazing bars and ends, as shown in Fig. 34.

raising plants and bringing them on as soon as possible. The one shown by Fig. 35 can easily be put together at quite a trivial cost. In appearance it resembles a miniature garden frame on legs, with a slanting glass roof, which can be raised or moved as required. It is heated by a paraffin-oil lamp, and is so constructed that no noxious fumes can reach the seedlings. The outside dimensions of the propagator are 2 ft. 7½ in. wide by 1 ft 10½ in. deep, and it stands 3 ft. 1 in. high at the back and 2 ft. 8½ in. at the front

Fig. 35.—Easily-made Propagator

The glass used in glazing the light should be 21 oz., sprigged and bedded in oil putty, care being taken to paint the rebates before glazing. An iron handle similar to that shown in Fig. 26 is screwed to the top rail, and will be found useful for moving the light. When complete the light should be painted with not less than two coats of good oil paint.

EASILY-MADE PROPAGATOR

Where a greenhouse or hotbed is not available, a propagator is very useful for

As will be seen on reference to the cross section (Fig. 36), the water tank, which measures 2 ft. 6 in. by 1 ft. 9 in. by 1½ in deep, rests on the top of the legs, and thus gives the propagating chamber a depth of about 1 ft. 2 in. at the back and 10 in. at the front.

To begin the construction, first cut four legs from a length of 2-in. quartering and square them off to each 1 ft. 8 in. long These should be then connected at the top by rails 2 in. wide by 1 in. thick which should be dovetail-keyed into the legs, as in Fig. 37. The rails should be brought flush with the outside face of the legs, and the dovetails worked parallel on the front face and made only $\frac{7}{8}$ in. long into the thickness of the latter. The legs and framing, which should now resemble Fig. 38, are next covered in on the under-

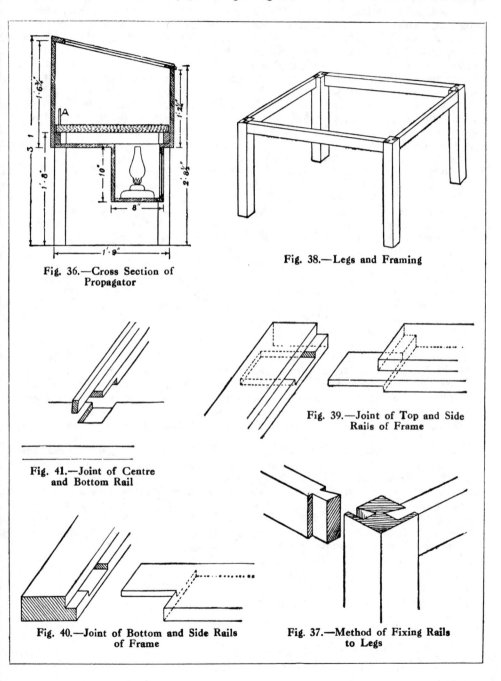

Fig. 36.—Cross Section of Propagator

Fig. 38.—Legs and Framing

Fig. 39.—Joint of Top and Side Rails of Frame

Fig. 41.—Joint of Centre and Bottom Rail

Fig. 40.—Joint of Bottom and Side Rails of Frame

Fig. 37.—Method of Fixing Rails to Legs

side of the rails with $\frac{3}{4}$-in. grooved-and-tongued boarding, leaving an opening 8 in. square at the centre of the front for the reception of the lamp chamber. This should be made 10 in. high of the same thickness boarding, nailed together at the angles and all round at the top to the edge of the opening in the bottom of the propagator. A glass panelled door should be hinged at the side of the front of the lamp chamber for the purpose of attending to the lamp, and a few $\frac{3}{4}$-in. holes made in the sides to allow air to enter and the fumes to escape.

The sides of the propagator are next cut from $\frac{3}{4}$-in. grooved-and-tongued boarding, the front measuring 1 ft. $2\frac{1}{4}$ in. high and the back 1 ft. $6\frac{3}{4}$ in. These are nailed together at the corners, and also to the framework at the top of the legs. It is of great importance to have well-seasoned boarding, and to see that the tongues are not broken away in places, causing bad joints, or the heat will escape at any gaps and cause trouble with draught to young seedlings.

The glass-framed top is of 1-in. stuff, and the top and two side pieces should be planed to $2\frac{1}{2}$ in. wide, and rebated throughout their length to a depth of $\frac{1}{2}$ in. each way. The front piece need only be $\frac{1}{2}$ in. thick and $2\frac{1}{2}$ in. wide. The four pieces should now be mortised and tenoned together, the top into the two sides as in Fig. 39, and the bottom piece as in Fig. 40. A centre rail 1 in. square and rebated on each side should be tenoned into the top and let in the bottom as in Fig. 41, and when the joints are ready, glued up and wedged in tightly between two lengths of batten, so that the joints come up quite close. With the addition of a couple of runners nailed to the top of the sides, this will complete the wood-

work of the propagator. The rebating should receive a coat of white-lead prior to bedding the glass in soft oil putty, or the latter will not stick properly, after which the whole should be painted with three coats of good oil colour to preserve the wood.

The tank to contain the water should be made of stout zinc well soldered together at the angles, and to prevent the top sagging in the centre, a few short pieces of zinc tubing should be soldered on the inside at intervals. A short length of tubing A (Fig. 36) should also be soldered at one of the sides, by which the tank may be emptied or filled. A good paraffin-oil lamp capable of holding sufficient oil to last at least a full day without requiring to be refilled will be needed to heat the tank, and the top of the glass chimney should be quite 2 in. or 3 in. clear of the bottom of the tank.

The best material with which to cover the top of the tank is undoubtedly cocoa-nut-fibre refuse ; but if this is not procurable or is too expensive, fresh sawdust will answer the same purpose. Whichever is used, it is imperative that the material be kept thoroughly moist throughout the entire depth. A thermometer should be fixed to one of the sides of the propagating chamber, so that it can easily be seen from without, and for general purposes an even temperature of about 60° should be maintained. The lamp should be first turned up as for giving light, and when once the heat is diffused throughout the propagating material it should be turned low. The chamber will then keep up an even temperature and the lamp will burn all night and day without needing replenishing or altering.

Greenhouses

PORTABLE GREENHOUSE : TENANT'S FIXTURE

A SPECIAL feature of the greenhouse shown by Fig. 1 is its portability. It is of simple construction, being formed of four principal parts, namely, top, side, and two ends, and these being connected together with screws, very little fixing to the wall is required. By this means the greenhouse would be a tenant's fixture, and, for removal, could be taken apart by undoing a few screws. Front and two end elevations are shown by Figs. 2, 3 and 4.

Good quality red deal will be the most suitable wood, and it will be more economical to buy it ready sawn to the following

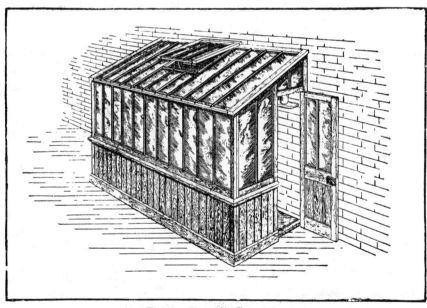

Fig. 1.—Portable Greenhouse

sizes : Bars for side, ends, and roof, 2 in. by 1 in., 120 ft. run ; stiles, rails, etc., for sides and ends, 3 in. by 2 in. 120 ft. run ; stiles and rails for roof and middle rail of side and ends, 4½ in. by 2 in., 50 ft. run ; bottom rail of roof, 4½ in. by 1¼ in., 13 ft. run ; ventilating skylight, 3 in. by 1½ in., 14 ft. run ; hinged sash in end, 2 in. by 2 in., 14 ft. run : matchboarding for lower part of framing including plinth, ⅞ in. by 6½ in., 130 ft. run ; middle and bottom rail for door, 7 in. by 2 in., 5 ft. run ; weathering strip, and stout bars in end and roof, 1½ in. by 2 in., 50 ft. run. The foregoing sizes are for the wood in the rough, the dimensions marked on the illustrations being those of the wood when planed. To prevent waste, care must be taken to purchase such lengths of wood as will cut up to the best advantage.

Saw the wood off to lengths ; all vertical parts such as stiles should be cut off 2 in. longer than required ; for the rail-pieces having tenons allow about ½ in. longer at each end. All the pieces should be planed

true on one side, then an edge planed at right angles, after which they should be gauged, and planed to the thickness and breadth indicated in the illustrations. It is advisable to set out and complete cne piece before attempting the second, so as to avoid mistakes through the pieces becoming mixed.

The principal parts lettered in Figs. 5, 6, and 7 are as follows : A, bottom rail ; B, middle rail ; C, top rail ; D, bottom rail of roof ; E, trimming bar ; F, top rail of roof ; G, wall-piece ; H, top rail of ventilating skylight ; M, fillet to hinge same to ; J, bottom rail of skylight ; K, plinth ; L, weathering strip or sill ; N, stile of side ; O, P, and T, stiles of end ; R and S, stiles of door ; U, matchboarding ; V, stop round door opening ; W, bar.

The setting-out and subsequent operations for the side will now be described. The two angle stiles should be placed

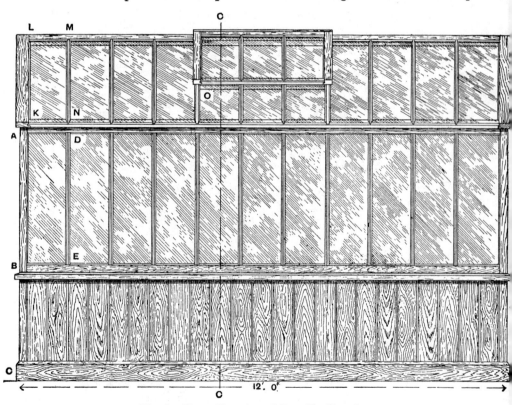

Fig. 2.—Front Elevation of Portable Greenhouse

together in pairs, the positions for mortises being shown in Figs. 8 and 9, and a halved joint (Fig. 10) should be marked across the edges ; as the mortises are to be made right through, the lines must be continued to the opposite edges. The top, middle, and bottom rails can next be placed together, and marked out for shoulders at each end (*see* Figs. 8, 9, and 10). They should also be set out for the mortises for the bars (Figs. 11 and 12). By referring to Figs. 8 and 9, it will be seen that the outer shoulder has to fit to the rebate, and therefore must be set out to the depth of the rebate longer than the inner one. The mortise gauge should now be set to suit the chisel that is to be used (one about $\frac{5}{8}$ in. will be the most suitable), then gauge the pieces for the mortises

and tenons. Next make the mortises in the stiles and rails ; in the former they go through, and in the latter they should be about $1\frac{1}{4}$ in. deep, as indicated in Figs. 11 and 12. The tenons can now be cut ; not the shoulders. The bars should next be set out and gauged, and the tenons cut. Each piece should now be gauged for the rebates. The rebating can be done with a side fillister ; but if this tool is not availa..e, a rebate plane can be very easily adapted for the purpose. Three pieces of wood are screwed to the plane ; one to only allow it to work a fixed distance " on," and two other pieces to prevent it going below the desired depth. Care must be taken to keep the iron projecting a little beyond the side of the plane, in order to produce clean rebates.

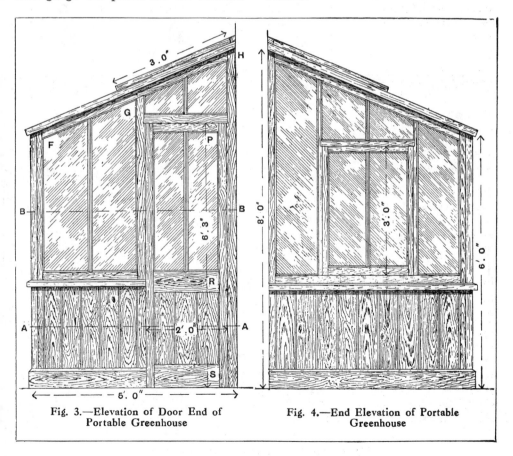

Fig. 3.—Elevation of Door End of Portable Greenhouse

Fig. 4.—End Elevation of Portable Greenhouse

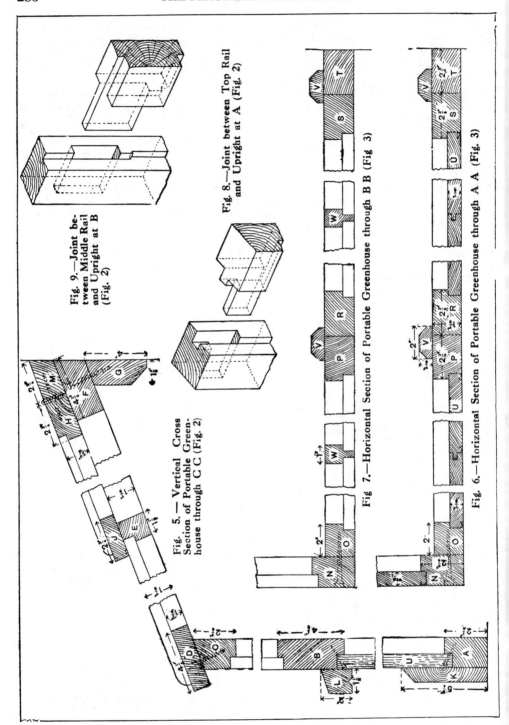

Fig. 9.—Joint between Middle Rail and Upright at B (Fig. 2)

Fig. 8.—Joint between Top Rail and Upright at A (Fig. 2)

Fig. 5. — Vertical Cross Section of Portable Greenhouse through C C (Fig. 2)

Fig 7.—Horizontal Section of Portable Greenhouse through B B (Fig 3)

Fig. 6.—Horizontal Section of Portable Greenhouse through A A (Fig. 3)

The shoulders of the tenons can now be cut. The tenons of the top and middle rails must be reduced to the shape shown in Figs. 8 and 9, forming a haunch. The under edge of the middle rail and the top edge of the bottom rail require to be rebated for boarding (*see* Figs. 5, 10, and 12). Now plane the upper edge of the top rail to the angle shown at Fig. 5. The rebate of the lower part of the stiles must be made deeper, so as to receive the edge of the board (*see* Fig. 5). Each tenon must now be fitted in its respective mortise, after which the whole should be put together and any necessary easing done. Then take two pieces, paint the joints, and put together. The tenons of the top and middle rails must next be

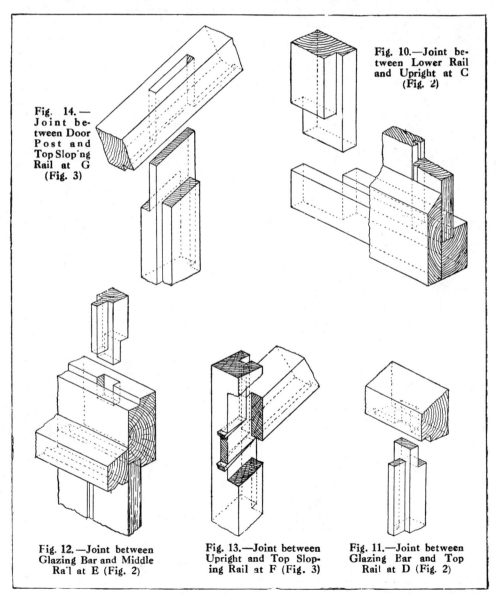

Fig. 14.—Joint between Door Post and Top Sloping Rail at G (Fig. 3)

Fig. 10.—Joint between Lower Rail and Upright at C (Fig. 2)

Fig. 12.—Joint between Glazing Bar and Middle Rail at E (Fig. 2)

Fig. 13.—Joint between Upright and Top Sloping Rail at F (Fig. 3)

Fig. 11.—Joint between Glazing Bar and Top Rail at D (Fig. 2)

wedged in the mortises, as indicated at Fig. 13. The bottom rail and stiles can be connected with two or three screws. Any unevenness between the surfaces of the stiles and top and middle rails should be planed away. It is important to keep the frame square until the boarding is fixed in the lower part ; that is, the stiles and rails must be held at right angles to each other. This can be done by temporarily nailing two strips of wood across the top angles. The matchboarding for the lower part can now be cut off to lengths and secured to the middle and bottom rails with 2-in. nails driven in

obliquely, as indicated in Fig. 5. The top of the stiles should be sawn and planed level with the top of the rails, and the ends of the tenons and wedges planed flush to the edges of the stiles.

Next prepare a board long enough to form the plinth (see K, Fig. 5). carefully mitre the ends, and secure by nailing to the boards and bottom rail. The weathering strip, or sham sill, L (Fig. 5) should be planed to the form shown ; the V-groove can be made with the rebate plane. The ends of the sill should now be mitred ; then nail the sill to its position as shown Secure the bars

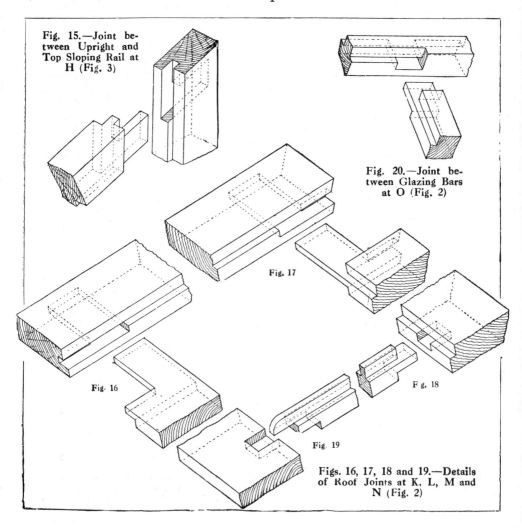

Fig. 15.—Joint between Upright and Top Sloping Rail at H (Fig. 3)

Fig. 20.—Joint between Glazing Bars at O (Fig. 2)

Fig. 17

Fig. 16

F g. 18

Fig. 19

Figs. 16, 17, 18 and 19.—Details of Roof Joints at K, L, M and N (Fig. 2)

to the top and middle rails with a small nail.

The lower parts of the ends are prepared in a similar way to that described for the side. But two points that must be kept in view are, that the mitre of the sill piece and the plinth must be made to project beyond the edges of the stiles of ends, a distance equal to the thickness of the stiles of the side framing (*see* Figs. 3 and 4). It will be found easier to make the joints for the lower part and fit them together first. The top rail can then be placed in position, and the shoulders marked on it at each end, and also the position of the mortises in the stiles can be determined, after which the pieces may be gauged and the mortises and tenons made ; the form of these is shown in Figs. 13, 14, and 15. The mortises for the bars in the top rail, also those for the pieces forming the top of the doorway and the hanging sash, should be set out and made. The ends can now be put together, and each bar laid on and marked for shoulders, then gauged ; the tenons and shoulders can then be cut, and the bars fitted into their respective positions. The method of completing each end will be almost exactly the same as described for the side. A good plan is to procure a piece of oak about 2 in. square for a threshold, and to connect

the stiles that form the doorway, as shown in Fig. 1.

The making of the roof and skylight should present little difficulty. The wood for the bottom rail should be planed up to dimensions, noting that the thickness of this is less than the stiles by the amount of the rebate. The several pieces should be set out for the joints, etc., which are shown by Figs. 16, 17, and 18, the one for connecting the stiles to the bottom rail requiring special notice. The form of joint between the bars and the bottom rail is shown by Fig. 19. By referring to Fig. 2 it will be seen that the bars supporting the ventilating skylight require to be rebated their whole length on one side, and only as far as the trimming piece on the other. It should also be noted that they are stouter than the other bars, and it will be as well to let their tenons pass through the top rail. The joint connecting the bars and the trimming pieces is shown by Fig. 20.

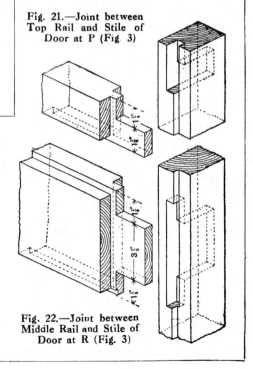

Fig. 21.—Joint between Top Rail and Stile of Door at P (Fig. 3)

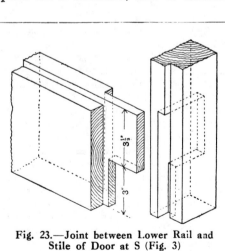

Fig. 23.—Joint between Lower Rail and Stile of Door at S (Fig. 3)

Fig. 22.—Joint between Middle Rail and Stile of Door at R (Fig. 3)

The tenons of the bars should be fixed to the top and bottom rails with a small nail, and the whole completed in a manner similar to that described for the other parts. The joints of the door are shown by Figs. 21, 22, and 23.

The method of fixing will now be described. The ground where the ends and a side are to stand should be levelled, and very suitable foundation would be formed by a course of bricks. One end and the side should be placed in position, and temporarily stayed until screwed together ; the other end should be fixed to the side in the same manner. The wall piece G (Fig. 5) should be prepared and cut off to the exact length. This should next be placed in position and firmly secured to the wall with 4-in. nails driven into the brickwork. The roof can now be lifted on and secured to the wall piece, ends, and side with 3½-in. screws, as indicated in Fig. 5. The stiles abutting to the walls should be secured by two or three holdfasts. Then plane the edges of the door and sash to fit into their respective openings and hinge them, and also the skylight on the top. A chamfered fillet, as shown in section at v (Figs. 6 and 7), should be prepared and fixed round inside the door opening and window in the opposite end.

The greenhouse will now be ready for a first coat of paint, after which it should be glazed and finally finished with two more coats of paint of any colour desired.

SMALL SPAN-ROOF GREENHOUSE

The matter of keeping the cost as low as possible has been consistently borne in mind when designing the span-roof greenhouses shown in side and end elevations by Figs. 24, 25, and 26, and to further this object in the actual construction it is not advised that the timber should be purchased in so many pieces cut to the lengths required, or it will cost more ; but rather that it should be bought in bulk, the worker cutting it up himself. The quantities required, with the various sizes and sections are given later.

The greenhouse is 12 ft. long by 7 ft.

wide, the height being 5 ft. to the eaves. The roof is of square pitch, that is, the rafters form a right angle at the top, and the whole structure stands on a foundation consisting of a single row of bricks as shown. The lower portion is boarded with 1-in. tongued-and-grooved boards, the upper part and the roof being glazed. The door is placed in the middle of one end of the house, thus leaving room for a stage down each side. Ventilation is provided for by the two ventilators at one side of the roof, and one at the other, thus forming a through current of air, which can be regulated as desired.

The necessary setting out and framing together is very simple. Figs. 27 and 28 show the framing of the door end and one side respectively. In these latter illustrations the posts A are the same. The corner posts must be mortised as in Fig. 29 to take the sills, the middle rails, and the top rails or plates. The whole of the mortises must be kept back from the face sides (that is the outsides) the thickness of the boarding to be used in the lower part, which will be ⅞ in. This will facilitate the making of the rebates to take the glass and the boarding, and also simplify the tenons on the various rails, etc., which have to fit to the posts. The intermediate posts in the sides and ends will be mortised to take the middle rails, as shown in Fig. 30, these mortises passing straight through. They will also be tenoned to fit into the top rails (plates), and cut as shown at the bottom to fit the sills. The reason of this latter cut, instead of an ordinary tenon, will be given later. The two door posts will be similar to the last mentioned, with the exception that instead of the tenon to fit into the top rails, mortises must be made instead, as shown in Fig. 31. These mortises must not be allowed to pass through the wood, or it will show in the doorway. Other similar mortises must be made higher up and on the opposite sides to take the door head, and the posts should be left to run up so as to cut off afterwards to fit the rafters when these are fitted and fixed.

The sills will need cutting, as in Fig. 32,

being kept less in width to allow the board to run down beyond them. The mortises take the form of slots, which accounts for the shape of the tenon at the bottom of the intermediate posts (Fig. 30). The tenons at the end of the sills, which fit into the corner posts, must be " bare-faced " ; that is, with a shoulder on the inside only, as shown on the left in Fig. 32. The top rails will be tenoned as in Fig. 33, to fit the corner posts ; also mortised to take the intermediate posts. These mortises should not go through the wood. The rail is shown wrong way up in the illustration, so as to show the mortises. The outside upper corner of

them stronger, they are each made nearly long enough to reach through the post, and each halved on to its fellow. Thus the rails will not only be pinned to the post, but will also be pinned together through the halving. The corner posts will need rebating to take the glass and boards at each side on the outside corners ; the intermediate posts will need rebating in the same way at each of the outer corners ; also the top rails on the under-side, and the middle rails both on the under and the upper sides. The rebates in all cases should be ⅜ in. deep, and reach to the mortise or tenon, as the case may be. Thus Fig. 33 is shown ready

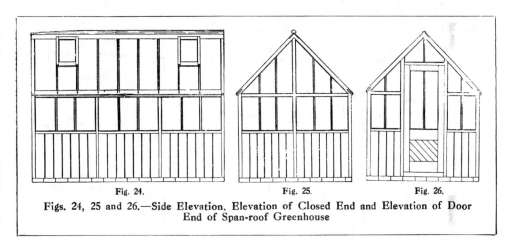

Fig. 24.   Fig. 25.   Fig. 26.

Figs. 24, 25 and 26.—Side Elevation, Elevation of Closed End and Elevation of Door End of Span-roof Greenhouse

these rails must be chamfered off to an angle of 45°, as shown in Fig. 28, to form a bed for the eaves board, and when the framing is put together the chamfers will be continued on the ends of the posts as shown. Fig. 34 shows the top rail for the end opposite the door (Fig. 25). The ends of the tenons are shown mitred so as to fit up to the tenons of the side rails in the corner posts, thus giving more hold for the pins when fixing together. The mortise for the middle post must, in this case, pass through the wood to take the continuation of the post. In the middle side rails (see Fig. 25) the tenons would be very short where they come to the intermediate posts, if cut in the ordinary way, therefore, to make

for rebating, and Figs. 34 and 35 are shown with one rebate made. The door posts will need rebating as above at one side ; but the door side will either need a deeper and wider rebate to take the door, or slips may be nailed on to answer the same purpose ; probably the latter will be found the better way. In all cases where a tenon comes to a mortise in a post or other part that has to be rebated, the outer shoulder must be left longer to fit into the rebate. Fig. 36 is a section of one side of the greenhouse.

When all the parts are cut correctly, the whole frame may be put together, carefully painting each mortise and tenon as it is fitted ; also the pins as they are driven in. The frame will then be ready for the roof, a section of which is shown by Fig. 37. Fig. 38 is an enlarged section at the eaves.

The outside rafters must be cut as in Fig. 39 and the intermediate ones as in Fig. 40 ; and the roof being of square outside rafters may be tenoned together ; or, if preferred, they can be halved, and fixed with screws ; or they may be mitred. The intermediate rafters will, as a matter of course, be mitred, and no ridge board is necessary. At the upper

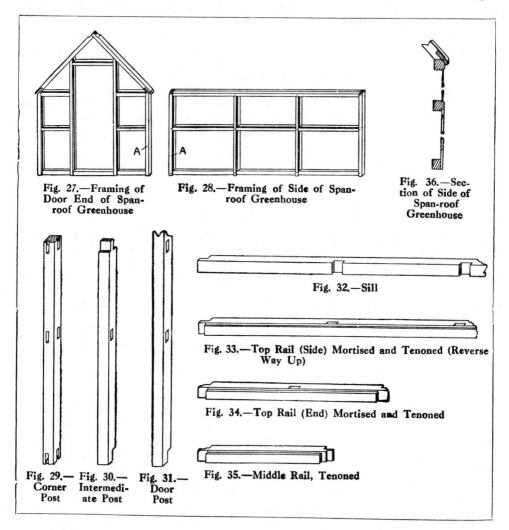

Fig. 27.—Framing of Door End of Span-roof Greenhouse

Fig. 28.—Framing of Side of Span-roof Greenhouse

Fig. 36.—Section of Side of Span-roof Greenhouse

Fig. 32.—Sill

Fig. 33.—Top Rail (Side) Mortised and Tenoned (Reverse Way Up)

Fig. 34.—Top Rail (End) Mortised and Tenoned

Fig. 35.—Middle Rail, Tenoned

Fig. 29.—Corner Post

Fig. 30.—Intermediate Post

Fig. 31.—Door Post

pitch, it follows that the angle at the bottom will be one of 45°. The point at A must come to the edge of the chamfer on the top rail, so that the plain surface B and the chamfer are continuous when the rafters are fixed, and form a bed for the eaveboard C. At the upper end the ends the tongues of the rafters must be cut away down to within about $\frac{3}{16}$ in. of the rebate, to take the boards D, which will fix to each pair of rafters on both sides of the roof, and the glass will fit up under them, as in Fig. 41. These roof boards may be anything from 3 in. to

5 in. wide by ¾ in. thick. They are nailed one on the other at the apex of the roof, the ridge roll E covering the joint. In fixing the boards, take care that the rafters are kept the correct distance between.

The two ventilators take the form of in a small house like the one being described, the top rail can be fitted and hinged to the ridge roll. The opening of the ventilators is done by means of a curved iron bar fixed to the bottom rail of the ventilator, and a cord passing over a pulley fixed in the cross trimmer

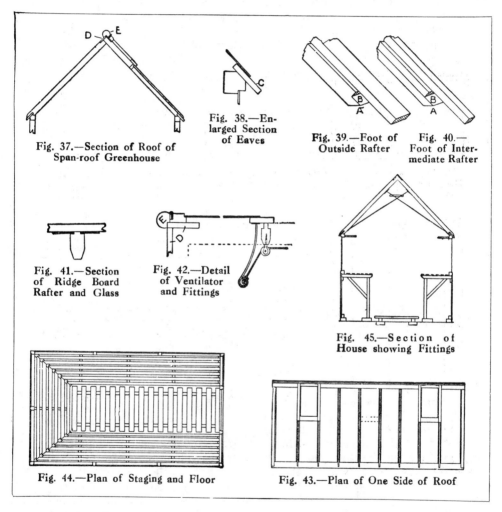

Fig. 37.—Section of Roof of Span-roof Greenhouse

Fig. 38.—Enlarged Section of Eaves

Fig. 39.—Foot of Outside Rafter

Fig. 40.—Foot of Intermediate Rafter

Fig. 41.—Section of Ridge Board Rafter and Glass

Fig. 42.—Detail of Ventilator and Fittings

Fig. 45.—Section of House showing Fittings

Fig. 44.—Plan of Staging and Floor

Fig. 43.—Plan of One Side of Roof

small sashes, made so as to cover one pair of rafters in width, and to reach about halfway between the ridge and the eaves in the length. A piece of rafter material is fixed between the pair of rafters, in the correct position for the bottom rail of the sash to rest on. When closed, and between the rafters. A section of the whole arrangement is shown by Fig. 42. The plan of one side of the roof (Fig. 43) shows the position of the two ventilators on that side; the dotted lines also show the position of the single ventilator on the opposite side. The bars in the sides and ends of the greenhouse, apart from the actual framing, may be cut to fit tightly and fixed with brads; or they may be tenoned into the middle rail and bradded to the top rail, if preferred. The fixing of the boarding round the greenhouse will present no difficulty, and the door can be simply framed up with mortise-and-tenon joints or halving joints. The door will be fixed with butt hinges, and should be fitted with a lock and key.

A plan of the inside fittings is shown by Fig. 44. The staging along each side is 2 ft. wide, and that across the end is 6 in. wider. It consists of battens 2 in. wide by 1 in. thick fixed to the bearers,

The whole should be kept down in width sufficiently to allow of the complete floor being turned up and taken out through the door when required. Shelves may be fixed along the top rail, supported by brackets, as shown in Fig. 45, and another one may be fixed in the top part of the roof. Solid shelves are shown as being more convenient for fixing; but if formed of laths in the same way as the staging, they will last longer. Iron tie rods, as shown in Fig. 45, should be fixed across the house in the middle lengthwise.

In conclusion, a specification of the materials required to build the greenhouse is here given, the various sections being shown by Figs. 46 to 56. Top rail (Fig.

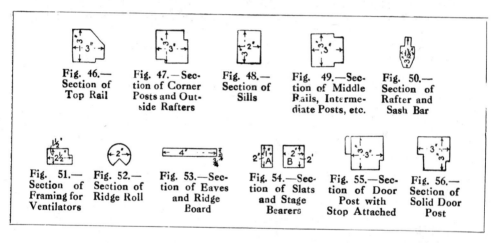

Fig. 46.—Section of Top Rail

Fig. 47.—Section of Corner Posts and Outside Rafters

Fig. 48.—Section of Sills

Fig. 49.—Section of Middle Rails, Intermediate Posts, etc.

Fig. 50.—Section of Rafter and Sash Bar

Fig. 51.—Section of Framing for Ventilators

Fig. 52.—Section of Ridge Roll

Fig. 53.—Section of Eaves and Ridge Board

Fig. 54.—Section of Slats and Stage Bearers

Fig. 55.—Section of Door Post with Stop Attached

Fig. 56.—Section of Solid Door Post

as shown in the section (Fig. 45), with a space of about 1 in. between. The ends of the bearers which come to the outside of the greenhouse rest on fillets screwed to the outer boarding as shown, the inner edge of the staging being supported by the braced legs. These latter should stand on a brick laid in the ground or firmly on it, and should be painted on the end grain before they are fixed. The floor, as shown, may be dispensed with if preferred; but the greenhouse will be found much more comfortable with it. It consists of two pieces of scantling 2 in. square resting on bricks at intervals in their length, the floor proper being slats 3 in. or 4 in. wide, spaced out as shown.

46), 24 ft. required; corner posts and end rafters (Fig. 47), 50 ft.; sills (Fig. 48), 40 ft.; intermediate posts and middle rails (Fig. 49), 70 ft.; intermediate rafter for glass 15 in. wide (Fig. 50), 120 ft.; stiles and top rails of ventilators (Fig. 51), 24 ft.; ridge roll (Fig. 52), 12 ft.; eave and ridge boards (Fig. 53), 52 ft.; slats and bearers for stage and floor (Fig. 54), 400 ft. for A and 100 ft. for B; door post (stop nailed on) (Fig. 55), 14 ft.; door post solid (alternative) (Fig. 56), 14 ft.; 1¼ squares of 1-in. tongued-and-grooved boarding; 14 ft. of 9-in. by 1½-in. for the door; 60 ft. of sash bar (as Fig. 50, but smaller); 300 ft. of horticultural glass; putty, paint, nails, screws, etc.

Doors and Windows

DOORS

Ledged and Battened Doors.—The simplest type of door is the ledged and battened door as shown in Fig. 1. The boards or battens should be tongued, grooved and beaded, or V-jointed.

It is usual to select the boards so that the width will build up to the required size. In Fig. 1 six 6½-in. boards are suitable. Cut the boards to length and cramp together. Measure the surplus width and divide it between the two outside boards. Cut away the surplus width. If the boards are not a convenient width, it may be necessary to make each board narrower and re-plough the groove to receive the tongue.

Prepare the ledges as shown. The top ledge is suitable for inside work, the middle and bottom ledge show two methods for outside

work, the latter being better because the throating throws off the water.

Construction.—Take one of the outside boards and mark on the back the positions for the ledges. Nail on the ledges firmly, taking care to have them at right angles to the edge.

Turn the ledges and board over so that the ledges lie flat and "out of twist" on the bench. Place the remaining boards in position and cramp up. Rule pencil lines where the nails are required. Nail every board securely and punch the nails.

Screws in the outside boards prevent them curling off, and paint should be applied between the ledges and boards.

Ledged and Braced Door.—This door (Fig. 2) is similar to the previous one with the addition of the braces, which prevent the door from

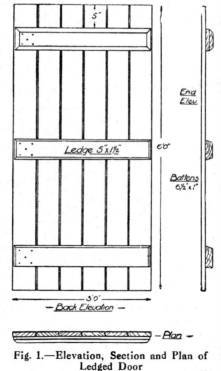

Fig. 1.—Elevation, Section and Plan of Ledged Door

dropping at the outer edge and rubbing on the floor.

The simplest method is to make the door exactly as Fig. 1, and then " let in " the braces ; these must be placed so that

3 in. away from the end of the ledge or the portion receiving the thrust will shear off.

Framed and Ledged Doors.—This makes an excellent door for hard wear.

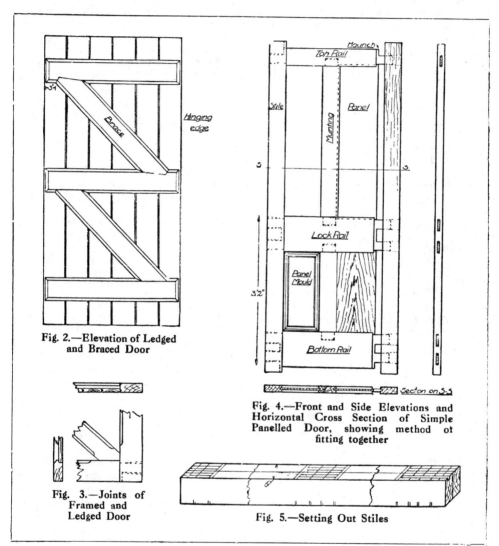

Fig. 2.—Elevation of Ledged and Braced Door

Fig. 3.—Joints of Framed and Ledged Door

Fig. 4.—Front and Side Elevations and Horizontal Cross Section of Simple Panelled Door, showing method ot fitting together

Fig. 5.—Setting Out Stiles

the bottom end is on the same side as the hinge.

The chamfers on the ledges and braces will require mitreing where they meet. Two ways of letting in the braces are shown. Keep the end of the brace about

It consists of stiles, head, ledges and boards. The stiles and head are equal in thickness to the ledges and boards together.

The ledges and head are tenoned into the stiles and the head is rebated for the

the casings is increased, and often framed and moulded panels are formed.

Frame for External Door. — For outside walls a much stronger frame is required, such as Fig. 16. It is formed of about 5 in. by 3 in.

In construction the stiles or jambs are tenoned into the head, which projects at each end to build into the wall in new work. The transom is shown prepared for an opening light. The fixing is done by wedging at the top and transom and by iron dowels driven into the foot of the jamb (Fig. 16). These dowels fit into corresponding holes drilled in the stone or concrete. The sectional plan shows the method of finishing for a 9-in. wall, and also for a thicker wall.

Garden Door. — The garden door shown in Fig. 17 is both simple and effec-

Fig. 17.—Trellised Garden Door

DOOR FRAMES

The form of a door frame depends upon the position in which it is placed. Fig. 14 is a common type used for inside work. It is formed of 6-in. by $1\frac{1}{2}$-in. casing stuff, which is stocked by most builders. The section Fig. 15 shows the method of fixing for a $4\frac{3}{4}$-in. wall. The wall is plugged and the casings nailed to the plugs. For better-class work, grounds are fixed to the brickwork (as shown), and the woodwork fixed to the grounds.

The stiles are housed into the head to the depth of the rebate. The horizontal and diagonal stays are to keep the casings square until they are fixed.

If the wall is more than $4\frac{1}{2}$ in. thick, the width is made up by wood linings or by plaster. In good work the width of

Fig. 19.—
Cross Section of
Part of
Panelling

Fig. 18.—Details of Construction of Garden Door

tive, and is especially suitable for reproduction in oak. The framework is framed up with an opening on each side of the door ; the door is framed together, and the lower portion is panelled, while the upper portion of the door and the openings at the sides are filled with an open trelliswork. It is suggested that the opening for the door be 7 ft. high by 3 ft. wide, and the openings at the sides 2 ft. 6 in. high by 1 ft. wide, and 3 ft. 6 in. above the ground level.

The door framework is $3\frac{1}{2}$ in. by $2\frac{1}{2}$ in., framed together with mortise-and-tenon joints ; it is rebated to receive the door and the edges are stop-chamfered. The trellis work at the sides is composed of bars 1 in. square in section, which are half lapped together and stump-tenoned in position. The door consists of two stiles and three rails. The stiles are 4 in. wide at the top, increasing to 6 in. in width at the bottom, by $1\frac{1}{2}$ in. thick ; the top rail is 10 in. deep at the ends and 6 in. deep in the middle by $1\frac{1}{2}$ in. thick ; the middle rail is 8 in. deep by $1\frac{1}{2}$ in. thick, and the bottom rail is 10 in. deep by $1\frac{1}{2}$ in. thick. The rails are tenoned into the stiles with joints similar to those indicated in Fig. 18. The panelling at the bottom is $\frac{1}{2}$ in. thick, and is in about five portions. The edges of each portion are slightly chamfered, and are tongued together, as shown by Fig. 19, and the panelling is rebated into the edges of the door frame as shown in the same illustration. The trellis work at the top is made up in a similar manner as that in the openings at the sides, and the edges of the door framework are slightly chamfered.

The door should be hung with three 3-in. butt hinges or with a pair of long flap wrought-iron hinges, and a suitable lock and handle should also be fitted.

WINDOWS

Windows are primarily intended to give light, but, in addition, it is nearly always necessary to arrange for ventilation, and sometimes for ornamentation. Very little guidance can be given with regard to the position or size, other than what may be found in any Local Bye Laws. It must be remembered, in designing, that there is a minimum size, dependant upon the size of the room in which the window is placed. Only the types of window which the average woodworker and amateur are likely to have to contend are dealt with here.

Fast-Sheet Windows.—Fig 20 shows

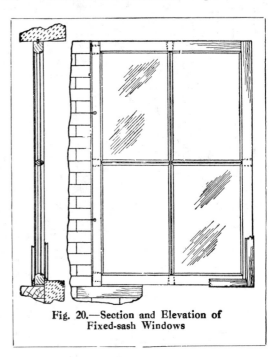

Fig. 20.—Section and Elevation of Fixed-sash Windows

in elevation and vertical section a fast sheet, such as is used in positions where ventilation is not required or has been otherwise provided for. The material generally used is known as sash stuff and may be obtained ready prepared to the following sizes, 3 in. by 2 in., 2 in. by 2 in. and 2 in. by 1 in. bar stuff, the latter being moulded and rebated on both sides. Very often thicker stuff, or a special mould, is required, in which case it is necessary to prepare the stuff in the ordinary way as explained in the section on doors.

Also, the bar stuff is often considered too thin, and 2 in. by 2 in. substituted and moulded on both sides.

The drawing shows the window fixed in position, with a portion of the linings on the inside, and the scotia on the outside. The window is divided into squares according to the size of glass required. The reason for having small squares is to diminish the cost of breakages, but it will be understood that the inclusion of bars adds very much to the labour of making. The stiles are mortised for the rails and bars. The mortise is not necessarily in the middle of the stuff, but depends upon the moulding. It should be placed on the square of the mould. The usual form is shown in Fig. 21, which also shows the method of making the joint between rail and stile. The dots show the easier method when making by hand, and it will be observed that instead of the mould being scribed through, only a small portion is scribed and the shoulder is left square ; therefore the haunch is on the stile instead of on the rail. If the stiles are 3 in. or more the usual haunch may be used exactly as described for the top rail in making a gunstock door. If there are several bars it is better to put them together by halved joints and mitre the moulding. The horizontal bar should run through on the rebate side, otherwise the rebate will probably break off.

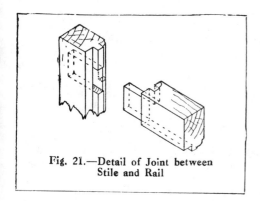

Fig. 21.—Detail of Joint between Stile and Rail

The window is fixed by means of the wedges at the top and bottom, and by holdfasts up the sides. An oak lath about 1 in. by ½ in. is shown in the sill, bedded in white-lead and oil. This preserves the wood. The linings may be mitred at the angles, but the usual method is as

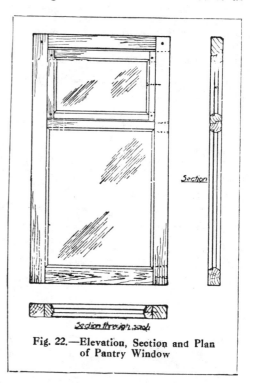

Section

Section through sill

Fig. 22.—Elevation, Section and Plan of Pantry Window

shown. The scotia is mitred on the outside. If the window is beaded for the glass, then the mould is placed on the outside of the window, as this obviates the difficulty of glazing the windows from the outside. When the mould has to stand the weather, the horizontal members should have the top edge bevelled instead of moulded to throw off the water. The tenons on the bars should run through the stiles and rails, then the bars can be straightened when wedging up. When driving in the wedges cast the eye along the bar and tap the wedges to keep the bar straight until it is all right, then drive in the wedges tightly. For outside windows use paint when putting together, for inside windows use glue

Pantry Windows.—Fig. 22 shows a small window, with top portion opening for ventilation, generally called a pantry window. The same type of window, but much larger, is generally used in mills and warehouses. The construction is the same as for the fixed sheet, but the stiles are slot mortised for the head, so that when the sash is hung, or pivoted, the head is regulated to the correct posi-

pivots or screws must be slightly above the centre and then the sash will close of its own accord. This method gives an open joint between the window stile and sash stile. If this is objected to, it is necessary to have rebates; then it is easier to hinge the sash to the transom and open with a quadrant or fanlight opener. The same

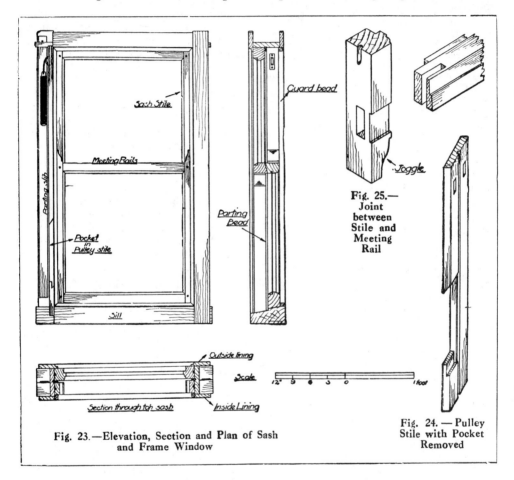

Fig. 25.—Joint between Stile and Meeting Rail

Fig. 23.—Elevation, Section and Plan of Sash and Frame Window

Fig. 24. — Pulley Stile with Pocket Removed

tion, and then pinned instead of wedged. The transom is rebated on the top edge for the sash, and the stiles, above the transom, have the mould taken off. The sash is pivoted, very often by an ordinary screw at each side, and opened by a length of picture cord which is attached to eyes in the top and bottom rail of sash. Pivots must be used for larger sashes. The

general principles of construction apply to any size of window, the only difference being the addition of bars.

Sash and Frame Windows.—Fig. 23 gives the details for a sash and frame window of the simplest form such as is usually found in cottage property. The window consists of a built-up frame and two sashes which slide up and down. The sashes are balanced by means of weights attached to the sashes by pieces of cord which pass over pulleys let into the sides of the frame.

The weights run in boxes formed at the sides of the frame, and the two weights to each sash should together approximately equal the weight of the sash. In order to ensure that the sashes keep in position, the weights of the bottom sash should be a little lighter than the sash, and those of the top sash a little heavier.

The frame should be constructed first. This consists of sill, $5\frac{3}{4}$ in. by 3 in.; pulley stiles and head, $4\frac{1}{2}$ in. by $\frac{7}{8}$ in.; outside linings, about $3\frac{1}{2}$ in. by $\frac{5}{8}$ in.; inside linings, $\frac{5}{8}$ in. narrower than the outside linings; guard-beads, $\frac{7}{8}$ in. by $\frac{5}{8}$ in.; parting beads, $\frac{7}{8}$ in. by $\frac{3}{8}$ in. or $\frac{5}{16}$ in. The above are finished sizes. It is usual to have parting slips to separate the weights; these are rough pieces about $1\frac{1}{2}$ in. by $\frac{5}{8}$ in., hanging loosely from the head to within a few inches of the sill. Also, back linings are nailed on the back edges of the linings to keep the boxes free from mortar, etc. The sill is trenched to receive the pulley stiles, which are wedged and nailed; it is also shouldered to receive the outside and inside linings, which finish flush with the sill. The head is trenched about $\frac{1}{4}$ in. deep, to receive the stiles, and secured by nails. A slot is also made at each end to receive the parting slips. The stiles are cut square to the necessary length and then prepared for the pocket pieces. Fig. 24 shows one method of preparing the pockets, but there are many ways in which this may be done. The pockets must be large enough to put the weights through. To prepare the pocket, as shown in Fig 24, commence with the bottom, and cut in half the thickness from the front with the sash chisel. Note that the cut is bevelled inwards. Then turn over and saw as deeply as possible to half the thickness with a dovetail saw, and finish off with the sash chisel. Saw down the groove for the parting bead with a pad saw, and then make the bevelled cut at the top with a dovetail saw. The top is then forced out until the pocket splits off at the bottom, when it is replaced, screwed in position and cleaned off with

the smoothing plane The sash chisel, which has a very thin and wide blade, should be dipped in water before using.

The pulleys must be let in on the centre line of the sash run, and about 3 in. from the top of the stile. Mortise for the body of the pulley and then let in the plate flush with the face of the stile. Everything is now ready to assemble. Commence with the sill and stiles. Wedge and nail the stiles firmly, taking care to have them out of twist, then put on the head. Lay the frame on a level surface, square, and fix temporarily. Then nail on the inside linings, avoiding nailing into the pockets. Turn the frame over, test again for squareness, and put on the outside linings. These project $\frac{5}{8}$ in. inside for the sash to run against. If they are moulded it is necessary to mitre for the mould. Make a gauge for the $\frac{5}{8}$-in. projection and use it whilst nailing on the linings.

The sashes present no difficulties, except at the meeting or middle rails, and Fig. 25 shows the method of making the joint. The rails are $\frac{5}{16}$ in. (the thickness of the parting bead) thicker than the rest of the sash. This increased thickness should be rebated as shown, to exclude the dust, etc., and to prevent the sash fastener being opened from the outside. The sash is much stronger if provided with joggles and also looks better in appearance.

The stiles are mortised in the ordinary way, and, in addition, are cut out about $\frac{3}{16}$ in., to receive a corresponding portion of the meeting rail, as shown in Fig. 25. Care should be taken that the wrong side of the stile is not cut out. For the top and bottom rail proceed in the ordinary way, as shown in Fig. 21. Wedge up and pin the sashes, clean off, then plough the groove for the sashcord, about two-thirds the length of the stile, as shown in Fig. 25. Fit the sashes into the frame, and at the same time put in the parting and guard-beads.

The sashes are hung, of course, after the frame is fixed, and the sashes glazed. They should be weighed after glazing in order to find what weights are required. Take out the beads and pockets. A ' mouse " is necessary (this is a piece of chain, lead or even a nail, bent to go through the pulley and attached to a piece of twine). Tie the twine to the sashcord, pass the mouse over the pulley, take hold of the mouse through the pocket, and draw the cord through. Then attach the weight securely, and pull the cord outside, until

into position. This is a usual source of trouble at first. Replace the beads for completion. Special nails known as clout nails are used for nailing on the cords. Fig. 24 shows the pulley stile mortised for the pulleys and with the pocket removed. Fig. 25 shows the joint between the meet-

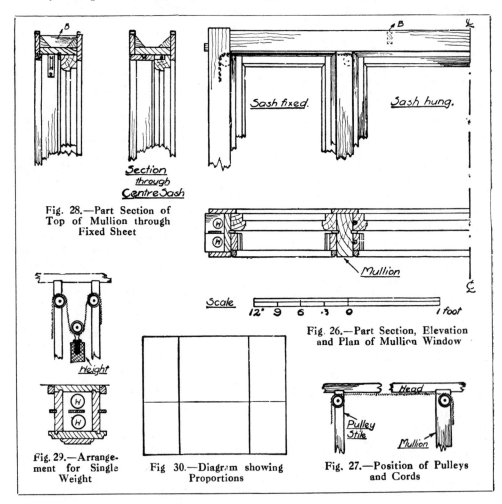

Section through Centre Sash

Fig. 28.—Part Section of Top of Mullion through Fixed Sheet

Sash fixed.

Sash hung.

Mullion

Scale
12" 9 6 ·3 0   1 foot

Fig. 26.—Part Section, Elevation and Plan of Mullion Window

Height

Fig. 29.—Arrangement for Single Weight

Fig 30.—Diagram showing Proportions

Head
Pulley Stile
Mullion

Fig. 27.—Position of Pulleys and Cords

the weight is near the top of the box, and temporarily nail the cord in this position to the frame. When all the cords are in position they may be cut to the correct lengths and nailed to the sides of the sashes. See that the cords for the bottom sash are long enough and the top cords short enough for the sashes to go

ing rail and stile, also the method of preparing the joggle and the groove for the cord.

It is necessary to draw the section and plan to full size, otherwise it is impossible to set out the stuff correctly for the sashes. The size of the window generally refers to the brickwork opening, so that when setting out the opening is marked first and then the outside lining is set out to the margin required.

Mullion Windows.—Fig. 26 shows the simplest type of mullion window. The chief advantage is that the narrow mullion does not exclude much light. Only the centre sashes are hung, the outside sashes being fixed. The constructional work procedure is similar to that of the sash and frame window, except for the arrangement of the pulleys, an extra pulley being required for each cord. It is necessary that the cord should run over the outside sashes owing to the weights being on the outside of the frame, and this necessitates the pulleys being at the top of the pulley stiles and mullions. Figs. 27 and 28 show the method of arranging the pulleys in the mullion. The mortise does not go any deeper than is necessary for the pulley and a narrow groove is made for the cord to pass through the remainder of the thickness. The ordinary pulleys may be used with the top flange broken off. The head holds the pulley securely at the top, so that the screw at the bottom is sufficient. Instead of breaking off the flange it may go into the head, or, if preferred, special pulleys may be purchased. The top fixed sash is rebated for the cord to pass over, and a wide guard-bead is used to cover the cords. The bead is removed in elevation to show the cord passing over the sash. This guard-bead is screwed so that it is easily removed for rehanging the sashes when required. The mullions are cut square to the same length as the pulley stiles. Triangular blocks are glued to the head and top linings as shown in section to strengthen the linings and also two strengthening blocks (B Fig. 26). Fig. 27 shows the arrangement of the pulleys and cord. If all the sashes have to be hung, the mullions must be framed for the weights, as on the outsides. The objections to this window are the labour it entails and the light it excludes, as the mullions have to be of sufficient width to take the four pulleys. Fig. 29 shows an alternative method, where one weight acts for two sashes, but this is very troublesome for rehanging. The weight is cast with lead and may be square or circular. A special pulley is inserted and a rivet passed through. Fig. 30 is a line diagram to show the proportions.

Yorkshire Light.—This window (Fig. 31) is easy to make and very satisfactory in every sense. The frame consists of two stiles, head and sill, formed of 5 in. by $2\frac{1}{2}$ in., and an upright bar in the centre of 2-in. by 2-in. sash stuff, or $2\frac{1}{2}$ in. by 2 in. specially prepared as in Fig. 32. One half of the frame is rebated for glass, and the other half is arranged for a sliding sash.

Both the sill (which should be of hardwood) and head run through, and the stiles are tenoned into them. Double tenons may be used if desired, but they entail a lot of labour ; and one big tenon, say $1\frac{1}{2}$ in. with two large nails to assist it, is quite good enough. The head is shown rebated for the sash to slide in, and the sill is ploughed for an oak or wrought-iron lath to act as a runner. An oak lath may be used at the top also in place of the rebate. In that case the guard-beads only serve to keep out the draught, and may be dispensed with if desired. That would mean a narrower frame. The sash is formed of 2 in. by 2 in., or one stile may be prepared, as shown in Fig. 32. The stiles run through, and the top and bottom rails are tenoned into them in the ordinary way. The bottom rail should be of hardwood, as there is considerable wear between the sill and bottom rail. Very often small pulleys are let into the bottom edge of the rail to ease the friction, the pulleys running on a strip of hoop-iron. Metal shoes are sometimes used running on a strip of wrought iron. If a lath is used at the top instead of the rebate, it is necessary to put the sash and lath in together, and then screw the lath to the head whilst regulating the sash for easy running. Bars may be used according to the size of glass required. The sash is secured by a thumb-screw, which passes through the loose sash and into the fixed upright bar. Fig. 32 is a section through bar of frame and stile of sash showing alternative methods.

Casement Windows.—These windows consist of the frame and one or more sashes, opening on hinges. If the casements or sashes come down to the floor, so that they may be used as doors, they are called French casements. With regard to details and design, no windows are as subject to variation as casement win-

often the sashes are all made to open inwards, but this generally gives trouble with the bottom rail of the bottom casements, owing to the rain beating in. Patent metal water bars are obtainable for the purpose of keeping out the wet. Sometimes the top sashes are arranged to open inwards and the bottom ones

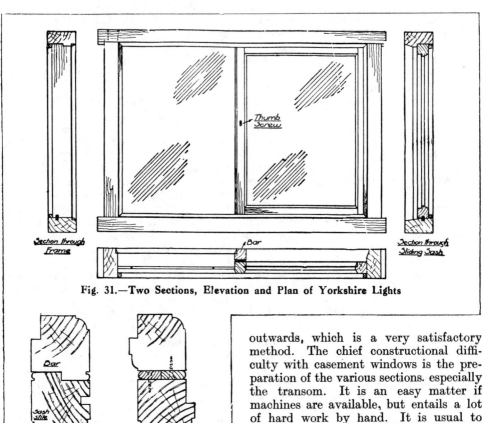

Fig. 31.—Two Sections, Elevation and Plan of Yorkshire Lights

Fig. 32.—Two Constructions of Sliding Bar and Stile of Yorkshire Light

outwards, which is a very satisfactory method. The chief constructional difficulty with casement windows is the preparation of the various sections, especially the transom. It is an easy matter if machines are available, but entails a lot of hard work by hand. It is usual to partly cut for the shoulders and tenons, and do the mortising before the moulding and rebating. If the tenons are finished completely before the rebating and moulding, it is difficult to get a seating for the planes, also the shoulders get bruised. This refers to making by hand. Casement stays are placed on the bottom rail of bottom casements, to prevent them blowing open, and also to fix them into any desired position. Casement fasteners are used to fasten them when closed. The top sashes are hinged to the head and a

dows, so that these makes are largely a question of individual taste.

Fig. 33 shows a simple type with a centre mullion. Four casements are shown, but it is not necessary for all of them to open. All the sashes in this window open outwards, and this necessitates the top ones being hinged to the head. Very

quadrant fixed at the transom. Leaded lights are usually put in the top sashes and are very effective. The drawings show plaster. It is usual to plough grooves for this purpose. The right-hand stile in plan (Fig. 33) shows an alternative method of

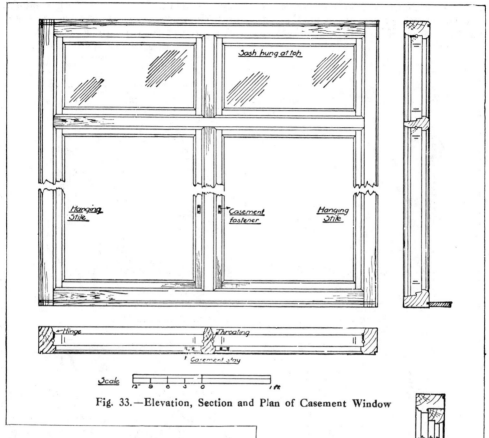

Fig. 33.—Elevation, Section and Plan of Casement Window

clearly all the details. Care must be taken with the various throatings, otherwise the rain will prove a source of trouble. Weep holes (shown by dotted lines) are bored in the top rails of the casements, to allow any water gathered in the throating to escape. Only one is required in the centre of each rail, but the groove should be slightly deeper at the weep hole than at the ends, so that the water will get away.

Fig. 34 is an enlarged detail of the hanging stile showing the method of letting in the hinges, and also the throatings, either or both of which may be used. The inside of the frame should be prepared for the window bottom and the linings or

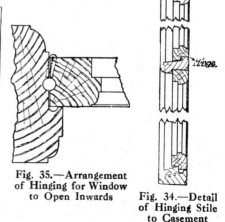

Fig. 35.—Arrangement of Hinging for Window to Open Inwards

Fig. 34.—Detail of Hinging Stile to Casement

forming a key for the plaster. If it is required to open the sashes inwards, the details necessary to make a satisfactory window are shown in Fig. 35. The water is certain to get through at the bottom rail, but the section of the sill will allow it to

Circular Framing.—When building up circular framing, it is generally better to build up by dividing the thickness into layers and crossing the joints, then gluing and nailing or screwing the several layers together. Fig. 36 shows this

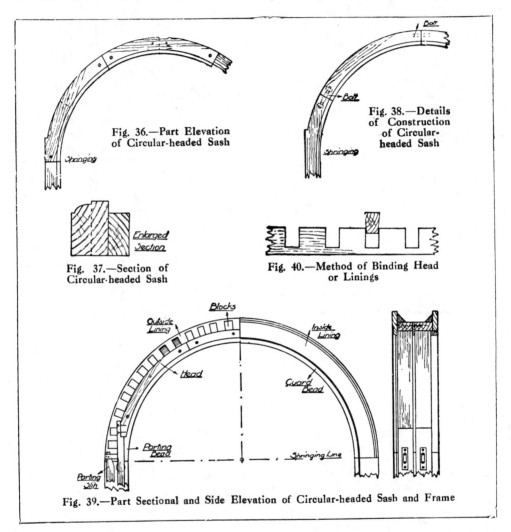

Fig. 36.—Part Elevation of Circular-headed Sash

Fig. 38.—Details of Construction of Circular-headed Sash

Fig. 37.—Section of Circular-headed Sash

Fig. 40.—Method of Binding Head or Linings

Fig. 39.—Part Sectional and Side Elevation of Circular-headed Sash and Frame

run out at the weep holes. The weep holes are bored with brace and bit, and then the holes are charred with a red hot iron, or filled in with brass tubing. In these details the top sashes are hung at the transom and opened by a quadrant at the top.

method very clearly. The section of the sash stuff is divided into two parts. The division is arranged according to the members. It should be as near to the centre of the stuff as possible, but the first consideration is the ease in sticking the mould. For instance. in Fig. 37 if the section is divided into two layers it is much better to divide as shown by the full line than by the dotted line, as the latter would entail the sticking of the mould on one piece and the rebate on the other, whereas the full line only requires a narrower ring to form the rebate. The number of the joints depends upon the radius of the circle and the width of the material available. The success of the work depends upon an intelligent division of the joints.

If the framing has to be cut out of the solid, the method of making the joints is by hammer-headed keys or by handrail bolts, sometimes assisted by dowels, as shown in Fig. 38. The latter is preferable for small work. The joints should radiate to the centre for striking the curves. In all circular work it is necessary to set out the work to full size and to cut thin templets for the various members required, so that they can be applied when cutting out the planks or boards. If the radius is not too small it is better to steam and bend any small section that is permanently fixed, such as the guard-bead in Fig. 39, which shows the circular part only of a circular-headed sash and frame. The lower portion is as already described for a sash and frame.

The chief difficulty is the circular head to the pulley stiles. Two methods are available. First by means of layers built up of three layers, the parting bead forming one layer. This method has been described already. The second method is very good and is more favoured by the majority of craftsmen. That is, to bend the head to the required shape. This may be done in two ways. If it is a large radius, the usual way is to cut out as shown in Fig. 40. Then bend to the required shape and fill in the notches with wedge-shaped pieces of pine, the length of which is equal to the width of the head. These pieces are well glued and driven in tightly, and the whole allowed to dry before being disturbed. It is necessary to prepare a temporary drum or saddle to bend the work round. For a semi-circular head or any work with a small radius it is better to commence with a piece sufficiently thin to bend round the drum and then glue

blocks on the back, afterwards gluing on canvas. The point where the bending commences is called the springing, and a few inches of material should be left on below the springing to secure to the stiles and to fix to the drum. With the second method the parting bead should be planted on, instead of arranging for a groove. Tongues entail a lot of labour and are not worth the increased cost. Glue and nail on the inside and outside circular linings, and then block well inside the head. In Fig. 36 one half of the inside lining is omitted to show the joint between the stile and the head. The stile runs up and screws are put through from the back. The method of fixing the parting slip is shown. A block is fitted in tightly between the linings, and slotted or mortised for the slip. It is necessary to prepare a stop on the sash and the frame, otherwise the sash would bang on the head at the crown and break the glass. This is shown on the elevation of the sash (Fig. 38), which is drawn separately for clearness. The sash may be prepared in concentric layers, as in Fig. 33, or by cutting the material out of the solid and jointing by means of handrail bolts or hammer-headed keys, as in Fig. 38. Concentric layers construction is easier for hand work.

For a segmental head the preparation would be the same for the frame, except for the joint between pulley stiles and head. In this case it is better to trench the head for the stiles as if it were a straight head. Also on the sash, the joint between head and stile would be an ordinary open mortise-and-tenon joint and pinned. For a very flat segmental arch, as is commonly found in cottage property, it is usual to keep the head to the pulley stiles straight, and follow the curvature of the brickwork with the outside lining only. This necessitates the top rail of the sash being wide, and the under edge cut to the same curvature as the lining.

Bull's-eye Windows.—This term is applied to small circular windows the sash of which opens as a whole on pivots (Fig. 41). The building up of the frame and sash is as previously described for circular work.

Both frame and sash should be divided into two thicknesses. The beads will be cut out of the solid. Prepare a board the same thickness as the width of the bead. Cut out the inside of the bead to the correct sweep, then work the bead by means of a router and cut off with a bow saw, or band saw if available. Part of the bead on each side fixes to the sash and the other part to the frame. The sash will open in at the top so that the bead at the top should be on the inside, and the bead at

the sash and beads, to give the required size, and glue them on to the frame.

If a straight surface is left on the frame when preparing, and the corresponding portion cut off the sash and beads when fitting, it is better for outside work as the small pieces glued on are apt to get broken off in time. Fix the pivot to the frame and the eye to the sash, then the groove, necessary to slip the sash into position, can be made in the bead so that it will not show when the sash is closed.

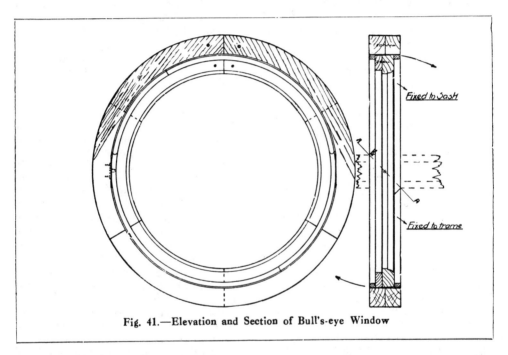

Fig. 41.—Elevation and Section of Bull's-eye Window

the bottom on the outside. The drawing shows the method of cutting the beads. Set out the sash and beads when open horizontally, as shown by dotted lines, then draw the line A A through the intersections of the two drawings. The cut for the beads is at right angles to the line A A, and from the points of intersection. The pivoting is rather a difficult operation. First it is necessary to have a plane surface on the frame at the centre, equal to the thickness of the window. The plane surface will be a square. For good work, the best method is to cut pieces off

Circular Louvre or Ventilator.— Fig. 42 gives the section and elevation of a circular ventilator. The frame should be prepared as in the previous example, either by cutting out of the solid and using handrail bolts or hammer-headed keys, or by building it up in two layers and crossing the joints.

The setting out for the louvres and the cutting of the louvres is an interesting geometrical exercise. The drawing shows the top surface of the top louvre developed, or the true shape to which the louvre is cut. Consider the front edge A A as an axis, and revolve the louvre about this axis until it is perpendicular.

In the section, this revolving is shown by the edge A 2, 3, 4, 5. It is turned vertically to A 5'. In the elevation the

frame together temporarily, fix the rods one on each side, and with a straightedge mark the positions of the louvres both on the face and the back of the frame. The rods B B, and the method of applying them,

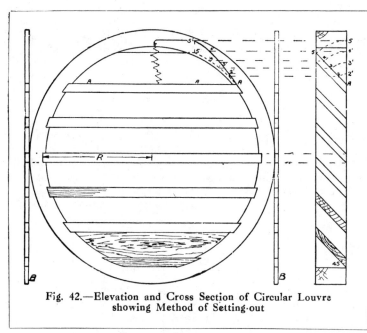

Fig. 42.—Elevation and Cross Section of Circular Louvre showing Method of Setting-out

Fig. 43.—Method of Setting-out Louvres

are shown in Fig. 42. Next, take a piece of cardboard, equal in width to the thickness of the louvres, set it to the marks on the front and back of the frame. Mark on each side of the cardboard, and this

point 5, when revolving, will follow a path at right angles to the axis until it reaches the same height as in the section. So from point 5 draw a vertical line, and the place where a horizontal line from 5' in the section cuts this vertical line will be the point required. Repeat for points 2, 3, and 4, and draw a curve through these points. This gives the true shape of the louvre.

By this method it is necessary to repeat for each louvre, which is very tedious, the practical method described below being much simpler. For this method set out two rods or boards, with the edges of the louvres marked on the edges of the rods. These rods will be exactly alike. Put the

gives the cuts for the louvres. Take the frame asunder and cut out to the marks to a depth of half an inch. Now put the frame together permanently. To cut the louvres, set out a quarter ellipse as shown in Fig. 43.

To obtain the axes, set out a line equal to R in Fig. 43. Draw a right-angled triangle with the hypotenuse at 45°, because the louvres are inclined at 45°. The hypotenuse is the major axis, and the base R is the minor axis. Draw the ellipse. Apply this templet in the grooves for the louvres until a portion is found to fit. Mark this portion and apply it to the louvre. Get the edge cut by means of a bevel for both front and back.

Dressers and Sideboards

MODERN KITCHEN CABINET OR DRESSER

A CABINET useful for kitchen or living room, and designed to hold all necessary utensils and materials for preparing food,

is shown by Fig. 1. It occupies very little space while affording the maximum amount of accommodation. It could be placed with ease in the recess formed at the side of a fireplace.

The lower portion is divided up into

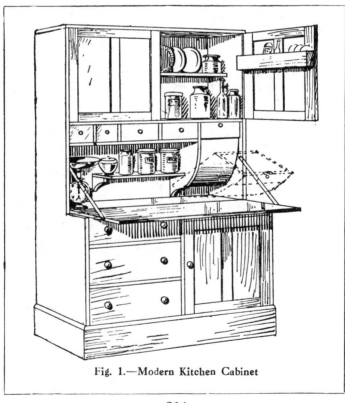

Fig. 1.—Modern Kitchen Cabinet

three drawers on the left side, the top one being for cutlery, and divided into three divisions and lined with green baize. On the right-hand side is a cupboard with shelf for storing pots and pans ; the pastry-board slides in a recess above the door. The upper part, enclosed by a hinged flap, contains two small and two large drawers for spices and such commodities as are used in cooking. On the

fixed two wooden trays for small articles. The shelf has a raised fillet to keep plates from slipping when standing on edge. The constructional work is of the simplest order, and only a few details need be outlined.

The sides should be $1\frac{1}{8}$ in. thick, tongued and grooved to the $\frac{7}{8}$-in. thick top. The drawer and door rails and bearers are $2\frac{1}{4}$ in. by $\frac{7}{8}$ in., and housed

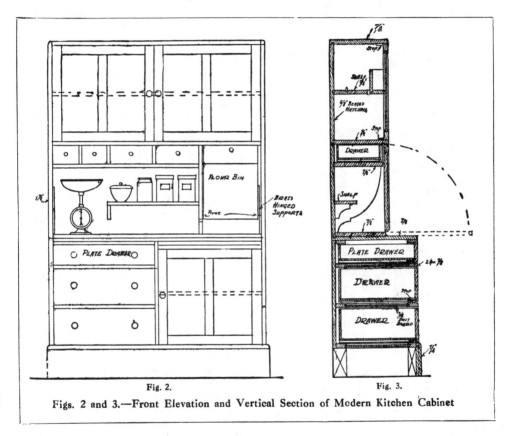

Fig. 2. Fig. 3.

Figs. 2 and 3.—Front Elevation and Vertical Section of Modern Kitchen Cabinet

right-hand side is a flour bin pivoted at the bottom, and kept in position when closed by a strong snap-catch. This bin when in use is lowered until it rests on the open flap and permits of easy access for removing the flour. Below the drawers is a small shelf for tins, etc., and on the left is space for a weighing machine. Above is another cupboard with shelf enclosed by two doors. On the doors are

into the sides. The doors are framed up with $2\frac{1}{4}$-in. by $\frac{7}{8}$-in. stiles and rails, and the panel-fillings of $\frac{5}{8}$ in. are tongued and grooved into framing. The drawers have $\frac{7}{8}$-in. fronts, lap-dovetailed to the $\frac{3}{8}$-in. sides. A plinth, $\frac{7}{8}$ in. thick, is tongued under the bottom bearer. A study of the scale drawings (Figs. 2 and 3) will render these instructions clear.

The general woodwork is deal, painted

white, the flap of teak and unpainted inside.

KITCHEN DRESSER WITH ENCLOSED MANGLE

In many small cottage homes a mangle is a necessity, but, as a rule, not an ornament, and the dresser shown by Fig. 4 has been designed to cover it whilst not in use. It will be understood that the mangle is

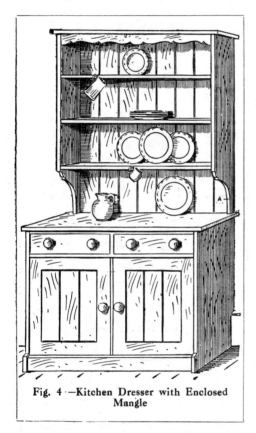

Fig. 4.—Kitchen Dresser with Enclosed Mangle

by nature of an accessory, and that with a little modification the dresser could be utilised for other purposes. Mangles are usually obtainable locally, and the general dimensions of them when folded are: Height from floor to top, 2 ft. 3½ in.; length of top, 3 ft. ½ in.; and 1 ft. 8½ in. wide. Should there be any variation from these sizes due allowance

would have to be made. Part front elevation and end elevation are shown by Figs. 5 and 6.

The upper part of the dresser, with shelves, is separate from the lower part, and is fixed with holdfasts and screws to the wall, the latter being drilled and plugged to receive the iron holdfasts. The lower part of the dresser (Figs. 7 and 8) is made with the ends to fold inwards against the front, which is made to imitate doors and drawers. Thus, when not in use it can be placed flat against a wall. The front and ends are kept in position by iron stays. The loose top simply rests on the front and ends. The height of the dresser top is about 8 in. higher than the mangle top, so that, if desired, any articles may be placed out of sight by simply raising the front edge of the top. The hollowing out of the lower ends of the upper part A in the end elevation (Figs. 4 and 6) allows for the handle of the mangle to turn.

The complete dresser may be made of pine or deal, painted or stained to match walnut or mahogany. The main dimensions are: Total height, 6 ft. 9 in.; height of lower part, 3 ft.; and extreme width across the front, 4 ft. The back of the upper part B in the part front elevation (Fig. 5) and the sham door panels are made of ½-in. matchboarding, and the remaining parts of 1-in. stuff, finishing when planed about ¾ in. full. The trouble of planing the wood may be avoided by purchasing good sound flooring boards and jointing them to the requisite widths. Most local timber merchants keep these in stock.

In making the dresser the top part with shelves may be first taken in hand. The ends have a rebate worked in the back edges to receive the matchboarded back. The shelves, of course, will be the thickness of the back, less in width than the ends. The latter must be dovetailed grooved across to receive the ends of shelves (Fig. 9). The groove in the ends must be stopped ¼ in. from the front edge, so that the dovetail will not show at the front. The top C (Fig. 5) may be grooved likewise to receive the top parts of the ends.

When the top, shelves, and ends are fixed with glue and nails, next fit in the match-boarding back B. This may pass down behind the top of the lower part. When fixing to the wall due regard must be paid to the weight of crockery it will be likely to contain. The front of the lower part, from the floor to the top. The double centre stile is tenoned into the top and bottom rails F and G. A plinth H, $\frac{3}{4}$ in. thick, with bevelled top edge, is planted on the bottom rail G. The imitation bearers J are strips about $\frac{1}{8}$ in. thick and $\frac{7}{8}$ in. wide, and are planted on the face of

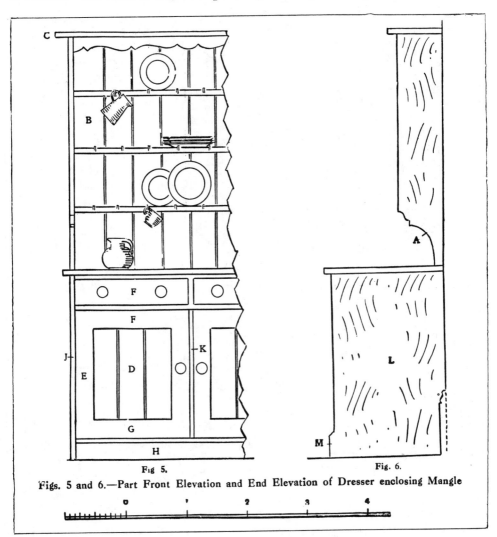

Fig 5.   Fig. 6.

Figs. 5 and 6.—Part Front Elevation and End Elevation of Dresser enclosing Mangle

in imitation of doors and drawers, should be framed together with mortises and tenons, grooves being ploughed in the stiles and rails to receive the panels D (Fig. 5). The two outer stiles E extend the framing and secured with glue and brads ; likewise K, about $\frac{3}{8}$ in. wide, $\frac{1}{2}$ in. round in section. The ends L have a piece M glued on the front edge, so that the plinth H can butt against them. The ends L (Fig. 6) are fixed to the front framing with hinges, as shown by Fig. 10. The iron angle stay (Fig. 11) may be made of stout wire, or, better still, by a smith, of $\frac{1}{4}$-in. iron rod, and connected to the front and ends with iron screw eyelets, which can be had from most ironmongers.

Four blocks O, or two battens about 2 in. wide, should be fixed to the underside of the top, as shown in Fig. 12. These will keep the top in the proper position. The dresser may be made 3 in. or 6 in. narrower or wider if desired. Knobs as shown (Fig. 13) may be used, or brass handles. Hooks

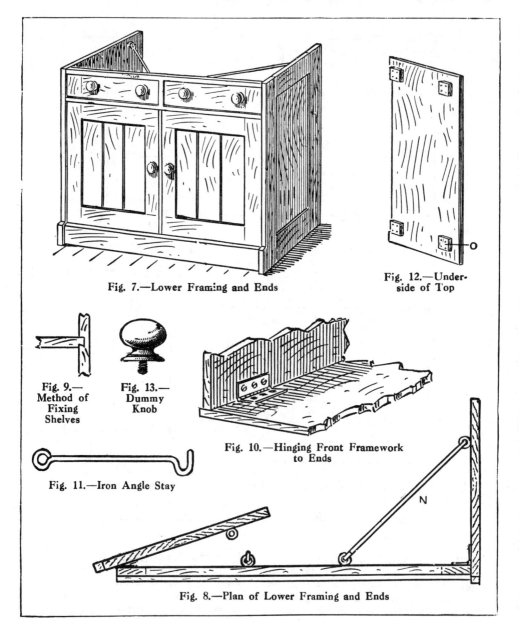

Fig. 7.—Lower Framing and Ends

Fig. 12.—Underside of Top

Fig. 9.—Method of Fixing Shelves

Fig. 13.—Dummy Knob

Fig. 10.—Hinging Front Framework to Ends

Fig. 11.—Iron Angle Stay

Fig. 8.—Plan of Lower Framing and Ends

Fig. 14.—Mangle Raised

Fig. 15.—Mangle Lowered

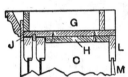

Fig. 19.—Section through Top Portion of Cupboard

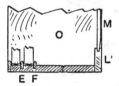

Fig. 18.—Section through Lower Portion of Cupboard

KITCHEN DRESSER WITH GLASS DOORS

Fig. 16 is a front elevation and Fig. 17 an end elevation, drawn to the scale of feet and inches. The extreme height is 7 ft., and the width outside the carcase ends is 4 ft., the top A projecting 1 in. at the front, back, and ends, and the plinth B $\frac{3}{4}$ in. at the front and ends. The depth of the top carcase C is 1 ft., and the lower carcase D 1 ft. 6 in. ; but these sizes may

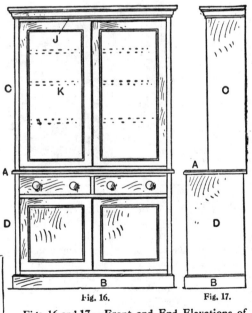

Fig. 16.   Fig. 17.

Figs. 16 and 17.—Front and End Elevations of Kitchen Dresser with Glass Doors

can be fixed to the front of the shelves according to requirements. If the ends of the lower part are panelled they will be less liable to warp than if made in one piece. Two illustrations of a suitable mangle are shown by Figs. 14 and 15.

be increased or diminished according to requirements, remembering that one door has to pass behind the other. To keep the doors in their right track, grooves E and F (Fig. 18) are ploughed in the bottom of the top carcase, and hardwood strips are inserted as shown. For the top of the doors a similar groove and strip are provided in the detachable cornice G (Fig. 19). The back of the inner door slides against the edge of the carcase top H, and the

shelves are fixtures, then matchboarding running from the top to the bottom will serve. In constructing the lower carcase (Figs. 16 and 17) the plinth B is detachable like the cornice, and the doors are pushed up from below and then dropped on the plinth. The fillet E (Fig. 18) coming between the two doors causes a gap extending from the top to the bottom ; this must be closed by a strip fixed to the inner side of the front door.

Fig. 20.—Kitchen Dresser before Alterations

front of the outer door against a fillet J (Figs. 16 and 19) fixed behind the cornice moulding. The doors are put in place, and the cornice is dropped over them and then secured with screws from the underside of the top H. If the shelves K are movable like a bookcase, it will be necessary to make the carcase back L (Fig. 19) in one large frame with a centre stile and a cross-rail, with $\frac{1}{2}$-in. thick panels M inserted in ploughed grooves, so as to make the top carcase rigid. But if the

To allow the doors to slide freely, rollers should be fixed to the bottom edges, and to make a substantial job the carcase ends and doors should be about $1\frac{1}{8}$ in. thick.

IMPROVED KITCHEN DRESSER

Utility should be the keynote of modern kitchen furniture, and with this object in mind a design is shown for the conversion of the ordinary kitchen dresser into a real labour-saving piece of furniture. Fig. 20 shows an ordinary type of kitchen dresser in process of transformation and which, actually (for the purpose it is supposed to fulfil) is more or less useless. The same dresser converted into a really useful article is shown by Fig. 21. It will be noticed that the front of the shelves has been filled with doors, and the shelves widened so that they are deep enough to hold plates flat. The drawers and cup-

flat chisel or a screwdriver to avoid breaking them, for the wood will come in useful in other places. Carefully note where the beading is bradded, and exert most pressure quite close up. Next fit two division boards cut from $\frac{3}{4}$-in. by 11-in. stuff as shown. Slots should be cut in these boards to allow of them being pushed right back to the wall. These slots will require careful marking out, and the best way is to commence with the top

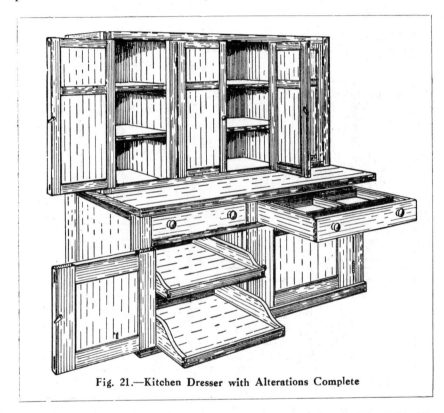

Fig. 21.—Kitchen Dresser with Alterations Complete

boards underneath are arranged to enable their contents to be reached without trouble, and, above all, the surface for dust collecting is reduced to a minimum. Front and end elevations are given by Figs. 22 and 23.

Commencing then with an ordinary dresser, as shown by Fig. 20, first remove all the beading placed on the front of the shelves to keep the plates in place. These pieces should be carefully raised with a

slot, as shown at a (Fig. 24). The distance to the line should be measured from the shelf, and the position of the groove determined by placing the board quite upright with the edge against the shelf; the thickness may then be marked off. To make sure that the shelf is quite at right angles, place the try-square on as shown in Fig. 20. If there is any inclination, this must be allowed for. The groove should be sawn out close up to the line and the waste carefully removed. When this groove is done, place the board in position and push the groove on the shelf, so that the second groove may be marked off. Cut this out in the same way, and finally the bottom one, if there is a third shelf, may be marked out and cut. The second division board may be marked off from the first if it fits, and any adjustment may be made. These boards should have a space of 2 ft. if the dresser is a 5-ft. length, used at any rate for the two division pieces. The latter pieces should be 2 ft. apart in the centre, leaving about 1 ft. 2 in. or so for the side openings, as shown by Fig. 25. This frame when placed against the division boards will leave a space at each end, as shown in the side view (Fig. 26) ; this space has now to be filled up. First of all screw or nail a length of the same material on to the top board of the dresser, as shown at B (Fig 27), and

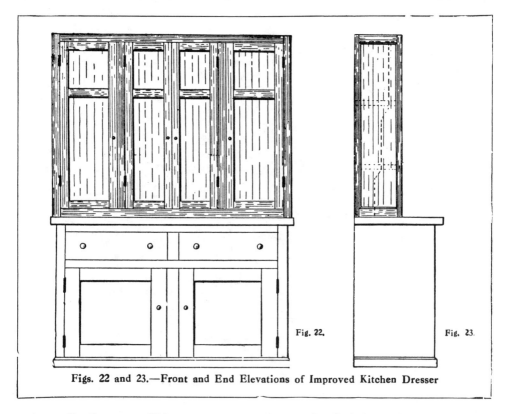

Figs. 22 and 23.—Front and End Elevations of Improved Kitchen Dresser

as is usually the case. If longer, a space of 2 ft. 6 in. would do.

The next stage is to make a framework to hold the doors. This should be made from 2¼-in. by 1¼-in. batten planed down to 2 in. by 1 in. Two lengths will be required for the top and the bottom, these being 2 in. longer than the distance between the uprights holding the shelves. Mortise-and-tenon joints are preferable for the corners, but halving joints may be also another length at the top, as at c. Next cut some lengths to fit between the two uprights, and shape them at the inside ends, with a corresponding sloping notch cut out of the sides. If it is not desired to cut the dresser—and in a rented house this may not be advisable—the pieces should be supported as shown in Fig. 28 ; but in each case the level of the top of the cross-rails must be on a line with the underside of the existing shelves. The front frame should be lightly bradded or screwed into position, with the division boards placed exactly in the centre of the division uprights, and then a thin board prepared to fit in the space at each end, as shown in Fig. 29. The boards should be about ¼ in. thick, and should fit tightly to allow for inevitable shrinkage.

The whole of the work may now be secured with nails and screws, but it

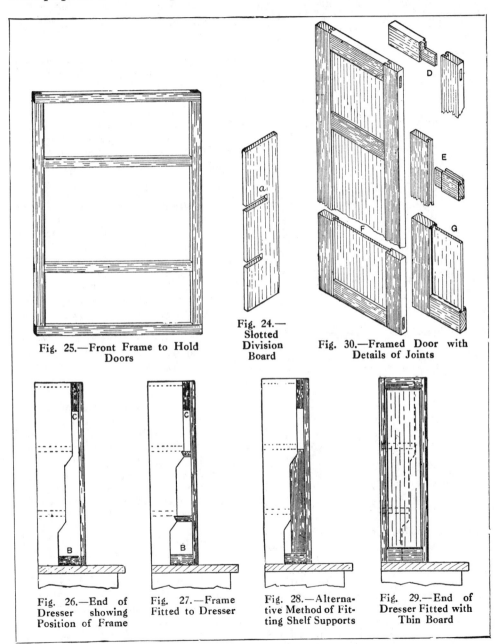

Fig. 25.—Front Frame to Hold Doors

Fig. 24.—Slotted Division Board

Fig. 30.—Framed Door with Details of Joints

Fig. 26.—End of Dresser showing Position of Frame

Fig. 27.—Frame Fitted to Dresser

Fig. 28.—Alternative Method of Fitting Shelf Supports

Fig. 29.—End of Dresser Fitted with Thin Board

would be easier to leave this until the doors are made and hinged, so that the hinge slots may be cut in the front frame.

The best form of door, and the one which will well repay for labour in appearance and wear, is the framed and panelled door, as shown in detail by Fig. 30. The joint for the corners is shown at D. It is

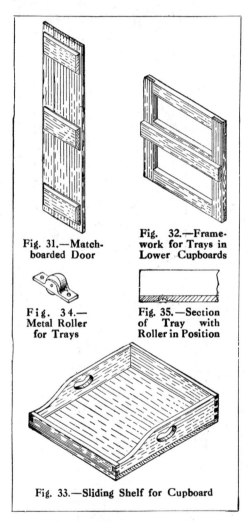

Fig. 31.—Match-boarded Door

Fig. 32.—Framework for Trays in Lower Cupboards

Fig. 34.—Metal Roller for Trays

Fig. 35.—Section of Tray with Roller in Position

Fig. 33.—Sliding Shelf for Cupboard

called a haunched mortise-and-tenon joint, and is no more difficult to make than the ordinary form; it only requires a little more care in setting out. The joint at E is an ordinary mortise-and-tenon.

There are two methods of fitting the

panel, the best being shown in section at F, where the panel of $\frac{1}{4}$-in. wood fits in a groove cut inside the framing. The alternative method, which is much simpler, is shown in section at G, the panel in this case being made to fit the inside of the frame and kept in position by beading. There are four doors to make, the centre opening being fitted with a double door, as shown in Fig. 22. Ordinary butt hinges and any kind of suitable fastening should be used. As an alternative to the framed door, the matchboarding door made as shown by Fig. 31 may be used. This is not so strong and does not look so workmanlike, but it will answer the purpose.

The shelves should now be made up to the full width of the space, and should rest on the lengths at each end already fixed in position, and on fillets of $\frac{7}{8}$-in. wood nailed on to the division boards. These shelves will be of varying widths, and probably of $\frac{7}{8}$-in. thick board to match the thickness of the original shelves. This will now complete the upper structure, and the lower portion may be tackled.

It is suggested that the drawers should be fitted with sliding compartments. The internal fittings should be arranged to fit in with the particular requirements of the house. The cupboards of these dressers are not usually convenient; they go back a fair depth, and it is not easy to get at the contents; therefore, the shelves are dispensed with and sliding shelves substituted. A framework flush with the door frames must be made and provided with runners, as shown in Fig. 32. The sliding shelves are made as in Fig. 33. These will run much more easily if fitted with rollers (Fig. 34), a section of the fitting in position being given by Fig. 35. No difficulty should be experienced here, as the work of making the trays will be quite easy. The advantage of these trays will be found when they are stocked with articles, such as tea-things, etc., for they may be washed up, placed on the tray, and put in the cupboard ready for use again. The lower portion of the cupboard doors may, if desired, be filled with a frame to hold various articles as suggested for the kitchen table; but, of course, the use to which the movable shelves will be put must be considered first to see if there will be room.

Figs. 36 to 41. The dresser should be made chiefly of good northern pine, the top of the lower portion being of birch.

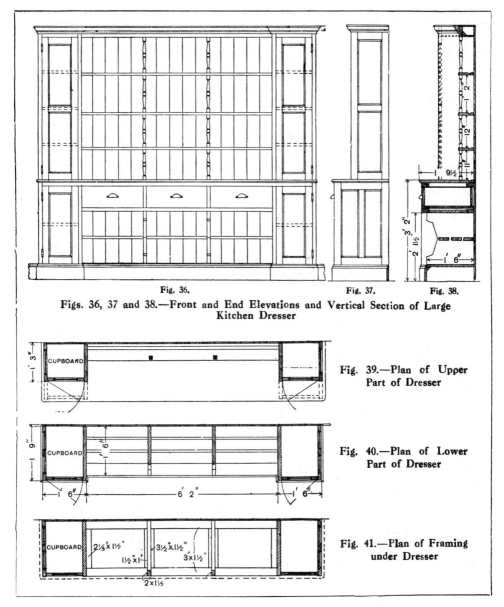

Fig. 36.

Fig. 37.

Fig. 38.

Figs. 36, 37 and 38.—Front and End Elevations and Vertical Section of Large Kitchen Dresser

Fig. 39.—Plan of Upper Part of Dresser

Fig. 40.—Plan of Lower Part of Dresser

Fig. 41.—Plan of Framing under Dresser

LARGE KITCHEN DRESSER

A kitchen dresser suitable for a town house or a country mansion is shown by

The material required for the following members is $1\frac{3}{8}$ in. thick, finished : The two plain ends to the top of the cupboard, shown in Fig. 30, and the ends of the lower part shown in Fig. 40, two standards, with shaped front, shown on section (*see* Fig. 38), and in the enlarged section (Fig. 42). The material required for pot-boards is as follows: One piece 6 ft. 4 in. by 18 in. by $\frac{7}{8}$ in. thick; and two pieces

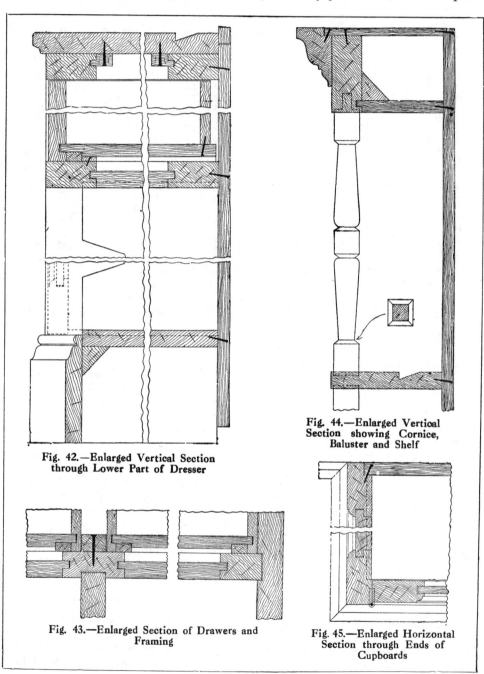

Fig. 42.—Enlarged Vertical Section through Lower Part of Dresser

Fig. 44.—Enlarged Vertical Section showing Cornice, Baluster and Shelf

Fig. 43.—Enlarged Section of Drawers and Framing

Fig. 45.—Enlarged Horizontal Section through Ends of Cupboards

1 ft. 5 in. by 20 in. by $\frac{7}{8}$ in. thick. The two shelves of the lower cupboard are each 1 ft. 5 in. by 20 in. by $\frac{7}{8}$ in. ; the six shelves for the top cupboard each 1 ft. 5 in. by 13 in. by $\frac{7}{8}$ in. The three panels in the framing, forming dust-proof divisions between the drawers and the lower cupboard, as shown on section (Fig. 38), and on the plan of the framing (Fig. 41) and enlarged section (Fig. 43), are each 1 ft. 11 in. by 16 in. by $\frac{7}{8}$ in. thick, finished ; three drawer bottoms, each 2 ft. 1 in. by 20 in. by $\frac{1}{2}$ in. thick, finished (see the enlarged vertical section illustrated by Fig. 42). The birch top should be cut off 2 in. longer than the required length, which is 9 ft. 4 in. by 22 in. by $1\frac{1}{8}$ in., finished thickness, as shown in Fig. 42. The whole is grooved for cross-tongueing, the groove in the birch top to be stopped 3 in. from each end. The eight balusters are turned, as shown in Fig. 44. The panels in the framing at the ends are flush on the inside, as shown in Fig. 45.

The trellis pieces at the open portion of the lower part of the dresser are cut in lengths fitting between the standards and ends of the cupboards, and are housed in $\frac{1}{2}$ in. at each end, as shown by Fig. 38. The bottom rails of the lower portion of the dresser are dovetailed at the ends. Fig. 46 shows the construction of the front and back rails of the dresser under the birch top, as well as the construction of the two inner ends of the cupboard. The top rail at front and back is dovetailed to the two outside ends. The lower rail at front and back under the drawers is tenoned and mortised ; the shoulder inside the rail being housed in the end to the same depth as the rail forming the runner. The two muntins between the three drawers are tenoned, mortised, and housed, as before described. The shaped standards are housed in the pot-board (stop-housing) at the front, as shown by dotted lines in Fig. 42. The pot-board of the two end cupboards is tongued as shown in Fig. 47. The shelves in the cupboards are housed in the ends as shown by dotted lines in Fig. 45.

The rail forming the runner for the drawers is grooved on the underside to

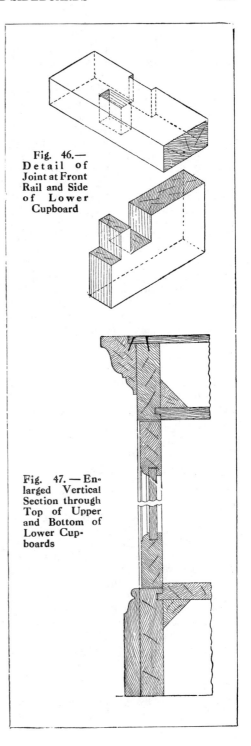

Fig. 46.— Detail of Joint at Front Rail and Side of Lower Cupboard

Fig. 47. — Enlarged Vertical Section through Top of Upper and Bottom of Lower Cupboards

receive the top end of the standard as shown in Figs. 42 and 43. The top rails under the cornice are dovetailed. The three shelves at the top portion of the dresser are sunk, as shown in Fig. 44. The three shelves are housed $\frac{1}{2}$ in. deep into the ends of the cupboards, the housing being cut to fit the sinking in the shelf. The two top balusters are tenoned into the top rail, and are housed in as shown in Fig. 44. The four ends of the lower cupboard run down to the floor, and three bearers, each 5 in. by $1\frac{1}{2}$ in., are fixed under the pot-board, and glue-blocked as shown in the various sections. The four ends of the top cupboard are housed $\frac{1}{2}$ in. into the top of the lower portion of the dresser, and stopped. The sinking for plates at the top (Fig. 42) is stopped between the two ends of the cupboard. The birch top is buttoned down, as shown in Fig. 42. The doors are hung with two 3-in. steel-butts, each door being fitted with a small mortise lock and drop handle, while each drawer is fitted with an ordinary grip handle or with turned wood-knobs. Stop-drawers at the front are shown in Fig. 42.

The front and ends of the dresser should be painted in three oils of an approved tint, or grained; the whole being twice varnished.

KITCHEN DRESSER WITH ENCLOSED CUPBOARDS

A kitchen dresser of a similar type to the one last described but of more simple construction is shown in front elevation by Fig. 48.

Figs. 49 and 50 show two vertical sections, and plans of the upper and lower parts are given by Figs. 51 and 52. This dresser could be adapted for a position against a blank wall or could be placed in a recess. Selected red deal or pitchpine would be suitable woods.

The lower portion consists of cupboards and drawers. The doors of the cupboards should be 1 in. thick framed up with panels moulded on the face, as shown in Fig. 53. The drawers should be fitted with 1 in. fronts, and the top above the drawers (see Fig. 54) should be 1 in. thick with plain

moulding on the edges secured to the framing below. The upper portion of shelving should preferably be made separate from the lower portion, as the dresser will then be more portable than if constructed in one piece. The sides of the shelving should be 1 in. thick, shaped as shown, and fitted with two tiers of shelving supported with turned balusters $\frac{3}{4}$ in. square. The top cornice (Fig. 55) should be cut out of $1\frac{1}{2}$-in. stuff, blocked at intervals for strengthening purposes. Below this are fixed cut and shaped heads $\frac{1}{2}$ in. thick housed into brackets and side cheeks. The back is covered with $\frac{1}{2}$-in. V-jointed boarding in narrow widths. The lower cupboards should be fitted with brass latches and the drawers with plain drop handles; brass hooks for cups and jugs should be fixed on the edges of the shelving. The dresser, when finished, should be either painted to match the existing woodwork or stained and twice varnished.

SMALL SIDEBOARD

A pleasing design for a single sideboard is shown by the half-tone reproduction (Fig. 56). Figs. 57, 58 and 59 show front elevation, vertical section and plan respectively. Of the four uprights the two at the back can be quite plain and finished about 2 in. by $1\frac{1}{2}$ in. The front uprights are 2 in. square (finished), and have chamfers, as at A in Fig. 60, stopped 12 in. above the floor B (Fig. 57) and running into the small turned finials at the tops. One of the latter is shown to a large scale in Figs. 61 and 62, the octagonal section formed by the chamfers being finished with a slight hollow, as at C in both figures. Above this the uprights are round-turned to the design given. At a height of 7 in. above the floor the front legs are sunk $\frac{1}{16}$ in. all round, and thence tapered downwards to $1\frac{1}{4}$ in. square. Three $\frac{7}{8}$-in. or $\frac{3}{4}$-in. shelves will be required, and they should be moulded, as in Fig. 63, on three sides. Along the front and ends they are supported by means of $\frac{7}{8}$-in. by 2-in. rails, as at D in Figs. 58 and 63. These rails are tenoned into the uprights, the front two

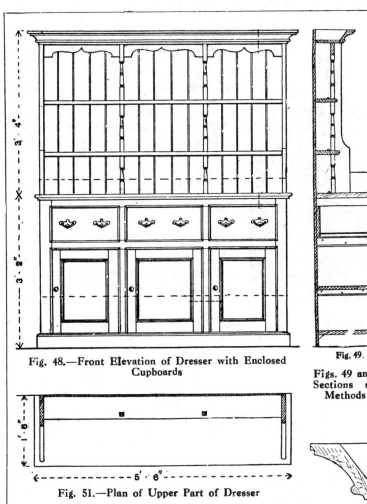

Fig. 48.—Front Elevation of Dresser with Enclosed Cupboards

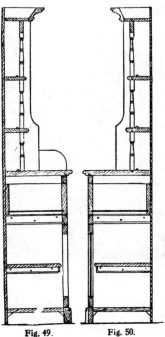

Fig. 49.   Fig. 50.

Figs. 49 and 50.—Two Vertical Sections showing Alternative Methods of Finish to Ends

Fig. 51.—Plan of Upper Part of Dresser

Fig. 52.—Plan of Lower Part of Dresser

Fig. 55.—Section through Cornice

Fig. 54.—Section of Top above Drawers

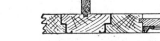

Fig. 53.—Section through Stiles of Doors

Fig. 56.—Small Sideboard

close intervals from behind, their ends being first halved or notched into the back uprights as in Fig. 59, and the whole finished flush at the back. The top shelf is treated in exactly the same manner, except that its rail F (Fig. 58) is 5 in. deep, and is finished with a small capping mould either rebated or planted in position and continued over the back uprights by means of flat, solid caps $3\frac{1}{2}$ in. by 3 in., moulded and mitred as required, and sunk underneath to fit $\frac{1}{4}$ in. over the posts.

SIDEBOARD DRESSER

A sideboard dresser which harmonises admirably with old-world interiors is shown by Fig. 64. From the point of view of utility it must be confessed that a sideboard dresser of this type is not so

of which take two rails at each level, the tenons being arranged as in Fig. 60, in order that the longest rails may be jointed the farthest into the uprights. When the rails and uprights have been framed up, the shelves can be cut away at the corners as necessary, carefully fitted into position, and s c r e w e d from the underside obliquely through the rails.

A skirting being desirable along the back edge of each shelf, this is made to take the place of the rail which would otherwise be necessary below the shelf to ensure the required amount of rigidity. For t h e t w o lower shelves this skirting takes the form of pieces $\frac{7}{8}$ in. by 3 in., having their lower edges flush with the undersides of the shelves E (Fig. 58), to which latter the rails are screwed at

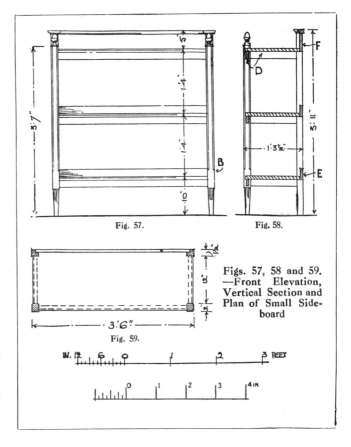

Fig. 57.

Fig. 58.

Fig. 59.

Figs. 57, 58 and 59.
—Front Elevation, Vertical Section and Plan of Small Sideboard

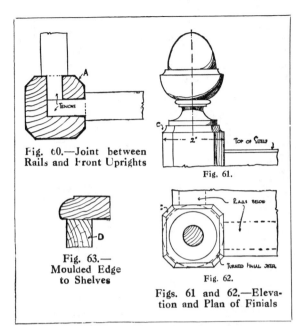

Fig. 60.—Joint between Rails and Front Uprights

Fig. 61.

Fig. 63.— Moulded Edge to Shelves

Fig. 62.

Figs. 61 and 62.—Elevation and Plan of Finials

satisfactory as one designed along Sheraton or Chippendale lines ; but it should be pointed out that many people prefer a good display of china to provision of cellaret drawers and other fittings. A sideboard dresser of this type provides a fair amount of drawer accommodation for linen and cutlery, and the cupboards in the top part serve admirably as receptacles of small articles of plate, cruets, etc.

The constructive features of the sideboard dresser shown in front elevation by Fig. 65 do not present any special difficulties. A half-sectional plan through the drawers is shown in Fig. 66, illustrating the construction of the divisions. It will be noticed that a clamp is fixed to the front of the division at each end of this and the corresponding one ; on the other half, tenons are cut which fit into the top rails and bottom of the dresser. The divisions should be grooved into the back and finally secured by screwing through. Fig. 67 shows the connection of the shelf to the legs. Both ends of the bottom part should be tenoned into the legs, and the span rail of the front should be tenoned to the bottom previous to tenoning this part into both the front and back legs. The insides

of the carcase ends should be grooved to receive the ends of the bottom. An enlarged detail of one corner of the drawer part, with broken corner mouldings fixed, is shown in Fig. 68. This detail also serves for the cupboard doors in the upper part.

To construct the top part, the best plan is to carry each end right through from top to bottom ; all shelves are then slip-dovetailed between the ends (see Fig. 69), and the cupboard bottoms dovetailed up. To bind the top part together the span rails are also slip-dovetailed between the carcase ends and made flush at the front. An enlarged detail is shown by Fig. 70 illustrating the method of fixing the cornice moulding round. The latter is allowed to project above the ends in order to receive the dust-board, which is screwed down and levelled off. The matched back with V joints is quite suitable for a sideboard of this type, and an enlarged detail of the matching is shown by Fig. 71. Fig. 72 shows the construction of the cupboard doors, made in one piece with

Fig. 64.—Sideboard Dresser

clamps at each end. Round the bottom of the top part a small half-round moulding should be rebated and mitred, which forms a neat finish between the upper and lower part.

The metal-work suggested for the sideboard is armour-bright iron. The handles could be of a ring shape as shown, or handles with pear-shape drops could be introduced with advantage.

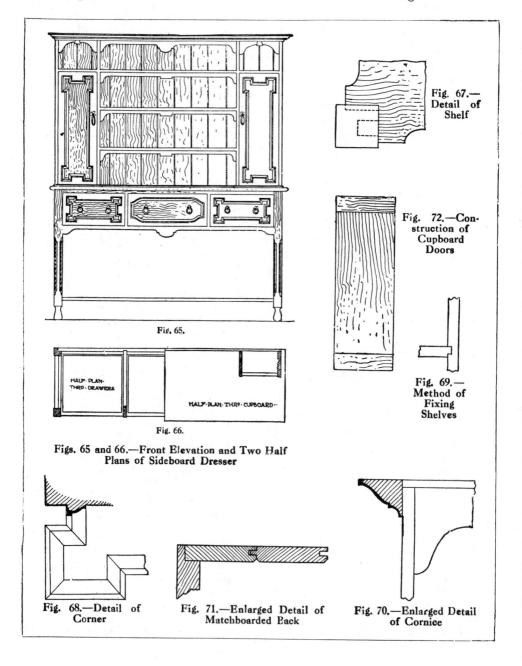

Fig. 65.

Fig. 66.

Figs. 65 and 66.—Front Elevation and Two Half Plans of Sideboard Dresser

Fig. 67.— Detail of Shelf

Fig. 72.—Con-struction of Cupboard Doors

Fig. 69.— Method of Fixing Shelves

Fig. 68.—Detail of Corner

Fig. 71.—Enlarged Detail of Matchboarded Back

Fig. 70.—Enlarged Detail of Cornice

ANOTHER SIDEBOARD DRESSER

The constructional work of the further example of sideboard dresser shown by Fig. 73 is on identically the same lines as the preceding one, and therefore no useful purpose would be served by giving details. This sideboard is simply included here as presenting an alternative design, and the tone reproduction (Fig. 74). Two elevations and an enlarged vertical section are shown by Figs. 75, 76 and 77.

The dresser is made in two distinct portions, the lower one having four front legs 2 in. or $2\frac{1}{4}$ in. square, but circular-turned at a point just above the floor, as in Fig. 78. There are also four 2-in. or $2\frac{1}{4}$-in. by $1\frac{1}{2}$-in. back legs, not turned at

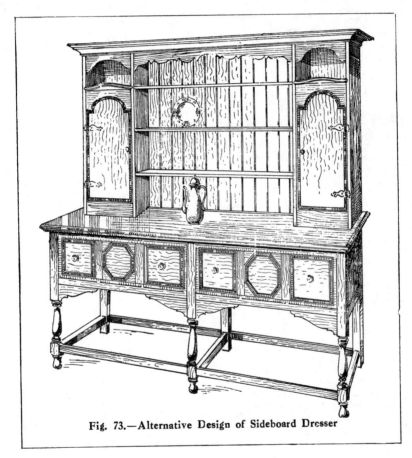

Fig. 73.—Alternative Design of Sideboard Dresser

craftsman who desires to make it should study the construction in conjunction with that just described.

DRESSER SIDEBOARD WITH SLIDING DOORS

An oak dresser, fitted at the top with sliding glazed doors, is shown in the half-

all. These eight legs are connected up by means of top and drawer rails at the front, back and ends, as at A and B in Fig. 78, and as shown in section by Fig. 77. The drawer spaces should be fitted with the necessary guides, runners, and drawers, the fronts of the latter being recessed when shut, and having a small moulding mitred round them. Panels should be

Fig. 74.—Dresser Sideboard with Sliding Doors

formed at the ends, as at C in Figs. 76 and 79, and mouldings applied to match the drawers, and ultimately ten small cut brackets should be fitted where shown. Near the floor the legs should be connected by means of $1\frac{1}{2}$-in. by 2-in. diagonal braces, as in Fig. 80, halved in the middle where they cross. Similar rails should be framed in as at D in the same figure, to take a central shelf about 1 ft. 3 in. wide. A $\frac{3}{4}$-in. moulded top will complete the lower half of the dresser.

The upper portion should be built up of sides, top and lowest shelf, finished about $\frac{3}{4}$ in. thick, the top moulded and made into a cornice by means of a small hollowed fillet, as at E in Fig. 77, which also shows at F the shaped outline for the sides. The latter should be housed $\frac{3}{8}$ in. deep into 2-in. by 1-in. moulded feet G (Figs. 77 and 78), the line of which is continued against the back by means of a moulded fillet as at H. If possible, the whole back should be panelled; but in any case the lower open portion should

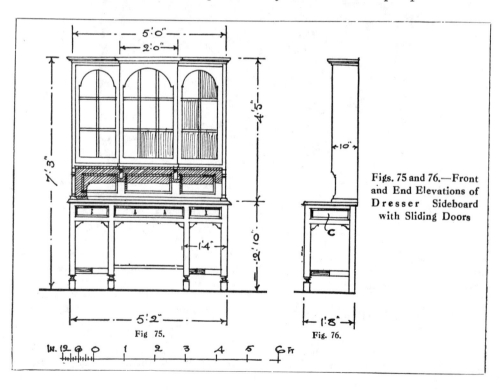

Figs. 75 and 76.—Front and End Elevations of Dresser Sideboard with Sliding Doors

Fig 75.

Fig. 76.

be in three moulded panels, set out to correspond with the glazed divisions above. Two cut brackets and a small top moulding J (Figs. 77 and 78) will complete this portion.

Dealing next with the glazed front, metal tracks will be best for these, although they can be grooved top and bottom to run on rounded oak tongues, as at K in Fig. 77, if desired. Fig. 81 is a detail part plan of this. The small top-rail at L (Fig. 77) as shown should run

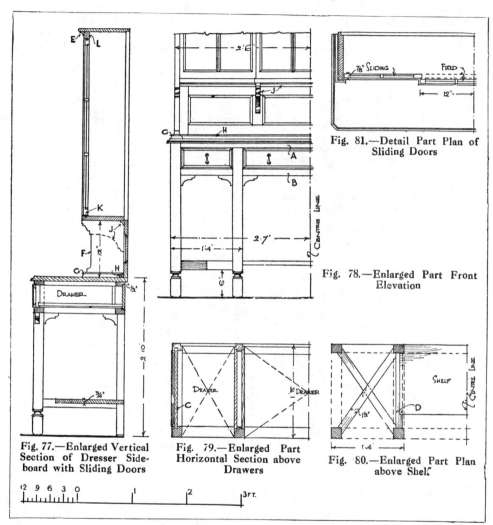

Fig. 81.—Detail Part Plan of Sliding Doors

Fig. 78.—Enlarged Part Front Elevation

Fig. 77.—Enlarged Vertical Section of Dresser Sideboard with Sliding Doors

Fig. 79.—Enlarged Part Horizontal Section above Drawers

Fig. 80.—Enlarged Part Plan above Shelf

this should be about $\frac{7}{8}$ in. thick, and all well framed in the ordinary manner. The side lights slide towards the centre behind the middle one, which is fixed and projects as shown, the top and bottom shelves being broken out to suit it. It should overlap the side lights $\frac{1}{2}$ in., and

right across behind the middle light, and it will be essential to make it exactly parallel to the lower shelf, in order to let the lights slide properly. By opening the side lights it will be quite simple to reach the spaces behind the fixed central portion. If possible, the shelves should coincide with the horizontal glazing-bars in level.

MAHOGANY SIDEBOARD

The eminently useful example of dining-room furniture illustrated in Fig. 82 (finished perspective view) has been designed to show the possibilities of a sideboard which does not involve very

shaped edges to the doors and frames. As will be seen from the various views, the shaping is based upon a "repeating" unit, and this detail, as well as the remainder of the design, shows much better in the actual material than in plain black-and-white.

The elevations of the sideboard show the projection of the top part of the back. This is necessary in order to allow for the

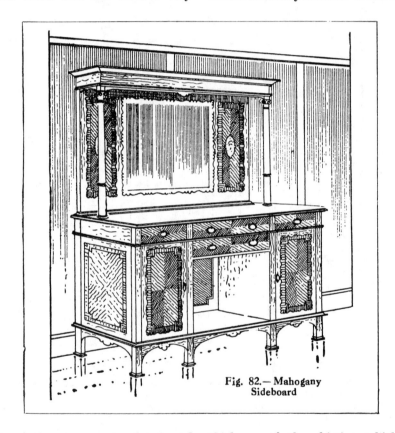

Fig. 82.—Mahogany
Sideboard

difficult practice or expensive detail, and readers will no doubt admit that the simple lines of the example introduced are much to be preferred to the " many-mirrored " type of sideboard. Front and end elevations are shown by Figs. 83 and 84 on the opposite page.

The decoration of this sideboard is chiefly obtained by the judicious arrangement of well-figured veneers, and an additional decorative feature consists of

thickness of the skirting which would otherwise prevent the top part fitting close against the wall. In some instances similar considerations necessitate making the whole of the bottom part flush at the back, in which case the curve shown on the leg would be omitted. This would not seriously affect the appearance of the sideboard, and has the effect of reducing the overhang or back projection of the top part. Two sectional views of the sideboard are shown by Figs. 86 and 87, which illustrate the construction.

A detail of the decorative shaping used on the doors and frames is also shown in Fig. 86, and this would be executed by

The first step in making the sideboard would be to prepare the four carcase ends, and to dowel the two outside ones into the legs. Before they are glued together, the insides of the ends should

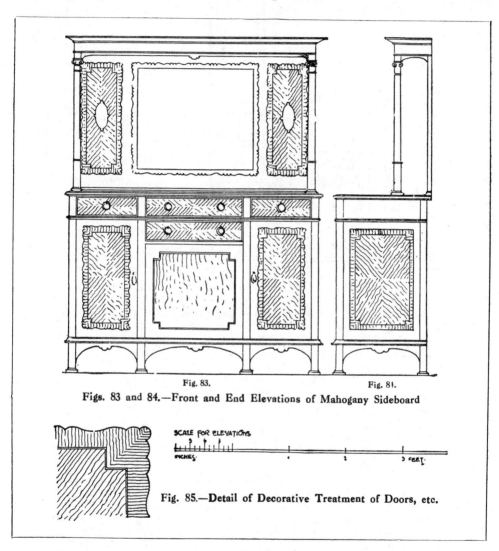

Fig. 83.

Fig. 84.

Figs. 83 and 84.—Front and End Elevations of Mahogany Sideboard

SCALE FOR ELEVATIONS

INCHES.

3 FEET.

Fig. 85.—Detail of Decorative Treatment of Doors, etc.

simply fret-sawing to the shape shown and finishing with fine files and glass-paper. The shaped part is, of course, only about 1 in. thick, and represents the projecting parts of the framing form-ing the rebate.

be trenched to receive the drawer runners, as shown in the first sectional view. The inside ends are then dowelled only into the front legs, as they are secured at the back to the main panelled back, there being only six legs. Both sides of the

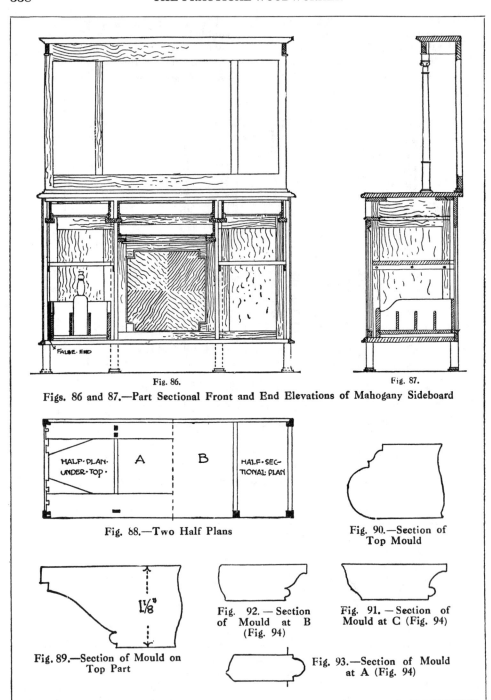

Fig. 86.

Fig. 87.

Figs. 86 and 87.—Part Sectional Front and End Elevations of Mahogany Sideboard

Fig. 88.—Two Half Plans

Fig. 90.—Section of Top Mould

Fig. 89.—Section of Mould on Top Part

Fig. 92. — Section of Mould at B (Fig. 94)

Fig. 91. — Section of Mould at C (Fig. 94)

Fig. 93.—Section of Mould at A (Fig. 94)

inside ends must be trenched to receive drawer runners, and the short drawer rails may then be tenoned in between the glued-up ends. The method of attaching the top rail is indicated at A in Fig. 88, from which it will be seen that the ends are pinned through the rails and the latter are dovetailed down into the carcase ends and legs. Triangular brackets are attached to the rails, these serving for

sitates the use of a false end (*see* Fig. 87). The sectional view (Fig. 86) shows the shaped ends for this part, and also the divisions which need not be made the same width of the ends. A necessary feature of a cellaret drawer is the lead lining which is usually soldered in after the woodwork has been completed. The shelf above the cellaret provides for cruets and small articles of plate, and the

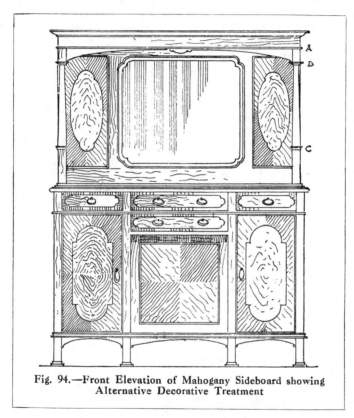

Fig. 94.—Front Elevation of Mahogany Sideboard showing Alternative Decorative Treatment

additional strength and economise the material. Reference to Fig. 87 shows the bottom running right through underneath the carcase ends. The legs should, of course, be housed to receive it, and the inside legs may be screwed to the carcase bottom underneath the moulding, the latter being fixed after the carcase has been glued together. At the bottom of the left-hand cupboard a cellaret drawer should be introduced; this necessitates the use of a false end (*see* Fig. 87).

right-hand cupboard proves useful for reserve bottles, knife-cases and like articles indispensable to a well-equipped dining-room.

The drawers are made in the usual way and veneered with quartered patterns. An added decorative touch is imparted to this part of the work by adding cocked beads which project beyond the face of the work. With cocked beads the face of the drawer front should be in exactly the same plane as the front legs, and the bead then breaks the joints between them, and also protects the edges of the veneer which would otherwise chip away through coming in contact with the drawer rails. The curved span rails at the bottoms should preferably be made in three pieces, and each one mitred up in order to obviate the short grain which would inevitably break away if the rails were cut from the solid. At the bottoms of the legs small moulded blocks are either screwed or dowelled on to act as feet.

The sectional view (Fig. 87) shows the groundwork of the back frame. This should be made of Honduras mahogany with square edges, and then the front part is faced up with Cuba mahogany. The cornice is made with three rails secret-mitred at the corners with frieze mouldings underneath. A moulded top is prepared to fit right over the frame, and this is secured by pocket-screwing through the insides of the cornice rails. The base moulding is worked in one piece moulded on three sides, and is screwed up to the back frame. To fix effectively the columns, the squares should run to the underside of the moulded top, and to effect this it is necessary to cut this away for the cornice which leaves a projecting horn which may be screwed to the rails. In cases where the top part must be made as a separate feature, a good plan is to mortise and tenon three base mouldings, which act as a sufficient tie or brace for the top part. The shaped rails underneath the frieze moulding are simply fitted in between and then glued up to the moulding.

The centre elliptical shapes in the panels are intended to be executed in curl veneer (described in a later section), and may be cut to the desired shape by placing the two pieces in between two pieces of quarter stuff with pins to secure the whole. The shape may then be fret-sawn and finished with fine files previous to separating them. The quartering should not present any special difficulties, and in this particular instance it would probably economise time to cut in the elliptical centre parts after the quartered veneers had been glued down. The back of the bottom part has necessarily to be made in one piece; this is indicated in the sectional view, from which it will be seen that the top rail has to be made wider in the centre part in order to make the proper margin. The square or broken corners can be added to the rails for purposes of economy. A panelled back of this kind is very strong, and when rebated into the legs, as shown at A in Fig. 88, and screwed to these and the carcase ends great rigidity is obtained.

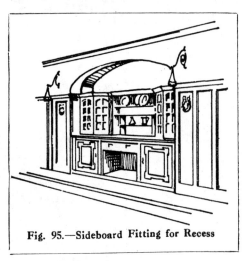

Fig. 95.—Sideboard Fitting for Recess

Details of the moulds are shown by Figs. 89 to 93.

An alternative decorative treatment is indicated in the second elevation shown in Fig. 94. The constructional features are almost identical to those in the first elevation. The veneered designs are different, and flush veneered-doors are substituted for the framed ones. These flush doors are made with clamps mortised and tenoned on, with cocked beads fixed as with the drawers after the veneering has been completed.

SIDEBOARD FITTING FOR A RECESS

Well-planned houses are now frequently arranged with a recess in the dining- or

Occasional Tables

SIMPLE OCCASIONAL TABLE

THE neat little occasional table shown by the half-tone reproduction (Fig. 1) is stronger in construction and better finished than the majority of such tables, yet it will be found very simple to make. The dimensions are given in the drawings of an elevation and plan shown by Figs. 2 and 3.

The first part to prepare is the top, which must be 1 ft. 8½ in. long by 1 ft. 2½ in. wide; that is, the size without the moulding on the edges. This will require to be in two pieces of board ¾ in. thick, jointed together by planing one edge of each perfectly straight and square, so that they fit together quite close like one piece of wood. These edges are warmed and fixed

Fig. 1.—Simple Occasional Table

together with hot, rather thin glue, rubbing together a little to work out the surplus glue, then left in accurate position in a dry place to set thoroughly. In the meantime the legs may be planed straight and square, each the exact length, 2 ft. 2½ in. by 1¼ in. square. Two pieces of stuff about ¾ in. thick are next required, 1 ft. 3½ in. long by 3½ in. wide, planed and squared on the top edge and the ends, the lower edge to be shaped to a slight curve. These are joined to the legs by ⅜-in. wood dowels, the outer surface of the rails being $\frac{1}{16}$ in. in from the outside surface of the legs. Two more rails similar to these are required, but only 9½ in. long, to be joined to the legs to complete the upper frame of the stand. In joining these the dowels should be a

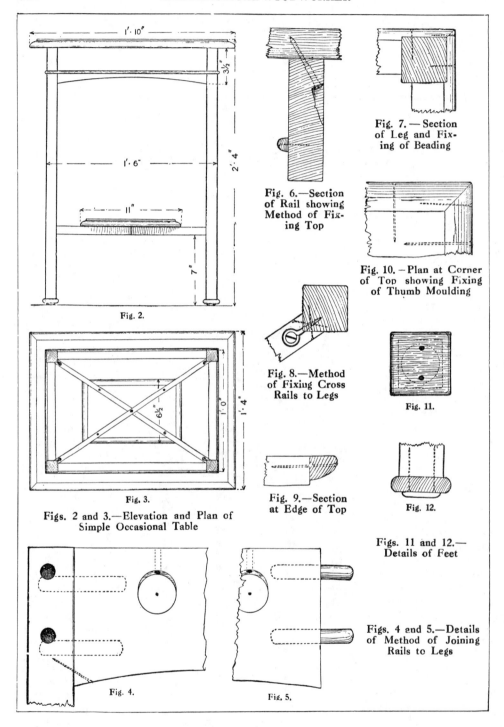

Fig. 2.

Fig. 6.—Section of Rail showing Method of Fixing Top

Fig. 7. — Section of Leg and Fixing of Beading

Fig. 10. — Plan at Corner of Top showing Fixing of Thumb Moulding

Fig. 8.—Method of Fixing Cross Rails to Legs

Fig. 11.

Fig. 3.

Fig. 9.—Section at Edge of Top

Fig. 12.

Figs. 2 and 3.—Elevation and Plan of Simple Occasional Table

Figs. 11 and 12.— Details of Feet

Fig. 4.

Fig. 5.

Figs. 4 and 5.—Details of Method of Joining Rails to Legs

little higher, to miss cutting through the others, but may just cut a little into them (*see* Figs. 4 and 5). These show the inner side of the rails, and it will be noticed that there is a circular impression made by boring on the slant with a 1-in. diameter centre-bit, and a screw-hole slanting through the upper edge of the rail. These are for fixing the table top (when it is ready), as in Fig. 6, which also shows the small beading fixed along the rails and round the legs, as further shown by Fig. 7. Glue and very fine panel pins are used for fixing. The beading can easily be made by a small smoothing plane.

Two cross-rails to support the shelf may next be fitted. They are of $\frac{7}{8}$-in. by $\frac{5}{8}$-in. section, halved into each other where they cross at the centre. The ends are fitted and fixed to the legs, as in Fig. 8, but should also be glued in addition to the screw-eye fixing and pins. The shelf can then be made 10 in. by $5\frac{1}{2}$ in. ; that is the size without the moulding. Both the shelf and the top should be planed on the top surface and edges perfectly level. The thumb-shaped moulding round the top is $\frac{3}{4}$ in. by $\frac{5}{8}$ in. in section, and can easily be made with the smoothing plane. It is shown in Figs. 9 and 10, fixed with glue and the fine pins. The shelf is done in the same way, but the moulding may be a little smaller. It is fixed in place by means of screws through the cross-rails, as seen in Fig. 3.

Four pieces of firm wood are now required, $1\frac{5}{8}$ in. square by about $\frac{1}{2}$ in. thick, to be rounded bead-like on the edges, and fixed on the ends of the legs with glue and two fine nails, as in Figs. 11 and 12, which also indicate a set of gliders that are put on finally. The table is now ready for finishing. It must be well smoothed with glasspaper, rubbing down slightly all very sharp corners. Pin-heads should be punched down a little and the holes filled with putty, also any other small defects that there might be.

CHESS AND DRAUGHTS TABLE

Devotees of the ancient game of chess will appreciate the small table shown by Fig. 13, with its top subdivided into the requisite number of squares, and a small cupboard underneath for tobacco sundries. An elevation and plan are given by Figs. 14 and 15.

Structurally it consists of four $1\frac{1}{8}$-in. square legs having their outer faces tapering downwards to $\frac{7}{8}$ in. square at the bottom. The upper ends of the legs can be stub-tenoned or dowelled to the table top, which will be described later. At a height of 1 ft. 4 in. above the floor they are notched to receive a square framework of $1\frac{3}{4}$-in. by $\frac{3}{4}$-in. stuff, mitred and halved or tenoned as at A in Fig. 16, which shows an

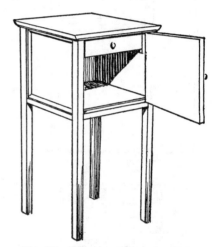

Fig. 13.—Chess and Draughts Table

angle cut out to suit the notch in one of the legs (indicated by dotted lines). This framework should finish flush with the legs, and is partially shown on plan at B in Fig. 17. This figure shows how, by means of small quadrant mouldings C, mitred round each of three sides, the sides of the cupboard can be fixed in position as at D without the necessity for grooves or rebates. These sides can be $\frac{1}{2}$ in. or even less in thickness, and when they are in position, a thin bottom, as at E in Fig. 18, can be fitted, its front edge serving as a stop to the door.

The door should be made to match the sides, with a moulding mitred round its outer edges, and if the small internal drawer is required, it must be hinged so as to open right back (*see* Fig. 19), and leave this free to be pulled out without encountering any obstruction. The table top can be a $\frac{7}{8}$-in. board with moulded edge projecting about 1 in. beyond the legs and having the quadrant mould fixed to its woods, such as sycamore and mahogany, and glued to a deal baseboard F, the edges being finished with a larger moulding than in the simpler case, mitred round.

A possible addition to the table would be a couple of thin hardwood slides to pull out from under the cupboard to take the

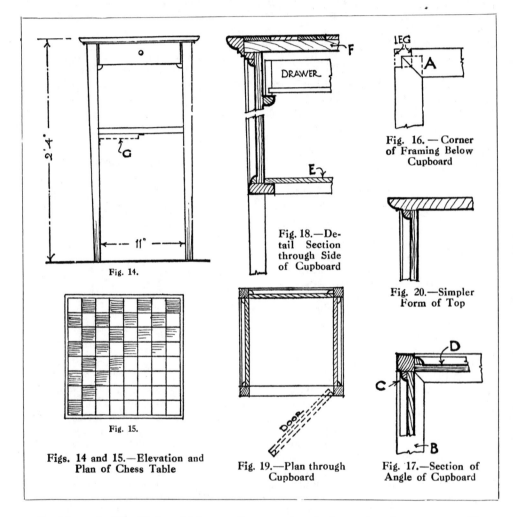

Fig. 16. — Corner of Framing Below Cupboard

Fig. 18.—Detail Section through Side of Cupboard

Fig. 20.—Simpler Form of Top

Fig. 14.

Fig. 15.

Figs. 14 and 15.—Elevation and Plan of Chess Table

Fig. 19.—Plan through Cupboard

Fig. 17.—Section of Angle of Cupboard

underside, as in Fig. 20, in which case the light and dark squares would probably be stained or painted on it. For a more elaborate piece of work, however, the arrangement shown in Fig. 18 would be preferable. Here the squares are each cut and fitted separately in two contrasting captured pieces of each opponent. These could slide in strips of brass bent and screwed in position, as at G in Fig. 14, on opposite sides of the table, and should have small stops on their undersides to obviate any chance of being pulled out too far.

SMALL TEA-TABLE WITH PANELLED FALLS

The construction of the useful little tea-table shown by Figs. 21 to 23 should offer no difficulties to the amateur woodworker. The table is arranged with two panelled falls, which when opened form an extension of the lower shelf.

The table is 2 ft. 5 in. high, and the top should finish $\frac{1}{2}$ in. in thickness, the legs being square wrought and 2 ft. $4\frac{1}{2}$ in. high by $1\frac{1}{4}$ in. square. The top rails should have a bead on the lower edge. The open ends should be framed together first, the joints, of course, being mortised and tenoned together and the legs mortised for the diagonal stretcher stub-tenons. The stretcher is halved together in the centre, and is fixed in position when the com-

Fig. 21.—Small Table with Panelled Falls

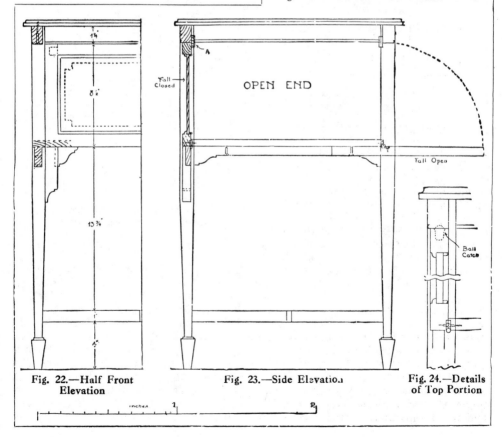

Fig. 22.—Half Front Elevation

Fig. 23.—Side Elevation

Fig. 24.—Details of Top Portion

plete frame is glued up, together with the lower shelf. This shelf should be fastened by screwing up through the spandrels on the ends. The top, which is 1 ft. 8 in. by 1 ft. 8 in., should project ½ in. beyond the frame all round, and should now be fixed in position. This is secured either with screws through the top rails, or with wooden buttons. If the latter are used, provision will have to be made for them, and the four top rails must be grooved inside before the table is put together.

Next proceed with the falls, and

they are closed, and a small brass knob should be screwed in to allow of easy opening. A check or box line in the top and panels are additions that tend to improve the design.

SMALL TABLE WITH RISING TRAY

A small table of somewhat novel construction is shown by Fig. 25. When the top (which is divided down the centre) is raised a tray or cellaret is lifted out of the

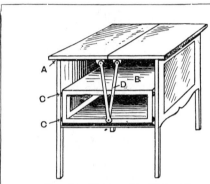

Fig. 25.—Table with Rising Tray with One Panel Removed

mortise and tenon these together, allowing for a stub-tenon on the two small brackets underneath the bottom rail. The fall should be ⅞ in. thick. The reason why the " horns " are left on the fall " uprights " or " stiles " is that when the falls are opened and in position, the horns swing under the lower shelf and effectively prevent the falls from dropping lower than shown in Fig. 21. When hinging the falls in position care must be taken to sink one half of the hinge in the fall, and the other half in the edge of the shelf, as shown in Fig. 24. The centre of the hinge knuckle must be exactly in line with the bottom edge of the fall and shelf. A wood stop (Fig. 23) should then be screwed into the top rail to prevent the fall from being pushed in too far. A small spring ball-catch should be fixed in the top edge of the falls to fasten them when

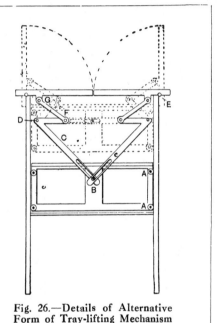

Fig. 26.—Details of Alternative Form of Tray-lifting Mechanism

hollow part of the table to the normal level of the table top. In the figure one panel of the table is removed in order that the interior arrangement may be seen. The illustration shows a table 2 ft. by 2 ft. The table rises 9 in., and the guide frame is 9 in. deep. The height of the table is 2 ft. 6 in. The top of the table opens in two flaps hinged on the outside at A. A sliding shelf B has a framework underneath, to each corner of which is fixed two roller wheels C to prevent friction when the shelf is raised and lowered. Four arms D, two on each side, work loosely on pivots attached to the frame. The upper ends of the arms are attached to the underside of the flaps as shown. The lifting of one flap would raise the two, thus preventing any tipping of the shelf. A spring catch (fixed in the front of the outer case and near the top) to shoot into or under the shelf when raised would prevent the flaps closing until required.

Fig. 26 shows another arrangement, in

pin D fixed to the inside surface of the table. The flaps are hinged at E, and connected to cranks by rods working loosely on centre pins F and G. A strong fixed iron pin B having a short piece of tube revolving thereon to form a roller projects from the sliding frame, and works through both the slots of the cranks. The top of the frame is solid to form a shelf. Two wheels A (eight in all) should be fixed close to the top and bottom corners of the frame to prevent friction. The centre of

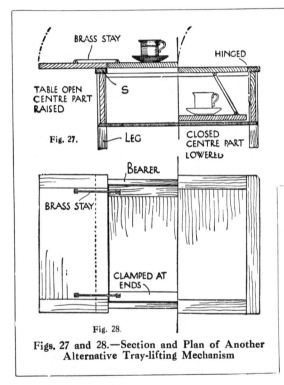

Fig. 27.

TABLE OPEN CENTRE PART RAISED

CLOSED CENTRE PART LOWERED

BRASS STAY

HINGED

S

LEG

BEARER

BRASS STAY

CLAMPED AT ENDS

Fig. 28.

Figs. 27 and 28.—Section and Plan of Another Alternative Tray-lifting Mechanism

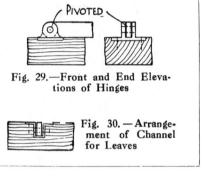

PIVOTED

Fig. 29.—Front and End Elevations of Hinges

Fig. 30.—Arrangement of Channel for Leaves

pin D to centre of F is twice that of centre of hinge E to centre of pin G; centres D to B are twice centres D to F. A spring catch should be fixed in front to shoot into the frame when raised to prevent the flaps falling.

Still another arrangement of the lifting-mechanism is shown by the part section and the plan Figs. 27 and 28.

Two strips S (Fig. 27) are secured by dowels or screws to the end bearers, and to these the leaves are hinged. Four pivoted brass stays connect these with the centre portion, so that when the table is open the section will be that shown in the left of Fig. 27. When the leaves are folded over, the centre part will descend until it assumes the position shown in the right of Fig. 27. In the plan of the device shown by Fig. 28, it will be seen that to avoid warping it is advisable to clamp the various portions at the ends.

which levers and cranks are used for raising the flaps of the table both at the same time, and consequently keeping the sliding shelf level as it rises and falls, leaving only a small part of the connecting levers exposed above the top when the flaps are open. Of course, the arrangement of levers here shown must be in duplicate, at the two ends of the table. In this figure C is a slotted crank made at an angle of 45°, and working on a centre

It must be noted that care must be taken to close the leaves simultaneously if the centre part is to be kept level while in motion, a condition essential if it is to carry tea-cups. Details of the brass stay are shown by Fig. 29. If the surface of the table is desired flush, the stays could be fitted into channels, as in Fig. 30, without interfering in any way with the movement.

obtained. Sufficient allowance should be made in length, width, and thickness for working. The sizes of the table shown by Fig. 31 are: top, 1 ft. 6 in. square by $\frac{5}{8}$ in. thick; legs, 2 ft. 4 in., tapering from $1\frac{1}{4}$ in. square at the top to $\frac{13}{16}$ in. square at the bottom; width outside the legs, 1 ft.

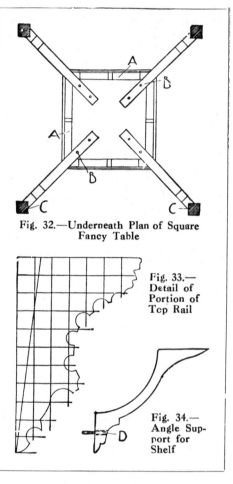

Fig. 32.—Underneath Plan of Square Fancy Table

Fig. 33.—Detail of Portion of Top Rail

Fig. 34.—Angle Support for Shelf

Fig 31.—Square Fancy Table

SQUARE FANCY TABLE

Suggested woods for the fancy table shown by Fig. 31 are birch for the legs and the other parts of pine and all finished in white enamel. If, however, the tables are required to match other articles of furniture, such as mahogany, American walnut, or satinwood, these woods, finished with french polish, would be quite suitable. First set out a full-size elevation of one side, and a plan of the design chosen from the dimensions given; then the sizes of the various parts can be

1 in. at the top and 1 ft. 5 in. at the floor line; deepest part of shaped top rails, 11 in. by $\frac{5}{8}$ in. thick. The central shelf is 8 in. square by $\frac{5}{8}$ in. thick, the top of the shelf being 1 ft. 1 in. from the floor. The top sides of the angle supports, where connected to the legs, are 9 in. from the floor. An underneath plan of the table is shown by Fig. 32.

To facilitate the copying of the curves of the shaped parts, the diagram Fig. 33 should be spaced out in lines at right angles to each other, forming 1-in. squares. The short spandrels A (Fig. 32) under the central shelf are $6\frac{3}{8}$ in. by $1\frac{1}{2}$ in. A moulding is worked round the upper edges of the table top. The shaped top rails under the top are tenoned into the legs, and stand back $\frac{1}{8}$ in. from the face of the legs. The top is secured with screws driven in a

Fig. 35.—Octagonal Fancy Table

slanting direction through the inside of the top rails and then into the table top. The shaped angle supports to the central shelf are screwed from the underside into the shelf, as shown at B (Fig. 32), and the opposite ends are fitted to the leg with a V-shaped end, as at C, and fixed with short dowels or screwed from the inside as at D (Fig. 34). The small spandrels of the central shelf are fitted between the angle supports and secured with glue, and are screwed from their under edges into the central shelf.

OCTAGONAL FANCY TABLE

Another fancy table, but of octagonal shape, is shown by Fig. 35. The design of this is based upon very similar lines to

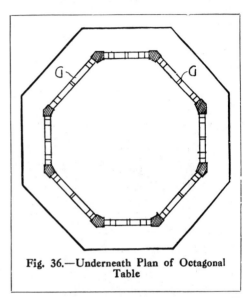

Fig. 36.—Underneath Plan of Octagonal Table

the last one described, and will lend itself equally well to the same treatment as regards material and finish, etc.

The general dimensions of this are:

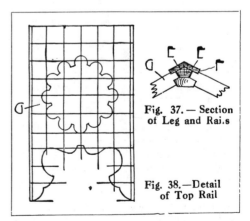

Fig. 37. — Section of Leg and Rails

Fig. 38.—Detail of Top Rail

Extreme width of top, 1 ft. 10 in.; sides, about 9 in.; thickness, $\frac{5}{8}$ in. The legs, shown in cross section in the plan (Fig. 36) and in detail section in Fig. 37, are 2 ft. 4 in. long; extreme width, $1\frac{3}{8}$ in.; thickness, $1\frac{1}{8}$ in. The two outer faces E (Fig. 37) are $\frac{3}{4}$ in. wide, and the sides F are bevelled to fit the right-angled shoulders of the shaped top rails G, which are shown enlarged by Fig. 38. Each angular face

$\frac{3}{16}$ in. deep into the sides of the legs, and the spindles housed their full thickness into the spindle rails and the shelf beneath.

HEXAGONAL OCCASIONAL TABLE

This useful table (Fig. 39) should be made in mahogany, oak or walnut.

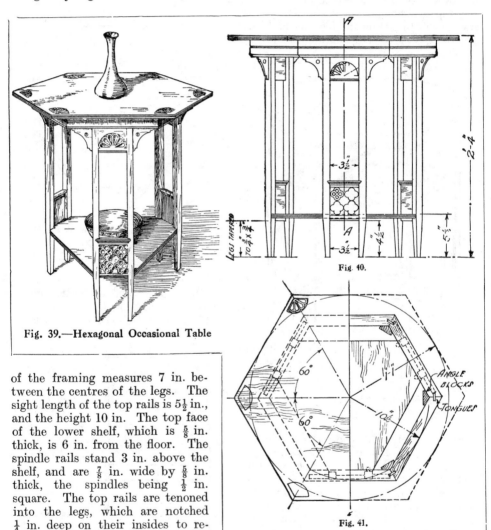

Fig. 39.—Hexagonal Occasional Table

Fig. 40.

Fig. 41.

Figs. 40 and 41.—Elevation and Sectional Plan of Hexagonal Table

of the framing measures 7 in. between the centres of the legs. The sight length of the top rails is $5\frac{1}{2}$ in., and the height 10 in. The top face of the lower shelf, which is $\frac{5}{8}$ in. thick, is 6 in. from the floor. The spindle rails stand 3 in. above the shelf, and are $\frac{7}{8}$ in. wide by $\frac{5}{8}$ in. thick, the spindles being $\frac{1}{2}$ in. square. The top rails are tenoned into the legs, which are notched $\frac{1}{4}$ in. deep on their insides to receive the full thickness of the shelf, the latter being cut away to receive the legs. The shelf is then secured with glue and slanting screws from the underside of the shelf. The ends of the spindle rails should be housed

All necessary dimensions and details of construction are given in the elevation and plan (Figs. 40 and 41) and the detail drawings. It will be seen that the hexagonal frame is tongued and glue-blocked at its angles (Fig. 41). It is also grooved on its inner face to receive the " buttons," and embellished with a small moulding and $\frac{1}{4}$-in. bead (Fig. 42). The three pairs of legs are tenoned to the frame, the full size of the leg ($1\frac{1}{8}$ in. by $1\frac{1}{8}$ in.) being let in to a depth of $\frac{1}{8}$ in., as are also the upper ends of the brackets and top carved panels. The leg tenons are 1 in. by 1 in. and 1 in. long (see enlarged section, Fig. 43), and the lower part of the legs are tapered on three sides to $\frac{3}{4}$ in. by $\frac{3}{4}$ in. The housing of the panels and brackets to the legs is indicated in the detail drawings (Figs. 44 and 45) by means of dotted lines, and should be no more than $\frac{1}{8}$ in. deep in each case. The panels have a shoulder formed $\frac{3}{16}$ in. back from the un-carved face, and the brackets also have a shoulder $\frac{3}{16}$ in. back from the face. The legs, panels and brackets are dowelled and glued together; and here it should be noted that the brackets must be fixed to the legs before these latter are assembled to the frame. A $\frac{1}{4}$-in. bead is run round the edges of the top and all visible edges of the undershelf. Six " buttons " hold the top to the frame, and the undershelf is fitted in between the legs and secured to each by means of a screw-eye and screw (see Fig. 42).

The carving to the panels and top is incised and recessed to a depth of about $\frac{1}{16}$ in., and the recessed portions either treated with a carver's punch to give a rough texture, or they may be worked to a smooth face according to taste ; but in no case should these surfaces be polished to a shine. They should either be left clean or treated with a dull polish in contrast to the rest of the work.

In the case of the panels the carved effect may be obtained by cutting out the design in $\frac{1}{16}$-in. fretwood, and applying this as an overlay to the panels, a method which is often employed where the edges of the overlay can be concealed. This

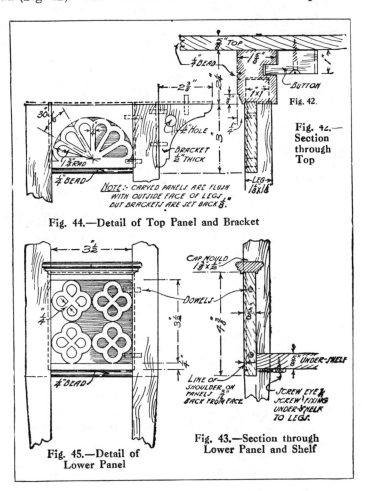

Fig. 44.—Detail of Top Panel and Bracket

Fig. 42.

Fig. 42.—Section through Top

NOTE :- CARVED PANELS ARE FLUSH WITH OUTSIDE FACE OF LEGS, BUT BRACKETS ARE SET BACK $\frac{3}{8}$.

Fig. 45.—Detail of Lower Panel

Fig. 43.—Section through Lower Panel and Shelf

cannot be done with the six ornamentations on the top, and it is advisable to carve these.

The moulded capping to the lower

the top is folded the whole answers as a side table. The wood for the top should be well seasoned, as, being connected to the table frame by a centre only, it is liable

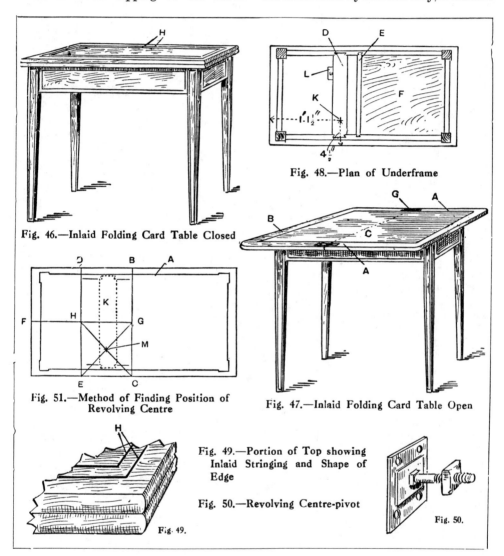

Fig. 46.—Inlaid Folding Card Table Closed

Fig. 48.—Plan of Underframe

Fig. 51.—Method of Finding Position of Revolving Centre

Fig. 47.—Inlaid Folding Card Table Open

Fig. 49.—Portion of Top showing Inlaid Stringing and Shape of Edge

Fig. 50.—Revolving Centre-pivot

Fig. 49.

Fig. 50.

panels is returned on the outer faces of the legs, as shown in the illustrations.

INLAID FOLDING CARD-TABLE

The card-table shown closed by Fig 46 and open by Fig 47 is made so that when

to warp if not thoroughly dry ; mahogany is suitable. The ornamental lines are inlaid (inlay and veneer work are dealt with in a later section) with satinwood or boxwood stringing, which can be obtained from most cabinet-makers or veneer merchants. Instead of the inlaying, the lines can be incised with a tool shaped like a **V**, or a small gouge. If not to be inlaid, the table could be made of pine, with birch legs, and afterwards stained, painted, or enamelled.

The following are the dimensions of the stuff required, allowing a little for working : Two pieces for the top, 3 ft. by 1 ft. 6 in. by 1 in. ; four legs, 2 ft. 5 in. by 1¾ in. by 1¾ in. ; two side rails, 2 ft. 9 in. by 4¼ in. by 1 in. ; two end rails, 1 ft. 4 in. by 4¼ in. by 1 in. ; two strips of veneer A (Fig. 47) for the top, 3 ft. by 2 in. ; strips B (Fig. 47) for gluing round the inside of the tops to form a recess for the cloth, 1 ft. 3 in. by 2 in. (endway of grain) ; one cross-rail D (Fig. 48), on which the top revolves, 1 ft. 4 in. by 3 in. by 1 in. ; one inside rail E (Fig. 48), which forms the inside end of the box for holding cards, etc., 1 ft. 4 in. by 3½ in. by 1 in. ; and one piece for the bottom of the box F (Fig. 48), 1 ft. 4 in. by 1 ft. 5 in. by ½ in. The bottom F can be kept in position with ½-in. strips nailed or screwed to the side and end rails.

To proceed with the making, plane the tops to thickness and take to length and width. Next mark, with a toothing plane, the inside face of the top, which makes the cloth and the veneer borders stick better. The veneer, A and B (Fig. 47), can then be laid, the end pieces being endwise, and the grain running the same way as that of the top. Then insert the stringing H (Figs. 46 and 49) in the uppermost side of the top when the table is closed ; the outer line should be 1½ in. from the edge and the inner line 2 in. from the edge. If desired, the corners of the top may be rounded as shown in Fig. 47. When the veneer and stringing are dry, the two outside edges and ends of the top can be rounded, as shown in Fig. 49, the two inside edges, which are hinged, being left square. The top should then be cleaned up and glass-papered ready for hinging, as shown at G (Fig. 47). The legs should be squared up to 1¾ in., and the side and end rails planed and taken to width. Before tapering the legs they should be mortised to receive the tenons on the ends of the rails. Allowing for the legs to stand in underneath the top 1¼ in. at the ends and ½ in. at the sides,

the length from shoulder to shoulder of the side rails will be 2 ft. 6 in., and of the end rails 1 ft. 1½ in. The legs should be tapered to 1¼ in. square at the bottom, beginning the taper 4¼ in. from the top. The stringing is inlaid in the legs ¼ in. from the edge, and in the rails ½ in. from the edge. Before gluing the frame together, the inside rail E (Fig. 48) should be fitted either with stub tenons or dovetails 1 ft. 5 in. from the end rail. The later rail is ¾ in. narrower than the other rails, which allows the bottom of the card-box to be screwed underneath it. The cross-rail D (Fig. 48) can be dovetailed into the side rails when the frame is together.

When the frame is together, the top should be hinged and the centre may be fixed. The hinges (*see* Fig. 47) and the revolving centre (Fig. 50) can be obtained of most ironmongers. The position for the revolving centre is shown at K (Fig. 48), 1 ft. 1½ in. from the end of the top and 4½ in. from the side. For instructions on fixing card-table hinges, see an earlier chapter. Folding and revolving card-table tops are, as a rule, made exactly square when open ; therefore, when closed, the width would be half the length. When this is the case, a ready way of finding the centre is as follows : Place the leaf (which is to be fixed to the frame) underside on the bench, the other leaf being hinged to it at the side E and C (Fig. 51). Next turn the table frame upside down, and adjust it to its exact position as regards projection at the sides and ends ; then mark round the frame with a pencil, as at A (Fig. 51). Now take off the frame, and divide the top at the centre of its length B C. Next bisect the half length at D E, and the width at F G. Draw diagonal lines G E and H C, and the intersecting point is the position of the centre on which the top revolves. The dotted lines on Fig. 51 show the position of cross-rail K through which the centre works. If the width of the top is not exactly half the length, mark the centre lines B C and F G as before. Now mark on line F G the point H at the same distance from G as from G to C. The line H E, drawn parallel to G C, and the diagonals as before, give the centre. The point M is transferred by measurement from the top to the frame.

The large plate of the revolving centre is screwed to the underside of the top, the should be pasted down after the table has been polished. Suitable baize or cloth can be obtained from dealers in upholsterers' materials. When applying the paste, see that it does not ooze through the baize.

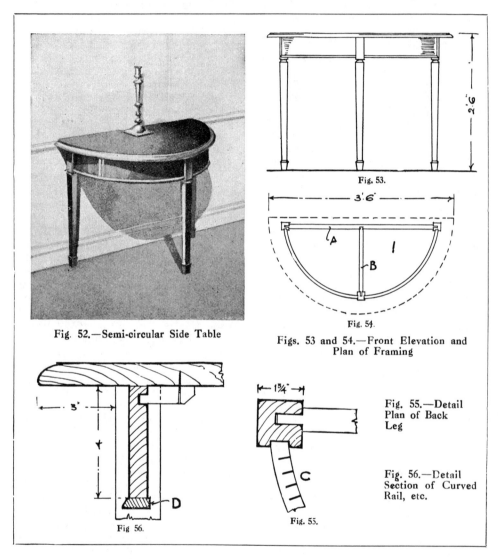

Fig. 52.—Semi-circular Side Table

Fig. 53.

Fig. 54.

Figs. 53 and 54.—Front Elevation and Plan of Framing

Fig. 55.—Detail Plan of Back Leg

Fig. 56.—Detail Section of Curved Rail, etc.

Fig. 56.

Fig. 55.

bolt goes through the rail D (Fig. 48), and the nut screws up underneath. To prevent the top turning too far when opened, as in Fig. 47, a piece of wood L (Fig. 48) about 1 in. wide is screwed to the underside of the top. The cloth C (Fig. 47)

SMALL SEMI-CIRCULAR SIDE TABLE

It is strange that tables of the type shown by Fig. 52, while often found in old houses, are not more extensively used at the present day. In form they are un-doubtedly simplified versions of the massive marble and gilt " console " of the palace and mansion, and are particularly graceful in appearance and convenient in shape for a variety of purposes. They are much associated with the work of the brothers Adams, whose characteristic type of ornament can very suitably be applied to their edges and framing, or they might be enriched in the style of Sheraton with inlay and banding.

In the example shown, and of which Figs. 53 and 54 are a front elevation and plan respectively, the top is an exact semicircle of 3 ft. 6 in. diameter, moulded on its periphery and overhanging the legs, to the extent of 3 in. The framing consists of three $1\frac{3}{4}$-in. square legs, tapered and worked to any desired extent, the back ones having a 4-in. by 1-in. rail tenoned into them, as at A in Fig. 54. In the centre of this rail, and at right angles thereto, is dovetailed a shorter one B,

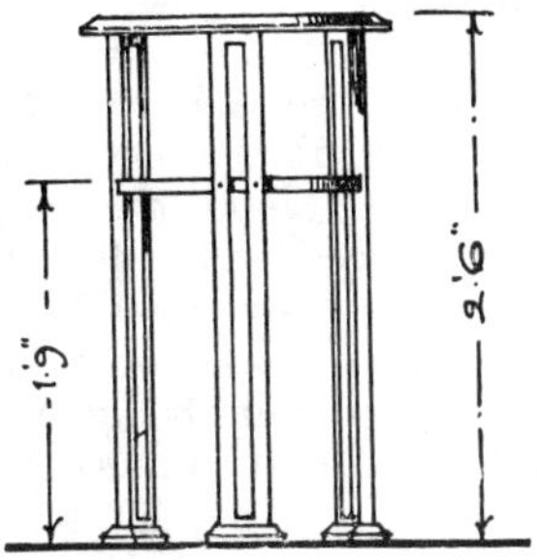

table edge. This is bent by means of a series of saw-kerfs on the inside, as at C in Fig. 55, and is finished with a thin

Fig. 57.—Miniature Occasional Table

moulded slip along the bottom, as at D in Fig. 56, which also indicates the fixing by means of rebates and oak buttons of the top to the various rails.

MINIATURE OCCASIONAL TABLE

The little occasional table shown in the photographic reproduction (Fig. 57) would look well in oak. It consists of a 1-in. circular top with chamfered edge, supported on three pairs of 1-in. square uprights. Elevation and plan are shown by Figs. 58 and 59.

Each pair of uprights has a 1-in. distance piece at top and bottom, as at A in Fig. 60, the upper ends being housed $\frac{1}{2}$ in. into the under-side of the table top, and the

Figs. 58 and 59.—Elevation and Plan of Miniature Occasional Table

Fig. 58.

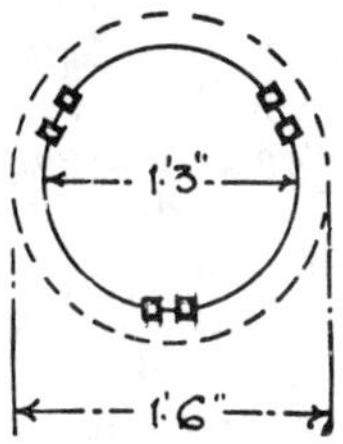

Fig 59.

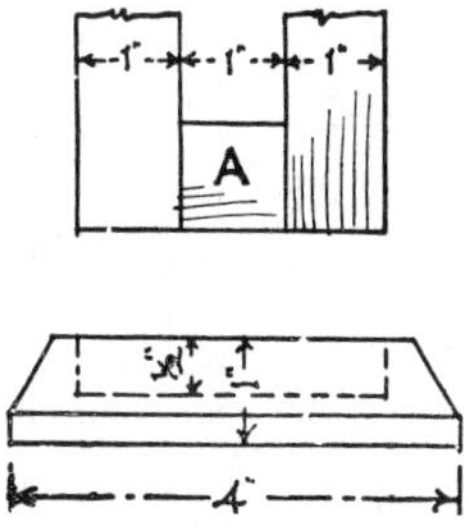

Fig. 60.—Detail of bottom of Leg

tenoned into the front leg. Connecting the legs and slightly housed into them is a curved 4-in. by $\frac{3}{4}$-in. rail parallel to the

bottoms similarly let into a 4-in. by 2-in. by 1-in. chamfered base next the floor. and screwed from below. About

8 in. below the top a shelf 1 ft. 3 in. in diameter is fitted in order to stiffen the uprights, to suit which it should be very accurately notched out at the six points required. The uprights can be nailed to this shelf and the holes stopped, or they may be secured with brass round-headed screws.

SMALL CIRCULAR TABLE

An occasional table, equally suitable for a circular or octagonal top, of exceedingly

Fig. 61.—Small Circular Table

simple construction is shown by Fig. 61. With a view to giving the worker as nearly as possible the exact style he happens to prefer, two alternative elevations are shown, the actual construction being identical in both cases. As will be seen, the alternative in Fig. 62 has turned legs, while that in Fig. 63 has simply square

tapered legs. In this latter case the ties or stretchers between the legs near the floor are shown of a different outline, which is, of course, interchangeable with the first.

Briefly reviewing the construction of the first alternative, this should consist of a circular top, $\frac{3}{4}$ in. or $\frac{7}{8}$ in. thick, 2 ft. 7 in. in diameter, with a moulded or simply a chamfered edge, and made up of, say, three widths cross-tongued together. This is supported on four legs turned out of, say, $1\frac{1}{2}$-in. stuff, which would in the majority of cases have to be bought ready or made to order, and are intended to be fixed in the positions denoted by small crosses in Fig. 64. Their upper ends are tenoned into horizontal bearers on top rails each about $1\frac{1}{2}$ in. square, as shown by the isometric sketch (Fig. 65). The positions of these bearers are indicated by the dotted lines in Fig. 64. They have shaped ends, and are halved together where they cross in the centre, as in Fig. 65. Their upper edges will need to be planed and tested until perfectly true, in order properly to take the top as first described. The ties might be about $4\frac{1}{2}$ in. above the floor level, and are placed immediately under the bearers. They should be kept light in section, say about 1 in. high and $\frac{3}{4}$ in. thick, each being cut out of one flat piece and notched in the centre to form a halved joint with the other, in the same way as shown for the bearers. Their ends are tenoned into the upright legs. The worker will probably have the turned legs prepared for him, and should have them kept simple and restrained in outline, as a lot of detail will only detract from the appearance of the table.

As previously stated, the construction for the alternative design need not differ from that already described; but the legs should be kept square, and tapered from about $1\frac{1}{2}$ in. at the top to 1 in. next the floor. Figs. 66 and 67 will be found to give full details concerning the setting-out of the work, the centres from which the curves of the ties are drawn, etc. The

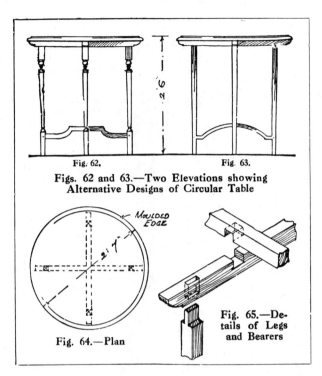

Fig. 62.   Fig. 63.

**Figs. 62 and 63.—Two Elevations showing
Alternative Designs of Circular Table**

Fig. 64.—Plan

Fig. 65.—Details of Legs and Bearers

are of the better kind. A good quality of mahogany should be chosen, especially as the quantity being small, the cost will not amount to much. The delicate construction requires a good sound material. If old mahogany is used, with good workmanship, they can be made to strongly copy genuine antiques. Fig. 70 shows how they may be made to take apart by screw threads being turned on the pins, though this is not really necessary. The stem of the table (Fig. 69) is turned in one piece, with a plain pin to fit into the top collar.

The first table (Fig. 68) is 1 ft. 8½ in. high, with a 1-ft. diameter tray top, and has an inlaid "fan centre." The second (Fig. 69) is 1 ft. 7¼ in. high, the top being 11 in. in diameter, ornamented by various details can be readily transposed from one design to the other, or replaced with other simple treatments of the same general construction.

COFFEE TABLES

The reproduced photographs (Figs. 68 and 69) show two different patterns of wine or coffee tables, as they are called. They will be of special interest to the woodworker who can do turning, as they are all lathe-work except the legs. Wood-turning is dealt with in a later section. There are a variety of patterns in these tables, but the two here to be described

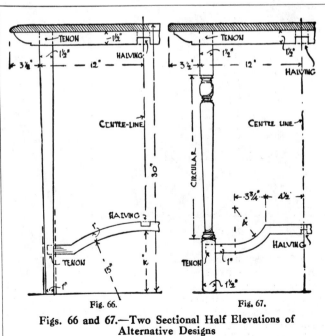

Fig. 66.   Fig. 67.

**Figs. 66 and 67.—Two Sectional Half Elevations of
Alternative Designs**

carving the marginal bead into sections. The line drawings given on page 843 are all to the same scale. Figs. 71 to 76 refer to

sional wood-turner, it will be necessary to make a cardboard pattern for the turned stems and collars, as shown by Figs. 71

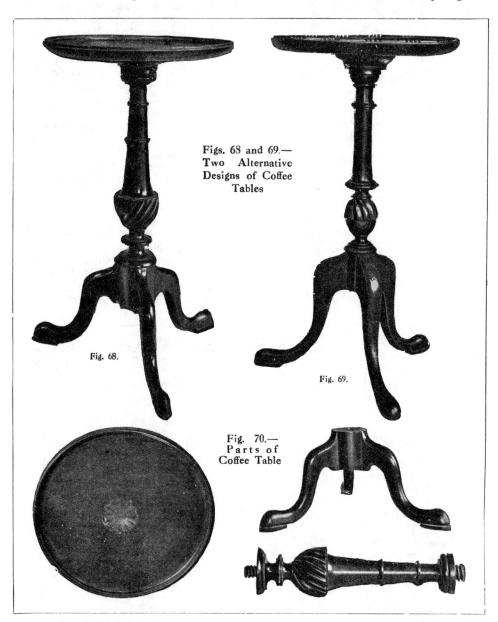

Figs. 68 and 69.—Two Alternative Designs of Coffee Tables

Fig. 68.

Fig. 69.

Fig. 70.—Parts of Coffee Table

the table (Fig. 68), and Figs. 77 to 81 refer to Fig. 69. Whether the worker does his own turning, or gets it done by a profes-

and 77 ; also for tops, as in Fig. 72. The stem (Fig. 71) will require 3-in. diameter material to finish $2\frac{3}{4}$ in.; and Fig. 77

requires 2-in. stuff to finish $1\frac{3}{4}$ in. The collars are 5 in. in diameter by 1 in. thick, and the tops are of the same thickness.

The patterns for the legs are easily drawn by ruling a piece of cardboard with 1-in. squares, and forming the curves as in Figs. 73 and 79. They must be cut out

(Fig. 71), and Fig. 81 is somewhat similar, but reversed, for the stem (Fig. 77). Fig. 78 shows the carved work on the top of the table (Fig. 69); but it is not essential, and may be left plain if preferred.

When the turning is done the next thing is to mark out the part of the stem

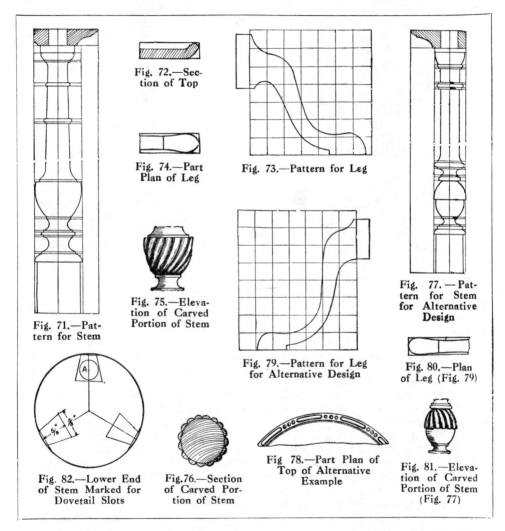

Fig. 72.—Section of Top

Fig. 74.—Part Plan of Leg

Fig. 73.—Pattern for Leg

Fig. 75.—Elevation of Carved Portion of Stem

Fig. 71.—Pattern for Stem

Fig. 77. — Pattern for Stem for Alternative Design

Fig. 79.—Pattern for Leg for Alternative Design

Fig. 80.—Plan of Leg (Fig. 79)

Fig. 82.—Lower End of Stem Marked for Dovetail Slots

Fig. 76.—Section of Carved Portion of Stem

Fig 78.—Part Plan of Top of Alternative Example

Fig. 81.—Elevation of Carved Portion of Stem (Fig. 77)

with a sharp-pointed knife, to be used for marking out on the 1-in. thick board. When the legs are cut, other patterns, as Figs. 74 and 80, are required for marking the shape of the feet. Figs. 75 and 76 show the carved work on the stem

to be carved. The carving is done simply with a $\frac{3}{8}$-in. bevelled paring chisel. The lower part of the stem must be set out for making the three dovetail slots for joining on the legs, as in Fig. 82. First find the three angle points on the circumference, and mark lines from these to the centre point. These lines must also be marked perpendicularly up the stem, and other lines $\frac{3}{8}$ in. at each side of them. The $\frac{3}{4}$-in. space

then be chiselled off to the shape, and the upper side of the leg rounded. With these legs the underside also is rounded, but oftener they are left flat. In any case

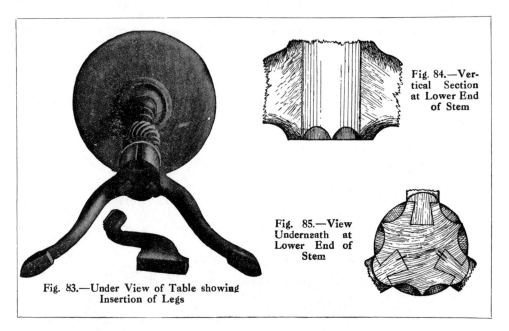

Fig. 84.—Vertical Section at Lower End of Stem

Fig. 85.—View Underneath at Lower End of Stem

Fig. 83.—Under View of Table showing Insertion of Legs

between these lines must be chiselled flat, and the centre lines marked again ; also other lines $\frac{3}{16}$ in. at each side of them. These latter indicate the narrow opening of the dovetail slot, which must spread to $\frac{5}{8}$ in. and $\frac{5}{8}$ in. deep. The waste is removed first by boring from the end, as shown at A (Fig. 82). They are then sawn at the lines and cleaned out with the chisel and mallet.

The trimming up and fitting of the legs is an interesting piece of work to a woodworker. First the dovetails should be marked on the part allowed for joining, and the cuts on the sides of the leg may be made. By fixing a wood hand-screw in the bench-vice the awkward handling is overcome. The point of the feet may

they require continual judging with the eye to obtain a pleasing shape. To form the shoe, they are cut with the fine saw $\frac{1}{16}$ in. deep, and pared with the chisel to make the line more distinct. The dovetail pins may then be sawn and trimmed carefully to fit. They should taper slightly, and be tried in place, but should not be driven in too tightly, to be taken out again for gluing. They must be marked before taking out to know their correct positions (Fig. 83), and both the slots and pins must be glued. The top is fixed with three screws through the collar. The square corner on the lower end of the stem between the legs is "thumb" notched with a $\frac{5}{8}$-in. gouge (Figs. 84 and 85).

Gate-leg Tables

OVAL GATE-LEG TABLE

THE construction of a gate-leg table as shown by Fig. 1 appears to be somewhat

it measures 3 ft. 6 in. by about 1 ft. 8 in., and when placed against a wall makes a convenient side or auxiliary table. The working diagrams are to the scale given on

Fig. 1.—Oval Gate-leg Table

complicated, but when carefully considered it is easily within the scope of the amateur woodworker.

The illustration shows a table 4 ft. 6 in. by 3 ft. 6 in. When both leaves are down

page 846. Figs. 2 and 3 show two elevations. The gate-leg principle is handy and decorative in smaller sizes, and the illustrations may be adapted by making a new scale. For dining-tables, 2 ft. 4½ in.

is the usual height, and for smaller occasional tables the height ranges from

draw the outlined oval of the top, make a horizontal line 4 ft. 6 in. long, and a

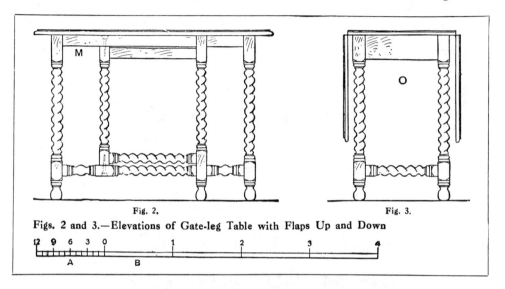

Fig. 2.   Fig. 3.

Figs. 2 and 3.—Elevations of Gate-leg Table with Flaps Up and Down

2 ft. upwards, according to requirements or special considerations.

central vertical line 3 ft. 6 in. long (*see* dotted lines in Fig. 4). With a radius of

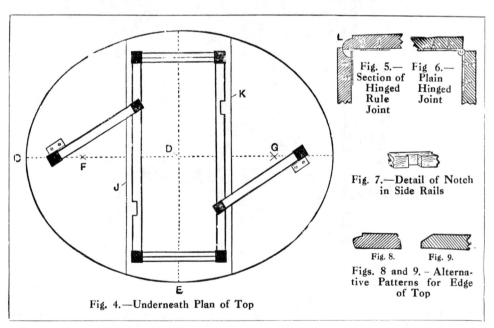

Fig. 4.—Underneath Plan of Top

Fig. 5.— Section of Hinged Rule Joint

Fig 6.— Plain Hinged Joint

Fig. 7.—Detail of Notch in Side Rails

Fig. 8.   Fig. 9.

Figs. 8 and 9. – Alternative Patterns for Edge of Top

First make full-size working drawings on sheets of paper gummed together. To

half the length, c to d, draw an arc, taking e as the centre, and where it cuts the horizontal line at F and G drive two nails through the paper and into the floor, and another nail at E. Stretch and tie a length of string extending round E, F, and G, forming a triangle. Remove the nail at E only, and draw the outline of the oval by keeping a pencil upright, pressing against the inside of the string. The above rule applies to an oval when the length and width are first decided on. The two vertical lines J and K, 1 ft. 6½ in. apart, represent the hinged joints of the leaves and the bed.

dowelled. When making up the widths of the leaves, a saving in length of wood may be made by noting where the joints come, and allowing for the gradual lessening of the oval end. If the hinged joints of the table are to be of the rule-joint kind, as in Fig. 5, then the projecting part L must be added to the bed. This joint is usually made with special planes; it has a very neat appearance, forming an ovolo moulding when the leaves are down. If the table is used only with the leaves raised, then the ordinary joint, as at

Fig. 10.—Another Example of Gate-leg Table

The legs may be about 2¼ in. square; for a 3-ft. 6-in. table about 2 in.; for a 2-ft. 6-in. table about 1⅝ in. The gate-legs may be about ¼ in. less than the corner ones, also the turned cross-rails. Before proceeding with the plan (Fig. 4) draw the side elevation (Fig. 2) and the end elevation (Fig. 3). It is advisable, before proceeding further with the table, to obtain the timber for the legs.

The table top should be of 1-in. stuff (¾-in. for smaller tables), the centre part and the leaves being made up of available widths of board jointed together and

Fig. 6, is sufficient. The side top rails M (Fig. 2) are dovetailed into the tops of the legs; the end rails O (Fig. 3) and the lower side and end rails have tenons fitting in mortises in the legs. Very thick screws may form the centres on which the gates move, the one at the top being inserted before the table top is fixed with screws to the under-framing. To allow for the gate-legs closing against the upper and lower side rails, the latter must be notched for nearly half their thickness, and the gate-legs to correspond (see Fig. 7). The table top may have a moulding, as in Fig. 8, or a simple bevelled edge, as in Fig. 9.

necessary elevations and plan are given by Figs. 11, 12 and 13. The main dimen-

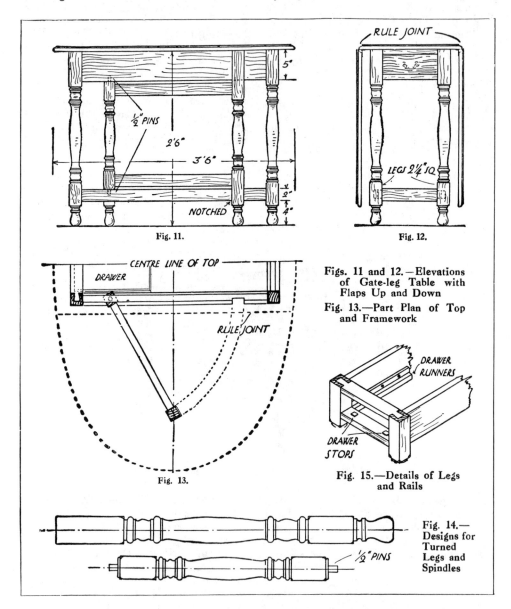

Fig. 11.

Fig. 12.

Figs. 11 and 12.—Elevations of Gate-leg Table with Flaps Up and Down

Fig. 13.—Part Plan of Top and Framework

Fig. 13.

Fig. 15.—Details of Legs and Rails

Fig. 14.—Designs for Turned Legs and Spindles

ANOTHER EXAMPLE OF GATE-LEG TABLE

Another gate-leg table of different design is shown by Fig. 10, while the

sions of the table are 5 ft. 9 in. long over all, 3 ft. 6 in. wide, and 2 ft. 6 in. high. The most suitable material for the table will be, of course, good-quality oak.

The legs, of which there are eight,

should be prepared first, the four main ones being $2\frac{1}{4}$ in. square and the legs of the two " gates " a little lighter—2 in. square. Fig. 14 suggests the patterns for the legs. The rails of both the table and the gates can be prepared, after which the actual construction can be commenced. Details of this are shown in Fig. 15, the central table being framed up in the usual way, the lower rails of 2-in. square stuff and the upper 5-in. by 1-in. The two gates, which are framed up with the ordinary mortise-and-tenon joints, swing between the rails of the centre portion, for which purpose $\frac{1}{2}$-in. pins are turned at each end of the hinging legs. The outer or meeting legs are notched or halved into the upper and lower rails of the table, so that the whole lies flush when the gate is closed. As the upper rail of the table is of only 1-in. material, a $\frac{3}{8}$-in. iron pin might be substituted for the one turned on the end of the hinging leg. In each case care must be taken that the centre of the upper pivot is vertically over the centre of the lower to ensure the gate swinging true. Provision is made for a drawer at one end of the table, the runners for which are screwed to the inner side of the rails (*see* Fig. 15). The drawer could, if desired, be partitioned off for cutlery.

The top, of $\frac{7}{8}$-in. material, is in three portions, the centre and two leaves or flaps, the shape of the whole being that indicated in the plan (Fig. 13). It is slightly fuller at the ends than a true ellipse, which, although possibly having a better appearance, would be less economical in material and accommodation than the shape suggested. The three portions will probably have to be jointed up from two or more widths of timber each, preferably being dowelled together. The rule joint shown in Fig. 12 is the best to employ when hinging the flap, as it presents a good appearance when it is folded down. This may, with care, be worked with a suitable pair of hollow and round moulding planes, and three strap hinges fitted to the underside as shown. The centre of the top is fastened to the framework by sinking channels on the inner side of the top rails with a gouge, and screwing from beneath. When the three parts have been fitted and hinged the whole top may be finished to shape and a simple thumb moulding worked on the edge. A couple of small wedge-shaped stops might be fixed to the underside of the leaves to keep the gates in their correct position, and the construction is completed.

Draw and Extending Dining Tables

MEDIÆVAL DRAW TABLES

THE dining table, so much in evidence now, is usually constructed on the telescope or dovetail-slide principle and, like others characteristic of European countries, the method of extension is based upon a telescope or dining-table screw.

justified, for by no other system can such a length be obtained so compactly, or be operated in such a simple fashion with a single or double screw. For tables, however, that are not required to extend to quite twice the length of the bed frame, it is extremely doubtful whether the dovetail slider or telescope

Fig. 1.—Elizabethan Draw Table with Carved Legs and Inlaid Rail

The advantages of this system lie in the great length to which these tables can be extended, and, conversely, to the comparatively small space they occupy when closed, it being no uncommon thing to manufacture tables which, when closed, occupy a space not more than 4 ft. long, and which may be extended to a length of 16 ft. or even 18 ft. It is in this way that the telescope system of extension is

system is the better. There are draw tables—so named from their peculiar construction—which dispose of the least satisfactory features of ordinary dining tables, and combine in a marked degree the essential feature of utility and the excellent feature of artistic merit. The latter is a difficult problem with modern table designers. The draw table is of considerable antiquity, although there are modern developments, patented, embracing a slight improvement in the slider action.

most furniture of the time, it is made in an extremely strong fashion, and stands

Fig. 2.—Elizabethan Table and Joint Stool

Figs. 1, 2 and 3 show three examples of the mediæval type, the constructional features of each being practically the same. Fig. 1 is a fine example of

to-day in almost the same condition as when it left the craftsman's hands four hundred years ago. The tops are framed together, the stuff is about $1\frac{3}{4}$ in. thick,

Fig. 3.—Draw Table with Bottle-shaped Legs

Elizabethan woodwork. It is essentially mediæval in character, and, similarly to

and in the large top there are six panels firmly mortised and tenoned together. A top of this character that has to stand alone, without any fixing to the framing rails, as is usual with ordinary dining tables, has, it will be obvious, to be

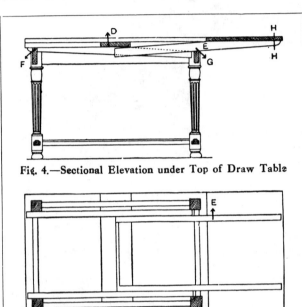

Fig. 4.—Sectional Elevation under Top of Draw Table

Fig. 5.—Plan Under Top of Draw Table

acorn shape. The leaf carvings on the legs are particularly good Elizabethan detail, as is also the inlay work on the side and end rails. Although the proportion between the carved cappings of the legs and the swelled part or shaft are at first sight disproportionate, a sympathetic study of this style will reveal in these unique proportions a massiveness and richness of effect which is eminently suited to dining-room furniture. Some modern furniture experts query the suitability of under-framing on dining tables, which, incidentally, can only be introduced in the fixed types, or with draw tables. It is generally agreed that mahogany tables to which a high degree of finish has been imparted, are spoiled by the continual action of boots upon the under frames. But where oak is the material employed, with a dull or fumed finish, no

specially well constructed in order to stand flat and be kept free from warping. Underneath the main top there are two smaller ones in leaves, to give them their correct designation (see Figs. 4 and 5). These also are specially constructed, being mitre-clamped together with mortise-and-tenon joints.

From the design point of view (Elizabethan) there is much to be learned from this piece and that illustrated by Fig. 2. The legs are those technically known as

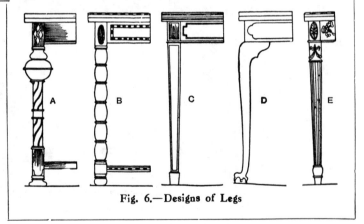

Fig. 6.—Designs of Legs

detrimental effect is produced by using them fairly as foot-rests. Many of these old types, and indeed nearly all of the mediæval draw tables, were provided with foot-rests, and the evidences of wear they exhibit testify to their appreciation by the users. Fig. 3 is another fine example

brackets are added underneath the rails, a detail peculiar to the Dutch types, a somewhat unnecessary detail, however,

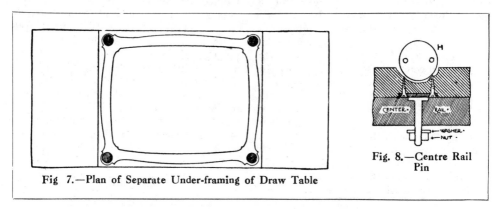

Fig 7.—Plan of Separate Under-framing of Draw Table

Fig. 8.—Centre Rail Pin

of a draw table in the Elizabethan style. The similarity between this and Fig. 1 will be noted, and it is interesting as showing the variation of details, with almost the same outlines and general treatment. The rails exhibit carved nulling, a popular detail in Elizabethan and Jacobean woodwork, especially the former. The acorn or bottle-shaped legs shown in the previous examples are Dutch in character, and were developed from the bulbous-shaped legs introduced into England from the Continent. Such an example is that shown in Fig. 3 ; it is

for dining tables, which are nearly always covered when in actual use. Gadrooning is another detail very much used in Elizabethan turning and carving. It resembles somewhat the nulled decoration of the rails, or it may be defined as inverted fluting. That shown in the legs in Fig. 1 is very good, the strapwork surrounding each inverted flute being a detail that should be particularly noted.

Although draw tables are chiefly made in the Elizabethan style, there is no specific reason why their production should be confined to these periods of

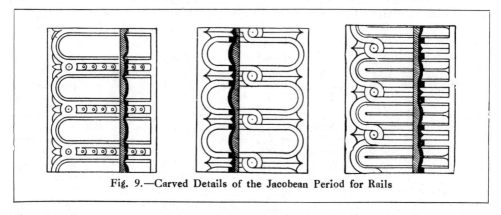

Fig. 9.—Carved Details of the Jacobean Period for Rails

a particularly good specimen. In addition to the leg and rail decoration it will be seen that small pierced or fretted

design. They can be produced to advantage in woods such as mahogany and Italian walnut, and give a good scope for the ingenuity of the designer in decorating them. The legs, for instance, can be turned, or even thurmed in square moulded legs, of which an example is shown by D (Fig. 6). A carved or recessed knee part adds to the general effect. A and B show two alternate treatments for turning suitable for furniture based on the eighteenth-century styles. They are also produced with twisted turning based on the Cromwellian and Early Queen Anne periods. When inlaid, with legs tapered and inlaid as at C (Fig. 6), they are quite in accordance with the delicacy peculiar to Sheraton work, whilst D shows a "Queen

structive feature of this example, which can be extended to a variety of other furniture, lies in the construction of a framed-up shape, made completely independent of the legs or rails, and secured to the legs by the toes. This is effected by stopping the legs immediately above the position of the under-framing, and boring a hole 1 in. in diameter about 2 in. into the bottom part of the leg. The toes or feet are turned up into corresponding pins or dowels in the solid, which pass through holes in the under-framing. When all are glued in position, a particularly strong job is effected.

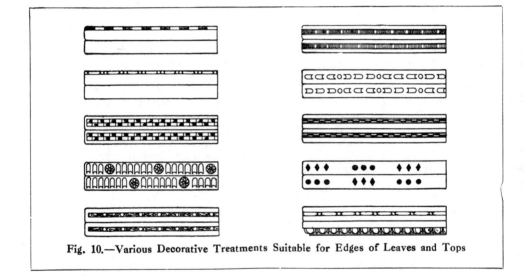

Fig. 10.—Various Decorative Treatments Suitable for Edges of Leaves and Tops

Anne" design, and E an "Adams" treatment. The essential factor to consider in designing these tables to harmonise with definite period work is proportion and ornament, and the former is not a difficult matter to a designer conversant with the historical periods. Under-framings would hardly be in line with the eighteenth-century periods; but when they are designed in William and Mary, Queen Anne and Early Georgian lines, they can be introduced with considerable effect. Fig. 7 shows the application of under-framing to an Early Georgian example executed in Italian walnut. The con-

Reverting to the photograph reproduced by Fig. 3, this fine specimen is of Dutch origin, and shows excellent bottle-shape legs. From this source, it should be noted, much furniture of the seventeenth century in England was developed. Considering the date of this piece, one is struck by the refined lines and detail of the design. A pleasing feature is the "thimble" carving on the knee part— and above the feet—of the legs; the brackets underneath the rails are also excellent detail.

Regarding the construction of these tables, reference should be made to

Fig. 4, in which is shown a longitudinal section through the table, illustrating the system of extension. It will be observed from this diagram that a centre rail D is fixed to the framework, and sliders E (Figs. 4 and 5) operate under the centre rail and above the end rails, these being notched out to receive them. The complete success of the action depends on these sliders, and, assuming that the top and leaves in this case are each 1¾ in. thick, the rail should be so notched at the part marked F (Fig. 4) to allow a clear space equal to the thickness of the top withdraw a leaf, it is simply pulled out, this causing the top to rise slightly, and where the leaf is pulled out to its fullest extent, the top will drop and rest on the bearer as shown in the sectional view. It should here be noted that the top is secured to the fixed centre rail with two card-table movements, consisting of a plate sunk into the underside of the top. A pin passes from this plate through the centre rail, and a nut screwed into same and carefully adjusted allows the top to be raised (Fig. 8). When it is required to close the table up, the centre top is raised

Fig. 11.—Extending Top Dining Table

that has been withdrawn. Or, again, the part G showing above the leg must equal the thickness of the top, and the slider or bearer at H must equal the space from underneath the top to the bottom of the notch in the rail.

The plan view (Fig. 5) shows how the two pairs of sliders are arranged. Two run inside the pair on the opposite side, and, to prevent them working apart, they are connected with a rail dovetailed into their ends. All sliders are screwed to the underside of the leaves or small tops, and blocks between the outside sliders and the rails facilitate their working action. To

slightly and one leaf can then be pushed in, the operation being repeated at the other end. The modern development of this action, previously mentioned, is a patent lever arrangement fixed under the leaves, by which means the centre top can be raised sufficiently to permit of the entry of a leaf. Two are, of course, fixed, one in each table ; the centre also has an action to facilitate the action of the sliders. With this it is necessary to also fix runners to the framework, these, together with the sliders, being channelled out to admit the insertion of small wheels. This latter development, while it certainly renders the opening and closing process somewhat easier, involves a good deal of extra labour, and, excepting the very large

illustrated and described. Fig. 10 shows various decorative treatments suitable for the edges of the top and leaves.

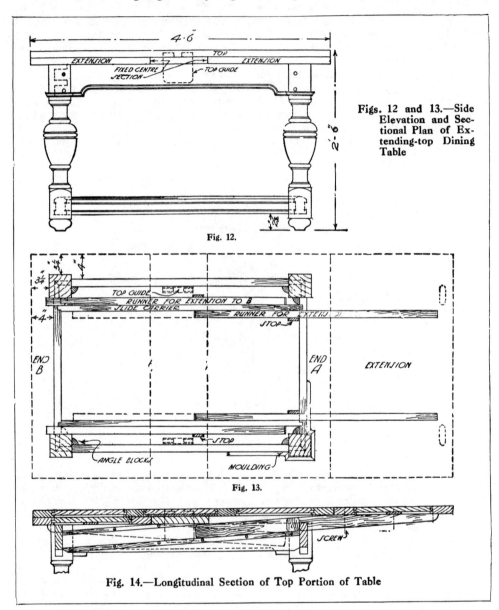

Figs. 12 and 13.—Side Elevation and Sectional Plan of Extending-top Dining Table

Fig. 12.

Fig. 13.

Fig. 14.—Longitudinal Section of Top Portion of Table

or heavy types, it is unnecessary. In Fig. 9 are shown various decorative details which could be employed to advantage on the rails of tables similar to those

EXTENDING-TOP DINING TABLE

The method of extension embodied in the table shown by Fig. 11 is a modern adaptation of the old-fashioned principle previously described. Modern constructional features are also introduced.

extending operation, the fixed centre section, and the two extensions. A plan and longitudinal section are shown by

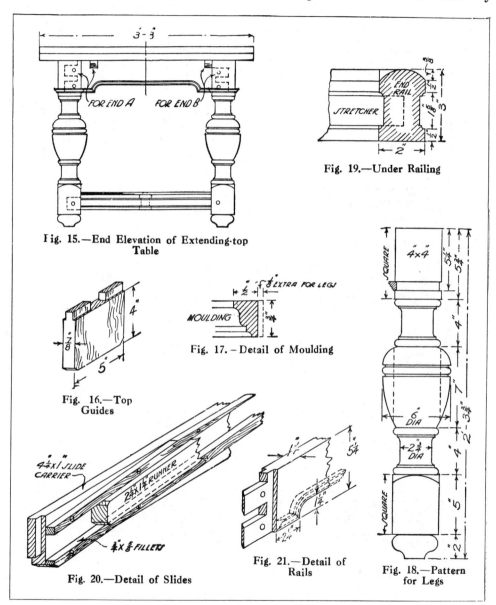

Fig. 15.—End Elevation of Extending-top Table

Fig. 19.—Under Railing

Fig. 16.—Top Guides

Fig. 17.—Detail of Moulding

Fig. 20.—Detail of Slides

Fig. 21.—Detail of Rails

Fig. 18.—Pattern for Legs

Fig. 12 is a side elevation of the table closed, and in this same figure appear the names on parts concerned, these being the top, which rises and falls during the

Figs. 13 and 14, and an end elevation by Fig. 15. To extend the table an extension is pulled out from the end, and it will be seen on reference to Fig. 14 that these are each carried on runners working in slides which are oblique, so that on the extension reaching its outward limit it will have member is fully out and the two parts become flush. The section shows the table with one end extended. The top

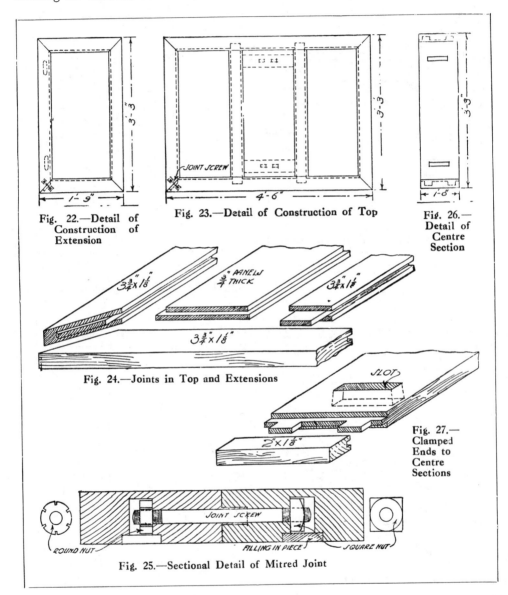

Fig. 22.—Detail of Construction of Extension

Fig. 23.—Detail of Construction of Top

Fig. 26.—Detail of Centre Section

Fig. 24.—Joints in Top and Extensions

Fig. 27.—Clamped Ends to Centre Sections

Fig. 25.—Sectional Detail of Mitred Joint

risen above its former level to the extent of the thickness of the top (in this case 1⅛ in.). During this operation the top is lifted by the moving extension, but falls back to its normal position when that guides, shown dotted in the illustrations and detailed in Fig. 16, are stub-tenoned into the underside of the top and work in slots cut in the fixed centre section to keep the top in position and ensure its falling correctly. Both ends of the table act similarly, and to close it the top must be lifted by hand sufficient for the introduction of the edge of the extension, which is then pushed in.

As regards the construction of the table, the legs and rails are framed together with haunched tenons, draw-bored and dowelled, and blocks are glued in angles to add strength. A slight difference occurs with the rail tenons for the end B, owing to the notches for the runners coming close up to the legs, and this is indicated in Fig. 15. The moulding, of which a detail is given (Fig. 17), is planted on the face of the rails and carried round the legs, these being recessed $\frac{1}{8}$ in. to receive it. Lines dotted on the detail of the turned legs (Fig. 18) show where the 4 in. by 4 in. must be packed out for turning to the larger diameter. The two end under-rails are tenoned and dowelled in place, and the long stretcher rail is tenoned to these, the rounding on the former members being stopped in the middle where the stretcher abuts (*see* Fig. 19). Fig. 20 is a detail of the slides, consisting of $4\frac{1}{4}$ in. by 1 in. slide carriers with a pair of oak fillets screwed to each side, one pair running up as shown, and the other pair running up from the opposite end. These must, of course, be very carefully set out full-size, as accuracy at this point is essential to the proper working of the table. The slope required is one that gives a rise of $1\frac{1}{8}$ in. in a distance of 1 ft. 9 in. The fact that the top fillet comes to a feather-edge is not of consequence, as the thrust from the runner when the extension is out is taken by the fixed centre section, the fillet at this point merely acting as a packing piece. Six screws are used to fix each extension to the hardwood runners placed where indicated in Fig. 14, and it will be observed that a packing piece is necessary under the middle screws as the extensions are not flush on the underside. Stops are fixed to each runner, those at the end A (Fig. 13) striking on the inner face of the rail and those at the end B striking on the legs. Both end rails have, of course, to be notched for the passage of their respective pairs of runners. A detail of the rails is shown by Fig. 21. The top, etc., above the rails will now be dealt with.

Dealing first with the top and extensions, the method of construction is shown in Figs. 22, 23, 24 and 25, and it will be seen that they consist of a frame of $3\frac{3}{4}$-in. by $1\frac{1}{8}$-in. stuff (finished) tongued and grooved at the mitres, and further strengthened at these joints with joint screws. The frames, including muntins in the case of the top, are grooved $\frac{3}{8}$ in. by $\frac{3}{8}$ in. to receive $\frac{3}{4}$-in. panels, all being flush on the top side. Two finger grips are sunk in the underside of the extensions where indicated, and packing pieces, 3 in. by $\frac{3}{8}$ in., are fixed across the middle panel of the top to obtain a deeper mortise for the fixing of the top guides.

Figs. 26 and 27 show the centre section which is of $1\frac{1}{8}$-in. stuff (finished thickness) throughout. It has both ends clamped and is, as previously mentioned, slotted in suitable position for the two top guides, the slots being a snug fit to these on the top side, but slightly tapered outwards at their ends towards the bottom, to allow for free movement of the guides when the top is lifted and in a tilted position. The centre section is fixed to the side rails with screws.

If casters are added to the table, the height of the legs should be reduced correspondingly.

SCREW-OPERATED DRAW TABLE

The telescopic dining table shown by Fig. 28 is the usual type in which the legs are moved with the top. The table shown is a fairly good size when drawn out, being 14 ft. long and 4 ft. 6 in. wide. It will bear a much greater weight than any other expanding table, but more material is required, consequently it is more expensive than other kinds. It is essential that the larger tables should be made completely of hardwood. The under-construction of the sliders, etc., bears a tremendous strain when the table is drawn out full size, and the sliders being composed of short lengths, must be sufficiently strong at those parts of lapping when the sliders are at the top. Fig. 29 shows a plan of the table without the top.

The legs having been chosen of the desired pattern should be $4\frac{1}{2}$ in. square at the top. These are joined together in pairs by the under-framing at the desired height of the table, minus the thickness of the table top and height of the caster-wheel. These rails A (Fig. 29) are $4\frac{1}{2}$ in. deep and $1\frac{3}{8}$ in. thick. The distance between the legs is 3 ft. 5 in., which is the same distance as the shoulders apart on

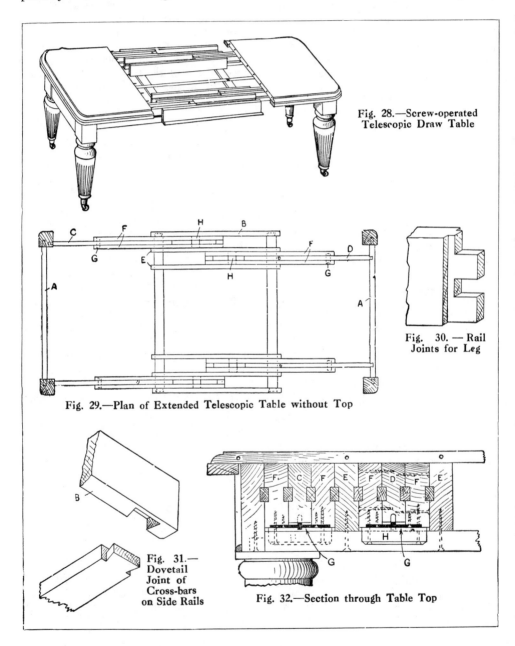

Fig. 28.—Screw-operated Telescopic Draw Table

Fig. 30. — Rail Joints for Leg

Fig. 29.—Plan of Extended Telescopic Table without Top

Fig. 31.—Dovetail Joint of Cross-bars on Side Rails

Fig. 32.—Section through Table Top

the rails. The tenon at each end will be 2½ in. long, so it is necessary to cut the rails to 3 ft. 10 in. long. Fig. 30 shows the method of making these strong joints. The tenon is ⅝ in. thick, and when driven

rail at the other end of the table. There are sixteen sliders, eight on each side, all of them being 1¼ in. thick. The four fixed sliders F are made the full depth of 3½ in., as shown in Fig. 32. These are

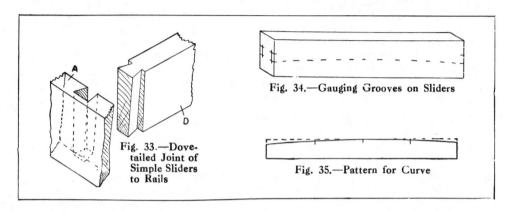

Fig. 33.—Dovetailed Joint of Simple Sliders to Rails

Fig. 34.—Gauging Grooves on Sliders

Fig. 35.—Pattern for Curve

together the face of the rail is ¾ in. beyond the face of the leg. The two side rails B (Fig. 29) are 3 ft. 6 in. long, 4½ in. deep, and 1⅜ in. thick, framed together by two cross-bars 3 in. by 1 in., which are dovetailed underneath about 2 in. from each end. The dovetails are 1 in. long and lapped into grooves ¾ in. deep, as shown in Fig. 31. The distance outside the rails B should be 4 ft. 1½ in. ; this will allow the side rails to be just within the face of the legs when closed up. The dovetailed frame gives a space above the cross-bars of 3½ in., in which the sliders work.

The sliders, excepting the four single

secured with screws through the cross-bars underneath. The double sliders E are ¼ in. less in depth (3¼ in.), and the single sliders ½ in. less (3 in.). The section of half the table (Fig. 32) shows them clearly. When all the sliders are prepared to size, they should be laid together in position and exact measurements taken for the joints of the single sliders. Those marked C are mortised and tenoned into the legs, as shown in Fig. 30. These should be draw-bored and pinned from the inside when finally fixed together, as these joints are in tension and have to receive great strain. The sliders

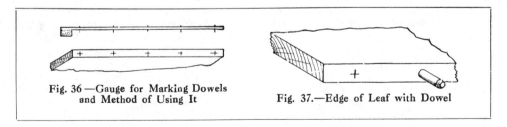

Fig. 36 —Gauge for Marking Dowels and Method of Using It

Fig. 37.—Edge of Leaf with Dowel

ones, are 3 ft. 6 in. long. The single sliders C are 2 in. longer to allow for a tenon into the leg at each side, and those marked D are 3¼ in. longer, because they are extended to make a fixing on to the

D are dovetailed to the rail, as in Fig. 33. The dovetails for these joints are ⅞ in. long and are slightly tapered as shown.

An important part in the making of the table is the grooving and tongueing of the sliders. This must be done so as to make the table top slightly arched shape when extended. By making the grooves in each piece a trifle convex at the top, the centre portion of the table will rise when drawn out to the extent of $\frac{1}{4}$ in. to $\frac{1}{2}$ in., according to the size of the table. This will counteract any tendency of the table to sag, which would be sure to take place if the grooves were made straight. The grooves should be $\frac{3}{4}$ in. wide by $\frac{1}{4}$ in. deep in the middle of the sliders. Fig. 34 shows one of the sliders gauged for the width and depth of the grooves on each side and end. The $\frac{3}{4}$-in. grooving plane is guided by a piece of wood temporarily nailed on. This piece of $\frac{3}{8}$-in. or $\frac{1}{2}$-in. boarding must be convex $\frac{1}{8}$ in. at the middle, and the curve must be regular. It is hardly possible to strike this portion of a circle in the usual way, so proceed to mark it as shown in Fig. 35. The length is divided into four parts, the ends are marked $\frac{1}{8}$ in. down, and the points between the middle and the ends $\frac{1}{16}$ in. below. This edge is rounded off with a smoothing plane. When all the grooves have been made in this way, prepare the hardwood tongues 3 ft. 6 in. long by $\frac{3}{4}$ in. by $\frac{1}{2}$ in. These are glued on both sides of the four single sliders C and D, and on the outsides of the double sliders. Short ends about $2\frac{1}{2}$ in. long are cut off the single sliders and fixed at the ends of the double sliders, as shown in Fig. 29. These are secured by screwing from the outside, with one or two pieces of paper packing each side to give freedom to the sliders.

The end rails and single sliders should now be smoothed up, glued, and cramped into the legs, after which the whole should be placed together and the pieces B secured by gluing and screwing on the cross-bars. The fixed sliders E are secured with screws through the cross-bars underneath. The stops should now be fixed to the sliders so as to allow them to lap about 14 in. when drawn full out. An iron plate G is screwed underneath the ends of the double sliders, and an iron pin driven in underneath the single slider to catch against the plate. This pin is adjusted to give the desired lap. The double sliders

have a block H screwed across underneath to catch against the cross-bar as required. At this stage the double winding screw should be obtained and fixed. The tongues of the sliders are blackleaded to make them work freely.

By allowing the table top to overhang the legs 2 in. at the sides and ends, the boards are cut off so as to finish 4 ft. 6 in. long and 2 ft. $3\frac{1}{2}$ in. wide. The number and widths of the extra leaves or flaps should be ascertained, all of which are cut off to a finish at 4 ft. 6 in. long. The undersides of all boards are then planed true, the edges being shot and planed to their correct widths. The ends are planed square, and all the boards laid together. Now mark for the dowels on each edge. These should be equally spaced, and the end ones about 2 in. from each end of the joint. Fig. 36 shows a gauge which should be made for marking the holes. A small block is fixed on to a strip of wood, and brads driven through at the required distances. Care should be taken to see that the dowels are marked from the same ends of all the boards. Then gauge from the undersides to half the thickness, and bore with a $\frac{3}{8}$-in. twist-bit, all the holes being 1 in. deep. Glue and drive in all the dowels, making sure they are driven in on the same edge, say the right edge of each board. Then cut them off so as to project $\frac{3}{4}$ in., and use a dowel rounder to trim off the corners (Fig. 37).

The table top is fixed with screws from underneath, holes being bored in the usual way through the rails A and the single sliders. There is $\frac{1}{16}$ in. of packing between the rails and the top to facilitate the free working of the curved tongues. This is done by gluing pieces of veneer on the top of the rails each side of the screw-holes. After the tops are screwed on the table should be screwed up tight, the top planed true, and the moulding worked and fixed on as required. The extra leaves are then placed in one at a time and finished off flush with the fixed top. When all are finished, place them in altogether, and scrape and glasspaper to a good surface. The casters are then screwed on, when the table is ready for polishing.

ANOTHER SCREW-OPERATED TELESCOPIC TABLE

The screw-operated extension table is still preferred by many people. The table shown by Fig. 38 is constructed with this system of operation. Fig. 39 is a side elevation of the table fully extended and with the extra leaves A in position, while Fig. 40 shows it in the act of being opened, and Fig. 41 is a plan with the top removed. A section is shown by Fig. 42.

The screw can be obtained from any large furnishing ironmonger.

In constructing the framework, first plane the stuff to the sizes given, and then set out the mortises of the legs and the tenons of the rails, as shown by dotted lines in Fig. 39. The mortises for the inner sliding rails are farther from the front edge of the legs than those for the outer rails, as shown in Figs. 41 and 45. The inner rails or slides C should be ploughed from their top edges, 1 in. wide and $\frac{1}{2}$ in. deep. This groove can be made with a $\frac{1}{2}$-in. plough-iron, or with a rebate plane by fixing a piece of wood at the right distance parallel to the top edge.

Fig. 38.—Screw-operated Telescopic Table

The table is of average simple construction and should be of mahogany, oak, or walnut. When closed this table is 6 ft. long, and it has been designed to extend to 9 ft. with the addition of two 1-ft. 6-in. leaves. The legs, if preferred, can be obtained ready turned, or can be worked as shown from stuff about $4\frac{1}{2}$ in. square. The outer rails for the framework may be solid, or the outside portion may be of $\frac{1}{2}$-in. stuff glued to a pine backing, as shown at B in Fig. 43. The inner rails or slides and the two cross-rails should be of cheap hardwood, such as beech or birch. The former are marked C in Figs. 39 to 43, and the latter D in Figs. 41 to 44 inclusive.

Pieces of hardwood should be planed so as just to fit in the grooves as at E in Figs. 43 and 45, and glued into the grooves of the inner rails. The moulding on the bottom of the outer rails F (Fig. 43) should next be fixed with glue and screws. The cross-rails D should be dovetailed to the inner sliding rails in one case and into the projecting moulding at F in Fig. 43, as sketched in Fig. 44, in the other. Care must be taken in making these dovetails, or the rails, not being parallel, will prevent proper working. When all the joints fit properly, those between the legs and the rails, and between the cross-rails and the latter, should be glued together, keeping

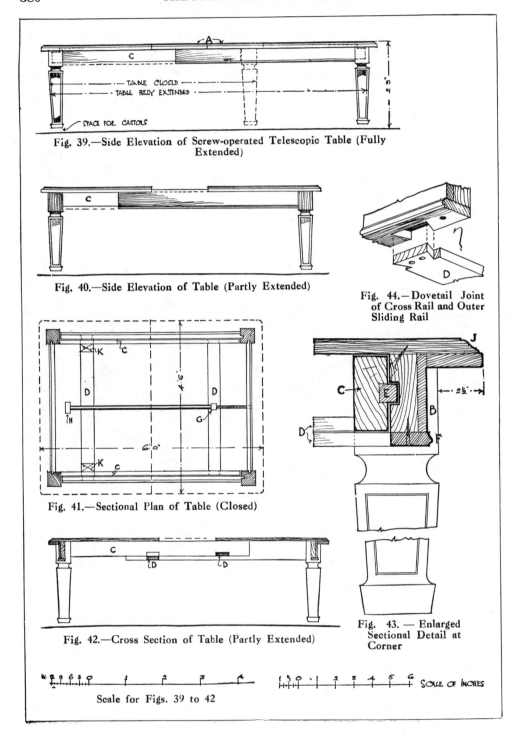

Fig. 39.—Side Elevation of Screw-operated Telescopic Table (Fully Extended)

Fig. 40.—Side Elevation of Table (Partly Extended)

Fig. 44.—Dovetail Joint of Cross Rail and Outer Sliding Rail

Fig. 41.—Sectional Plan of Table (Closed)

Fig. 42.—Cross Section of Table (Partly Extended)

Fig. 43. — Enlarged Sectional Detail at Corner

Scale for Figs. 39 to 42

SCALE OF INCHES

the legs and rail square. The cross-rails should also have a couple of screws inserted, as shown in Fig. 44.

The table top must be of well-seasoned material. If it can be obtained in about 1-ft. 6-in. widths, each half will require only one joint. The leaves are also 1 ft. 6 in. wide. The top should be dowelled and glued, and the undersides of the top and leaves trued up. Next join together the two portions of the permanent top and the two leaves, and dowel them with hardwood pins about

other end of the barrel being secured at H to the underside of the top, to which it may be necessary to fix a wood block for this purpose. Next tighten the screw a little so as to hold the top firmly together, plane the top and leaves, and work the moulding round the edges shown at J in Fig. 43. The thicknessing fillet shown fixed round the edge of the table top in Fig. 43 should next be prepared. It should be mitred at the angles (which might alternatively be formed as in Fig. 47), fitted round the tops of the legs, and

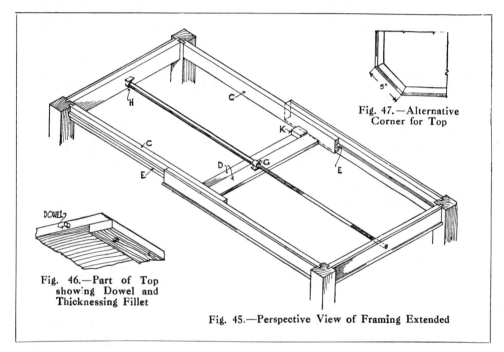

Fig. 47.—Alternative Corner for Top

Fig. 46.—Part of Top showing Dowel and Thicknessing Fillet

Fig. 45.—Perspective View of Framing Extended

$\frac{3}{8}$ in. in diameter, projecting about $\frac{5}{8}$ in. (*see* Fig. 46). The whole should then be stretched out to its full length, as shown in Fig. 39, turned bottom side up, and the framework fastened to the two permanent parts of the top with screws inserted obliquely, as shown in Fig. 43.

The screw and barrel should now be fixed, the handle end of the screw being secured to the end rail of the table. The box in which the screw works, and which holds one end of the barrel, can be fixed to the cross-rail at G (Figs. 41 and 45), the

fixed with glue and screws. It is best to have the two side pieces long enough to reach from end to end, thus taking in the two leaves, afterwards cutting with a fine saw where the joints of the leaves should occur. Two stops K (Figs. 41 and 45) prevent the framework moving too far. This table would be firmer if it extended to 8 ft. 6 in. only, the leaves being then only 1 ft. 3 in. wide ; but at the same time is quite suitable under ordinary conditions for the full-length extension of 9 ft. previously mentioned. The legs are shown square, tapered and simply shaped, the panel effect being produced either by means of an inlaid banding or a sinking on

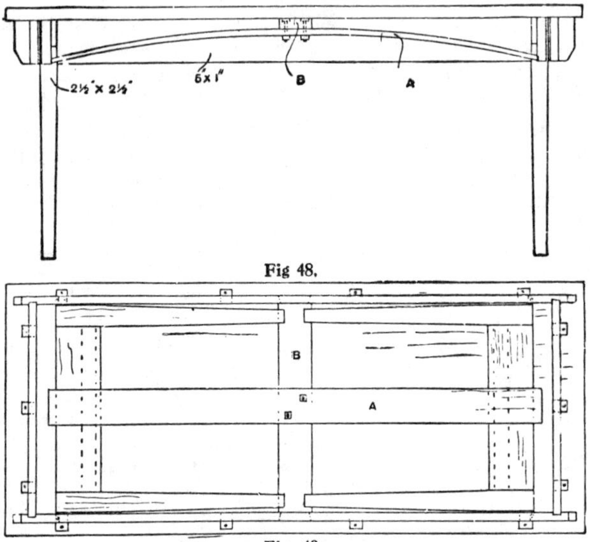

Fig 48.

Fig. 49.

Figs. 48 and 49.—Sectional Elevation and Plan (Legs Folded) of Underside of Collapsible Table

the outer faces of each leg. In setting out the legs, allowance must be made for the casters in calculating the total length.

COLLAPSIBLE DINING TABLE

This dining-table is made so that the legs can be folded up within the depth of the side rails, thus making it portable and convenient for stacking away when not in use. The legs are secured, when the table is in use, or when folded up, by means of a wooden spring. The table is an ordinary one in appearance ; but the sectional elevation as shown by Fig. 48 illustrates the wooden spring A for strutting the legs to a rigid position. Fig. 49 is a plan of the underside of the table when folded up. The sizes given are of a table 6 ft. long and 2 ft. 6 in. wide, which is nearly the minimum in length to allow folding space for the legs. If a table of a larger or different size be required to act on this principle, the members of the table should vary accordingly.

Whatever timber is used for the table,

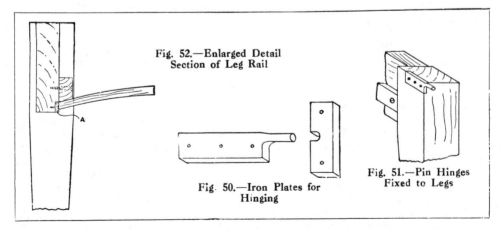

Fig. 52.—Enlarged Detail Section of Leg Rail

Fig. 50.—Iron Plates for Hinging

Fig. 51.—Pin Hinges Fixed to Legs

The invisible type, working in a slot cut in the end of each leg, are to be recommended.

it is essential to use oak for the spring A. It is a straight piece of wood 4 in. wide, ¾ in. thick in the middle, and is made thinner to $\frac{1}{2}$ in. at the ends. The length, for the present, should be cut so as to fit between the end rails. This spring is fixed with two $\frac{3}{8}$-in. bolts to the cross bearer B, which can also be of oak, 4 in. by 1 in., dovetailed to the top edges of the side rails before the table top is fixed. The legs, although shown square, can be turned to any shape required, and framed together in pairs by means of rails, as shown in Fig. 49. The rails should be as wide as the side rails, about 5 in. or more, and jointed strongly into the legs, so as to ensure the table being rigid. The plan (Fig. 49) shows the legs folded in with about 2-in. clearance at the ends, and about $\frac{1}{2}$-in. space between the legs and the side rails. The space between the leg rails and the end rails is about $2\frac{1}{2}$ in. to 3 in. The arrangements for hinging the legs are shown by Fig. 50. The hinge plates are made of 1-in. by $\frac{3}{8}$-in. iron. A round end or pin $\frac{3}{4}$ in. long and $\frac{3}{8}$ in. in diameter is filed on the longer piece, and a notch is made to receive this pin on the other piece as shown. The plate with the pin is fixed with screws to the inner top corners of the legs, as shown in Fig. 51,

and the notched plate is let in flush on the side rails. It will be seen that the open notch is uppermost, allowing the leg frames to be lifted out when the table top is off.

The leg rails have a fillet on the inside to make a rebate to receive the wooden spring, which should be fixed $\frac{5}{8}$ in. from the bottom edge of the rails. An iron plate 6 in. long by $\frac{1}{2}$ in. by $\frac{1}{8}$ in. is let flush into the rails, and screwed so as to take the thrust of the spring when the table is erected. Fig. 52 shows a section of leg rail with the fillet and the small iron plate A. Now fix on the table top by the usual method or by means of small iron plates, as indicated in Fig. 49. These plates can be let in flush on the top of the rails, and project over to take a screw for fixing the top. If the pin hinges are fitted properly, the legs should not open beyond the vertical position. The ends of the spring should then be cut off, so as to give a tight thrust to the legs when in position.

To fold the table it is only necessary to lift the spring from the recess of the leg rails.

Chairs

TWO DINING-ROOM CHAIRS

THE chair shown by the half-tone reproduction (Fig. 1) is slightly more difficult to make than the one illustrated by Fig. 2, which is of a somewhat simplified form. Two elevations of this latter are shown by Figs. 3 and 4. The differences may be pointed out, and the reader left to adopt whichever scheme he may prefer, or feel best qualified to undertake.

In the half-tone the two back rails are very slightly curved in plan, and the front of the seat is also curved a little, thus adding somewhat to the finish and appearance of the chair, although these details are not actually essential for its comfort. In this case, also, it will be observed that the lower rails which connect the legs in the simpler design (Fig. 2) do not appear, thus making the whole construction

depend for strength on first-class workmanship in the joints between the legs and seat rails.

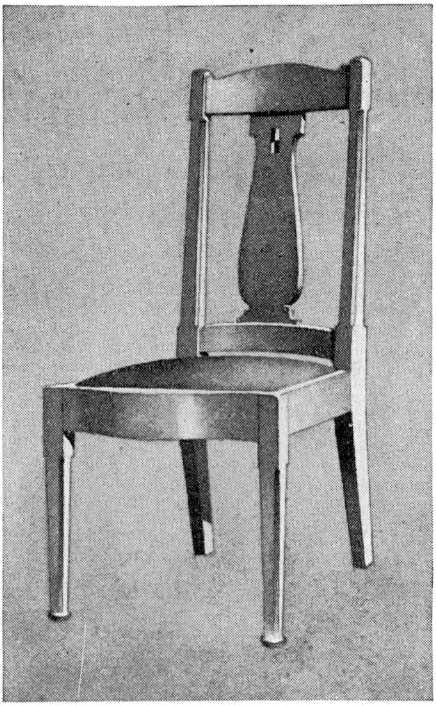

Reverting to the chair shown by Fig. 2, the front legs should be $1\frac{1}{2}$ in. square (finished sizes are given throughout), splayed at the angles as at A in Fig. 5, the splays or chamfers widening downwards, and the four square sides tapering, until just above the floor the legs form in section an octagon contained in a square of 1-in. sides as at B. Below this each leg curves out to a circular foot of about $1\frac{1}{2}$ in. diameter, as clearly indicated in the same figure.

Each back leg should be worked up from a piece $2\frac{1}{4}$ in. by $1\frac{1}{2}$ in. and 3 ft. 7 in. long, the sides of which are shown by the dotted lines at C in Fig. 5, which shows the lower half of one back leg in side elevation. At seat level, and measuring from the dotted line on the left, the

Fig. 1.—Dining-room Chair

384

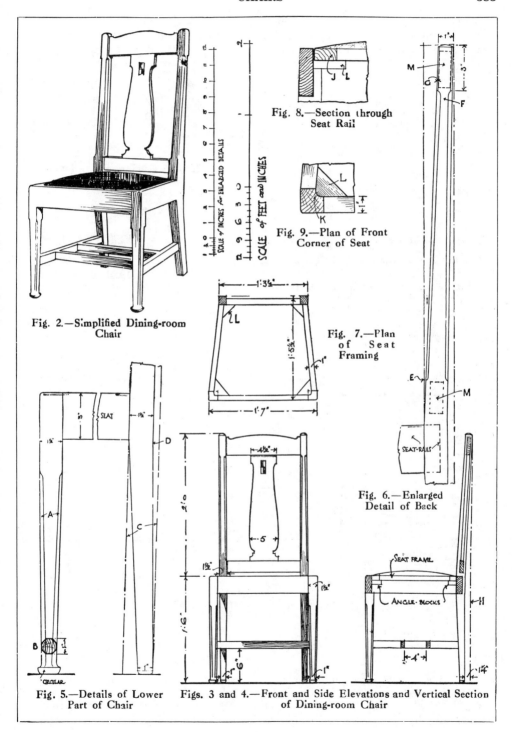

Fig. 8.—Section through Seat Rail

Fig. 9.—Plan of Front Corner of Seat

Fig. 2.—Simplified Dining-room Chair

SCALE of INCHES for ENLARGED DETAILS

SCALE of FEET and INCHES

Fig. 7.—Plan of Seat Framing

Fig. 6.—Enlarged Detail of Back

Fig. 5.—Details of Lower Part of Chair

Figs. 3 and 4.—Front and Side Elevations and Vertical Section of Dining-room Chair

leg is 1½ in. wide, whence it tapers downwards to the extreme right of the 2¼ in. width as shown. Next to the floor it to a very slight curve, as at D. In front elevation, the back leg is 1½ in. wide at seat level, and it tapers down to 1 in.

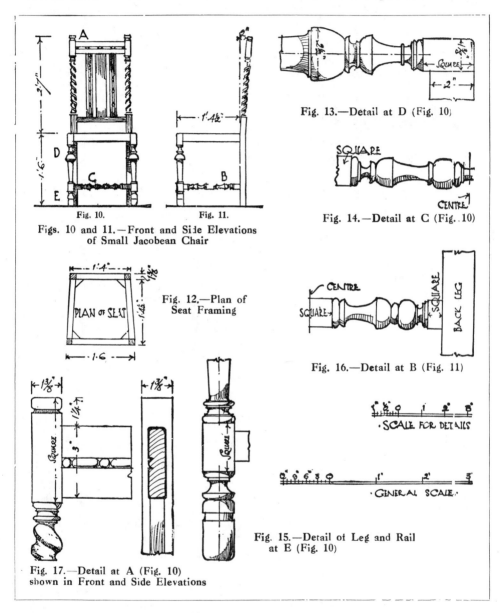

Fig. 13.—Detail at D (Fig. 10)

Fig. 14.—Detail at C (Fig. 10)

Figs. 10.   Fig. 11.

Figs. 10 and 11.—Front and Side Elevations of Small Jacobean Chair

Fig. 12.—Plan of Seat Framing

Fig. 16.—Detail at B (Fig. 11)

·SCALE FOR DETAILS·

·GENERAL SCALE·

Fig. 15.—Detail of Leg and Rail at E (Fig. 10)

Fig. 17.—Detail at A (Fig. 10) shown in Front and Side Elevations

is 1 in. wide, and rounded underneath to obviate the need for casters. It should be noted that while the left-hand or front edge is straight, the back edge is finished next to the floor, as clearly shown on the left-hand side of Fig. 3.

The upper part of each back leg is rather more elaborate, being tapered from $1\frac{1}{2}$ in. square at seat level to 1 in. square at the extreme top, the end being slightly rounded, as in Fig. 6. In addition to this tapering, the edges are chamfered as shown, the chamfers being very slight at their start 3 in. above the seat rail E (Fig. 6), and increasing until the leg is nearly octagonal in section at the level of F. Above this the leg is square, but very slightly chamfered off as at G. The method of stopping the larger chamfers by means of a quadrant curve outwards will be noticed. When framed up the back legs slope back as in Fig. 4, the top overhanging the bottom to the extent of $1\frac{1}{4}$ in., as explained by the dotted line H, this being vertical.

The four seat rails are 3 in. by 1 in., and set out in accordance with Fig. 7, tenoned joints being used. Removable padded seats upholstered in leather, etc., on a $1\frac{1}{2}$-in. by $\frac{3}{4}$-in. frame J (Fig. 8) should be adopted for this class of chair. They should be very accurately fitted into the opening formed by the seat rails, the inner angles of the front legs being cut away to suit them, as at K in Fig. 9, and they should be supported on small angle-blocks housed into the latter, as at L in Figs. 7, 8, and 9. The four small rails connecting the legs should be about $1\frac{1}{4}$ in. by $\frac{7}{8}$ in. or $\frac{3}{4}$ in., stub-tenoned in position. Two horizontal rails are required for the back, the lower one 2 in. by $\frac{7}{8}$ in., and the top one $2\frac{1}{2}$ in. by $\frac{3}{4}$ in., this one being shaped, as in Fig. 3, to a very slight curve on the top. Both should be tenoned centrally into the back legs, as at M in Fig. 6, and between them is stub-tenoned a shaped centre slat, 5 in. across at the widest point, $\frac{1}{2}$ in. thick, and relieved with a spot of inlay, as in Fig. 3. Finally the top edges of the front legs and outer angles of the seat rails should be rounded slightly.

SMALL JACOBEAN CHAIR

The characteristic features of the Jacobean style have been retained in the elaborate turning and spiral turning, and the tall, almost upright, back of the chair shown by the two elevations (Figs. 10 and 11). A plan of the seat framing is shown by Fig. 12. There is no curved work, and the framing together will be found quite straightforward. Particular care should be devoted to the turning (*see* later section), as it is on this that the effect will depend. It will be noticed that the spirals of the back uprights both wind outwards, or in other words, wind in opposite directions. The back legs are shown square and plain in order to simplify the work ; but in old work they are usually turned.

Enlarged details of the turning are given by Figs. 13, 14, 15 and 16, the portions left square being noted in all cases. The rail B in the side elevation (Fig. 11) occurs at each side, while that at C in the front elevation (Fig. 10) crosses from side to side in the centre of the two rails at B. The back has a filling of one wide and two narrow uprights with inch spaces between, the narrow ones as well as the top rail having a sunk beaded ornament incised as in the detail, Fig. 17. Alternatively, a narrow cushion might be contrived on the back of the chair : it should be long so as to suit the outer uprights.

The seat might very appropriately be filled in with rush-work, or removable seats, consisting of light padded frames, upholstered with leather or leather-cloth, could be made or obtained, the angle-blocks to support them being indicated on the plan of seat.

Walnut and oak will be found suitable materials.

BEDROOM CHAIR

Lightness and simplicity of design are the usual characteristics of bedroom chairs, and, in their making, any difficulty of construction that may present itself is merely due to the necessity of securing sufficient strength consistent with lightness. The chair shown by Figs. 18 to 21 has been designed with these requirements in view, and their achievement has been chiefly secured by the inclusion of the lower rails, which materially add to the strength of the chair, but do not give it any appearance of clumsiness as would be the case if heavier material was used. As regards the actual construction, this follows almost good depth (2½ in.) is allowed for the upper rails in order to secure strength, but the deep appearance of these is relieved by the curved lower edge of the

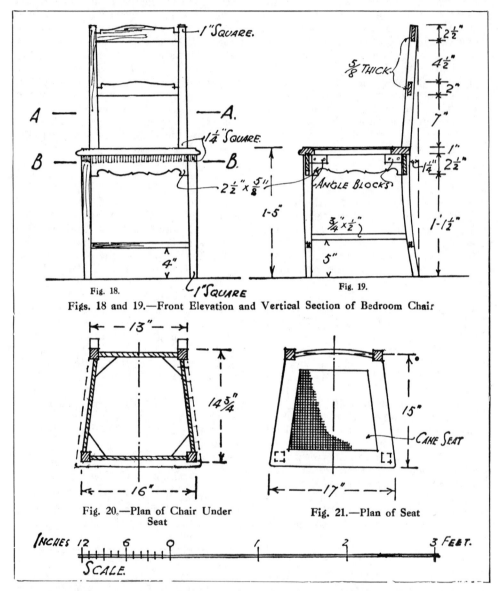

Fig. 18.

Fig. 19.

Figs. 18 and 19.—Front Elevation and Vertical Section of Bedroom Chair

Fig. 20.—Plan of Chair Under Seat

Fig. 21.—Plan of Seat

exactly upon the lines as the chair described earlier in this section (Fig. 2), and therefore repetition is unnecessary. All dimensions are given in the figures. A rail. In order not to unduly weaken the legs the front and side lower rails are placed on two levels at heights of 4 in. and 5 in. respectively.

A cane seat is shown (Fig. 21), and the fitting of this will probably be beyond the sphere of the worker, but it will be an easy matter to get done, or as an alterna-

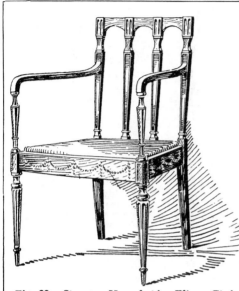

Fig. 22.—Sheraton-Heppelwhite Elbow Chair

tive one of the many prepared seats could be fitted.

TWO SHERATON-HEPPELWHITE ELBOW CHAIRS

Figs. 22 and 23 are modest examples of elbow chairs of the Sheraton style, late eighteenth century, which is no doubt the nearest to our present-day taste. The designs of the Sheraton school are, without question, worthy to rank with other earlier masters, such as Chippendale, Heppelwhite, and Adam. These Sheraton chairs are usually executed in mahogany with satinwood inlay. Light and graceful in construction they are sometimes found with round legs, fluted or reeded, and, as in the example shown, with square tapered legs and toe. Similar designs were also executed with loose upholstered seats covered in various silks.

The general proportions of the various members may be gleaned from the front and side elevations, Figs. 24 and 25, and Figs. 26 and 27. The part plans (Figs. 24 and 26) show the framing and shaping of the seats. Throughout the whole of the framing all the joints should be neatly executed with mortise and tenons of the greatest practicable length according to situation. Due regard, of course, must be observed in the shaping of the various members, viz., arms, back, and seat framing.

SHERATON DINING-PARLOUR CHAIR

Fig. 28 illustrates a fine example of what was known as a dining-parlour chair, also of the Sheraton style. As will be seen the two front legs are not square and tapered as in the two preceding designs, but round and fluted, tapering

Fig. 23.—Alternative Design for Sheraton-Heppelwhite Elbow Chair

to toe, while the two back legs are of square section. Here also will be noted a suggestion of Heppelwhite in the semi-circular detail of the back, with tapered

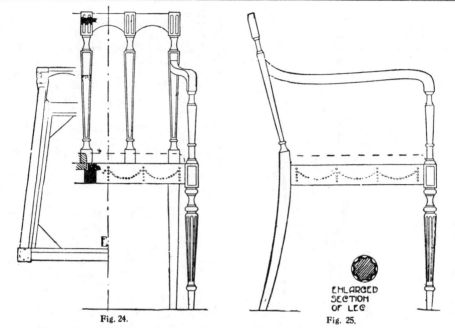

Fig. 24.

Fig. 25.

ENLARGED
SECTION
OF LEG

Figs. 24 and 25.—Part Plan and Part Front Elevation and Side Elevation of
Elbow Chair (Fig. 22)

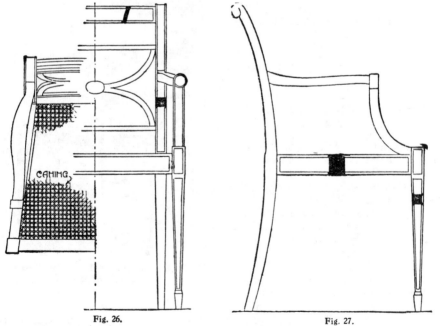

CANING

Fig. 26.

Fig. 27.

Figs. 26 and 27.—Part Plan and Part Front Elevation and Side Elevation of
Elbow Chair (Fig. 23)

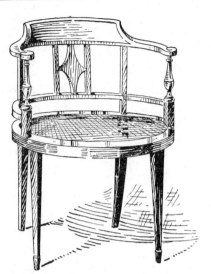

Fig. 28.—Sheraton Dining-parlour
Chair

uprights, ornamented with flutes and sinkings. As shown in front elevation (Fig. 29) the framing of the seat is delicately enriched with inlays of satinwood, or coloured woods, festooned, or in many instances hand-painted decorations are applied. The seat in this example is a thinly upholstered loose seat covered in silk, which should sink almost flush with the top of framing. A side elevation is shown by Fig. 30.

CHAIR WITH ADJUSTABLE SEAT AND BACK

An adjustable chair of simple design that could easily be made by anyone with a little knowledge of woodworking is shown by Fig. 31. Front and side elevations and plan are given by Figs. 32, 33 and 34 respectively.

There are four short legs, connected

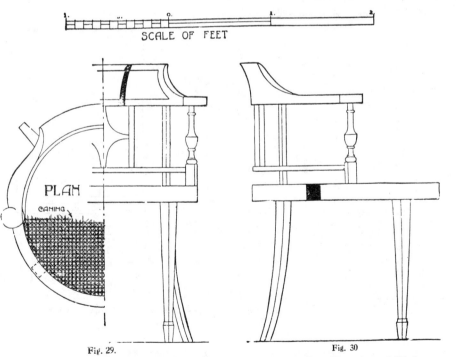

SCALE OF FEET

PLAN

CANING

Fig. 29.   Fig. 30

Figs. 29 and 30.—Part Plan and Part Front Elevation and Side Elevation of Dining-parlour Chair

at the tops by four rails and at the centre by stretchers. Four supports for the arms are fixed at the corners of the lower framing. The arms are given additional over the stuffing. Along each top rail of the seat framing four rollers are pivoted, on which the seat slides (Fig. 35). The back of the seat is pivoted to the bottom

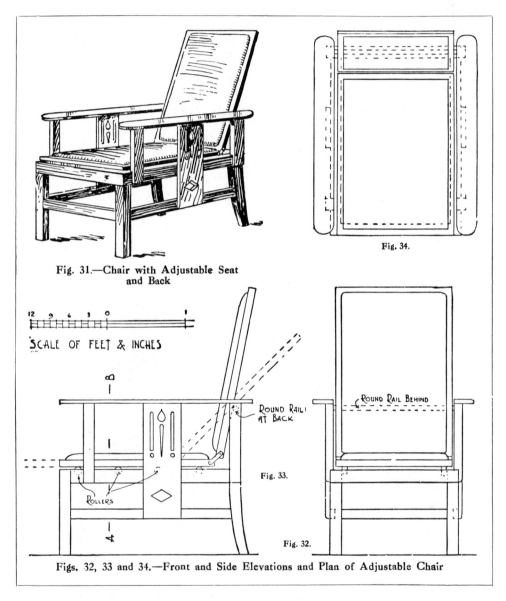

Fig. 31.—Chair with Adjustable Seat and Back

Fig. 34.

SCALE OF FEET & INCHES

ROUND RAIL AT BACK

ROUND RAIL BEHIND

Fig. 33.

ROLLERS

Fig. 32.

Figs. 32, 33 and 34.—Front and Side Elevations and Plan of Adjustable Chair

support in the middle by the two decorated brackets shown. The seat and back consist of wooden frames with webbing underneath and a suitable covering tacked edge of the back. The seat may therefore be brought forward to any position, and the back adjusted to any inclination. In order to keep the seat in the desired position, a removable peg could be inserted through one of the arm supports to fit into a series of holes bored along the edge of the seat. A better method would be to make a number of saw-teeth-like indentations in the back, and make the back rail of a suitable section to fit into them. By simply lifting the back, sliding the seat forward and lowering the back, the chair could be adjusted and fixed in the desired position.

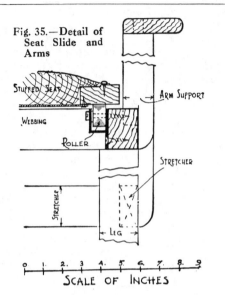

Fig. 35.—Detail of Seat Slide and Arms

TWO QUEEN ANNE CHAIRS

During recent years there has been a marked tendency to go back to the old styles in furniture, and not without good reason. It would seem that popular taste had been degenerating. For good design, comfort, and conscientious workmanship it is necessary to go back from fifty to two or three hundred years. Although the old styles are being copied they are usually modified, with a view of keeping them as inexpensive as possible,

Fig. 36.

Fig. 37.

Figs. 36 and 37.—Side and Back Views of Queen Anne Chair

Fig. 38.—Front View of Queen Anne Chair

thickness. It is fitted with the ordinary stuffed loose seat to fit in the rebate, indicated by dotted lines in Figs. 43 and 44. The seat frame is of beech, mortised and tenoned together in the usual way, webbed, canvased, hair-stuffed, and covered with leather. That, of course, is a detail, as it might be covered in tapestry or in any other suitable material.

To make such a chair frame, it is recommended first to draw full half elevations of the front, back, and side parts, also plan, and cut out cardboard patterns to same. The back uprights, top rail, splat and back seat rail may be cut out in the solid and worked approximately to the shape for jointing together, the veneering to be done afterwards. Fig. 46 shows the shape it should be when veneered, at a point about the middle of the first curve above the back leg, from whence it tapers to the top. The joint to the shaped top rail is shown

to comply with modern requirements. At present, one of the most popular styles for furniture suites is that known as the Queen Anne style. The name applies principally to the chair frames, the couch and "easy" chairs being generally of the stuff-over make, showing nothing but the legs in woodwork.

In the first instance details of a genuine old chair will be given, followed by the necessary instructions for making a replica. Figs. 36, 37 and 38 show various views of the old chair, Fig. 39 gives a more detailed view of the carved leg, and Figs. 40, 41 and 42 are enlarged views of the carving. On many of the old chairs the carving is much simpler, and others again are quite plain. The principal measurements are given in Figs. 43, 44 and 45. Solid walnut is the wood used, the back being cross-veneered with " figured " walnut of about $\frac{1}{10}$ in.

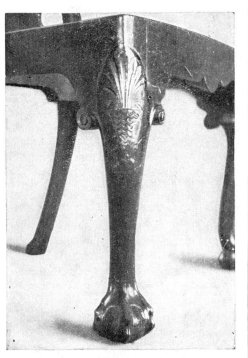

Fig. 39.—Detail View of Carved Leg

by Figs. 47 and 48 ; but the back seat rail must first be mortise-and-tenon lower edge (*see* Fig. 38) ; but the upper edge is quite straight to receive the

Fig. 40.—Detail View of Carving on Leg

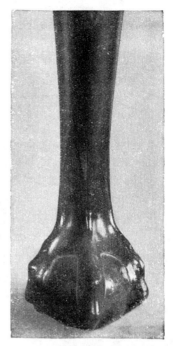

Fig. 41.—Detail View of Foot

Fig. 42.—Detail View of Carving on Top of Back

jointed in position. The shape of the back rail is a simple curve cut out of the moulded base piece for the splat. This is seen in Fig. 43. The splat is jointed

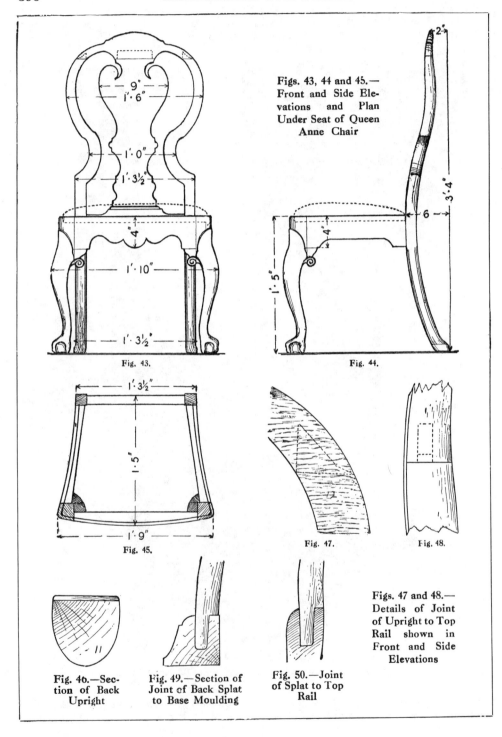

Fig. 43.

Figs. 43, 44 and 45.—
Front and Side Ele-
vations and Plan
Under Seat of Queen
Anne Chair

Fig. 44.

Fig. 45.

Fig. 47.

Fig. 48.

Figs. 47 and 48.—
Details of Joint
of Upright to Top
Rail shown in
Front and Side
Elevations

Fig. 46.—Sec-
tion of Back
Upright

Fig. 49.—Section of
Joint of Back Splat
to Base Moulding

Fig. 50.—Joint
of Splat to Top
Rail

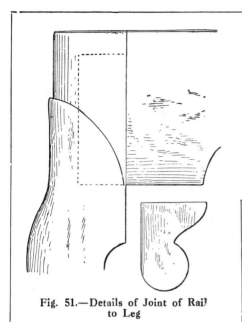

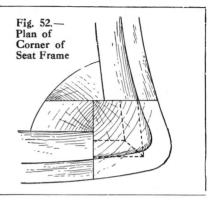

Fig. 52.—Plan of Corner of Seat Frame

Fig. 51.—Details of Joint of Rail to Leg

into it, as shown in Fig. 49. The upper end of the splat is jointed in a similar manner to the top rail (see Fig. 50). The uprights and rails may be jointed permanently to be trimmed when set to the correct shape before gluing the splat with base in place.

The front legs will require to be cut out of stuff $2\frac{3}{4}$ in. square, to be mortise-and-

Fig. 53.—Modern " Queen Anne " Chair

Fig. 54.—Detail View of Leg

tenon jointed to the front rail, the scroll blocks being cut separate (*see* Fig. 51). Before being glued, the joints of the side

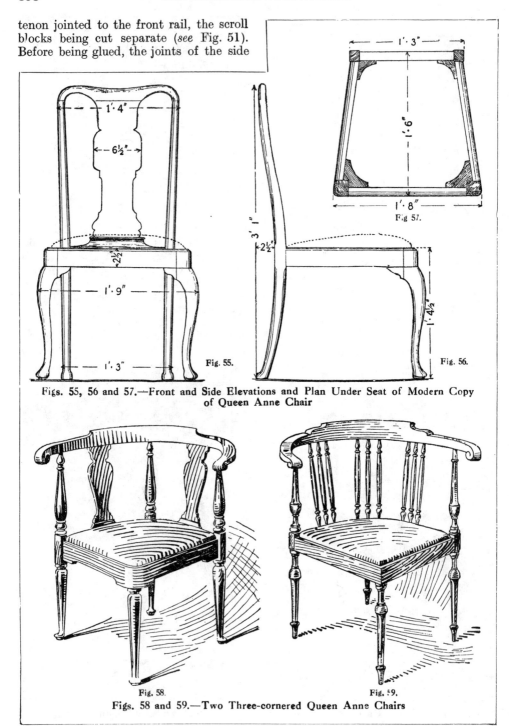

Fig. 55.

Fig 57.

Fig. 56.

Figs. 55, 56 and 57.—Front and Side Elevations and Plan Under Seat of Modern Copy of Queen Anne Chair

Fig. 58.

Fig. 59.

Figs. 58 and 59.—Two Three-cornered Queen Anne Chairs

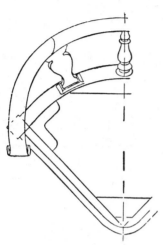

Fig. 61.—Part Plan of Three-cornered Chair (Fig. 58)

Fig. 60.—Another Design for Three-cornered Queen Anne Chair

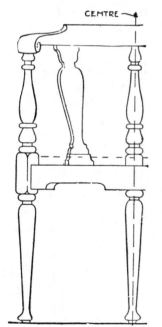

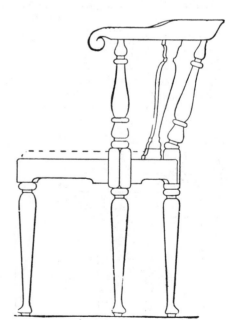

CENTRE

Fig. 62.

Fig. 63.

Figs. 62 and 63.—Part Front Elevation and Side Elevation of Three-cornered Chair (Fig. 58)

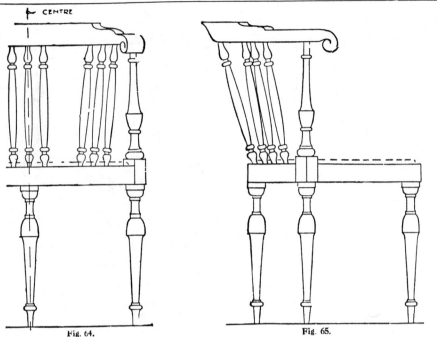

Figs. 64 and 65.—Part Front Elevation and Side Elevation of Three-cornered Chair (Fig. 59)

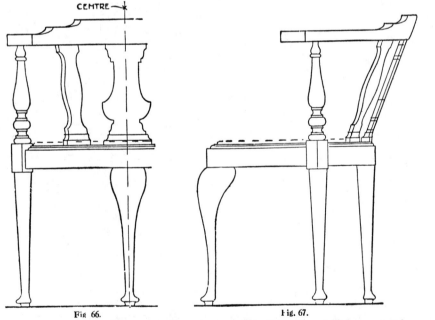

Figs. 66 and 67.—Part Front Elevation and Side Elevation of Three-cornered Chair (Fig. 60)

rails must be made, and the rebating done to all three rails and tops of the legs, also the carving. When they are glued up, the scroll blocks may be carved to something near the mark to be carefully fitted, toothed, and well glued in place, to be trimmed to the finished shape when thoroughly set. To give further support, the blocks which are glued in the corners must come well down behind them. These blocks also give strength and rigidity to the frame (see Fig. 52), which also shows how the tenons should fit inside the legs.

The finished work should be carefully trimmed up and french-polished.

Fig. 53 shows a modern copy of a much plainer design, made in mahogany. The loose seat was upholstered in green morocco leather. Fig. 54 gives a more complete view of the leg. The method of construction may be as described for the old chair, the measurements being given in Figs. 55, 56 and 57.

THREE THREE-CORNERED CHAIRS

The three-corner, or what are known as "roundabout" chairs, illustrated by Figs. 58, 59 and 60, are after the Queen Anne style. These chairs appeal to many for their charm of simple design and solid construction, remarks which apply generally to the furniture of that period. The prevailing wood for furniture construction of the Queen Anne period was walnut, as oak was for earlier times. The reproduced drawings (Figs. 61 to 67) are to scale and provide a sufficient guide to the intending constructor.

A characteristic of the design shown by Fig. 65 is the splay or rake given to the splats, which overhang the framing of the seat some six inches. This not only adds to the comfort but also to the general character of the design. .In some instances these splats were shaped so as to fit the shoulders, and certainly gave additional comfort. In each case the chair is fitted with a loose frame seat which is upholstered and covered in various materials.

CHILD'S HIGH CHAIR WITH HINGED TABLE

The chair shown in the photographic reproduction (Fig. 68) is constructed of oak. The seat and legs are of 1-in. stuff, three small panels of $\frac{1}{4}$-in. stuff, the frame of the table of $\frac{1}{2}$-in. stuff, and the rest of $\frac{3}{4}$-in. stuff. The sizes given are suitable for a child of average size, and the footrest can be unscrewed and lowered

Fig. 68.—Child's High Chair with Hinged Table

as required. The drawings are to scale, and from these the work should be set out on a board full size, and the angles and lengths measured from it. The seat is fixed with four brass screws, whose heads are sunk into the rails underneath (inside). Fig. 69 is a front elevation with the table

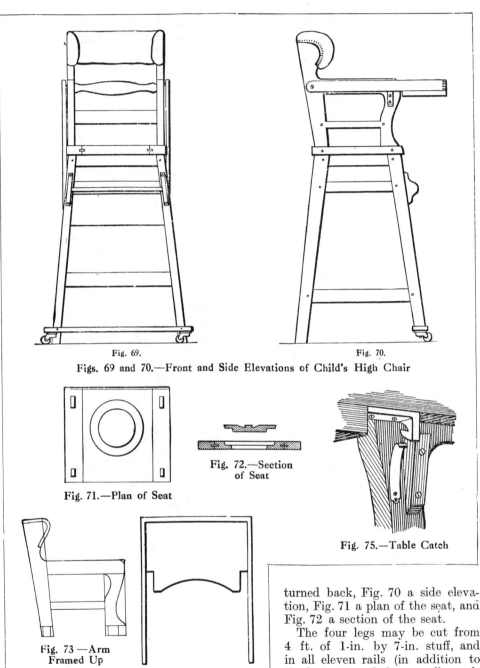

Fig. 69.

Fig. 70.

Figs. 69 and 70.—Front and Side Elevations of Child's High Chair

Fig. 71.—Plan of Seat

Fig. 72.—Section of Seat

Fig. 75.—Table Catch

Fig. 73 —Arm Framed Up

Fig. 74.—Plan of Table

turned back, Fig. 70 a side eleva-tion, Fig. 71 a plan of the seat, and Fig. 72 a section of the seat.

The four legs may be cut from 4 ft. of 1-in. by 7-in. stuff, and in all eleven rails (in addition to the footrest) and three small panels will be required. In framing up, the parts are all draw-bored and pegged, the tenons not coming quite through except in the case of the seat and the bottom front rail for the casters. The two arms are framed up as in Fig. 73,

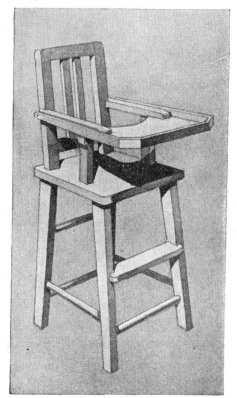

Fig. 76 —Another Design for Child's High Chair

and the curves afterwards cut with the bow-saw. The piece which comes out at the elbow is glued on again higher up, and a rebate $\frac{1}{2}$ in. wide is sunk $\frac{1}{8}$ in. for the upholstery. The turned rail in the back forms a convenient handle for moving the chair, but it may be replaced by a plain straight rail if necessary. The table (Fig. 74) swings on two stout brass screws, and drops on to stops on the arms. To prevent the child from lifting the table, a catch is fitted outside one arm. Fig. 75 shows its arrangement, and to lift the table the spring is pressed in by the thumb; simply dropping the table fastens it down. This fitting may

be made up in brass; let the spring be well hammered, and make the holes as low down it as possible.

When all the parts are put together, the sharp edges should be carefully removed, more especially above the seat, and the finishing should be three coats of good oil varnish.

ANOTHER DESIGN FOR CHILD'S HIGH CHAIR

Probably the most essential portion of the high chair shown by the half-tone reproduction (Fig. 76) is the actual seat, as it is into this that both the upper and lower framings are tenoned.

Front and side elevations are shown by

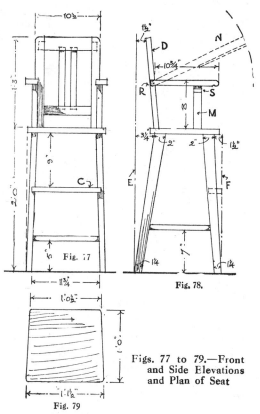

Figs. 77 to 79.—Front and Side Elevations and Plan of Seat

Figs. 77 and 78. The seat should be shaped, as in Fig. 79, out of wood at least 1 in. thick, and can be left quite flat or

slightly " dished " in the centre as preferred. The under-framing consists of
several rails and four legs, the latter 1 in.
thick, tapered from 2 in. to 1½ in., and
fixed sloping as in Fig. 78, and sloped
slightly outwards towards the bottom as
seen from the front (Fig. 77). They are
intended to be fixed ⅞ in. from the back
and front edges and ¾ in. from the sides,

Figs. 77 and 78, of each leg. Oak or
ash rods of ¾-in. diameter are employed
to connect the legs at the levels indicated.
They can be tapered slightly at the ends
and should be tightly fixed into sockets
about ½ in. deep. At the level of c in
Fig. 77 is a 3-in. by ¾-in. footrest, let
into grooves in the front legs, and rounded
on the front corners.

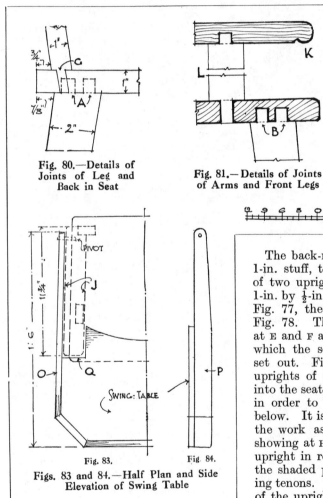

Fig. 80.—Details of
Joints of Leg and
Back in Seat

Fig. 81.— Details of Joints
of Arms and Front Legs

Fig. 82.—Plan
of Corner of
Seat

Figs. 83.   Fig. 84.

Figs. 83 and 84.—Half Plan and Side
Elevation of Swing Table

The back-rest is composed of 1½-in. by
1-in. stuff, tenoned together in the form
of two uprights and two rails, with two
1-in. by ½-in. slats down the centre as in
Fig. 77, the whole sloping as at D in
Fig. 78. This figure incidentally shows
at E and F a couple of vertical lines from
which the several slopes can readily be
set out. Fig. 80 shows at G how the
uprights of the back should be tenoned
into the seat, this operation requiring care
in order to avoid the joints of the legs
below. It is accomplished by setting out
the work as in Fig. 82, which is a plan
showing at H the outlines of a leg and an
upright in relation to one another, while
the shaded portions indicate the projecting tenons. It will be seen that the tenon
of the upright is cut back on the left, in
order to almost completely avoid the back
tenon of the leg ; and as the latter does
not go right through the seat, the actual
overlapping of the two joints is negligible.
Arms 2 in. by 1 in. should be arranged

by means of double-stopped tenons ⅝ in.
long, as at A in Fig. 80 and B in Fig. 81,
the joints being carefully adjusted with
the bevel to suit the two slopes, as in

as dotted at J in Fig. 83, parallel to the sides of the seat, notched into the sloping uprights, and shaped on the front ends as at K in Fig. 81, which shows at L the method of fitting upright supports as at

necessary adjunct, and is explained by Figs. 83 and 84. It consists of $1\frac{1}{2}$-in. by $\frac{1}{2}$-in. arms, as at O and P, fixed to a $\frac{3}{8}$-in. flat table-top, curved on the inner edge and cut away to clear the arms of the

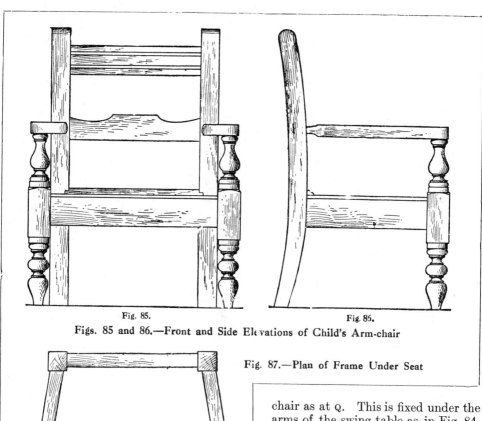

Fig. 85.

Fig. 86.

Figs. 85 and 86.—Front and Side Elevations of Child's Arm-chair

Fig. 87.—Plan of Frame Under Seat

chair as at Q. This is fixed under the arms of the swing table as in Fig. 84, these arms forming a ledge to it on the sides. The ledge is carried round the outer edges in the form of a beading to match the arms, strengthened, if necessary, at the mitres with small brass plates screwed on. The arms of the swing table are pivoted on oak dowels in the chair arms at R, and have stops to keep it level as at S, both in Fig. 78, and a catch might be provided to fasten it down when required.

M in Fig. 78. These are stop-tenoned into the undersides of the arms, and through-tenoned into the seat, where in this case they can be kept well away from the leg joints below.

A swing table, as at N in Fig. 78, is a

57—N.E.

CHILD'S ARM-CHAIR

Figs. 85 and 86 show two elevations of a child's small arm-chair of very sturdy construction.

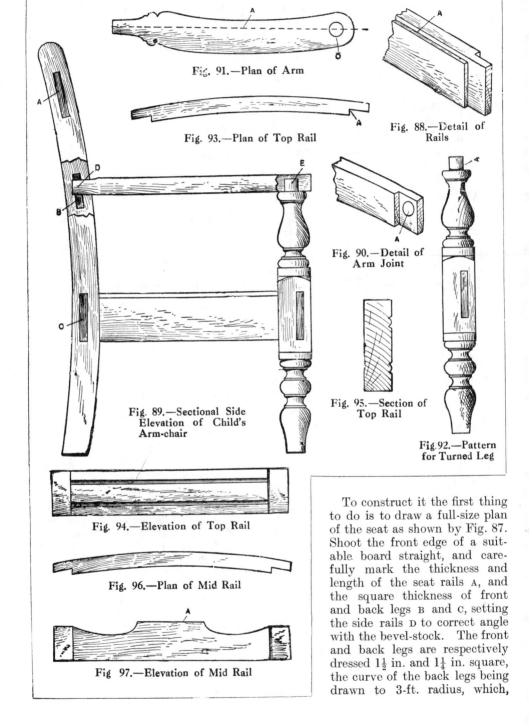

Fig. 91.—Plan of Arm

Fig. 93.—Plan of Top Rail

Fig. 88.—Detail of Rails

Fig. 90.—Detail of Arm Joint

Fig. 89.—Sectional Side Elevation of Child's Arm-chair

Fig. 95.—Section of Top Rail

Fig. 92.—Pattern for Turned Leg

Fig. 94.—Elevation of Top Rail

Fig. 96.—Plan of Mid Rail

Fig 97.—Elevation of Mid Rail

To construct it the first thing to do is to draw a full-size plan of the seat as shown by Fig. 87. Shoot the front edge of a suitable board straight, and carefully mark the thickness and length of the seat rails A, and the square thickness of front and back legs B and C, setting the side rails D to correct angle with the bevel-stock. The front and back legs are respectively dressed 1½ in. and 1¼ in. square, the curve of the back legs being drawn to 3-ft. radius, which, failing a proper trammel, can be drawn with a thin lath of wood pivoted on a bradawl. The finished size of the seat rails is 1⅞ in. by ⅞ in. thick. The framing is prepared with 5/16-in. mortise-and-tenon joints, glued and cramped together. The front rail and side rails are also rebated on the inside upper edges to take the bottom as shown at A (Fig. 88). Fig. 89 is a section of the chair showing the setting out of

the centre for prong-and-poppet chucking to turn the tenon ends, and the tenons are turned ⅝ in. in diameter, also the beading, as shown at B, and the hole C bored with a ⅝-in. centre-bit to suit the front leg tenon A (Fig. 92).

The top back rail is ⅝ in. thick and 2 in. deep, sawn out, as in Fig. 93, to a curve of 2-ft. radius, the tenons being shouldered to the front side as at A. It is finished

Fig. 98.—Chair-table in the Seventeenth-Century Style

the back-rail mortises A and B and seat-rail mortise C, and how the arm tenon D pins into the back leg through the back-rail tenon (as indicated by the hole A in Fig. 90); also the method of fixing to the front leg by the pin E. The arms, a plan view of which is shown by Fig. 91, are of ¾ in. thick stuff, the pieces being 2 in. wide before turning and sawing out to the curved shape. The dotted line A indicates

with flush scratched beadings as shown in Fig. 94, and also in the enlarged section of the top rail (Fig. 95). The mid back rail (Fig. 96) is similarly sawn out, but from 1¾-in. stuff, and afterwards finished to the shape shown in Fig. 97, the upper part A being smoothly rounded both for appearance and to prevent it hurting the child's back.

In putting the chair together, the back

leg mortises and back-rail tenons are brushed with hot glue of medium thickness, and quickly but carefully cramped together. Any exuded glue should at once be wiped off with a hot, damp rag. The front legs and front rail being similarly treated, the job may be placed aside to let the glue set; or the side rails can be at once glued in and the frame made ready for the bottom, which for strength should be about $\frac{7}{16}$ in. thick, and if possible in one solid width.

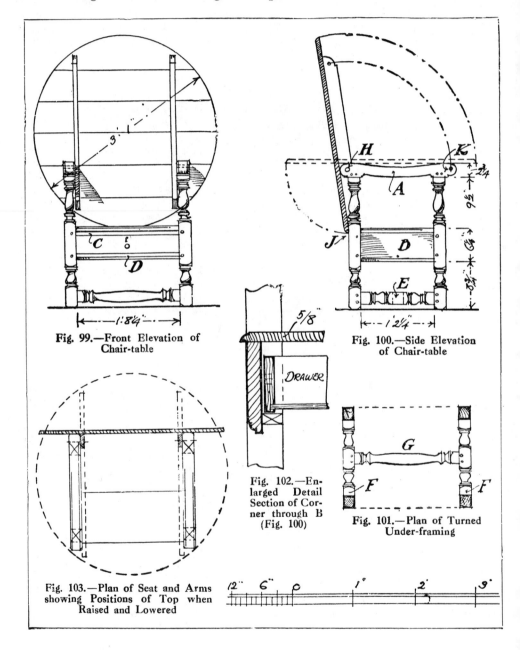

Fig. 99.—Front Elevation of Chair-table

Fig. 100.—Side Elevation of Chair-table

Fig. 102.—Enlarged Detail Section of Corner through B (Fig. 100)

Fig. 101.—Plan of Turned Under-framing

Fig. 103.—Plan of Seat and Arms showing Positions of Top when Raised and Lowered

CHAIR-TABLE IN THE SEVEN-TEENTH-CENTURY STYLE

What is sometimes known at South Kensington Museum as the " miser's chair "—probably owing to the facilities it offers its occupant for guarding the contents of the drawer below the seat— is a substantial oaken piece of furniture, having a circular back pivoted in such a way that it can be lowered until it rests in a horizontal position on the arms at each side. The photographic reproduction (Fig. 98) shows the chair-table from the front with its top just slightly raised from the level position. It being thought that the idea involved might appeal to a number of readers in search of something a little unusual, therefore it is proposed to describe the chair-table as it exists.

The main supports consist of four upright legs each $2\frac{1}{4}$ in. square, shown in elevation by Figs. 99 and 100, and in plan at the corners of Fig. 101. It may here be mentioned that the square corners at the end of each part left square are rounded off a little. Each pair of legs is tenoned at the tops into the underside of a shaped arm-rest, as at A (Fig. 100), with its top slightly rounded in section, the joints here and throughout the job being secured with oak pegs, and the arms made so that the flat top will rest evenly on them, as shown by the dotted horizontal lines in Fig. 100. Under the arms, and at each side of the actual seat, pieces as at B (Fig. 100), are fixed by tenoning into the legs flush with them; it is beaded along the bottom outer edge and measures $5\frac{5}{8}$ in. wide by 1 in. A similar piece, without bead, is fixed at the back. An enlarged detail section through B is given in Fig. 102 showing a $\frac{5}{8}$-in. seat (which is in two pieces, as indicated in Fig. 103) with rounded projecting edges on the top, a drawer-runner marked with a diagonal cross, and the side of an ordinary drawer in oak with a 1-in. front, small lock and round knob. In the front above the drawer is a bearer C 2 in. by 1 in. high for the edge of the seat, while below is a piece D tenoned and pegged in position, about $1\frac{1}{2}$ in. by $1\frac{1}{4}$ in. high, at the same level as, and beaded to match, the lower edges of the side pieces B.

The third connection between the front and back legs on each side is made $\frac{3}{4}$ in. above the floor by a $2\frac{1}{4}$-in. square rail E (Fig. 100) and F (Fig. 101), tenoned at each end as before and partially circular-turned in the manner shown. The square central portion is left to receive a tie G (Fig. 101), almost the whole of which is turned, as will be seen from the photograph, and this completes the main framing, leaving the top to be described.

The top consists of an approximate circle of 3 ft. 1 in. diameter, having a rounded edge and being made up of six widths of $\frac{1}{2}$-in. oak on a couple of ledges of a somewhat eccentric cut outline. These are shown in Fig. 100 in a simplified form, and are pivoted by means of oak centre-pins driven tightly through the arms, as at H (Fig. 100), with ends projecting about $1\frac{1}{2}$ in. on the insides, on which projections the two ledges of the top work loosely. The whole is so arranged that the bottom edge of the top overlaps the back of the seat at J (Fig. 100) about $\frac{1}{2}$ in. when the top is upright. At the front extremes of the arms are small holes, as at K (Fig. 100), with corresponding ones in the ledges, so that by the insertion of a pin the top may be fastened in its horizontal position when desired.

Hanging Cupboards and Cabinets

SMOKER'S CABINET

A CERTAIN amount of quaintness of design is shown in the smoker's cabinet illustrated by Fig. 1.

Wainscot oak, left clean without stain or polish, is a suitable wood to use. The sides, shelves, and brackets are of ½-in. stuff. The small inner shelf is of ¼-in. stuff, and the front arch piece and also the back are ⅛-in. fret-wood (all finished thicknesses). As an essential preliminary to the commencement of the job, a full-size setting-out of the front elevation (Fig. 2) should be made, this being drawn accurately to a vertical centre line. From this full-size diagram the exact length of the shelves and also the angle formed by the sloping sides can be taken, and if care is taken at this

stage of the work it will save possible trouble later on. A side elevation and vertical section are shown by Figs. 3 and 4 on the next page.

The top may be made by gluing two blocks to the ½-in. stuff, as indicated by dotted lines on the front elevation, afterwards cutting and working to shape ; or it may be cut from one solid block. The objection to the former method is the possibility of the joints showing, unless the pieces of oak are carefully matched and the joints well made. The second method is therefore recommended, even though it entails rather more work. The sides are housed into the top to a depth of $\frac{3}{16}$ in. and glued and bradded, and the two shelves are similarly fixed to the sides ; but in the case of

Fig. 1.—Smoker's Cabinet

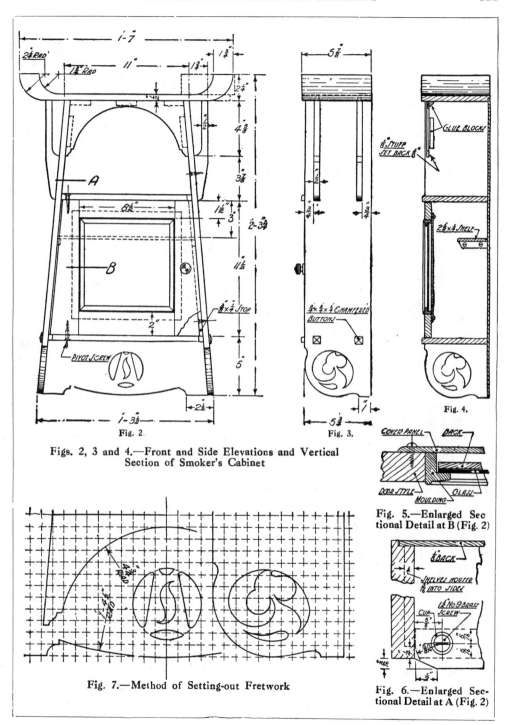

Figs. 2, 3 and 4.—Front and Side Elevations and Vertical
Section of Smoker's Cabinet

Fig. 7.—Method of Setting-out Fretwork

Fig. 5.—Enlarged Sec
tional Detail at B (Fig. 2)

Fig. 6.—Enlarged Sec-
tional Detail at A (Fig. 2)

these members two $1\frac{1}{2}$-in. No. 8 screws are used at each joint. The screw-heads should be well countersunk, and so placed that they are concealed by the brackets at the top and by the " buttons " at the bottom. All the housings should be stopped within $\frac{1}{4}$ in. of the front edges of the sides and glued. The back edges of the sides and top are rebated to receive the $\frac{1}{8}$-in. back, which is secured in position with brads. The upper ends of the four brackets are housed and glued to the top, and the lower parts of these are secured to the sides with 1-in. No. 4 screws, as indicated on the front view. Five angle-blocks are glued behind the front arch-piece, and a little glue is used on the three straight edges of it. This feature is set back $\frac{1}{8}$ in. from the front edges of the sides, and the top projects $\frac{1}{8}$ in. in front of these. The two shelves project $\frac{3}{16}$ in., and are bevelled back flush at their ends (see Fig. 5).

The door, of $\frac{5}{8}$-in. stuff, is framed together with mortise-and-tenon joints, and if no suitable planes are available with which to work the moulding on the stiles and rails, a neat picture moulding may be obtained and mitred and glued into same, as shown in the enlarged detail (Fig. 6). A picture serves as a panel ; but if so desired, a mirror or wood panel (carved or plain) may be used. The detail (Fig. 6) shows the method of fixing the picture or mirror, and in any case the $\frac{1}{8}$-in. fret-wood cover-panel ($9\frac{1}{4}$ in. by $9\frac{3}{4}$ in.) should be fixed as a finish. Sixteen $\frac{3}{8}$-in. No. 2 brass round-headed screws are required for this. A plain moulding such as that shown, and not more than $\frac{1}{2}$ in. or $\frac{5}{8}$ in. wide across the face, should be used in preference to an elaborate moulding.

As the door has sloping stiles, it must be pivot hung, this being accomplished by means of two $1\frac{1}{2}$-in. No. 9 brass screws working in the brass cups ordinarily used for screws in hardwood. From the enlarged detail (Fig. 5) it will be seen that the upper pivot screw is $\frac{5}{8}$ in. from the door edge, and the correct position of the lower pivot must be obtained by squaring off the lower shelf, so that a line running through both pivots will be at an

exact right angle with the shelves. The " hanging " stile is planed to a $\frac{5}{8}$-in. radius for clearance when opening, and the " shutting " stile (fitted with a knob) shuts on a $\frac{3}{8}$-in. by $\frac{1}{4}$-in. stop, which is screwed to the inner face of the side.

Two $\frac{1}{2}$-in. diameter holes bored in the back board, about $8\frac{1}{2}$ in. apart and 1 in. below the underside of the top, will provide ready means for hanging the cabinet.

An enlarged setting out of the fretted work is given (Fig. 7), and the central perforation in the lower part of the back should be backed with silk. The inner shelf is optional, but is very useful for the accommodation of small articles. Should it be desired to fit a catch to the door, one of the small bullet pattern would be most suitable.

SIMPLE HANGING SHELVES AND CUPBOARD

The small set of shelves shown by the half-tone reproduction, Fig. 8, and in front elevation by Fig. 9, can be made in a very simple manner from wood $\frac{3}{4}$ in. or even less in thickness. The four shelves are housed $\frac{1}{4}$ in. into the upright sides, which are shaped top and bottom as in Fig. 10, the whole being stiffened by means of a couple of back uprights 2 in. wide, as at A in Figs. 9 and 11. Each of the three lower shelves is notched at the back to receive these uprights, which run up to the underside of the top shelf, and are bradded or screwed to the shelves and sides, and shaped at the bottom as shown.

The pierced and shaped back B (Fig. 9) can easily be added, as can also a thin filling to the back of the cupboard, fixed to small angle fillets as in Fig. 12.

The door of the cupboard can be framed up, or simply made as in Figs. 13 and 14, with thin strips planted on a good piece of three-ply, a method by which a small door can be made quite substantial in appearance, although for anything larger it would be worse than useless. In lieu of a wood panel to the door, it might be preferred to insert a repoussé copper or other form of decorated panel, as shown in the illustration of the finished shelves. The door is hung between a couple of stiles 1½ in. wide, as at c in Figs. 9 and 14, and the whole supported in position by means of four brass wall plates screwed on the back.

and horizontal sections are shown by Figs. 16, 17 and 18. The instructions for making the cupboard just described are equally applicable for this one, and therefore need not be repeated. Details of construction are shown by Figs. 19 to 23.

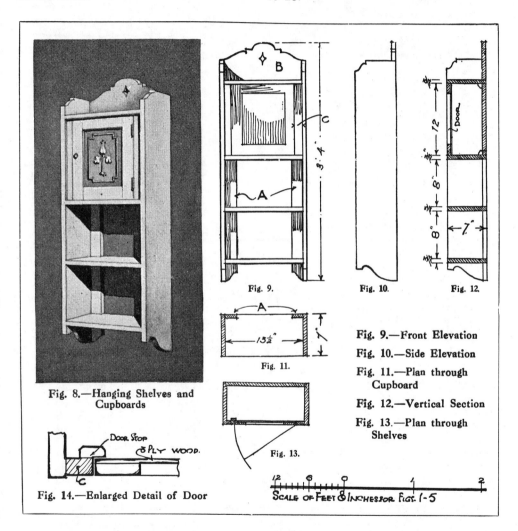

Fig. 8.—Hanging Shelves and Cupboards

Fig. 9.

Fig. 10.

Fig. 12.

Fig. 11.

Fig. 13.

Fig. 14.—Enlarged Detail of Door

Fig. 9.—Front Elevation

Fig. 10.—Side Elevation

Fig. 11.—Plan through Cupboard

Fig. 12.—Vertical Section

Fig. 13.—Plan through Shelves

Scale of Feet & Inches for Figs. 1-5

GLAZED CUPBOARD WITH SIDE SHELF

A cupboard equally as simple as the preceding one, and constructed on practically identical lines, is presented by Fig. 15. A front elevation and vertical

CUPBOARD WITH SHELVES OVER

Fig. 24 shows still another cupboard which is perhaps a little more elaborate than the two former ones. A front elevation and two sections are shown by Figs. 25, 26 and 27 respectively. The

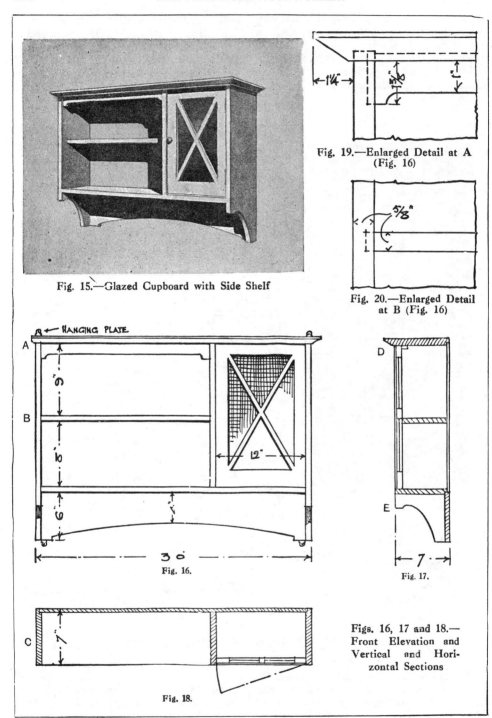

Fig. 15.—Glazed Cupboard with Side Shelf

Fig. 19.—Enlarged Detail at A (Fig. 16)

Fig. 20.—Enlarged Detail at B (Fig. 16)

HANGING PLATE

Fig. 16.

Fig. 17.

Fig. 18.

Figs. 16, 17 and 18.—Front Elevation and Vertical and Horizontal Sections

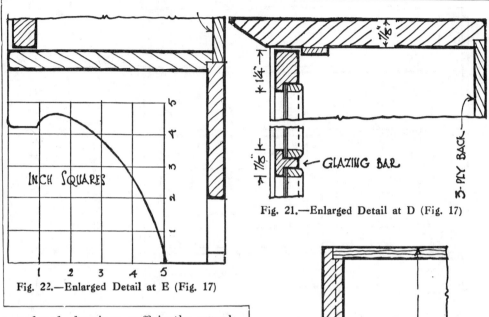

Fig. 22.—Enlarged Detail at E (Fig. 17)

INCH SQUARES

Fig. 21.—Enlarged Detail at D (Fig. 17)

← GLAZING BAR

3-PLY BACK

reproduced drawings sufficiently reveal the construction, and if studied in conjunction with the instructions given for making the first example of this class of cupboard, the worker will experience no difficulty. The design and method of setting out the ends are shown by Figs.

SHELVES STOP HOUSED TO ENDS

Fig. 23.—Enlarged Detail at C (Fig. 18)

Fig. 24.—Cupboard with Shelves Over

31 and 32. Fig. 33 is an enlarged horizontal section at one end, and clearly shows the construction of the doors and back of cupboard. A further detail of the doors is shown by Fig. 30. An enlarged sectional elevation at F (Fig. 25) is shown by Fig. 28, and an enlarged plan at G (Fig. 25) by Fig. 29. The finish may be according to the worker's taste.

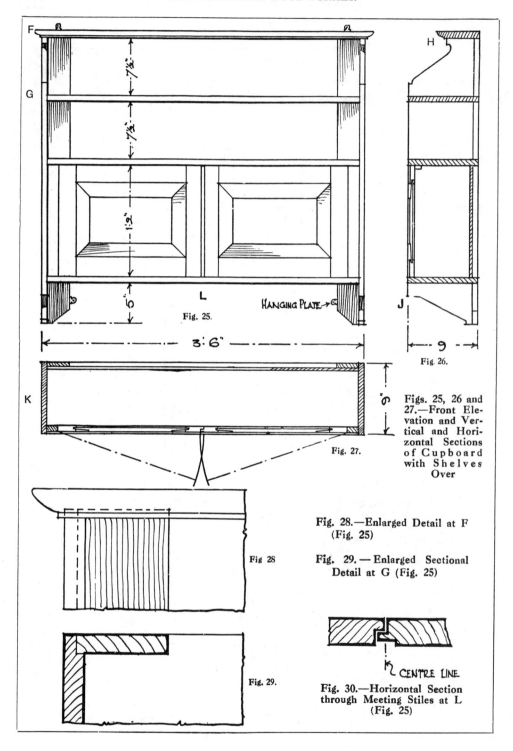

Fig. 25.

Hanging Plate →

Fig. 26.

Fig. 27.

Figs. 25, 26 and 27.—Front Elevation and Vertical and Horizontal Sections of Cupboard with Shelves Over

Fig 28

Fig. 28.—Enlarged Detail at F (Fig. 25)

Fig. 29. — Enlarged Sectional Detail at G (Fig. 25)

Fig. 29.

Centre Line

Fig. 30.—Horizontal Section through Meeting Stiles at L (Fig. 25)

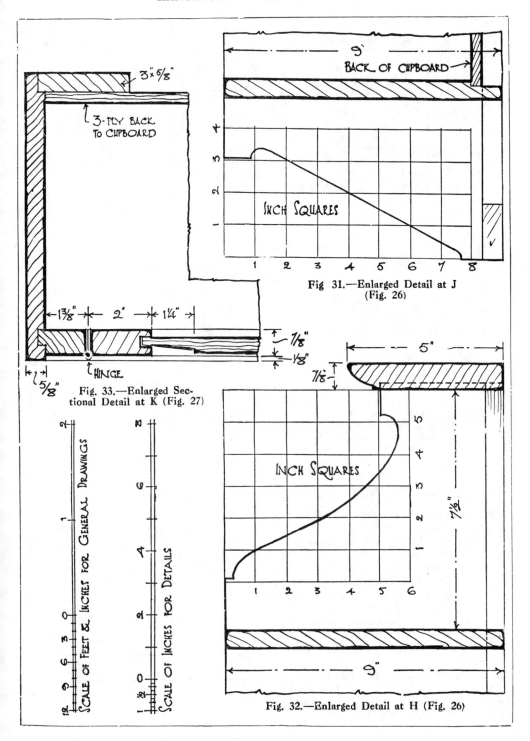

Fig 31.—Enlarged Detail at J
(Fig. 26)

Fig. 33.—Enlarged Sectional Detail at K (Fig. 27)

Fig. 32.—Enlarged Detail at H (Fig. 26)

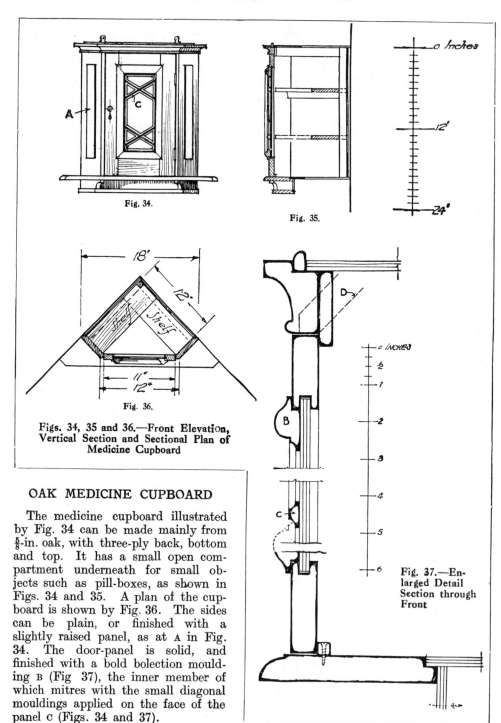

Fig. 34.

Fig. 35.

Fig. 36.

Figs. 34, 35 and 36.—Front Elevation, Vertical Section and Sectional Plan of Medicine Cupboard

Fig. 37.—Enlarged Detail Section through Front

OAK MEDICINE CUPBOARD

The medicine cupboard illustrated by Fig. 34 can be made mainly from ⅝-in. oak, with three-ply back, bottom and top. It has a small open compartment underneath for small objects such as pill-boxes, as shown in Figs. 34 and 35. A plan of the cupboard is shown by Fig. 36. The sides can be plain, or finished with a slightly raised panel, as at A in Fig. 34. The door-panel is solid, and finished with a bold bolection moulding B (Fig 37), the inner member of which mitres with the small diagonal mouldings applied on the face of the panel C (Figs. 34 and 37).

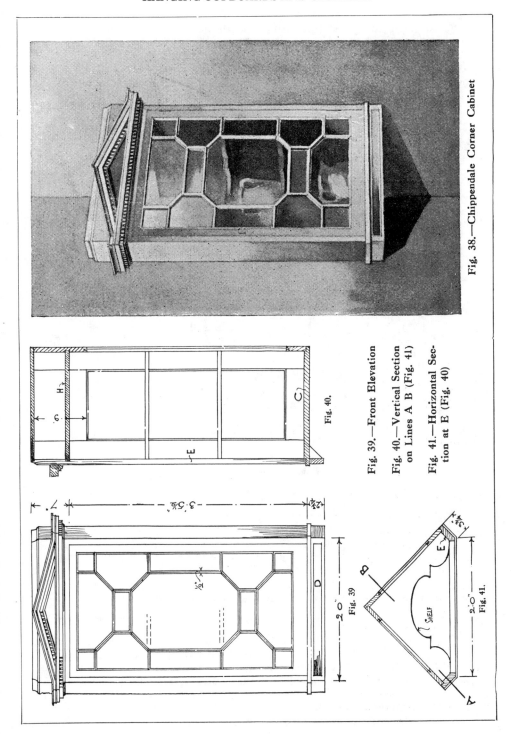

Fig. 38.—Chippendale Corner Cabinet

Fig. 39.—Front Elevation

Fig. 40.—Vertical Section on Lines A B (Fig. 41)

Fig. 41.—Horizontal Section at E (Fig. 40)

Fig. 40.

Fig. 39

Fig. 41.

The dotted lines at D on the latter figure explain the relationship of the sides to the door which is intended to project about $\frac{1}{8}$ in. when in the closed position as shown in Fig. 34.

on the geometric pattern of the glazing-bars. Fig. 39 shows a front elevation.

The actual framing of the cupboard starts from a 1-in. bottom shelf C (Fig. 40), rebated $\frac{1}{4}$ in. deep all round and intended

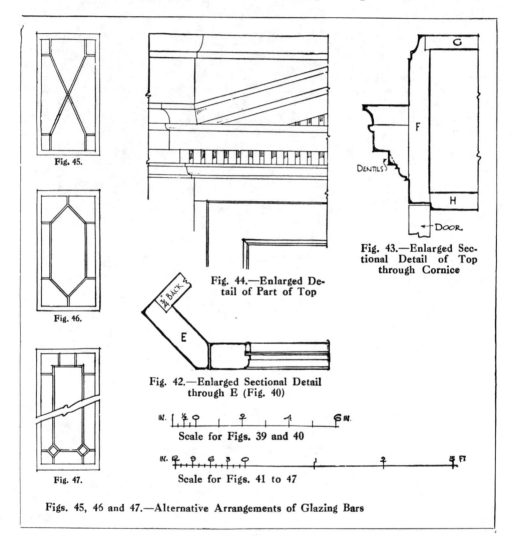

Fig. 45.

Fig. 46.

Fig. 47.

Fig. 44.—Enlarged Detail of Part of Top

Fig. 42.—Enlarged Sectional Detail through E (Fig. 40)

Fig. 43.—Enlarged Sectional Detail of Top through Cornice

Scale for Figs. 39 and 40

Scale for Figs. 41 to 47

Figs. 45, 46 and 47.—Alternative Arrangements of Glazing Bars

CHIPPENDALE CORNER CABINET

The cabinet illustrated by the halftone reproduction (Fig. 38) is specially designed as a corner fitting, though if desired it could be adapted to a rectangular plan. Its interest depends very largely

to project $\frac{3}{16}$ in. beyond the finished work. It can be of hardwood or merely pine faced along the front edges with strips of mahogany, etc. The 2-in. apron at D in Fig. 39 is not constructional; it is sunk $\frac{1}{16}$ in. on the face, and fixed with angle-blocks as in Fig. 40. The door stiles E (Figs. 40, 41 and 42) extend right up to the extreme top, where they are connected by a rail as at F in Fig. 43, mitred in position and of the same thickness as the door, the whole being moulded as shown, and rebated for a light top board G. An inner top, as at H in Figs. 40 and 43, is desirable, fixed at the necessary level to form a rebate for the door (see Fig. 43), and housed $\frac{1}{4}$ in. to the stiles and the two backs. The latter should be panelled and flush on the inside, rebated at the back corner (see Fig. 41), and having a 9-in. top rail (see Fig. 40), so that they may show an equal margin all round their exposed portions.

Shelves can be fitted as required, but it is suggested that they be made to line with the horizontal glazing bars where dotted on Fig. 39. If shaped on plan as in Fig. 41, they will add to the interest of the whole design.

In order to contrive the pediment in the simplest possible manner consistent with the style, the cornice may be in two sections, as in Fig. 43, the lower portion taken horizontally round the three exposed faces, and also fitted on the rake to form the lower mouldings of the triangular pediment (see Figs. 39 and 44), the top portion being mitred and fitted round last of all. The dentil course will serve to emphasise the cornice, and should be finely cut. The dentils on the raking portion should have their sides vertical (not at right angles to the slope) as shown, and their width measured horizontally (not on the rake) should equal that of the dentils below. Alternative suggestions for the glazing bars are shown by Figs. 45, 46 and 47.

Cabinets and Cupboards

CABINET WITH CUPBOARDS AND SHELVES

ALTHOUGH suited to other positions, the cabinet shown by Fig. 1 would be particularly appropriate in a recess on one side of a fireplace. Practically any kind of wood can be employed in its construction. Various modifications of detail can be introduced to meet special requirements, or the whole thing can be taken as merely a suggestion on the outline of which to fashion some fresh design. The simple inlay on the back can—if constituting a difficulty—be omitted or done professionally, the small oval if adopted forming possibilities for a little quartered veneering. Another way would be to treat this back as a piece of narrow framing enclosing a panel.

For a painted finish, leaded glazing in the cupboard doors would be most suitable. If, however, hardwood (especially mahogany) be selected, very narrow wooden bars would be more appropriate to the material. In any case, the division of the glass into small panes as shown should be retained, as without this the work loses much of its interest and proportion. Leaded glazing can easily be obtained to order, and should have leads of a flat section, not less than $\frac{1}{4}$ in. wide. The chief dimensions are shown on the elevations, Figs. 2 and 3. Figs. 4 and 5 show a vertical section and a sectional plan respectively.

In order to carry out the work in accordance with the illustrations, the pieces enumerated in the following list will be necessary. The sizes given are those of the various

Fig. 1.—Cabinet with Cupboards and Shelves

422

parts when approximately ready for jointing together, and in cutting or ordering the wood small allowances should be made for sawing and planing.

For the uprights and shelves : (1) Two end uprights, 9 in. by ¾ in. by 3 ft. 2⅝ in. ; (2) two intermediate uprights as at A (Fig. 2), 8¼ in. by ¾ in. by 1 ft. 1½ in. ;

central back piece, 1 ft. 3½ in. by ¾ in. by 1 ft. 9 in., made up of two widths dowelled or tongued together, and fixed with grain upright or horizontal, as convenient ; (8) two backs to top cupboards, 9½ in. by ⅜ in. by 1 ft. 1 in. ; (9) one back to extend across lower cupboards and central division, made up of two

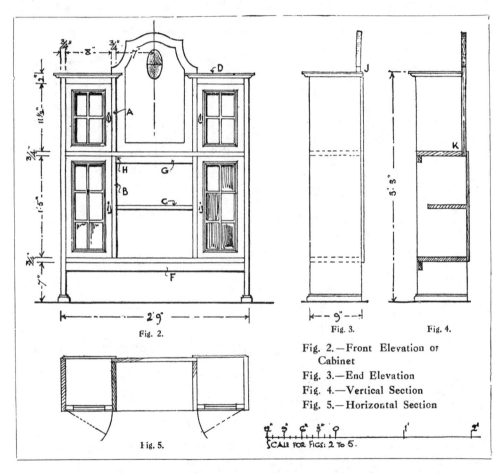

Fig. 2.

Fig. 3.   Fig. 4.

Fig. 2.—Front Elevation of Cabinet

Fig. 3.—End Elevation

Fig. 4.—Vertical Section

Fig. 5.—Horizontal Section

Fig. 5.

SCALE FOR FIGS. 2 TO 5.

(3) two intermediate uprights as at B, 9 in. by ¾ in. by 1 ft. 5⅜ in. ; (4) two main shelves, 9 in. by ¾ in. by 2 ft. 8¼ in. ; (5) one smaller shelf C (Fig. 2), 7 in. by ½ in. by 1 ft. 2 in. (1 ft. 2¼ in. if housed into uprights) ; (6) two top shelves as D (Fig. 2), 10⅜ in. by ¾ in. by 11½ in., moulded as at E (Fig. 6) on three edges.

For the back, doors, etc. : (7) One

or three pieces with grain horizontal, total size, 1 ft. 6 in. by ⅜ in. by 2 ft. 9 in. ; (10) two doors, 8 in. by 11½ in., composed of 1-in. by 1¼-in. stuff, tenoned halved or mitres at the angles, rebated ⅜ in. for glazing, and either moulded on the outer face in the usual way, or kept square as in Fig. 7 ; (11) two similar doors, 8 in. by 1 ft. 5 in. ; (12) one strip as at F

(Fig. 2), 1½ in. by ¾ in. or ½ in. by 2 ft. 7½ in. (or 2 ft. 8 in. if housed into the upright ends); (13) two similar strips above doors to top cupboards, but 1 in. deep and 8 in. or 8½ in. long; (14) one strip, 1 ft. 2 in. or 1 ft. 2½ in. long, as at G (Fig. 2). Alternatively this might be a curved spandrel, as in the illustration of the completed article, in which

joints ⅜ in. deep, stopped 1 in. back from the front edges as in Fig. 9, the only exception to this being the junction at H (Fig. 2), which can be as in Fig. 10. The fillet there shown will be concealed by the strip or spandrel (No. 14 in list of parts), which together with Nos. 12 and 13 should be fixed, either with or without housed ends as noted, ⅛ in. back from the

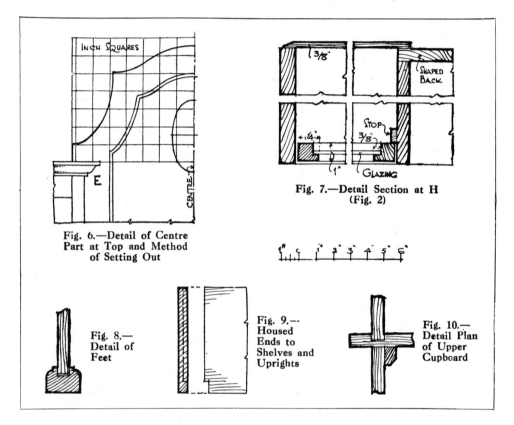

Fig. 6.—Detail of Centre Part at Top and Method of Setting Out

Fig. 7.—Detail Section at H (Fig. 2)

Fig. 8.—Detail of Feet

Fig. 9.—Housed Ends to Shelves and Uprights

Fig. 10.—Detail Plan of Upper Cupboard

case it should be cut to a flat curve from a piece 2½ in. wide; (15) two feet for the end uprights, 2 in. by 1½ in. by 9⅝ in., moulded as in Fig. 8, and grooved ½ in. deep to take the housed ends of uprights. In addition to the above parts, there will also be required some small glazing beads for the cupboard doors, and a few small fillets for door-stops, etc.

To construct the cabinet, the uprights and shelves should be put together as shown in Fig. 2, by means of housed

front edges of the shelving. Note that the moulded top shelves overhang ⅜ in. at the back J (Fig. 3). The back piece No. 7, when shaped as in Fig. 6, is fixed to the intermediate uprights as in Fig. 5, the upper long shelf being cut away in the centre to suit it as at K in Fig. 4, as are also small pieces of the moulded shelves. The ⅜-in. back pieces (Nos. 8 and 9) can then be applied as in Figs. 4 and 5, and will stiffen the whole work. They may be bevelled off as in Fig. 7, which also shows one of the small doors, these being hinged to fit $\frac{1}{8}$ in. back from the edges of shelving, and fitted with small latches and drop handles. The two feet (No. 15) should be screwed to the uprights from below.

SIXTEENTH-CENTURY CABINET IN OAK

The cabinet shown by the half-tone reproduction (Fig. 11) is based upon the

sions so as to work out conveniently in accordance with English lineal measurements, and it might be mentioned that sizes and thicknesses generally may be slightly reduced if economy is desired, work of this type having been executed at a time when oak was more plentiful than at present. Front and end elevations are shown by Figs. 12 and 13, and a vertical section and two sectional plans by Figs. 14, 15 and 16.

Fig. 11.—Sixteenth-century Cabinet in Oak

design of a fine specimen of sixteenth-century Flemish cabinet-work from the Steen Museum, Antwerp, and has an additional interest for the English craftsman by reason of the general resemblance which examples of this period bear to those of the Tudor style.

In preparing the drawings, some slight alterations have been made in the dimen-

The cabinet is constructed of oak throughout, the corner uprights being 2 in. square, with a quirked bead worked on three sides (Fig. 17). To these the heads, $2\frac{1}{4}$ in. by $1\frac{1}{4}$ in., and middle bearers, 2 in. by $1\frac{3}{4}$ in., are framed, both the latter having a similar bead worked along the lower angle. The intermediate frames for the cupboard doors are 2 in. by $1\frac{1}{4}$ in.,

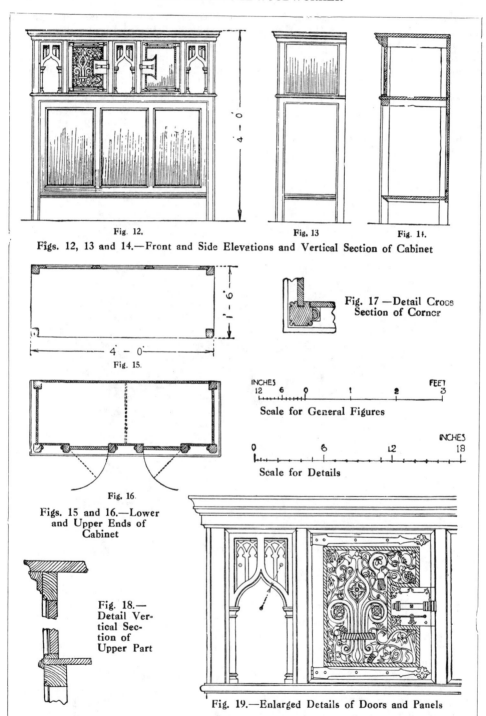

Fig. 12.

Fig. 13

Fig. 14.

Figs. 12, 13 and 14.—Front and Side Elevations and Vertical Section of Cabinet

Fig. 15.

Fig. 17.—Detail Cross Section of Corner

INCHES
12 6 0   1   2   FEET 3

Scale for General Figures

INCHES
0   6   12   18

Scale for Details

Fig. 16.

Figs. 15 and 16.—Lower and Upper Ends of Cabinet

Fig. 18.—Detail Vertical Section of Upper Part

Fig. 19.—Enlarged Details of Doors and Panels

and are rebated to receive the small pierced panels. The panelled back of the lower portion should not be less than ¾ in. thick, with panel moulds worked on the solid. The top is ⅞ in. thick, with a cavetto mould worked on the edge, and under this is planted on a mould out of 2 in. by 1¼ in., completing the cornice effect (Fig. 18). The bottom shelf is constructed in a similar way, except that the shelf is ⅝ in. thick and the small mould

Fig. 20.—Drawing-room China Cabinet

under 1 in. by ¾ in., the shelf being let into the corner posts and mortised to the back. The small traceried panels are made in two distinct parts, the framing of the arch (which is struck from three centres as shown out of ½-in. stuff), and the tracery infilling, which, being fine, might best be cut out of ⅛-in. fretwood or three-ply.

The arch framing has a small quirked bead worked on the angle ; to simplify, a plain chamfer might be substituted. The half columns are, of course, turned, with square top members to the cap and the base. The doors, as shown in the illustration (Fig. 19), are of a somewhat uncommon form of construction. Instead of a framed panel in the manner usual nowadays, they are in one solid piece rather more than ¾ in. thick, probably being made thus to facilitate carving the wood and fitting the lock-plate. This is one reason for the use of the long "cross garnets" in place of ordinary modern butt hinges, as the grain of the wood being all one way (vertical) the doors would have a tendency to split if unsupported by long iron hinges. In the original, only one panel is carved, as shown, and whether one, or both, or neither be so treated is a matter for individual taste. If, however, the carving be attempted, an endeavour should be made to realise the flamboyant character of the work, as indicated on the detailed drawing of the panel. The locks will hardly be possible of reproduction as in the original, so judiciously selected turn-buckles in wrought-iron or copper, with drop handles, might reasonably be substituted.

A small mould, ⅞ in. by ½ in., is planted on below the cupboards, and serves to cover the joint between the shelf and the frame. It need hardly be added that the cupboards may have a vertical division as indicated by dotted lines on the plan, if this be desired.

DRAWING-ROOM CHINA CABINET

The centre cabinet illustrated by Fig. 20 can be made of mahogany inlaid with satinwood, various parts being kept as light as possible in order to produce a graceful effect. It will be noticed that, while each side is the same in appearance, one of them is constructed as a door (Figs. 21 and 22).

Such a cabinet may be made of any required size, the dimensions shown being: total height 4 ft. 9 in., width 1 ft. 9 in. The sides of the glazed cabinet are made

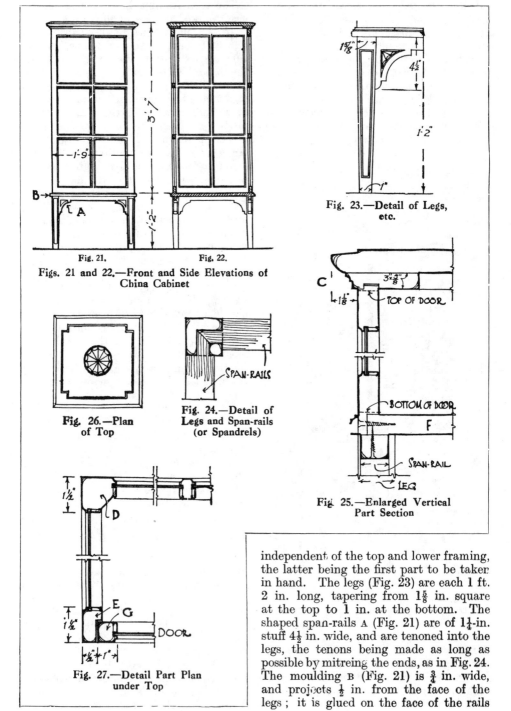

Fig. 21.   Fig. 22.

Figs. 21 and 22.—Front and Side Elevations of China Cabinet

Fig. 26.—Plan of Top

Fig. 24.—Detail of Legs and Span-rails (or Spandrels)

SPAN-RAILS

Fig. 23.—Detail of Legs, etc.

C — TOP OF DOOR

BOTTOM OF DOOR

F

SPAN-RAIL

LEG

Fig. 25.—Enlarged Vertical Part Section

DOOR

Fig. 27.—Detail Part Plan under Top

independent of the top and lower framing, the latter being the first part to be taken in hand. The legs (Fig. 23) are each 1 ft. 2 in. long, tapering from $1\frac{5}{8}$ in. square at the top to 1 in. at the bottom. The shaped span-rails A (Fig. 21) are of $1\frac{1}{4}$-in. stuff $4\frac{1}{2}$ in. wide, and are tenoned into the legs, the tenons being made as long as possible by mitreing the ends, as in Fig. 24. The moulding B (Fig. 21) is $\frac{3}{4}$ in. wide, and projects $\frac{1}{2}$ in. from the face of the legs ; it is glued on the face of the rails and legs and mitred at the corners. Before finally gluing together, the satinwood stringing on the outer faces of the legs and the fan pattern at the ends of the rails should be inlaid.

The top of the cabinet projects $1\frac{1}{8}$ in. all round. It is of 1-in. stuff, and underneath are 3-in. by $\frac{5}{8}$-in. strips mitred at the corners, these forming the lower member of the cornice when moulded,

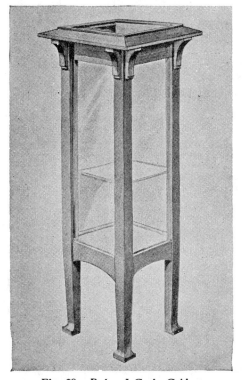

Fig. 28.—Pedestal Curio Cabinet

as at c in Fig. 25. These strips are well screwed to the underside of the top. On the upper face is a line of stringing $1\frac{1}{2}$ in. from the edge, breaking inwards $1\frac{1}{2}$ in. at the corners (see Fig. 26). In the centre is a fan-shaped patera 6 in. in diameter. This ornament is obtainable from inlayers, or it might be omitted.

The carcase now remains to be made, and it will be found that its jointing together requires neat and careful work-

manship. The corner posts on the side opposite the door are $1\frac{1}{2}$ in. square, with the inside corners bevelled off, as at D in Fig. 27. Those right and left of the door are $1\frac{1}{4}$ in. by $\frac{7}{8}$ in., as at E (Fig. 27), and the door stiles are 1 in. by $\frac{7}{8}$ in. The glazing bars are $\frac{3}{4}$ in. on the face and $\frac{7}{8}$ in. thick. The top rails are 2 in. by $\frac{7}{8}$ in. on the three fixed sides, worked as at c in Fig. 25, to fit a rebate on the top. The corresponding bottom rails are the same thickness and $2\frac{5}{8}$ in. wide, rebated to fit the pine bottom F (Fig. 25) $\frac{7}{8}$ in. thick.

The door has similar rails, but, of course, less by the amount of the rebates at the top and bottom (see the dotted lines in Fig. 25). Its stiles G (Fig. 27) are 1 in. by $\frac{7}{8}$ in. To receive the glazing a $\frac{3}{16}$-in. rebate is worked on the bars and framing, the edges next to the glass being hollowed with a quarter-circle moulding, as shown on the details. A line of satinwood stringing would be an improvement in the middle of the bars, and on the stiles, posts, and rails.

Two shelves will be required level with the horizontal glazing bars. They may be of pine covered with a suitable shade of velveteen (the bottom being covered with the same material); or of plate-glass with polished edges, fixed on small brackets at each corner.

The outside glass should be fixed with narrow beads as shown. Three small butt hinges and a very narrow lock will complete the cabinet.

PEDESTAL CURIO CABINET

The pedestal curio cabinet here illustrated might very suitably be executed in mahogany, and will have the general appearance shown in Fig. 28. It consists of a framework about 9 in. square and 3 ft. high, finishing with a top 1 ft. 1 in. square with small curved brackets under. All the sides and the top are glazed, access to the interior being obtained when required by lifting off the top and sliding out one of the glass sides. The intermediate shelves would be spaced at the correct distances to suit the in-

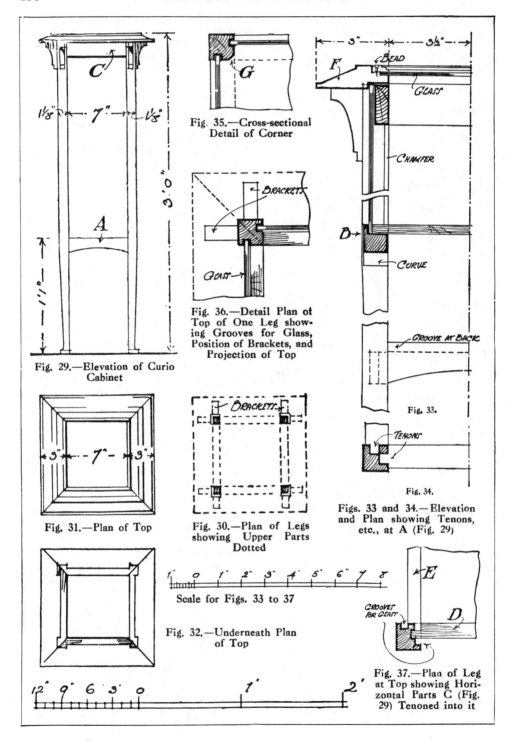

Fig. 29.—Elevation of Curio Cabinet

Fig. 35.—Cross-sectional Detail of Corner

Fig. 36.—Detail Plan of Top of One Leg showing Grooves for Glass, Position of Brackets, and Projection of Top

Fig. 31.—Plan of Top

Fig. 30.—Plan of Legs showing Upper Parts Dotted

Figs. 33 and 34.—Elevation and Plan showing Tenons, etc., at A (Fig. 29)

Scale for Figs. 33 to 37

Fig. 32.—Underneath Plan of Top

Fig. 37.—Plan of Leg at Top showing Horizontal Parts C (Fig. 29) Tenoned into it

tended contents, and should be of light plate-glass with polished rounded edges.

Fig. 29 is a side elevation, and three plans are shown by Figs. 30, 31 and 32. The elevation shows the main legs, which are intended to be 2 ft. 11¼ in. long, and about 1⅛ in. square finished sizes. From about 12 in. above the floor they are tapered off on their outer faces only to ¾ in. square, being simply finished thus, or curved out again to form feet 1⅛ in. square as shown, at the discretion of the craftsman. Four bearers, as at A (Fig. 29), are then prepared 1¾ in. by 1 in. and 7¾ in. long, being tenoned into the legs ⅜ in. at each end, cut to a slight segmental curve on their undersides, and worked with a rebate ¾ in. wide and ⅜ in. deep along their top back edges. One of these is shown in section in Fig. 33, with the tenons required at each leg. A plan is shown by Fig. 34. The method of supporting the bottom (which can be fitted afterwards, and would be about ⅜ in. thick) is shown in Fig. 33, care being taken that it allows the glass sides to slide right home at B. It will require to be cut to fit closely at the angles, as at G in Fig. 35, the chamfer on the leg at this point being mentioned later.

Before any of the work is fixed together, narrow grooves should be worked up the inner faces of each leg to take the glass, starting from the point B in Fig. 33, and continuing right to the top. These grooves should be about ¼ in. back from the outside faces of the legs, and the glass should fit as closely as possible ; they are shown in Figs. 35, 36 and 37. The other connection between the legs is made by means of four horizontal pieces, as at C (Fig. 29), also shown in section in Fig. 33, from which it will be seen that they are intended to be 1¼ in. deep and sufficiently thin to avoid obstructing the glass. Two of these on opposite sides (that is, parallel to each other) should first be tenoned into the legs as at D on the part plan in Fig. 37, and the two others fixed as at E afterwards. The next step will be to prepare a length of moulding something like that shown at F in Fig. 33, 3 in. wide and 1 in. deep, having a double rebate along the inside top edge. The first or lower rebate is for the glass top, and the second to receive a small moulded bead as shown, either screwed or bradded in position, to secure the glass. The underside has another rebate not more than ¼ in. deep, and just sufficiently wide to take the horizontal pieces below and the top of the glass along each edge.

After the moulding has been mitred together like a picture-frame with an opening 7 in. square, the rebate on the underside should be extended at the corners, as indicated in Fig. 32, in order to fit closely over the top ends of the legs. When this has been done, the eight cut brackets may be prepared out of, say, ⅝-in. or ¾-in. stuff, each 3 in. long, and secured to the legs as closely as possible under the top portion, but, of course, not actually fixed to it, although, if desired, small catches of the hook-and-eye variety can be fixed under the top so that it is held down to a couple of the brackets. But it would not do to attempt carrying the case about by means of the top, unless special precautions are adopted to allow for this. For a very good job it might be worth while to house each of the brackets ¼ in. into the legs.

The intermediate glass shelves can easily be arranged for by slightly chamfering off the inside angle of each of the legs, as at G in Fig. 35, and putting in small brass screw-eyes to support the corners at the required levels.

CROMWELLIAN CABINET AND A MODERN VARIATION

Dating from the first half of the seventeenth century, the massive oaken cabinet shown by the half-tone reproduction (Fig. 38) forms a good example of English work of its period. The elaboration —or, rather, profusion—of its ornament is somewhat too overpowering to be desirable in a modern reproduction ; but in the deep tones of the original they are not at all obtrusive. A careful inspection of the illustration will show that while the construction itself is direct enough, every possible opportunity has been seized to introduce a band of strap-work, a guilloche, or some rather primitive carving, all exhibiting the Jacobean influence. This decoration, it is assumed, would be eliminated in work inspired by study of the cabinet, the result being more restful and, indeed, more refined drawers below and two shallow ones above, while at the top is a recessed part (as shown by the half plan, Fig. 41) in the shape of three cupboards, in front of which a pair of the characteristic columns or balusters of the time support a frieze, and this in turn a cornice mitreing

Fig. 38.—Cromwellian Cabinet

in consequence. For explanatory purposes rather than as working drawings, Figs. 39 and 40 show the side and half-front elevations respectively of the cabinet almost as it stands, although a certain number of modifications have been introduced. It consists of a large cupboard with a pair of doors, having two deep round projecting brackets or trusses. The end elevation (Fig. 40) is of interest as showing that the idea of concentrating all the work on the front is of fairly ancient date. The framing is square and perfectly plain; the explanation of the curious appearance of the right-hand stile is that this is the side view of the 4-in. stile showing on the front, this being 4 in. by 1¾ in. and substantial enough, although it would scarcely be considered satisfactory in appearance.

The principal modifications introduced in these first figures are as follows : (1) A reduction of the upright division between the large doors A (Fig. 39) to 4 in. wide similar to those at the outsides, instead of as in the original, which is 7½ in. wide and has a carved band down it, and incidentally is really a sham, being actually attached to the left-hand door and opening with it. (2) Altering the bottom drawers to keep them central with the doors above, and not as in the half-tone. (3) Improving the design of the fat balusters and reducing their bulk. (4) Substituting a pair of plain brackets for each of the three in the half-tone, which are of varying widths.

Of course, for modern purposes this piece of furniture is open to criticism, more especially because of its great size and consequent weight, and also on account of the inaccessibility of the upper drawers ; but given such an example as a pattern, there is much to be gathered from it, and many different ways in which it can be varied, retaining, however, the old character. In Figs. 42 and 43 there is such a variation, itself liable to receive similar treatment. This design shows a cabinet of 1-ft. 6-in. projection and 4-ft. 10½-in. width, standing 6 ft. 7 in. over all, as compared with 1 ft. 10 in. by 5 ft. 9 in. by 7 ft. 2 in. in height, as in the first ; and these reduced dimensions (together with the fact that the work can be made in three independent parts) bring it within reasonable limits. Needless to say, four drawers might be substituted for the two shown, and the top cupboards might have larger doors ; or these could be solid, with pieces planted on to form the arrangement first shown (Fig. 39) ; and the extra mitres in the main cornice, as well as the enriched moulding, can be varied to suit. Material is largely a matter of choice, pine or oak being the most suitable, and in the latter case the thicknesses throughout can be reduced.

Reviewing the construction of this second scheme in detail, the lower part (up to the level of B, Fig. 42) is formed at the ends with ordinary square panelled framing tongued into a groove in a 4-in. by 1¼-in. upright stile C (Fig. 44), decorated on the face with two sinkings $\frac{1}{16}$ in. deep, separated from the angles and in the centre by plain bands ⅝ in. wide. This stile is framed up in the usual way with horizontal rails D and E (Figs. 45 and 42) about 2¼ in. deep, E having, in addition, a rough continuous piece F (Fig. 45) fixed below to bear on the floor, this applying to the ends also, the whole being finished by the application of a moulded skirting 3½ in. high kept up just clear of the floor as shown. The central upright is 2¼ in. wide, and has one sinking similar to those on the ends. and it has a piece of plain stuff fixed on each side G (Fig. 42), which also occurs at the outer ends to keep the moulding to the drawer clear of it. The side framing is rebated at the back H (Fig. 44) to receive a stout back, which should be panelled if possible, and which will serve to make rigid the whole work if properly fixed, a point which is further secured by making the boarded bottom to the cupboard above as a part of this piece of the structure, fitting it partly into a rebate worked on D (Fig. 45), and running the grain from back to front rather than lengthwise.

The drawers will be made in the ordinary way, but with a moulding about 1 in. wide mitred round their fronts. They must slide on grooved runners blocked out to suit, as in Fig. 46. A small moulding J (Fig. 45) is mitred round the top of this part, projecting a little above the top of D.

The next stage of the design is that situated between B and K on Fig. 42, and continues with similar construction to that described for the base, namely, a plain side or end in six panels tongued to C (Fig. 44) as before, and fitted to a stout panelled back ; C is framed up with horizontal pieces L (Fig. 45) in front 1¾ in. by 1¼ in. below, and 2 in. by 1¼ in. at the top M (Fig. 47). The central upright is *fixed* (not as in the old) between

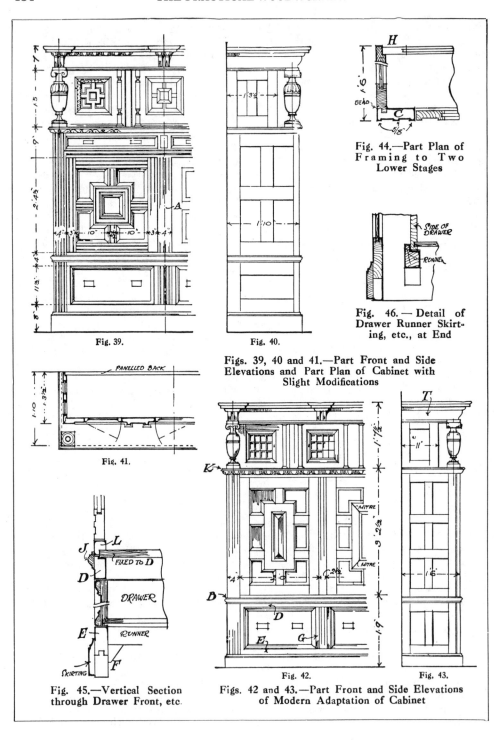

Fig. 39.

Fig. 40.

Fig. 44.—Part Plan of Framing to Two Lower Stages

Fig. 46. — Detail of Drawer Runner Skirting, etc., at End

Figs. 39, 40 and 41.—Part Front and Side Elevations and Part Plan of Cabinet with Slight Modifications

PANELLED BACK

Fig. 41.

FIXED TO D

DRAWER

RUNNER

SKIRTING

Fig. 45.—Vertical Section through Drawer Front, etc.

Fig. 42.

Fig. 43.

Figs. 42 and 43.—Part Front and Side Elevations of Modern Adaptation of Cabinet

these, and has strips planted down it on the inside to form stops to the doors. The latter are of 1-in. framing, 3 in. wide next the edges, the inner pieces being $2\frac{1}{4}$ in. Each door is in seven panels as shown, with small mouldings mitred round, and the middle panel bevelled or raised if desired. The framing surrounding it should be mitred at the angles, as indicated on the right of Fig. 42. This work might be carried out in the manner adopted for the little top doors in the original cabinet, where it is all made up of thin stuff planted on the face of a plain square panel; and this will simplify the work, which will, however, lose a certain value as regards the sincerity of its construction.

The second stage should be finished with a top cross-tongued together as one piece N (Fig. 47), with a wide shallow rebate and a moulded edge projecting about $1\frac{3}{8}$ in. on the three exposed sides, finished as shown with a bold moulding carved if possible, although a plain quadrant section would look well. Probably this part as a whole would seldom be taken off the base, to which it will be seen to fit securely without fear of movement by reference to L (Fig. 45), and would apply at this part equally as a section through the ends.

The top stage still remains to be described, and is shown in detail by Figs. 47, 48 and 49. It has a panelled back rebated into a square end, all as below, except that the end is only 11 in. wide and is mitred into the end of the front O (Fig. 49). In order to make the frieze come properly over the column (which must be kept central with the stile below), the face of the end framing must be set back $\frac{1}{2}$ in. from that below, as noted on Fig. 49; but as the stile at O should be kept central with the column, it is consequently reduced to 3 in. in width, and may be plain or sunk on the face as desired. It should be about $1\frac{3}{8}$ in. thick, rebated as shown in Fig. 49, to take a piece of $\frac{7}{8}$-in. framing P arranged to show a margin of 2 in. all round the small cupboard door. Three of these margins will be required tongued

into uprights 5 in. by $1\frac{1}{4}$ in., as at Q, sunk on their faces, which will each show 4 in. similarly to the stiles in the lower part of the cabinet. Each upright is finished with a plain piece about 1 in. square, as at R (these are turned balusters in the old work).

The cupboard doors are simply fairly bold mouldings mitred together and rebated for panels or leaded glazing, which latter would be a pleasing introduction. A small stop will be required as at S (Fig. 49), and when completed neat little mouldings as caps and bases should be mitred round the pieces R, as shown in Fig. 49.

The columns, which are 5 in. in diameter and $13\frac{1}{2}$ in. long, can be turned for a distance of $10\frac{3}{4}$ in., leaving a square base and also a block for the cap. The turned part is finished plain surface or having the upper part of the body carved to the fluted design shown in Fig. 48. It will not be a difficult matter to set out the volutes of the caps $1\frac{3}{4}$ in. deep, and to carve them to shape, sloping the front decidedly, as on the side view (Fig. 47), and forming alternate wide and narrow ridges, as are there indicated. While the columns are proposed to be made removable, the cornice and fascia should be fixed to the cupboard framing, the end part of which should be connected to a piece T (Fig. 43) $1\frac{1}{4}$ in. thick and 5 in. deep, its end shaped as at U (Fig. 47), the front fascia being jointed into it as in Fig. 50, which also indicates one of the brackets planted on (V); these latter can be plain or sunk on face. An abacus or block $3\frac{1}{2}$ in. square is arranged to come centrally over each column (Fig. 48), and a small bead is planted along the fascia in a line with it. A piece of filling-in is tongued on the top of the framing surrounding the cupboard doors W (Fig. 47) to make it level with the top of the fascia. A thin soffit X (Fig. 47) is fitted in with the aid of angle-blocks and a small bead, and the top boarding is put on with the grain running from back to front overhanging the fascia $2\frac{1}{2}$ in., and broken out farther over the brackets if desired. Its edges are finished with a square slip and moulding as at Y, making the projection about $3\frac{1}{2}$ in., and a good-size bed-mould, which should be returned round the brackets. It will be a simple matter

The fitting up of the interior depends so much on the destined uses of the cabinet, that no suggestions bearing on this work are put forward.

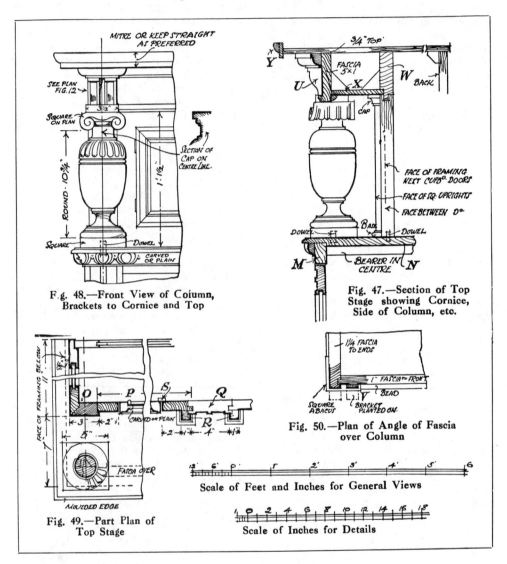

Fig. 48.—Front View of Column, Brackets to Cornice and Top

Fig. 47.—Section of Top Stage showing Cornice, Side of Column, etc.

Fig. 49.—Part Plan of Top Stage

Fig. 50.—Plan of Angle of Fascia over Column

Scale of Feet and Inches for General Views

Scale of Inches for Details

to fix dowels in the top of the middle part of the cabinet, fitting into holes in the bottom of the work just described, to keep same in position, and its own weight will be sufficient to keep it rigid if this is properly done.

CABINET FOR THE DINING-ROOM

The cabinet shown by Fig. 51 would, if executed in mahogany, harmonise quite well with Chippendale furniture, and the design is such that with slight modifications it could be made to match existing inlaid furniture. The shaped edges of the doors could be substituted with inlaid stringing. The particular arrangement of this cabinet is that of glazed cupboards at the sides, with an enclosed cupboard in the centre part. It may be desired to have all the cupboards with glazed doors, in which case the centre door can be

furniture it will be found most economical in the long run to make a full-size drawing on some ceiling or lining paper, and for this purpose the scale drawings will be found invaluable. Two elevations are shown by Figs. 52 and 53. The scale shown should be transferred to a slip of paper, so that the true sizes may be taken off, and then half the whole elevation

Fig. 51.—Dining-room Cabinet

readily adapted to a design harmonising with the side doors. It does not necessarily follow that a centre door with " barred " design should exactly resemble the side doors, because in actual practice it will be found that a simple centre door, designed in good proportion and without curved bars, will give a certain relief to the side ones, and obviate an overcrowded appearance.

When making practically any piece of

should be drawn. A scale sectional elevation (Fig. 54) is given, which should be drawn full size at the side of the half elevation. With such a drawing it should be quite an easy matter to obtain all the sizes required when making. Fig. 55 is a vertical section.

The construction is fairly simple, as the whole piece may be regarded as four separate parts, namely, stand or base, carcase, frieze, and top. After cutting

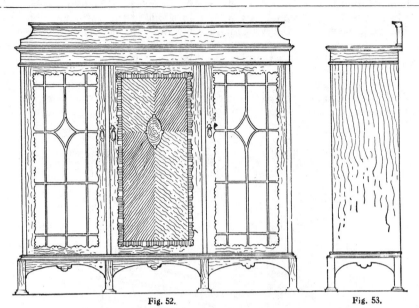

Fig. 52.

Fig. 53.

Figs. 52 and 53.—Front and Side Elevations of Dining-room Cabinet

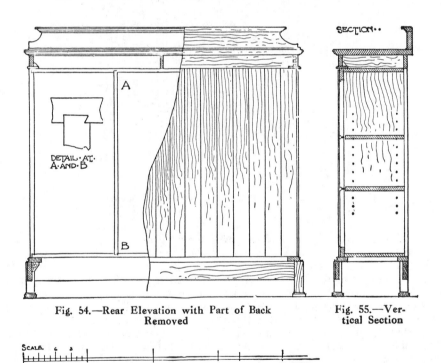

DETAIL·AT·
A·AND·B

A

B

SECTION··

Fig. 54.—Rear Elevation with Part of Back
Removed

Fig. 55.—Ver-
tical Section

SCALE
INCHES
1   2   3 FEET

out and planing up all the pieces required to make the whole job, it would be best to begin making the stand. The long back and front rails are therefore mortised and tenoned into the outside legs, and this is followed up by tenoning the short end rails into the legs. When this part has been completed the inside legs may be bridled over the front rail. This is effected by cutting away a groove on the front of the rail just the width of the legs, and then the remaining thickness of the rail is cut out of the leg in order to form a prong or fork which fits into the rail. If machinery is employed, all the rails can then be taken out, and the front and end ones shaped. It is inadvisable to cut the shape near

and B (Fig. 54). This is generally called slip-dovetailing, and the partitions should be made ¼ in. longer at each end for the slip dovetail. It is best to cut the slip dovetails in the top and bottom first, stopping them ¼ in. from the front edge, and then shoulders and dovetails should be cut on the partitions to fit the socketed parts. Alternatively the partitions may be pinned or tenoned through the top and bottom, in which case it is customary to wedge the tenons after the job has been glued together. Both the top and the bottom should be lap-dovetailed to the carcase ends. A matched back is indicated in the back view, which is quite good for a strong carcase of this type. The joints would, of course, be grooved

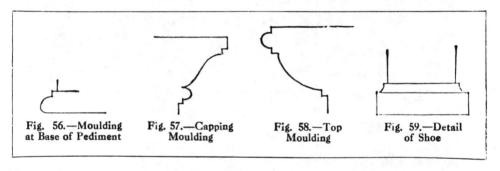

Fig. 56.—Moulding at Base of Pediment   Fig. 57.—Capping Moulding   Fig. 58.—Top Moulding   Fig. 59.—Detail of Shoe

the legs, as this short grain may break away. A little wood should therefore be left on these parts, and finally taken down to the finished shape when the stand has been glued up. If executed by hand, the shapes may be cut with a bow-saw, and then finished as indicated above.

After the stand has been glued up, the legs may be cut off level with the rails and the whole planed perfectly level. A centre cross-rail can be introduced with advantage. The mouldings are then mitred round to the section shown in the sectional view, and the blocks indicated glued to the mouldings and the rails at intervals of about 3 in. in order to strengthen the whole stand.

The construction of the main carcase is fairly straightforward. An enlarged detail is shown of the joints used at A

CUTTING LIST FOR CABINET

No.	For.	Lgth. ft. in.	Wh. in.	Th. in.	Wood.	Pcs.	Remarks.
1	Legs ..	6¾	1	1¾	mahog.	6	Straight grain
2	Front rail ..	4 3	3¼	1¼	,,	1	,, ,,
3	End rails ..	1 1¼	3.	1¼	,,	2	,, ,,
4	Back rail ..	4 3	4¼	1¼	,,	1	,, ,,
5	Cross rail ..	1 1¼	2¼	⅞	wh'w'd	1	,, ,,
6	Moulding ..	7 0	⅞	⅞	m. hog.	1	Cuts 3 lengths
7	Carcase ends..	2 9¼	12¼	½	,,	2	Figured stuff
8	Back ..	2 10	3¼	⅜	wh'w'd	17	Vee-jointed
9	Top..	4 2	11½	⅞	,,	1	
10	Bottom ..	4 2	11¼	⅞	,,	1	
11	Divisions ..	2 9¼	12¼	⅞	mahog.	2	Straight grain
12	Door stiles ..	2 10¾	1¾	⅞	,,	6	,, ,,
13	Rails ..	1 2	1¾	⅞	,,	2	,, ,,
14	Centre rails ..	1 4¼	1¾	⅞	,,	2	,, ,,
15	Panel ..	2 7¼	14	⅛	,,	1	Plain for veneering
16	Frieze front ..	4 3	2¼	⅞	,,	1	
17	Ends ..	1 1	2¼	⅞	,,	2	
18	Back ..	4 3	3	⅝	wh'w'd	1	
19	Mould'ng ..	6 6	2¼	½	mahog.	1	Cuts 3 lengths
20	Moulded top ..	4 3¼	14¼	⅞	,,	1	Figured
21	Pediment ..	4 2¼	3¼	⅞	,,	1	
22	Top mould'ng	4 0	1⅞	⅞	,,	1	
23	Base ..	4 3¼	1⅜	⅝	,,	1	

and tongued, and the inside parts V'd to give the necessary finish. Two screws

Fig. 60.—Cabinet in Ebony

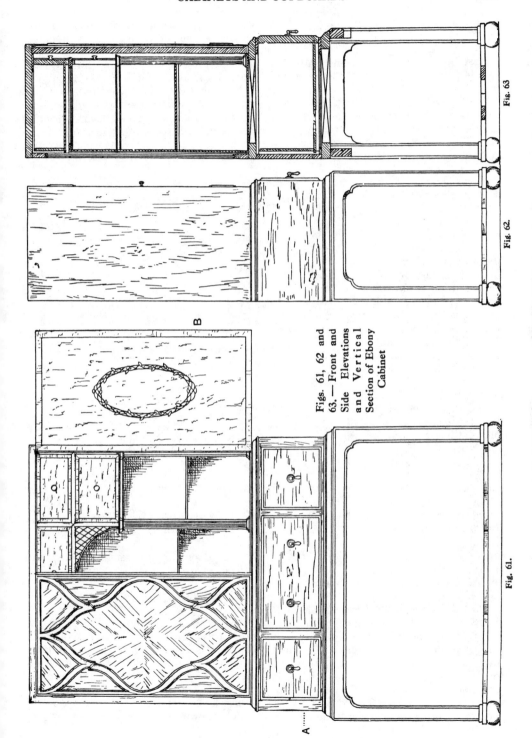

Figs. 61, 62 and 63. — Front and Side Elevations and Vertical Section of Ebony Cabinet

Fig. 61.

Fig. 62.

Fig. 63

should be used to secure each board at the top and bottom, and particular care must be exercised in order to keep the carcase quite square whilst the matching is being fixed, or an untrue carcase will result.

The frieze box can next be made. This should be of solid mahogany, and the front corners mitre-dovetailed. The back can be lap-dovetailed, as indicated in the back view. It will be seen that the back rail is made rather wider, so that the bottom edge will be level when the mouldings are mitred round. The moulded top is next made and secured to the frieze by pocket-screwing from the inside. The pediment does not present any special difficulty, it being simply shaped as shown with base and capping mouldings attached. Details of the various moulds, etc., are shown by Figs. 56 to 59.

The doors should be mortised and tenoned together, then rebated, and the slats fitted to receive the bar mouldings. Each door should have the slats first fitted in all straight lengths, stub-tenoning the ends into the doors, and halving the slats where they cross. Separate curved diamond centres should then be prepared by fitting curved pieces round a diamond shape, and keying the corners with veneer. When these are dry they can be taken off the blocks, and cut into the straight bars with V'd joints. For additional strength small slips of silk or linen should be glued into the angles, and the bars can be mitred over the slats. The usual bar is astragal; but with this design a plain rectangular one can be introduced, with the front corners slightly rounded. The

curved edges can be cut and finished after the bars have been glued on. The shelves for this bookcase should rest on fillets, so that the front edges coincide with the second and third bar from the bottom.

The veneering of the centre door should be effected by fitting and gluing the pieces down to stiff paper, and then veneering the panel with a caul, the paper being removed after the veneering is dry. Bullet or French catches should be used

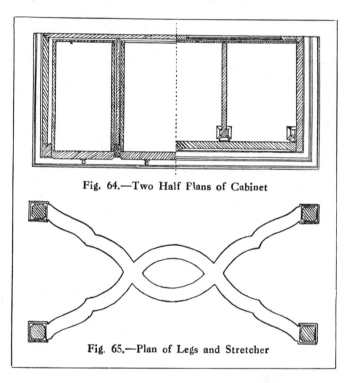

Fig. 64.—Two Half Plans of Cabinet

Fig. 65.—Plan of Legs and Stretcher

for the doors in preference to locks and keys.

CABINET IN EBONY

In the cabinet shown by Fig. 60 the same idea has been followed as used in the Queen Anne periods and in a good deal of Spanish work, namely, a closed cabinet with drawers, etc., inside, the whole on a stand. The woods used are ebony and an uncommon coromandel of a rich brown colour, and a broad figure something like walnut, the whole having a rich though perhaps a quiet effect. On opening the doors an interesting change is obtained by the interior being lined with satinwood, inlaid with ivory. Front and end elevations are shown by Figs. 61 and 62, and two half plans by Fig. 64. A vertical section is presented by Fig. 63, and a plan of the legs stretcher by Fig. 65. The two half plans are on the levels A and B (Fig. 61). The reproduced drawings are to a scale of 1 in. to 1 ft.

The constructional part is in mahogany. The top carcase is secret dovetailed at the angles, the inside fittings (the drawers are made in cedar) being worked in with the carcase. It is perhaps worthy of note that the doors are of one plain piece, with no clamps; this has stood perfectly.

The shaped mouldings are applied. Though on the drawing the ends, etc., appear to be bare, actually the figure of the wood overcomes that. The three deep drawers in the lower carcase project with a simple moulding on the corners. All the large mouldings are frames faced with ebony. The stand is on plain ebony legs, with an ovolo moulding worked on each edge, and is held at the bottom with a shaped stretcher, the four diagonals of which are framed into the centre piece. The whole stands on ball feet. All arrises are protected by small ebony corners. The handles and hinges are oxidised, and the interior knobs are of ivory.

The outside sizes are : height 5 ft. 1½ in., extreme width 3 ft. 1 in., extreme depth 1 ft. 4 in.

Fancy Boxes

INLAID TRIPLE WORK-BOX

AN effective triple work-box inlaid in mother-of-pearl with ornamental brass hinges at the sides that enable it to

A very simple method of jointing together the corners of the trays is suggested, a skilled worker, however, being quite at liberty to adopt a more elaborate system.

A convenient size for the work-box

Fig. 1.—Inlaid Triple Work-box

open out into three trays is shown by Fig. 1. The box is shown open by Fig. 2, this illustration rendering clearly the working of the hinges, there being nothing in the construction of the box and hinges that an amateur could not undertake.

would be 10½ in. by 8½ in. by 7 in. deep, the trays measuring 2 in. deep in each case and the lid 1 in. deep. Mahogany or satin walnut would be the most suitable material for making the box, a thickness of ⅜ in. being required for the sides,

444

and thinner material serving for the top of the box and the bottom of the trays.

Begin by preparing the material for the sides of the trays and lids. Cut six pieces measuring $8\frac{1}{2}$ in. by 2 in., six pieces $10\frac{1}{2}$ in. by 2 in., two pieces $8\frac{1}{2}$ in. by 1 in., and two $10\frac{1}{2}$ in. by 1 in., and plane up all carefully to the exact measurements. The corners are mitred together, the next item being therefore to plane them all to an angle of 45°, as shown by A (Fig. 3). Mark a line $\frac{3}{8}$ in. from one edge, and then carefully plane away the corner up to that line as indicated by B. Before joining together the corners it will be necessary to cut a rebate in the top and bottom of each piece forming the sides of the trays, so that they nicely fit into one another. Fig. 4 shows how the sides of the three trays are cut. A rebate is made in the top edge of each, measuring $\frac{1}{4}$ in. by $\frac{1}{4}$ in., and at the bottom on the inner face measuring $\frac{3}{8}$ in. by $\frac{1}{4}$ in., this being made a little deeper to allow for fitting in a bottom $\frac{1}{8}$ in. thick. An ordinary marking gauge, with the point substituted by a sharp cutter, will serve for cutting the rebates if one does not happen to possess a rebate plane. Clean up with a glass-paper block, slightly rounding off the tops as indicated. A similar rebate is cut in the sides of the lid, omitting, of course, to cut one round the top edges.

A simple method of jointing, and one that yields a good appearance if neatly done, is by keying the corners together (see Fig. 5). Two saw-cuts are made in each corner as indicated, then a strip of $\frac{1}{16}$-in. beech, coated with glue, is hammered in. In order to obtain a good fit of the trays, the complete article should be carefully squared up and tied together with strong string before the saw-cuts are made, the glued strips being then driven in and the work allowed to dry.

For the bottom of the trays prepare three pieces of $\frac{1}{8}$-in. fretwood measuring $10\frac{1}{4}$ in. by $8\frac{1}{4}$ in., and glue into the rebate at the bottom of each tray. A nice piece measuring $10\frac{1}{2}$ in. by $8\frac{1}{2}$ in. by $\frac{1}{4}$ in. should be prepared for the top, this not being glued in place until the small amount of inlaying has been done.

Fig. 6 gives the patterns of the hinges on an enlarged scale, the three parts being next drawn out to the required size. These are sawn out of brass of about the thickness of a sixpence, the little engraved work included in the design being done afterwards. Care must be taken that the screw-holes for fixing the hinge are set out in line (see Fig. 7) to ensure it working properly, it being observed that the greater the slope given to the plates the wider the trays will open. Having obtained a pattern on thin paper, paste on to the metal, and saw out with a fret-saw with fine teeth, truing up with a needle file on completion. When the engraving is completed run a little sealing-wax into the lines, and then clean up with fine emery-cloth and oil. The hinges are then fixed with $\frac{1}{4}$-in. large-headed screws, leaving enough play for the plates to easily move.

Fig. 8 gives the pattern of the mother-of-pearl fish which is inlaid in a piece of brass of elliptical form in the centre of the lid. Obtain a piece of brass about 3 in. by 2 in., and a piece of mother-of-pearl slightly smaller of the same thickness, and gum together with a piece of paper in between. The two materials are cut out at the same time, the pattern being pasted on the upper one. Thus, after sawing out, one will fit into the other when separated, if a vertical cut has been made all round. Mark out the form of the ellipse on the lid, and then cut to the same depth as the thickness of the brass, taking care, in chiselling out, to obtain a level bottom and a recess no deeper than the brass. Cement in with glue and whiting, then when dry level off. The two fish on the front of the trays are inlaid similarly, the patterns being given by Figs. 9 and 10.

Fig. 11 gives the pattern of the hinged clasp, the design of which is based on seaweed. For making this, a piece of metal measuring $4\frac{1}{2}$ in. by $1\frac{1}{2}$ in. will be necessary for the lower part, and a piece 4 in. by $\frac{3}{4}$ in. for the upper. For the hinge obtain a $1\frac{1}{4}$-in. length of small brass tubing, and solder to the edge of the upper half (Fig. 12). Divide this

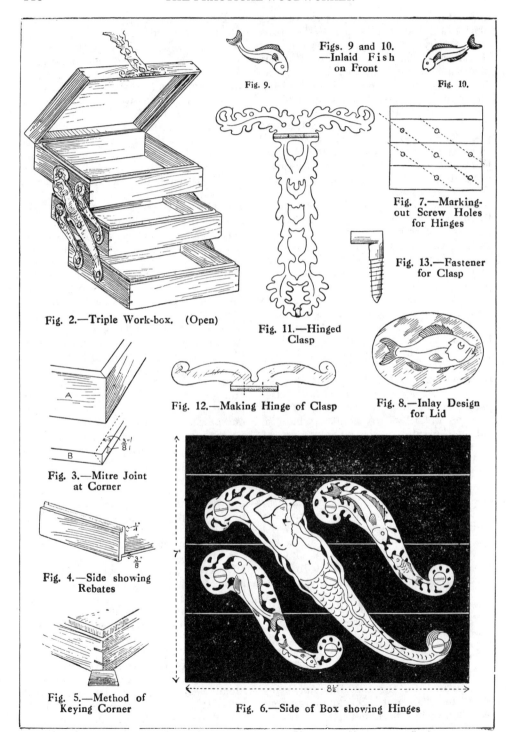

Figs. 9 and 10.
—Inlaid Fish
on Front

Fig. 9.

Fig. 10.

Fig. 7.—Marking-out Screw Holes for Hinges

Fig. 13.—Fastener for Clasp

Fig. 2.—Triple Work-box. (Open)

Fig. 11.—Hinged Clasp

Fig. 8.—Inlay Design for Lid

Fig. 3.—Mitre Joint at Corner

Fig. 12.—Making Hinge of Clasp

Fig. 4.—Side showing Rebates

Fig. 5.—Method of Keying Corner

Fig. 6.—Side of Box showing Hinges

into three, and then saw away the middle section as shown. This being soldered to the edge of the other section of the clasp and a pin put through the whole, the hinge is complete. Screw the upper plate to the lid with $\frac{1}{4}$-in. screws, and then file a screw, as shown by Fig. 13, for fastening the clasp, the screw being turned upwards when it is required to unfasten it.

Glue on the top of the lid, which is hinged with a pair of $\frac{3}{4}$-in. brass hinges, then the work-box is complete and ready for polishing.

VENEERED MAHOGANY WORK-BOX

The work-box illustrated by Fig. 14 has been designed with a view to showing a good application of veneering. It depends for its decoration on well-arranged figured veneers of contrasting colours. The interior of the box is shown in Fig. 15. A section and interior plan are given by Figs. 16 and 17.

As is indicated in the diagrams showing the arrangement of the top and sides (Figs. 18 and 19), the three veneers selected are : " well-figured Cuba mahogany " veneer, " curl " veneer, and " fiddle back." The curl veneer should be the darkest in colour, and the fiddle back the lightest. The various veneers vary in colour according to the age of the wood, and care must be exercised in the preliminary selection to ensure the necessary contrasts of colour. It is usual in first-class work of this character to accentuate or diminish the colours of the various veneers by slightly staining some before polishing the whole. To obtain a successful result, however, this must be done by an experienced polisher, as otherwise the sharpness of the design is likely to be spoiled. If the veneers are well chosen in the first instance, the finished job can be stained all over with bichromate of potash stain, which darkens all the veneers without making the lightest of them very dark in colour. As the effect so much depends on the relative colour values of the various veneers, it will be

found a good plan to make up a small piece of veneering together with the box, which may be usefully experimented on before the box is stained and polished.

The interior of the box is fitted with a tray containing two spaces, one being fitted with a lid. The inside of the lid is intended to be padded with silk, the necessary thickness being made up with wadding, with the silk buttoned down at intervals to produce the cushioned effect. The main box or groundwork for the veneering is made with secret dovetailed corners, as is indicated in Fig. 20. It will be seen from A and B in Fig. 20 that a wide pin is introduced near the top. This is made larger, so that when the lid is cut away from the bottom part, the proper shoulder or half-pin is left on each part. The box sides, back, and front should be rebated at the bottom as indicated, in order to receive the bottom. This feature can also be introduced to advantage at the top in order to obviate the end grain for veneering on. When the parts have been dovetailed together and the insides cleaned up, the top and bottom should be fitted and glued in position. When thoroughly dry the whole is planed up perfectly square and true, and then toothed sized before veneering. The sizing can be done with weak glue well rubbed into the grain of the wood, using a short-haired glue-brush. When the size has quite dried, any excess should be removed by toothing down with a very fine toothing plane.

The next step is the preparation of the veneer (*see also* section on veneering), and it must be emphasised that veneers should be well shrunk before they are worked up and laid. Veneer is usually cut from solid wood in a more or less moist condition, in order to reduce the risk of splitting. Should the veneer not be well dried before laying, shrinkage takes place and shows itself by frequent cracks on the surface. This is particularly the case in regard to curl veneers, this particular kind shrinking a good deal. Many otherwise excellent pieces of furniture veneered with " curl " show cracks in the surface after a few months, and to prevent this shrinking before laying is absolutely essential. Curl and other figured veneers also require flatting, which is done at the same time as shrinking. It

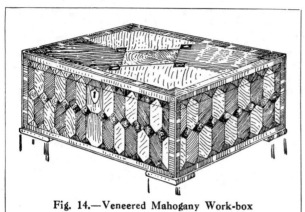

Fig. 14.—Veneered Mahogany Work-box

is a good plan to moisten the veneer first if it is very buckled in order to prevent splitting it when pressed flat. After the veneer is moistened in small sheets, $\frac{1}{2}$-in. pinewood pieces are made very hot on a plate or over a shaving blaze. The veneers are then placed between them, and the whole lightly hand-screwed together. This is repeated three or four times until all the moisture has been drawn out of the veneer, and it will be readily understood that the pressure and heat, in addition to properly shrinking the wood, will have made the veneer leaves absolutely flat. If the veneers are exposed to the air again they will have a tendency to buckle. To obviate this they should be laid on the bench with a covering board and a weight.

The veneers being properly prepared, the next step is to take the veneering in hand. Cartridge paper should first be damp-stretched on an old drawing or other flat board, a margin

about $\frac{1}{2}$ in. wide only being glued. When the paper has thoroughly dried, a line-drawing should be made of the top, sides, and front. A sharp, hard pencil should be used in order to ensure absolute accuracy. All the lines indicated in the parts should be shown with the exception of the $\frac{1}{8}$-in. edging. The crossbanding, it should be noted, should run to the extreme edges in the first instance. The line-drawings having been prepared, the lozenge-shaped pieces can be partly prepared by gauging off strips as indicated in B[1] in Fig. 21. A small mitre cut is then prepared as indicated in diagram D[1] in order to facilitate cutting the ends. The procedure necessary to complete the veneering is almost identical with the various parts.

As an example, the front will first be

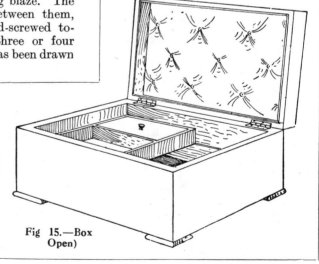

Fig 15.—Box Open)

considered. A length of cross-banding should first be gauged off the fiddle-back veneer, mitred at each end, and then lightly glued down to the drawing.

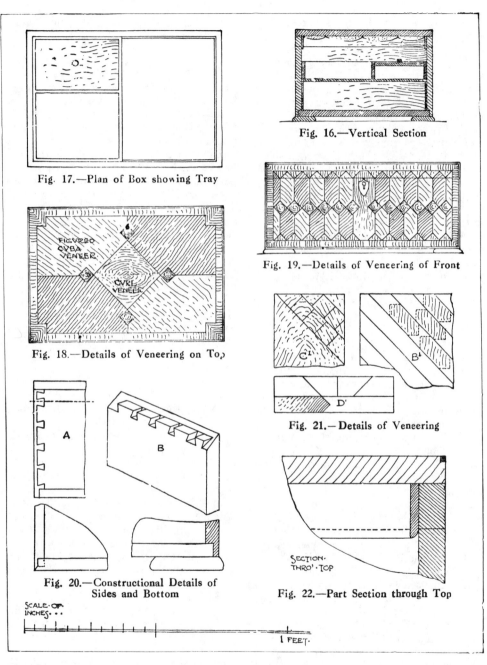

Fig. 17.—Plan of Box showing Tray

Fig. 16.—Vertical Section

Fig. 19.—Details of Veneering of Front

Fig. 18.—Details of Veneering on Top

Fig. 21.—Details of Veneering

Fig. 20.—Constructional Details of Sides and Bottom

Fig. 22.—Part Section through Top

Should it not be possible to obtain each length in one piece, butt-joints between various short pieces should be made with a very sharp chisel. Each piece is then glued down to the paper, and if the joints have been carefully made they will hardly show. Diagram c^1 in Fig. 21 indicates the preliminary step with regard to the small curl squares. The strips should be gauged off at an angle of 80° with the centre line of the curl, and then the squares can be gauged off to the exact size required. These pieces should all be marked, so that when glued down they will be in the same relative position as when in the leaf. A mixture of shades and colour is thus avoided. A half square is then prepared and glued in the corner. Then a half lozenge shape is fitted, if necessary, with a shoulder plane and shooting board to the exact shape. A whole square of curl is then glued down, and so on piece by piece until each side, etc., is finished. The work takes some time to complete, and when stood aside a board should be placed on the veneer in order to prevent possible buckling. When quite dry the paper is cut round and each design shows complete with paper on one side.

To veneer the box, one side is well glued, and after the glue has chilled, the veneer is pinned in position with the paper uppermost. A wooden caul is then heated and then cramped and handscrewed down. Each veneered surface is treated in this way, and then all the paper is toothed off the veneer. The square edges are next inlaid by cutting small rebates to receive $\frac{1}{8}$-in. square lines. These should be glued in, and the box bound round with tape until the glue is dry.

After the box is thoroughly dry it should be scraped and properly glasspapered up prior to gauging and sawing off the lid. The edges are then planed to fit, and beads are fitted inside the lid as shown in the section through the top (Fig. 22), which ensures the surface of the box remaining exactly level when the lid is down.

Special hinges should be used to attach the lid. They are called box hinges, and allow the lid to fall back a little beyond the perpendicular. A box lock is next fitted, and then the feet. The escutcheon is intended to be cut out of either mother-of-pearl or ivory with a fret-saw, and then inlaid. The tray is quite simple in

character, and may be slid from side to side on the thin fillets shown.

JEWEL-BOX AND HAND-MIRROR

The two half-tone reproductions (Figs. 23 and 24) show a jewel-box made in mahogany, inlaid with satinwood. Later the making of a hand-mirror to match this box is described.

The finished measurements of the box are $7\frac{1}{2}$ in. by $4\frac{1}{2}$ in. and $3\frac{1}{2}$ in. high. A part elevation and section of the box are shown by Fig. 25, and a plan by Fig. 26. The four sides are of $\frac{3}{8}$-in. thick mahogany and the top and bottom of $\frac{1}{4}$ in. For the sides, a piece is prepared in one length 2 ft. by $2\frac{1}{4}$ in., and on each long edge a slip of the sycamore is glued, to be finished to $\frac{1}{8}$ in., which will make the sides $2\frac{1}{2}$ in. wide. When the piece is cleaned up on both sides and evenly thicknessed and the edges planed straight to the correct width it may be marked across square for the four box sides, which may then be cut. They are to be dovetailed together in the way known as " mitre-dovetail " or " secret-dovetail." In this case, it is as if the wood box sides were of $\frac{1}{4}$ in. thickness, ordinary dovetailed and covered on the outside with wood of $\frac{1}{8}$ in. thickness, mitred at the corners. But it is worked in the solid as in making lap dovetails, with the laps $\frac{1}{8}$ in. over to be mitred. If the setting out is done correctly, there need be little chance of failure ; but, of course, neat fitting is indispensable. The cross marks shown in Fig. 28A (p. 1047) indicate waste, and the dotted lines show where the box will have to be cut through to form the lid, which it is necessary to consider in setting out the dovetail pins.

When the joints are all made, they may be glued up, and after observing that it is quite square and true, may be left in a very dry place to set. In the meantime the bottom and top of $\frac{1}{4}$-in. thick mahogany must be prepared. They are glued in place and secured with screws ($\frac{3}{4}$-in. No. 4), three to each edge, the heads being countersunk flush with the bottom ; but sunk $\frac{1}{16}$ in. below the surface of the top, in view of the satin-wood banding which has to be inlaid round the margin, and covers the screws.

The centre of the lid is inlaid with a

Fig. 23.—Jewel-box (Closed)

fan-oval ornament of satinwood and green sycamore. This and the banding are stock patterns, which can be bought for so small a sum that it would not pay to make one. It is shown in Fig. 26. The banding is inlaid first, by making a cut with the cutting gauge $\frac{1}{8}$ in. on the margin and $\frac{1}{16}$ in. deep, and another $\frac{3}{8}$ in. (the width of the banding) inside it. The waste between is then pared out and scraped level with a $\frac{1}{4}$-in. chisel, to allow the banding to lie in quite neatly and nearly level, the corners being cut to a mitre. For inlay work it is essential to have the glue in good working condition ; it should be hot, strong and thin enough to run freely. It is also an advantage to warm the work. The glue is run plentifully into the groove, and the banding laid in quickly and pressed down with a suitable flat iron or other weight to squeeze out the glue. It is advisable to keep going over it until no part shows any tendency to rise.

The fan-oval may then be inlaid. It has paper glued over it at one side to keep it together and this must be the outside. To get it true in position, the lid should be pencil-lined lengthwise and across the centre, to correspond with the lines on the oval, as shown in Fig. 26, therefore it must be marked on the paper

side. Whilst being held in position, it is marked round with the sharp point of a knife, then cut to about $\frac{1}{16}$ in. deep, and the waste pared away as was done for the banding. When it is ready for gluing in, the place for it should be warmed and glued, and the paper side of the oval wetted with hot water and immediately placed in and pressed with the hammer to work out the superfluous glue. In doing this the paper gets rubbed off, and sometimes some of the sections have an inclination to rise ; but it must be persevered with, and it might be necessary to place over it a piece of paper, then a well-heated flat piece of wood cramped or weighted down. After about ten hours' rest in a dry, warm place to set, the wood may be removed ; but the inlay should be allowed as much time as convenient to set—at least several days—before being cleaned up with the steel scraper and glasspaper.

When this is done the square corners should be rounded off with the glass-paper wrapped over a cork rubber ; then the sides may be marked $\frac{5}{8}$ in. from the top surface, and cut through square and

Fig. 24.—Jewel-box (Open)

true with a fine saw, to form the lid. The sawn edges will require lightly plan-ing, and the lid can be hinged with box-hinges, so that it can only open upright and cannot fall back. The lock also can be put on, and an oval of satinwood is let in at the key-hole.

Under the bottom, slips are put on, to stand forward about $\frac{1}{8}$ in. as a beading.

They are of 1-in. by $\frac{3}{16}$-in. section, mitred at the corner and fixed in place with glue and screws. Under these at each corner ball feet of brass are screwed on (see Fig. 25). The box should now be rubbed

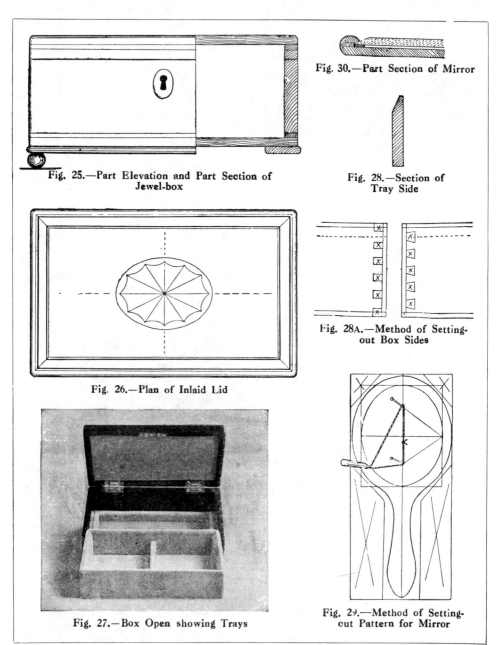

Fig. 25.—Part Elevation and Part Section of Jewel-box

Fig. 30.—Part Section of Mirror

Fig. 28.—Section of Tray Side

Fig. 26.—Plan of Inlaid Lid

Fig. 28A.—Method of Setting-out Box Sides

Fig. 27.—Box Open showing Trays

Fig. 29.—Method of Setting-out Pattern for Mirror

all over with linseed oil, and left a few days to dry in, when it can be french-polished.

The box is fitted with two trays, as shown in Fig. 27, lined with a good quality grey velvet. The bottom tray is $\frac{1}{2}$ in. deep, and the other one rests on it, and of accurate depth so that the velvet-covered sides stand up about $\frac{1}{4}$ in. higher than the mahogany box sides to go up into the lid, which also is to be lined on the underside. The upper tray is made to fit fairly close so as to seem permanent and keep the lower place secret ; but by a steady pull gripping the centre division piece it can be lifted out (*see* Fig. 27). It cannot be pulled out hurriedly on account of the vacuum. The velvet inside the lid when closed presses over the edges of the tray, keeping it dustproof and practically airtight. The bottom tray is composed of four slips of wood, $\frac{3}{8}$ in. by $\frac{1}{4}$ in. in section, for the sides and a bottom of thin stiff cardboard. The velvet is glued on before they are fixed together with fine wire nails. The method is to cut the cardboard for the bottom, and fit in the slips of wood, allowing for the thickness of the velvet, which may then be cut for each piece. For the slips it must be cut about $1\frac{3}{4}$ in. wide and about 1 in. over long. To fix it, the slips should be glued on the under edge and inner side, and the velvet put on ; then they may be fixed together with the fine pins or nails. The velvet must be glued on the cardboard bottom the net size, and it may be fixed on with $\frac{3}{8}$-in. fine wire nails. The outer sides of the slips may then be glued and the velvet drawn over, neatly fitting it at the corners and clipping off the surplus, except the over-width, which must be glued under the bottom. It should fit in place fairly tight, unless it is intended for lifting out. In that case it should be slightly loose, and would require a silk-ribbon loop at the centre of each end by which to raise it ; the loop may be fixed by gluing on the bottom. To give a finished appearance to the bottom, it may be covered with velvet or paper.

With the other tray, the short sides are $\frac{1}{4}$ in. thick, with the top edge bevelled on the inner side to $\frac{1}{8}$ in. (*see* Fig. 28). The long sides are $\frac{1}{8}$ in. thick, and the bottom of cardboard. The method of making the tray is the same as for the bottom one, the division piece being put in and fixed just before the outer sides are glued for drawing over the velvet. For the lid a piece of cardboard is cut, allowing for the velvet to turn over the edges, to be glued on the back about $\frac{1}{2}$ in., and it is glued in place. The trays should be allowed plenty of time in a dry place for the glue to dry thoroughly and the box may have the fittings put on and the polishing finished.

To make the mirror, first a piece of cardboard should be obtained and cut to a true oblong 12 in. by $5\frac{1}{2}$ in., to make a pattern. On this, a pencil line is made lengthwise and one across, dividing the space into four equal parts. A true oval (ellipse, strictly speaking) is then struck out on one half of the cardboard, the diameters being $5\frac{1}{2}$ in. by $4\frac{1}{2}$ in. To do this, an oblong that size should be first marked out, with lines across dividing it into four smaller ones to find the centres. The best way to describe the ellipse is by means of three pins, a piece of string and a pencil (*see* Fig. 29). To ascertain the exact points for the two pins shown, take half of the length-wise diameter line, which will be $2\frac{3}{4}$ in., and two lines that length may be ruled from the end of the short diameter line as shown. At that point a third pin may be inserted for the purpose of tying the piece of string so as to bring it to the right tension. Another oval is made $\frac{1}{2}$ in outside, which is to be the outline of the frame ; and the handle may be drawn freehand or with the compasses. The other lines shown mark the waste (indicated by cross marks), which may be cut away. With a sharp-pointed knife, the inner oval should be cut out clean and true, the waste piece to be given as a template in ordering the bevelled silvered plate to be made to it.

The other part is the pattern for the woodwork, but is not yet cut to the

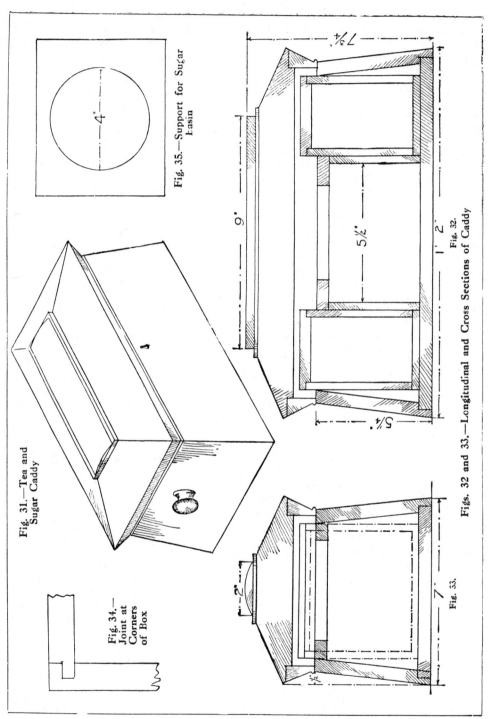

Fig. 35.—Support for Sugar Basin

4"

Fig. 31.—Tea and Sugar Caddy

Fig. 34.—Joint at Corners of Box

9"

7¾"

5½"

1' 2"

5¼"

Fig. 32.

2"

7"

½"

Fig. 33.

Figs. 32 and 33.—Longitudinal and Cross Sections of Caddy

true outline. Three pieces of wood are now required to be cut to the roughed-out outline of the pattern. Two of them must be of mahogany fully $\frac{3}{16}$ in. in thickness, and one of sycamore $\frac{1}{8}$ in. thick, all to be planed straight and even to lie together as close as possible. The sycamore may then have the oval cut out with a fret-saw, neatly to take the glass. It is then glued to one of the pieces of mahogany, and it is advisable to cramp it well to a level piece of board.

The other piece of mahogany must have the oval cut out $\frac{1}{8}$ in. inside the line, as it has to be glued on the front of the sycamore when the glass is in place to cover the edge of the bevel all round. When it is cut, it must be trimmed and neatly rounded with the spokeshave and glasspaper, and the rounded edge should be rubbed with a linseed-oil rag, and polished, as it is much easier to do now than when in place on the front of the glass.

The cardboard pattern for the glass should be taken and $\frac{1}{4}$-in. strip cut off all round the edge in one piece. This is to be placed in behind the glass to form an air space and keep it from the wood, to prevent any chance of rubbing. The mahogany front may then be tried in place to see that it fits quite well. and is glued and cramped as before.

Several days in a dry place should be allowed to set, and the cardboard pattern may be cut to the correct outline from which to mark, the wood being then cut out with the fret-saw and nicely rounded with the spokeshave to the section shown by Fig. 30. When smoothed up with No. 2 and No. 1 glasspaper it is ready for polishing.

TEA AND SUGAR CADDY

The caddy shown by Figs. 31 to 33 should be made either of oak, mahogany, or black walnut.

The box is made of $\frac{1}{2}$-in. material, with the sides sloping inwards, as shown in Fig. 32. The corner joints are tongued and grooved as in Fig. 34. The sides are rebated to take the bottom board,

which is fitted between. Before the box is glued together, two small stop grooves are cut in the front and in the back pieces. These grooves are for the two $\frac{1}{4}$-in. partitions, between which the tea boxes slide (see Fig. 32). Allowance of $\frac{3}{8}$ in. is made on the top of these partitions for the piece into which the sugar basin fits (see Fig. 35). The corners of the box should be glued and cramped, then the partitions slid in from underneath. The bottom should then be glued and bradded.

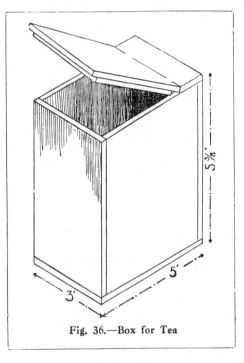

Fig. 36.—Box for Tea

When the glue is dry the sides should be smoothed and glasspapered.

A cross section of the lid is shown in Fig. 33. The mounted top is made with the rebate plane, the rounded piece being glued upon the top. The lid is also bevelled and rebated underneath to take the framed fillet that fits over the inner boxes. This framed fillet is first mitred, then beaded and bevelled with the bead and rebate planes ; it is then glued and bradded. The lid is fixed with brass butt hinges.

The boxes for the tea and sugar are shown in Fig. 36. They are made of ¼-in. material, and are made to slide in. The corners are neatly bradded, the lids being fixed with very small brass hinges. If a lock is required, it should be fixed before the piece (Fig. 35) is fixed. A turned knob is screwed on each of the simply as antiques ; but something better than a mere box can be made of them. They vary in style and are well made, the workmanship far surpassing the present-day machine production, and in most cases are worth restoring. The bands and lines of those that are veneered can often be matched, and if the veneer

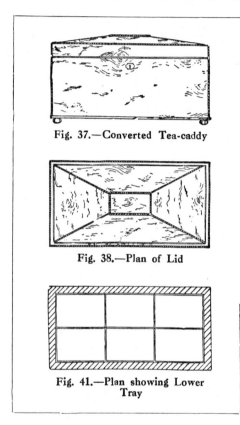

Fig. 37.—Converted Tea-caddy

Fig. 38.—Plan of Lid

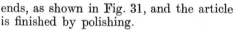

Fig. 41.—Plan showing Lower Tray

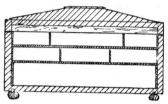

Fig. 39.—Vertical Section showing Partitions

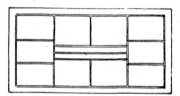

Fig. 40.—Plan showing Upper Tray

is not worth patching, a whole side is a small matter to renew. No attempt should be made to add feet where the original had none, or an extra bead to " improve " it.

The work of restoring a veneered caddy is far easier than one would anticipate. Sometimes they are found covered with dirt, and not even the kind of wood can be recognised ; but a judicious use of soap and water will often bring to light a piece of workmanship that very little beyond furniture cream is required to revive. At other times perhaps a coat of varnish has to be removed before the grain of the wood is discovered. Generally the french-polish must be cleaned off, and this may be done with a pad of calico soaked in methylated spirit. Having removed the polish, go over all the angle bands and remove any

ends, as shown in Fig. 31, and the article is finished by polishing.

CONVERTING OLD TEA-CADDY INTO JEWEL-CASE

Old tea-caddies such as that shown in elevation and plan by Figs. 37 and 38 are now more often kept as ornaments than used for the purpose for which they were originally intended. Where the interiors are damaged, or the cut-glass sugar basin is missing, they are not worth preserving

that are loose, scraping off the old glue before re-gluing. Cut lengths to fit in the spaces where any are missing. These joints should be cut slightly on the bevel to make a neat joint. Any veneer that is loose should be re-glued, and small damaged places cut out and re-instated with wood to match as nearly as possible. Should the wood be dark mahogany, a solution of permanganate of potash and water will often produce the required tint. Both the bands and the veneer with which the restoration is done will be thicker than the old work, and will no doubt appear to be a very patch-work job at first; but after the glue has been left to harden for a day, the use of a steel scraper will soon produce an even surface, which can be finished with fine glasspaper, and prepared for repolishing.

Some caddies have an interlining and partitions mitred at the corners and just slipped in. This is most useful when it is to be converted into a jewel-case, for two pieces 1 in. wide cut off all round form the sides for the two trays (see Figs. 39, 40 and 41). These should be reduced sufficiently to allow the trays to slip in with ease. For the bottom of the trays, thicker wood should be used; that sold for fretwork is very suitable. The partitions for the trays are of the thin wood, and fitted with a **V**-joint and glued. When the tray is completed the top edges should be rounded with fine glass-paper, and then french-polished. The outsides of the tray should also receive a few coats of polish. Make another lining of the thicker wood, and fit into the bottom to support the trays. The top tray will rest on the lower one. Treat the lower lining and bottom in a similar way to the outside of the trays before putting in. It is better than lining with material, and makes a neater finish.

The lining for the compartments of the trays should be of velvet; dark green is one of the best colours for the purpose. First cut out pieces of brown paper as shown, and these should be slightly smaller than will cover the space, as the velvet takes up some of the room. Cut the velvet in squares slightly larger than the paper. Glue the paper, and press the velvet on it. When dry cut out the pieces not required, and glue down the edge that is turned over. At the same time they may be creased to form little boxes, slightly glued round the top edges, and put into position. The compartments for rings are made with similar paper. Two rolls are covered with velvet, and pressed into each space; these should be just firm enough to hold the rings securely. Keep the velvet slightly below the top of each space, so that a small edge of wood is visible.

THREE SMALL FANCY BOXES

The three small boxes illustrated in the photographic reproductions (Figs. 42, 43 and 44) are made up from scraps of mahogany $\frac{1}{4}$ in. thick. They are just the kind of receptacles ladies delight in for stowing away their trinkets and the other small objects—hairpins, hat-pins, etc.

The oblong box (Fig. 42) measures $10\frac{1}{2}$ in. long by $3\frac{3}{4}$ in. wide, and its height is $3\frac{3}{8}$ in. As it is covered with fabric there is no need for dovetailing the angles. They are put together with glue and long brass pins. Iron pins are a mistake for work of this kind, because in time their heads rust, and rusty marks are communicated to the fabric. The lid, which overhangs some $\frac{3}{16}$ in. all round, has the edges bevelled. The covering fabric is old brocade in pink and silver. Owing to the thickness of the material it is rather intractable, but the difficulty may be got over in the following way: A length of material is cut in one piece to cover all four sides, with an overlap of $\frac{1}{4}$ in. at the top and bottom. This is glued on, the glue being used sparingly, so as to preclude the possibility of any of it coming through the silk. The one vertical joint is at one of the back angles, where the overlapping piece is turned in and glued down, thus making it safe against fraying.

The overlap at the bottom is glued down, pieces being taken out at each corner to make it sit snugly, and over all is glued a piece of billiard cloth. The overlap at the top is dealt with as follows : Along the centre of each edge of the side boards a saw-cut $\frac{1}{4}$ in. deep is made, as shown in Figs. 45 and 46. Glue is worked

Fig. 42.—Box Covered with Silk Brocade

into these saw-cuts with a knife, and the material is then forced down into them. using the blade of a penknife. The result is as shown in Fig. 46. Before covering the lid, a piece of springy wool serge, as used for curtains is cut to the size defined by the inner edges of the bevels and glued in place, after which the brocade covering is applied

Fig. 43.—Box with Inlaid Miniature

and stretched over the serge and bevels, and carried under the lid, where it is glued down, $\frac{1}{2}$-in. overlap having been allowed for the purpose. The underside of the lid is then lined with white silk, the edges of the latter being turned under. The best way to manage this lining is to paste the silk to a piece of thin card or stout paper, cut to the desired size, and to turn the margin over all round and paste it down to the other side of the backing. When the paste is dry the lining may be glued in place.

The box and lid having been covered with brocade, the latter is secured to the former with two small brass hinges. A clasp fastening is made from stout

brass wire in the form shown by Fig. 47, and a small plate with central stud is fixed to the front of the box and adjusted so that the clasp will snap over it. The wires are soft-soldered together.

The inside of the box is left with the mahogany surface untreated ; but if desired it might be enamelled white. In decorating boxes with applied fabric, the great point is to see that there are no loose ends or edges that may become frayed, otherwise with very little use they develop into unsightly wrecks.

The box (Fig. 43) is made in the following manner : The bottom is cut to shape, the front and back edges being arcs of a circle (see Fig. 48). The sides are cut so that the grain of the wood should run vertically, which facilitates the bending of the two which form back and front. These are soaked in hot water, and then glued and nailed in place. The ends are then added, and lastly the top, so that at this stage the box is entirely closed. All surfaces are made smooth with glass-paper, the corners being rounded. The top is pared away

Fig. 44.—Box with Shell Inlay

with the chisel to give it a certain amount of convexity, a central space being left flat for the miniature and its frame (see Fig. 49). Then a gauge line is run round at a point where the lid is to be separated from the box proper, and the line cut through with the dovetail saw.

As the lid is not to be hinged, it is necessary to add a lining to the box part, which should stand up above the line of separation of the box and lid.

The measurements of the box are $6\frac{1}{2}$ in. long by $3\frac{1}{4}$ in. wide at the widest part,

put in in four pieces, those conforming to the curved sides first, and those for the two ends afterwards. Fig. 48 shows these details.

At this stage the polishing of the box may be undertaken. It only remains to add the miniature. The frame is turned from a ring of ivory. Miniature and glass are secured to the frame by

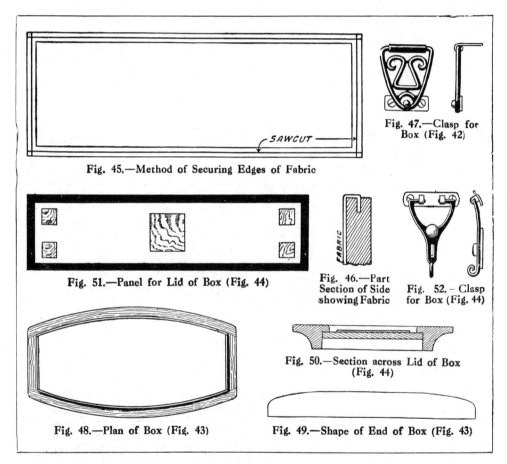

Fig. 45.—Method of Securing Edges of Fabric

Fig. 47.—Clasp for Box (Fig. 42)

Fig. 51.—Panel for Lid of Box (Fig. 44)

Fig. 46.—Part Section of Side showing Fabric

Fig. 52. – Clasp for Box (Fig. 44)

Fig. 50.—Section across Lid of Box (Fig. 44)

Fig. 48.—Plan of Box (Fig. 43)

Fig. 49.—Shape of End of Box (Fig. 43)

the ends narrowing down to $2\frac{3}{8}$ in. The depth of the box is 2 in. Sizes, however, are not material, as dimensions can be adopted which may suit the purpose for which the box is intended. The lining stands $\frac{1}{4}$ in. above the top edge of the box, and is made of two thicknesses of stout mahogany veneer glued together. The grain runs vertically. The lining is

gluing a circle of Bristol board over the back of the frame, the rebate of which is made of such a depth as to ensure the back of the miniature standing flush with the back of the frame. The frame then is sunk in the cavity already made for it and secured with glue. It will always be found that the lid fits the box best when it is put on in the way it stood when the box and lid were in one piece. It is well, therefore, to add some little mark to the box and the lid as a guide to their proper relationship. Two small black dots would suffice, or a small ornamental device might be painted on the front of the box and the lid, say in gold-size, and gold-leaf applied.

The bottom of the box should be covered with billiard cloth. It gives a good finish and prevents scratches to table tops.

The box shown by Fig. 44 is $8\frac{3}{8}$ in. by $2\frac{3}{8}$ in. by $1\frac{5}{8}$ in. deep externally, exclusive of the lid, which, it will be seen, overhangs considerably. The box and lid in this case are made separately. The former is put together with glue and pins, and all four sides are brought to a fair surface. The lid is framed together by mitreing. A length of mahogany strip $\frac{13}{16}$ in. by $\frac{1}{2}$ in. is prepared to the section shown in Fig. 50. This is cut to the proper lengths, and the mitres are joined with glue without nails. Then a panel is prepared. This measures 8 in. by $2\frac{1}{4}$ in. (the inside dimensions of the box). The opening left after mitreing the four pieces of the lid measures $7\frac{1}{2}$ in. by $1\frac{11}{16}$ in. A piece of stout mahogany veneer is cut $\frac{1}{4}$ in. less in length and width than this opening, and glued down on the prepared panel. This is shown in Figs. 50 and 51.

The decoration of this panel consists in inlaying five squares of polished shell. The pieces of shell are rubbed flat on a Washita stone, and to the same thickness as the veneer. They are then shaped with the file until truly square, after which their outlines are scribed out on the surface of the veneer, the pattern being as shown in Fig. 51, and the shapes so defined are cut away, the veneer only

being removed. The further treatment of the panel consists in french-polishing the veneered portion to a dull silvery lustre, by using aluminium powder with the polish in the manner already described, but using white polish. This does not work quite so well as the ordinary french-polish, and some degree of practice is required to get a good surface with the aluminium powder. The process is facilitated, however, by dusting the surface of the panel with the powder after applying the polish, removing all loose powder, and then polishing it over a second time. When a satisfactory result is attained the squares of shell may be glued into their respective cavities.

The lid is secured with two small brass hinges. The catch employed is shown by Fig. 52. It is cut from sheet brass, and a bead of silver is soldered in.

There is an infinite amount of scope for the tasteful treatment of these little boxes. The coloured lacquer effect can be varied as regards tint by using various dry pigments with the french-polish, and designs in gold or aluminium leaf may be added to the polished surfaces. If Japanese patterns be used, the resemblance to actual lacquer work may be made very close. There are many classes of objects which may be applied by way of decoration, amongst which may be mentioned cameos, carvings in ivory, small oil paintings, pierced metal-work (watch clocks and the like), semi-precious stones like onyx, agate, cornelian and jade, with or without metal settings. Also such objects as butterflies' wings, snake and lizard skins, amber, tortoise-shell and even fancy hardwoods may be worked in.

Writing Furniture

SMALL MAHOGANY WRITING-TABLE

THE design of the small mahogany writing-table shown by Fig 1 is of the late Georgian period. Its attractive appearance is apparent in the photographic reproduction. Front and side elevations are shown by Figs. 2 and 3, whilst Fig. 4 represents a section at c (Fig. 2) and shows the division of the top drawer. It will be noticed that the drawers can be opened from each end, a feature seldom met with in present-day furniture.

Supporting the body of the desk are four tapering square legs cut out of $1\frac{1}{4}$-in. material, shaped as shown in Fig. 5, and connected at the top by pieces $\frac{3}{4}$ in. thick cut according to sizes given. The desk sides are of $\frac{3}{4}$-in. material,

Fig. 1.—Small Mahogany Writing-table

having a bottom $\frac{1}{4}$ in. thick. It is again divided by a $\frac{1}{8}$-in. piece of mahogany forming a runner for the top drawer. This member, together with the bottom, is moulded with a half-round bead on three sides only, the back being square.

The top is made of two pieces, the lower portion being fixed, and the top hinged so as to fall back and form one flush writing-surface, as shown in Figs. 3 and 5. Fixed along the top edge of the hinged part is a cock bead moulded and cut, as shown in Figs. 6 and 7. The top sides of the fixed part and the under side of the hinged portion are covered with green baize, leaving a margin of 1 in. round the four sides of the whole top when open. Both the hinged and fixed portions of the top are moulded on three sides, as in Fig. 5.

The top drawer is made of $\frac{3}{4}$-in. ends, with small half-round bead running round the outside edges, the side being of $\frac{1}{4}$-in. material and the bottom $\frac{1}{8}$ in. thick. The fittings are uncommon, as will readily be seen by reference to the illustrations. The lower drawer has no fittings or handles, and forms a secret drawer, access to the same being obtained by pressure from each end. It is made of the same thickness material, and finished with half-round bead at the ends similar to the top drawer.

OAK WRITING-DESK

The most suitable wood for the desk shown by Fig. 8 (p. 1086) is oak. Figs. 9 and 10 show front and side elevations, and in Fig 13. The handle and escutcheon plates are of polished brass, and give a striking contrast to the dark colour of the oak.

The legs are of 2-in.-square material

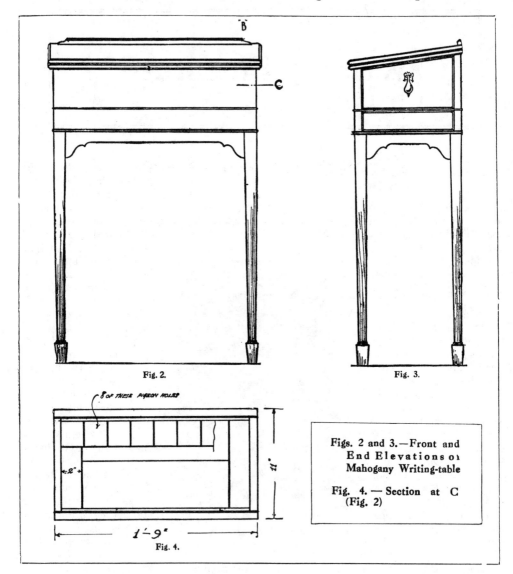

Fig. 2.

Fig. 3.

Figs. 2 and 3.—Front and End Elevations of Mahogany Writing-table

Fig. 4. — Section at C (Fig. 2)

two half-plans and a part back elevation are shown by Figs. 11 and 12.

The top is of $\frac{3}{4}$-in. material ($\frac{5}{8}$-in. finished thickness) in two pieces, and moulded at the front and sides as shown (finished), and turned as shown in Fig. 13. The axis of the circular portion not being vertical, but at an angle pointing inwards, the outside edge, which corresponds with the outside corner of the square portion,

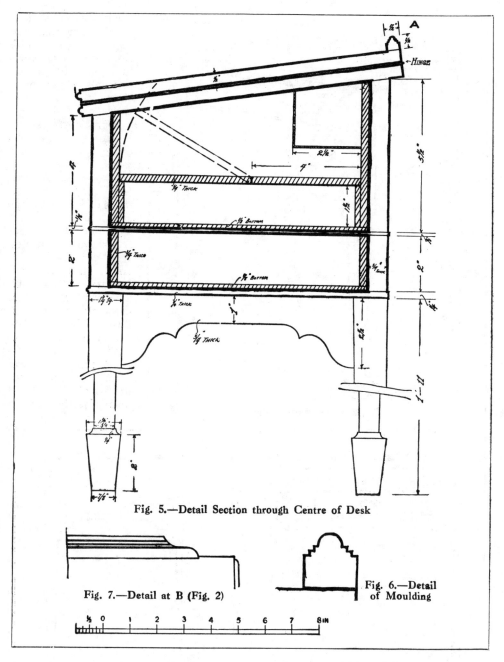

Fig. 5.—Detail Section through Centre of Desk

Fig. 7.—Detail at B (Fig. 2)

Fig. 6.—Detail of Moulding

is vertical and parallel to the square portion (*see* Fig. 13).

The front is composed of two rails of $\frac{7}{8}$-in. by $\frac{3}{4}$-in. material (finished), and a shaped portion $\frac{3}{4}$ in. thick (finished size), both tenoned and dowelled into the legs and flush with the outside surface of the legs. The sides and back are of $\frac{3}{4}$-in.

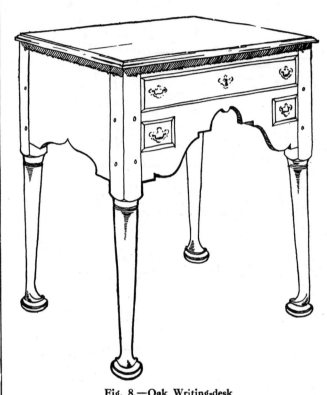

Fig. 8.—Oak Writing-desk

thick material (finished) tenoned and dowelled into the sides, shaped as shown in Figs. 9, 10 and 12, and finished flush with the outside surfaces of the legs.

Fig. 11 gives a section through the drawers. The top one, which occupies the whole length between the front legs, is 3 in. deep overall, and the small ones at each side are $2\frac{1}{2}$ in. The fronts are of $\frac{3}{4}$-in. material (finished), and the ends, sides and bottom of $\frac{1}{4}$-in. stuff. The surface of the drawers when shut is flush with the remainder of the front, with a $\frac{1}{8}$-in. half-round moulded bead running round the drawer at the front and projecting beyond

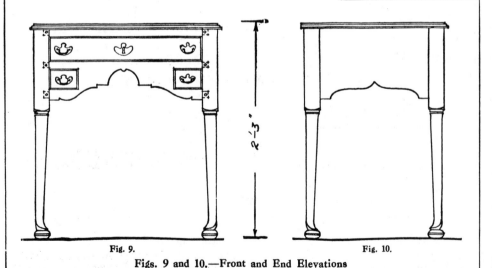

2'-3"

Fig. 9.

Fig. 10.

Figs. 9 and 10.—Front and End Elevations

the main surface. The drawer runners are of soft wood, and four are tenoned are tenoned into the front and back. In Fig. 11, which gives two half plans

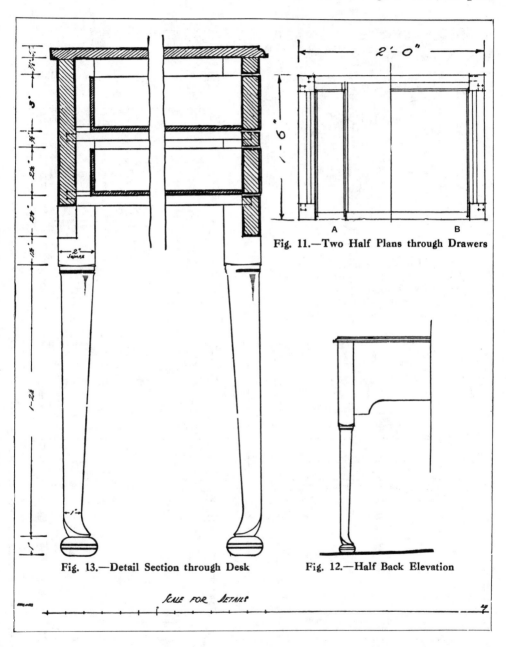

Fig. 11.—Two Half Plans through Drawers

Fig. 13.—Detail Section through Desk

Fig. 12.—Half Back Elevation

SCALE FOR DETAILS

into the legs, and the remaining two for the interior edges of the lower drawers through the drawer line, A is top drawer and B is bottom drawer.

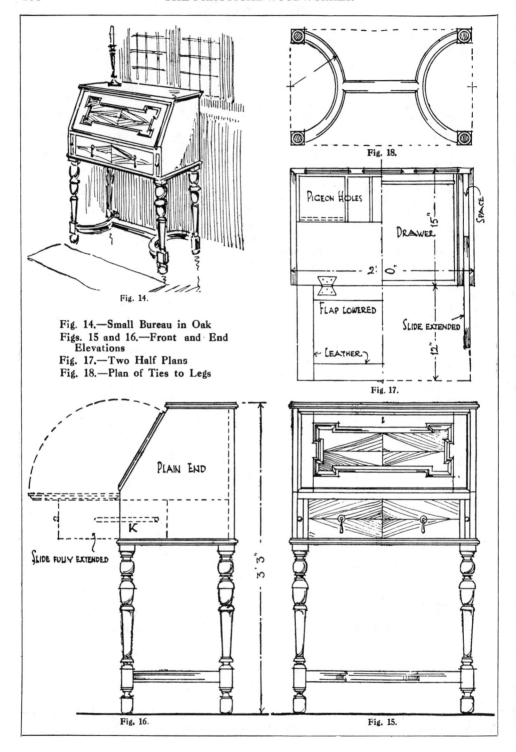

Fig. 18.

Piceon Holes

Drawer   15"   Space

2' 0"

Flap Lowered   Slide Extended

12"

Leather

Fig. 17.

Fig. 14.

Fig. 14.—Small Bureau in Oak
Figs. 15 and 16.—Front and End
  Elevations
Fig. 17.—Two Half Plans
Fig. 18.—Plan of Ties to Legs

Plain End

K

Slide Fully Extended

3' 3"

Fig. 16.

Fig. 15.

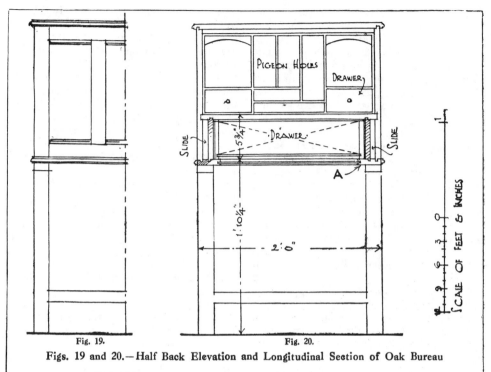

Fig. 19.

Fig. 20.

Figs. 19 and 20.—Half Back Elevation and Longitudinal Section of Oak Bureau

Fig. 21.—
Cross
Section

SMALL BUREAU IN OAK

Designed for a dining-room, the bureau shown by Fig. 14 (p. 1088) may be carried out in oak, selected for the best possible figure and grain. At the same time it would look extremely well executed in dull-polished Italian walnut, and its small proportions might be increased consistently throughout, in the event of a larger article being required. In addition to the general illustrations (Figs. 15 to 19), reduced reproductions of the full-size working details are given.

What may perhaps be termed the key to the whole construction is a piece of horizontal framing, shown in section at A in Figs. 20 and 21, and also at B in Fig. 22. This consists of 4-in. by 1-in. oak mortised and tenoned together and grooved for a thin panel, the whole measuring 2 ft. by 1 ft. 3 in. overall, and serving as a base to the upper half of the work. Below and sub-tenoned into it there are four legs, round-turned to a very carefully con-sidered profile (as in Fig. 22) out of 2¾-in. square oak. The widest portion is in-tentionally arranged at c, and the small portions remaining square should be very accurately reduced, the upper one to 2⅛ in. on each face, and the lower one to 1¾ in. The ties near the floor are set out as in Fig. 18, and worked to the section given at D in Fig. 22, the sunk top sur-face being very effective in such a posi-tion. As the size is small, each curved portion might be worked out of one solid piece ; or it might be preferred to build them up, each in two lengths, halved accurately in the middle and tenoned into the legs at the ends. The straight central rail could be dovetailed from below into the curved portions, the sunk top being worked when the whole tie has been put together.

The shell or carcase of the upper part of the bureau is composed of the follow-ing parts : First, two plain ends as in Fig. 16, mitred as in Fig. 23, to a simple back framed up in three panels (Figs. 19 and 24), the whole being tongued into grooves in the horizontal framing already referred to as the key to the situation, as at J in Fig. 22. Similarly they are tongued into the underside of a top piece 1 in. thick, and moulded on all four edges (Fig. 25). Next, with its upper surface 2 ft. 4 in. above floor level, there should be arranged a shelf as at H (Fig. 21), ⅞ in. thick, stop-housed slightly into the ends, and butted against the inside of the back.

At each end of the drawer space now formed there should be contrived a cavity for a pull-out slide, by means of a piece as at J (Fig. 22), secured by means of tongues and grooves as shown, except on the actual face of the work. Each slide should be arranged to pull out 8 in. only, by means of a groove worked in it, as at K in Fig. 16, and a peg fixed on the inner face of the end and projecting into the groove. The width overall of the slide compartment should equal that of the top of the leg. The slide should close quite flush on the face, be fitted with a tiny turned-oak knob, and covered on its top edge with felt or soft leather. The bottom edge should be ultimately finished by means of a moulded strip as at L (Fig. 22), mitred all round, and the drawer can be made in the usual manner, but with a piece of oak applied as at M, to reduce the friction and wear on the framing below. The drawer front is in-tended to be veneered in quarters, and to be rebated for and finished with a narrow bead mitred round, as in Fig. 26.

Like the rest of the work, the flap should be carefully set out on paper as a preliminary to the actual work. It must finish the same thickness as H (Fig. 21), in order to bear properly upon the slides, and consists of framing 2¾ in. wide and having a small moulding worked round its outer edges, as at O in Fig. 25, from which all its particulars can be gleaned. The framing is cut away on the face to suit the mitred arrangement of the panel moulding, but on the inside remains a simple rectangle. The panel is almost flush on the inside, allowing for a morocco-leather lining to be glued in place, while on the outside it is finished with another quartered arrangement of selected veneer (Fig. 27). The flap is fixed with small best-quality brass counter-flap hinges, in the position shown in Fig. 26, which gives its position in relation to the sloping top of the end-piece. Under the front edge of the top it should meet a small splayed piece, as shown by Fig. 28 (seen also at R in Fig. 21), and it should be supported in its closed position by moulded strips housed into the end pieces as at S (Fig. 25), these making a good finish to the appear-ance when open.

The pigeon-holes and small drawers in-corporated with them can be in very thin oak, holly, or satinwood, set out as indi-cated in Figs. 20 and 21. In the best work they are built up separately and inserted complete. Antique oxidised drawer-handles and a good lock will complete the work.

OAK JACOBEAN WRITING-BUREAU

The oak Jacobean writing-bureau shown by Fig. 29 (p. 1092) is made up with three drawers, above which are pigeon-holes

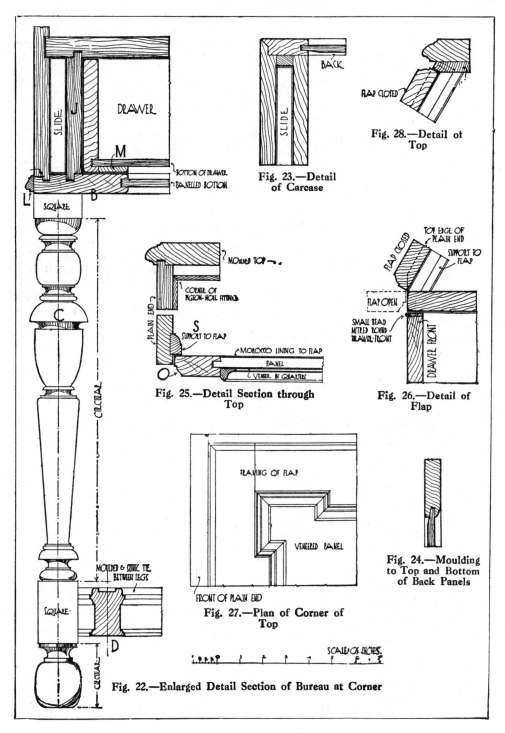

SLIDE

DRAWER

J

M

L

B

SQUARE

BOTTOM OF DRAWER

PANELLED BOTTOM

Fig. 23.—Detail
of Carcase

BACK

SLIDE

FLAP CLOSED

Fig. 28.—Detail of
Top

CIRCULAR

C

MOULDED TOP

PLAIN END

CORNER OF
PIGEON-HOLE FITTINGS

S

SUPPORT TO FLAP

O

MOROCCO LINING TO FLAP

PANEL

VENEER IN QUARTERS

Fig. 25.—Detail Section through
Top

TOP EDGE OF
PLAIN END

FLAP CLOSED

SUPPORT TO
FLAP

FLAP OPEN

SMALL BEAD
MITRED ROUND
DRAWER FRONT

DRAWER FRONT

Fig. 26.—Detail of
Flap

Fig. 24.—Moulding
to Top and Bottom
of Back Panels

FRAMING OF FLAP

VENEERED PANEL

MOULDED & SUNK TIE
BETWEEN LEGS

SQUARE

D

CIRCULAR

FRONT OF PLAIN END

Fig. 27.—Plan of Corner of
Top

SCALE OF INCHES

Fig. 22.—Enlarged Detail Section of Bureau at Corner

Fig. 29.—Oak Jacobean Writing Bureau

enclosed by a hinged flap. The latter, when opened and supported on two slides, forms a writing space. Front and side elevations are given by Figs. 30 and 31.

The main features of construction are apparent in the section (Fig. 32). The sides are prepared out of 1-in. stuff and finished $\frac{7}{8}$ in., the rails being $2\frac{1}{4}$ in. by $\frac{7}{8}$ in., dovetailed and grooved into the sides. The drawer bearers are of 1-in. stuff and $\frac{7}{8}$ in. finished. The back is framed and panelled, framing $2\frac{1}{4}$ in. by $\frac{7}{8}$ in. with a panel $\frac{5}{8}$ in. thick, grooved. The framing is grooved and tongued into the top and bottom rail. The drawers have $\frac{7}{8}$-in. thick fronts, moulded on the edge,

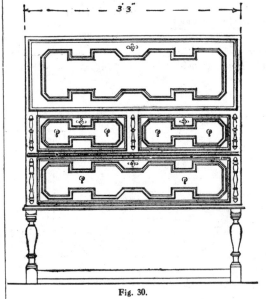

Fig. 30.

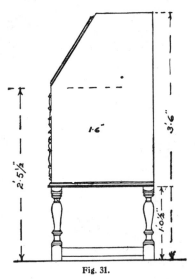

Fig. 31.

Figs. 30 and 31.—Front and End Elevations

SCALE OF FEET

and rebated over the rails and stiles, with a moulding planted on to form the raised and shaped panels. The sides of the drawer are dovetailed to the front, and the usual construction of a well-made drawer as shown gives the necessary finish. The top is mitred and rebated to

suitable sinking to take it, but this would be a matter of taste. The flap would be fixed by brass counter-flap hinges sunk. The handles should be of a good pattern. Those suggested are drop handles and are a little later in style than Jacobean, but, nevertheless, are very suitable. The lock-

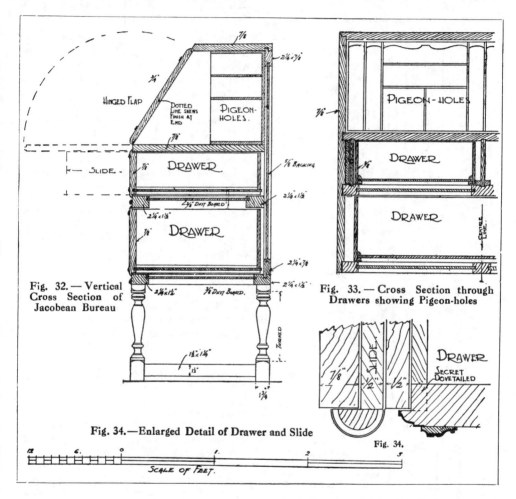

Fig. 32. — Vertical Cross Section of Jacobean Bureau

Fig. 33. — Cross Section through Drawers showing Pigeon-holes

Fig. 34.—Enlarged Detail of Drawer and Slide

sides as shown. Details of the drawers are shown by Figs. 33 and 34.

The slides to support the flap are masked by the turning to which they are fixed. The flap is solid, but could be framed if wished, the panel mouldings covering the joints, and also, if desired, it can have a leather cover inside with

plates should be open strap-work or fretted ; a number of suitable designs can always be selected from at a good iron-monger's shop.

The pigeon-holes are formed of ¼-in. wood, and can be built up to meet requirements. Those shown are of useful dimensions for stationery. Small drawers can also be introduced ; but these should be raised 2 in. or 3 in. above the writing surface to clear all loose papers.

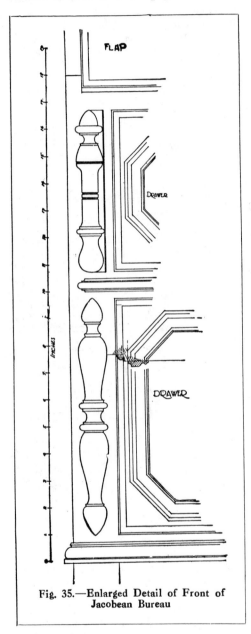

Fig. 35.—Enlarged Detail of Front of Jacobean Bureau

The legs supporting the whole should be carefully turned to a simple pattern, the mouldings small, in keeping with the period, and the struts slightly rounded on the top corners. An enlarged detail of the front is given by Fig. 35.

The most suitable finish would be to stain and wax-polish.

COMBINED WRITING-TABLE AND CABINET

The combined writing-table and cabinet shown by Fig. 36 is 4 ft. 6 in. high, 2 ft. 2 in. wide, and 1 ft. 3 in. deep. The top portion serves as a china cabinet, the doors having leaded lights and copper fittings. Below the cabinet is a nest of pigeon-holes, and under this is a drawer, which, when partly drawn out, forms a rest for the writing flap above. The lower portion is fitted with two shelves for books.

Oak would be the best material to use, but the nest of pigeon-holes would look better in satinwood or holly. The leading dimensions are given in the drawings (Figs. 37 and 38). Fig. 37 shows alternative designs for the leaded lights of the cabinet. A full-size section of the whole cabinet should be prepared before beginning the construction.

First get out the two ends, which are 1 ft. 3 in. in the widest part, and therefore would probably have to be jointed up. As the upper portion of the ends is 8 in. wide, the best position for the joint would be in continuation of this width. Shoot the back and top and bottom edges, and mark the outline and the positions of the housings. Work a rebate on the inside back edges, as shown at A (Fig. 39), for a length of 2 ft. 4¼ in. from the top. Next cut out the housings for B, C, D, and the two shelves E (Fig. 38), B, C, and E being dovetailed, as shown by Fig. 40, and B and D plain-housed. The frame D is mortised and tenoned together, as shown by Fig. 41. The back edge is rebated, and a hollow is worked on the front edge (see also F and G, Fig. 42). Having prepared the shelves B, C, E, and the framework D (Figs. 38 and 42), cut their ends to fit into the corresponding housings, and work a scotia moulding on the front edge of the shelf B.

The top of the cabinet should now be prepared, and housings cut to enable it to fit over the ends. A rebate is worked on the back under edge, as shown at H in Fig. 42. The top is afterwards moulded. Care should be taken, when preparing the ends, not to chip off the wood between the housings and the outer edges. The two ends are housed into the feet or bearers J (Figs. 37 and 38), which are of 3½-in. by 1½-in. stuff, shaped as shown.

Next to be taken in hand are the doors of the cabinet, the writing flap, and the drawer. The doors are mortised and tenoned together in the usual way, and are rebated on the inside to receive the leaded-glass panels, which are held in position by small beading sprigged to the frame. The two meeting-stiles are re-bated, and a bead is run along the face of one, as shown in section at Fig. 43. A small bead is secured round the cabinet, as shown at M (Fig. 42), to form a stop for the doors. The correct width for the writing flap should be ascertained by measurement; this would come out at about 1 ft. 0¼ in. The frame is mortised and tenoned together. A tongue is worked on the panel edges, fitting into corresponding grooves on the inside of the frame (see Fig. 42). The inner surface of the panel should be a trifle below that of the frame, as it has to be covered with green baize, which is glued over the panel. This covering may be dispensed with if desired, in which case the panel should be flush, as shown. A thumb moulding is worked on the edges as shown. The flap, when closed, rests on two strips screwed to the ends (see Figs. 36 and 42). The drawer is constructed in the ordinary way, and does not require any special description. A narrow strip of baize should be glued along the top edge of the front, to prevent the surface of the flap from being scratched when it is rest-ing on the drawer, and two drawer stops O (Fig. 42), 1½ in. long, should be screwed to the framework D to prevent the drawer being pushed too far back. The span rail K is got out of 3-in. by ⅝-in. stuff, and should be shaped as shown in Fig. 37;

this may be secured by simply butting against the ends, but it would be better to let it in.

The framework D (Fig. 42) and the shaped span rail K should be blocked at the angle, as shown in Figs. 38 and 42. The back, which should be screwed to the shelves, sides, etc., is made up of ½-in.

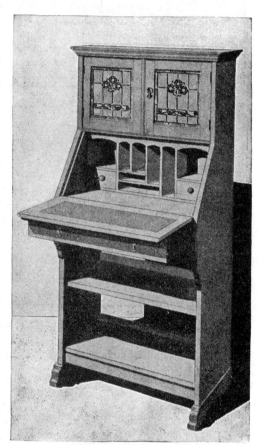

Fig. 36.—Combined Writing-table and Cabinet

boards grooved and tongued together. The doors are hung with ordinary 1½-in. brass butt hinges. One keyplate only is necessary, but two look better. Suit-able drawer handles should be fixed, and a keyplate should be screwed both to the drawer front and to the face of the flap.

The nest of pigeon-holes, shown in elevation by Fig. 44, is made separately

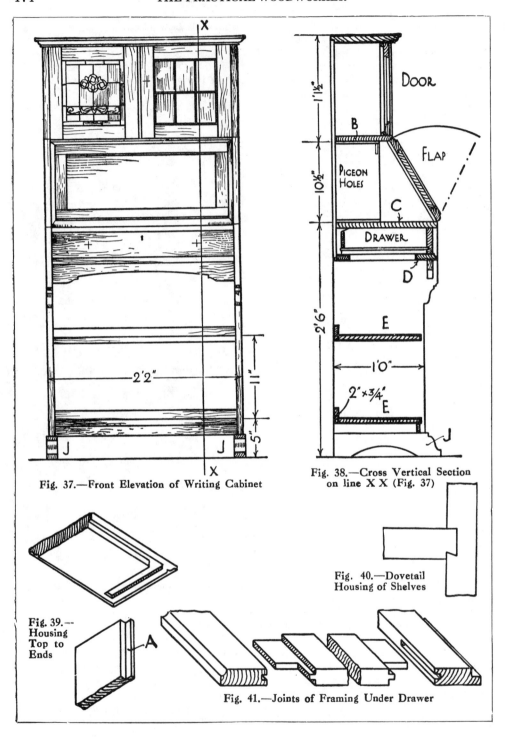

Fig. 37.—Front Elevation of Writing Cabinet

Fig. 38.—Cross Vertical Section on line X X (Fig. 37)

Fig. 39.—Housing Top to Ends

Fig. 40.—Dovetail Housing of Shelves

Fig. 41.—Joints of Framing Under Drawer

and slipped in from behind, the depth from back to front being 6 in. Material $\frac{1}{4}$ in. thick should be used for this. The bottom corners are fitted with drawers, as shown in Fig. 44. The arched pieces L should be well glued in last of all.

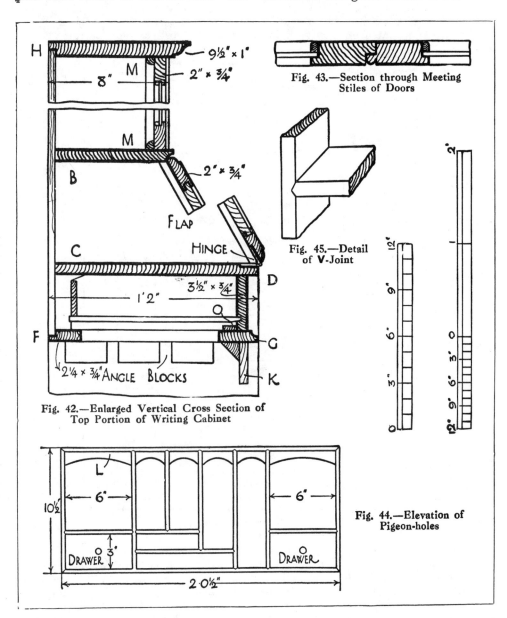

Fig. 43.—Section through Meeting Stiles of Doors

Fig. 45.—Detail of V-Joint

Fig. 42.—Enlarged Vertical Cross Section of Top Portion of Writing Cabinet

Fig. 44.—Elevation of Pigeon-holes

corners are mitred together, the V-ends of the division pieces fitting tight into corresponding grooves (see also Fig. 45). The

The cabinet may be fumigated and wax-polished, or stained, the former method being the more suitable.

RECESSED BOOKCASE-SECRETAIRE

The use of a recess for a fitted bookcase which has an escritoire or writing attachment is a feature which will no doubt be appreciated in many dining-

the considerable advantage of being in a fairly warm part of the room, a feature which should not be ignored.

A secretaire of the type shown in the perspective drawing (Fig. 46) not only economises space, but considerably reduces the cost, as only narrow ends are

Fig. 46.—Recessed Bookcase-secretaire

rooms. In most small houses and flats there is hardly room for a bookcase, if the sideboard, dining-table, and dinner-wagon receive the space they deserve for appearance and comfort. In such circumstances a bureau-bookcase is really desirable, and, fitted as suggested in a recess at the side of the fireplace, it has

required, and a back can be dispensed with if the wall is moderately level and in good condition. As will be seen from the illustration, the most is made of the available space. The two side cupboards are invaluable for ink, spare pens, extra stock of stationery, and old correspondence, which is usually untidy if not definitely provided for, whilst the centre part is fitted up for a few necessary works of reference or much-used volumes. The arched cupboard part is quite a decorative feature if furnished with one or two pieces of pottery or pewter.

But the main feature, and the one most appreciated, is the secretaire writing-part fitted with drawers and pigeon-holes, and provided with a fall-down writing-flap. This flap is certainly the most difficult part of the job, but the exercise of ordinary care and accuracy should ensure success. The large cupboards underneath the writing part are invaluable for the storage of small portfolios, part numbers, and general impedimenta. In this instance the carcase ends should extend from underneath the dustboard at the top right down to the floor, and, as will be seen in the elevation (Fig. 47), all the main divisions can be fixed between the carcase ends, so as to form the necessary divisions. An important point to bear in mind is that the cornice rail runs right through, it being necessary to cut away the carcase ends just the thickness of the rail for this purpose. The top of the carcase is set back for this reason, as indicated in the sectional view (Fig. 48).

The table shelf must be shaped on the front edge, as shown in Fig. 49. Ordinary brass back-flap hinges are used to connect the flap with the table shelf, and if the edges are shaped as shown, the flap will fall level with the shelf. Having prepared the cornice board to the section indicated, and also the table shelf, these parts and also the three other main horizontal divisions can be slip-dovetailed in between the carcase ends. Both the main vertical divisions can next be slip-dovetailed in position. Should the total width of the whole job exceed, say, 3 ft., it is a good plan to introduce a vertical division in the bottom part. This should be arranged to fit behind the doors, so that rebated action of the fall and shelf can be arranged.

After the main carcase has been glued up and set, the doors and flap should be proceeded with. The top doors should be made with a small stuck moulding

forming a rebate to receive the panel, and the bottom doors should be made as shown by Fig. 50. Long and short shouldered joints are necessary. The mouldings are then fitted in as shown to receive the panel.

The flap or fall should be made rather like an ordinary three-panelled door, which means that the framing should be mortised and tenoned together with the panels grooved in with bare-faced tongues. These should be carefully fitted so that they come flush on the inside. The panels should, of course, be veneered and cleaned up on the outside before being glued in, and in this connection it should be mentioned that if ordinary oak is used for the framing and nicely-figured oak for the side panels, the centre quartered device should be made from some well-marked pieces of pollard-oak veneer. The small pieces are intended to be of either rosewood or ebony.

The inside of the fall should have a veneer lipping about 1 in. wide glued round in order to receive the leather lining. This can easily be laid with a hammer, and should be cut to the exact width required with a cutting gauge after it is dry, the superfluous veneer being removed with a chisel.

The cornice rail and frieze moulding should next be attached, and the carcase may then be fitted and fixed in the recess. The cornice moulding may then be attached, one end of the moulding being returned on itself, as shown in the perspective view. This gives the necessary rebate to receive the dustboard, which can next be fitted and glued down.

In the sectional view (Fig. 48), a back to the upper part is shown, but the introduction of this part is quite optional. Should it be decided on, three-ply wood $\frac{3}{8}$ in. thick is quite suitable. The arch should now be fitted with the columns as shown, with small square caps and vases to finish off the latter.

To complete the fall part, the frame should be fitted in the opening, and the small curved piece D (Fig. 49) attached as shown. Then the bottom edge of the fall is rebated, and the hinges cut in. It is

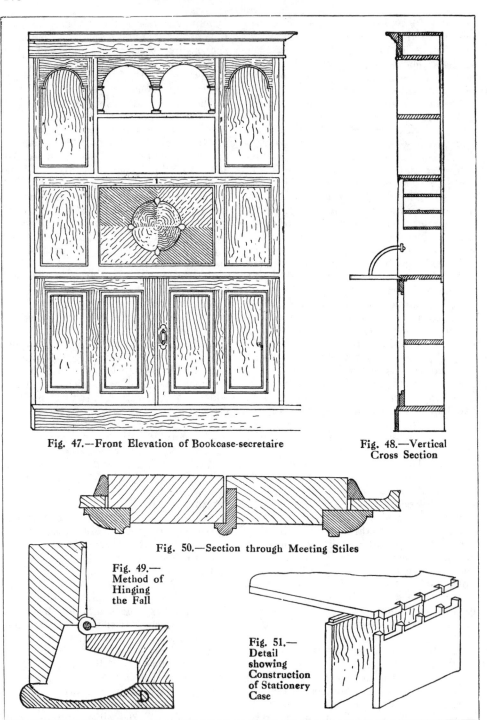

Fig. 47.—Front Elevation of Bookcase-secretaire

Fig. 48.—Vertical Cross Section

Fig. 50.—Section through Meeting Stiles

Fig. 49.—Method of Hinging the Fall

Fig. 51.—Detail showing Construction of Stationery Case

important to note that the centre of the back flap-pin should coincide exactly with the corners of the flap and the shelf, in which case the former is bound to turn correctly, as on an axis, and, more important still, the inside surface will be level when the flap is lowered. The skirting should next be fitted, and then the bottom doors. Quadrant stays are used to support the falling flap.

The construction of one corner of the stationery case is shown by Fig. 51. All the vertical and horizontal divisions should be slip-dovetailed. This part should be completed by making the small centre door and the small drawers.

An open-grained finish to oak is desirable, this being effected by means of stain and slightly french-polishing. This should have a final rubbing with wax, which imparts a desirable tone to the work.

COMBINED WRITING-DESK AND BOOKCASE

The combination of a writing-desk and bookcase, both of which are desirable features in every home, are means by which economy of space is attained.

A design for a piece of furniture of this description is shown by Fig. 52. The lower portion is designed for the writing-desk, and the upper portion that of the bookcase. Drawers, trays, and cupboards are fitted in the two arms of the writing-desk; the drawers to accommodate small books, while the trays can be utilised for the indexing of catalogues, letters, or the storage of loose papers, as required. These trays are a saving on ordinary drawers, both in labour and material, their construction being very simple and light. The long cupboards will conveniently take rolls, etc. Between these two arms immediately below the writing-desk a rack is fitted, which can be utilised for keeping ledgers or other ponderous books.

The desk itself is provided with a slightly sloping top, and forms the cover to a large shallow drawer suitable for the storage of large papers which require to be kept flat. A locker comes directly

behind this desk, and can be used for storing documents of a private nature, so that they are always close at hand if wanted. A flap is provided to close the locker. The desk could be easily fitted up as a roll-top desk, if desired, by securing runners to the panels at the side of the desk; and the roll cover could be fixed inside the locker just mentioned, the flap being omitted.

Fig. 52.—Combined Writing-desk and Bookcase

The end compartments of the bookcase are provided with shelves, adjustable to any desired position. This is effected by fixing to the framing strips of brass which are holed to receive small hardwood pegs. These pegs are removed to the required place, and the shelves are rested on them. In these end compartments can be stored books which are not often in use, while the centre portion is for books more frequently wanted. This

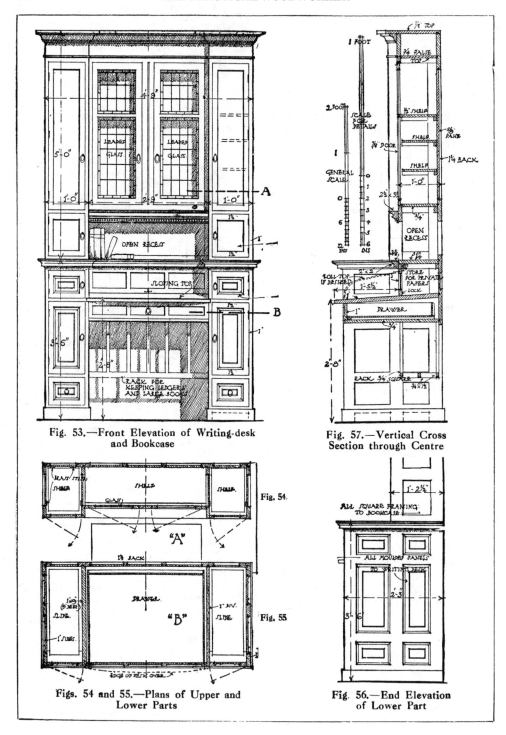

Fig. 53.—Front Elevation of Writing-desk
and Bookcase

Fig. 57.—Vertical Cross
Section through Centre

Figs. 54 and 55.—Plans of Upper and
Lower Parts

Fig. 56.—End Elevation
of Lower Part

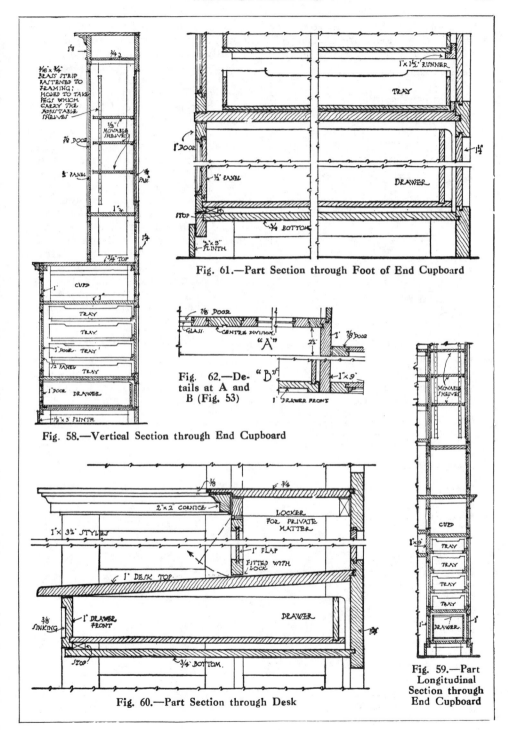

Fig. 61.—Part Section through Foot of End Cupboard

Fig. 62.—Details at A and B (Fig. 53)

Fig. 58.—Vertical Section through End Cupboard

Fig. 60.—Part Section through Desk

Fig. 59.—Part Longitudinal Section through End Cupboard

centre cupboard is fitted with ordinary shelving, and the doors are glazed with plain, clear leaded-glass in small squares.

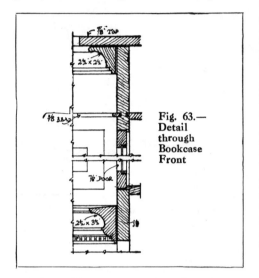

Fig. 63.—Detail through Bookcase Front

Below this centre cupboard and over the locker previously mentioned is an open recess, meant for putting books which are in everyday use. The recess is left open at the back, the coloured wall showing through, lending relief to the whole. This design, of course, is meant to be executed in hardwood, and would look exceedingly well in polished mahogany, while the cornice and plain leaded glazing are very pleasing. If variety is desirable, inlaid panels may be fixed, and the small bead shown in the panels omitted.

The illustrations may be described as follows : Fig. 52 a perspective sketch, Fig. 53 a front elevation, Fig. 54 a plan at A (Fig. 53) and Fig. 55 a plan at B (Fig. 53), Fig. 56 a part side elevation, Fig. 57 a vertical section through the centre, Fig. 58 a vertical section through the end cupboard, Fig. 59 a part longitudinal section through the end cupboard, Fig. 60 a part section through the writing-desk, Fig. 61 a part section through the foot of the end cupboard, Fig. 62 details at A and B (Fig. 53), and Fig. 63 a detail through the bookcase front (Fig. 57).

OFFICE FURNITURE

Writing furniture and fitments possessing a characteristic style pertaining to the office are dealt with in a later section under the title of Office Furniture.

Wardrobes

SMALL WARDROBE WITH LEADED LIGHT

THE small hanging wardrobe shown in three elevations by Figs. 1, 2 and 3, and simple as possible. Figs. 1 and 2 give the principal dimensions.

The construction may be divided into three parts, the main carcase, the framed-up base or stand, and the cornice. In

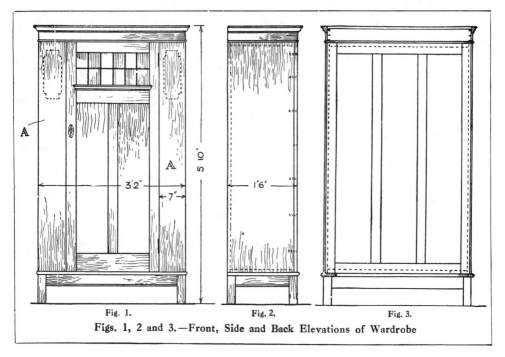

Fig. 1. Fig. 2. Fig. 3.

Figs. 1, 2 and 3.—Front, Side and Back Elevations of Wardrobe

of which a photographic reproduction is given by Fig. 4, would be most suitable for construction in oak. An attempt has been made to keep the construction as the main carcase, the ends, top and bottom are of $\frac{7}{8}$-in. material lap-dovetailed together in the usual way. The back should, if possible, be framed up, as in

Fig. 3, and screwed into rebates in the ends. Coming to the carcase front, the two pilasters A (Fig. 1) are dowelled to the ends and at the top and bottom, and are decorated by the inlaying of a suitable mosaic banding (a banding of ebony and boxwood looks well in oak).

The base is 8 in. high, the 2½-in. by 1-in. bearers being tenoned into the legs, which are 2 in. square. These legs are shown plain, but they could have a slight chamfer taken off the edges, or could be turned.

The cornice is a dovetailed frame, faced up and fitted with a cornice moulding, dustboard and frieze moulding, as shown in the section (Fig. 5).

Details of the door are shown in Fig. 6. A leaded light is introduced into the upper part, but to simplify construction, both this and the strip of moulding planted beneath it could be dispensed with, a plain wooden panel being used instead.

The interior fitting can be treated in a variety of ways. In the first place, coat hooks could be screwed to battens about 4 in. wide secured to the carcase back and ends, while triple hooks could also be screwed into the carcase top. As an alternative, lengths of brass tubing could be supported on ledges near the top, from which coat hangers are suspended. A similar arrangement lower down could be used for trousers. The most suitable method of finishing would be to fume the oak (or, as this is likely to be inconvenient, to achieve a similar result by means of a spirit stain), and polish with wax.

4-FT. 6-IN. WARDROBE

The wardrobe to be described is, according to the usual practice and for the sake of portability, designed to be made in three sections, namely, surbase, carcase and cornice. Figs. 7 and 8 show the

assembled wardrobe and give the main dimensions, which, of course, may be varied to some extent to meet individual requirements.

To describe the job in the order in which the work should be undertaken, the surbase (Figs. 9, 10 and 11) claims first attention. This is built up on four 1½-in.

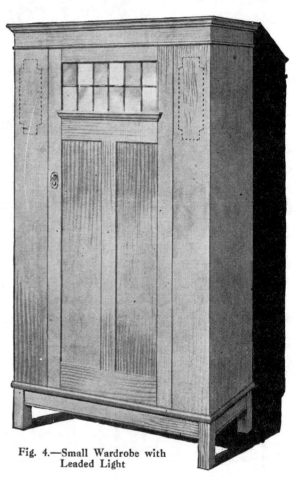

Fig. 4.—Small Wardrobe with Leaded Light

by 1½-in. angle-posts, the lower portions of which are packed out to a size suitable for turning to form the feet, the maximum diameter of which is 3 in. The top rail is dovetailed to the posts as shown in the plan, and the bottom rail and the back board are tenoned into these, the sides being tongued and glued in place. The bottom board has its ends housed to

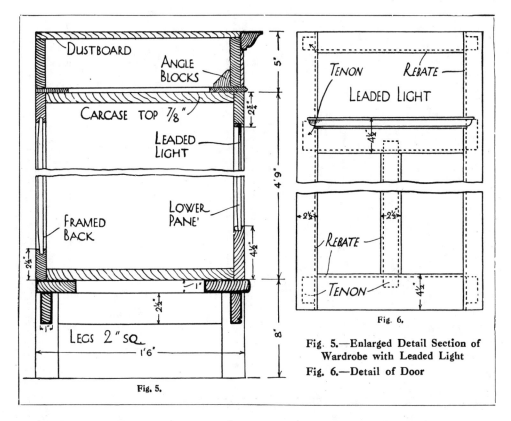

DUSTBOARD

ANGLE BLOCKS

CARCASE TOP 7/8"

LEADED LIGHT

FRAMED BACK

LOWER PANE'

LEGS 2"SQ.

1'6"

5"

2½"

4'9"

4½"

2½"

1"

2½"

8"

1"

Fig. 5.

TENON   REBATE

LEADED LIGHT

4½"

REBATE

2½"   2½"

TENON   4½"

Fig. 6.

Fig. 5.—Enlarged Detail Section of
Wardrobe with Leaded Light

Fig. 6.—Detail of Door

the sides, and, together with the rest of the structure, is stiffened where indicated by a liberal number of angle-blocks. Four fillets and two stops must be fixed where shown in preparation for the drawer, and the two ⅜-in. mouldings planted on the front and both sides. These mouldings are of similar section to that shown on the top frame, and in fixing, it should be borne in mind that the upper member is placed ⅛ in. below the top surface of the bottom rail, to avoid its being damaged and possibly wrenched off with the working of the drawer.

The top frame is mortised and tenoned together, moulded on its three exposed edges, and is held in its place on the surbase with dowels and angle-blocks.

Figs. 12, 13 and 14 deal with the construction of the drawer, the front, back and sides of which are dovetailed together.

The bottom rests in a groove in the drawer front (Fig. 13) and in grooved fillets glued to the sides (Fig. 14), and it is further supported in the middle by the grooved rail which is housed to the drawer front and screwed to the bottom edge of the drawer back. The bottom should be bradded at its back edge only, so as to ensure freedom for possible shrinkage. A suggestion for veneering the drawer front is given in Fig. 7, and the fixing of lock and drawer pulls completes the surbase.

For the next section—the carcase—reference must be made to Figs. 15 to 25, from which it will be seen that the top board is dovetailed to the sides, the bottom board being similarly assembled. The partition is dovetail-housed to the top and bottom boards, and the panelled back (Figs 16 and 17) is screwed to all back edges of the carcase, and keeps this square and rigid. Four locating blocks

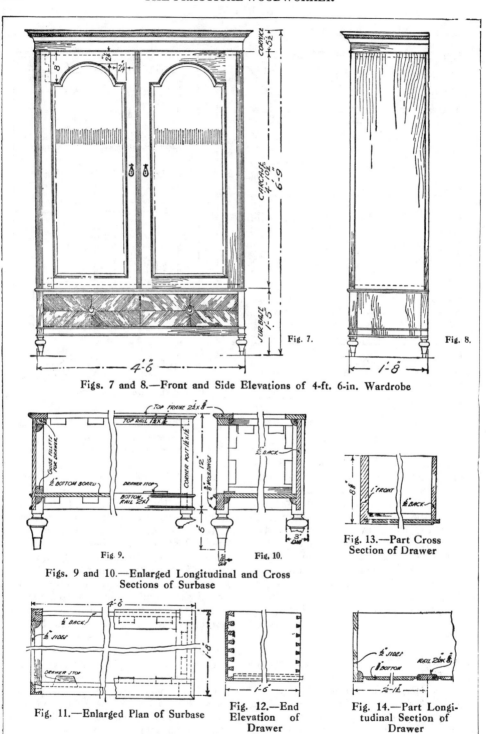

Figs. 7 and 8.—Front and Side Elevations of 4-ft. 6-in. Wardrobe

Fig. 7.

Fig. 8.

Fig. 9.

Fig. 10.

Figs. 9 and 10.—Enlarged Longitudinal and Cross Sections of Surbase

Fig. 13.—Part Cross Section of Drawer

Fig. 11.—Enlarged Plan of Surbase

Fig. 12.—End Elevation of Drawer

Fig. 14.—Part Longitudinal Section of Drawer

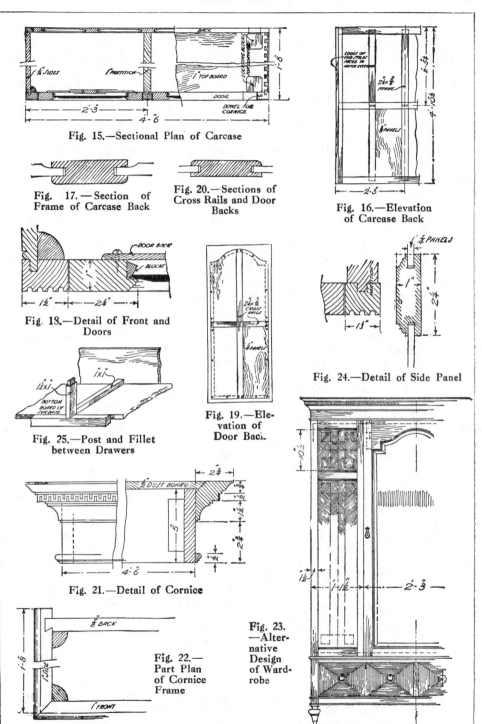

Fig. 15.—Sectional Plan of Carcase

Fig. 17.—Section of Frame of Carcase Back

Fig. 20.—Sections of Cross Rails and Door Backs

Fig. 16.—Elevation of Carcase Back

Fig. 18.—Detail of Front and Doors

Fig. 24.—Detail of Side Panel

Fig. 25.—Post and Fillet between Drawers

Fig. 19.—Elevation of Door Back

Fig. 21.—Detail of Cornice

Fig. 22.—Part Plan of Cornice Frame

Fig. 23.—Alternative Design of Wardrobe

are glued and bradded to the underside of the bottom, and so placed as to fit in the angles of the top frame of the surbase, thereby locating the carcase in correct position on that section. Four similar blocks are placed in suitable positions on the carcase top, for the purpose of fitting on the cornice section. These latter blocks are shown in Fig. 15, as are also the two dowels which further secure the cornice in place.

Details of the front and doors are given in Fig. 18, and it will be seen that the partition is faced with a fluted member to match the end pilasters.

The doors are framed together with haunched tenons—two at the top rails— the moulding being mitred at the angles, and each door is hung on three 2-in. brass butt hinges and fitted with a wardrobe latch. Wedge-shape blocks are pinned at intervals in the rebate to hold the bevelled plate-glass mirror, and here it should be noted that it is advisable to blacken the rebate with stain, to avoid a conspicuous reflection of the rebate surfaces when the glass is in position.

Backs for the doors are constructed as shown in Figs. 19 and 20. A vertical bar runs through with two cross-rails tenoned into it, and the panels fit into grooves in these. The bar and rails must, of course, be halved over the door frame to allow the panels to be screwed down, this being effected with four round-head brass screws placed where indicated. Figs. 21 and 22 give details of the cornice section. This is built up on a frame which may have its front angles mitred and blocked, or, if made of pine, dovetailed and the frame afterwards faced with hardwood. The back rail is dovetail-housed to the sides. The enrichment on the cornice may be fretted out of $\frac{1}{16}$-in. fret-wood, and applied to the moulding by gluing.

Fig. 23 shows an alternative design, being an arrangement for one central door and two drawers, and Figs. 24 and 25 are details relating to this alternative scheme, which may be further varied by moulding the stiles of the side framing as well as the rails, and substituting plain raised panels with chamfered margins about

$\frac{3}{4}$ in. wide in place of the veneered work, in which case the veneering should be omitted from the drawer fronts also. These side frames are fixed with dowels and glue, the wardrobe sides being beaded where they abut.

As regards material, the job would look well in walnut, oak, or mahogany. If, however, the choice of timber is quite open, and a suggestion on the matter would be helpful, walnut, finished with a wax-polish, is recommended. In practice it is customary to use oak and occasionally pine or American whitewood for the interior or unexposed work such as the carcase back, partition, top and bottom boards, door backs, and all parts of the drawer excepting the front, and there is, of course, no need for this to be of the superior hardwood, if the suggestion for veneering is adopted. Well-seasoned deal will serve for the dust-board to the cornice, the bottom board of the surbase and the top frame to same, this latter having the hardwood moulding planted on its edges.

WARDROBE WITH DRAWERS AND TRAYS

The wardrobe shown in Fig. 26 is known as a bachelor's wardrobe, and differs from the usual kind inasmuch that there is no hanging space, the whole being utilised by drawers and trays for holding folded clothing. Fig. 27 is a front elevation, and Fig. 28 shows the interior fittings. Suitable woods are mahogany, oak, ash, etc., if it is to be french-polished ; pine or American whitewood if for painting, etc.

The principal measurements are : Extreme height, 6 ft. 10 in. ; width across the front of the carcases, 3 ft. 6 in. ; width of the ends, including the thickness of the doors, 1 ft. 8 in. to 1 ft. 10 in., according to requirements. If hardwood is used, a saving in cost can be made if all the out-of-sight parts are constructed of pine or American whitewood. It is usual, however, no matter what kind of hardwood is selected, to make the inside parts of baywood or Honduras mahogany. In getting out the wood the portions made of 1-in. stuff are : Carcase ends, tops, and bottoms, drawer fronts, tray fronts (*see* Fig. 29), bearers D (Fig. 27), frieze E (Fig. 27), moulding F (Fig. 27), separating the top and bottom carcases and the grooved muntins for the carcase back G (Fig. 30). The parts constructed of ½-in. stuff are : Door panels H (Fig. 31),

(Fig. 28), and then veneer the outer faces. Another method of avoiding veneering is to secret-dovetail the corners. The top and bottom of the upper carcase are dovetailed into the ends, the latter being 3 in. less in width than the lower carcase.

In making the lower carcase containing the drawers, wood can be saved by using

Fig. 26.—Wardrobe with
Drawers and Trays

drawer and tray sides, backs, and bottoms, and grooved slips K (Figs. 32 and 33), frieze moulding L (Fig. 34), carcase backs M (Fig. 30), and the dustboards or divisions N (Fig. 35). The doors are of 1¼-in. stuff, finishing about 1⅛ in. thick.

First make the frieze E (Fig. 27). It is usual to dovetail the front and end pieces together the same as shown in the tray

bearers (Fig. 30), and jointing angular pieces P to them. The arrangement and method of fitting together of bearers, drawer runners, and dustboards between each drawer will be seen clearly in Fig. 35. The division between the two short drawers is tenoned into bearers above and below. The plinth moulding C (Fig. 27) is mitred at the corners as shown

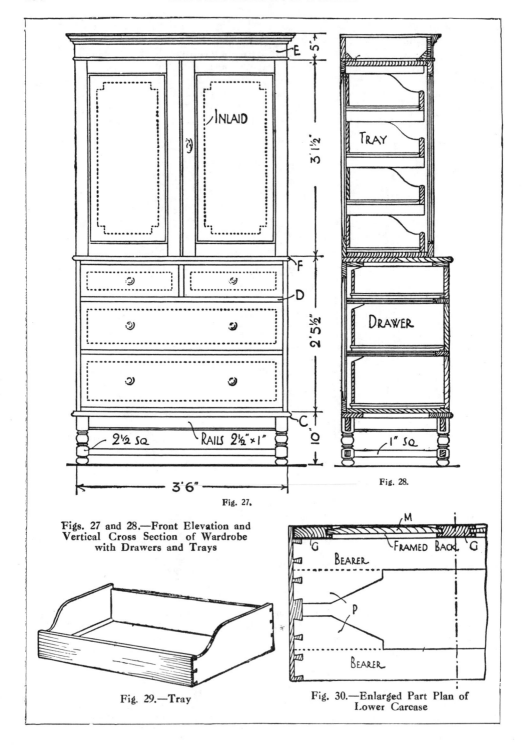

Fig. 27.

Fig. 28.

Figs. 27 and 28.—Front Elevation and Vertical Cross Section of Wardrobe with Drawers and Trays

Fig. 29.—Tray

Fig. 30.—Enlarged Part Plan of Lower Carcase

(*see also* enlarged section, Fig. 36). The mouldings F (Fig. 27) and L (Fig. 34) are treated in the same way ; Fig. 37 is an enlarged section of F (Fig. 27). The cornice moulding can be faced with hard-wood and backed with pine (*see* section in Fig. 34), and then mitred at the corners. To prevent dust lodging on the top of the cornice, a ½-in. board (Fig. 34) can be

in position, allowing them to be drawn out the same as drawers.

The doors are mortised and tenoned to-gether, and an ovolo moulding is worked on the inner edges, as shown in Fig. 34 ; or a rebated moulding could be fixed along the edges of the stiles and the rails, and mitred at the corners. The bead which divides the centre stiles of the

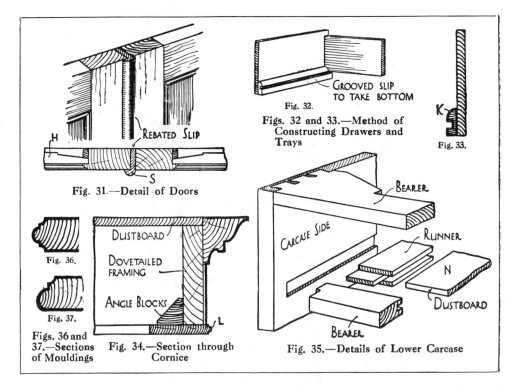

Fig. 31.—Detail of Doors

Figs. 32 and 33.—Method of Constructing Drawers and Trays

Fig. 32.

Fig. 33.

Figs. 36 and 37.—Sections of Mouldings

Fig. 34.—Section through Cornice

Fig. 35.—Details of Lower Carcase

fixed ; it also serves to place any suitable ornaments.

The fronts of the trays for the upper carcase are about 3½ in. wide, and the sides are about 9 in. wide (*see* Fig. 28), the latter being shaped down to the front. This figure also shows the method of dove-tailing the trays together. Figs. 32 and 33 illustrate the grooved strips K in which the bottoms of the trays slide. The drawers in the lower carcase are con-structed in the same way as the trays. Between the lowest tray and those above, strips of ½-in. stuff are screwed to the carcase ends, and serve to keep the trays

doors is shown at s (Fig. 31). The full thickness of the bead is first glued to the stile, and then it is rebated to receive the other stile. The door panels are decor-ated by inlaying a mosaic banding as indicated in the elevation (Fig. 27). The drawer fronts are treated in a similar manner. The left-hand door will re-quire flush bolts top and bottom, and the right-hand door a spring lock, with a handle to work the latter.

The stand upon which the wardrobe rests is tenoned together in the usual way, the legs are turned from stuff 2½ in. square, the upper rails being 2½ in. by 1 in., and the lower 1 in. square. The lower carcase is secured to this by pocket screwing from the inside of the rails.

4-FT. WARDROBE WITH MIRROR PANELS

Fig. 38 is a conventional view of a wardrobe which has mirror panels, and which,

A front elevation, a vertical section, and two half-plans are shown by Figs. 39, 40 and 41 respectively, Fig. 40 being on the lines B B and Fig. 41 on the lines A A of the front elevation. Another vertical section, this time of the hanging portion, on the lines C C of Fig. 39 is shown by Fig. 42. The arrangement of the shelves, etc., is clearly indicated in Fig. 43. The

Fig. 38.—4-ft. Wardrobe with Mirror Panels

except for this detail, embodies practically the same constructional work as the three-piece wardrobes described in the preceding pages. It may be mentioned that this wardrobe agrees in design fairly well with a dressing-table and washstand described in a later section.

back of the wardrobe is as shown in the back elevation (Fig. 44). A detail of the top of the door is given by Fig. 45. A detail section of the front on the line L L (Fig. 39) is given by Fig. 46. The construction of the three sections of which the wardrobe is built is made

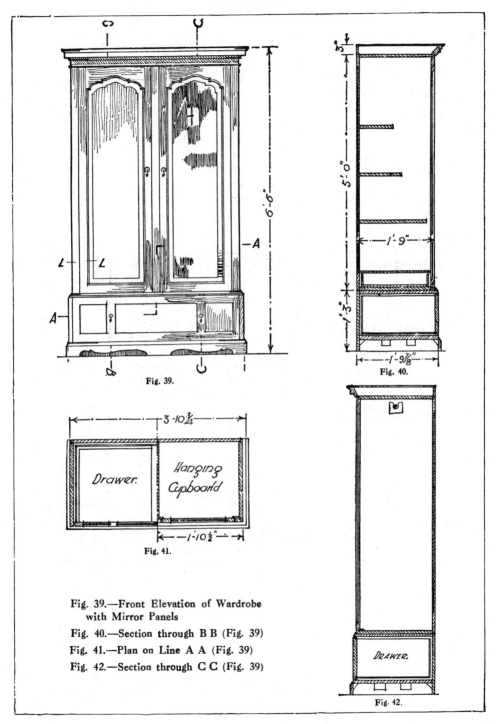

Fig. 39.

Fig. 40.

Fig. 41.

Fig. 39.—Front Elevation of Wardrobe with Mirror Panels

Fig. 40.—Section through B B (Fig. 39)

Fig. 41.—Plan on Line A A (Fig. 39)

Fig. 42.—Section through C C (Fig. 39)

Fig. 42.

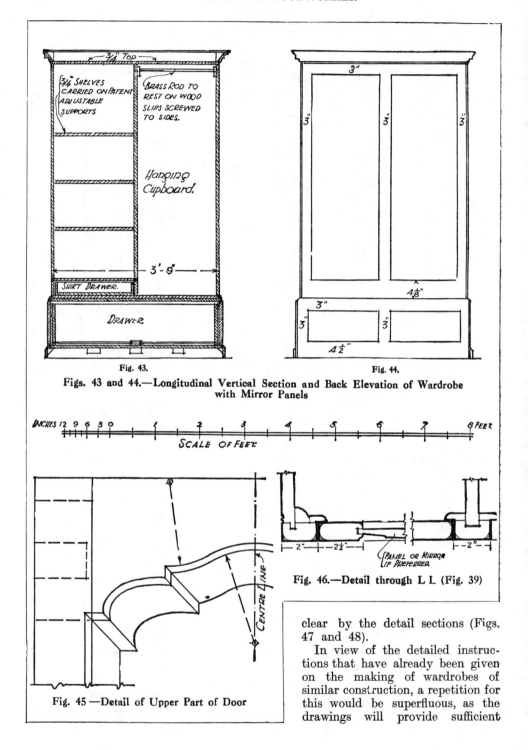

Fig. 43.

Fig. 44.

Figs. 43 and 44.—Longitudinal Vertical Section and Back Elevation of Wardrobe with Mirror Panels

Fig. 46.—Detail through L L (Fig. 39)

Fig. 45 —Detail of Upper Part of Door

clear by the detail sections (Figs. 47 and 48).

In view of the detailed instructions that have already been given on the making of wardrobes of similar construction, a repetition for this would be superfluous, as the drawings will provide sufficient information if studied in conjunction with examples already given.

HANGING WARDROBE

As a substitute, at a comparatively moderate cost, for the ordinary form of

whitewood, or deal, the panels being flush on the top side so as to leave no traps for dust.

The construction of the top is shown in Figs. 50, 51 and 52. The two upper members of the cornice are glued and pinned in place, and the 2½-in. by ⅝-in.

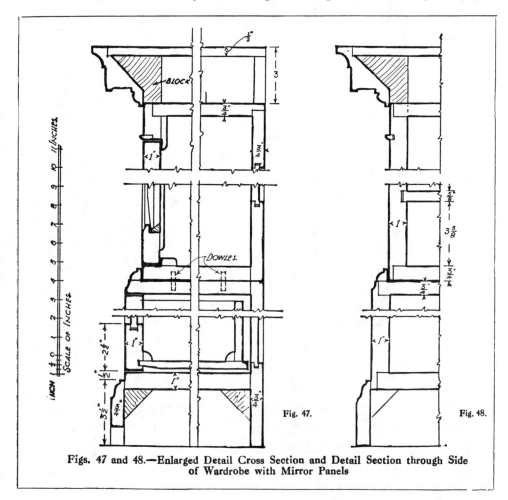

Fig. 47.   Fig. 48.

Figs. 47 and 48.—Enlarged Detail Cross Section and Detail Section through Side of Wardrobe with Mirror Panels

wardrobe, the arrangement shown by Fig. 49 may be of interest to many who experience the need for additional hanging accommodation, particularly for items of ladies' attire.

The pillar, feet, and cornice members of the top are intended to be of hardwood, but the top may be framed up in pine,

moulded fillet is secured by screwing through the top, the mitred angles being strengthened by glue-blocks as shown in Fig. 51. A 9-in. by 9-in. by ⅞-in. chamfered block is screwed diagonally to the underside of the top to add strength in the fixing of this to the pillar, and four brass brackets of the strong cast type

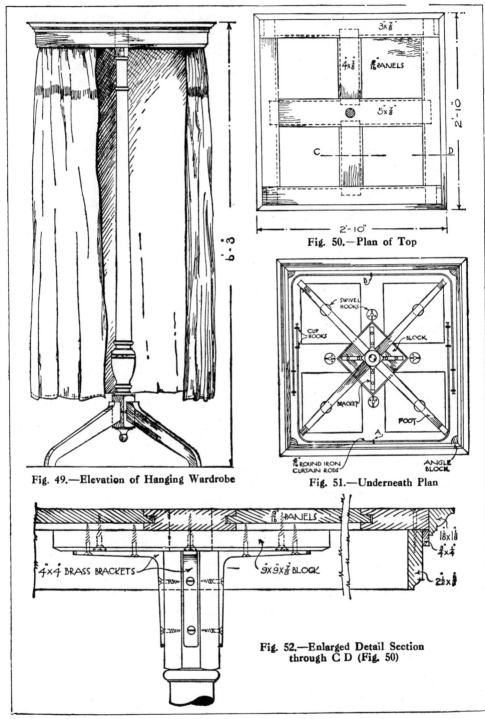

Fig. 49.—Elevation of Hanging Wardrobe

Fig. 50.—Plan of Top

Fig. 51.—Underneath Plan

Fig. 52.—Enlarged Detail Section through C D (Fig. 50)

are added to afford further support for the top, which, as will be seen from the illustrations, carries the hooks on which the clothes are hung. The angles of the upper squared part of the pillar are planed away to form a face, just wide enough for the fixing of the brackets.

Fig. 53 shows the pillar and feet in detail; the latter being tenoned and pinned to the lower squared part of the pillar which is turned from some $2\frac{3}{4}$-in. by $2\frac{3}{4}$-in. stuff. The dotted lines indicate where the stuff must be packed out for turning

Fig. 54.—Recess Wardrobe Fitment

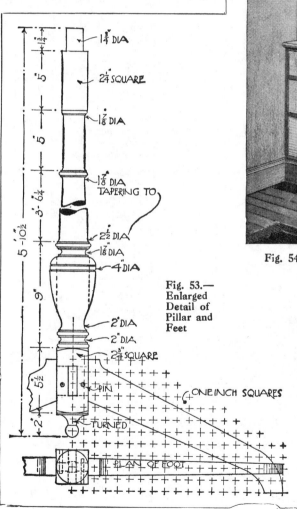

Fig. 53.—Enlarged Detail of Pillar and Feet

to 4 in. in diameter. This method saves material.

As an alternative to the turned pillar, a square pillar tapering from $2\frac{3}{4}$ in. at the bottom to 2 in. at the top may be used, the angles being chamfered and stopped, say, within 2 in. of the top of the feet, and the same distance from the bottom of the brass brackets.

The curtain rods are of $\frac{5}{16}$-in. round iron, and supported on brass cup-hooks of suitable size, these hooks being closed with pliers when the rods are in position, so as to prevent their being dislodged. It will be seen by reference to Fig. 51 that the rods run by each other at their ends, so as to allow the curtains to lap at their edges, and sufficient clearance must be allowed between the two sets of hooks for the rings of both curtains to pass.

For access to the wardrobe, the cur-

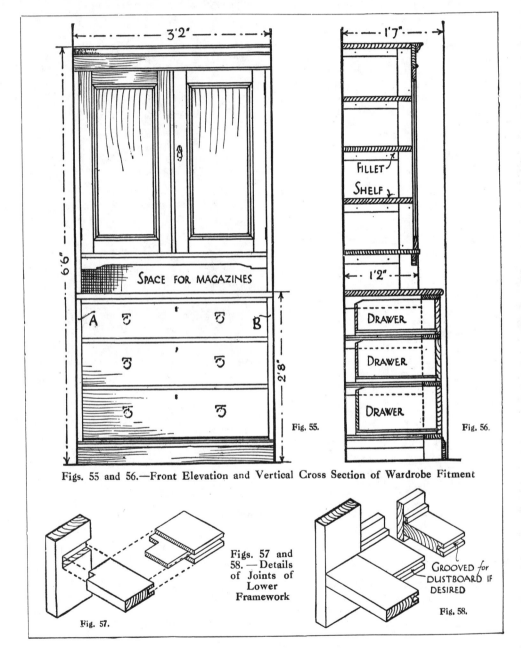

Figs. 55 and 56.—Front Elevation and Vertical Cross Section of Wardrobe Fitment

Figs. 57 and 58. — Details of Joints of Lower Framework

tains are drawn back to the central cup-hooks at A and B. Eight double brass wardrobe-hooks with back plates are fillets nailed to them, which are in turn nailed to the side walls. The whole of this lower framework should be fitted

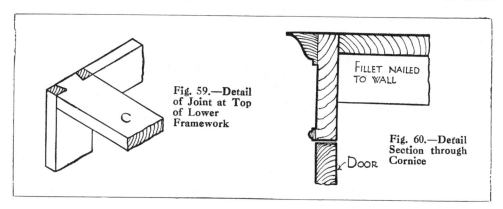

Fig. 59.—Detail of Joint at Top of Lower Framework

FILLET NAILED TO WALL

Fig. 60.—Detail Section through Cornice

DOOR

fixed where shown in Fig. 51, four being on the panels and four on the frame.

RECESS WARDROBE FITMENT

The half-tone reproduction (Fig. 54) shows a fitment designed to fill one of the recesses found in most bedrooms. The dimensions given on Figs. 55 and 56 are for a recess 3 ft. 2 in. wide and 1 ft. 7 in. deep ; but the worker will, of course, modify the dimensions to suit his own particular case. The majority of the work is from 1-in. material.

There will in most cases be an existing skirting-board, to which the lower framework will need careful adjustment. In this framework the two stiles A and B (Fig. 55) have the drawer rails and runners tenoned into them (see details, Figs. 57 and 58), and are connected at the top by the rail C dovetailed into them (see Fig. 59). The runners have 3-in. by $\frac{5}{8}$-in.

together temporarily before being inserted into the recess and nailed, during which process the runners should be carefully adjusted to a horizontal position. The top of the drawers, which has a moulded or rounded front edge, can now be prepared and fitted into position. The plinth should be so fitted that it continues the lines of the existing skirting board (see general view, Fig. 54). The drawers are constructed in the usual manner, and guide strips for them should be fitted in the angles formed by the fillets and runners (Fig. 58).

The upper framework for the cupboard should present no difficulties. Fig. 60 shows the arrangement of the cornice. Between the lowest shelf of the cupboard and the top of the drawers a clear space is left. The cupboard doors are framed up with mortise-and-tenon joints, and a moulding is mitred round and pinned on.

DRESSING-TABLE AND WASHSTAND

Dressing - table. — The dressing-table shown in Fig. 1 is designed on the usual lines, the jewel drawers being underneath in order to leave the top as clear as possible for toilet requisites. Two elevations and a part sectional plan are shown by Figs. 2, 3 and 4, whilst a vertical section is given by Fig. 5.

The table is constructed with four $1\frac{5}{8}$-in. square legs tapering to $1\frac{1}{4}$ in., with front and side rails out of 9-in. by $\frac{3}{4}$-in. material, the back rail being $6\frac{1}{2}$ in. by $\frac{3}{4}$ in. The front and side rails are cut to the shapes as shown in Figs. 2, 3 and 6, and are tenoned to the legs as shown in

Figs. 7 and 8. In order to make the table perfectly rigid, it is advisable to frame to the feet of the legs the $1\frac{1}{4}$-in. by $1\frac{1}{2}$-in. rails shown in Figs. 2 and 5.

The construction of the drawers and bearers is detailed in Figs. 6 and 9, Fig. 9 being a detail plan of the drawer, etc., and Fig. 6 being a section through same viewed from the front. The drawer runners ($\frac{3}{4}$ in. by $1\frac{1}{2}$ in.) are stub-tenoned to the front and back rails, and have small guide fillets planted on the top, the two members above the drawers (Fig. 6) being necessary to prevent the drawer tilting when withdrawn. The table-top is 1 in. thick, and is fixed with buttons screwed to same from the underside and tongued to the rails (see Fig. 6).

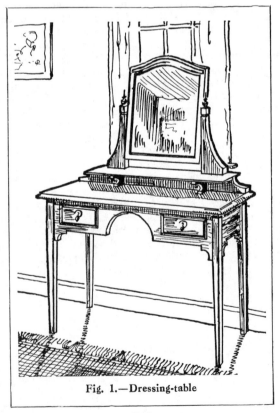

Fig. 1.—Dressing-table

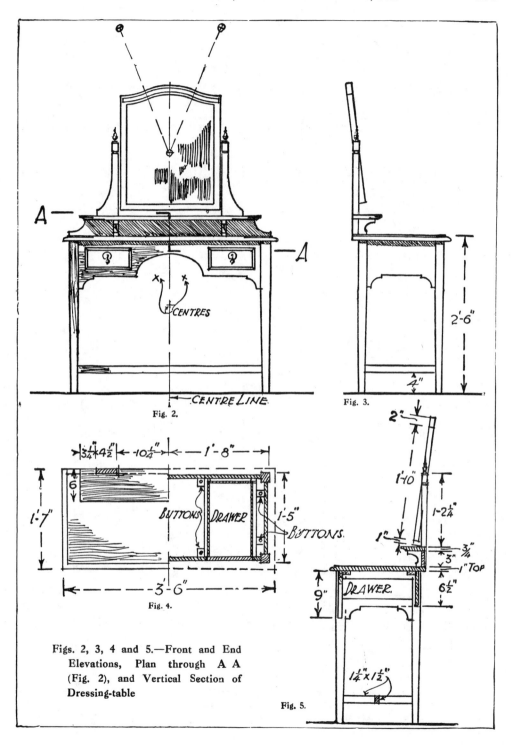

Fig. 2.

Fig. 3.

Fig. 4.

Figs. 2, 3, 4 and 5.—Front and End
Elevations, Plan through A A
(Fig. 2), and Vertical Section of
Dressing-table

Fig. 5.

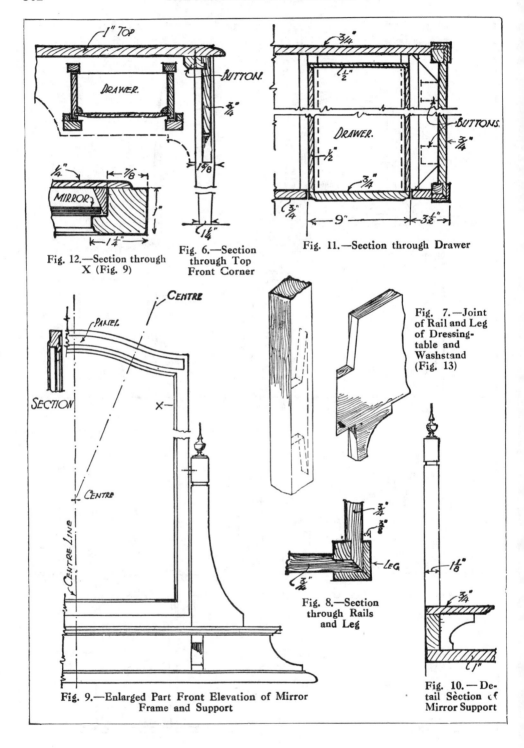

Fig. 12.—Section through X (Fig. 9)

Fig. 6.—Section through Top Front Corner

Fig. 11.—Section through Drawer

Fig. 7.—Joint of Rail and Leg of Dressing-table and Washstand (Fig. 13)

Fig. 8.—Section through Rails and Leg

Fig. 9.—Enlarged Part Front Elevation of Mirror Frame and Support

Fig. 10. — Detail Section of Mirror Support

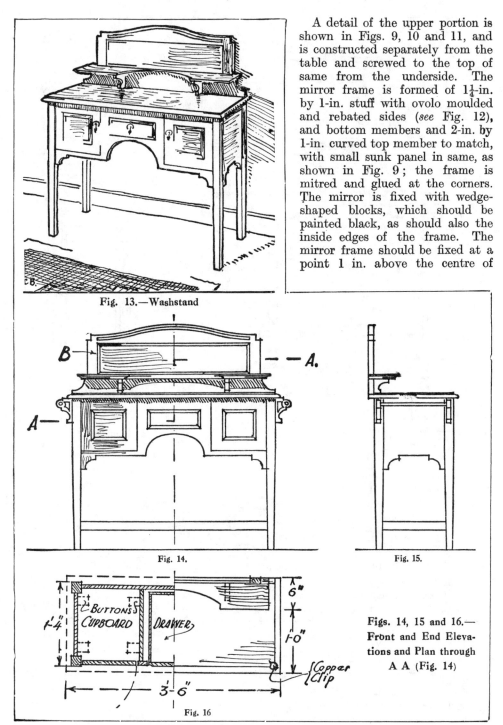

A detail of the upper portion is shown in Figs. 9, 10 and 11, and is constructed separately from the table and screwed to the top of same from the underside. The mirror frame is formed of $1\frac{1}{4}$-in. by 1-in. stuff with ovolo moulded and rebated sides (see Fig. 12), and bottom members and 2-in. by 1-in. curved top member to match, with small sunk panel in same, as shown in Fig. 9; the frame is mitred and glued at the corners. The mirror is fixed with wedge-shaped blocks, which should be painted black, as should also the inside edges of the frame. The mirror frame should be fixed at a point 1 in. above the centre of

Fig. 13.—Washstand

Fig. 14.

Fig. 15.

Fig. 16

Figs. 14, 15 and 16.— Front and End Elevations and Plan through A A (Fig. 14)

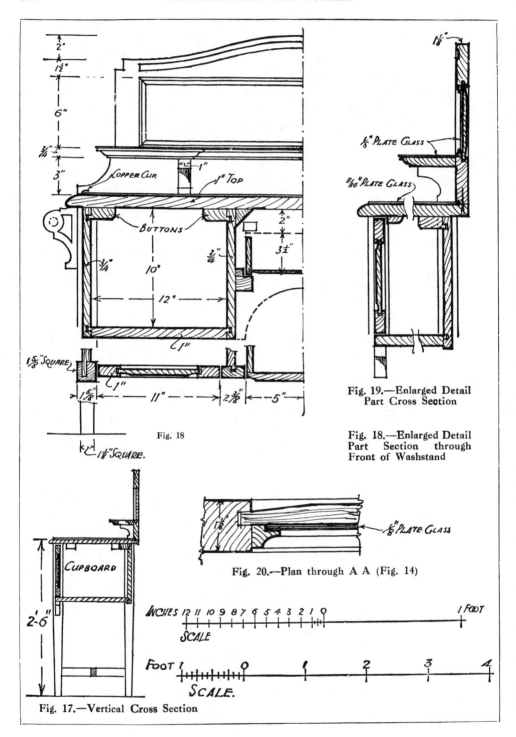

2"
1½"
6"
3/16"
3"

COPPER CLIP.
1" Top
1"
BUTTONS
2"
3/4"
3¼"
¾"
10"
12"
1"
¾"

1⅝" SQUARE
1"
1⅝"
11"
2⅜"
5"

Fig. 18

1⅛" SQUARE.

⅛" PLATE GLASS

3/16" PLATE GLASS

Fig. 19.—Enlarged Detail Part Cross Section

Fig. 18.—Enlarged Detail Part Section through Front of Washstand

CUPBOARD

2'-6"

⅛"

⅛" PLATE GLASS

Fig. 20.—Plan through A A (Fig. 14)

INCHES 12 11 10 9 8 7 6 5 4 3 2 1 0   1 FOOT
SCALE

FOOT 1   0   1   2   3   4
SCALE.

Fig. 17.—Vertical Cross Section

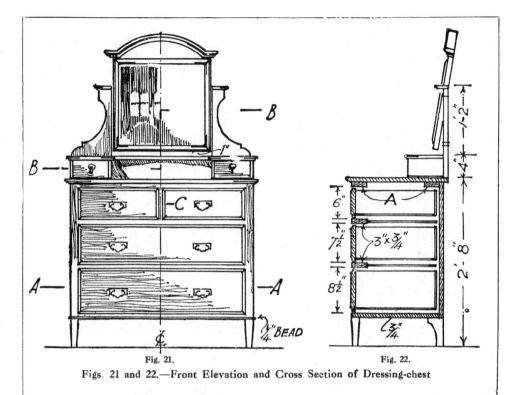

Fig. 21.

Fig. 22.

Figs. 21 and 22.—Front Elevation and Cross Section of Dressing-chest

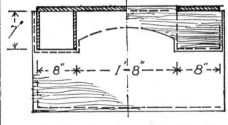

Fig. 23.—Plan through B B (Fig. 21)

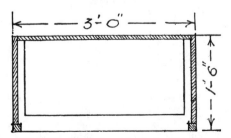

Fig. 24.—Plan through A A (Fig. 21)

the same with pivots in the usual manner.

Washstand.—The washstand is shown by Fig. 13. It is designed *en suite* with the dressing-table already described, being of similar construction in many respects. The principal members are of the same dimensions, and therefore need not be mentioned again. Two elevations and a sectional plan are shown by Figs. 14, 15 and 16, and a vertical section by Fig. 17.

The legs, side, back, bottom rails and table-top should be loosely framed together first and the side toilet cupboards, etc., framed to them as shown in Figs. 18 and 19. The centre of front with perforation for drawer is tongued and grooved to the cupboards and fixed to the table-top. The small curved end pieces which are required in order to match the outline of the dressing-table front are planted on to the bottom of the cupboards and housed to the legs.

The table-top and shelf is covered with clear plate-glass with ground edges, and

fitted into the panel of the back screen, as shown in Fig. 20. This method of covering the exposed parts with glass is very effective in practice, allowing as it does the grain of the wood to be clearly

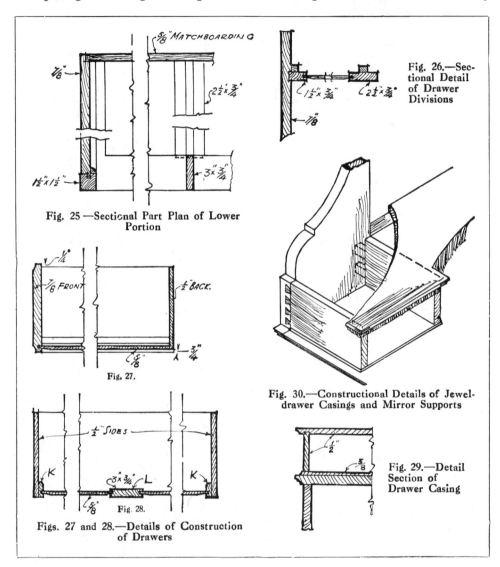

Fig. 25 —Sectional Part Plan of Lower Portion

Fig. 27.

Figs. 27 and 28.—Details of Construction of Drawers

Fig. 26.—Sectional Detail of Drawer Divisions

Fig. 30.—Constructional Details of Jewel-drawer Casings and Mirror Supports

Fig. 29.—Detail Section of Drawer Casing

is secured at the back by a small rebate in the bottom of the vertical screen (Fig. 19), and at the front corners with small ornamental copper clips screwed to the table-top. A sheet of similar glass is also

seen, and at the same time providing an easily cleansed surface.

The back screen is framed with $1\frac{1}{8}$-in. material with mortise-and-tenon joints at the corners, and a $\frac{1}{4}$-in. panel in the centre with a small moulding planted round (Fig. 20). The shelf is screwed to the screen from the back, and also to the small brackets which rest on the top of the glass. These latter are not fixed to the table-top, so that it is unnecessary to cut the glass round the feet of same.

DRESSING-CHEST

The dressing-chest shown by Figs. 21

treated. The back is of $\frac{5}{8}$-in. match-boarding let into the sides, as shown in Fig. 25, and screwed to them.

The drawer divisions are framed together with $\frac{3}{4}$-in.-thick material grooved for the $\frac{3}{8}$-in. panels, the whole being housed, glued and blocked to the sides and back, as shown in Figs. 25 and 26. The drawers are constructed as shown in Figs. 27 and 28, the fronts, sides and backs being dovetailed together, and the

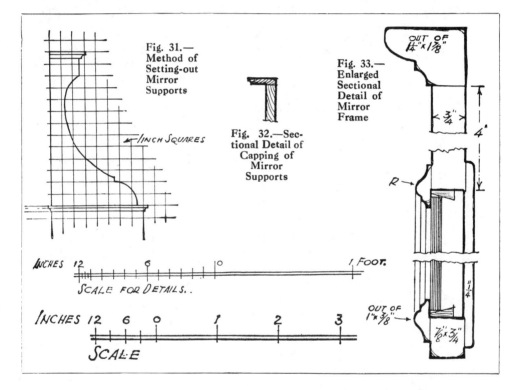

Fig. 31.—Method of Setting-out Mirror Supports

Fig. 32.—Sectional Detail of Capping of Mirror Supports

Fig. 33.—Enlarged Sectional Detail of Mirror Frame

to 24 is a very useful piece of bedroom furniture where space is valuable, combining as it does the purposes of a chest of drawers and washstand.

The lower portion is composed of $\frac{7}{8}$-in. sides tongued into the $1\frac{1}{2}$-in. square front legs, with a small fillet glued to the inside-front corner, shown in Fig. 25. The back legs are in one piece with the sides. The $\frac{3}{4}$-in. bottom is dovetailed at the ends to the sides, the two 3-in. by $\frac{3}{4}$-in. top members (marked A on Fig. 22) being similarly

bottom panels being housed into fillets (K in Fig. 28), which are screwed to the sides; the long drawers have an additional support in the centre, as shown at L in Fig. 28.

The top is $\frac{7}{8}$ in. thick with moulded front and side edges, as shown in Fig. 29, and is fixed by being screwed from the underside through the members A (Fig. 22).

The jewel drawers at the sides and the mirror supports are constructed separately and screwed to the top from the

Fig. 34.—Easily-constructed Chest of Drawers

underside, the drawer casings being constructed as shown in Figs. 29 and 30, and the drawers in the usual manner with $\frac{1}{2}$-in. fronts, sides and backs.

The mirror bearers can be set out as shown in Fig. 31, there being a small capping at the top as shown in Fig. 32. The detail of the mirror frame is given in Fig. 33, and is $\frac{3}{4}$ in. thick with mitred and glued angles, the moulding R being planted on. The mirror is fixed with wedge-shaped blocks, which should be painted black, as should the inside edges of the frame. Various types of fittings are obtainable for fixing the mirror frame to the supports.

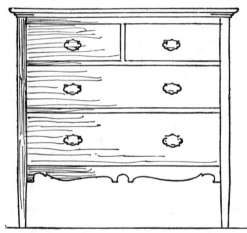

Fig. 35.

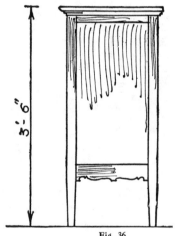

Fig. 36.

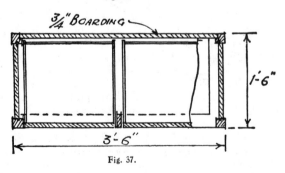

¾" BOARDING

Fig. 37.

Figs. 35, 36 and 37.— Front and End Elevations and Sectional Plan of Chest of Drawers

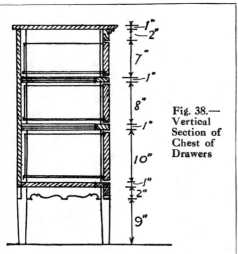

Fig. 38.—Vertical Section of Chest of Drawers

EASILY CONSTRUCTED CHEST OF DRAWERS

With the chest of drawers shown in perspective by Fig 34 an endeavour has been made to obtain a simple but well-proportioned effect, and at the same time to keep the construction as straight-forward as this will allow. The drawers are kept well clear of the floor in order to facilitate cleaning, a point which most housewives will appreciate.

Figs 35 and 36 show the front and side elevations respectively, and Fig. 37 shows a plan through the top drawers. Fig. 38 is a vertical section. Details of construction are given in Figs. 39, 40 and 41.

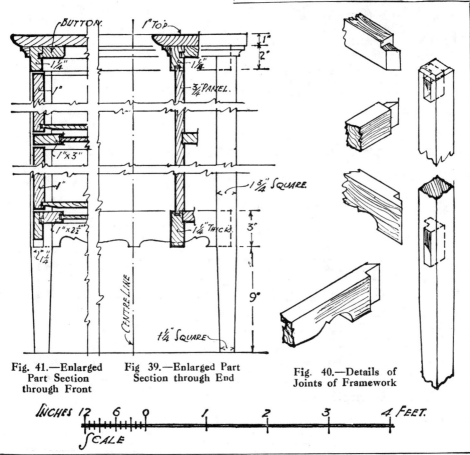

Fig. 41.—Enlarged Part Section through Front

Fig 39.—Enlarged Part Section through End

Fig. 40.—Details of Joints of Framework

Fig. 42.—Queen Anne Chest of Drawers

The framework is composed of four $1\frac{3}{4}$-in. legs tapered at the feet, as shown in Fig. 39, with 2-in. by $1\frac{1}{4}$-in. rails tenoned to same at top of front, and sides with similar rails out of 3 in. by $1\frac{1}{4}$ in. at the bottom, these being cut to the curves as shown on Figs. 35 and 36. The posts and side rails are grooved for the $\frac{3}{4}$-in. panel as shown in Fig. 39. The tenoned joints of the rails and posts are shown in isometric view in Fig. 40. The back is covered with boarding let into rebates in the posts and screwed to same.

The drawer divisions are constructed of 3-in. by 1-in. framing with $\frac{3}{8}$ in. panels, the whole being housed, glued and blocked to the sides. The 1-in. top has a rounded front and side edges, with a small cavetto moulding planted under it,

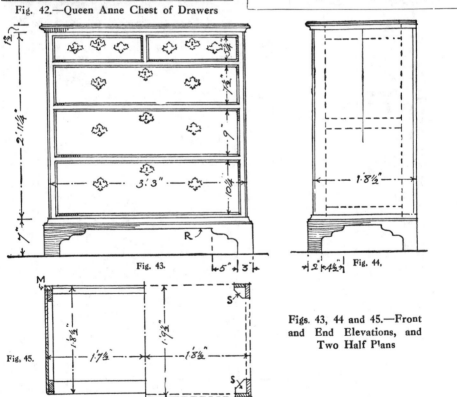

Fig. 43.

Fig. 44.

Fig. 45.

Figs. 43, 44 and 45.—Front and End Elevations, and Two Half Plans

and it is fixed with small buttons screwed to the top from the underside and tongued to the top rails, as shown in Figs. 39 and 41. The drawers are constructed in the usual manner with 1-in.

QUEEN ANNE CHEST OF DRAWERS

The chest of drawers shown by the half-tone (Fig. 42) is a reproduction of a

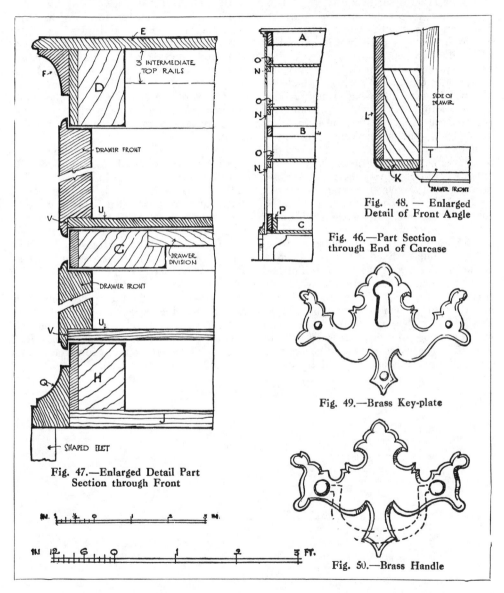

Fig. 47.—Enlarged Detail Part Section through Front

Fig. 46.—Part Section through End of Carcase

Fig. 48. — Enlarged Detail of Front Angle

Fig. 49.—Brass Key-plate

Fig. 50.—Brass Handle

fronts, and ½-in. sides and backs, dovetailed at the corners with ⅜-in. bottoms tongued to the sides.

similar piece of furniture of over two hundred years of age. The worker will note the liberal and convenient depth from front to back, the projecting fronts of the drawers, and the general simple lines of the whole structure.

Two elevations are given by Figs. 43 and 44, and two half plans by Fig. 45.

The ends are framed up with uprights front and back and three rails, all as dotted in Fig. 44 and in approximately $2\frac{1}{2}$-in. by 1-in. pine. At the back they are connected by similar rails A, B and C (Fig. 46), the spaces between which are afterwards filled in rather roughly with thin boarding. Along the top front edge is a pine rail $1\frac{1}{4}$ in. by 2 in., faced with oak D (Fig. 47), and supporting three intermediate rails introduced to stiffen the oak top E, which is just over $\frac{1}{4}$ in. thick, moulded on the projecting edges and finished with a cavetto moulding as at F. Three $2\frac{1}{2}$-in. by 1-in. drawer rails faced with oak and rebated for the divisions G (Fig. 47) are framed between the ends, and also a $1\frac{3}{4}$-in. by $1\frac{1}{4}$-in. bottom rail H, beneath which is fixed a rough bottom J.

The front faces of the ends are finished with moulded strips as at K (Fig. 48), covering the $\frac{1}{4}$-in. oak sides L, which are in two widths with a central butt-joint. The back angles are similarly finished with $1\frac{1}{4}$-in. by $\frac{1}{2}$-in. oak strips, as at M in Fig. 45. The three drawer divisions are stiffened next the ends by fillets under-

neath as at N (Fig. 46), and larger ones above as at O, the latter serving as guides for the drawers. At the bottom is a piece as at P, its upper surface coinciding with that of the rail H in Fig. 47.

The plinth is surmounted by an oak moulding Q (Fig. 47) mitred round and extending to the line R in Fig. 43. Below this are triangular blocks as at S (Fig. 45), dowelled in position and faced with $\frac{3}{4}$-in.-shaped oak feet as in Figs. 43 and 44. The faces of the latter being in the same plane as the lowest face of the moulding Q, there is a butt-joint where they meet at R.

The fronts of the drawers are 1 in. thick and are rebated and moulded all round on the solid, as in Fig. 47. The sides and back are a trifle less than $\frac{1}{2}$ in. thick, and are dovetailed together and to the fronts at T (Fig. 48). Their lower edges all finish level with the lines marked U in Fig. 47, and $\frac{5}{16}$-in. bottoms are bradded on from below without grooves or rebates. It will be noticed from Fig. 47 that the drawer bottoms extend right out to the carcase face at V, thus presenting one smooth wearing-surface.

The key and handle plates should be cut out of thick brass and have bevelled edges. Suitable designs for these are shown by Figs. 49 and 50.

Roll-top Desk

THE principal views of a 5-ft. roll-top desk are shown by Figs. 1 to 8.

Fig. 1 shows the desk in perspective, and elevations and half plans are given by Figs. 2, 3 and 4.

Roll-top desks as commonly known are more often made of oak than any other wood, probably on account of so many being made abroad, where the particular kind of oak is plentiful and cheap, besides being of a very suitable texture; but, of course, there is no reason why any other hardwood should not be used, the only question being one of expense. Some of the superior specimens sometimes seen are constructed of mahogany, and have a very beautiful appearance.

With these introductory remarks the worker will be left to use his own judgment and taste in selecting the material. The following methods and principles of construction are suitable for any wood.

For a job of this character working drawings of a full-size horizontal section (a half section is shown in Fig. 4) and vertical section (Fig. 5) should at least be made, and will be found of great advantage for setting out the parts.

The following is a list of the sizes of material required for the various parts:

Lower Framing of Carcase of Desk.—Four front corner stiles F S (Fig. 3), 2 ft. 6 in. by $2\frac{5}{8}$ in. by 2 in.; four angle stiles A S (Fig. 3), 2 ft. 6 in. by $1\frac{1}{8}$ in. by $2\frac{5}{8}$ in.; two inner stiles I S (Fig. 3), 2 ft. 6 in. by $1\frac{1}{8}$ in. by $2\frac{5}{8}$ in.; one bottom rail for back B R (Fig. 4), 4 ft. 11 in. by $3\frac{1}{2}$ in. by $1\frac{1}{8}$ in.; two bottom rails for kneehole framing, 2 ft. 5 in. by $3\frac{1}{2}$ in. by $1\frac{1}{8}$ in.; one middle rail for back M R (Fig. 2), 4 ft. 11 in. by $3\frac{1}{8}$ in. by $1\frac{1}{8}$ in.; two middle rails for kneehole framing, 2 ft. 5 in. by $3\frac{1}{8}$ in. by $1\frac{1}{8}$ in.; one top rail for back T R (Fig. 2), 4 ft. 11 in. by $2\frac{5}{8}$ in. by $1\frac{1}{8}$ in.; two top rails for kneehole framing, 2 ft. 5 in. by $2\frac{5}{8}$ in. by $1\frac{1}{8}$ in.; two top rails for ends T R (Fig. 4), 2 ft. 5 in. by $2\frac{5}{8}$ in. by $1\frac{1}{8}$ in.; fourteen lower muntins for back, ends, sides, and kneehole framing, 1 ft. $3\frac{1}{2}$ in. by $3\frac{1}{8}$ in. by $1\frac{1}{8}$ in.; fourteen upper muntins for back, ends, sides, and kneehole framing, 8 in. by $3\frac{1}{8}$ in. by $1\frac{1}{8}$ in.; four lower panels for back, 1 ft. $1\frac{1}{2}$ in. by $6\frac{1}{2}$ in. by $\frac{3}{4}$ in.; three lower panels for back, 1 ft. $1\frac{1}{2}$ in. by $6\frac{1}{2}$ in. by $\frac{3}{4}$ in.; moulded on each side; seven middle panels for back, $6\frac{1}{2}$ in. by $5\frac{1}{2}$ in. by $\frac{3}{4}$ in.; six lower panels for ends, 1 ft. $1\frac{1}{2}$ in. by $7\frac{1}{2}$ in. by $\frac{3}{4}$ in.; six upper panels for ends, $7\frac{1}{2}$ in. by $5\frac{1}{2}$ in. by $\frac{3}{4}$ in.; six lower panels for kneehole framing, 1 ft. $1\frac{1}{2}$ in. by 7 in. by $\frac{3}{4}$ in.; six upper panels for kneehole framing, $5\frac{1}{2}$ in. by $7\frac{1}{2}$ in. by $\frac{3}{4}$ in.; one plinth for back, 5 ft. 2 in. by $4\frac{1}{8}$ in. by $\frac{3}{4}$ in.; two plinths for ends, 2 ft. 8 in. by $4\frac{1}{8}$ in. by $\frac{3}{4}$ in.; two plinths for kneehole, 2 ft. $6\frac{1}{2}$ in. by $4\frac{1}{8}$ in. by $\frac{3}{4}$ in.; one plinth for back of kneehole, 2 ft. 1 in. by $4\frac{1}{8}$ in. by $\frac{3}{4}$ in.; two plinths for front, 1 ft. 8 in. by $4\frac{1}{8}$ in. by $\frac{3}{4}$ in.; eight division rails between drawers D R (Fig. 5), 1 ft. 4 in. by 2 in. by 1 in.

Framing for Outer Edge of Desk.—

For the top T F (Fig. 5) two pieces 5 ft. 4 in. by $3\frac{3}{4}$ in. by 1 in., and two pieces 2 ft. 10 in. by $3\frac{3}{4}$ in. by 1 in. will be required.

Panel for Top Framing.—As this is usually covered with leather or similar material it may be made of the best pine; but whatever wood is used it must be obtained thoroughly well seasoned. It will following runners and panels may be of deal or pine; Fourteen runners, 2 ft. $4\frac{1}{2}$ in. by $1\frac{1}{2}$ in. by 1 in.; and six panels, 1 ft. $1\frac{1}{2}$ in. by 2 ft. by $\frac{3}{8}$ in. It should be noted that the straight grain runs the short way of these panels, therefore they will require to be made of probably three boards jointed up. One panel under

Fig. 1.—Roll-top Desk

probably have to be made of two or three boards jointed up. The size of this panel will require to be 4 ft. 10 in. by 2 ft. 3 in. by $\frac{3}{4}$ in. There will be required: Two pull flaps, 1 ft. 6 in. by 1 ft. 3 in. by $\frac{3}{4}$ in.; two clamps for same, 1 ft. 3 in. by $2\frac{1}{4}$ in. by 1 in.; and one rail over kneehole drawer, 2 ft. $3\frac{1}{2}$ in. by $1\frac{5}{8}$ in. by $\frac{3}{4}$ in. The central drawer, 1 ft. 11 in. by 2 ft. $2\frac{1}{2}$ in. by $\frac{1}{2}$ in., is also required.

Upper Carcase Framing of Desk.—Four angle stiles A S (Fig. 4), 1 ft. 10 in. by $2\frac{5}{8}$ in. by $1\frac{1}{8}$ in.; one bottom rail to back B R (Fig. 2), 4 ft. 11 in. by $2\frac{5}{8}$ in. by $1\frac{1}{8}$ in.; one middle rail to back M R (Fig. 2), 4 ft. 11 in. by $3\frac{1}{8}$ in. by $1\frac{1}{8}$ in.; one top rail to back T R (Fig. 2), 4 ft. 11 in. by $2\frac{5}{8}$ in. by $1\frac{1}{8}$ in. ; two bottom rails for ends B R (Fig. 4), 2 ft. $4\frac{1}{2}$ in. by $2\frac{5}{8}$ in. by $1\frac{1}{8}$ in. ; and two middle rails for ends M R (Fig. 2), 1 ft. 7 in. by $3\frac{1}{8}$ in. by $1\frac{1}{8}$ in. The curved rail and piece of top rail will receive special attention later. There are also required : Six lower muntins for back, 11 in. by $3\frac{1}{8}$ in. by $1\frac{1}{8}$ in. ; six upper muntins for back, 9 in. by $3\frac{1}{8}$ in. by $1\frac{1}{8}$ in. ; four lower muntins for ends, 11 in. by $3\frac{1}{8}$ in. by $1\frac{1}{8}$ in. ; two upper muntins for ends, 9 in. by $3\frac{1}{8}$ in. by $1\frac{1}{8}$ in. ; seven lower panels for back, 9 in. by $6\frac{1}{2}$ in. by $\frac{3}{4}$ in. ; seven upper panels for back, 7 in. by $6\frac{1}{2}$ in. by $\frac{3}{4}$ in. ; four lower panels for ends, 9 in. by $7\frac{1}{2}$ in. by 1 in. ; and two upper panels for ends, 7 in. by $7\frac{1}{2}$ in. by 1 in. The four special panels at the ends can be got out of about 2-ft. run of 8 in. by 1 in.

It will be seen that the top is formed of two thicknesses as shown by T and M (Fig. 5), the portion M being framed together. For this the following will be required : Two pieces, 5 ft. 3 in. by $2\frac{1}{2}$ in. by $1\frac{1}{8}$ in. ; two pieces, 1 ft. 3 in. by $2\frac{1}{2}$ in. by $\frac{1}{8}$ in. ; and one 5 ft. 3 in. by 1 ft. 2 in. by $\frac{5}{8}$ in.

Drawers.—By reference to the illustrations it will be seen that there are two deep bottom drawers, which have the appearance of four drawers. The following pieces will be required for the drawer fronts, 1 ft. $2\frac{1}{2}$ in. by 1 ft. by $1\frac{1}{8}$ in. ; two drawer fronts, 1 ft. $2\frac{1}{2}$ in. by 1 ft. by $1\frac{1}{8}$ in. ; made in two pieces, one drawer front over kneehole, 2 ft. $1\frac{1}{2}$ in. by $3\frac{1}{2}$ in. by 1 in. ; eight drawer sides, 2 ft. 2 in. by $5\frac{3}{4}$ in. by $\frac{1}{2}$ in. ; four drawer sides, 2 ft. 2 in. by 1 ft. by $\frac{1}{2}$ in. ; two drawer sides for kneehole drawer, 2 ft. 2 in. by $3\frac{1}{2}$ in. by $\frac{1}{2}$ in. ; four drawer backs, 1 ft. $2\frac{1}{2}$ in. by $5\frac{1}{4}$ in. by $\frac{1}{2}$ in. ; two drawer backs, 1 ft. $2\frac{1}{2}$ in. by $11\frac{1}{2}$ in. by $\frac{1}{2}$ in. ; one drawer back for kneehole drawer, 2 ft. $1\frac{1}{2}$ in. by 3 in. by $\frac{1}{2}$ in. ; six drawer bottoms, 2 ft. $1\frac{1}{2}$ in. by 1 ft. 2 in. by $\frac{3}{8}$ in., which will be jointed up in about three pieces, the straight grain running the short way of the wood ; and one drawer bottom, 2 ft. 2 in. by 2 ft. 1 in. by $\frac{1}{2}$ in.

Roll.—For this will be required three boards about 5 ft. long, 11 in. wide, and $1\frac{1}{4}$ in. thick, and one slamming rail for roll 5 ft. by 3 in. by 1 in.

Drawer Pulls.—For these eight will be required, 7 in. by 2 in. by 1 in., and two 5 in. by $1\frac{1}{4}$ in. by 1 in.

Locking Arrangement.—This will require four pieces 2 ft. by $1\frac{1}{4}$ in. by 2 in., two pieces 1 ft. 3 in. by 2 in. by $1\frac{1}{4}$ in., and two blocks 5 in. by $2\frac{1}{2}$ in. by $\frac{1}{2}$ in.

The sizes given are from the saw, and allow only a fair margin for planing. The next procedure will be to face up and plane square the edge of each piece, and then gauge and plane to thickness and breadth to the finished sizes. After this the setting out can be proceeded with.

The four angle stiles joining the back and side framings should be placed in pairs face to face, and set out on the edges for mortising, haunching, and mitreing as shown by Fig. 6. By reference to the illustrations it will be seen that the moulding, which is made on the solid of the framing, is as wide on the face as the depth of the plough groove to receive the panels. Therefore the distance A A (Fig. 6) shows the full breadth of the rails, the distances A B the depth of the plough groove and width of moulding, and at the upper end of the stiles the distance C A shows the width for the haunching. A mortise gauge should now be set to $\frac{5}{16}$ in., and so that the fixed tooth is the same distance from the face of the work as the front arris of the plough groove. Fig. 7 shows the stile mortised, and Fig. 8 the stile ploughed, moulded, mitred, and shouldered.

Taking the piece for the bottom rail for back, say, the edge, face, and back should be set out for shoulders of tenons, mortises for tenons of muntins, mitreing, etc., as shown in Fig. 9. By reference to the illustrations it will be seen that the front mouldings project beyond the back shoulders the exact distance of the breadth of the moulding. Special attention must be given to this matter throughout the setting out of the framing, otherwise a mistake is very liable to occur, by not allowing for this prolonging of the front shoulders, and thus making the rails too short. The mortises for the tenons of the muntins

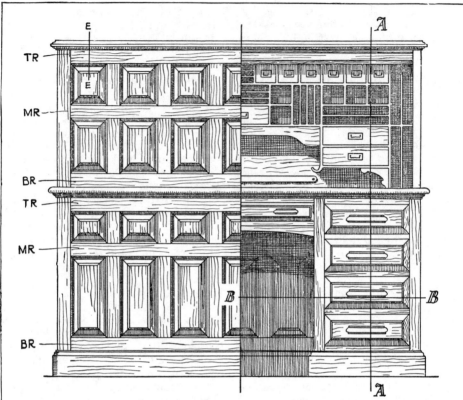

Fig. 2.—Half Back and Half Front Elevations of Roll-top Desk

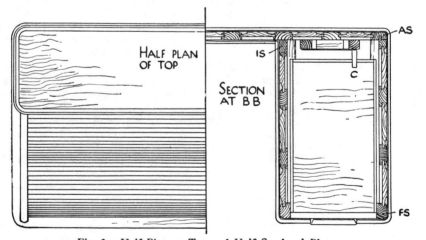

Fig. 3.—Half Plan at Top and Half Sectional Plan

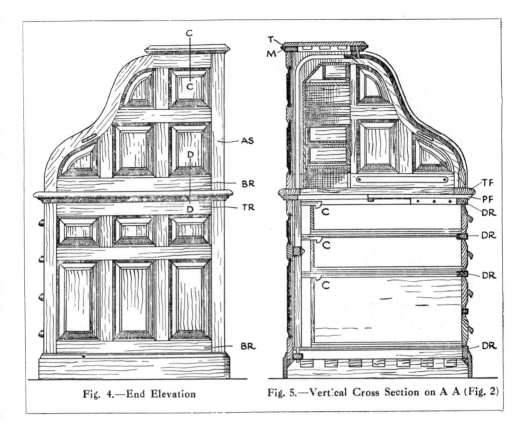

Fig. 4.—End Elevation   Fig. 5.—Vertical Cross Section on A A (Fig. 2)

should next be set out as shown in Fig. 9, the distance A A being the full breadth of the mouldings, and thus shows the beginning of the mitres, whereas B B shows the breadth of the mortises in each case. Fig. 10 shows the end of the bottom rail mortised and the tenon cut, and Fig. 11 shows the end of the bottom rail completed.

The bottom rail, middle rail, and top rail should be placed together with their face edges outwards, and the top and middle rails thus set out from the bottom rail. Having set out one edge of the middle rail, the line should be squared across the face and continued on the opposite edge. Now take one of the upper muntins, and mark off from a stile the exact distances for the front and back shoulders, and from these set out the shoulder lines on the face side and back side, as shown in Fig. 12. The remaining upper muntins should be placed face to face and with the one set out on the top. Then the face edge of each should be scribed down from the one already set out, and then the shoulder lines scribed on each in turn. Fig. 13 shows a muntin tenoned and moulded, and Fig. 14 shows a completed muntin. The procedure for setting out the lower muntins will be precisely similar to that just described for the upper muntins. The gauging for the mortising and tenoning can now be done.

The setting out for the stiles, rails, and muntins for the ends can next be proceeded with if desired, and in method will not differ from what has been described for the back framing. It will be clear that the two front corner stiles, and also the two stiles of the kneehole, form part of the framing of the ends and the kneehole respectively. The setting out for mortising, etc., for the edges of the stiles which

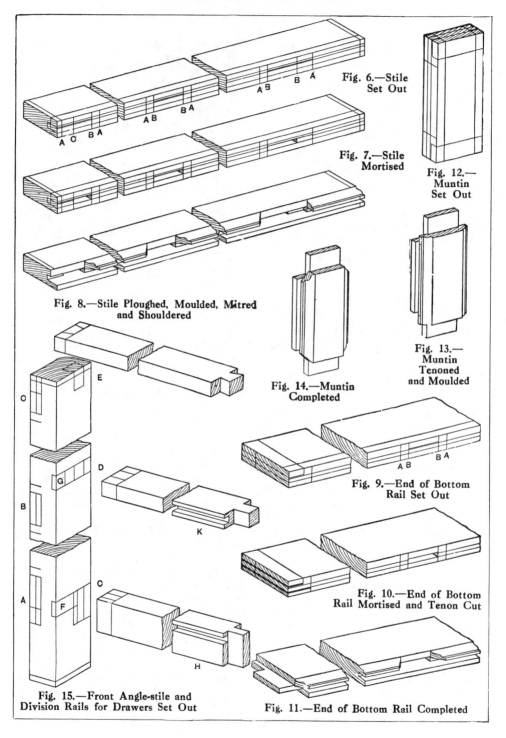

Fig. 6.—Stile Set Out

Fig. 7.—Stile Mortised

Fig. 12.—Muntin Set Out

Fig. 8.—Stile Ploughed, Moulded, Mitred and Shouldered

Fig. 13.—Muntin Tenoned and Moulded

Fig. 14.—Muntin Completed

Fig. 9.—End of Bottom Rail Set Out

Fig. 10.—End of Bottom Rail Mortised and Tenon Cut

Fig. 15.—Front Angle-stile and Division Rails for Drawers Set Out

Fig. 11.—End of Bottom Rail Completed

are to be part of the panel framing is shown at A, B and C (Fig. 15). The form of the completed stile is shown in Fig. 16. The setting out for rails, muntins, and kneehole framing can next be proceeded with, and should present no difficulty.

Taking one of the front stiles, it should be set out on its proper edge for mortises to receive the tenons of the bottom and top, and two horizontal divisional rails for the drawers. The proper relation for this setting out to the adjacent edge of framing is shown at C, D, and E (Fig. 15). A shallow housing is shown set out at F and G for the reception of the ends of the runners. It will be seen in Fig. 15 that the top rail is connected with the stile by a dovetail joint ; this is a better method than having simply a mortise and tenon. The setting out of these front rails is comparatively a simple matter, as the front and back shoulders are of equal length.

The front stiles for the kneehole will require setting out for the two rails which are to receive the drawer. It should be observed that the faces of these rails are set back from the face of the stiles about ¾ in., as shown in Fig. 17, so that the circular corner of the stile may be continued to the underside of the top. All the necessary gauging for mortising and tenoning may now be completed.

All the mortises should next be made, and, as a rule, the depth of these should be about two-thirds the breadth of the material, except, of course, the middle rails, where the mortises should be made right through, working half from each side. Of course, great care should be taken to make the mortises parallel to the face of the wood, otherwise there will be a difficulty in keeping the surfaces of the material truly in plane when fitting them together.

The tenons should next be sawn, carefully observing to stop sawing at the proper shoulder line at the front and back. The shoulders should not be sawn at this stage.

A mortise gauge should be set to the exact width of the plough iron, and all the pieces gauged. This will be found to obviate the chances of ragged edges, which are liable otherwise to be left from the plough iron where the stuff is cross-grained. All the pieces should now be ploughed to the proper depth.

Of course, it is important that the plane required for moulding the edges of the framing should have been at hand before any setting out was done. If the worker has not one already in stock, it may be necessary to make one ; but there should be no difficulty in purchasing a new one, or even a second-hand one, and care should be taken to adjust or make it so as to be in proper working order. Then a short length of moulding should be worked on a spare piece of wood, and from this two gauges should be set, one for the exact distance it works on the face, and the other for the exact distance it works down. All the stiles, rails, and muntins should now be gauged with these two gauges A stile, rail, and muntin are shown gauged in Figs. 6, 9, and 12 respectively.

The shoulders of the tenons should be cut with a fine tenon saw. The best method for the front shoulders will be to saw just a shade from the scribe line, and then slightly inclining the saw inwards. Then the remaining slight amount of waste should be removed by means of a metal shoulder plane. This will leave the greater part of the shoulder as a square surface for fitting against the shoulders of the stile or rail, as the case may be.

The moulding in front of the mortises should be cut away by paring a little from what will be the finished mitres, and a square shoulder made so that its outer arris and that of the moulding are in one and the same line as shown. Then with a mitre template and a freshly ground chisel

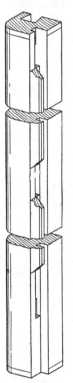

Fig. 16.—
Front
Angle-stile
Completed

(*see* Fig. 18) all the mitres can be pared exactly to the setting-out marks made on each of the stiles, rails, and muntins. These parts when completed will have the appearance shown in Figs. 8, 11, 14 and 19. The two parts forming each joint of the framing should now be fitted together

used on the face ; then the panels may be set out as shown in Fig. 20. If desired, the sunk surfaces may be moulded as shown, for which a plane will have to be made or obtained. But if simply a flat splayed surface is required, a skew-mouth rebate plane will be found most suitable

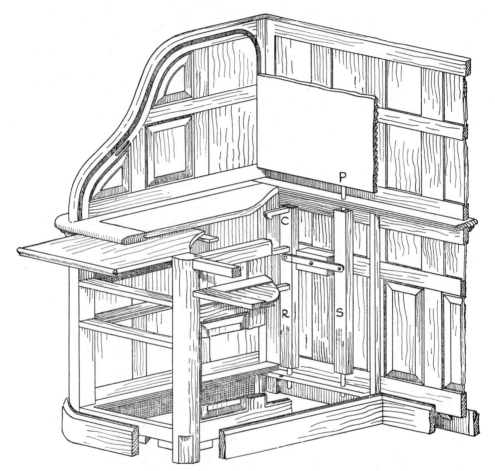

Fig. 17.—Details of Construction of Carcase

and numbered. The tenons of the top rails will require to be reduced in breadth, so as to form the haunchings.

The panels should first be trued up exactly to length and breadth. Then a gauge should be set to the distance of the sinking, the edges gauged, and another gauge set to the breadth of the sinking and

for the purpose, especially when being used against the grain. In working the sinkings it will be found to be the best to work the two across the grain first, as shown in Fig. 21, and the two with the grain afterwards. If the small hollow is to be worked on the edge of the field of the panel, it will be found an advantage to also work the two arrises at the ends before the sinking is done for the sides of the panel, as shown in Fig. 21. Fig. 22 shows the moulding with the grain completed. It will be observed that the three lower

found to fit satisfactorily the joints should be glued and cramped up in the usual manner. The next process will be to true and smooth off the front of each piece of framing.

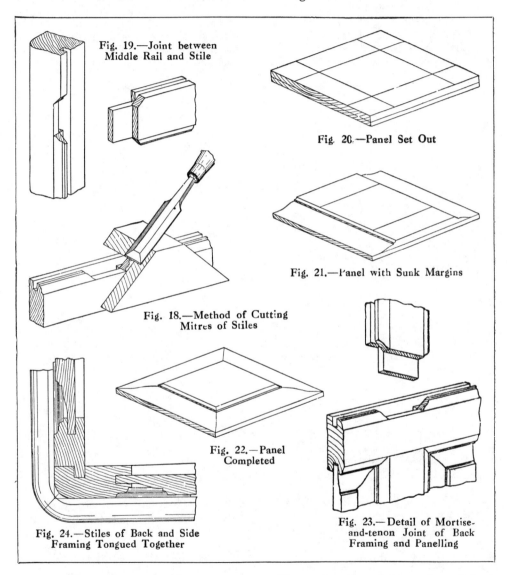

Fig. 19.—Joint between Middle Rail and Stile

Fig. 20.—Panel Set Out

Fig. 21.—Panel with Sunk Margins

Fig. 18.—Method of Cutting Mitres of Stiles

Fig. 22.—Panel Completed

Fig. 24.—Stiles of Back and Side Framing Tongued Together

Fig. 23.—Detail of Mortise-and-tenon Joint of Back Framing and Panelling

panels at the back are moulded on each side. A conventional view of a portion of the back framing is given in Fig. 23.

The next thing will be to fit in all the panels, and when the different parts are

The angle-stiles of the ends and back which meet should be ploughed and tongued, so as to fit together, as shown in section by Fig. 24. The stiles of the knee-hole framing adjacent to the back should be fitted, and these parts prepared to fit together with two or three hardwood dowels. The divisional rails for drawers should be tenoned and ploughed for receiving the panels as indicated at H and K (Fig. 15). Having proceeded thus far, the several pieces can be glued together, forming the main portion of the carcase. A few small blocks should be glued in the angles between the back and end framings as to form a bed for these triangular pieces glued on the back of the plinth, as shown by the section (Fig. 26). The top edge of each piece of plinth should now be moulded. The circular ends should now be worked to within a little of the finished size, and the top edges moulded. The carved portions of the mouldings will, of course, have to be worked by means of a chisel and gouge. The plinth should next

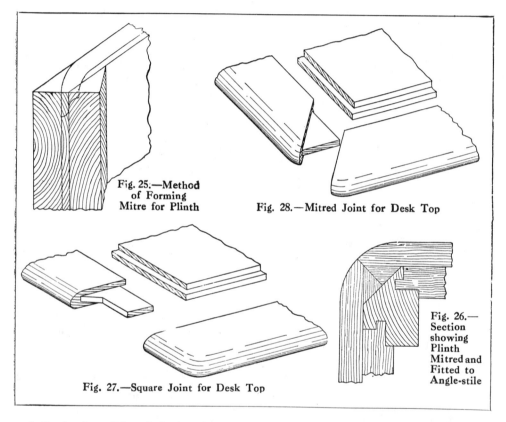

Fig. 25.—Method of Forming Mitre for Plinth

Fig. 28.—Mitred Joint for Desk Top

Fig. 27.—Square Joint for Desk Top

Fig. 26.—Section showing Plinth Mitred and Fitted to Angle-stile

and the back and kneehole framings, as shown in Fig. 5.

The pieces for the plinth should be fitted round and mitred. Then at the angles a triangular piece should be prepared so that its grain is running in the same direction as the piece of the plinth, and then glued on the back of same, as shown in Fig. 25. Next the bottom portion of the angle-stiles should be pared away carefully to a surface angle of 45°, so

be fixed. This may be done by gluing, holding in position by hand screws, and the insertion of a few screws from the back of the stiles.

The desk top is formed by two rails and stiles with a panel which is nearly flush with the top of the rails. The reason of this sinking is to allow for the thickness of the leather or cloth with which the top is to be finished. In Fig. 27 is shown the ordinary method of forming the joint between the stile and rail where a square shoulder is used for the rail. Fig. 28 shows the method by which the stiles and rails would be mitred and tenoned together. Of course, in each case the stile and rails should be ploughed to receive the tongue of the panel as shown. Four strips should next be prepared, mitred, moulded and fitted, and fixed on the top of the car-

little difficulty. The only part where such might occur will be in the curved rail, and for this the worker is strongly advised to make a full-size elevation of the end, from which a mould should be made for the curved rail. Having prepared and fitted together the three pieces of the framing, the groove for the roll should be made. This, of course, will have to be

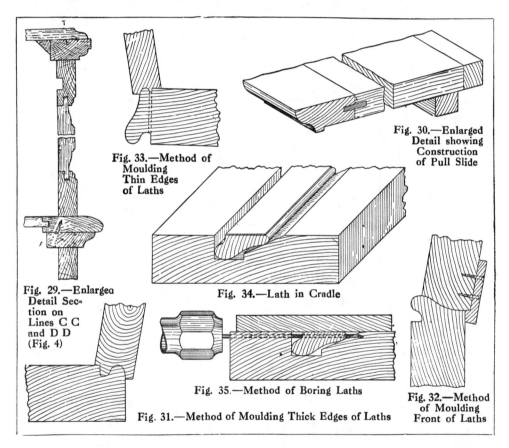

Fig. 33.—Method of Moulding Thin Edges of Laths

Fig. 30.—Enlarged Detail showing Construction of Pull Slide

Fig. 29.—Enlarged Detail Section on Lines C C and D D (Fig. 4)

Fig. 34.—Lath in Cradle

Fig. 35.—Method of Boring Laths

Fig. 32.—Method of Moulding Front of Laths

Fig. 31.—Method of Moulding Thick Edges of Laths

case immediately under the desk top. This is shown in section at A (Fig. 29). It should here be observed that a portion of this moulding forms the front edge of the pull flap. An enlarged detail of the construction of the flap A (Fig. 17) is given by Fig. 30.

After having made the framing for the lower part of the desk, the preparing of the framing for the roll top should present

principally done by gauging, and then cutting and paring out with a chisel, working the groove to an even depth by using a router. The groove is shown in section in Fig. 29.

Probably the simplest method of preparing the moulded laths for the roll will be to obtain a good, straight-grained, and mellow board, whose thickness is a little more than the breadth the laths will be when finished. Then by altering an old bead plane, or making one, the thicker edge of the laths can be worked, as shown in Fig. 31. An old round or a rebate plane can be adapted with a fence screwed on it, as shown in Fig. 32, for working on the edge. Of course, a gauge must be used, so as to work down to exactly the right distance. Then an ordinary small bead plane can be used for working the small rounded edge, as shown in Fig. 33. Now, taking the quirk as a guide, the strip can be sawn off. The edge of the board can be re-shot, and the process above described repeated for each lath in turn.

For backing off and getting the laths exactly to a thickness a cradle can be made by ploughing and splaying a piece of

bored through, as shown in Fig. 35. The second method, which perhaps may prove the best, will be to obtain three or four strips of $\frac{5}{8}$-in. by $\frac{1}{16}$-in. untempered steel, which should be drilled and countersunk for $\frac{3}{8}$-in. No. 3 screws. The distance apart, of course, should be equal to the breadth of the strips of the roll, so that the steel is then fastened by the screws to each strip (*see* Fig. 36).

The back of the roll may be covered by gluing on canvas. Of course, great care must be taken not to allow the glue to get between the joint of the strips. A good method of obviating this will be to coat with moderate thin glue one side of a few sheets of thin drawing paper, then when dry cut them into strips about $\frac{1}{4}$ in. wide.

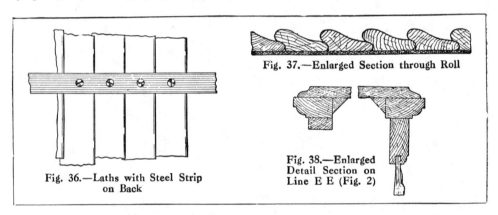

Fig. 37.—Enlarged Section through Roll

Fig. 36.—Laths with Steel Strip on Back

Fig. 38.—Enlarged Detail Section on Line E E (Fig. 2)

board, so that the laths can rest in, just to the proper depth. Then the upper surface of the cradle will be an exact guide for planing down to the proper thickness, as shown in Fig. 34.

The length of the desk being 5 ft., it will not be well to depend solely on the canvas backing for keeping the laths properly together, therefore the two following methods are offered : All the laths may be bored with four holes and cords passed through. Each of the holes will have to be at the same distances in all the laths. The cradle which was used for planing to thickness can be bored at the proper intervals and distance from the top with a fine bit. Then each lath in turn can be held firmly in the cradle, and the four holes

The glued side should then be damped, and stuck over all the joints at the back whilst the roll is laid on a flat surface. The strips of paper should be allowed to stand an hour or two to dry, after which the canvas should be glued and applied to the back of the strips and pressed to them, taking care not to disturb the paper strip. Thin american cloth, although more expensive, has its advantages over canvas, because the fabric side can be glued without the glue running through to the other side. The ends of the roll should be sawn off true to size, and they should afterwards be fitted into their respective grooves in the sides, and, of course, any necessary easing done. An enlarged section of the roll is shown by Fig. 37. When this is satisfactory, the side and back framings should be fitted together, the shutter being inserted, and the desk top screwed from its underside into the bottom edges of the framing.

The top can next be prepared and fixed on ; an enlarged section of this is given in detail by Fig. 29. A section through the front and back of the top is given in Fig. 38. For connecting the upper part of the desk to the lower, a few screws should be inserted upwards through the moulded fillet, which was fixed to the top of the carcase, as shown at A (Fig. 29), into the underside of the stiles and rails of the desk top. Thus it will be seen that for the purpose of removal, etc., the roll top portion of the desk can be separated from the pedestal portion.

It will be seen that by an ingenious con-trivance when the roll top is open the drawers are unfastened ; but immediately the roll is drawn the drawers are fastened at the back. This arrangement is clearly shown in Figs. 5 and 17, where it will be observed that the edge of the roll strikes a projection pin P, forcing it down, and at the same time the sliding piece S, which is connected by a metal lever working on a pivot at its centre as shown. This causes a second sliding piece R to rise, and at the same time raises hardwood or metal clip fasteners C, which are fixed to it, as shown in Figs. 3, 5 and 17. These clips when down engage in the back of the drawers as shown ; but on the slide being raised they dis-engage themselves from the back of the drawers, thus allowing them to be opened. To bring about this action properly the sliding piece R must be considerably heavier than S.

The fronts of the drawers should be carefully fitted in by the usual method, and the sides connected to these and the back by dovetailing.

Timber: Varieties and Uses

THE following list of timbers is arranged in alphabetical order for ease of reference. The colour, characteristics and uses are given for each.

Acacia. Another name for the wood, Locust, which see.

Acajou. (*See* CEDAR, CIGAR-BOX, and MAHOGANY.)

Acle (*Pithecolobium acle*), a fine dark-brown heartwood, resembling walnut, with whitish sapwood. It is moderately hard and heavy, and has a decidedly peppery smell when worked. It is a native of India and the Philippines, where it is used for house- and boat-building; but, although as yet unknown in English trade, both it and several allied species of *Pithecolobium* would be well suited for furniture. It has been confused with the much heavier Pyingadu (*Xylia xylocarpa*).

Ailantus (*Ailanthus glandulosa*), native to Northern China, grown in Japan, in some parts of France and near Odessa, but in England and the Eastern United States for ornament only. Has a greyish-orange heart, much resembling ash when in cross section, is moderately heavy and hard, though somewhat brittle, and durable. It is used for firewood, charcoal, and joinery in France; but, having a beautiful satin-like lustre, is appreciated by cabinet-makers. It grows rapidly to a considerable height, but seldom reaches much more than 1 ft. in diameter. Its oriental name, "Ailanto," is said to mean "Tree of Heaven"; in French it is "Ailante" or "Vernis du Japon," in Russian "Pajasan," and in Chinese "Chou-chun."

Alder (*Alnus glutinosa*), with no heart, is a soft, smooth, and fine-grained wood. White when alive, it turns to a deep red or pink when cut, and dries to a pinkish brown. Weighing from 50 lb. to 60 lb. per cubic foot when green, it loses at least a third of its weight and about a twelfth of its bulk in drying, but does not subsequently warp, split, or splinter. It is recognisable by its pith, which in cross section is triangular with rounded angles; by the few broad, nearly straight compound pith-rays with very many fine simple ones between them; by the faint boundaries of the annual rings bending slightly inward at the broad rays; and by frequent brown pith-flecks that are often concentric. The wood seldom reaches large dimensions. It is liable to the attacks of the larva of a small beetle; but if wholly submerged is very durable. It is said to have been used in ancient times for boats. Vitruvius states that Ravenna was founded upon piles of this wood, and Evelyn says that those of the Rialto at Venice and those of Amsterdam were made of the same material. It is still so employed in Holland. Old trees full of knots, when cut into plank, have all the beauty of curled maple and the colour, though not the density or lustre, of mahogany. In Scotland this wood is sometimes immersed in peat water, to which lime is added, for some months, and is then used for table-tops which require varnishing. Newly felled alder can be readily stained to imitate ebony ; or, being rich in tannin, will, if left long in peat, become equally black. Its non-splintering causes it to be used for the staves of herring-barrels, shovels, knead-ing-troughs, wheelbarrows, stone-carts and bobbins : the alder poles from the German Baltic ports were mainly bought by the Lancashire clog-makers ; and in France, after being hardened and pro-tected from the boring beetle by being smoked. The wood is suitable for turnery and plywood.

THE AMERICAN ALDER (*Alnus incana*) is a similar but inferior wood ; and the large RED, OREGAN, or WESTERN ALDER (*Alnus rubra*) of the Pacific slope has a light brownish wood which is similarly employed. The name WHITE ALDER (*Platylophus trifoliatus*) is applied in Cape Colony to a hard, tough, durable, lustrous yellowish-white wood, often with a fine twisted grain, known to the Boers as " White Els."

Alerce. (*See* THUYA.)

Amaranthe. (*See* PURPLE-HEART.)

Amboyna-wood, the burrs of Kiabooca, probably *Pterospermum indicum*, native to Amboyna and other Molucca islands and New Guinea, known also as Lingoa-wood. The burrs are sawn off in slabs 2 in. to 8 in. thick, and up to 9 ft. in diameter, though generally much smaller, light reddish-brown to orange, beautifully mottled and curled, fragrant, very hard, and taking a good polish, and very durable, weighing about 39 lb. per cubic foot. Much used in the eighteenth century for inlaying, etc., but now rare and generally superseded by Thuya or Totara burrs from Algeria and New Zealand respectively.

Anjan (*Hardwickia binata*), native to Southern India, dark red streaked with black or purplish ; one of the hardest, heaviest, and most durable of Indian timbers, is very strong and does not warp, but is liable to splitting ; used for bridge-building, railway sleepers, etc., and, though resinous, also for cabinet work.

Apple (*Pyrus Malus*), a dark brown wood, generally with a red tint, with broad rings, invisible rays, and no pith-flecks, close-grained, very hard, and sus-ceptible of a good polish, but brittle and warping badly in drying. It weighs about 50 lb. per cubic foot. As the fruit-bearing trees are now generally discarded whilst comparatively young, this timber is neither common nor of any considerable dimensions ; but it is sometimes used for tool-handles, mallets, etc. The writer has known croquet-mallets and balls to be turned in this wood.

Ash (*Fraxinus excelsior*), the most valuable of European woods, is a light brown, much resembling light oak ; but though its annual rings are well marked, the pith-rays are hardly visible. Of moderate weight and hardness, it is, when well grown, very even and close in grain, lustrous, and susceptible of a good polish, whilst it is the toughest and most pliable of European woods. Though the tree will grow in almost any soil, it produces the best wood when grown quickly in rich loam and in a moist climate. Few trees become useful so early, since it is fit for walking-sticks or whip-handles at four years' growth, for hop-poles or lances at five or six, for spade handles at nine, and reaches its full value per cubic foot when 3 in. in diameter. For small wood it is frequently coppiced, being then known as maiden or ground ash. In the Potteries it is largely used for crate-making, for which purpose it is cut every five or six years. As the wood can be steamed or heated and readily bent into any curve, without injury, it is invaluable for hoops. Larger wood is much used by the wheel-wright and carriage-builder, especially for felloes, and there is a constant demand for this wood in arsenals for the building of artillery wagons. Its combination of lightness, flexibility, and toughness makes it in great request for the construction of aeroplanes. For such a purpose, how-ever, it is essential that the wood should be bright—a sign of soundness—and capable of standing the severest tests of its flexibility and strength. For this it should be valley-grown, winter-felled, and quickly converted into plank or board and seasoned. It is then very durable, but otherwise rapidly deteriorates.

The slower-grown Ash of Northern Europe, of mountains, or of poorer soils, is commonly darker in colour and may become " black-hearted," as also does the wood of pollard trees. In the north-east of England, wounds or " cankers " in the heart are attributed to bees, the wood being known as " bee-sucken ash " ; and billets of ash imported from Austria and Hungary often exhibit contortion of the fibres, producing figure, known as " ram's-horn " or " fiddle-back " ash. Pyrenean Ash also exhibits figure, and is imported as veneers. These malformations detract from the flexibility, though not from the hardness of the wood. As ash does not splinter readily, it is admirable for chopping-blocks or shop-boards requiring frequent washing, or for billiard cues or oars ; but its flexibility unfits it for architectural work. In Russia the ash grows soft and kind, and is accordingly much used by the joiner and cabinet-maker in house-fitting and furniture. As there is no bitter principle in ash comparable to the tannin in oak, the wood is liable to be attacked by the larvæ of beetles, and requires, therefore, to be painted.

THE AMERICAN or WHITE ASH (*Fraxinus americana*) is the lighter-coloured wood of a quick-growing species which occurs from eastern Canada to Carolina in damp ground. It is about a third lighter than English Ash and fully as much less elastic, so that, although employed in America for all the purposes to which we put European Ash, the wood, when imported here, is put to very different uses. It comes, in part, from Quebec in partly square logs 18 ft. to 35 ft. long and 10 in. to 18 in. square, or in planks, or partly manufactured, as oars, etc. The whitest logs, which are considered the best, are in great demand for bedroom and other furniture, carriage-panels, etc., and the inferior darker logs for carcase work and drawers, for which European Ash is never used. It is kind, soft, very easy to work, and stands well in panelling when thoroughly dried. Several other species are

in use in North America, of which the best is, perhaps, the Blue Ash (*Fraxinus quadrangulata*) of the lower part of the Wabash Basin and the central United States.

ASH, BLACK. Another name for Cabinet Ash (*see* below).

CABINET ASH, the English trade name for the black-barked, or Nova-Scotia Ash (*Fraxinus nigra*), which grows in swamps from Newfoundland and Winnipeg southward, and yields a dark wood, inferior to white ash, and " burls," or wart-like swellings, forming valuable veneers ; and for the red or brown-barked ash (*F. pennsylvanica*), which is somewhat inferior.

JAPANESE ASH, the English trade name for a wood with some resemblance, but no real relationship to ash, known in Japan as " Sen," in China as " Tzu-Chin " (*Acanthopanax ricinifolia*), the plant being now common in our gardens and greenhouses, though there not of timber size. It reaches 60 ft. in height and 3 ft. in diameter, and its wood is hard, glossy, and fine-grained. It has been used for spears, tool-handles, the bottom-boards of boats, and for the fittings of railway carriages. A valuable true ash (*Fraxinus sieboldiana*), known as " Shui chü liu " in China, is not yet known in our commerce.

QUEBEC ASH. Another name for American or White Ash, which see.

Asp. (*See* ASPEN, below.)

Aspen (*Populus tremula*), a soft, light, dingy white or reddish-brown wood, which warps and cracks but little, does not splinter, and is fairly durable if kept dry, is tender and easily split or turned. It is imported in small quantities from the ports on the south side of the Baltic, mainly for cooperage, being used for milk-pails, butchers' trays, pack-saddles, and herring-barrels, and also for blindwood, clogs, matches, and paper-pulp. In France it is employed for sabots and for flooring. A similar North American species (*P. tremuloides*), often called the American or Quaking Asp, is used for cooperage, flooring, " excelsior " (wood-shavings used for packing), and paper-pulp; but for this last purpose aspen is inferior to spruce.

Assegai-wood (*Curtisia faginea*), a South African species, sometimes known as "Cape Lancewood," or in Zulu as "Umguna" or "Umnoiso," though not in English trade, is a valuable wood. Bright red, but becoming dull on exposure, it is heavy, close-grained, strong, tough, elastic, and durable. The tree reaches 40 ft. to 80 ft. in height and 1 ft. to 4 ft. in diameter, and the wood is used for assegai-shafts, tool-handles, spokes, felloes, and wagon building. It might well be imported for turnery.

Basswood (*Tilia americana*), native to the east of Canada and the United States, not distinguished in commerce from White Basswood (*T. heterophylla*) of the Middle and Southern States, is very similar to the closely related Linden of Europe (*T. europœa*). It is white or light brown, sometimes with a reddish tinge, without the lustre of the maples, light, soft, close-grained, tender, and not strong, shrinking considerably in drying, but durable if kept dry. It is extensively used, especially in the northern United States, where the Tulip-tree does not grow, for the seats of Windsor chairs, carriage-panels, cheap office and bedroom furniture, toys, general carpentry, turnery and cooperage. It is also worked up by the rotary veneer machine into thin board as long as the log and as much as 100 ft. broad for the manufacture of three-ply wood. In the London cheap furniture trade this wood is often confused with canary whitewood.

Bay-wood. A trade-name for Mahogany (Honduras), which see.

Beech (*Fagus sylvatica*), native to Central and Southern Europe and to the southern parts of Britain, and giving their names alike to Bukovina, Buckingham, and Betchworth, is one of our more generally useful woods. It can be obtained in straight logs of considerable length and diameter and, though varying considerably in colour, has various uses for its different qualities. It varies, according to the soil upon which it has been grown, from red to yellow, or white, the redder, grown upon richer soil, being the better. In Germany the wood is known as red beech in contradistinction to

that of the hornbeam, known there as white beech. Newly-felled beech is often reddened by steaming, as in the Sheffield tool trade. The annual rings are distinct and wavy, while the very wide pith-rays give a satiny lustre. The wood weighs from 41 lb. to 56 lb. per cubic foot, but usually 43 lb. to 44 lb. It is hard and as strong as oak, and even tougher—hence its use for wheel cogs—but it is much less stiff. It is close, even and silky in grain, cleaving readily along the rays, and is very suitable for turnery, being manufactured into tool-handles, wooden screws, shoe-lasts, wedges, tent-pegs, shovels, etc. The wrest-boards of pianos must be of English beech. The wood is grown and used on a large scale for the "Windsor" chair-making industry of Buckinghamshire and for the bentwood furniture of Vienna, its freedom from any oily secretion rendering it suitable for the staining usual in the latter trade. It is very durable under water, as is seen in the logs on which the foundations of Winchester Cathedral were laid in A.D. 1202 ; but it cannot, unless treated with preservatives, stand alternations of wet and dry conditions. Most of the complaints as to the perishability of beech—often attributed to soil or situation—are, in fact, due to the wood not having been seasoned or treated immediately after felling.

In France and Germany beech is considered the best of all woods, except walnut, for sabots and wooden soles ; but for this purpose it is smoked over a fire of branches and chips of the same wood so as to become saturated with pyroligneous acid and very impermeable. In its natural state the wood, having numerous vessels, is very porous ; it is possible to blow out a candle through a jack-plane of beech ; and it is partly on account of this structure that beech forms so excellent a fuel, burning with a clear, bright flame ; and for the same reason it absorbs large quantities of liquid preservatives. It is largely used for railway sleepers in France, after treatment with copper sulphate ; and has been successfully used, after creosoting, for wood-paving.

In North America this species, though

reaching large dimensions, has generally more sapwood, and—under the name of WHITE BEECH—is recognised as much inferior to the Red Beech (*Fagus ferruginea*), which is used for the same purposes as English beech, but is somewhat inferior to it.

Of allied southern species belonging to the genus *Nothofagus*, the evergreen NEGRO-HEAD BEECH or Myrtle (*N. Cunninghamii*) of Tasmania and Victoria reaches large dimensions and is a satiny reddish-brown wood, susceptible of an excellent polish, used for pier-decks, ball-room floors, piano carcases, furniture, fretwork, etc. Fine burrs occur on its stems. *N. betuloides*, another evergreen species, occurs from Tierra del Fuego northward, and is known in Argentina by the vague name Roble (Oak). Its handsome, fine-grained, easily-worked wood has been extensively used for the panelling of railway carriages.

For BLUE or WATER BEECH and the ORIENTAL BEECH, *see* HORNBEAM.

The name Beech is also applied to many woods, in different parts of the world, in no way related to the true beeches. Of these, the white beech of N.E. Australia (*Gmelina Leichhardtii*) is fine-grained, easily-worked wood used for decks, flooring and carving.

Beef-wood is a name applied to various deep red furniture woods. Of these, *Lophira alata* from Lagos and the Gold Coast, also known as African Oak, is very heavy, hard, and coarse-grained, weighing about 70 lb. per cubic foot. In Trinidad the name is applied to *Rhopala montana*, a valuable wood; and in Australia to the allied proteaceous *Grevillea striata*, also known as Silvery Honeysuckle, *Banksia integrifolia* (or Coast Honeysuckle), and *Stenocarpus salignus* (or Silky Oak); and also to various species of *Casuarina*, also known as She-oak, Forest Oak, or Swamp Oak. Of these, *C. torulosa* (Forest Oak) is used for furniture and veneers, *C. suberosa* (Erect She-oak) for mallets and handles and formerly for boomerangs.

Birch (AMERICAN BIRCH) is the trade name for the imported wood which is the product of four or five species from Canada and the North-eastern United States, but chiefly of *Betula lenta*, which is variously known as Sweet, Black, Cherry or Mahogany Birch or Mountain Mahogany. This reaches larger dimensions than European birch. When first sawn the sapwood is distinctly yellow, the heart a brownish red; but after seasoning the sapwood fades to a cream white and the heart to a pinkish red, though often darker in parts and handsome. The rays are wider than in other species, the pores large and pith-flecks rare, and the wood takes a beautiful satiny polish and presents the " roll-figure " seldom seen in any other wood. It weighs from 37·5 lb. to 48 lb. per cubic foot, and is hard, strong, close-grained, not very liable to insect attack, and, for a birch, fairly durable. It is largely used in America for furniture, being sometimes stained to imitate mahogany or cherry. It is imported in slightly waney logs, 6 ft. to 20 ft. long. and 1 ft. to 2½ ft. square, and in sawn planks seldom more than 9 in. wide, the best coming from Quebec. Here it is used in carriage-building, chair-making, and bedroom furniture. *Betula lutea*, the Yellow, Grey, Tall or Silver Birch, chiefly used for very small woodware, yields tough burrs from which mallets are made; and *B. papyrifera*, the Canoe, White or Paper Birch, has a curl in the grain at the base of its branches which is in request for cabinet veneers in Boston; but this and other perishable and weak species are mainly converted into paper-pulp.

EUROPEAN BIRCH (*Betula alba*) varies from yellowish or reddish white to light brown, with distinct rings and rays, and generally numerous pith-flecks near the centre of the stem. It weighs from 32 lb. to 49 lb. per cubic foot, and is moderately hard, even-grained, difficult to split, but easily worked. It is not a strong wood; and, being rich in sugar when young and destitute of tannin or other bitter principle, is so liable to a fungoid fermentative decay or to the attacks of insects as to be far from durable. Occurring, however, as a rapidly-growing weed of timber lands throughout the north of Europe and Asia, **it is** in many lands the cheapest native hard wood, and is largely used for cooperage, turnery, furniture, fuel, and charcoal. In Yorkshire it is made into clogs, and in France it is one of the chief materials for sabots. Birch logs have been imported in considerable quantities from the Baltic, mostly with the bark on ; but are very apt, especially if felled in spring, left on the ground, kept too long on the voyage, or stored without ventilation, to become " doated " or foxed by incipient decay. A very extensive industry has arisen within recent years in the manufacture of ply-wood. The timber is cut rotarily, and two, three, or more thicknesses are then glued back to back with their grains n different directions so as to correct warping. This wood is largely exported to Ceylon and India, where soft wood is scarce, for tea-chests, and is now applied to a variety of purposes, such as carriage-building, where lightness combined with moderate stability is desirable. Burrs with a valuable marbled wood occasionally occur on the stems of birch ; in Lapland these are turned into cups. Unlike the wood, the bark of the birch is rich in tannin and very durable, and is used for an immense variety of purposes, boats, boxes, boots. cordage, baskets, dyeing and tanning, the coppice-wood, with the young bark on, being also put to many of these uses.

BIRCH, TASMANIAN. (*See* LIGNUM-VITAE.)

Blackwood is a name applied to several valuable woods in different regions. Indian Blackwood (*Dalbergia latifolia*), also known as Malabar Blackwood, or as Indian, Bombay or Rosetta Rosewood, has the smell of rose-water, and burns with a smoky flame smelling of tar. Its sapwood is narrow and yellow, the heart dark brown or purple to greenish-black, often with darker or lighter longitudinal streaks, taking a fine polish. It weighs from 46 lb. to 66·75 lb. per cubic foot, and is very hard, tough, close, and cross-grained, the difficulty of working it being intensified by calcareous secretions in the wood. It is used for sleepers, gun-carriages, cartwheels, agricultural implements, and tool-handles ; but is the best furniture wood in India. It is exported for furniture to Hong-Kong and Canton and, via Bombay, to London.

AFRICAN BLACKWOOD (*Dalbergia melanoxylon*), also known as Senegal Ebony or " Congo-holz " (the latter German). a native of Tropical West Africa, has a jet-black or brownish-black heart and is used as ebony in turnery.

TASMANIAN BLACKWOOD (*Acacia melanoxylon*), also known as Black, Silver, or Hickory Wattle, is one of the most generally useful of Australian timbers, an excellent substitute for American walnut. Dark brown, with a beautiful figure. sometimes fiddle-back, in the older wood, hard, close, and even in grain, but easily worked, it takes an excellent polish. When newly sawn it is sticky with resin-veins, and, unless very carefully seasoned, will warp. It is used for beer barrels, oil-casks, gun-carriages, gunstocks, and tool-handles, and the sounding-boards of pianos ; whilst the figured wood is cut into veneers for billiard tables and other furniture, or for railway-carriage panels.

In Cape Colony the name Blackwood, the Boer " Zwartbast " or Zulu " Umcaza " (*Royena lucida*), a small ebenaceous tree, is used in wagon-building, though it is fitted for higher uses in turning or for furniture-making.

Box (*Buxus sempervirens*). A light yellow wood, hard and difficult to split, more uniform in grain than any other known wood. With neither rings, rays nor vessels distinct, it is almost horn-like in its homogeneity, planing almost equally well in any direction. It only occurs in small dimensions, and is apt to split in drying. Box was used in ancient Rome for turnery and veneers, and was made into flutes, and it is still used for " strings " in inlaying. At St. Claude, in the Jura, where the largest boxwoods in Europe occur, the wood is turned into small boxes, beads, spoons, etc., for which purposes the wood is stored in the dark for from three to five years, soaked, boiled, and buried in bran. While box is invaluable for mathematical instruments, its chief use from the fifteenth to the nineteenth century was engraving. For this purpose it is chiefly imported from Asia by way of Constantinople, Smyrna, and Odessa in billets 3 ft. to 8 ft. long and 3 in. to 12 in. across. Large blocks for engraving were built up of small pieces. In spite of the general employment of other methods for engraving, there is still a great demand for box, and no completely satisfactory substitute for it has been found.

The Balearic species (*B. balearica*) is larger, but somewhat coarse in grain. The South African *B. Macowani* is suitable for turnery ; but hardly for engraving. The name is also applied to Kamassi (*which see*) and to an excellent West Indian wood, *Tecoma pentaphylla*, the Jamaica Box, White Cedar, Cogwood, or Roble blanco of Tropical America. China Box (*Murraya exotica*), the Malay " Kamuning," growing in Queensland, the Philippines, Burma, and India, and used for tool-handles and walking-sticks, is a similar very heavy and hard yellow wood, suggested as a substitute. In Australia the name Box is applied to various species of *Eucalyptus*.

Box-Elder. (*See* MAPLE, ASH-LEAVED.)

Boxwood, CAPE and EAST LONDON. (*See* KAMASSI.)

Brazil-wood or Braziletto, is the hard, heavy, dark red wood of *Cæsalpina brasiliensis* and several allied Tropical American species. It takes a high polish and forms the material of violin-bows. These woods are mainly employed as red dyeing materials, and are imported from the Bahamas.

Butternut. (*See* WALNUT, GREY or WHITE.)

Buttonwood. (*See* PLANE.)

Calamander-wood or Coromandel-wood (*Diospyros quæsita* and allied species) is one of the most beautiful of cabinet woods. It is a native of Ceylon, belonging to the ebony family, but is now scarce. A red hazel-brown or chocolate colour, with handsome black stripes, and susceptible of a high polish, it is somewhat intermediate in appearance between the nearly allied zebra-wood and rosewood. It is intensely hard and close-grained, so as to be difficult to turn or work. It is light in weight for an ebony, weighing, as

it does, 57 lb. per cubic foot. It is sometimes employed in veneer.

Camphor-wood (*Cinnamomum Camphora*), a native of China, Japan, and Formosa, of moderate dimensions, moderately hard, not very heavy, reddish, often prettily marked, rather coarse-grained but easily worked, fragrant, and, owing to the large amount of camphor it contains, durable. It was formerly used in China for coffins and the keels of junks, for sleepers, and even as fuel ; but, being now scarcer, is used for high-class furniture, and, owing to its insect-proof character, for entomological cabinets. In Manila many cabinets are made of soft wood treated with camphor oil, in imitation of this wood.

The wood of the Bornean Camphor or " Kayu Kapor Barus " (*Dryobalanops aromatica*), a large tree, is light red, resembling bay-wood, not fragrant but straight-grained, and has been used for planks, beams, and piles and imported for wood-paving.

Canary Whitewood and American Whitewood are the English trade names for the wood of the magnoliaceous Tulip-tree (*Liriodendron tulipifera*) and the closely allied Cucumber-tree (*Magnolia acuminata*), often called Yellow or Virginian Poplar in the United States. It is a native of the Eastern States and reaches large dimensions. It is a light lemon-yellow, greenish olive-tinted or brownish, weighs about 25 lb. or 26 lb. per cubic foot, soft, close and straight in grain, firmer than most woods which are as soft, taking a satiny polish, stain, or paint very well, and easy to work. In America it is largely used as a substitute for pine in building, for joists, rafters, doors and wainscot, and for the seats of chairs, boxes, and turnery. Canary Whitewood is imported in waney logs and in large planks and boards, the latter being often planed on both sides to save freight. The planks and boards are often the somewhat harder and coarser cucumber-tree, which is also distinguishable by its wider sapwood. The wood is in great request for panelling, shop-fitting, carriage building, and cabinetwork, especially for ebonising or staining, but is often inexcusably confounded with basswood.

Cedar, a name applied in different parts of the world to a great number of woods, most of which are brown, even-grained, moderately hard, and easily worked and fragrant. They include many coniferous woods belonging to the genera *Cedrus Juniperus, Cupressus, Thuya,* and *Libocedrus,* and several entirely unrelated species of the meliaceous broad-leaved genus *Cedrela,* Lebanon Cedar (*Cedrus Libani*), with a pleasant odour obnoxious to insects, and therefore of great repute in ancient times for durability, but rather brittle; was used for coffins nearly three thousand years B.C., and later for internal work, carving and cabinets. In England it is only known as an ornamental tree ; but at Warwick Castle there is a room panelled with the wood of wind-fallen Lebanon Cedars from the grounds of the Castle. The wood of the closely-related Mt. Atlas Cedar (*Cedrus atlantica*) of North-west Africa is the Numidian Cedar, of which the beams of the Temple of Apollo at Utica, stated by Pliny to have been sound after nearly 1,200 years, were made. It is known to the French as Lebanon Cedar. The Deodar Cedar (*Cedrus Deodara*), the chief timber of North-west India, is only known in England as an ornamental tree, it being introduced here in 1831.

PENCIL CEDAR in English commerce now means only *Juniperus Virginiana,* the Red Cedar of the United States. It reaches considerable dimensions, may be rose-red, and has no resin ducts. It was formerly much used for shipbuilding by the Spaniards in Florida, for coffins in the Southern States, for cooperage in Philadelphia, and even for railway sleepers and fencing, and in England until about 1860 for cabinets, work-boxes, etc. It is now, however, too dear for any use but pencil making, for which several million cubic feet are cut annually. Bermuda Cedar (*J. bermudiana*) and Barbadoes Cedar (*J. barbadensis*) are closely related forms, and Rocky Mountain Red Cedar (*J. scopulorum*) and Western Juniper or Yellow Cedar (*J. occidentalis*) have very

similar woods, as also has the gigantic East African Cedar (*J. procera*), which occurs from Abyssinia to British East Africa.

WHITE CEDAR is a useful American trade name for the light brown woods of *Cupressus, Thuya,* and *Libocedrus.* Oregon or Port Orford Cedar (*Cupressus Lawsoniana*), reaching large dimensions, hard, strong, and durable, is one of the most valuable timbers of North America, and is largely cut for boat-building, fencing, flooring, etc. The white cedars of the Eastern States (*Cupressus thyoides* and the more fragrant *Thuya occidentalis*) are valuable timbers for many purposes, as also is the Californian Incense Cedar (*Libocedrus decurrens*) ; but perhaps the most important is *Thuya plicata,* otherwise known as *T. gigantea* or *T. Lobbi,* and as Western Red Cedar, Yellow Cedar, or Canoe Cedar. This species, which grows from Alaska to California, was the only wood used by the Red Indians of the North-west for their canoes ; it is the chief shingle wood of the United States, nearly 75 per cent. of the 15,000 million shingles used annually on American roofs being of this wood ; it is also used for internal fittings, coarse furniture and paving, and is now being very extensively planted. The Cedar of English commerce is, however, the Cigar-box Cedar (*Cedrela odorata*), also known as West Indian, Cuba, Havana, Honduras, Jamaica, or Mexican Cedar, which is a broad-leaved tree related to the mahoganies. This valuable wood, which can be obtained from 18 ft. to 40 ft. long and 1 ft. or 2 ft. square, is much softer than mahogany, weighs from 27 lb. to 47 lb. per cubic foot, is bitter, fragrant, but somewhat peppery in smell, and is now so scarce as only to be used for the boxes of the better qualities of cigars, African mahogany being used for cheaper brands. Few woods are more useful to the amateur craftsman than Cigar-box Cedar. Allied species, *C. guianensis* and *C. brasiliensis,* from the Guianas, Brazil, and the Argentine, are also used.

MOULMEIN CEDAR, Indian Mahogany or Toon, the Cèdre de Singapore or Cèdre rouge of the French, the Thitkado of Burma, or Calantas of the Philippines are names under which several valuable, closely-related, pale reddish, light and soft woods, durable and proof against termites, are confused. They are now referred to the genus *Toona* (*T. serrata*, *T. ciliata*, *T. febrifuga*, and *T. calantas*), nearly allied to *Cedrela* ; reach a large size ; and are fragrant, straight-grained, and easily worked. They sometimes exhibit a beautiful curl near the root or branches, suitable for furniture veneers, and are used for tea-chests, cigar-boxes, carving, and, in Queensland, for boat-planks.

The " Fragrant Chun," " Frêne odorant," or " Hsiang Chun," of China (*Cedrela sinensis*), lemon-scented, and beautifully marked with red bands on a yellowish brown, is an abundant, quick-grown, and valued allied species.

Cherry (*Prunus Avium*) is a moderately hard and heavy, light yellowish-brown wood, fine and even-grained, but not durable. After soaking for several days in lime-water the wood becomes a beautiful brownish red and can be used as a substitute for mahogany. It is used in inlaying, and is valued for turnery. The Perfumed Cherry, the fragrant, hard, red-brown, or green-streaked wood of *Prunus Mahaleb*, is grown in Austria for walking-sticks and the long stems of German tobacco-sticks ; and the larger but scarce American Wild Black or Rum Cherry (*P. serotina*) is a similar pink or reddish wood, moderately hard and durable and susceptible of a good polish, which is also stained to imitate mahogany and is employed with that wood for cabinetwork, furniture, and interior decoration.

Chestnut, often spoken of as Spanish Chestnut, to distinguish it from the unrelated Horse-Chestnut (*Æsculus Hippocastanum*), is the wood of a tree (*Castanea vulgaris*), sometimes reaching large dimensions, which is a native of the Mediterranean area, though long grown in England. It is brown, resembling oak, but distinguished from it by the absence of broad pith-rays. Though moderately hard, it is lighter and far softer than oak, for which reason it may be recommended to the wood-carver. It is rather coarse-grained, not very strong, but fairly durable. It is

largely grown for hop-poles and fencing ; but as it takes glue well it is one of the best carcase-woods for veneering. The ancient roofs alleged to be of this wood, such as those of Westminster Hall, Beaulieu Abbey, Leycester's Hospital, Warwick, etc., are, without exception, oak.

The AMERICAN CHESTNUT of the Eastern United States (*C. dentata*) is closely related and a very similar wood, employed for a variety of purposes, but now threatened with extermination by the ravages of a fungoid disease. The smaller Chinquapin Chestnuts (*C. pumila*) and in the Western States *Castanopsis chrysophylla*, yield rather darker, heavier, stronger, and more durable woods, and there are allied species in the Eastern Himalayas and in Southern China.

The MORETON BAY CHESTNUT (*Castanospermum australe*) of North-east Australia, named from the resemblance of its seeds, is, however, in no way related. It is a dark brown, prettily-streaked wood, somewhat like walnut, used for gunstocks, veneers, and furniture.

Chikrassi. (*See* MAHOGANY, EAST INDIAN.)

" Christmas Tree." (*See* SPRUCE, COMMON.)

Cocobola-wood, a species of *Humiria*, from British Guiana, is a hard, heavy, coarse-grained wood of a deep orange colour with jet-black linear markings, which is used in Tunbridge Wells ware and other inlaying and turnery.

Cocus-wood, also known as American, Green, Jamaica, or West Indian Ebony (*Brya Ebenus*), is a very heavy, dark greenish-brown or purplish wood, very fine and even in grain, of small dimensions, used in the manufacture of flutes and flageolets, for inlaying, and, though not well fitted for the purpose, for bows.

Cornelian-wood. (*See* DOGWOOD.)
Coromandel. (*See* EBONY.)
Cottonwood. (*See* POPLAR.)
Crocus-wood. (*See* SAFFRON-WOOD.)
Cucumber-tree. (*See* CANARY WHITE-WOOD.)

Cypress is not a wood often employed in Europe at the present day under that name. The fragrant. reddish, very fine-grained, and practically indestructible wood of *Cupressus sempervirens*, a native of South-west Asia and the Mediterranean area, was used by the ancient Egyptians for mummy-cases ; for the doors of St. Peter's and for the gates of Constantinople, both of which were destroyed in the fifteenth century after some eleven hundred years' existence ; and, according to Evelyn, for harps and organ-pipes.

The soft, reddish, fine-grained, durable wood of the DECIDUOUS CYPRESS of the Southern United States (*Taxodium distichum*), formerly used in Louisiana for canoes and house-building, is still extensively employed for roof-shingles, door and window frames, the drawers of mahogany furniture, fencing, and railway sleepers. It is closely similar in character and uses to the woods of the Redwoods (*Sequoia*) of the West.

Cypress-pine the general name for the species of the genus *Frenela*, the East Australian representatives of the Cypresses, brown woods, often with pinkish or darker streaks, and beautifully figured, with a camphor-like smell that renders them largely proof against termites and teredo. They are easily worked, take a good polish, and are durable. They are used for telegraph poles, piles, building, sleepers, and furniture. The chief species are *F. robusta*, *R. Endlicheri*, *F. rhomboidea*, and *F. Parlatorei*.

Dagame, or Degame Lancewood (*Calycophyllum candidissimum*), a native of Cuba, yellow, moderately heavy, and hard, and very fine and close in grain, is used as lancewood.

Date Plum. (*See* PERSIMMON.)

Deal, though now often used as a synonym for pine or spruce wood, is properly merely a name for 9-in. planks of such wood not more than 4 in. thick. The country of their origin and their colour is often indicated by a prefix. Thus the Northern Pine (*Pinus sylvestris*) yields Dantzic, Red or Yellow Deals ; the Spruce (*Picea excelsa*) White Deals ; and most Canadian and New Brunswick Spruce Deals are *Picea nigra*.

Dogwood in England is the name for two shrubs (*Cornus sanguinea* and *Rhamnus*

Frangula), formerly used for skewers or "dags," and now largely employed for gunpowder charcoal. In North America the name is used for two larger species related to the first-named, *Cornus florida* and *C. Nuttalli*. *C. florida* is known commercially as Cornel, Cornelian wood, or Boxwood, and *C. Nuttalli* as Western Dogwood. Reddish-brown, heavy, very hard, and fine-grained woods, they are used for engraving, cogs, tool-handles, mallets, and turnery, In the manufacture of shuttle-blocks, blocks of these woods, measuring 2 in. square, are compressed by hydraulic power to $1\frac{5}{8}$-in. square, a test that very few woods can stand without rupture of their fibres.

Douglas Fir, or Oregon Pine (*Pseudo tsuga Douglasii*), one of the most valuable and most widely distributed of American timbers, is native to the whole extent of western North America from the Tropic of Cancer to 55° N. lat., but reaches its greatest dimensions in Oregon, round the shores of Puget Sound, and in southern British Columbia. Reaching sometimes a height of 300 ft., free from branches for 200 ft. from the ground, and diameters of 6 ft. to 12 ft., or more, it comes to market in clean, straight spars 40 ft. to 110 ft. long and 9 in. to 32 in. in diameter. The wood resembles that of the larch or that of Canadian red pine (*Pinus resinosa*), its well-defined darker bands of autumn-wood placing it commercially with " hard pines " not only in appearance, but also in quality. The tree varies much in its rate of growth, according to situation, and tests made by the United States Forest Service show that rapidly grown wood (less than eight rings to the inch) is relatively weak, the best material having twelve to sixteen rings per inch, though that with twenty-four rings was the strongest. The wood with narrow growth-rings is known in its country of origin as " yellow fir," being reddish-yellow in colour, light, soft, easy to work, straight and fine in grain, uniform in texture, firm, tough, and elastic, but not at all liable to warp.

The more rapidly grown wood, known as " red fir," is a dark reddish colour, uneven in texture, with weak open spring-wood and flinty autumn-wood, coarse-grained, difficult to work, and heavier in weight. Employed in America for house-building, engineering work, and even for fuel, it is more used than any other wood down the Pacific coast of both North and South America. It is excellent for the lower masts, yards, and cross-arms of ships, and is largely used for sleepers.

The Californian or Pacific variety or Green Douglas Fir (var. *macrocarpa*) is grown in Britain in preference to the Colorado or Blue Douglas Fir (var. *glauca*), which is much slower in growth and is recognised by its shorter, stiffer, bluer leaves. The flagstaff at Kew, erected in 1861 with its butt end in a brick vault, but taken down in 1914 in an unsound condition, to be replaced by a larger one, is not perhaps a good advertisement of the durability of Douglas Fir.

Ebony, the very dense, hard, black heartwood of species of *Diospyros* and the allied genera *Maba* and *Euclea*. Any member of the family *Ebenaceæ* may furnish ebony if its heartwood is sufficiently developed, and it seems impossible to distinguish the woods of the various species microscopically. Many are so small as to be of little commercial importance. Some of the streaked woods, such as the Cala-mander-wood of Ceylon, already described, the Marblewood or Zebra-wood (*Diospyros Kurzii*) of the Andamans, and the Bolon-geta (*D. pilosanthera*) and Camagon (*D. discolor*) of the Philippines, are more beau-tiful than the dead black ; but they are less in demand and are sold as " bastard ebony." Most of the ebony of British India is the produce of *D. Melanoxylon*, known as " Coromandel " or " Godavery Ebony," reaching good sizes and some-times beautifully streaked with purple. That of Ceylon is mostly *D. ebenum*, which also reaches a good size in that island, though seldom in India. Most of the ebony of the Philippines is the wood of the smaller *Maba buxifolia ;* but it is stated that the streaked woods of Bolongeta and Camagon are rendered uniformly black by being buried in the salt mud of mangrove swamps. In Mauritius, ebony is the pro-duct of *D. tessellaria ;* in Madagascar, of

D. haplostylis and *D. microrhombus ;* at Zanzibar, of *D. mespiliformis ;* in West Tropical Africa, of *D. Dendo ;* and in South Africa, of *Euclea pseudebenus.* The East African ebonies weigh from 50 lb. to 60 lb. per cubic foot ; but the East Indian from 75 lb. to 80 lb. The fine-grained character of ebony and the filling up of its elements with a tannate of iron render the wood very free from shrinkage or warping, so that it is much used, not only for fine furniture, cabinetwork, inlaying, walking-sticks, and brush-backs, but also for pianoforte keys, the string-holder of violins, and foot-rules.

The Corsican ebony of ancient Rome, the false ebony of the French, is the dark green-ish brown wood of the Laburnum (*which see*) ; and the green ebony of the West Indies has been described under its other name of Cocus-wood. The name ebony is extended in various countries to woods in no way related to the true ebonies, such as the leguminous Mountain Ebony (*Bauhinia acuminata*) of Indo-China, the Queensland Ebony (*Bauhinia Hookeri*) and some species of Acacia and Blackwood.

ARTIFICIAL, or GERMAN EBONY, is the dyed wood of box, pear, or yew, and can nearly always be distinguished by its much lighter weight, whilst its colour is usually only superficial. Holly is often " ebonised " for the handles of teapots, and Canary whitewood is stained black for furniture ; but these imitations are hardly ever susceptible of the fine polish of true ebony.

EBONY, FALSE (FRENCH), (*see* LABUR-NUM).

EBONY, FIGURED (*see* MARBLEWOOD, ANDAMAN).

EBONY, GREEN (*see* COCUS-WOOD).

EBONY, SENEGAL (*see* BLACKWOOD, AFRICA).

EBONY, WEST INDIAN (*see* COCUS-WOOD).

Elm, the ENGLISH ELM (*Ulmus cam-pestris*), is a handsome, strong, and in many respects valuable wood. It reaches a great height (80 ft. to 90 ft.) and a diameter of 3 ft. or more. The narrow yellowish sapwood is as strong and durable as the dark brown heart. This latter is hard, firm. tough, and susceptible of a high polish, and, when dry, 1 cub. ft. weighs about 44 lb. The wood, being sweet, is liable to be worm-eaten, and is, therefore, not suitable for building. As it wears smooth and does not splinter, it is used for butchers' blocks, pulleys, the naves of cart-wheels, the seats of chairs, and the sides of ammunition boxes. If kept thoroughly dry or wet it is so durable that hollowed elm-stems were formerly used as water pipes : the Rialto at Venice is said to be built upon 12,000 piles of this timber, and it is still used in building pumps. In China, under the name of "Yii," it is in request for tables, furniture, general turnery, axles, and other parts of carts ; but with us it is now chiefly employed for coffins. The loose hold the tree has upon the soil causes large numbers to be blown over by storms, so that the supply of the wood and its price are subject to considerable fluctuations. It is liable to twist while seasoning. Elm has also been most successfully employed for paving blocks where traffic is heavy, but it is too good a wood for such a purpose. Burrs are frequent on old elms and yield fine cabinet veneers.

AMERICAN ELM is a name under which, unfortunately, several species are imported indiscriminately. The small CORK-WINGED ELM (*U. alata*) of the south-east United States yields a light brown, heavy, fine-grained wood used for hubs and blocks, but seldom exported.

THE RED, MOOSE, or SLIPPERY ELM (*U. fulva*) of the north-eastern States and south-east Canada is larger, darker, coarser grained, readily split, and therefore used locally for fence rails and, when steamed, for the ribs of boats ; but little of it comes to England.

THE WHITE or WATER ELM (*U. americana*) of the eastern States has of late years been largely exterminated by the ravages of beetles. It is a very large, light-brown, coarse-grained wood, inferior to English elm, but employed for boat-building, wheel-hubs, tool-handles, and most of the purposes to which English elm is put in this country. When imported, however, it is used chiefly for keels.

ROCK or HICKORY ELM (*U. racemosa*),

of Canada and the central United States, reaches less diameters than the last-mentioned, and is a slower-grown wood, averaging only 1 in. in diameter in fourteen years ; but, though less flexible than slippery elm, it is harder and probably much the best of American elms. It is imported in logs 20 ft. to 40 ft. long and 11 in. to 16 in. square, which are liable to split on drying. Used in America for chair-making, sleepers, door and window sills, and all the other uses of elm, it is largely imported to England for coach-building, wheels, and boat-building, being one of the best timbers for bending.

SCOTCH or WYCH ELM (*Ulmus glabra*) is a lighter coloured, softer, straighter-grained wood, more easily split than English elm. It is the common species north of the Trent. Many of the fine old linen-chests usually taken for oak are of this wood, "Wych" being apparently the early English "Hwæcce," the French "huche," a chest, our modern "hutch." At High Wycombe the wood both of this and of the last-mentioned species is used for the backs of Windsor chairs, and this species seems to be specially known as chair elm. Its wood is so flexible and tough that it was formerly used for long bows, and it is now used for shafts and many other purposes to which ash—a more costly wood—is applied, and, when steamed, for boat-building. It is distinguishable from oak by its narrower, less prominent, and darker-coloured rays.

Fir is a name used very loosely, both in commerce and in botany. White Fir or "Baltic White," and other species of *Picea*, are dealt with under the head of Spruce ; Oregon Fir or Pine has been treated under that of Douglas Fir ; and all the various names for our Scots Fir (*Pinus sylvestris*), derived mostly from the ports of shipment, such as Dantzic, Memel, Riga, Norway, Swedish, Red or Yellow Fir, come more suitably under NORTHERN Pine, where they will be found described. The name Fir is restricted to the genus *Abies*, and, though several of the species are well known in our arboreta as ornamental trees, and are employed locally in their native countries, the only kind at all important as a wood in use in England is the Silver Fir (*Abies pectinata*) of Central Europe. This is of a yellowish or pinkish-white, without distinct heart and with few resin-canals, but with regular circular, well-defined annual rings, light, soft, lustrous, easily worked, but not durable. As it takes glue well, it is used in its native countries for general carpentry, for toy-making, carving, paper pulp, and especially for packing-cases and small boxes which are largely exported from Switzerland and the Tyrol.

THE HIMALAYAN SILVER FIR (*A. Webbiana*) is used locally for building. *A. Veitchii*, the best Fir in China, is also used for telegraph poles, matches, and paper pulp ; the tall SILVER FIR (*A. grandis*) of Oregon and British Columbia, and, better still, the RED FIR, LARCH FIR, or NOBLE FIR (*A. nobilis*), of the Western States, light, but hard, strong and durable, are used for internal carpentry.

For PRINCE ALBERT'S FIR (*see* HEMLOCK SPRUCE).

Fustic, the name applied to two entirely distinct woods, both mainly employed as yellow dyes. The smaller, " Young " or " Zante Fustic," is that of the Venetian Sumach or Wig-tree (*Rhus Cotinus*), well known as a garden shrub, belonging to the family *Anacardiaceæ* Old (that is, larger) Fustic, the " Fustete " or " Palo narango " of Spaniards and " Bois d'orange " of the French, is that of *Chlorophora tinctoria*, var. *Xanthoxylon* or *Maclura tinctoria*, a member of the mulberry family, native to Brazil, Guiana, the West Indies, and Bahamas. It reaches 20 ft. in length and 1 ft. in diameter, is a canary-yellow colour, light, tough, and hard, and is used for spokes and for the bellies of long bows, or the middle of three-wood bows.

Greenheart (*Nectandra Rodiœi*), a very valuable timber, native to the north-west of South America and the West Indies. It yields timber 40 ft. to 70 ft. long and 1 ft. to 2 ft. square ; is dark greenish or chestnut in colour, often nearly black at the centre ; is fine, even, and straight in grain, with indistinguishable annual rings, and is very heavy, hard, tough, strong, and durable. Its weight is usually from 60 lb. to 76 lb. per cubic foot. It is somewhat liable to heartshake, but its heartwood is very teredo proof. It is in request for dock-gates, jetties, piles, bridge-building, keelsons, etc. The lock-gates of the Manchester Ship Canal, the Panama Canal, and the Liverpool Docks are of this wood, and some of the latter have been found perfectly sound after thirty years' use. The imported logs are sometimes 60 ft. long and have " snape " or tapered ends to facilitate their being drawn out of the forest. These ends are useful for carriage shafts, motor-wagon spokes, fishing rods, etc.

The so-called AFRICAN GREENHEART from Nigeria, a species of *Piptadenia*, belonging to the entirely unrelated family *Leguminosæ*, has proved not to be durable, and is, therefore, worthless as a substitute for true greenheart.

Gum, the BLACK GUM (*Nyssa sylvatica*), of the eastern United States, is harder, heavier, and stronger than the related " Tupelo " or " Sour Gum " ; but is used, as they are, for hubs, handles, and wooden shoes. They are imported in sawn boards and used for linings in cheap cabinetwork.

BLUE GUM (*Eucalyptus Globulus*), native to Victoria and Tasmania, and now largely planted, as a supposed preventive of malaria and as a quick-growing source of firewood or mine-timbers, in South Africa, California, the Philippines, etc. The tree reaches 200 ft. to 350 ft. in height and from 6 ft. to 25 ft. in diameter, and its wood is pale straw colour, grey or light brown, with darker streaks, hard, very heavy, moderately strong, tough and durable, partially immune from teredo, planing well but with a curled and twisted grain. It is used in India and Ceylon, whither it is extensively exported, for sleepers, bridge-building, and house-beams ; and in its native country for fences, telegraph poles, carriage and ship-building. It is the most durable hardwood in Tasmania, and it is preferred to Jarrah or Karri for the piles driven in advance of the shield in tunnelling ; in Dover harbour works piles of this timber 70 ft. to 100 ft. long and 18 in. to 20 in. square have been employed. The various gum trees of Australia are often wastefully felled at from 3 ft. to 12 ft. above the ground to save trouble ; but their stumps often exhibit beautiful curled or wavy grain suitable for cabinet-work.

RED GUM (*Eucalyptus rostrata*), of Eastern Australia, known also as Flooded Gum, Yellow-jacket, and aboriginally as " Yarrah " (not to be confounded with Jarrah), is the most valuable hardwood in Victoria. It does not reach the gigantic dimensions of blue gum, but is a large tree. Its wood is dark red, often with a pretty curly figure. It is not quite as heavy as blue gum, but is exceedingly hard and most difficult to work when dry, which is against its use for furniture, although it takes a fine polish. Like most of the eucalyptus woods, it is liable to twists and shakes during seasoning ; but is very durable, termite-and teredo-proof. It is the chief wood used for paving in Melbourne ; is preferred to blue gum for sleepers ; and is in request for piles, bridge and house-building, ships' beams, posts, etc. It must not be confounded with the next wood in the list.

SWEET GUM (*Liquidambar styraciflua*), belonging to the American Wych-hazel family (*Hamamelidaceœ*), and no more related to the walnut, pine or hazel than to the Australian gum-trees than to the walnut, pine or hazel. It is known in America as " Bilsted " or " Red Gum," and reaches 100 ft. to 140 ft. in height, 4 ft. to 5 ft. in diameter, and weighs on the average about 38 lb. per cubic foot. The sapwood is cream-white ; the heart irregular, reddish-brown, often beautifully marked with dark false rings, moderately hard, close grained, tough, free from knots but splintery, taking a satiny polish, but warping and twisting badly in drying, unless it be first steamed. Although little suited for paving, it has been sold for that purpose under the designation of Cali-fornian Red Gum ; but it grows in the eastern States, especially in the Lower Mississippi Valley, and is shipped from New Orleans. In the timber trade it is com-monly supposed that " Hazel Pine " is a trade name for the sapwood and " Satin Walnut " for the heart ; but, as a matter of fact, the so-called hazel pine is the whole

wood of the same species as satin walnut, but grown in low-lying swampy districts where the dark colouring-matter is not developed. It is the hygroscopic char-acter of the gum that fills the vessels of this wood which makes it liable under changes of temperature both to longi-tudinal twisting and to transverse warping, for which reason it is better fitted for cheap bedroom furniture than for use in rooms in which fires are lit. The hazel pine is largely imported in planed boards which are used for the lining of cheap furniture, competing with the lower grades of canary whitewood. The satin walnut, which is undeniably a beautiful wood, makes hand-some veneers.

Gurjun, or wood-oil tree (*Dipterocarpus turbinatus* and *D. alatus*), red, moderately hard woods of large dimensions, native to India and Burma, and used for house-and boat-building, are recommended for sleepers, and have some figure, so that when treated by the process known as Powellising they resemble African mahogany.

Hackmatack. (*See* LARCH.)

Hawthorn (*Cratœgus Oxyacantha*) is a hard, heavy, flesh-coloured wood of slow growth and seldom of any size, known chiefly as used for walking-sticks, though it is the best substitute for box for the purposes of the engraver that has yet been discovered.

Hazel (*Corylus Avellana*), a reddish-white wood with no heart, resembling beech, but soft, very elastic, only of small dimensions and not durable, is used chiefly for barrel-hoops, walking-sticks, and alpen-stocks. The TURKISH or CONSTANTI-NOPLE HAZEL (*C. Colurna*), native to the Balkan peninsula and much of Central Asia, reaches much larger dimensions and is suitable for small furniture work, for which purpose it is employed in China.

Hemlock Spruce (*Tsuga canadensis*), often spoken of simply as " Hemlock," or as " Eastern Hemlock," although specially valued for its bark, which yields a tanning extract, is an abundant and useful timber of eastern North America. It grows to more than 100 ft. in height and from 3 ft. to 6 ft. in diameter, and is a light reddish, lustreless grey or brown wood, with little distinction of heart and few resin-passages, light, soft, and stiff, but brittle, coarse-grained, splintery, shrinking and warping considerably in seasoning, wearing rough and not very durable, but retaining nails firmly, and employed for sleepers, laths, rafters, and fencing.

THE WESTERN HEMLOCK (*Tsuga heterophylla*), which grows from Alaska to Oregon and is known in arboreta as " Prince Albert's Fir " (*Abies Albertiana* or *A. Mertensiana*), is larger and yields a heavier and harder timber, which, however, is not so strong. The Chinese species (*T. chinensis* and *T. yunnanensis*) are both known as " Tieh sha," a name signifying Iron Fir, and are valued for planking and roof-shingles.

Hickory, the wood of species of the North American genus *Hicoria*, formerly known as *Carya*, which is nearly related to the Walnuts, though the woods are very different. When stripped of their characteristic barks, the hickories are not readily discriminated. They are slender trees, sometimes reaching from 70 ft. to 120 ft. in height, and 2 ft., 3 ft., or even 5 ft. in diameter. The sapwood is broad and white, the heart a reddish nut-brown, often not unlike ash. All the species are very heavy, ranging in specific gravity from ·75 to ·84, weighing, that is, from 47 lb. to 52 lb. per cubic foot ; they are very strong, tough, and elastic, rather coarse, but smooth, and straight in grain, with large pith but indistinct rays. They dry slowly, shrinking and splitting considerably in the process ; and, in addition, they are found to be very liable to insect attack and are not durable in contact with soil or exposed to the weather. The reddish-brown streaks often seen in the sapwood are due to the attacks of birds.

Hickory is unsuitable for house- or boat-building, but is of great value in carriage-building, for axles and spokes, axe and other tool-handles, screws for presses, chair-making, coach-whips, bows, and cask-hoops. It is harder, heavier, and tougher than ash, which it closely resembles in its general properties and uses. Nearly all American-made carriage-wheels imported into this country have their spokes and felloes of this wood, which, however, is better suited to the dry air of the States than to ours.

The best species are PIG - NUT or BROOM HICKORY (*Hicoria glabra* or *Carya porcina*), SHELL - BARK or SHAG - BARK HICKORY (*H. ovata* or *C. alba*), MOCKER-NUT HICKORY (*H. alba* or *C. tomentosa*), and BIG or THICK SHELL-BARK HICKORY (*H. laciniosa* or *C. sulcata*). These differ but little in value, and are hardly distinguished from one another commercially. Pig-nut Hickory is said to be the best for axles and axe-handles ; Mocker-nut Hickory, for whip-handles and the back bows of Windsor chairs ; and the Shell-barks are most largely imported for spokes, bows, etc. Mocker-nut Hickory is white when young, and the Thick Shell-bark is slightly lighter in weight and darker in colour than the others here named. The other species, of which the chief are the PECAN, NUTMEG, BITTERNUT, and WATER HICKORIES (*H. Pecan, H. myristicæformis, H. minima,* and *H. aquatica,* formerly known as *Carya olivæformis, C. myristicæformis, C. amara,* and *C. aquatica*), are lighter in weight, softer, and more brittle, and are chiefly used as fuel.

Holly (*Ilex Aquifolium*) does not reach a large size, seldom exceeding 40 ft. in height or 1½ ft. in diameter. It is a beautiful white wood, except in old trees, which are apt to be brownish, very fine, and close in grain, more nearly approaching ivory both in colour and texture than any other wood, and susceptible of a high polish. It weighs about 47½ lb. per cubic foot, and is hard, but readily turned. It is sometimes difficult to prevent its shrinking, warping, splitting, and becoming spotted or stained in drying. For this reason it should be cut into the form required, whether into veneer planks or round blocks for turning, as soon as felled and boiled in water for many hours. This removes the sap and enhances the whiteness of the wood. The pieces are then packed closely together and covered up for several weeks so as to cool and dry slowly, and are then stored in dry air, without being allowed to touch one another. Besides the use of small Holly for whip-handles, the wood is considerably used for engraving, especially in calico-printing and in veneer for inlaying, as in Tunbridge ware, and for white or stained strings in furniture and cabinet-work. For staining, dyeing, or ebonising, Holly is unequalled. The AMERICAN HOLLY (*Ilex opaca*) of the Eastern States is a very similar wood and is employed for the same purposes.

Honeysuckle-wood, a name sometimes applied in America to the wood of the Plane (*Platanus occidentalis*) when cut radially so as to expose the beautiful grain which makes it a first-rate wood for fretwork. In New Zealand the name is applied to the beautiful Rewa-rewa (*which see*) ; but it is, perhaps, most used for the Australian species of *Banksia, B. marginata, B. serrata,* and *B. integrifolia.* These belong mainly to the south-east, and are of moderate dimensions. They require careful seasoning, and are liable to become worm-eaten ; but have beautiful figure, and are susceptible of a high polish. The two first named are a dark mahogany-like red ; while the third, known as Coast Honeysuckle, is lighter-coloured. (*See also* BEEF-WOOD.)

Hornbeam (*Carpinus Betulus*), generally of moderate lengths and not more than 1 ft. in diameter, is a yellowish white, heavy, hard, close-grained, and somewhat lustrous wood which, owing in part to its wavy growth-rings, is of exceptional toughness. This renders it the best wood for the bearers of printers' rollers and for cogs, mallets, skittles, etc., for which purposes it is imported by us from France. It is also excellent fuel.

There is a species in the eastern Mediterranean region (*C. duinensis*) and one in eastern North America (*C. caroliniana*), with similar timber, though the latter is, perhaps, slightly inferior. All three trees are confused with the beeches from general resemblances of bark, bud, leaves and, to some extent, wood. Thus the German name for our species is "Weiss-buche," that is, White Beech ; *C. duinensis* is sometimes dubbed Oriental Beech ; and the American species is also called Blue or Water Beech.

The Hop-hornbeams of Southern Europe and the east of North America (*Ostrya carpinifolia* and *O. virginica*) are closely related woods, similar in structure, but browner or redder in colour, which are tolerable substitutes for the true hornbeams.

Horse-chestnut (*Æsculus hippocastanum*), a very quick-growing, light, soft, white wood, reaching considerable dimensions, and resembling willow or poplar in character. It has neither strength nor durability, and is grown chiefly for shade and ornament ; but is a cheap substitute for other white woods. It warps but little, so is suitable for flooring and still more for the lining of carts and wheelbarrows, packing-cases, blind-wood in cabinetwork, moulds for castings, and the backs of scrubbing brushes. In France it is used for sabots, and might be employed, as are the woods of the related Buck-eyes in the United States, for artificial limbs. It is in no way related to the true, sweet, or Spanish chestnut.

Huon-pine (*Dacrydium Franklinii*), known also as Macquarie Pine, a light-yellow, coniferous wood from a Tasmanian tree 80 ft. or 100 ft. in height and 3 ft. to 6 ft. in diameter. It is light, close-grained, and tough, but easily worked, susceptible of a good polish, and often beautifully marked with dark wavy lines and small knots. It is, perhaps, tougher than any other pine ; and when seasoned is harder than Baltic or American pine. It is durable, and very free from the attacks of insects, and has been used for bedroom furniture, and especially for boat-building ; but is now quite scarce.

Ironwood, a name applied to many widely different woods in various countries, often to several in one region. As most of these woods have other local names, it will avoid confusion if, when they come into English commerce, this name be not used. In the United States it is sometimes applied to the Bitternut Hickory (*Hicoria minima*) or to the Hornbeam and Hop-hornbeam (*Carpinus caroliniana* and

Ostrya virginica). In South and East Africa the name is applied to the Mopane (*Copaïfera Mopane*) ; various species of Olive (*Olea*), the " Olivenhout " of the Dutch, dark, heavy, dense woods, nearly equal to Lignum-vitæ and used as guides for the stamps in gold-crushing, are known as Black Ironwood ; and the name White Ironwood is applied to the Umzimbit (*Toddalia lanceolata*), and Mauritius White Ironwood or White Milkwood, to the very heavy greyish-yellow *Sideroxylon inerme*, used for telegraph poles and construction work. As the name *Sideroxylon* is merely the Greek equivalent of ironwood, the species of this genus have, perhaps, the best right to the English name. *S. nitidum*, in Java ; *S. ferrugineum*, the " Tuak-tuak " of the Malay Peninsula ; and *S. tomentosum*, of the Coromandel coast, are known as Ironwood. The " Bilian " of Borneo (*Eusideroxylon Zwageri*) ; the " Tampinis " (*Sloetia sideroxylon*) of the same region ; the "Nagesah" (*Mesua ferrea*), of India, Ceylon, and Malaya ; the " Ipil " (*Intsia bijuga*), " Mirabow " (*Intsia Bakeri*), and " Pynkadu " (*Xylia xylocarpa*), allied dark-coloured leguminous woods, widely distributed in the East Indies, are among the chief " ironwoods " of the East Indies. In New Zealand the myrtaceous Rata (*Metrosideros robusta* and *M. lucida*) and the allied *M. tomentosa* are given this name, as is *M. vera*, the Kayu besi of Malaya or Nani of Amboyna.

In Australia the name Ironwood is applied to Marblewood (*Olea paniculata*) ; to the allied and similar Native Olive (*Notolœa ligustrina*) ; to several species of Wattle or Myall, such as *Acacia excelsa* and *A. stenophylla* ; and to the Swamp Oak or Beef-wood (*Casuarina equisetifolia*), the Kayu ru of Malaysia. For Kaffir Ironwood, *see* UMZIMBIT. This by no means exhausts the list of ironwoods.

Jack (*Artocarpus integrifolia*), an East Indian wood, sometimes known from its colour as " Orange-wood," and used as a dye, is moderately hard and takes a good polish ; but is coarse and crooked in grain, generally warping seriously, and brittle. It is used in the East for house- and boat-building, furniture, and the backs of musical instruments, and in this country in turnery, marquetry, and for the backs of brushes. It is much improved by being Powellised, its colour and figure being well brought out.

Jarrah (*Eucalyptus marginata*), perhaps the most valuable timber of South-west Australia, where it is fairly plentiful. Growing 90 ft. to 150 ft. high and 3 ft. to 5 ft., or even 10 ft. in diameter, it yields timber 20 ft. to 40 ft. long and 1 ft. to 2 ft. square, of a deep red mahogany-like colour, sometimes with some mottling and ornamental curl in the grain, very heavy, hard, close-grained, taking a good polish, working smoothly, very uninflammable, and, owing to the astringent gum it contains, very durable. It requires, however, careful seasoning, being liable otherwise to twist and split. In ship-building it can be used without copper sheathing, and can be imported into India at a cost below that of teak. It is largely used for piles, telegraph poles, sleepers, and especially for paving-blocks. Its chief drawbacks for such purposes are its liability to split during the process of conversion, and its wearing to a polished surface. The engineer must also bear in mind that the tree is often unsound at the centre and that large gum-cavities, which seriously affect the strength of the log in the round, also frequently occur. The ornamental varieties are used for furniture, and large and beautiful burrs sometimes occur.

Jarul (*Lagerstrœmia speciosa*) and other related species, known by this name in Bengal, as " Pyinma " in Burma, " Muruta " in Ceylon, and " Banaba " in the Philippines, is the most valuable timber of North-east India, and second in value only to teak in Burma. It reaches a large size, is moderately hard and heavy, reddish in colour, and durable, whether dry or under water. It is used in building, for gun-carriages, wagon-building, wheels, and boats, often yielding compass timber suitable for knees. It is also used in the east in wharf-building, for piles and for sleepers.

Juniper (*Juniperus communis*), little more than a shrub, yields wood of small dimensions, tough, durable, and fragrant when burnt. It is used on the Continent for whip-handles and for vine-stakes. The woods of this genus closely resemble those of the related genera *Cupressus* and *Thuja*, and produce similar ornamental burrs. *J. excelsa* may reach 100 ft. in height, and forms pure forests in the Crimea, the wood of which may prove valuable for sleepers. The nearly related Indian Juniper (*J. macropoda*), the only valuable timber near Quetta, is used both for building and carpentry. *J. pseudosabina* in Northern Turkestan and Siberia yields good timber, and several species are employed in China. The American species are alluded to under the name of Pencil Cedar.

Kamassi (*Gonioma Kamassi*), also known as Cape Boxwood, Knysna Boxwood, or East London Boxwood, names liable to confuse it with the similar but unrelated *Buxus Macowanii*, from the same region, is one of the best woods of South Africa, though only small. It is heavy, hard, close-grained, and tough, and is used for cabinetwork, planes, and other tools, but would also be suitable for engraving.

Karri (*Eucalyptus diversicolor*), from South-west Australia, huge timber, occurring over a large area between Albany and the Blackwood River, though not nearly so abundant as Jarrah. It reaches 300 ft. to 400 ft. in height and 12 ft. in diameter ; but an average tree will be 200 ft. high and 4 ft. in diameter. It is a reddish wood, weighing from 50 lb. to 72 lb. per cubic foot, slightly wavy or curled in grain, but with no ornamental figure, hard, tough, strong, and elastic ; but not so easily wrought as Jarrah, frequently having large gum-cavities and liable to star-shake, durable under water, but not between wind and earth, comparatively non-inflammable, but more liable to dry-rot than Jarrah. It is much used in Australia for wheels. boat-building, piles, bridge-building, and wagons, and is now largely exported and used almost indiscriminately with Jarrah for paving.

Kauri Pine (*Agathis australis*) has been described by an impartial expert as " undoubtedly the best of all soft woods." It unfortunately grows only in the north of the North Island of New Zealand, and is slow in growth. It reaches 120 ft. to 140 ft. or even 200 ft. in height, and 4 ft. to 10 ft. or even 15 ft. or 20 ft. in diameter at the base, so that planks 20 ft. long and 4 ft. to 5 ft. wide without knot or shake are readily obtainable. The wide sapwood is very resinous, copiously exuding the well-known Kauri gum. The heart is yellowish-white to brown, very clean, straight, fine and close in grain, moderately hard for a pine, very firm, strong, and elastic, generally sound or with only a slight heart-shake, shrinking very little in seasoning, planing up well, with a beautiful silky lustre like the plainer samples of satinwood, taking a good polish or staining well, and wearing even, without splintering. It is thus unrivalled for masts and spars, and, owing to its freedom from knots or splintering, for the decks of yachts. Except when exposed to the teredo, it is more durable than any other pine, and has been used for sleepers, telegraph poles, and house-building. Being sometimes richly curled in grain, it is also used for joinery and carving. It is imported in sawn planks ; but its scarcity and the heavy freightage on soft wood brought from so great a distance limit its use.

QUEENSLAND KAURI, the allied *Agathis robusta*, and *A. Palmerstoni*, also known as Dundatha Pine, is a somewhat smaller tree with a yellower, softer, but useful wood, largely used in North-east Australia by joiners, cabinetmakers, builders and pattern-makers.

Laburnum (*Cytisus Laburnum*) is the Faux ebénier (False Ebony) of the French and the Corsican Ebony of ancient Rome. Its broad yellow sapwood contrasts markedly with its dark brown, slightly greenish heart. It is very hard and capable of a high polish, and is used in turnery and inlaying. In England the tree is so exclusively considered as an ornament to the garden that its wood is seldom seen in commerce.

Lacewood, a name sometimes applied in America to the wood of the Plane or Buttonwood (*Platanus occidentalis*) when cut radially so as to display the darker silver-grain against the lighter groundwork. It is also known as Honeysuckle-wood, and is cut into veneer and used for fretwork.

Lancewood, chiefly imported from Guiana, where it is known as "Yari-yari," is *Duguetia quitarensis*. It is yellow, light, hard, elastic, and fine-grained, and is used for carriage-shafts, fishing-rods, bows and arrows. The closely allied *Guatteria virgata* of Honduras, known locally as "Yaya," is imported under the same name. *See* also under MYRTLE.

LANCEWOOD, CAPE (*see* ASSEGAI-WOOD).

LANCEWOOD, DEGAME (*see* DEGAME).

Larch, the rapidly grown, light, even-grained, soft, tough, and very durable woods of the ten or twelve species of the coniferous genus *Larix*, especially *L. euro-pœa*. The common larch may reach 80 ft. or 100 ft., or even 120 ft. in height, with a diameter of 2 ft. to 4 ft. at its base. The heartwood is yellowish-white, or reddish-brown in alpine regions, generally straight-grained and therefore easily split, though sometimes rather coarse. The annual rings are slightly waved and sharply defined by broad, dark autumn-wood. It shrinks and warps still more in seasoning, and afterwards, which militates against its use for boat-building ; but its lightness, its great durability (owing to its richness in tannic and phenolic antiseptic substances), and its comparative non-inflammability have recommended its use for building from early times. Much of Venice was built originally on larch piles, which are still sound. It is largely used for sleepers, pit-props, scaffold-poles, and ladders ; and, being more free from large and loose knots than spruce, is much in demand for carpentry. It works up fairly well and has a lustrous surface. Owing to the ravages of the larch canker-fungus (*Dasyscypha calycina*, formerly known as *Peziza Willkommii*), which, while only sporadic in the early ripened woods of the mountains, becomes epidemic in our lowland woodlands, the Japanese species, *L. leptolepis*, was recommended to British foresters as likely to prove quicker in growth and more immune from the attacks of this fungus than the European. This species, found chiefly in Nippon, is redder, heavier, and harder than European larch.

It has, however, been proved experimentally in Bavaria that, when twenty years old, the European species has outgrown *L. leptolepis ;* and experiments are consequently being carried out with the more northern *L. kurilensis.*

In Eastern Siberia and Manchuria there is a species, *L. dahurica*, apparently closely similar, which is employed for coffins, pillars in temples, masts and telegraph poles, as well as for sleepers, and is thought superior to Oregon Fir for shipbuilding. There are several species in China, of which *L. Potaninii*, of North-west Szechwan, is valued : the Himalayan *L. Griffithiana* is soft and not large, and but little used ; whilst *L. sibirica*, of W. Siberia, is closely similar to the European species.

Larches in the United States are commonly known as TAMARACKS or HACK-MATACKS. *L. pendula*, also known as *L. americana*, *L. microcarpa*, and *L. laricina*, the Black Larch of the North-east United States or "Epinette rouge" of the French Canadians, is similar in dimensions, structure, and uses to European Larch, though lighter and perhaps harder. It has been described as resembling Hard Pine in appearance, quality, uses, equalling European Larch in strength and oak in durability. It is one of the best American timbers for sleepers ; it is used for interior finish ; its straight growth makes it valuable for telegraph-poles, though crooked pieces are available for ships' knees ; and it is very durable when in contact with the soil.

The WESTERN TAMARACK, or Larch (*L. occidentalis*), the largest species in the genus, sometimes reaching 250 ft. in height and 4 ft. to 8 ft. in diameter, is stronger than all other American conifers, and redder, heavier, and harder but somewhat coarser in texture than *L. pendula*. Though used chiefly for sleepers, fencing, and fuel, it is sometimes beautifully coloured and is suitable for interior finish. It grows mainly in Montana, Idaho, Oregon, and Washington, extending into British Columbia, and accompanied by *L. Lyalli*.

Laurel, Cape. (*See* STINKWOOD.)

Letter-wood, or Leopard-wood, the "Lettre moucheté" of the French or

" Pao de letras " of the Portuguese, is the straight-grained specimens of the mottled wood of *Brosimum Aubletii* of Guiana. It is known in English commerce as " Snake-wood." The heart is very heavy and hard, and takes a splendid polish ; but it only squares about 20 in., of which not more than 6 in. exhibits the characteristic mottling, and is difficult to work and full of defects. It is imported in very small quantity for the bellies of bows, walking-sticks, and inlay.

Lignum-vitæ, a name belonging properly to the Tropical American species of the genus *Guaiacum*, especially *G. officinale, G. sanctum,* and *G. arboreum.* The first named of these, native to Jamaica, Cuba, Hayti, Venezuela, and Colombia, shipped mainly from Jamaica and St. Domingo, is not a large tree, its height ranging from 20 ft. to 40 ft., with a diameter of 1 ft. or 2 ft. Lignum-vitæ is one of the heaviest known woods, ranging from 60 lb. to 83 lb. per cubic foot. The dingy yellow, non-resinous sapwood is as durable as the heart, and part of it is consequently left on, to preserve the rest from splitting. The heart is blackish, with a greenish tinge : the pith rays are indistinguishable and the annual rings nearly so, whilst, owing to the oblique direction of the fibres, both radially and tangentially, the wood can hardly be split. Though very close-grained and strong, it is liable to cup-shake when more than 10 in. in diameter. The presence of from 25 per cent. to 26 per cent. of the gum resin, which renders the wood so valuable medicinally as to have given it the names of Palo santo (holy wood) or Lignum-vitæ (wood of life), renders it almost imperishable. It is imported in lengths of from 6 ft. to 12 ft. up to 10 in. in diameter, or from 3 ft. to 6 ft. when wider. It is used for ships' blocks, pulley-sheaves, pestles, mortars, skittle-balls, police truncheons, croquet-mallets, rulers, string-boxes, etc.

BAHAMA LIGNUM-VITÆ (*G. sanctum*) occurs in Florida and the Bahamas, and is sometimes 26 ft. long, otherwise resembling *G. officinale.* MARACAYBO LIGNUM-VITÆ (*G. arboreum*), occuring from Paraguay to Venezuela, sometimes from 60 ft.

to 70 ft. long, with a diameter of 1 ft. or 2 ft., is brown, but almost as heavy and hard as the other species. The name Lignum-vitæ is sometimes given by the French to the coniferous *Tetraclinis articulata* (*see* THUYA) ; in New Zealand to species of *Metrosideros* (*see* RATA), and in Australia to several different woods, including an Acacia (*A. falcata*), a Myrtle (*Myrtus acmenioides*), and a Gum-tree (*Eucalyptus polyanthema*).

As the true Lignum-vitæ is becoming scarce, mention may be made here of two of the most practicable substitutes for it, namely the myrtaceous *Xanthostemon verdugonianus* (*see* MANCONO), and the sapindaceous *Dodonæa viscosa.* This latter is a shore plant widely distributed throughout the tropics, but usually small. It is known as Ake-ake in New Zealand, as Birch in Tasmania, as " Banderu " in the Philippines, as " Apiri " in Tahiti, as " Varal " in Ceylon, and as " Switch-sorrel " in Jamaica. It has white sapwood and a dark-brown or greenish-black rose-streaked heart, very hard, close-grained and durable. It is used for walking-sticks, tool-handles, turnery, and engraving.

Lime. (*See* LINDEN, below.)

Linden, the preferable name for the wood of *Tilia cordata, T. platyphyllos,* or *T. vulgaris,* often known as Lime, a name corrupted from Line and belonging rather to one of the Orange tribe. It is pale yellow, white, or reddish-white, very light, weighing only about 30 lb. the cubic foot, soft and close-grained. It is liable to become worm-eaten, and will not stand exposure to weather ; but stands fairly well when thoroughly dried and varnished or painted. Used in Japan for sandals, and on the Continent sometimes for sabots, Linden is chiefly turned into small boxes for druggists, carved into toys or used for the sounding-boards and blind-wood in pianofortes. For this latter purpose it is imported from Lithuania It might, however, be more extensively employed for furniture, coach-building, and plywood, being closely similar to the nearly related American Basswood (*T. americana*), which, as already mentioned, is largely used for such purposes. Leather-cutters' planks are of linden, and no wood lends itself better to carving in high relief for decorative work where light weight is an object. The beautiful work of Grin-ling Gibbons, best represented at Windsor, Chatsworth, Trinity College, Cambridge, and the choir of St. Paul's Cathedral, is mostly in this wood. Grinling Gibbons lived at one time in La Belle Sauvage Yard —where this work is printed and published. Here it was, according to Horace Walpole, that " he carved a pot of flowers which shook surprisingly with the motion of the coaches that passed by."

Lingoa Wood. (*See* Amboyna-wood.)

Locust, a name not often used in Eng-land. In the United States it is, with the names Black or Yellow Locust applied to *Robinia pseudacacia*, the tree commonly called the Acacia in this country. This species, a native of the south-eastern United States, reaches considerable dimen-sions and is of fairly rapid growth, forming heartwood in five-year-old shoots, which is, perhaps, earlier than any other tree. It is valued as a shade tree in North China, and for planting on railway banks on the continent of Europe, its moist foliage serv-ing to quench sparks and thus protect forest from fire, while the coppice-shoots are eagerly eaten by cattle. The heart-wood is yellowish-brown streaked with red and green, weighing about 46 lb. per cubic foot, hard, strong, tough, and very durable, especially in contact with soil. It shrinks considerably in seasoning, which unfits it for furniture or building ; but it is used for sleepers, and especially for trenails, fence-posts, and wheel-spokes. As it has of late years been found very suitable for the spokes of motor-cars, it might well be grown more than it is. Fence-posts of this wood will last fifteen or twenty years.

The nearly allied Honey Locust, or Three-thorned Acacia (*Gleditschia tri-acanthos*), from the same region, yields a similar wood, which, however, is not quite so heavy. In the West Indies and in Demerara the name Locust is applied to the allied but superior wood of *Hymenœa Courbaril*, also known as " Courbaril,"

or in Spanish as " Algarrobo," a fine red-dish-brown wood with darker streaks, very heavy and hard, close and even in grain, easily worked, taking an excellent polish and not warping. It is used in shipbuilding, engineering, and cabinet-work, for trenails and for cogs.

Logwood (*Hæmatoxylon campechianum*), a native of Central America, naturalised in Jamaica, comes to market in logs from 3 ft. to 4 ft. long, of a deep dull brownish-red, very heavy and hard, and with a violet-like perfume ; but is used exclu-sively as a red or black dye, or as an ingre-dient of ink.

Mahogany, a name belonging origin-ally to the West Indian *Swietenia Maha-goni* and *S. macrophylla*, now known dis-tinctively as Spanish or Cuba Mahogany, but extended in the East Indies and in Africa to numerous other members of the sub-family *Swietenioideæ* and sometimes to the West Indian genus *Cedrela* and the allied East Indian genus *Toona*, belonging to the sub-family *Cedreloideæ* in the same family, *Meliaceæ*, and (less justifiably) in Australia to certain species of *Euca-lyptus* and similar woods. The Cedrelas and Toonas are often known as Cedars or Cigar-box woods, and the Australian woods ought at least to be distinguished as Bastard, Forest or Swamp Mahoganies.

The name Borneo Mahogany is some-times applied to Poon, and the trade name Philippine Mahogany is most misleadingly used for at least three entirely distinct woods, none of which is a true Mahogany, namely Calantas (*Toona calantas*), Padouk (*Pterocarpus indicus, P. dalbergioides, P. echinatus*, and *P. macrocarpus*) and Tanguile (*Shorea polysperma*).

True Spanish Mahogany reaches large dimensions, yielding accurately squared timber 18 ft. to 35 ft. long and 11 in. to 24 in. square, very solid at centre, rarely affected by cup- or star-shake, and with insignificant heart-shake. Its weight is about 53 lb. per cubic foot, which is very heavy, and it is very hard, close, and straight in grain, and susceptible of the most perfect polish, with a beautiful satiny lustre. When freshly felled it is a light reddish-brown, soon darkening on exposure to light to a cinnamon brown. Its fine but distinct pith-rays are deeply coloured, and a variety of wavy figures occur, yielding the valuable "roe," "mottle," "cross-mottle," "dapple," "fiddle - back," "plum - pattern," and "curl mahogany." It does not as a rule shrink or warp, and is, perhaps, superior to all other woods in taking a firm hold of glue. It is almost non-inflammable and very durable. *Swietenia macrophylla* is rather lighter and softer than *S. Mahagoni.*

From the early days of the Spanish Conquest down to the eighteenth century mahogany was used as an oak substitute in shipbuilding for beams, planks, and stanchions, whilst figured specimens soon attracted attention for furniture. Thus in Spain, in the Spanish Netherlands, as at Ghent, and in Spanish America, as at Lima, we see cathedral stalls of this wood. In England, whilst oak was used almost exclusively down to 1625, and from 1625 to 1688 or into the reign of Queen Anne there was the "Age of Walnut" in furniture (though that wood had been considerably employed on the Continent for two or three centuries), the "Age of Mahogany" is dated from 1688. The admirable designs of Chippendale, Heppelwhite, and Sheraton, mostly executed in mahogany, gave this wood the popularity throughout the eighteenth century in England that satinwood then had in France. Its very extensive use for diningtables, piano-cases, wardrobes, and other large articles, although latterly these have been very generally veneered, rendered Spanish mahogany scarce and costly.

ST. DOMINGO MAHOGANY was similar in quality to the Cuban, or even harder and almost horny, and was mostly figured, presenting a rich curl at the bases of its branches; but it was much smaller, being generally 8 ft. to 10 ft., though sometimes 25 ft., long and 12 in., 13 in., or rarely 15 in. square; and it now appears almost exhausted

The mahoganies of the Central American mainland, which form the bulk of the shrinking American supply, and are known as Honduras, Tabasco, Bay-wood, Colombian, Panama, Mexican, or Bermuda mahogany, are all probably the woods of species of the allied genus *Cedrela.* They are considerably lighter than Cuban mahogany, often weighing not more than 35 lb. per cubic foot; and they are also correspondingly softer.

HONDURAS MAHOGANY, shipped from Belize, Trujillo, and Tabasco (the largest logs coming from the last-mentioned port, but frequently affected by heart-shakes), yields logs 25 ft. to 40 ft. long and 12 in. to 24 in. square, or even larger. It is seldom figured, and is apt to become brittle and to develop star-shake on drying; but under the general trade name of Bay-wood, it is largely used by cabinetmakers, especially as ground for veneers. Guatemalan mahogany is generally classed with, and sometimes sold as, Honduras; but Mexican, though reaching the largest dimensions, squaring 36 in. or even 48 in., is generally somewhat soft and spongy at the centre.

AFRICAN MAHOGANY, first imported about 1833, and in rapidly increasing quantities since 1886, is the product of a considerable number of species of the genera *Khaya*, *Trichilia*, and *Entandrophragma*, all nearly related to the West Indian genus *Swietenia*, distributed down the West Coast from Senegal to Angola and represented also by newly discovered species, in which a trade may develop, in Central and Eastern Tropical Africa. The main difficulties as to the supply of this wood are the facts that the trees occur scattered among a host of less valuable species in the confusion of a tropical jungle, that their great weight makes it very difficult to get them to waterways, and that the coast surf in many places much hinders their shipment. The wood reaches England in logs hewn square from 10 ft. to 29 ft., but mostly 15 ft. to 20 feet long, and from 13 in. to 52 in., but mostly 20 in. to 30 in. square. It is mostly lighter in weight and often in colour than West Indian mahogany; but it varies from yellow to brown, with dark zones: it is sometimes even a darker red-brown than that from Cuba, and it may be so beautifully figured as to fetch the very highest prices for veneers. Some of the finest veneer and counter-top wood comes from the French Ivory Coast ports of Assinee and Grand Bassam. Here, and in the neighbourhood of the Gold Coast ports of Axim and Sekondi, the wood is mainly the produce of *Khaya senegalensis* ; from Lagos to Benin (South Nigeria), of *Trichilia Pricuriana*, excellent cabinet wood ; and from Benin eastward to Sapeli, of *Entandrophragma Candolleana* or some other species of that genus, fine, large, well-squared, and scented like a cedar.

EAST INDIA MAHOGANY is a name generally used for *Soymida febrifuga*, a large tree of Central and Southern India, nearly related to the true mahogany, but yielding a darker blood-red wood, heavier and harder than that wood, somewhat cross-grained and brittle, but used for furniture and carving, though scarce. The name is also applied to the related and similar, but lighter and more cedar-like, Chikrassi (*Chukrassia tabularis*), a fragrant, hard wood with a fine satiny lustre, liable to warp in hot weather.

MAHOGANY, INDIAN (*see* CEDAR, MOULMEIN).

MAHOGANY, MOUNTAIN (*see* BIRCH, AMERICAN).

MAHOGANY, PHILIPPINE (*see* PADOUK).

Mancono(*Xanthostemon verdugonianus*), a myrtaceous wood, probably the heaviest and hardest wood in the Philippines, being about the same weight as, but even harder than, Lignum-vitæ, appears immune to the attacks of termites and teredo ; and being of crooked grain and difficult to split, seems, on the whole, to be the best substitute for that timber as yet discovered.

Mango (*Mangifera indica*), widely cultivated in the East Indies and introduced elsewhere in the Tropics, yields the cheapest light wood obtainable in Madras. It is dull grey, becoming a light chocolate colour, and porous, and holds nails faster than any other wood. It can be readily treated with preservatives : when Powellised it takes an excellent polish and it can also be creosoted. It is used for planking, packing-cases, blindwood, ground for veneers, canoes, solid cart-wheels, etc.

Manzanita (*Arctostaphylos pungens*), a fine-grained, small, heavy reddish-purple wood, with lighter streaks, native to the United States and employed in turnery.

Maple, the wood of various species of the genus *Acer*, exclusive of *A. Pseudoplatanus*, the Sycamore. The only British species, the Common, Field, or Hedge Maple (*A. campestre*), is a small tree, rarely yielding wood more than 9 in. or 10 in. in diameter. This wood is light brown or reddish-white, heavy, hard, fine-grained, and tough, with a beautiful satiny lustre. It is sometimes marked by dark pith-flecks and not uncommonly has a curled or speckled (bird's-eye) grain. Besides its use for fuel or charcoal, the wood is valued in France for turnery and cabinetwork. The curled and bird's-eye specimens when cut into veneer by the rotary knife are equal to those imported from America. The wood of the root is often beautifully mottled and dark, and the handsome " mazer " bowls, formerly turned and mounted in silver, were probably mostly from this part of the tree.

The NORWAY or PLANE MAPLE (*A. platanoides*), widely distributed on the Continent, is a much larger tree, yielding a moderately hard, heavy, and tough wood, which is easily worked, takes a fine polish owing to the satiny pith-rays characteristic of the group, but is apt to crack and warp. It is used in turnery, for musical instruments, gunstocks, etc., and in wagon-building, being nearly identical with sycamore ; but its greyish tinge detracts from its value, fashion decreeing that sycamore must be pure white.

Though there are species locally valuable in the Himalaya (*A. Campbelli*, used for planking and tea-boxes, and *A. lævigatum*, for beams), in Manchuria (*A. tataricum*, " Sê," used for furniture), and in Japan, and one species from the Pacific slope is important, eastern North America presents the greatest variety of maples.

OREGON or CALIFORNIA MAPLE (*A. macrophyllum*) is moderately heavy, hard, strong, and close-grained, and sometimes reaches 4 ft. in diameter. It is used locally for axe- and broom-handles, snow-shoe-frames, and furniture, the occasionally occurring " fiddle-back " curl being especially valuable for the latter purpose.

This waviness of the grain, though rarely noticeable in the growing tree or on a transverse section, produces transverse corrugations visible when the bark is removed and varying in width from one to several to the inch. On all planed longitudinal or oblique sections this figuring appears, and so closely resembles the light and shadow on an undulating surface that it is difficult to believe it smooth.

The most valuable species of eastern North America is *A. barbatum* (also known as *A. saccharum*), the ROCK, HARD or SUGAR MAPLE. This grows to a good size and yields a pale buff, heavy, very hard, fine, and close-grained tough wood, with a satiny lustre and susceptible of a fine polish. In New England it is used as an oak substitute, in preference to beech, birch, or elm, for boats' keels, houseframes, flooring and interior finish, chairs and other furniture, axles, spokes, shoelasts, saddle-trees, etc.; and also largely for fuel. Blister, landscape, bird's-eye or pin, fiddle-back, and curly figures all occur in this species, the first two being almost confined to it. " Blister " is produced by wart-like prominences on the wood beneath the bark. The minute pittings or rudiments of buds known as bird's-eye appear as " eyes " in a tangential section and in a transverse direction as " pins." These figurings seldom extend more than 6 in. or 8 in. from the surface. They are cut by a rotary lathe into veneers the length of the log and running spirally inwards, and these figured veneers are the chief form in which this wood is imported. They are now largely used to face three-ply wood for panelling.

A " bog maple," dug out of peat, of a beautiful pale blue colour, is also cut into veneer and used in cabinetwork.

The SILVER, WHITE or SOFT MAPLE (*A. saccharinum*) is a redder, lighter, softer wood than the last, sometimes curled, which is used for flooring, interior finish, cheap furniture, and turnery. The red-flowered SWAMP or WATER MAPLE (*A. rubrum*) produces a similar wood, used in chair-making and turnery and for fuel, or, when curled, for gunstocks and veneers ; but it is rarely exported. The ASH-LEAVED MAPLE, or

Box-elder (*Negundo aceroides*, formerly *Acer Negundo*), well known in a variegated form in our suburban gardens, produces in the United States a soft white or yellowish wood, chiefly employed for paper pulp. In Australia the name Maple is applied to some totally unrelated woods.

Marblewood, Andaman (*Diospyros Kurzii*), also appropriately known as Figured Ebony or Zebra-wood, is handsomely streaked black and grey in alternating layers, and is very heavy, hard, and durable. It has been used for handles, but is valuable for furniture or walking-sticks, as a substitute for the scarce Calamander wood derived from related species in Ceylon.

Milkwood, White. (*See* IRONWOOD.)

Mirabow (*Intsia bakeri*, formerly *Afzelia palembanica*), a shade lighter in colour than Shoondul or Ipil (*I. bijuga*), but otherwise indistinguishable, the wood of these two species being one of the best in the Malayan region. *I. bijuga* occurs on the coasts from Madagascar to the Sandwich Islands, whilst *I. bakeri* is an inland species of narrower range. These trees yield timber 30 ft. to 40 ft. long, from $1\frac{1}{2}$ ft. to $2\frac{1}{2}$ ft. in diameter, reddish-brown, very heavy, so hard as to be known as Ironwood, fine and even in grain, working freely and taking so fine a polish as to resemble mahogany, very tough, termite-proof, and otherwise durable, and sometimes prettily figured. It is in demand for bridge-building, telegraph-posts, the corner-posts of houses, and furniture, for which last purpose it is sent to Europe.

Molavé (*Vitex littoralis, V. pubescens,* etc.), yellow, reddish-brown, or olive-brown woods, very heavy and hard, close-grained, strong and durable, with a figure resembling satinwood and not shrinking or splitting in seasoning, are among the finest woods of the Indo-Malayan area, being apparently fully equal to teak for many structural purposes, bridge, dock, house and shipbuilding, piles, mine-props, joists, planking, sleepers, paving-blocks, wheels, axles, wedges, etc., while they might well be used in cabinetwork.

Mora (*Dimorphandra excelsa*), a native of Guiana and Trinidad, is a tree 100 ft.

or more in height, yielding logs 18 ft. to 35 ft. long and 12 in. to 20 in. square. The wood is chestnut-brown or red, very heavy and hard, straight-grained, tough, strong and durable, but very subject to star-shake. It takes a good polish and has sometimes a beautiful curled figure. It is used for ships' beams, and, especially when red and figured, as a mahogany substitute for furniture.

Mulberry (*Morus alba*), a native of China, introduced into Europe, as a food for the silkworm, in the fifteenth century, is a tree of moderate size, having a yellowish-brown heartwood, somewhat similar to that of *Robinia*, but becoming reddish, like old mahogany, heavy, hard, tough, flexible, and lustrous. It is used by the Chinese for agricultural implements and furniture, and is occasionally used in Europe for veneers and inlay. The woods of *M. indica*, native from Japan to the Himalaya, used for tea-boxes and furniture, and *M. rubra*, of the Eastern United States, used for fence-posts and cooperage, are very similar to that of *M. alba*.

Myall, an aboriginal name applied in Australia to various species of wattle (*Acacia*), especially *A. pendula*, a small tree, native to the north-east of the continent. Its wood is a rich dark brown, beautifully marked resembling briar-root, very heavy, hard, close-grained, and, when unpolished, violet-scented, for which reason it is often known in England as Violet-wood. It is used for boomerangs, tobacco pipes, fancy boxes, and veneers ; but is sometimes imitated by artificially scenting the wood of other species.

Myrobalan (*Terminalia belerica*), the Behara or Bohera of India, Bulu of Ceylon, or Thitsein of Burma, is a yellowish-grey wood, without heart, hard but not durable, readily becoming worm-eaten, though improved by steeping in water. It is used for coffee-boxes, packing-cases, planking, and canoes.

Myrtle, a name applied to the Evergreen Beech (*Nothofagus Cunninghamii*) of Tasmania and to various Australian myrtaceous trees. Of these the most important, perhaps, is *Backhousia myrtifolia*, the Scrub, Grey, or Native Myrtle of north-

east Australia, also known as Lancewood, a small tree yielding a light yellow wood with pretty dark brown walnut-like streaks, hard, close-grained, tough, and durable. It is used for bows and turnery, mallets, tool-handles, etc.

Nan-mu (*Machilus nanmu*, with other species of the genera *Machilus* and *Lindera*) affords one of the most valuable woods in China. It was formerly obtained in logs 82 ft. long and over 4 ft. in diameter ; but now reaches Shanghai in planks 8 ft. long and 14 in. across. It is greenish and brown, close-grained, easily worked, fragrant, and very durable, and has been used in building the palaces in Pekin.

Nettle-tree (*Celtis australis*), the " Micocoulier " of the French and " Zürgelbaum " of the Germans, is a tree of moderate size, native to the Mediterranean and Temperate and Tropical Asia, having a yellowish grey wood with dark streaks, heavy, hard, compact, strong, and elastic, taking a high polish, and, when cut obliquely, resembling satinwood. It was used for the early Greek statues of the gods, and is now employed to some extent for furniture, but chiefly for whip and tool-handles, walking-sticks, flutes, and other turnery.

Oak, a name which should be restricted to the woods of the species of the genus *Quercus*. Upwards of three hundred of these species are known to botanists, none of which occur south of the Equator, except in and near Java ; but many of these are not used as timber even locally, while the number in general commerce is quite small. On the other hand, there are great variations in the quality of the woods obtained from the same species in different districts. Oak wood is generally yellowish-brown to brown, with distinctly visible pith-rays, either all fine or some wide and others narrow. It is moderately or very heavy and hard, with a strength that is exceptional in its proportion to the weight ; but, as has been truly said, it is neither the hardest and heaviest, nor the most supple and toughest of woods, but it combines in a useful manner the average of these qualities. Oak, in most species, is subject to star- and cup-shakes and warps and shrinks slightly in the process of seasoning ; but when once thoroughly dried, changes less than almost any wood. For fencing or staves, oaks generally split readily with a moderately smooth surface ; and, for ornamental purposes, they are susceptible of a high polish, and may exhibit handsome mirrors or silver-grain if quartered.

The chief species of oak grown in North Africa and Europe—to adopt as the most convenient a geographical enumeration—are *Quercus Robur*, *Q. Ilex*, the Holm Oak ; *Q. Cerris*, the Turkey or Mossy-cup Oak ; and *Q. Mibeckii*, the Zeen Oak ; though there are twenty others. The COMMON, BRITISH, or EUROPEAN OAK (*Q. Robur*) ranges from Mount Atlas and from Syria to lat. 60° N. It is a somewhat variable species, three somewhat inconstant types being recognised in Britain, namely, *pedunculata*, *sessiliflora*, and *intermedia*.

The PEDUNCULATE OAK (*Q. Robur pedunculata*) derives its name from the long stalks or peduncles to its acorns, for which reason also the Germans call it " Stieleiche," whilst from the situations in which it grows they term it " Thaleiche," Valley Oak, and from its early production and shedding of its leaves it is called " Früheiche," Early Oak, or " Sommereiche," Summer Oak. It is generally quick-growing, and its wood is denser, more compact, tougher, and lighter in colour than that of the other varieties, the French name " Chêne blanc " referring to this last characteristic.

The SESSILE-FLOWERED OAK (*Q. Robur sessiliflora*) has long stalks to its leaves, but not to its acorns, and is known by the French as " Chêne rouge," and by the Germans as " Rotheiche," " Bergeiche," or " Spateiche," Red, Hill, or Late Oak. It produces greater lengths of clear stem than *Q. Robur pedunculata*, but its wood is generally darker in colour, less dense, and more liable to shakes. From a supposed greater resemblance to the wood of the chestnut it is sometimes called " Chestnut Oak."

The DURMAST OAK (dark-acorned) (*Q. Robur intermedia* or *Q. Robur pubescens*) is uncommon. It has short stalks to both leaves and acorns. and its leaves are downy on their under surfaces. Its dark-brown wood is considered inferior ; but it must be admitted that in the absence of any external evidence as to the source of the wood, timber-dealers cannot discriminate between the produce of these varieties. Slow-grown, unthrifty oak from poor soil or severe climatic conditions, though often beautifully figured, is generally softer than quick-grown thrifty wood from good soil and a favourable climate ; while stunted, rock-grown trees or coppice-wood is often crooked in grain and difficult to split. There is, perhaps, greater difference between the oak of this species imported from various parts of the Continent than there is between the varieties just named. French oak, largely *pedunculata*, grown in Brittany and Normandy, is generally smaller, but shrinks and splits less in seasoning than does English wood ; and, being equally strong, tough, elastic. and durable, would seem to be a better all-round wood.

DANTZIC OAK, largely *sessiliflora* mostly brought down the Vistula from Poland to Dantzic, Memel, or Stettin, but sometimes shipped from Odessa, is brown, straight, and clean in grain, and free from knots, and is sometimes so figured as to be classed as " wainscot-oak," for furniture. It comes to market either as staves for casks ; in logs 18 ft. to 30 ft. long and 10 in. to 22 in. square ; or in planks about 32 ft. long, 9 in. to 15 in. wide, and 2 in. to 8 in. thick. It is so pliable and elastic as to be capable, when steamed, of being bent into almost any curve without fracture, but is inferior in strength to good English oak.

RIGA OAK. from the Western Dwina, is a very similar wood, probably of the same variety as that from Dantzic ; but only comes to market in wainscot logs of moderate dimensions for furniture or veneers, for which purposes it is the finest quality in the trade. Excellent oak, the product of this variety, occurs in Styria, Croatia, Hungary, Bosnia, Serbia, Rumania, etc., and is imported as " Adriatic " or Serbian.

Throughout Europe, and more especially in Britain, oak, mostly of this species, was employed for every purpose, both of naval and civil architecture, to the exclusion of all other woods, until about the beginning of the eighteenth century, when pine was first largely imported from the Baltic and North America. In our dockyards oak continued to be in large demand until about 1865, all other hard and heavy woods used in shipbuilding being compared with it as a standard and classed as "oak substitutes." With the introduction of armour-plating and steel ships, wood of any kind has become far less important in shipbuilding, and teak has largely superseded oak. In civil architecture, though the greater lightness, ease of working, and cheapness of coniferous timber have led to its being now generally preferred, oak is still in request where strength and durability are objects, though the picturesque partial collapse of old buildings is now avoided by the use of built-up beams in preference to those cut from the solid log, or, as the Americans term it, "box-hearted."

The durability of oak timber is undoubtedly much affected by the season at which it is felled, winter-felled wood containing least water and sap or fermentable matter. The "life" of a railway sleeper of good young oak, not treated with any preservative, is estimated at seven to ten years; if creosoted, at fifteen; or if treated with zinc chloride, at sixteen years; but the piles of Old London Bridge, sound when taken up in 1827 after six and a half centuries, or those sunk through the peat under Winchester Cathedral in 1079, probably without any preservative treatment, are still more striking evidences of durability. Bog Oak, blackened by the action of the iron salts in peat on the tannin of the wood—forming a natural ink—shows still greater periods of durability. The acid character of the wood, however, while securing it very largely from insect attack, has a very destructively corrosive effect upon iron in contact with it.

The harder qualities of oak are still largely in request for gate-posts, stair-treads, parquet floors, palings, and wheelwrights' work; whilst for wainscoting, furniture, and carving the softer, more figured varieties are required. For these purposes much American oak is now employed.

Veneers cut to the fortieth or fiftieth of an inch are sometimes used for wallpapers. Even when discoloured by the incipient decay of the aged but still growing tree, oak may fetch a high price for its deep coloured veneers, though, perhaps, in some cases this Brown Oak may be sound and owe its colour to the soil.

It may be suggested to the craftsman that, if he is not particularly anxious that his carvings shall endure for untold centuries, he may secure an effect almost equal to that of oak with about a tithe of the effort by working in chestnut. Attention has been directed to the widespread error of describing old roofs or buildings as chestnut which, on examination, prove invariably to be of oak.

The wood of the HOLM OAK (*Q. Ilex*), an evergreen species, native to the Mediterranean region, is not large, becomes with age a deep brown or jet-black, and is hard, horny, difficult to saw or work, and so liable to shakes as to be unsuitable for planks. Some Italian and Spanish oak formerly imported probably belonged to this species; but though common as an ornamental tree in England, its wood does not come into the market.

The TURKEY or MOSSY-CUP OAK (*Q. Cerris*) is a tall species with straight, clean stems producing a red-brown wood, which in the Mediterranean area is hard, but very liable to shakes and does not resist insect attacks. Some of the oak classed as Adriatic belongs to this species.

The ZEEN OAK (*Q. Mibeckii*) of North-west Africa covers a large area in Tunis. It reaches a very large size; its wood is yellowish or reddish, with broad pith-rays, and is heavy, straight-grained, and very durable; and, like most evergreen species apparently, of a horny texture, but liable to shakes and warping. When winter-felled and well seasoned it is a valuable timber for bridge-girders, piles, railway sleepers, and barrel staves.

The North American oaks are numerous, and fall naturally and commercially into three groups—"white," "red" or "black," and "live," that is, evergreen.

WHITE OAK (*Q. alba*), a native of South-eastern Canada and the Eastern United

States, ranges from 28° to 46° N. lat., and reaches large dimensions. Its wood is reddish as compared with European Oak, heavy, hard, tough, close and straight in grain, and durable in contact with the soil. It is one of the most generally useful and commercially important of American hardwoods ; but though the dominant species in extensive woodlands, its growing scarcity has made a market for Japanese wood.

QUEBEC OAK is the trade name for an excellent quality, fetching 20 per cent. more than the slower-grown Baltimore Oak, mainly because it reaches larger dimensions. The wood is largely used in boat- and house-building, for the frames, door-sills, and interior finish of houses, for barrel staves, railway sleepers, piles, fence-posts, carriage-building, agricultural implements, and fuel ; whilst when quarter-sawn it is beautifully figured and largely employed for furniture. When steamed, it is so elastic that planks cut from it may be bent into almost any form, and it is free from knots and shrinks and splits very little in seasoning, though it may twist to some extent. It is shipped in logs 25 ft. to 50 ft. long and 11 in. to 28 in. square, or in thick or thin planks. It is inferior to the best European Oak.

BURR OAK (*Q. macrocarpa*), a rich brown though rather more porous than the last-named species, is more durable in contact with soil than any other American Oak, but is both used and classed as White Oak.

POST OAK (*Q. minor*), Chestnut Oak or Rock Oak (*Q. Prinus*) and Basket or Cow Oak (*Q. Michauxii*) are similar brown, heavy, hard, durable woods, classed and used as White Oak.

RED OAK (*Q. rubra*), so called from its leaf-tints, known in commerce as Canadian Red or Black Oak, reaches large dimensions, though it is a slow-growing species. It is light or reddish-brown with indistinct pith-rays, and is heavy, hard, and strong, though inferior to White Oak, both in strength and durability. It is coarse-grained, but easy to work, and shrinks moderately without splitting in seasoning, and is quite suitable for much constructive work ; but is so porous as to be unfit for the staves of barrels to hold liquids. It

is used for flour- and sugar-barrels, clapboards, panelling and furniture, and is imported to England for the two last-named purposes.

The TEXAS RED or SPOTTED OAK (*Q. texana*), the Scarlet Oak (*Q. coccinea*), the Willow Oak (*Q. Phellos*), the Pin Oak (*Q. palustris*), and the Water or Punk Oak (*Q. aquatica*) are more or less similar oaks, varying in weight, which are classed as red oak and are at most not superior to it.

The LIVE OAK of the Southern States (*Q. virginiana*) reaches large dimensions and produces a dark golden-brown heartwood, with distinct pith-rays, which is very heavy, compact, hard, tough, strong, and durable, and takes a superb polish ; but is often crooked in growth, somewhat twisted in grain, and consequently difficult to work. It is, perhaps, stronger than any known oak, and is used by wheelwrights and millwrights, and for interior finish, mallets, and tool-handles. The California Live Oak or Maul Oak (*Q. chrysolepis*) is similar.

Several species of evergreen oak occur in Southern Japan, including " Aka-gashi " (*Q. acuta*), dark red-brown, very hard and heavy ; " Shira-gashi " (*Q. vibrayeana*), greyish-white ; " Ichii-gashi " (*Q. gilva*), also light-coloured ; and " Urajiro-gashi " (*Q. myrsinœfolia*). These are used in wagon- and boat-building. The genus is said to be represented by sixty species in China. On the Yalu River *Q. crispula* and *Q. dentata* reach a good size and yield hard, durable wood which used to warp and split considerably in seasoning, but is now steam-dried in Japan and is employed for shipbuilding, sleepers, casks, axles, oars, etc. In Southern China oak is found to be subject to termite attack, and none of the wood from this country appears to be equal in quality to *Q. Robur*.

In the Himalayas there are also a considerable number of species growing at altitudes of from 50 ft. above sea-level in Bengal up to 3,000 ft., 8,000 ft., and 10,000 ft., most of them being evergreen. Among them are the Holm Oak (*Q. Ilex*) ; the Grey or Himalayan Ilex (*Q. incana*) ; *Q. lappacea*, of the Khasia Hills, and *Q. lanceœfolia*, of the Garrow Hills, and Assam, which resemble English oak, but are harder; *Q. Griffithii*, of the Khasia Hills, Sikkim, and Bhotan; and *Q. serrata*, ranging into China and Northern Japan, brown woods much resembling English oak; and *Q. fenestrata*, at lower altitudes, which is somewhat inferior.

The SHE OAK, possibly a corruption of an aboriginal name "shiok," or possibly from some resemblance seen in the broad pith-rays, is a name applied in Australia to various species of *Casuarina*, by no means closely related to Oak. They are also known as Forest, Swamp, or Botany-bay Oak, and some of them as Beef-wood or Ironwood. They are mostly a mahogany like, red or reddish-brown, often prettily mottled with dark longitudinal bands, heavy, hard, tough, close-grained, easily worked, and very durable, but liable to split in drying. Formerly used for boomerangs and for the forks used by Fijian cannibals, and now locally for roof-shingles (whence the name Shingle Oak), fences, and handles, several species, especially *C. stricta* and *C. torulosa*, are also employed for furniture and veneers.

SILKY OAK, the north-east Australian name for the red-brown, hard, close-grained woods of *Grevillea robusta* and some other related species of the Family *Proteaceæ*. They sometimes have a beautiful wavy figure, and, as they are now becoming scarce, are employed in veneers, or for walking-sticks.

For AFRICAN AND FOREST OAK see BEEF-WOOD.

Olive (*Olea europœa*), native to the Mediterranean region, seldom of any considerable size, is a heavy, very close- and fine-grained wood of a light yellowish-brown, without distinguishable annual rings or pith-rays, but with handsome, irregular, wavy dark lines and mottlings, resembling box in texture, but not so hard and rather brittle. It takes an excellent polish, and is chiefly employed in turnery and carving for small articles, such as fancy boxes, paper-knives, etc. The Indian species, *O. cuspidata*, is very similar, and several others are used in turnery in different parts of the world.

OLIVE, WILD (*see* SUMACH, VENETIAN).

Orange (*Citrus Aurantium*), probably a native of India, but now cultivated for its fruit in most tropical and sub-tropical countries, has small, light yellow, heavy, hard, close-grained wood, used in the West Indies for cabinetwork, and for tool-handles in Szechuan, made into toothpicks in Madeira and at Rio de Janeiro, and imported from Algeria for walking-sticks. "Black Orange" and "Congo Oak" are, however, names used in the walking-stick trade for the stems of the common Broom (*Cytisus scoparius*), imported from the same country. *See also* JACK.

OSAGE ORANGE (*Toxylon pomiferum*, formerly known as *Maclura aurantiaca*), from Arkansas and Texas, is known as Bow-wood (French, "Bois d'arc"), having been used by the Redskins for their bows, just as the related and similar wood of the mulberry was by the aborigines of China. The tree reaches a considerable size, and its wood is brown when cut transversely, yellow longitudinally, but soon turning greyish on exposure. It is very heavy, hard, flexible, and durable in contact with soil, but shrinks considerably in drying. It is used in America for sleepers, mine-props, paving-blocks, fence-posts, etc., and is not common in trade, but might be employed in turnery or for carving.

Orham-wood is a Canadian elm, brown, soft, coarse-grained, twisting badly in seasoning, and not durable, which has been considerably imported to Liverpool as a cheap cabinet-wood.

Padouk (*Pterocarpus macrocarpus, P. indicus, P. dalbergioides*, and *P. echinatus*), ranging from Southern India, Southern China and the Andaman Islands to the Philippines, Sunda, and Fiji Islands, and variously known as Andaman Redwood, Tenasserim or Philippine Mahogany, and Burmese Rosewood, are a series of large, very heavy, hard, red woods. They vary in colour, being either dark red, brick red, or streaked with black, and sometimes beautifully figured; are heavier than mahogany and slightly aromatic, susceptible of a high polish, durable, and termite proof. Some trees yield timber squaring 2 ft. in the side and 60 ft. in length, or they may be 5 ft. in diameter. The wood takes two years for natural seasoning, may fade somewhat on exposure to light, and does not take glue like mahogany. In India it has been used for gun-carriages and for furniture ; in Burma for cart-wheels and for musical instruments ; and in the United States in the building of Pullman cars, for parquet floors, counter-tops, and furniture. It is unquestionably one of the most valuable Eastern furniture woods. The wood of the roots and of some parts of the stem is sometimes exceptionally dark and variegated, and is manufactured into small ornamental boxes. The name " AFRICAN PADOUK " has been applied to *Pterocarpus erinaceus* and *P. angolensis*. (*See* ROSEWOOD, African.)

Pai'cha (*Euonymus Hamiltonianus*), a native of China, is a yellowish, soft, close, and fine-grained wood, used for carving and for wooden type.

Palisander-wood, imported from Bahia and other Brazilian ports, is a handsome chocolate-brown wood, marked by deep black veins and bands, very heavy and hard and somewhat brittle. Though, perhaps, once the bignoniaceous *Jacaranda brasiliana*, it is probably now *Dalbergia nigra*, or some species of the allied leguminous genus *Machœrium*, otherwise known from their faint rose-water smell as Brazilian rosewood. The best figured variety comes from Bahia in roughly hewn semi-cylindrical half-logs, never sound at the centre. That from Rio de Janeiro is less unsound and in round logs, but less figured. It is a very valuable wood, both solid and in veneers, for furniture and cabinet-work, especially pianoforte cases.

Pear (*Pyrus communis*), the comparatively small wood of the well-known fruit tree, has no true heart, but is a light pinkish-brown, moderately heavy, hard, close-grained-firm material, easily cut in any direction, taking a satiny polish, and very durable, if kept dry. It is highly valued for turnery, cabinetwork, T-squares, set-squares, calico-printing blocks, coarse wood engraving, or, when ebonised, for picture frames. As a kind wood of pleasing natural colour and stable, it can be recommended to the craftsman. A Chinese species, *P. sinensis*, is used for wood engraving and for the manufacture

of combs, which are dyed yellow with the fruit of a gardenia so as to resemble box.

Peppermint. (*See* REDWOOD.)

Persimmon (*Diospyros virginiana*), native to the Eastern United States, is a tall ebony, not exceeding 2ft. in diameter, with a very broad creamy-white sapwood, sometimes extending over sixty rings, and a sharply contrasted dark brown or black heart, very heavy, weighing 50 lb. per cubic foot, hard, close-grained, strong and tough, resembling hickory, but finer in grain and taking a fine polish. Known also as "Date Plum." It is used for wagon-shafts, mallets, shoe-lasts, plane-stocks, etc.

Pine should be a general name for the woods of the species of the northern genus *Pinus*, as distinguished from Spruce, the wood of the species of *Picea* and Fir, which should be that of *Abies*. It is, however, extended to the woods of such allied genera as *Sciadopitys* and *Pseudotsuga* in the northern hemisphere, and to *Agathis, Frenela, Araucaria, Dacrydium, Podocarpus,* and *Prumnopitys* in the southern. Curiously enough, also, the wood of the various local varieties of the Northern Pine (*Pinus sylvestris*) imported from Baltic ports, such as Dantzic, Memel, and Riga, is known in trade as fir or deal, while the name Pine is used for that of other species of the genus imported from North America.

Deal, it may be explained, should properly mean only wood in the particular form of planks 9 in. broad and not more than 4 in. thick. The relatively simple and uniform structure of the wood of the genus *Pinus* makes it easy to work. The different species occur in pure forests— forests, that is, made up mainly of a single species—over wide areas in the north Temperate zone or on the mountains of the northern tropics. Their woods are, also, quick-grown, and, for these reasons, are cheap. They season rapidly, but with little shrinkage ; are never too hard to take a nail ; are, when seasoned, protected by their resin from the attacks of boring insects and are otherwise durable ; occur in long, straight-grown logs ; and are, in proportion to their lightness, very stiff and strong. These reasons combine to render them the most generally useful, and by far the most extensively used of all woods. Although many of them are harder than some of the woods of broad-leaved trees, such as poplars, willows, horse-chestnut, etc., all coniferous woods are conventionally known as " soft woods "; but the Pines fall into two natural groups known as Hard Pines and Soft Pines. The Hard Pines are heavier, darker-coloured, ranging from yellow to deep orange or brown, and—owing to the autumn wood forming a much broader proportion of the annual ring—harder ; while they also generally show a more abrupt contrast between heart and sapwood. This group includes the greater number of species, both in Europe and in North America, which latter area is the home of about three-fifths of the seventy species of the genus. The Soft Pines range in colour from white to light-red ; are lighter in weight ; and have a narrow zone of autumn wood merging gradually on its inner surface into the spring wood.

Deferring the description of the allied genera the wood of which is known as Pine, an arrangement will be followed as far as possible, both natural and geographical, beginning with the Hard Pines, and, among them, with those of Europe, but dealing only with the more important. NORTHERN PINE is the best general name for *Pinus sylvestris*, the only species indigenous in Britain, where it is commonly known as Scots Fir. It has a wide range over Northern Europe, reaching altitudes of 700 ft. above sea-level in Northern Norway and 6,500 ft. on the Sierra Nevada of Southern Spain, and occurring as far as 68° N. lat. As its branches are in whorls the knots serve to distinguish the wood from larch, in which they are scattered. The characters and quality of the wood vary much, according to climate and soil. Conversely to what is the case with oaks, the more slowly grown pines of high latitudes or mountains, having narrower annual rings with a proportionally smaller amount of spring wood, are heavier, denser, and stronger than those of the south, or of plains, or from rich soils.

English-grown pine of this species is thick-baited, carrying a large amount—often 4 in.—of sapwood, and is consequently of comparatively little value, not being nearly as durable as larch. Scottish-grown wood is of better quality and has been largely imported into the North of England, chiefly as mine-timber. Pine imported from foreign countries is known by various names, such as Red-wood, Red Deal, or Yellow Deal, or, according to its origin, as White Sea, Baltic, Petersburg, Riga, Memel, Dantzic, Gefle, Soderhamn, Swedish or Norway Fir. The White Sea wood, shipped from Arch-angel and Mezen especially to Peterhead and Leith, is close-grown, less resinous, but perhaps the strongest and most durable imported, though subject to heartshakes and surface-splitting. It is most suitable for joinery. Swedish wood from Gefle and Soderhamn is of high quality ; but much of the wood from that country is yellowish white and liable to various shakes, whilst it seldom exceeds 35 ft. in length or 16 in. square. It furnishes much cheap building material, deals for rough carpentry, matchwood and firewood.

Most Norwegian Pine comes over in cheap prepared flooring, matchboarding, door and window frames, and firewood. Large, heavy, hard, resinous wood, good for sleepers, paving-blocks, masts, beams and planks, comes from the Southern Baltic ports. Riga Fir, from the Dnieper and Western Dwina, has few knots, but has a slight tendency to heartshake, making it more wasteful in conversion, and is lighter than, and on the whole inferior to, Dantzic. This last, floated down the Vistula, comes to market in lengths of from 18 ft. to 50 ft., squaring 11 in. to 20 in. ; in deals from 2 in. to 5 in. thick, and in irregularly grown logs for sleepers. It is light, moderately hard, even and straight-grained, tough, elastic wood, easily worked, and useful for planking, beams, joists, scaffolding, masts, and spars. This pine is the chief timber used in house-building in the north of the continent of Europe. The houses are framed of hewn logs, the walls are built up of logs in the round, covered with clap-boards externally and with panelling within, all of this species. In Russia logs of it are used for corduroy roads, and it is used to an enormous extent as fuel on railways, and steamboats and in private houses.

Baltic Pine was imported to our east-coast towns for flooring, wainscoting, and joinery in the fifteenth, sixteenth, and seventeenth centuries, when oak was the chief timber employed over England generally. The high price of foreign timber during the Napoleonic Wars led to the clearing of the indigenous pine forests of Scotland and the north of England ; but the easy working and great durability of pine gradually broke down the prejudice in favour of oak and led to the great consumption of this timber, especially in Eastern Britain, and of the Yellow Pine (*Pinus Strobus*) of North America in the west.

The STONE or UMBRELLA PINE (*P. Pinea*) of the Mediterranean region is a whitish, very light, and moderately resinous wood, used locally though the tree is most especially valued for its edible seeds or " nuts." It does not reach a very large size.

The CLUSTER PINE (*P. Pinaster*) sometimes known as *P. maritima*, of the same region, and also of moderate dimensions, yields a reddish, soft, coarse-grained, very resinous, but not very durable wood. Planted on the landes of Bordeaux to check the drifting of the sand-dunes, this tree is there a valuable source of turpentine, charcoal, and lamp-black ; but a million loads have been annually imported into South Wales for mine-timbers. The wood is also used for coarse carpentry, packing-cases, etc.

The AUSTRIAN PINE (*P. nigra*, var. *austriaca*), or black Austrian Pine, the chief source of pine wool and pine oil, yields timber much used for building on the Continent, similar to that of the Northern Pine, but rather coarse in grain and apt, when grown in poor soil, to be knotty.

The CORSICAN PINE (*P. nigra*, var. *Poiretiana*, often known as *P. Laricio*, or Larch Pine) is a closely related lofty species (growing to 80-100 ft.), producing wood which is creamy-white when freshly cut, but becomes brownish-yellow when seasoned, very resinous, durable, and obnoxious to insects, equal to Northern Pine of good quality.

The ALEPPO PINE (*P. halepensis*) of the Mediterranean region, which has been introduced into Australia, was used for the flooring, doors, and ceiling of the Temple at Jerusalem, and was probably the " Ash " or " Fir " of Isaiah xxxvii. 24, and xliv. 14. Its yellowish-white, fine-grained wood is now valued locally for telegraph-poles, joinery turnery, and fuel, and the tree is also a source of turpentine. Largely used at one time for ships' decks.

The JAPANESE BLACK PINE (*P. Thunbergii*), the Sung-shu of Western China, O-matsu, or Kuro-matsu of the Japanese, occurring also in Corea, reaching large dimensions, and growing up to altitudes of 4,000 ft., has a close-grained and resinous wood which is durable only when grown at high altitudes. It is used in house-building. for furniture, and as fuel.

The JAPANESE RED PINE (*P. densiflora*), or " Aka-matsu," a somewhat smaller species, is used locally for all kinds of carpenters' work.

In the Philippines the SALENG (*P. insularis*) is a hard pine which is very resinous and of considerable local importance for house-building and planking.

Among American hard pines the best is, perhaps, the CANADIAN RED PINE (*P. resinosa*), known as Norway Pine in Canada, as Yellow Pine in Nova Scotia, and in European trade as American Red. It reaches 100 ft. in height and 2 ft. to 4 ft. in diameter, weighs from 30 lb. to 44 lb. per cubic foot, and is a buff or straw colour to a pale reddish-tan colour, light, hard, tough, elastic, fine-grained, with a silky lustre, working up well and very resinous, and does not shrink or warp much in seasoning. When of small dimensions and consequently largely sapwood, it is not durable ; but the heart is so. The wood is excellent for piles, spars, boat-building, and flooring ; but, being more expensive than Baltic Pine, has never been very largely imported.

The CAROLINA or SHORT-LEAF PINE (*P. echinata*), of the Eastern United States, is commonly known as Yellow Pine in America, but as Carolina or New York Pine at Liverpool, to which port it comes from North Carolina. It reaches a good size ; is a gold-ochre to a pale buff-yellow in colour, rather heavy, weighing 34 lb. to 38 lb. per cubic foot, hard, coarse-grained, compact, strong, not difficult to work, and durable, much resembling Long-leaf Pine—the pitch pine of our market—and little inferior to it in hardness or strength. It is used in house-building, flooring, and interior finish, and very largely in American dockyards for decks and spars.

The LOBLOLLY PINE (*P. Tœda*) of the Southern United States is generally confounded with the long-leaf pine, though it is softer, lighter, coarser in grain, wider in its annual rings, weaker, and less durable than that species. Its ready reproduction, rapid growth, easy felling and conversion, cheapness and suitability for many purposes, combine to render it the most valuable tree in Maryland, Delaware, and Virginia. It is so rich in resin as to be known as Torch or Frankincense Pine, and is, of course, excellent as fuel. It is known as Yellow Pine in the northern markets in the States.

The WESTERN YELLOW or BULL PINE (*P. ponderosa*) of the Western United States reaches a very great size, being sometimes 300 ft. in height and 15 ft. in diameter. In spite of its name it varies very much in weight, strength, and durability ; but is generally hard, brittle, resinous, and not durable in contact with soil. It is the chief hard pine of the region and is largely used for sleepers, mine-timbers, building, and fuel. The AMERICAN BLACK PINE (*P. Jeffreyi*), growing at altitudes of over 6,000 ft. in Oregon and California, is a closely related wood generally confused with *P. ponderosa*.

The PITCH PINE (*P. palustris*), known in America as the Longleaf Pine or as the Southern or Georgia Pine, is the most abundant and commercially most valuable of American pines. It reaches a good size and weighs from 37 lb. to 45 lb. per cubic foot, which is often nearly twice the weight of Yellow—the American white—pine. It

is exported from South Carolina, Georgia, and Alabama, being known, according to the port, as Savannah, Darien, Pensacola, etc., and comes in logs and planks, 20 ft. to 45 ft. long, squaring 11 in. to 18 in. or 3 in. to 5 in. thick and 10 in. to 15 in. wide. The wood is reddish, the redder quality—known as Red Pine in the northern American dockyards—being valued as more durable, especially against teredo. Though it resembles Northern Pine, it is somewhat heavier and more resinous, the broad zone of autumn wood having a somewhat greasy appearance. It is tough, compact, clean, and straight in grain, but varies from fine to a rather coarse texture ; it is susceptible of a high polish, but is rather difficult to work, and often has heart and cup shakes. It is, however, stiff, hard, and strong to a higher degree than any other American species on the market, and is very durable especially when any shaky portions are removed by quarter-sawing. It is stated that in piles and jetties, exposed to sea-water and weather, it will last twice or thrice as long as Memel or Dantzic fir.

In America it is largely used for fencing, sleepers, mine-timbers, building, flooring, and rafters, wood-paving and fuel, as well as for decks, planking, and spars and other dockyard purposes. Three-quarters of the paving-blocks used in the States are said to be " Southern Yellow Pine." This may include Short-leaf, Cuban, and even Loblolly Pine, since there is no sure method of discriminating them except by a microscopic examination which is impracticable in commercial transactions ; but the Long-leaf Pine is, undoubtedly, the species demanded. In England large quantities of this wood are used for wainscoting, church and school fittings, figured specimens being in request for cabinet-work. This species is the chief source of turpentine.

The CUBAN PINE (*P. heterophylla*) is smaller and coarser in grain, and has wider sapwood than the last named ; but is classed with it in Florida and is but little inferior.

Among the Soft Pines of America, none of which are as heavy, as hard, or as durable as the Hard Pines, the FOX-TAIL PINE

(*P. Balfouriana*) of California is used for mine-timbers.

The SUGAR PINE (*P. Lambertiana*), of Oregon and California, the loftiest species of the genus, reaching a height of 300 ft. and a diameter of 20 ft., has a very light, soft, straight, but coarse-grained, compact, fragrant, white wood, easily worked, but not cracking or warping. It is not distinguished commercially from the woods of *P. monticola* and *P. flexilis*, all being known alike as Western White Pine. It is used for indoor carpentry, cooperage.

The WESTERN WHITE PINE (*P. monticola*) is a large tree, growing at high altitudes in Idaho and other Pacific States, valuable in local commerce, but inferior to the White Pine of the Eastern States (*P. Strobus*) which it closely resembles.

The FLEXIBLE PINE (*P. flexilis*) of the eastern slopes of the Rocky Mountains is a small tree, abundant and important locally.

The WHITE PINE (*Pinus Strobus*) is unquestionably the most important of all Soft Pines. It is known also in America as Pumpkin Pine and in our English timber trade as Yellow Pine; whilst, when grown in England, it is called Weymouth Pine, from a Lord Weymouth, who planted it largely at Longleat about 1720. This species extends from Newfoundland and Quebec to Georgia, and has been known to reach 180 ft. in height, 100 ft. to its lowest branch, and from 6 ft. to 8 ft. in diameter. Its heartwood is pinkish-yellow to pinkish-brown; its weight is only 20 lb. to 30 lb. per cubic foot; and it is straight grown, very soft, compact, almost free from resin, easily worked, and susceptible of a fine polish, but liable to shakes and to a sponginess at the centre in old trees, and not durable in contact with soil. Its rapid growth, heavy yield of timber, easy management as a crop, and general utility render it the most valuable species of the Eastern United States. It is employed for every description of joinery, doors, sashes, blinds, interior finish, laths, roof-shingles, clap-boards, cabinetwork, and fuel. For masts or spars it is, however, much inferior in strength and durability to the Hard Pine of the Baltic; it cannot be relied upon for more than eight or ten

years, especially in the tropics, and should be carefully seasoned and then painted, the paint being renewed almost every year.

Sawmills having been started in 1623, and the exportation of this timber in 1635, all trees suitable for masts were protected by law in our American colonies early in the eighteenth century. A century later it is stated that 70 per cent. of the houses in North America were of wood, and that, of these, about 75 per cent. were built of this species. It has now practically disappeared from the States of New England and New York, and very nearly from Pennsylvania and other States, having been recklessly cut and burnt, so that the supply both in its own country and for exportation is much less than it was.

In the Himalaya the BHOTAN or BLUE PINE (*P. excelsa*), growing at altitudes of 6,000 ft. to 12,000 ft., is the most valuable species. Its light-red wood is light, moderately hard, compact, close-grained, very resinous and durable, and is used for railway sleepers and for planking. It should, however, be treated, sleepers lasting from two to two-and-a-half years when unprocessed, and ten or even thirteen years when creosoted.

The MANCHURIAN PINE of Northern China and Corea (*P. manchurica*) reaches 4 ft. in diameter, but does not exceed 80 ft. in height. Its reddish-white wood is used in house- and junk-building and for coffins, and in South China for piles and pit-props, but is found in that region not to be termite-proof or durable.

The CEMBRA PINE (*P. Cembra*), growing from Kamchatka to the Urals, Carpathians, and Alps, and known also as the Siberian Cedar or Swiss Stone Pine, though now valued mainly for its edible nuts, has wood very similar to that of *P. Strobus* and covers large areas of forest. It is used largely for wainscoting and turnery and lining chests.

The UMBRELLA PINE (*Sciadopitys verticillata*) of Japan, the native name of which is Kôya-maki, belonging to the Cypress group, produces a wood of good dimensions, varying in colour from nearly white to yellowish or reddish, straight-grained and strong, which is brought by water to the port of Osaka.

OREGON PINE (*see* OREGON FIR).

In the Southern Hemisphere, New Zealand is exceptionally rich in its variety of pine-like coniferous timbers, some of which have reached our markets in spite of the necessarily heavy freightage. For Kauri (*Agathis australis*) and Queensland Kauri (or Dundatha Pine (*A. robusta*) *see* KAURI.

NEW ZEALAND WHITE PINE (*D. excelsum* and *D. ferrugineum*), related species of this genus of the Yew family, are known to the Maoris as Kahikatea. They reach 150 ft. or 180 ft. in height, sometimes 60 ft. to the lowest branch and 4 ft. to 5 ft. in diameter, yielding timber 20 ft. to 60 ft. long, squaring 12 in. to 30 in., and weighing 27 lb. to 35 lb. to the cubic foot. The wood is white, soft, straight and even in grain, easily worked, but not durable when exposed or in contact with soil. It is thus in many respects comparable to American White Pine (*Pinus Strobus*). Used locally for building, cheap furniture, packing-cases, and paper-pulp, it has come specially into request with the great Australasian demand for butter boxes ; and, as it can be obtained of a large size, it may well compete not only with white pine, but also with Canary whitewood.

For NEW ZEALAND RED PINE (*Dacrydium cupressinum*) *see* RIMU, and for MACQUARIE PINE *see* HUON PINE.

WESTLAND or SILVER PINE (*D. Westlandicum*) is heavier, harder, tougher, and more durable, and is well adapted for sleepers or piles. Its Maori name is "Manao."

BLACK PINE is a name applied in New Zealand to two woods, both of the Yew family, *Prumnopitys spicata*, of which the Maori name is "Matai," and *Podocarpus ferruginea*, the Maori "Miro." The former reaches 80 ft. in height and 2 ft. to 4 ft. in diameter, weighs 35 lb. to 49 lb. per cubic foot, and is a cinnamon-brown colour, close, smooth, and even in grain, easily worked, strong and durable. It is used for piles, sleepers, house-building, and millwrights' work. Miro is rather less in diameter, heavier, reddish-brown, hard, planing up well, and taking a good polish,

durable in contact with salt water but not with soil. It is sometimes nicely figured, and, though used for piles, suited for cabinetwork or turnery.

For the *Podocarpus Totara, see* under TOTARA.

CELERY-TOPPED PINE, or "Tanekaha" (*Phyllocladus trichomanoides*), is about the same size as Black Pine, yielding timber 18 ft. to 70 ft. long, squaring 10 in. to 16 in., yellowish-white, heavy, close and straight in grain, working up well, very strong and durable, and employed for piles, bridges, sleepers, mine-timbers, masts, decks, and building.

The CELERY-TOPPED PINE of Tasmania, also known as Adventure Bay Pine, is the allied and similar, but smaller and more slender *Phyllocladus rhomboidalis*.

For HUON PINE (*Dacrydium Franklinii*) *see* HUON PINE.

NORFOLK ISLAND PINE (*Araucaria excelsa*), reaching 200 ft. in height and 7 ft. in diameter, yields excellent timber, but is now scarce.

MORETON BAY PINE (*A. Cunninghami*), occurring in north-east Australia and New Guinea, reaches nearly an equal size, yielding spars 80 ft. to 100 ft. in length, weighing 30 lb. to 33 lb. per cubic foot. It is light-coloured, straight-grained, hard and strong, working easily and sometimes exhibiting a figure produced by small knots. It is durable if kept constantly wet or dry, and is the chief soft wood in Queensland, being in request there for flooring, carpentry, and even cabinetwork ; but it is not equal to European or American Pine.

For the Australian species of *Frenela see* CYPRESS PINE.

In South America the CHILE PINE (*Araucaria imbricata*), familiar in our gardens as the Monkey-puzzle, reaches 100 ft. in height and 6 ft. or 7 ft. in diameter at base, and yields a yellowish and sometimes beautifully veined wood, susceptible of a fine polish, used locally for masts. Another species, *A. brasiliensis*, is now being worked on a considerable scale in Southern Brazil. For the South African species of *Podocarpus, see* YELLOW-WOOD.

Plane, properly the wood of species of the genus *Platanus*. The wood of the

Levantine species (*P. orientalis* and its forms), a good-sized tree, valued for its shade, is but little used. It resembles beech, but is softer, very apt to warp and split and become worm-eaten. The American or Western species (*P. occidentalis*) and the Californian *P. racemosa* are rather more important, being also known as Buttonwood, or when cut radially as Lacewood or Honeysuckle-wood (*which see*). It is used for tobacco-boxes, wooden bowls, butchers' blocks, cooperage and blind wood in cabinetwork; but the cabinetmakers of Philadelphia object to it that it warps when in plank. This defect would probably be remedied by some years soaking under water. A good deal of confusion has arisen from this wood being sometimes known as Sycamore, whilst that of the Great Maple or Sycamore (*Acer Pseudo-platanus*) is known as Plane in Southern Scotland.

Plum (*Prunus domestica*), a small tree, probably native to Western Asia, has a deep brownish-red heartwood, resembling mahogany, heavy and hard, but not very durable, used in cabinetmaking and turnery.

Poon, an Indian trade name applied to the wood of several species of *Calophyllum*, especially when in the form of spars. Some twenty species of the genus are known in Malaysia as "Bintangor." The widely distributed *C. inophyllum*, the "Penaga" of Telugu and "Palo Maria" of the Philippines, occurs from Madagascar to the Fiji Islands, may exceed 80 ft. in height, and reach 5 ft. in diameter, and weighs from 35 lb. to 63 lb. per cubic foot. It is red-brown, with a pretty, wavy figure, whence its name of Borneo mahogany, fairly hard, coarse-grained, very strong and durable, and is used in India for sleepers, although suitable for joinery or furniture. *C. tomentosum*, of Ceylon, Queensland, etc., is similar, and is employed for tea-chests and spars.

Poplar, the wood of species of *Populus*, known in America, from their hairy seeds, as "Cottonwoods." These woods are very quick grown, white or pale grey, yellowish or brown, very soft and light, not splintering or splitting when nailed, but holding a nail well, and easily worked or turned. As they shrink in drying, they require prolonged seasoning, and are neither strong nor durable; but it has been found that they are much improved by Powellising. There does not seem to be much difference in the quality of the woods in different species, so that preference has been given in planting to those that give the most rapid yield. The wood is mainly used for paper pulp and cellulose, matches, packing-cases, sugar-barrels, and blind wood, but also for boards for winding silk; clothes-pegs, turned ware, pails, sabots, high heels for shoes, or the bottoms of brick carts and other wagons, churns, coach panels, brakes for railway wagons, etc. The polishing wheels used by glass-grinders are made of horizontal sections, across an entire stem.

The WHITE POPLAR (*P. alba*) is used for matches in Japan, and for building junks and carving in Shan-tung. On the Continent the GREY POPLAR (*P. canescens*) is considered superior. In Manchuria *P. suaveolens*, and in West Hupeh *P. villosa*, are used for building, furniture, and carving. In the United States the BALSAM POPLAR (*P. balsamifera*) and *P. grandidentata* are used; but the wood exported to Liverpool as cottonwood is mostly that of the so-called BLACK ITALIAN, CANADIAN or CAROLINA POPLAR (*P. deltoidea*). A hybrid recently raised by Professor Henry and named *P. generosa* promises to surpass all others in rapidity of growth. For VIRGINIAN and YELLOW POPLAR *see* CANARY WHITEWOOD. (*See also* ASPEN.)

Porcupine-wood (*Cocos nucifera*).— The wood near the outside of the base of the stem of the Coco-nut Palm being crowded with dense black-brown fibro-vascular bundles resembling the quills of the porcupine, is very hard, strong, and durable. It has been used for spear-handles in India and for walking-sticks in England, but is generally seen as a veneer for work-boxes or other small fancy articles.

Purple - heart, Violet-wood, Amaranthe, or Paoroxo, the wood of several species of the leguminous genera *Peltogyne* and *Copaifera*, large trees native to Brazil, the Guianas and Trinidad, closely related and of nearly equal value and confused commercially. That from the mainland yields timber 20 ft. to 120 ft. long and squaring 18 in. to 30 in. ; that from Trinidad not more than 25 ft. long or 15 in. wide. The wood is brownish or a beautiful purple when freshly cut, but blackens with age. It is very heavy, hard, strong, easily worked, taking a fine polish, and durable. It is used for works of construction, house-frames, gun-carriages, furniture, and fretwork.

Quassia (*Picrœna excelsa*), a native of Tropical America, yielding logs 6 ft. to 10 ft. long and 6 in. to 10 in. in diameter, of a yellow, light, soft, fine-grained wood, intensely bitter, used medicinally as a tonic, being sometimes turned into drinking-cups which impart their taste to water. Often called " Bitter-wood." It is also used as a garden remedy against aphides.

Queenwood, a name applied to two ornamental leguminous woods : *Daviesia arborea*, native to North-east Australia, streaked with pink, hard, close-grained, and susceptible of a fine polish, and *Piptadenia rigida*, a Brazilian species, also known as " Angico," reddish or dark brown with black lines, hard and suitable, as is the other, for cabinetwork and turnery.

Raspberry-jam Wood (*Acacia acuminata*), a native of West Australia, 30 ft. to 40 ft. high, and weighing 54 lb. to 78 lb. per cubic foot, reddish-brown, hard, close-grained, with a smell like raspberry jam. Sometimes called " Jam-wood," and " Myall." It has been used for weapons and fence-posts, but is now used for furniture.

Redwood, a name very variously applied in different countries. In the English timber market it refers to Dantzic Fir (*Pinus sylvestris*). The Californian Redwood (*Sequoia sempervirens*), having been unsuccessfully introduced as a furniture wood under this name, is now known as Sequoia (*which see*). In India, Andaman Redwood is a name for Padouk (*Pterocarpus*), and Coromandel Redwood or Indian Redwood for East India Mahogany (*Soymida febrifuga*). In Jamaica the name is applied to *Erythroxylon areolatum*), the scientific name of which has the same signification, a handsome mahogany-like wood, also known from its hardness as Ironwood, durable in water and used for cogs and mill-frames, though its figure entitles it to other uses. In Cape Colony this name, or its Boer equivalent " Roodhout," is given to *Ochna arborea*, also called Cape Plane, a small tree with a hard, strong, durable wood used for wagon-building and furniture. In Eastern Australia *Eucalyptus piperita* is variously known as Peppermint, Blackbutt, Messmate, White Stringybark, or Redwood. It is a large, very heavy, red wood, difficult to work, very subject to shakes, but durable, and is used for posts, roof-shingles, and rough building.

Rengas. (*See* ROSEWOOD, BORNEO.)

Rewa-rewa (*Rymandra excelsa*), a beautiful New Zealand wood, known also as Honeysuckle-wood. It is large and heavy, becomes foxy unless thoroughly seasoned, and will not stand exposure ; but on a radial section it is a lustrous golden-yellow with pretty warm, red-brown silver-grain, very effective in inlaying and cabinetwork. The finest figure is known as Tiger grain.

Rimu (*Dacrydium cupressinum*), or New Zealand Red Pine, is a fine tree, yielding timbers 20 ft. to 80 ft. long, squaring 10 in. to 30 in., chestnut brown at centre, lighter outwards, figured with light-red or yellow streaks, weighing 33 lb. to 45 lb. per cubic foot ; hard, fine, uniform and straight in grain, working well, and taking a good polish ; strong, but not durable in contact with soil. It is the most widely distributed tree in the Dominion and the most extensively used for beams, panelling, fencing, sleepers, paving-blocks, furniture, and carpentry. Working as readily as birch, but with a strength comparable with oak, it might well replace satin walnut, which it somewhat resembles, as a cabinet-wood, being far more reliable than that wood, so that it should have an assured future in our market.

Roble, though properly the Spanish for Oak, is very loosely used, especially in South America, where it is applied in Chile to the Beech (*Nothofagus obliqua*), and in Argentina to the evergreen *N. betuloides*. This latter is a small tree yielding a straight, very fine-grained, handsome wood, somewhat resembling American Oak, very easily worked and now extensively used for panels in railway carriages.

Rosewood, a name applied to upwards of thirty different woods, mostly tropical, heavy, and dark-coloured. Many of them belong to the *Leguminosæ*, especially to the genera *Dalbergia*. *Machærium*, and *Pterocarpus*, and some contain a resin or oil, the resemblance of which in perfume to rose-water is their only connection with the rose. Much of the rosewood in commerce comes from Brazil, including that of Bahia, the best, Rio, the second best, and San Francisco, and derived from *Dalbergia nigra* ; or, in part, from *Machærium scleroxylon, M. firmum*, and *M. legale*, all four species being known as " Jacaranda." This wood comes in half-round logs 10 ft. to 20 ft. long, seldom more than 14 in. in diameter. It is dark chestnut or ruddy brown, richly streaked with black resinous layers, with the rose-water perfume, weighing 53 lb. to 65 lb. per cubic foot, taking a fine polish, but frequently hollow or with heart-shake and fading with age. It is a very valuable cabinet-wood, both solid and in veneer for furniture, especially pianoforte cases. Honduras and Nicaragua Rosewoods are apparently species of *Dalbergia* ; and East Indian or Bombay Rosewood is *D. latifolia* and *D. Sissoo.* (*See* BLACKWOOD, INDIAN and SISSOO.)

BURMESE ROSEWOOD is Padouk (*Pterocarpus indicus*, etc.). AFRICAN or GAMBIA ROSEWOOD, known also as African Padouk, is *Pterocarpus erinaceus*, which reaches 70 ft. in height and 5 ft. in diameter, but has often a spongy centre. It is red-brown and hard ; but fades on exposure to light. Unrelated rosewoods are those of Seychelles, Borneo Australia, and the Canaries. That of Seychelles is *Thespesia populnea*, a widely distributed Malvaceous tree of moderate size, known as " Faux bois de rose," " Bois de rose de l'Océanie," and other names. It is dark red or claret colour, resembling mahogany, smelling like roses when rubbed, hard, and strong ; and is used in India for spokes, gunstocks, furniture, and carriage-building.

BORNEO ROSEWOOD, or Rengas, is the product of various species of the Anacardiaceous genera *Melanorrhea* and *Swintonia*, beautiful red woods with purple streaks, darkening with age, very hard and heavy, and used for furniture, but containing a dangerously poisonous dark gum. In Australia the name is applied to some of the Myalls, Pencil-cedars, and Bastard Sandalwoods, but especially to the Meliaceous *Synoum glandulosum*, of the north-east, a wood of moderate size, deep red, rose-scented when fresh, firm, easily worked, taking a fine polish, and long valued for furniture.

CANARY ROSEWOOD (which comes from the Canary Islands) is a very different material, being the rhizome or underground stem and base of the aerial stem of several species of *Convolvulus*, which have a strong scent of roses and are distilled for the ethereal oil of rosewood, an adulterant of attar of roses.

Sabicu (*Lysiloma Sabicu*), a large and heavy West Indian timber, coming in logs 20 ft. to 35 ft. long, squaring 11 in. to 24 in. and weighing 43 lb. to 62 lb. per cubic foot. It is dark chestnut-brown, sometimes with a curled figure, resembling rosewood, hard, strong, elastic, close-grained, seasoning slowly, but shrinking little in the process, working up well, taking a high polish, and durable. The staircases of the Great Exhibition of 1851 were of this wood, and wore well, and it was used in shipbuilding and for furniture, being imported from Cuba ; but it is a wood of which little is heard to-day.

Saffron-wood (*Elæodendron croceum*), known also as " Safforan-wood " and " Crocus-wood " ; a native of South Africa, of moderate dimensions, reddish-brown, beautifully grained like walnut, heavy, hard, and tough, used for furniture and for wagon- and boat-building, wheelwrights' work, beams, and planks.

Sal (*Shorea robusta*), one of the most valuable gregarious species of the *Dipterocarpeæ* of the Indian region, forming vast forests, almost purely of the one species at the foot of the Himalayas from Assam to the Punjab and in Central India. Known also as " Saul." A large tree, 100 ft. to 150 ft. high and 7 ft. or 8 ft. in diameter, it yields timbers 20 ft. to 60 ft. long and from 1 ft. to 2 ft. in diameter, weighing 29 lb. to 52 lb. per cubic foot. The wood is brown, finely streaked with dark lines, hard, coarse, and cross-grained, elastic, tough, comparing favourably as to strength with teak, next to which it is classed in Lloyd's Register, warping and splitting considerably in seasoning, but almost unrivalled for durability, its whitish, aromatic resin protecting it from termites. It is the most extensively used timber in Northern India for piles, bridges, sleepers, beams, planks, gun-carriages, blocks, wedges, cogs, tool-handles, etc. ; but, being too heavy to float, it is expensive.

Saleng. (*See* PINE.)

Sandalwood, the fragrant wood of *Santalum album* and other species of the genus, or of the nearly related genera *Fusanus, Exocarpus,* and *Osyris. Santalum album* occurs in India, chiefly in the south, and Malaysia. It reaches a height of 30 ft. and a diameter not exceeding 2 ft., and weighs 56 lb. to 71 lb. per cubic foot ; but is sold in crooked billets weighing from 50 lb. to 90 lb. each. Yellowish-brown, heavy, moderately hard, close-grained, and fragrant, the heartwood increases in fragrance with age. It is largely used in India in the manufacture of carved and inlaid boxes, fans, walking-sticks, etc., burnt as a perfume, ground into powder as a cosmetic, and distilled for its oil. In the Sandwich Islands, *S. freycinetianum* and *S. paniculatum ;* in Fiji, *S. Yasi ;* in New Caledonia, *S. austro-caledonicum ;* and in Eastern Australia, *S. obtusifolium* and *S. lanceolatum* are collected. The scarce *Fusanus spicatus* of Southern and Western Australia is not very fragrant, but is exported to Singapore and China.

EAST AFRICAN SANDALWOOD, from Portuguese East Africa, is the small, brown, heavy crooked wood of *Osyris tenuifolia*. It is sometimes called " Mucumite."

BASTARD SANDALWOOD, in Australia, is the small, but very fragrant, brown and

beautifully mottled, hard woods of *Myoporum platycarpum* and the allied *Eremophila Mitchelli*, which take a fine polish and yield handsome furniture veneers. Known also as " Rosewood."

The Bastard Sandalwood of India is *Erythroxylon monogynum*, a dark brown, very hard and very fragrant wood, taking a fine polish. *E. laurifolium*, of Mauritius, and *E. australe*, of Queensland, are similar woods.

Two woods belonging to the *Meliaceæ, Epicharis loureiri* and *Lepidaglaia bailloni* are sold and used as Sandalwood in Burma and Cochin China.

Sanders Wood, Red (*Pterocarpus santalinus*), a native of Tropical Asia, known also as Red Sandalwood, to the Germans as Caliaturholz and possibly the Hebrew " Almug " of the Bible, is a small, deep orange-red wood, with lighter zones, turning to claret colour or black, very heavy and hard, fine-grained, and taking a beautiful polish. It is used for images, carving, furniture, turnery, etc., but chiefly as a source of the beautiful salmon-pink dyeing principle santalin, which is soluble in alcohol but not in water. The name is sometimes applied to *Adenanthera pavonina*, known also as Coralwood. Redwood, or Condori-wood, a large tree with beautiful coral-red heartwood with darker stripes when freshly cut, but apt to turn dark-brown or purple, like rosewood, on exposure, very heavy, hard, close-grained, and durable. It is used in house-building, for cabinetwork, and as a dye.

Sappan-wood (*Cæsalpinia Sappan*), a native of the East Indies, sometimes known as Redwood or Brazil-wood, small, dark, orange-yellow or brownish-red, very heavy, fine-grained, and taking a good polish, and thus useful for cabinetwork and inlaying, though almost exclusively used as a dye.

Sassafras (*Sassafras officinale*), a lauraceous tree of large dimensions, widely distributed in North America, with dull orange-brown heartwood and a slight characteristic smell ; light, soft, weak, but durable. An essential oil is distilled from the roots. The name is extended in various countries to other *Lauraceæ* and to members of the allied Family *Monimiaceæ*, several of which are yellow and fragrant.

Satin Walnut. (*See* GUM, SWEET.)

Satine. (*See* WASHABA.)

Satinwood, in India and Ceylon, is the Meliaceous *Chloroxylon Swietenia*, a light orange wood of good dimensions, sometimes with a beautiful curl, heavy, hard, close-grained, taking an excellent polish, with the lustre that gives it its name, durable, but liable to darken unless varnished. Weight 49 lb. to 65 lb. per cubic foot. The wood is used in India for sleepers, oil-mills, agricultural implements and furniture, the beautiful figured variety being imported into Europe for the backs of hair-brushes, turnery, cabinetwork, strings in inlay and fretwork. In the eighteenth century it was fashionable for harpsichords, coach-panels, or cabinets. These were generally decorated by paintings, with which the names of Cipriani and Angelica Kauffmann are specially associated.

WEST INDIAN SATINWOOD (*Fagara flava*), a similar but entirely unrelated wood, being a member of the Rue Family, is imported in considerable quantity from Bermuda, the Bahamas, Porto Rico, St. Domingo, and Jamaica, in logs 10 ft. long, 8 in. wide, and 8 in. thick. In the Bahamas it is known as Yellow-wood, and its Spanish name is Aceitillo. It is hard, close, and even in grain, like box, and has a smell like that of coco-nut oil. It is used for high-class bedroom furniture, brush-backs, and cabin fittings.

AUSTRALIAN SATINWOOD, or Thorny Yellow-wood (*Zanthoxylum brachyacanthum*) is nearly allied to the last-mentioned.

AFRICAN SATINWOOD is a name applied to a bright canary-yellow wood from Southern Nigeria, derived from a large tree of the leguminous genus *Cassia*. It is close-grained and firm and suitable for cabinetwork.

Sequoia (*Sequoia sempervirens*), one of the most valuable of Californian softwoods, known in its native country as Redwood, is restricted to the coast range and has considerably appreciated from the heavy felling of the last thirty years. The tree may attain more than 350 ft. in height, and 75 ft. to 100 ft. to its lowest branch, commonly reaching 80 ft. in height and 16 in. in diameter in thirty years. Old trees reach 20 ft. in diameter. The wood is almost identical with that of the Deciduous Cypress (*Taxodium distichum*) of the Mississippi, a related but deciduous tree. It is maroon to terracotta or deep brownish-red, darkening on exposure, light, soft, brittle, close but short-grained, non-resinous, not strong, but very durable in contact with soil. It dries rapidly, losing all vitality, and is thus extremely stable. In California it is largely used for doors, panelling, and carpentry ; sleepers, telegraph-poles, and furniture ; but having no ornamental figure, it is too monotonous for a high-class furniture-wood in England, and is now used mainly for cabinet drawers and blind wood.

Service (*Sorbus domestica*), a small tree, native to Central Europe, known generally as " Cormier," but sometimes as " Sorbier," in France, yielding a fawn-coloured, very hard, fine-grained wood, resembling pear, but sometimes beautifully figured ; in request for cabinetwork, turnery, cogs, screws, planes, and engraving.

Shoondul (*Intsia bijuga*), the Indian name for a moderate-sized tree, native to tropical shores from Madagascar to the Sandwich Islands, and yielding a valuable timber known under various scientific and vernacular names. It is the " Pyingadu " of Burma, " Ipil " of the Philippines, and " Vesi " of Fiji. A member of the Family *Leguminosæ*, it has dark reddish-brown wood, very hard, close-grained, termite-proof, and durable. In India it is employed for bridge- and house-building, sleepers, and electric-light poles ; it is the best timber in the Fijis, where the natives use it for canoes, pillows, kava-bowls, and clubs, and it is exported to Europe as a furniture wood.

Silk-cotton (*Ceiba pentandra*), a large tree, widely distributed in the tropics, producing light, soft, white wood, weighing less than 18 lb. per cubic foot, and used for rafts, canoes, floats, packing-cases, and toys. The huge flat buttress-roots of this and other species are sometimes utilised for gold-pans by prospectors.

Siris, Pink (*Albizzia Julibrissin*), a moderate-sized leguminous tree of the Old World Tropics, yielding a dark brown to black wood, prettily mottled, very heavy, and capable and susceptible of a good polish, which is valued for house- and boat-building, and for furniture.

Sissoo (*Dalbergia Sissoo*), a large tree of Northern India, yielding logs 10 ft. to 15 ft. long. It varies from light brown to a dark red-brown with darker longitudinal veins, being at least as variable in colour as mahogany, very heavy, hard, close and even in grain, strong, elastic, seasoning well without warping or splitting, durable. It is rapid in growth and is one of the most valuable of Indian timbers. Being sometimes almost as beautiful as its relatives the rosewoods, it is valued for furniture ; but it is unrivalled for the naves and felloes of wheels having to withstand heavy loads. It proved satisfactory for the spokes of heavy motor-wagons in the South African War, and is now being used in India in conjunction with Sundri-wood, but is unfortunately not plentiful.

Snakewood, in English commerce, is the crooked-grained condition of Letter-wood (*Brosimum Aubletii*), (*which see*) ; it is used for inlaying and the bellies of bows.

Sneezewood (*Pteroxylon utile*), the Boer " Neishout," perhaps the most valuable of South African timbers. It grows only 20 ft. to 30 ft. high, but reaches 2 ft. to 4 ft. in diameter, and weighs 65 lb. to 67½ lb. per cubic foot. The wood is handsome, with a beautiful grain resembling Satinwood, and takes a fine polish ; but is not only very hard, but irregular in growth, so as to be difficult to convert. It is so little affected by moisture as to be superior to lignum-vitæ, iron, or brass for bearings, and is both termite- and teredo-proof, ranking with Jarrah and Greenheart as one of the most durable woods in the world. The gum-resin, which causes its dust to produce sneezing, renders it very inflammable. It is used for engineering work,

furniture, agricultural implements, and carpentry.

Spindle-tree (*Euonymus europœus*), a British hedgerow shrub, producing a yellowish-white, hard, tough, fine-grained light wood ; difficult to split and not splintering, but easily cut. It is used for shoe-pegs and spindles, and yields a fine crayon charcoal ; but its poisonous character makes it unsuitable for skewers.

Spruce, a name originally applied to the European *Picea excelsa* from Pruce or Prussia, whence it was obtained, but now extend d to all the score or so of species of the genus *Picea*, evergreen cone-bearing trees of the north temperate zone. Though varying in durability according to the soil upon which it is grown, the woods of the various species are closely similar. Of a whitish colour, with no distinct heart, light in weight, only slightly resinous, straight and even in grain, easily worked, with a fairly lustrous surface, elastic and resonant, they are generally superior to the firs and at least equal to the soft pines as timber, not very valuable as fuel, but useful for paper-pulp and unequalled as resonance-wood for sounding-boards and violins. In Europe the chief species is the Norway, or Baltic Spruce or White Fir (*Picea excelsa*), though there are also Serbian and Caucasian species ; in Asia, though twenty species have been recorded from China and the Himalayan (*P. Morinda*), Siberian (*P. Maximowiczii*) and Thian-Shan species (*P. Schrenkiana*) are locally important, the Japanese and Yesso species (*P. hondoensis*) and (*P. ajanensis*) are, perhaps at present, of most consequence ; but in North America the Red, Black, or Canadian White and Sitka species (*P. rubra*, *P. mariana*, *P. alba*, and *P. sitchensis*) are, for flooring, carpentry, and paper-pulp, among the leading woods of the Continent.

The COMMON SPRUCE (*P. excelsa*) ranges from the Altai and Urals to the Alps and Pyrenees, and is well known as a timber-tree in Britain, although not indigenous. Young specimens are familiar as Christmas trees. Reaching 125 ft. to 180 ft. in height and 3 ft. to 6 ft. in diameter, it is the loftiest of European trees. Its wood, known as Baltic whitewood, White Deal, or, in the musical instrument trade, as Swiss Pine or Violin-wood, is sometimes yellowish or reddish. When dry, it weighs only 28 lb. to 32 lb. per cubic foot. If often has many small, hard knots, and it shrinks and warps slightly in seasoning ; but it contains some resin (known as Burgundy Pitch), and is durable. It is mostly imported from Norway, in logs 30 ft. to 60 ft. long and 6 in. to 8 in. in diameter, with the bark on ; but that from Petrograd is the best ; that from Riga, Memel, and Dantzig, large, but coarser ; that from the White Sea excellent ; whilst that from Moldavia and Transylvania is of great average length, but coarse in grain. Spruce is used for scaffolding, ladders, telegraph-posts, spars, roofing, packing-cases, the sounding-boards of pianos, the bellies of violins, dressers, and kitchen tables. In Central and Southern Europe it is commonly employed for flooring : for toys, specially wide-ringed, that is, quick-grown, wood is preferred ; and in Saxony and elsewhere it is largely used for paper-pulp.

HIMALAYAN SPRUCE (*P. Morinda*), growing at from 6,000-ft. to 11,000-ft. altitudes, is not a durable wood, but is largely used in Simla for packing-cases, carpentry, planking, and fuel.

HONDO SPRUCE (*P. hondoensis*), from the mountains of Central Japan, known locally as " Tohi," and in China as " Sha," seldom exceeds 120 ft. in height. It is yellowish-red, very light and soft, fine-grained and glossy, and is used in house-building and carpentry, for masts, telegraph-poles, pillars, beams, match-boxes, and paper-pulp.

BLACK SPRUCE (*P. mariana*, commonly known as *P. nigra*) ranges from 53° N. in Alaska to Newfoundland, and 44° N. in the North-Eastern United States. It does not exceed 80 ft. in height. Its wood, exported as American, Canadian, New Brunswick, St. John's, or Double Spruce, or Spruce Deals, is a very light buff or ruddy, light, weighing about 28¼ lb. per cubic foot, soft, elastic, and compact, with a satiny lustre. It is tougher,

stronger, more elastic, and more durable than Yellow Pine (*Pinus Strobus*) ; but, being only slightly resinous, is not so good as fuel. It is so similar to Baltic Spruce that in England each is used on that side of the country nearest to its origin, and the price of the one affects that of the other. The Canadian wood is, however, harder, more liable to loose knots and inferior in strength and durability to the European. The best is shipped from Quebec and St. John's, that from the lower ports being inferior. Trees with wide rings are confused by lumbermen with the White Spruce (*P. alba*). Black Spruce is used for flooring, spars, piles, and oars ; the best, quarter-sawn, for pianos and violins ; and immense quantities in Newfoundland for paper-pulp, for which it is, perhaps, the best material. In Manchester and Birmingham the wood is largely employed for packing-cases.

RED SPRUCE (*P. rubra*), of South-Eastern Canada and the Eastern United States, is said to be the most valuable timber of the district, being larger than the Black Spruce, reaching 80 ft. to 100 ft. in height and 3 ft. in diameter. Its wood is pale buff, light, soft, even-grained, but fairly strong. The best quality is used for the sounding-boards of pianos, the rest for flooring, carpentry, and paper-pulp ; but in export trade it has been confused with the Black Spruce.

WHITE or SINGLE SPRUCE (*P. alba*), with a geographical range nearly identical with the Black, and extensively planted during recent years in Jutland, is a slightly inferior wood, pale yellowish buff in colour, reaching large dimensions (150 ft. in height and 4 ft. in diameter), but not strong and mainly employed for inferior finish or paper-pulp.

SITKA SPRUCE (*P. sitchensis*), said to be the best of the American Spruces, ranges from 57° N. in Alaska to 40° in California, ascending the Rockies to 2,300 metres, and sometimes called " Californian Coast Spruce." It sometimes attains 250 ft. in height and from 6 ft. to 12 ft., or even 15 ft. in diameter ; but its wood weighs only 26¾ lb. per cubic foot. It is a light yellowish-brown, tinged with red, soft, straight-grained, compact, and strong, and is used in house- and boat-building, carpentry and cooperage; the lightness and elasticity render it peculiarly valuable in the construction of aeroplanes.

Stinkwood (*Ocotea bullata*), known also as Cape Laurel or Cape Walnut, reaches 70 ft. in height and 3 ft. or 4 ft. in diameter, and weighs over 50 lb. per cubic foot. It is a golden-brown, often mottled and resembling walnut, and sometimes iridescent. It gives off a strong, peculiar smell when worked, and is extremely tough, being little inferior to Teak in strength or durability, and more ornamental as a furniture-wood. Used in South Africa for house- and wagon-building and for gunstocks, but is now very scarce.

Stringybark (*Eucalyptus macrorrhyncha, E. obliqua,* and other species of Gum-trees of South-East Australia and Tasmania). *E. macrorrhyncha,* known also as "Ironbark," is 50 ft. to 100 ft. high and 2 ft. to 4½ ft. in diameter. Its wood is light brown, tinged with deeper red-brown, sometimes figured with yellow and brown stripes, hard, strong, close-grained, capable of a good polish, and durable. It is used for fencing, flooring, and carpentry, but is suitable for furniture. *E. obliqua,* which occurs in Tasmania, and is sometimes known as "Tasmanian Oak," is known in Victoria as "Mess-mate" from its resemblance to and association with the last-named species. It reaches far greater dimensions, even 250 ft. to 300 ft. in height and 15 ft. in diameter. It has been successfully introduced in the Nilgiri Hills. Its wood, like the last-named, weighs over 60 lb. per cubic foot. It varies from light to dark brown, with a wavy figure near the base of the stem ; is hard, straight but rather coarse in grain, very strong, and tough. It is liable to shakes and gum-veins, and warps if not well seasoned, but is very durable. It is probably the most generally used of all Eucalypti, being employed for fencing, house-building, beams, joists, flooring, roof-shingles, docks, wharves, piles, bridges, girders, ships' keels, mine-timbers, railway sleepers, and paving blocks, and is exported for such purposes to India and South Africa. For WHITE STRINGYBARK, *see* REDWOOD.

Sumach, Staghorn or **Virginian** (*Rhus typhina*), a native of Canada and the North-Eastern United States, is small wood, citron-green to greenish gold-ochre, with darker autumn zones, handsome, slightly aromatic, soft, light and lustrous, used as a dye or in small pieces in inlaying.

VENETIAN SUMACH (*R. Cotinus*), known also as "Young" or "Zante Fustic," or "Wild Olive," is a Mediterranean wood of a similar character, but harder, imported from Greece as a yellow dye for leather or wool.

Sundri (*Heritiera fomes*), which gives its name to the Sunderbunds of Bengal, but ranges to Borneo, yields timber 15 ft. long and 1 ft. in diameter, weighing 50 lb. to 58 lb. per cubic foot, brown, very hard, elastic, strong, durable, and tougher than any other Indian wood. It is now used for handles, the spokes of heavy artillery wheels, and, in Calcutta, for firewood.

Switch-sorrel. (*See* LIGNUM-VITÆ.)

Sycamore, a name belonging originally to the Levantine Fig-Mulberry (*Ficus Sycomorus*), a shade-tree with strong wood, used from at least 1600 B.C. by the Egyptians for mummy-cases. In the sixteenth century the name was transferred in English use to the Great Maple (*Acer Pseudo-platanus*), a totally different, but shady, tree from the same region. This reaches 60 ft. in height and 3 ft. in diameter ; and its white wood, which becomes yellowish with age, or slightly brown in the centre, weighs, when dry, 29 lb. per cubic foot. The fine, but distinct pith-rays, with the satiny lustre so general among maples, distinguishes it from linden-wood, and when cut radially this "fiddle-mottle" is in request for violins. The wood is compact, firm, fine-grained, and tough, though not hard ; it is easily worked, and is susceptible of a high polish, but requires careful seasoning, as it shrinks a twelfth of its bulk and has a tendency to warp and crack. When seasoned, however, it is durable, if kept dry, and is generally left free from insect attack. When of large size, British-grown Sycamore commands a higher price than any British timber, except cricket-bat willow. Large wood is sought after for calico-printing rollers, and when quartered and white, for those of washing-machines. At Glasgow it is largely used for bread-platters, butter-dishes and moulds, reels, shoemakers' cutting-boards, coach-panels and bobbins ; as veneer, it is employed for the interior of railway carriages ; and on the Continent it is in request for turners, toymakers, and carvers. It is known as Plane in Scotland, whilst in New England the Plane (*Platanus occidentalis*) is called Sycamore.

Tallow-wood (*Eucalyptus microcorys*), known also as "Forest Mahogany," a large tree of Eastern Australia, producing an excellent yellow or yellowish-brown wood, strong and durable, though very greasy when freshly cut, liable to shakes, and generally hollow. It is used for piles, girders, ballroom floors, and wheelwrights' work, and is one of the best of Australian woods for paving.

Tamarack. (*See* LARCH.)

Tamarind (*Tamarindus indica*), the large and very heavy wood of the slow-growing Indian medicinal fruit-tree. It is yellowish-white, with an irregular heart of dark purplish-brown blotches resembling ebony or tulip-wood, and weighs 80 lb. per cubic foot. It is very hard and difficult to work, and the tree is apt to be hollow ; but the wood is durable and free from insect attack, so that it is used for oil and sugar-mills, rice-pounders, mallets, and turnery.

T'an-mu, apparently a *Dalbergia*, is a reddish-black wood full of fine veins, very hard, tough and durable, used in China for wheels, shafts, and fine cabinetwork.

Teak (*Tectona grandis*), the most generally useful, durable, and valuable of Indian timbers, is a member of the verbena family, and is native to Southern India, Burma, the Shan States south of the Menam watershed, the Malay Peninsula, Sumatra, Java, and Celebes, whilst it has been largely planted in Ceylon and in parts of India where it is not wild. It may exceed 100 ft. in height and reach 8 ft. in diameter, yielding logs 23 ft. to 50 ft. long, squaring 10 in. to 30 in.

Its weight, when it is green, being more than that of water, is the reason for girdling the trees—that is, cutting a complete ring round the tree through its bark and sapwood, so as to kill it—some three years before felling them, so that they can be floated down to the port of shipment. The wood is straight-grown, light straw-colour to a brownish-red, when fresh, but darkening on exposure. In the Deccan it is sometimes beautifully veined, streaked, and mottled, and old trees occasionally produce burrs resembling Amboyna-wood. When fresh cut, teak is very fragrant, so as to resemble rose-wood, owing to the presence of an oleo-resin which renders it obnoxious to insects and even keeps off rust from iron in contact with it ; but, when seasoned, it has an unpleasant smell, like old shoe-leather. As at least a year usually elapses between the felling of this timber and its arrival in England, it arrives sufficiently seasoned and but very little shrunken, warped, or split ; but the rapid drying induced by girdling is said to render the wood inelastic, brittle, and less durable, so that it splits too readily for use in gun-carriages. It is a moderately hard wood, clean, straight, and even in grain, but varies considerably according to the conditions under which it is grown, that of Malabar being darker, heavier, and rather stronger than that of Burma, although not so large. Though not splitting from their circumference, teak logs have nearly always a heart-shake, which, owing to a twist in the growth, may often be at right angles at the top of the tree to its position at the butt ; this, however, while seriously interfering with conversion, may very little affect the use of the timber in bulk. In the shakes and larger vessels of the wood there is generally a secretion of white masses of apatite or calcium-phosphate, which will turn the edge of most tools. Teak owes its superiority for shipbuilding over pine and oak partly to its freedom, when once seasoned, from any change of form, even under the extremes of a monsoon climate.

As the Indian Forest Department plant several thousand acres annually, there is little fear of the supply becoming exhausted, and the wood of cultivated trees is said to be better than that of natural forests. Teak is used in India for bridge-building, sleepers, and other purposes ; but is little exported except to this country, where it is used for backing armour-plates, for deck-planks, railway wagons, greenhouses, etc. That from Moulmein drawn from the valleys of the Salwen and Thungyen Rivers, is rather shorter, but less shaky, than that shipped at Rangoon from the Irawadi Valley ; that from Java is excessively hard and gritty.

The name of so valuable a timber has naturally been applied to various very heavy and hard woods in no way related to it or to one another. The " Biji " of India, " Gammala " of Ceylon (*Pterocarpus Marsupium*), is known as Bastard Teak. It is a good-sized tree, with very heavy and hard yellowish-brown, dark-striped heartwood, taking a fine polish and very durable if not exposed to wet. It is heavier than most teak, and harder and darker than its ally Padouk ; but is expensive to work. It is used for sleepers, furniture, etc.

JOHORE TEAK (*Parinarium oblongifolium*), a very heavy and hard, dark-brown, termite-proof rosaceous timber, used for piles at Singapore and exported to Colombo for the breakwater, is now unobtainable. So, too, is the so-called AFRICAN TEAK (*Oldfieldia africana*), a euphorbiaceous wood from Western Tropical Africa, formerly used in ship-building. For New Zealand Teak or " Puriri " (*Vitex littoralis*), see MOLAVE.

Tenasserim. (*See* PADOUK.)

Tewart (*Eucalyptus gomphocephala*). known also as " Tuart," " Touart," and " White Gum," of West Australia, reaching a height of 150 ft. and yielding timber 20 ft. to 45 ft. long, squaring 11 in. to 28 in., weighing 60 lb. to 78 lb. per cubic foot, is one of the strongest and toughest of known woods, hard, twisted, or curled in grain, so as to be difficult to cleave or work, but apparently imperishable. It is used for keelsons, capstans, piles, dock-gates, etc.

Thingan (*Hopea odorata*), the Burmese name of a valuable wood of great length ranging from India to Borneo. It is said to combine the good qualities of oak with the durability of teak. It is yellowish-brown, moderately heavy and hard, easily worked, and not subject to insect-attack, and is in demand for building. It and allied diptero-carpaceous woods form part of the Yacal used for sleepers in the Philippines and known as " Ballow " in the Singapore market.

Thuya (*Tetraclinis articulata*), a small Cypress native to Algeria and Morocco, producing reddish-brown, fragrant burrs, resembling Amboyna-wood. This very durable wood is the " Alerce " of the Alhambra and the roof of Cordova Cathedral, and is known as " Lignum-vitæ," by the French. The Thyine-wood of the Apocalypse and the enormously costly Citron wood of ancient Rome were probably the burrs, the name of which is pronounced in our English market as Thoo'ee.

Toon. (*See* CEDAR, MOULMEIN.)

Totara (*Podocarpus Totara*), or New Zealand Yew, next to Kauri the most valuable timber in the Dominion and far more abundant. It grows 40 ft. to 70 ft. or even 120 ft. in height, sometimes 40 ft. to its lowest branch and 2 ft. to 6 ft., or even 12 ft. in diameter, so that its timber is in 20-ft., 45-ft., or greater lengths, squaring 10 in. to 22 in. It weighs 28 lb. to 37 lb. per cubic foot. It is deep red, moderately hard, straight, close, fine and even in grain, very easily worked, not warping or twisting, strong, teredo-proof, and very durable. It is used for piles, sleepers, paving-blocks, telegraph-poles, bridges, and building ; but might well be employed for interior finish or furniture, and should have a good future in our market. It sometimes produces Amboyna-like burrs.

Trumpet-tree (*Cecropia peltata* in Jamaica and *C. palmata* in Brazil and Guiana), small trees producing very light, resonant wood, used for floats and razor-strops, whilst hollow stems are converted into trumpets and drums.

Tulip-wood, in Europe (*Physocalymma scaberrimum*), a Brazilian wood, known locally as "Pao de rosa," rose-coloured, beautifully striped and used for inlay and turnery. In Queensland the name is given to the similar but unrelated black and yellow woods of *Harpullia pendula*, one of the *Sapindaceæ*, and *Owenia venosa*, one of the *Meliaceæ*. These handsome woods are heavy, hard, and close-grained ; and, taking an excellent polish, are valuable for cabinetwork. (*See also* CANARY WHITEWOOD.)

Umzimbit (*Millettia Caffra*), an intensely hard leguminous wood in South Africa with yellowish-white, durable sapwood, contrasting sharply with the dark reddish-brown heart. Known also as "Kaffir Ironwood." It is used for walking-sticks, but will serve for machine-bearings, spokes, gunstocks, and furniture.

Violet-wood, a name sometimes applied, on account of its colour, to the Purple-heart (*which see*) of Tropical America, sometimes, on account of its perfume, to the Australian Myall.

Walnut (*Juglans regia*), a native of Northern and Western China and Persia, introduced in early times into Greece and Italy, and thence into the rest of Europe. It may reach 50 ft. in height and 3 ft. in diameter, and its wood, when dry, weighs 46 lb. or 47 lb. per cubic foot. The dark-brown or black-brown heartwood is often "watered," exhibiting dark wavy lines and zones of great beauty. It is hard, fine, and close in grain, splitting but little in the process of seasoning, but may be readily split artificially, taking a beautiful polish and singularly free from any tendency to splinter after being worked up. It is durable if kept dry, especially when dark or figured ; but its sapwood is very liable to become worm-eaten. It can, however, be rendered resistant by being smoked over a beech-wood fire or by boiling in the juice of its own green fruits.

English-grown walnut, coming mostly from good soil in lowland situations, is pale, coarse, but little figured, and perishable ; French is better ; that from Austria, Serbia, etc., known as Black Sea, which is imported in waney logs 6 ft. to 9 ft. long, squaring 10 in. to 18 in., is still more valuable ; whilst that from Italy,

which comes in 5-ft. to 12-ft. planks, 10 in. to 16 in. wide and 4 in. to 9 in. thick, is the best. Walnut was considerably used in France for carving in the round during the fourteenth, fifteenth, and sixteenth centuries. At the beginning of the eighteenth century it became very fashionable as a furniture wood, its use being the first departure from the universal employ ment of oak.

The severe winter of 1709 killed most of the walnut trees of Central Europe, and the dead trees were bought up by the Dutch, who thus secured a "corner" in this wood. By 1720 it had become so scarce in France that its export was prohibited, and mahogany, imported by Dutch and Spaniards, largely replaced it as a furniture wood. No wood, however, equals walnut for the manufacture of gunstocks, so that the wars of the eighteenth century created a great dearth of this wood, and one reads of France consuming 12,000 trees a year in 1806, and of as much as £600 being paid for a single tree. European walnut is still in use for the best gunstocks ; and Swiss carvings are mostly in this wood. Good walnut is used for repairing and copying Queen Anne furniture ; plainer wood for the solid parts of furniture, turnery, musical instruments, etc. ; but it is now so scarce as to be largely replaced for all purposes by the inferior American species.

Burrs, often 2 ft. to 3 ft. across and over 1 ft. in thickness, beautifully mottled and weighing 5 cwt. or 6 cwt., occur on Italian and Black Sea wood, and are highly valued for veneers for the pianoforte and cabinet trade. Before the war they were largely imported from Turkestan.

AMERICAN WALNUT (*J. nigra*), a larger tree, has wood more uniform in colour, darker, duller, less liable to insect attack, and, therefore, more durable. Formerly used for many unworthy purposes, it is now too valuable as a cabinet and veneer wood, and for rifle-stocks, to be employed for anything else. Before the middle of the last century it was only used in England for carcase work and frames for veneering ; but now it is more used than European walnut, its uniform colour recommending it to shop-fitters as a basis for surface ornamentation in the cabinet trade. It is imported to Liverpool in 10-ft. to 21-ft. logs, squaring 15 in. to 50 in., in planks and in boards.

GREY or WHITE WALNUT, or Butter-nut (*J. cinerea*), is a very beautiful and durable American wood of good size, but lighter than the preceding, and is seldom imported.

MANCHURIAN WALNUT (*J. manchurica*) and JAPANESE WALNUT (*J. Sieboldiana*) cover large areas in Irkutsk, Transbaikal, and Yakutsk, and yield large, hard wood, suitable for gunstocks.

AFRICAN WALNUT is a Liverpool name for several woods from Tropical Africa of varying quality. One, *Boswellia Klainei.* is an inferior, light, coarse-grained wood. Another, from Benin, a species of *Trichilia* or *Pseudo-cedrela*, though a mahogany rather than a walnut, is a good but monotonous dark brown, easily worked furniture wood, of large diameter, weighing $32\frac{1}{2}$ lb. per cubic foot. A third, also known as "Owowe," is a large species of *Albizzia*, similar to the next and quite a useful substitute for walnut.

EAST INDIAN WALNUT is a name given in the London market on account of its colour to *Albizzia Lebbek*, a leguminous wood of wide range in the Tropics from Africa to Australia, known as "Siris" in Bengal, "Koko" in the Andaman Islands, and "Ki-toke" in Java. It weighs 41 lb. to 56 lb. per cubic foot; is dark brown, with darker streaks and a wide, light sapwood; hard, coarse-grained, polishing well and durable; and is used for building, wheelwrights' work, and mill-rollers, as well as for cabinetwork.

For SATIN WALNUT, see SWEET GUM; and CAPE WALNUT, see STINKWOOD.

Washaba (*Ferolia guianensis*), a rosaceous wood native to Guiana, known also as "Satiné," "Bois de féroles" or "Bois marbré," and as "Washiba" or "Waciba." It is exported in logs 14 ft. to 28 ft. long, squaring 13 in. to 15 in., and is red or red-brown, splashed with yellow, hard, solid tough, elastic, and susceptible of a beautiful polish. It is used for bows, fishing-rods, and cabinetwork.

Wattle, the general Australian name for the species of *Acacia*, from their use by the early colonists in wattling their huts. Among them, *A. binervata*, unfortunately known as Hickory as well as Black Wattle, is valued for axe-handles and bullock-yokes in the north-east of Australia; *A. mollissima*, known as Black Wattle or Silver Wattle in the south-east, formerly used for boomerangs, mulgas, and spears, is now employed in Tasmania for cask-staves; but the only species reaching this country are those known as Myall (*which see*, also BLACKWOOD, TASMANIAN). Many of the species yield valuable Wattle Gum.

Whitewood. (*See* CANARY WHITE-WOOD and SPRUCE.)

Willow, a name used only in Europe and America for species of the genus *Salix*. These hybridise freely among themselves, producing plants of very distinct characters. Many species and their hybrids are cultivated under the name of osiers for the manufacture of wicker-work. Others are treated as pollards, the small wood derived from their lopping being valuable for hurdles, hoops, hay-rakes, etc. Only two species are employed as sources of larger wood, the Crack Willow (*S. fragilis*) and several forms of the White Willow (*S. alba*).

CRACK WILLOW, also known as Open-bark Willow, grows to heights of 50 ft. to 90 ft. and to diameters of 4 ft. to 7 ft. Its wood, when dry, is salmon-coloured, light, tough. and elastic, and is used for cricket-bats, but is inferior to Close-bark Willow.

WHITE WILLOW (*S. alba*) ranges from North-West India and North Africa north-westward, and reaches almost the same dimensions as the last mentioned. Its heart-wood has a brownish tinge and weighs from 24 lb. to 35 lb. per cubic foot. It is soft and smooth-grained, does not splinter, shrinks one-sixth of its bulk in drying; but is very durable, either dry or wet. It was formerly used for cottage flooring, and is still employed for wheelbarrows, especially in ironworks, as it does not split or warp when heated, or take fire readily on friction. It is also used for brake-blocks on railway wagons, for paddles of steamboats, the strouds of water-wheels, shoemakers' lasts and cutting-boards, toy-making, druggists' boxes, etc. The polishing wheels used by glass grinders are made of complete horizontal sections of the stem. By far the most important use of willow wood, however, is the manufacture of cricket bats. These should be made of the wood of the variety known as Close-bark Willow (*S. alba* var. *cœrulea*) ; and large sound trees of this fetch very high prices.

Wych. (*See* ELM, SCOTCH or WYCH.)

Yellow-wood, though occasionally applied to Fustic and in Australia to various unrelated woods, is a name referring generally to South African woods of the Coniferous genus *Podocarpus*, especially *P. Thunbergii* and *P. elongata*, both of which are known as " Geel Hout " by the Boers ; but the former as " Umceya," the latter as " Umkoba," by the Zulus. They are tall trees, 2 ft. to 5 ft., or even 8 ft. in diameter, yielding pale yellow wood, weighing 30 lb. to 45 lb. per cubic foot, soft and close-grained, easily worked, but somewhat liable to warp and split. They are used for building, roof-shingles, flooring, and furniture, and, when creosoted, for railway sleepers. (For THORNY YELLOW-WOOD, *see* SATINWOOD, AUSTRALIAN.)

Yellow Jacket. (*See* GUM, RED.)

Yendaik (or **Yendike**) (*Dalbergia cultrata*), a moderate-sized leguminous blackwood in Burma, weighing 64 lb. per cubic foot, black with purple or light streaks, straight grown, very hard, tough, elastic, and durable, full of shakes, but not cracking or altering after conversion, sometimes called " Blackwood " and confused with Ebony. It is excellent for spokes, bows, tool-handles, spears, and carving.

Yew (*Taxus baccata*), generally of small height, but reaching 100 ft. in the Himalaya, and of all diameters up to 19 ft., produces a reddish-brown, non-resinous wood, resembling mahogany and weighing 40 lb. to 57 lb. per cubic foot. Often incorporating many ascending branches with separate centres in its stem, the resultant wood appears irregular in growth. It is very hard, close-grained, tough,

flexible, and elastic ; is susceptible of a high polish ; and is insect-proof and more durable than any other European wood, it being proverbial that a post of yew will outlast a post of iron.

The twelfth-century framework of the feretory of St. Manchan at Boher in King's County, made of yew, is still quite sound. Yew was employed for the early Greek statues of the gods ; it is, however, as a material for bows, on account of its combined toughness and elasticity, that yew has been best known from early times. Though home-grown wood was used in England for this purpose in mediæval times, that imported by Venetian traders from Italy, Turkey and Spain was of better quality. Small branches are used for walking-sticks, and the wood is employed to some extent in chair-making and on the Continent in turnery. It is also stained black as German Ebony. Old trees produce Amboyna-like burrs, veneers of which were commonly used towards the close of the eighteenth century for tea-caddies, punch-ladles, etc. The wood of *T. cuspidata*, the Japanese form, was used by the aboriginal Ainu for bows, though nowadays chiefly employed for furniture and pencils.

Zebra-wood, a name applied to many different woods, mostly tropical, heavy, hard, susceptible of a good polish, and so striped or streaked as to suggest the name. They are mostly employed for walking-sticks or veneers. Among them are the very rare " Hyawaballi " of British Guiana (*Connarus guianensis*), a large tree, with reddish-brown wood ; the " Arariba " (*Centrolobium robustum*), a large, leguminous wood, exported from Rio ; the " Sea-coast Teak " (*Guettarda speciosa*), a small, Rubiaceous, light reddish-yellow wood, resembling box, known as " Ronron " in Honduras and as " Bua-bua " in Fiji ; the Andaman Marble wood (*which see*) or Figured Ebony (*Diospyros Kurzii*), beautifully streaked with black and grey ; and the " Cuius-cuius " (*Taxotrophis ilicifoliæ*) of the Philippines, belonging to the Mulberry Family, which is streaked with greenish dark-brown or almost black, with dark spots.

Index

May we introduce other Ten Speed books that you will enjoy . . .

The Complete Woodworker
Edited by Bernard E. Jones

The first new edition in decades of one of the great classics in the field. This is a book about the old ways of working with wood (before power tools) which can make it possible for the contemporary craftsman to see and understand the traditional methods as they were originally presented.

6 × 9 inches   416 pages   One Thousand Illustrations
$8.95 Paper $14.95 Cloth

Before You Build
by Robert Roskind, The Owner-Builder Center

Before You Build provides the essential tool owner-builders have needed as a comprehensive guidebook and housebuilding checklist based on the experience of the recognized leaders in the field of "hands-on" education in the country — The Owner-Builder Center in Berkeley, California.

8-1/2 × 11 inches   192 pages $11.95 paper

Building Your Own House
by Robert Roskind

A housebuilding book that recognizes that people want clear, direct, well-illustrated and thorough instruction on the whole process from start to finish. Robert Roskind has taken his experience and developed a book unique in its step-by-step presentation of the first stage of building a house.

8-1/2 × 11 inches   320 pages $19.95 paper

Sound Designs
by Reinhold Banek and Jon Scoville

A totally unique book with plans and instructions for making over 50 musical instruments. Many of the designs in this book are versions of simple folk instruments from around the world — also included are some unique instruments invented along the way.

6 × 9 inches   224 pages   Illustrated $8.95 paper